SELLTIZ, WRIGHTSMAN AND COOK'S

Research Methods in Social Relations

FOURTH EDITION

Louise H. Kidder
Department of Psychology
Temple University

Published for the Society for the Psychological Study of Social Issues (SPSSI)

Holt, Rinehart and Winston
New York · Chicago · San Francisco · Dallas · Montreal · Toronto · London · Sydney

ISBN 0-03-043566-8

Copyright © 1981 by Holt, Rinehart and Winston
Copyright © 1951, 1959, 1976 by Holt, Rinehart and Winston, Inc.
All rights reserved
80-21977
Printed in the United States of America
5   6   7   8   016   9   8   7   6

*To Bob, Graham, and Charin, who let me do my work
and also gave me good reasons to stop.*

Publisher: Ray Ashton
Acquiring Editor: Dan Loch
Managing Editor: Jeanette Ninas Johnson
Senior Project Editor: Arlene Katz
Production Manager: Pat Sarcuni
Art Director: Renee Davis

Grateful acknowledgment is made to the following for the use of copyrighted materials:

Academic Press for text from Donald T. Campbell, Prospective: Artifact and control. In R. Rosenthal & R. L. Rosnow (Eds.), *Artifact in behavioral research.* New York: Academic Press, 1969.

Academic Press for text from David Glass & Jerome Singer, *Urban Stress: Experiments on Noise and Social Stressors,* 1972.

Addison-Wesley Publishing Co. for text from E. E. Maccoby and N. Maccoby, The interview: A tool of social science. In G. Lindzey (Ed.), *Handbook of Social Psychology* (Vol. 1), 1954.

American Psychological Association for text from *Ethical Principles in the Conduct of Research with Human Participants.* Washington, D.C.: American Psychological Association, 1973.

Donald T. Campbell, for text from Prospective: Artifact and control. In R. Rosenthal & R. L. Rosnow (Eds.) *Artifact in behavioral research.* New York: Academic Press, 1969.

Donald R. Cressey for text from *Other People's Money: A Study in the Social Psychology of Embezzlement,* New York: Macmillan Publishing Co., 1953.

David Glass and Jerome Singer for text from *Urban Stress: Experiments on Noise and Social Stressors,* New York: Academic Press, 1972.

Foreword

TRADITION AND PROGRESS

Since its inception in 1936, SPSSI has been concerned with the application of social science research methods to significant social problems. Given the historical perspective of SPSSI, the organization has been influenced by two opposing forces: the forces of tradition and the forces of progress. This fourth edition of *Research Methods* mirrors both. Its perspective and concern for social issues and the utilization of diverse methodologies reflect the traditional aims of the Society. While contemporary social scientists consider methodology to be a key component of their training, this has not always been the case. As recently as 1935, in Murchenson's *Handbook of Social Psychology*, research methods were not considered an important part of graduate training or textbooks. Not until 1950, with the publication of the first edition of this text by Jahoda, Deutsch, & Cook, was research methodology seen as having an important role in the study of social behavior. Thus, the first edition of this text helped initiate the tradition of modern social science research methodology.

Current concerns for applications and social problems emanate from one of the founders of SPSSI, Kurt Lewin. Interested in the major social issues of his time, Lewin translated his concerns into research on such topics as intergroup conflict, worker productivity, and leadership. He saw these projects as "action research," combinations of experiments and applications. Lewin felt this research could benefit society, and advance scientific knowledge as well. Thus, the study of social issues was the other major traditional goal of SPSSI. Throughout its discussions of methodology, this text reflects these traditional SPSSI aims and principles.

SPSSI is also very much concerned with progress. While the motivating forces and principles are traditional, the approaches must be progressive. This progress in methodological sophistication is amply demonstrated in this revision. Louise Kidder has included a broad range of modern methodologies. For example, the inclusion of evaluation research in this revision reflects SPSSI's concern that students be exposed to the latest research trends in the field. Thus, this text reflects SPSSI's traditional concern for good methodology and sensitivity to social issues, and furthers SPSSI's objectives of educating social scientists in the best and latest research methodologies.

One of the more unique features of our Society is that authors of SPSSI-sponsored texts contribute their labor. Louise Kidder and the other contributors to this fourth edition are owed a vote of thanks from the Society for developing this fine text.

As one of the contributors to the third revision, I am familiar with the challenges of working on a widely read and respected research text. In reviewing this textbook, I am gratified by its scholarship and its readability, and impressed by its apt blending, without compromise, of tradition and progress.

Leonard Bickman, President, SPSSI
1980

Preface

"Elementary, my dear Watson," said Sherlock Holmes as he deftly unravelled puzzles, and elementary they were once he found the solution. Like the reasoning of a detective, the work of a social scientist combines elementary logic and an elusive "aha" experience. The lessons in this book are lessons in logic because they can be taught. The aim of the book is to have students become deft in exploring the problems of the social world so that they too can find solutions.

The chapters on research *Design* present alternative detection strategies, ranging from controlled experiments to uncontrolled participant observation. The chapters on *Measurement* present multiple methods of gathering data. The chapters on *Results* show how to analyze data and prepare a report to make the conclusions clear and convincing. No single chapter explicitly instructs students how to achieve the insight that leads one to exclaim "aha," because that cannot be directly taught. Instead, students will learn how to use multiple research methods to explore the social world in various ways and maximize their chances of unravelling mysteries.

Ethical issues are not addressed in detail until the final chapter, but they pervade every chapter. How we ask questions, whose criteria we use in evaluating programs, and which theories we use to explain outcomes all have ethical implications. Locating causes for social problems is like laying blame on something or someone. Examining how organizations work means looking backstage and making private actions public. Research is not neutral, and we examine this fact.

I have tried to address this book to a wide audience of students in the social sciences. I hope each will find something familiar enough to feel at home with the terms and the topics but also something novel enough to feel stretched and informed about other ways of asking and answering questions. Most of all I want to teach students to explore, to ask previously unasked questions, and to find answers, so that we all may learn.

THIS EDITION AND ITS PREDECESSORS

Like a snake shedding its skin and taking on a new outer covering as it grows, this book has grown and donned a new cover four times. Each time it has grown, some things have changed while others have remained the same. An important feature of the book which has remained constant since its first appearance in 1950 is the sponsorship of The Society for the Psychological Study of Social Issues (SPSSI). The examples we have selected are again mainly social issues, and the analyses are largely psychological. The research methods presented, however, are appropriate to the study of political, economic, educational, and social welfare issues as well as sociological and psychological questions. In preparing this edition I have tried to keep in mind the same wide audience that previous editions have appealed to: undergraduates, graduates and in-service professionals in a variety of disciplines.

This edition, the fourth, represents the most radical growth spurt of all previous revisions because three-fourths of the contents are new. In early 1979 approximately 900 users of the third edition were surveyed by questionnaire to prepare for the revision. The fourth edition tries to address their needs and respond to their suggestions for changes in coverage. I have written six new chapters (1, 2, 3, 5, 6, and 7) and five other contributors have each written a new chapter: Daryl Bem on "Writing the Research Report," Marianne LaFrance on "Observational and Archival Methods," Leonard LoScuito on "Questionnaires and Interviews," Michael Milburn on "Data Analysis," and Leo Rigsby on "Survey Research Designs." Stuart Cook revised his chapter on "Ethical Implications" from the previous edition, and I revised three other chapters from the third edition (Chapters 9, 10, and 12). The focus of this edition is on causal analysis as a central theme.

ANCILLARY PACKAGE

For the first time RESEARCH METHODS is accompanied by an Instructor's Manual and a Student Study Guide. Both are being made available in direct response to the needs of the users of the third edition whom we surveyed.

The *Instuctor's Manual*, by John J. Hummel and George L. Hampton of the University of Houston, is designed to make course preparation more efficient for the instructor. Each chapter contains a summary, a list of key concepts, four lecture aids consisting of exercises and demonstrations, suggestions for covering problem issues, 12 discussion questions and 30 multiple-choice test items.

The *Student Study Guide*, by Francis C. Dane of The State University of New York — Oswego, organizes each text chapter for the students and helps them retain the subject matter. Each Study Guide chapter contains a list of key terms, 10 short answer questions, two exercises to demonstrate principles, a practice test of 25 multiple-choice questions and challenge material designed to show different methods to analyze results.

Louise H. Kidder
December, 1980

Acknowledgements

There are several circles of friends and colleagues whose help I want to acknowledge. The first are colleagues who agreed to serve as an Advisory Committee, giving time and assistance without ever having to attend any meetings. Each member of the advisory group read and commented on at least one chapter. They are Charles Atherton, Leonard Bickman, Howard Becker, Marilynn Brewer, William Brown, David Elesh, Eugene Erikson, David Kenny, Jeanne Marecek, Clara Mayo, John McCarthy, Richard McCleary, Joseph McGrath, Ralph Rosnow, Jeffrey Rubin, Jack Sawyer, Claire Selltiz, Harry Triandis, Lawrence Wrightsman, and Robert Wyer. Their work is felt on every page.

I am particularly indebted to four members of this group. Marilynn Brewer and Jeff Rubin read every word I wrote and most of the words I rewrote, and without their gentle prodding, concern, and criticism I would not have finished my work. They did this in their capacity as co-chairpeople of the publications committee for SPSSI and as friends and advisors. Larry Wrightsman and Len Bickman read through the entire manuscript in their capacity as past and present presidents of SPSSI.

Readers who were not members of the Advisory Committee also gave me the benefit of their reactions. They are George Balch, Thomas Berndt, Charles Judd, David Kipnis, Joan McCord, Neil McGuffin, Jerome Singer, and John Sweeney. And two classes of research students, taught by Jerry Greenberg and Rob Folger, gave feedback from the users' perspective.

Three mentors led me to the point of writing about research methods. Philip Brickman suggested I do it, and Howard Becker and Donald Campbell earlier had taught me how. Most of what I know about research methods and social science I learned from these three teachers.

Many people participated in the development of this edition at Holt, Rinehart and Winston. I thank Dan Loch, my Acquiring Editor at Holt, for his over-all supervision of *Research Methods*. Lauren Bahr, my Developmental Editor, paid close attention to each step in the progress of the manuscript toward a finished book. My special gratitude goes to Arlene Katz, who saw the book through the day-to-day nitty-gritty of production under the pressure of a tight schedule. Others at Holt who deserve credit include Rene Davis for her talented design efforts and Pat Sarcuni for his careful shepherding of the manuscript during composition, printing, and binding.

My families enabled me to do this work. In addition to giving me good counsel and support, they gave me expert advice. My father, Erasmus Hoch, gave me a careful reading of the chapter on "Reliability and Validity" and nourished my early interests in psychology and writing. My husband, Bob Kidder, read numerous chapters from a sociologist's perspective and gave me good examples. My mother, Catherine Hoch, and my children, Graham and Charin, showed me how to put the book in perspective and put it aside on occasion. To all of them I am thankful.

L.H.K.

Contents

Ethical Implications **365**

Appendix: An Introduction to Sampling **418**

part 1

Design

Exploring the Social World

THE PLAN OF THE BOOK
Design
Measurement
Results

VALIDITY AND RELIABILITY IN RESEARCH DESIGNS
Internal Validity
Construct Validity
External Validity
Reliability

THEORIES AND HYPOTHESES
Hypothesis Testing and Hypothesis Generating
Scientific Theories and Superstitious Beliefs
Testing Competing Theories

ON PRACTICING SCIENCE

SUMMARY

We invite you to explore the social world in new ways. Research methods in social relations can extend your vision to see the causes behind events, the meanings behind actions, and the social organization behind group activities. The research methods you choose will determine what you see because each method charts a different route and reveals different relationships. Research methods are as different from one another as are modes of transportation. Crossing the country on foot, in a car, or by plane — each gives you a different perspective on what the country looks like. Air traffic routes, highways, and footpaths are ways of traversing the country in very different styles, and they do not all lead to the same places. Some places can be reached only by foot; others are more accessible by car or plane. So too with research methods. Each provides a different perspective on the social world, and some aspects of the social world can be reached with only one method.

Our goal is to familiarize you with a variety of research methods so that you can choose methods most appropriate for the explorations you plan. The first section of the book introduces you to various modes of designing research. The second section introduces various methods of measuring the characteristics you choose to study. The third describes how to assemble, analyze, and write about the results, as well as how to address the ethical issues that accompany research from start to finish.

THE PLAN OF THE BOOK

Design

We introduce four modes of designing research: experiments, quasi experiments, surveys, and participant observation. Each is useful in a different setting and is best suited to answer a different type of question. Experiments are designed to answer questions about causes and effects. They require the experimenter to exercise control over what happens to whom. Experimenters randomly assign people or other units such as classes of students to different conditions and measure the effects of the treatment.

Quasi experiments are designed to answer questions about causes and effects in settings where experiments cannot be done. A researcher who cannot randomly assign people to treatment conditions can design a quasi experiment to determine whether a treatment has an effect.

Surveys can be designed to answer questions about relationships, including cause and effect relationships, but they are better suited to answer questions of fact and description. A researcher who wants to learn factual details such as what percentage of voting age people in the United States oppose the construction of nuclear energy plants can do so with a survey.

Participant observation is useful for studying social organization in settings ranging from small groups to large institutions. A researcher may use participant observation to study a street corner group or a city bureaucracy. It is useful for learning how groups form and function and how people learn to play roles.

We have a fifth chapter on evaluation research, which is not a different research method because evaluation researchers can use any of the other four modes. Evaluation research differs from the others in that it is purposely applied research, undertaken to determine whether social programs are working as they should. Evaluation research has a direct connection with social policy and political decisions, and therefore it raises some unique questions about whose interests are served and whose point of view should be represented in the research design.

In spite of the fact that each mode of designing research has its own forte, we examine how each method handles causal analysis, traditionally the forte of experiments. All of the nonexperimental methods are also used to study cause-effect relationships, and researchers often have cause-effect questions in mind when they conduct any study. For these reasons, we have made causal analysis a theme in all of the chapters on research design even though that is not the main purpose of every method. We begin our discussion of research design in Chapter 2 with true experiments, and in subsequent chapters we compare each method with true experiments. We could have proceeded in the opposite direction, beginning with participant observation and making participation and rapport the central themes. Had we done that, we could have examined the quality of the researchers' participation with the people they study in each of the other research methods. However, rather than carry that theme through every chapter on research design, we have reserved it for the concluding chapter on ethics.

We introduce you to this variety of research techniques so that you can become adept at exploring the social world in numerous ways. We give equal time to the different approaches — from the "hard" quantitative experimental methods to the "soft" qualitative participant observation methods. If, on occasion, it sounds as though we are selling one method as superior to the others, that signals our enthusiasm for the method under discussion rather than a disdain for other methods. We could have tried to erase all shows of enthusiasm, but that would have made a bland book. You should, therefore, read enthusiasm as an endorsement of the method under discussion and not an indictment of other methods.

Measurement

We introduce three general techniques for measuring characteristics of the social world: direct questionnaires and interviews, indirect assessments, and observational and archival measures. Each has a different set of procedures for measuring characteristics of people or social groups, but they must all meet the same requirements of good measurement: reliability and validity. Reliable measures are repeatable and consistent. Valid measures are accurate representations of the characteristic they are intended to tap.

Measuring characteristics of the social world is like shooting an arrow in the dark at a moving target. The targets are abstract concepts, so we cannot see the bull's-eye. Archers can demonstrate how accurate their aim is by measuring how far from the bull's-eye the arrow lands. They can demonstrate how reliable their aim is by repeating the shot ten times. Social researchers can measure their accuracy only with reference to other arrows shot in the dark aimed at the same abstract target. They can demonstrate how reliable their aim is by aiming in the same direction a second time; but if the arrow lands in a different location, they cannot be sure whether the target moved or their aim was off. As a way of dealing with what may be moving targets in the dark, the techniques of social science measurement set stringent requirements for what constitutes evidence.

Results

The exploration of the social world continues in the data analysis stage of research. We outline the steps for processing data by computer and for analyzing data by hand. New techniques of exploratory data analysis permit you to ask questions that had not occurred to you when you began designing the research and gathering data. Writing the research report is the last step in your exploration. In choosing what to emphasize and how to explain the patterns you have found, you give final shape to your research.

Throughout the research process ethical issues arise. The question you set out to answer may be value-laden. The methods you use may hurt the people you study. And the results of your research may have implications that please some persons and displease others. Social science research, therefore, is not value-free, and each decision you make can have ethical implications.

The people whose thoughts and behaviors are studied in social research occupy different roles in different studies, so we refer to them by various names. When they are subjected to experimental treatments and observations, we call them "subjects." When they are responding to survey interviews and questionnaires, we call them "respondents." And when they are members of a group whom the researcher studies as a participant observer, we call them "participants." The research methods described in this book treat people in all three manners. Your choice of research methods may depend on how you want to treat people in your research.

In choosing a research method, you select on the basis of what you are equipped to do, where you want to go, and what suits your taste or temperament. In this book we equip you to use a variety of methods. Where you want to go and what methods suit your taste are for you to decide.

VALIDITY AND RELIABILITY IN RESEARCH DESIGNS

Research is valid when the conclusions are true. It is reliable when the findings are repeatable. Reliability and validity are requirements for both the design and the measurement of research. At the level of research design, we examine the conclusions and ask whether they are true and repeatable. At the level of measurement, we examine the scores or observations and ask whether they are accurate and repeatable. In this chapter we discuss the validity and reliability of research designs and conclusions. In Chapter 7 we discuss the validity and reliability of measurements.

There are many ways to classify the validity of research designs and conclusions (Cook and Campbell, 1979; Judd and Kenny, in press; Chronbach, et al., 1972). We have chosen the following: internal validity, construct validity, external validity.

Internal Validity

Research has internal validity when it accurately identifies causal relationships. If you wish to say that one event was the cause of another, you must be able to rule out rival explanations to demonstrate that your conclusion is valid. For instance, if you conclude that a course in English composition improves college freshmen's writing skills, you must demonstrate that they would not have improved naturally during that time simply as a result of becoming older or writing term papers for their other courses. If some other events such as maturation or writing papers in other courses could explain the improvement, your research lacks internal validity because there are other explanations for your outcomes besides the writing course.

Construct Validity

Research has construct validity when it properly identifies or "names" the variables under study. For instance, if you found the remedial composition course improved students' essay writing and if you could rule out maturation and term paper assignments as rival explanations, you would still have to determine whether it was the instruction in composition or the unofficial group therapy that took place when students discussed their writing problems that caused the improvement. Was it the attention to rules of grammar or the attention to the students' fears about not being great writers that was the real cause? To discuss your findings in a theoretically meaningful way, you must be able to say which of these elements of the course produced the effect. The more complex the treatment, the more difficult it is to specify the cause and name the construct involved.

External Validity

Research has external validity when it shows something that is true beyond the narrow limits of your study. If the findings are true not just for the particular time, place, and people in your study but are generally true of other times, places, and people, your research is externally valid. Most psychological research is conducted with college students as subjects, yet the results are not intended to be true only of college students. For instance, research on the effects of noise on people's ability to solve problems was conducted with college students because they were a convenient population, but the results of that research were supposed to be true of all people (Glass and Singer, 1972). The experimenters believed the disruptive effects of uncontrollable noise are a human phenomenon, not limited to college students or to the particular college students they recruited for their study.

External validity requires that the conclusions be true not only across people but also across conditions. When Glass and Singer studied the effects of noise on cognitive performance, they wished to extend their findings not to similar noise conditions in other laboratories, but to many forms of "urban stress." They used noise as a "convenient device for studying antecedents and consequences of analogues of urban stressors" (Glass and Singer, 1972, p. xii). How reasonable is it to generalize from their laboratory studies of the effects of noise on college students' cognitive performance to the effects of urban stress? We can make a subjective assessment of the external validity of research by examining the procedures and the subject population and deciding whether it seems "reasonable" to generalize the research findings beyond the particular people and procedures of that study. But what seems reasonable to one judge may seem unreasonable to another. The only way we can objectively assess external validity is to see if the results can be repeated in another time and place with different people and procedures. The more variations in places, people, and procedures a piece of research can withstand and still yield the same findings, the more externally valid the conclusions. External validity is similar to reliability. We demonstrate both by repeating or replicating findings.

Reliability

Reliable research findings are repeatable: the conclusions can be generalized beyond the particular conditions in the initial research. To show that research is reliable, we must show that it can be repeated or replicated. However, scientists are seldom rewarded for simply repeating research, either their own or someone else's. Faithful replications are less creative and interesting than are new discoveries; consequently, researchers find it difficult to publish or recieve recognition for work that replicates previous research.

The less a piece of research looks like a mere repeat or exact duplication of previous work, the more interesting it becomes. Research that repeats the *ideas* or *concepts* rather than the procedural details of previous studies serves two purposes. It provides some new discoveries about another set of events, and it provides a *conceptual replication* of previous ideas. Of course, the less similar the two studies are, the less sure we can be that one is a replication of the other. For instance, in Chapter 2 we describe a laboratory experiment and a field experiment that were not intended to duplicate one another but that in fact reached similar conclusions. The laboratory experiment was a study of the effects of uncontrollable versus controllable noise on college students' ability to solve puzzles. The field experiment was a study of the effects of uncontrollable versus controllable visits by strangers on the physical and mental health of residents in a home for the elderly. These studies differ in every detail, but their findings and conclusions are similar. They found people who could predict or control what would happen to them did better than people who could neither predict nor control. Without having been designed to duplicate one another, these studies are conceptual replications. Both demonstrate that people benefit from having control over events in their lives.

Replicating a finding in a different setting and with different procedures is the same as demonstrating that the research has external validity and can be generalized across different people, places, or conditions. Exact replications of procedures and results demonstrate that the results are reliable. Conceptual replications of ideas and conclusions demonstrate that the research is externally valid.

THEORIES AND HYPOTHESES

A theory is a large body of interconnected propositions about how some portion of the social world operates; a hypothesis is a smaller body of propositions. Hypotheses are small versions of theories. Some are derived or born from theories. Others begin as researchers' hunches and develop into theories. For instance, a theory that was at one time popular in social psychology, cognitive dissonance theory, states that people try to reduce dissonance when it arises in their experiences. Dissonance arises when a person has contradictory beliefs, or behaves in a way that contradicts personal values, or makes a decision without being convinced it was the right decision. In these and other instances where there are contradictions in a person's life, dissonance theory states that the person will change one or more beliefs or values to remove the contradiction.

This theory makes reasonable and seemingly obvious assertions. Some of the hypotheses it has spawned are less obvious, more counterintuitive. One hypothesis is that people who are offered a small sum of money to make speeches opposed to their own attitudes will change their attitudes more than people offered a large sum. This hypothesis is derived from the theory as follows. If a person makes a counter-attitudinal statement and receives a large payment for doing so, she can justify her statement by the payment, saying, "I did it for the money," and walk away from the speech holding onto her original attitudes. If, however, she makes statements that contradict her attitudes for very little payment, she cannot justify her behavior in terms of the payment. She experiences a contradiction between her behavior and her attitudes and reduces the dissonance by changing her attitudes.

The hypothesis that small rewards for counterattitudinal behavior produce more attitude change than large rewards has been tested in many experiments, and most times the prediction has been borne out. Does this mean the hypothesis is true? And if this and other hypotheses derived from cognitive dissonance theory are "true," does that make the theory true? Not necessarily. Scientific method has a conservative bias that makes it impossible to verify hypotheses and theories or conclude that they are definitely true. It is possible only to disconfirm hypotheses and theories and conclude that they are false. We cannot say that we have verified a theory because there is always the possibility that some future research will disconfirm it or that some other theory will account for the same results. Theories, therefore, are always tentative. They represent the best of our knowledge for the time being but they do not represent some absolute truth. They await revision or replacement.

Hypothesis Testing and Hypothesis Generating

Hypotheses are used differently in the various research methods. Experimentation is primarily a hypothesis-testing method. Experimenters derive a hypothesis from a theory, design an experiment, and gather data to test the hypothesis. Participant observation is primarily a hypothesis-generating method. Participant observers record their observations and begin to create hypotheses and develop a theory to explain the data. Hypothesis testing is called *deductive* research; hypothesis generating is called *inductive* research. The former proceeds from hypotheses to data; the latter, from data to hypotheses. In practice, researchers often do both. Experimenters may test some of the hypotheses they began with but then develop new hypotheses when they see their data. Participant observers create hypotheses from their data, but they also began their data collection with some hunches that serve as hypotheses to guide their work. Quasi-experimenters and survey researchers begin their work with hypotheses, but through exploratory data analysis they also generate hypotheses (see Chapter 13.) Seldom is research purely deductive or purely inductive.

Hypotheses are almost inevitable in scientific research. Even if you set out to do purely exploratory research, not guided by any known theory, you will probably find yourself generating and testing hypotheses. By simply poking at elements in the social world, you are testing some rudimentary hypothesis of the "if . . . then" form. Your choices of what to poke and what to look at to see the effects of the poke are based on hypothetical reasoning such as the following: "If someone repeatedly cries 'Wolf!' bystanders will stop reacting." Simple observations also frequently have rudimentary hypothetical reasoning behind them. For instance, if you watch people in a singles bar enter alone or with a friend of the same sex and then leave with a partner of the opposite sex, you may begin to observe patterns. You may become adept at predicting which people are likely to find a new partner or even which partner or type of partner someone is likely to choose. Perhaps you base your predictions on dress styles or height or hair styles. Your observation of a pattern can translate into some hypotheses about similarity and attraction or about nonverbal communication. Whether stated formally or not, hypotheses enter into almost all research.

Scientific Theories and Superstitious Beliefs

The philosophy of science decrees that we can only falsify, not verify, theories because we can never be sure that a given theory provides the best explanation for a set of observations. In practice, however, scientists are often reluctant to discard a cherished theory. If they have prior data that support a theory, they do not consider the theory falsified the first time they or someone else fails to replicate the results. Instead, they point to procedural flaws in the replication effort and say that, given a fair test, the theory will again be supported. They may be right.

Superstitious beliefs often have the same tenacity and immunity to disproof. Rather than say the belief was wrong, the believer says the circumstances were not right. The following story from a collection of *Letters of an Indian Judge to an English Gentlewoman* (1978) illustrates such faith. The letter writer was working as a judge for the British government in Burma when the Burmese began a rebellion against the British. Among the rebels were young boys who went to battle wearing charms to protect them from harm. The vendors of the charms gave the boys a trial demonstration:

> . . . after binding the spells upon these youths' arms, it is the custom for the vendors of this uneasy magic to fire at them three or four times from a blank-cartridge pistol, after which the initiate, seeing he is unhurt, is imbued with a great courage [*Letters of an Indian Judge to an English Gentlewoman*, 1978, p. 122].

Equipped with their charms, tin helmets, and spear tips made from Burma oil cans, the young rebels rode their ponies into battle against Britsh policemen armed with guns. One of the youths who was shot and lying in the hospital still clung to the belief in his charms. He explained why:

> "In my case, the medicine was not good. There was something amiss. Perhaps I bound on my charms on a date that was inauspicious. The others," he said, "they are gun and knife proof. You shall see." [*Letters of an Indian Judge to an English Gentlewoman*, 1978, p. 123].

The vendors had previously demonstrated that the charms worked. This one failure to replicate those effects did not weaken the youth's belief. He found a procedural flaw in the replication—the charm was tied on on an inauspicious date. The youth was committed to a cause, and he had few other resources with which to fight, so he clung to his belief in spite of the evidence. Scientists sometimes also cling to beliefs or theories in spite of the evidence because they, too, have commitments. Their commitments may not be political causes but personal investments in research careers. Therefore, they do not always follow the rule that says data can falsify but not verify theories. A failure to replicate is not always taken seriously, and theories survive many such failures.

Testing Competing Theories

Rather than test a single theory at a time, it is better to pit competing theories against one another. If theories make different predictions, data can falsify the theory whose predictions are not borne out. It is rare to find theories that make clearly competing predictions, but this is the ideal way to proceed. The following hypothetical illustration shows how data can falsify one theory when two theories make competing predictions.

An experiment that we discuss in more detail in Chapter 6 was conducted to see whether a delinquency prevention program would have beneficial effects. According to one theory (we can call it the "optimistic theory"), the results of the program should have been positive; boys who received special counseling, summer sports programs, and guidance from professional social workers should have done better as adults than boys who received no special attention. According to a competing theory (the "labeling theory"), the results of the program should have been negative; boys who were assigned to the special services would get into more trouble and have dimmer futures than boys who were left alone because the boys in the program were labeled as needy. The label would convey to them that they were inadequate and become a self-fulfilling prophecy.

The results showed few differences between the two groups after they reached adulthood, but each of the differences that did appear was negative. Men who had been in the treatment program had more serious criminal records, poorer health, and lower occupational standing than those who had not been treated. This finding disconfirms the optimistic theory. Does it mean the labeling theory is correct? Not necessarily. The results may be accurate and reliable but the explanation may be wrong. The men may have suffered not because they were labeled but because the program gave them unrealistic expectations about what life would hold (McCord, 1979). The unsolicited help that they received as boys may have led them to expect that the world was full of kindly counselors; but that was true only for the duration of the experiment. That is a rival explanation, which we call the "theory of unrealistic expectations." There are others, too, that can explain the same outcome. The men in the treatment program may have suffered because they did not learn how to control what would happen to them. The help they received was unsolicited; they did not learn to request help or to compete for services. By being handed help or given a free lunch, they did not learn how to take control. This is another possible explanation which we call the "theory of control."

Because each of these three alternative theories makes the same prediction and explains the same results, we cannot accept the original labeling theory. We can only reject the optimistic theory because it made competing predictions that were not borne out. To test and choose among theories, we must pit competing theories against one another. We could not test the labeling theory and the theory of unrealistic expectations and the theory of control with the data from the delinquency prevention program because they make compatible rather than competing predictions.

To reject one or more of these theories, we must design another study in which they make opposite predictions.

Science progresses by rejecting false ideas and providing tentative support for the ideas that have survived current tests. Theories can be proved wrong; they cannot be proved correct; but they are considered innocent until proved otherwise.

ON PRACTICING SCIENCE

Practicing science is one of many ways of exploring the social world. Practicing art and practicing religion are other ways. Why learn research methods and why practice science?

One reason is to be able to *predict* correctly how people or nations will behave, to foresee the future. In 1948 political forecasters tried to predict who would be elected President of the United States, and they were wrong. They conducted a survey of a sample of voters, but they erred in their research methods; they drew their sample from a telephone directory, and, as it turned out, people with telephones were not representative of the voting population at large. The telephone directory sample said they would vote for Thomas E. Dewey; the people who went to the polls elected Harry Truman instead. Social and political forecasters can usually predict the future more accurately than can crystal ball gazers or palm readers, but to do so they must use correct research methods.

Another reason to learn research methods and practice science is to *understand* how the social world works by discovering the causal connections. Crystal ball gazers make predictions, but they do not usually give causes for events. They do not develop theories about causes and effects and are not interested in providing workable frameworks so that their customers can make predictions themselves. Their work is secret—only *they* can see into the future in inexplicable ways. Much of social science research is carried out not only to foresee the future but also to provide explanations that make the causal links clear. The goal is to demystify. We understand how something works when we can both predict what will happen and explain why. The causes of social behavior may be human intentions, or they may be forces beyond the human will. Natural disasters, social structures, and the distribution of wealth or power are also causes of social behavior. Discovering cause-effect relationships is best done with scientific methods.

A third reason for practicing science is to learn how to *control* events. Most of our existing institutions are set up to control human behavior—schools, prisons, hospitals, and factories are all arranged to control their occupants. Many of the consequences are unintended and even undesired, but they are still under the control of the institution. Some social science is practiced to learn how to control and produce intended effects.

Science does not have a monopoly on prediction, understanding, and control. Religious prophets make predictions, religious texts present a different way of understanding, and religious leaders try to control their followers. Practicing science does not guarantee that the end product—the prediction, understanding, or control—will produce the greatest good for the greatest number of people, but neither does religion. Each can be used to serve various interests. What science can promise is that the outcome will be the most accurate mapping of the empirical world that can be achieved with our current state of theories and methods. Whether you like that mapping and whether it serves your interests are separate questions, answered by you and not by scientific methods.

SUMMARY

We began by saying that research methods provide various ways of exploring the social world. Our goal is to make you versatile in these ways so that you can choose a method or methods appropriate to the question you ask and the manner you prefer. If you pursue research beyond the end of this book, you may find that you will change the kinds of questions you ask and the methods you prefer. You can experiment with the use of research methods themselves. By becoming versatile now, you need not follow a single path. Do not claim allegiance to one method because no one is best. Each has its forte, and you will find each useful for exploring a different terrain and reaching a different destination. Hiking on footpaths can delight your senses and let you discover life you have never seen before, but driving is sometimes necessary, and flying may be the most sensible way to cover great distances. So, too, with research methods.

Causal Analysis and True Experiments

CONTROLLING AND MANIPULATING VARIABLES

RANDOM ASSIGNMENT

INTERNAL VALIDITY AND THE PROBLEM OF RIVAL EXPLANATIONS

EXAMPLES OF TRUE EXPERIMENTS
A Laboratory Experiment
A Field Experiment

INDEPENDENT AND DEPENDENT VARIABLES
Experimental Versus Correlational Studies

EXPERIMENTAL DESIGNS
Design 1. Randomized Two-Group Design
Design 2. Before-After Two-Group Design
Design 3. Solomon Four-Group Design
Design 4. Factorial Design
Repeated Measures Designs: One Solution to the Numbers Problem

THE STRENGTHS AND WEAKNESSES OF TRUE EXPERIMENTS

SUMMARY

True experiments are highly specialized tools, and, like any tool, they are excellent for some jobs and poor for others. They are ideally suited for the task of causal analysis. No other method of scientific inquiry permits the researcher to say with the confidence of an experimenter, "This caused that to happen." In reading scientific reports, you find many guarded, qualified, and indirect causal statements such as "X seems to be a factor in determing Y" or "it would appear that there is a relationship between X and Y." The conclusions sound indirect and the words carefully chosen because the writers cannot make definitive causal assertions. They cannot make bold causal statements if they have not conducted true experiments.

We do not intend this chapter to stand as a tribute to true experiments, for they have their weaknesses. We point out their strengths and their weak points and show how they differ from other research approaches. The chief strength of true experiments is their internal validity. The greater the control an experimenter has, the greater the internal validity of the experiment. The same feature that promotes internal validity can jeopardize external validity. The more control an experimenter has over the subjects and the many variables that could influence the results, the more unnatural the study. Maximum control approximates an isolated laboratory with research conducted in a vacuum. The more the experimental conditions differ from real-life situations, the more difficult it is to generalize the results to naturally occurring social processes, and the lower the external validity of the research. Let us examine what it means to have control in an experiment.

CONTROLLING AND MANIPULATING VARIABLES

All research requires the manipulation or measurement of **variables.** Variables are qualities the researcher wants to study and draw conclusions about. For instance, if you want to study people's political behavior and understand why they vote as they do, their votes are a variable you must measure. *Variables*, as the name suggests, must vary and have at least two values. Therefore, to understand people's political party preference, you must study people who vote for at least two different candidates or parties. If everyone in your study said he or she would vote for Barbara Jordan for president, you would no longer have a variable. For most research, you have not just one but two variables, and you look at the relationship between the two. For instance, in a study of voting behavior, you could include people's religion as a second variable and examine the relationship between religion and voting preference. Political scientists and polling organizations already know a lot about the relationships between religious preference and political party preference and can often predict which candidate will win in which districts because they know the religious makeup of different parts of a city or state. Clearly there are many other variables besides religion that influence how a person will vote. A person's education, parents' party preference, income, and attitudes about specific issues such as abortion or gun control also determine how that person will vote. If you wanted to be able to *predict* people's votes, you would try to include as many of these variables as possible in your research. If, on the other hand, you wanted to understand the influence of a single variable, to see whether it affects voting, you would try to *control* all the other variables. The former is the strategy of survey researchers. The latter is the strategy of experimenters.

Experimenters ask questions like "what is the effect of televised appearances on people's votes for candidates?" Notice that the question refers to a variable the experimenter can possibly control — televised appearances. Experimenters study variables that either they or someone else can *manipulate* — like the timing or content or amount of televised political advertisements. These are called *experimental variables*. The variables we discussed earlier, such as religion, income, education, and parents' party preference are all variables that people bring with them to a study. These are called *subject* variables, or *organismic* variables. They are properties that people already possess. By contrast, experimental variables are properties that an experimenter can manipulate or expose people to. This is a major difference between experimenting and conducting nonexperimental or quasi-experimental research. Experimenters can control the variables they wish to study the effects of, or they can control who is exposed to those variables.

Experimenters may also control the influence of variables that are extraneous to the purpose of the study. For instance, if you wanted to study the influence of television advertising on voting behavior and were not interested in the effects of education, religion, and parents' party preferences, you could control for the effects of those variables in your experiment in one of two ways.

1. *Hold the other variables constant.* You can turn the variables of religion,

gender, education, and attitudes into constants by choosing only Catholic men with a college education and antiabortion attitudes as participants for your experiments. This approach to controlling other variables is like the approach frequently used in natural science. If you try to study the effects of some varieties of plant food on the growth of plants, you might select a field of white pine seedlings in a particular field in Maine and feed four varieties of plant food to trees in the four quadrants of the field. You have held constant the soil type (we assume the field has the same soil type in its four quadrants), the climate and the plant variety and the season. You know that all of these variables affect how fast plants grow, and you have controlled them in your study by limiting the experiment to one soil type, climate, plant, and season. This is an effective way to study the growing powers of your four varieties of plant food because you know the only difference between plants in the four quadrants is the type of food they received. This experiment has high internal validity — you can say quite confidently that the plant food caused differences in growth if you find differences between the quadrants. By confining your experiment to such a narrow range of conditions, however, you have sacrificed its external validity. You do not know whether the best plant food for white pines would also be best for red oaks or for trees in warm climates. The more you hold such other conditions constant, the lower the generalizability of your results. This technique of controlling other variables maximizes internal validity at the expense of external validity, and you may, therefore, choose not to hold all other variables constant. In the case of studying voting behavior, you could study the effects of television advertising on white, Catholic, college-educated men who opposed abortions if you believed that this group of people would respond to televised political advertisements in the same way as any other group. If, however, you thought they would be influenced in ways different from the larger population to which you wish to generalize, you should not try to control for the influence of religion, education, and the other variables by holding them constant. You should choose the second method instead.

2. *Randomly assign subjects to experimental conditions.* You can conduct an experiment with a heterogenous assortment of people (or plants or voting districts) and still control for the influences of the many extraneous variables those people possess by randomly assigning people to the experimental conditions. We shall refer to the units in experimental studies as "subjects," whether they are people, plants, or collectivities like voting districts. If you include in your study people who differ in education, religion, parent's preferences, and attitudes toward abortion, you can eliminate the influence of those variables by randomly assigning people to your experimental conditions. To compare the effects of different television campaigns — one that interviews the candidate and another that interviews supporters — you can draw the subjects' names out of a hat and assign the first to watch the candidate, the second to watch the supporters, the third to watch the candidate, and so on. Provided you have the names all written on similar slips of paper and have shuffled the slips sufficiently, you have a random assignment procedure as good as any. Random assignment controls for the influence of all the extraneous subject variables that you do not want to study but also do not want to hold constant because holding them constant limits the generalizability of your study. It is the defining feature of a true experiment.

RANDOM ASSIGNMENT

Random assignment is the best way we have of equating two or more groups before an experimental treatment begins. This is essential for making causal inferences about the effects of an experimental treatment because the experimenter must be reasonably confident that the differences that appear at the end of the experiment between two treatment groups are the result of the treatments and not the result of some preexisting differences between the groups.

Random assignment (also called randomization) is not the same as random sampling (also called random selection). **Random assignment** is a procedure you use after you have a sample of subjects and before you expose them to a treatment. It is a way of assigning subjects to treatments so that the groups do not differ before the treatment begins. It is a "fair" procedure, whereby all subjects have an equal chance of being assigned to condition A or condition B. Drawing names out of a hat is the prototype and works as well as more sophisticated techniques such as using a table of random numbers (for example, Myers, 1966) or using a computer-generated list of random numbers. *Random sampling* is the procedure you use to *select* the subjects you will study. Random sampling serves not to equate two or more experimental groups but to make whatever subject group you study representative of a larger population. It is also a "fair" procedure whereby all subjects in a given population (for example, the population of people over 21 living in North America) have an equal chance of being included in the study. Random sampling allows you to say that what you have found in this sample is true of people in the larger population. It maximizes the external validity of research. Random assignment, on the other hand, enables you to say, "X caused Y" with some degree of certainty. It maximizes the internal validity of research. We will not discuss random sampling further in this chapter; it will appear again in the chapter on survey research and the Appendix on sampling. We introduced it here to inform you that it is different from random assignment, and it is the latter that defines true experiments.

To appreciate what random assignment accomplishes and what its limitations are, consider the following experiment. You are hired by a publishing company to determine whether students learn more about research methods from attending lectures or reading a research methods book (the one the publisher is about to put on the market). The publishing company draws a random sample of undergraduate students from across the country, brings them together in your city, and pays them to take part in your study. You, therefore, do not have to worry about the representativeness or cooperation of the students. Your only concern is to determine whether students learn more from a textbook or from lectures. The simplest way to design this experiment is to assign students randomly to one of two conditions: Group T, which will read the textbook and not attend lectures, and Group L, which will attend lectures but not read the textbook. You measure how much they have learned by giving them all the same examination at the end of the semester. Assume for the sake of this example that the examination is an accurate and fair measure of how much people know about research methods.

By randomly assigning students to groups, you assume you have created equivalent groups. This is an assumption rather than a fact or a guarantee because there is a possibility that the groups you created were actually different, just by chance. When you toss a coin ten times, you expect to get five heads and five tails if the coin is unbiased. You know that it is possible, however, to get nine heads and one tail even from an unbiased coin. The chances of this occurring are small, but they exist. The same is true for random assignment to groups. The probability of the groups' being significantly different is small, but it is a probability we must acknowledge. We acknowledge it by reporting the *probability level*, or *p* level, associated with our statistical test performed at the end of the experiment. For instance, if you find the group that read the textbook scored higher on the final examination than the group that only attended lectures, you would report the probability level associated with that difference. Probability levels for statistical tests are reported as $p < .05$ or $p < .01$. These mean that the chance of creating a difference that large through random assignment alone is less than five in 100 or less than one in 100, respectively. Another way to think of this is to imagine you *started* your experiment with people's final examination scores in hand. If you randomly assigned their examination scores to two groups, labelled Group T and Group L, and computed the differences between the averages of those groups, you would find a difference as large as the difference obtained in your true experiment only five times in 100 (at the .05 level) or one time in 100 (at the .01 level). Therefore, random assignment is a rather reliable method for creating equivalent groups; only five times out of 100 would it fail (if we use the .05 level of significance). Of course, generally we do not know for sure whether the particular instance we are studying is one of those five; but most experimenters accept the .05 level of uncertainty. (Chapter 13 discusses this further.) Randomization is the best method we have for creating equivalent groups, even though it is not a 100 percent guarantee. Random assignment enables an experimenter to rule out threats to internal validity, particularly the threat of *selection* differences, as seen in the following discussion.

INTERNAL VALIDITY AND THE PROBLEM OF RIVAL EXPLANATIONS

To illustrate the problems of making causal inferences and maximizing internal validity, we use a hypothetical problem in which you may take the role of the researcher to experience the problems of identifying the real cause of an event. Making causal inferences is what doctors do when they try to diagnose the cause of a patient's discomfort or what detectives do when they identify the cause of a death. The researcher, doctor, and detective must each rule out a list of rival explanations to arrive at the most probable cause. The rival explanations are **threats to the internal validity** of the research proposition.

The problem.   You go to a high school reunion and find your group of high school friends has changed—become more conservative than you remembered. You compare their attitudes with the attitudes of people you now associate with, and they seem decidedly different. What is the cause of the difference between these two groups of friends?

One possibility is that growing older makes people more conservative. This alternative is called *maturation* in a list of threats to validity developed by Campbell and his colleagues (Campbell and Stanley, 1963; Cook and Campbell, 1979). If this is true, it should be true of your current group of college friends, too; have they, too, become more conservative than they were? Without knowing how liberal or conservative your current college friends were three years ago, you do not know what maturation has done to their attitudes and whether it is a plausible explanation.

Another possible explanation is that the changing economic and political climate has made your friends more conservative. This rival explanation is called *history* in the list of threats to validity. If you are sure that those friends and your current classmates began with similar attitudes, you can rule out history as an explanation if the two have been exposed to the same historical trends.

Is it possible that it is not your friends who have changed, but you? If you have changed, your friends would seem more conservative because you have shifted your own attitudes, and you are now measuring their attitudes against your own new standards. This explanation refers to a change in the measuring instrument, or *instrumentation*. To rule out this possibility, you might try assessing the attitudes of other people whom you also knew in the past — your neighbors or relatives. If they all seem more conservative now, it is plausible that it is you rather than they who have changed; but if they seem no different than before, you can rule out instrumentation as the explanation.

Perhaps your high school friends seem more conservative now only because your previous assessment of them came from a time when they were at a peak of liberalism. Were they extreme in their liberalism? If so, there would be no way for them to move but down, in which case their new attitudes do not reflect a real change but a statistical artifact known as *regression toward the mean*.

Understanding regression toward the mean requires an understanding of *correlation*. If two measures are perfectly correlated, it means that the person receiving the highest score on the first measure also receives the highest score on the second measure, that the person receiving the lowest score on the first receives the lowest score on the second, and that each of the other people in between the extremes retains the same position from one measure to the next. It is rare to find this degree of commonality between two measures. More frequently, people shift their positions, and the student who received the highest grade on the midterm exam may receive the second highest grade on the final. The student who received the lowest grade on the midterm is usually not the lowest on the final, and vice versa. Does this mean that the best students become worse over the course of a semester and the poorest students become better? No, it means merely that the instruments we have to measure any variable, including school performance, are imperfect. Some portion of the measurement — in this case, the midterm and final examinations — is irrelevant and introduces errors into our measurement. Therefore, even if the individuals truly remain in their original positions from one test to the next, the measures we obtain show people shifting positions because of measurement error. As a consequence, the correlation between the two tests is not perfect, and we find people whose initial scores were extremely high or low shifting away from those extremes. The highest score can only move down; the lowest can only move up. This is known as *regression toward the mean*, and it produces an apparent rather than real change, called a *regression artifact*. Returning to the study of your high school friends, if your original measure and memory of them came from a time when they were all speaking and acting in an extremely liberal way, they could only seem more conservative on subsequent measures if the measures were not perfect and not perfectly correlated. If you can demonstrate that they were not an extreme group to begin with, you can rule out regression as a rival explanation. (Chapter 5 includes further discussion of regression effects.)

If your original hunch or hypothesis was that going to college makes people more liberal, you must decide whether any of these other alternative explanations is plausible. Causal analysis requires ruling out these other rival explanations or threats to internal validity. One remaining rival explanation that we want to mention here is the possibility that your high school friends and your college friends were simply different types of people to begin with, with different political attitudes even before their educational paths diverged. Because they were not randomly assigned to the college and no-college groups, but rather *selected* their own paths or had their paths selected for them by admissions committees, school counselors, and other advisers, there is no guarantee that they were similar to begin with. Such *selection* effects are serious threats to the internal validity of studies in which there is no random assignment. Whenever people select their own treatments or are selected by others for treatments or end up in different treatment groups by some unknown process instead of by random assignment, we have no assurance that the people in different groups were equivalent to begin with. Chances are they were not because the very fact that they selected or were selected for different treatments indicates that they were different types of people, with different preferences, different abilities, or some other characteristics that made them seem more suitable for one treatment rather than another.

Selection differences appear wherever we study naturally occurring groups. Students in small rural colleges probably differ in important ways from students in big urban universities even before they set foot on their campuses. Any comparison of small college graduates and big university graduates must take this into account — the differences between those graduates may have little to do with the college experience itself and much to do with the preexisting differences between the groups.

By using experimental designs and random assignment of people to conditions, an experimenter can rule out many of these threats to internal validity. Random assignment is particularly effective in ruling out the threat of preexisting *selection* differences. It is not a cure-all, however, and we shall see that even laboratory experiments do not yield airtight causal inferences.

EXAMPLES OF TRUE EXPERIMENTS

To be a true experiment, a study need not be conducted in a laboratory. Experiments can also take place in real-life settings. The two examples we discuss in this section test the same theoretical proposition, one in the laboratory and the other in the field. The theoretical proposition is that people benefit from having a feeling of control over what happens to them and suffer from a lack of control. The settings range from a laboratory, in which everything else is controlled and the experiment is conducted in a social vacuum, to retirement homes, where many events in addition to the experimental treatment affect the subjects.

A Laboratory Experiment

David Glass and Jerome Singer conducted over two dozen laboratory experiments that they have published under the title *Urban Stress: Experiments on Noise and Social Stressors* (1972). They state in the preface that they were not interested in the effects of noise per se: "It is clear that most of our two dozen or so studies center around noise; yet we never considered this a 'noise' book. The use of noise stimuli in our research was simply a convenient device for studying antecedents and consequences of analogues of urban stressors" (p. xii). Noise in the laboratory was a substitute for urban social stressors such as "bureaucratic harassment and arbitrary discrimination" (p. xii). They did not study bureaucratic harassment and arbitrary discrimination directly because they would have lost the experimental control that they had in their laboratories. They wanted to maximize the internal validity of their research, possibly at the expense of external validity. How reasonable is it to generalize from the effects of noise in a laboratory to the other physical and social stressors of urban life? Each reader may have a different judgment about the generalizability or external validity of this research. The researchers themselves were "confident that the model and procedures used in our research apply equally well to all of these domains of study" (p. xii).

They examined the effects of two variations in the noise produced by an electronic noise generator. The first variation was predictability; they exposed subjects to either predictable intermittent or unpredictable intermittent noise. The experimenters measured the listeners' physiological reaction and their ability to solve graphic puzzles after being exposed to the noise. The second variation was perceived control: listeners who perceived they had control could press a button to turn off the noise, though they were encouraged not to use it unless it was absolutely necessary. Another group of listeners had no way to turn off the noise.

These variations represent two different types of control. Being able to predict when the noise will come gives some modicum of control in the sense that you are not taken by surprise. Being able to press a button to turn off the noise gives more control, though in this case the experimenters succeeded in persuading the listeners not to use the buttons. People who had the buttons were actually exposed to as much noise as those without buttons, but the former knew that they could terminate it if they wished. The experimenters called this *perceived* rather than actual control.

The subjects were randomly assigned to treatments—they were not permitted to choose one form of noise presentation over another. The experimenters measured the listeners' physiological reactions and cognitive performance after they were subjected to one of the noise conditions. The physiological measures included palmar sweating, a sign of arousal or anxiety. The cognitive measures included solving graphic puzzles and persistence in working on puzzles that the subjects believed could be solved but that, in fact, were insoluble; persistence was taken as a measure of frustration tolerance. The experimenters also gathered other data, including the listeners' ratings of how irritating, distracting, and unpleasant the noise was.

The unpredictable intermittent noise lowered the listeners' frustration tolerance; they worked for a shorter time at the insoluble puzzles after being exposed to random noise than to predictable noise. There were no effects of the predictable versus unpredictable noise on physiological reactions. Perceived control had an effect, however. Having access to a button to turn off the noise made a difference in both the listeners' physiological reactions and their frustration tolerance. Subjects who had such control sweated less (that is, were less anxious or aroused) and persisted longer on the graphic puzzles. Those subjects also rated the noise as less irritating, distracting, and unpleasant. Glass and Singer (1972) concluded from over two dozen experiments like these that the disruptive and disturbing effects of stress can be reduced if subjects can either predict when the stress will strike or believe they can control it by turning it off if they so choose.

Glass and Singer prefaced their book by saying it is not a book about noise but a book about urban stress. They relied on analogies, however, to study urban stress. Is the laboratory noise a good analogy for the physical and social stressors in cities? And are the physiological measures of palmar sweating and the cognitive performance measures of persistence at insoluble puzzles good analogies of the effects of urban stress? These laboratory procedures are all **operational definitions** of the abstract concepts such as "urban stress," "anxiety," and "frustration tolerance." An operational definition is a procedure used by the researcher to manipulate or measure the variables of the study. All research contains operational definitions of abstract concepts; they are not unique to laboratory experiments. If we were to study urban stress by going to people's neighborhoods and measuring the noise levels and asking them to rate on a scale from 1 to 100 how anxious the noise makes them and how much it affects their frustration tolerance, those measures would also be operational definitions of the more abstract concepts of "stress," "anxiety," and "frustration tolerance." Constructing good operational definitions requires appropriate and accurate procedures to measure and manipulate variables. The art of finding suitable procedures cannot be taught with a set of rules but is acquired by experience. Glass and Singer's use of noises produced in a laboratory to represent physical and social stressors produced in cities is persuasive at least to this author. Their conclusions seem to be generalizable to the world outside the laboratory. The real test of external validity, however, rests on the confirmation of those findings in other settings.

Glass and Singer's experiments have high internal validity. The effects are clearly attributable to their manipulations — to the predictable versus unpredictable noises and the controllable versus uncontrollable noises. Because Glass and Singer assigned subjects to experimental conditions, it is not likely that the effects were produced by *selection* differences (the likelihood is five in 100). Maturation is not a plausible rival explanation because there is no reason to believe that people aged or tired differentially in the different experimental conditions. Nor is *instrumentation* a plausible explanation — the groups did not differ in how or when they were tested. *History* was constant for all of the groups because they were kept in the same laboratory conditions. And *regression toward the mean* can be ruled out because the subjects were not initially selected with extreme tendencies on any of the measures. Normally, we would not even bother to go through this entire list of rival explanations to assess the internal validity of a true experiment. Random assignment and careful control of experimental conditions safeguard against most of these threats to validity.

It is the *external validity* of laboratory experiments that is questionable. The best test of external validity is a replication of a study—a demonstration that the results can be repeated with different subjects, different procedures, and different experimenters.

A Field Experiment

Richard Schulz (1976) conducted a study of the effects of control and predictability on the physical and psychological well-being of people in a retirement home. He did not set out to replicate the Glass and Singer research, and he does not talk about noise or urban stress, but he repeated some of the same ideas. We can, therefore, test the generalizability of Glass and Singer's laboratory research by seeing whether their ideas apply in another setting, an institution for elderly people.

Schulz began his experiment with the premise that "from the very young to the very old and dying, persons strive to control their environments. . . . Typically, however, retirement and old age precipitate an abrupt decline in control. Retirement means the loss of one of the most meaningful sources of instrumental control in life, the work role. . . . In addition . . . many aged individuals experience further declines in their ability to manipulate and control the environment as a result of institution-alization" (1976, p. 563). He asked residents in a retirement home if they would serve in a study of the "daily activities of aged individuals" (p. 566). Forty people agreed, and he randomly assigned them to one of four conditions. He tried to include people in the study who were not in daily contact with one another to prevent them from comparing notes and thereby arousing suspicion or contaminating the results of the study. Three of the four groups were visited by undergraduate students. The students explained that they were interested in getting to know some elderly people because they were taking a course on aging and thought they should get some first-hand experience. They also added that the experimenter thought the residents "might enjoy having someone to talk to." The experimental manipulation was the degree of control the residents had over the timing and duration of the visits. There were three variations and a fourth comparison group:

1. *Control-visitor group.* These residents controlled both the frequency and duration of the undergraduates' visits. They called the visitors when they wanted them to come and determined how long they stayed. In the initial visit, during which the undergraduates introduced themselves, they ended by saying, "Let me write down my name and phone number for you. If you ever just feel like talking, give me a call and I'll be over."

2. *Predict-visitor group.* These residents knew when their visitors would appear, but they could not control either the occurrence or the duration of the visits. Instead, the visitors told them at the beginning of each visit approximately how long they would stay and informed them by phone when they would visit again. To make these visits comparable to the control-visit group, each visitor in this group was paired with a visitor in the control-visit group and kept a similar visiting sched-ule. Thus, if a resident who could *control* the visitor's appearances requested daily visits of two hours each, Schulz selected a visitor from the *predictable* group to make similar appointments every day for two hours. If another resident in the controlling group requested visits only once a week for one-half hour each, a visitor in the pre-

dictable group followed the same schedule. This ensured equivalent amounts of visiting in the two groups, and the only difference was whether the residents controlled the timing of visits or were simply able to predict when they would occur.

3. *Random-visitor group.* Residents in this condition could neither control nor predict the timing of their visits. They were visited as frequently and for the same length of time as the other residents because each visitor in this condition was also paired with a visitor in the control-visit group and kept the same schedule but did not inform the resident of the time or duration of any visit. The visits were unpredictable from the resident's point of view, with the visitor stopping in unannounced and saying, "I decided to drop by and pay you a visit today."

4. *No-visit comparison group.* These residents had no undergraduate visitors, but they were interviewed at the beginning and end of the study. The interviews measured the residents' health, psychological well-being, and activity level.

The results of Schulz's experiment confirm the idea that having control over one's environment produces physical and psychological well-being. The predict- and control-visitor groups scored consistently higher on the measures of physical and psychological well-being than did the random- and no-visit groups. The control-visitor residents did not show any greater benefits than the predict-visitor residents, however, contrary to the idea that more control causes more well-being. Schulz says this "suggests that the relatively positive outcome of the predict and control groups is attributable to predictability alone."

It is difficult to interpret Schulz's finding of no difference between control and predictability. One of the cardinal rules of experimental research is that negative findings are often uninterpretable because they could be the result of many things — imprecise measurement, weak manipulations of the independent variable, careless procedures. Many negative findings are unreported because it is not clear why there were no differences. When differences between groups do emerge, however, and when there are no plausible rival explanations, the experimenter can conclude the differences were caused by the independent variables. Random assignment and experimental designs enable the experimenter to rule out most rival explanations, and positive findings in true experiments permit the experimenter to say, "This caused that." Schulz's field experiment partially replicates Glass and Singer's earlier laboratory experiments demonstrating that people benefit when they can predict and control events in their environment. This confirmation in another setting adds to the external validity of the laboratory studies.

INDEPENDENT AND DEPENDENT VARIABLES

In true experiments we study the relationship between two types of variables — **independent** and **dependent variables.** Independent variables are the *causes* and dependent variables the *effects*. In Schulz's experiment, the visiting manipulation is the independent variable or cause. It is one variable with four values: controlled visits, predictable visits, random visits, and no visits. If the independent variable had only one value and did not vary, it would be impossible to know if it caused anything. For instance, if Schulz had introduced visitors only in the control-visitor condition and measured the residents' health and psychological well-being after such visits, he would not have been able to conclude anything about the effects of the visits because he would have had nothing with which to compare those residents' reactions. For this reason, an experimental manipulation requires at least one experimental group and one comparison group—thereby creating an independent *variable* because there are two values, treatment and no-treatment.

Schulz used several *dependent* variables or measures of *effects*. He had several measures of health status: number of types of medication used per day, quantity of medication used per day, number of trips to the infirmary per week, and a subjective assessment by the director of the home. He also used several measures of psychological well-being: the residents' reports of how much of the time they felt lonely, how much of the time they felt bored, how happy, hopeful, useful they felt, and the activities director's rating of each person's "zest for life." Each of these measures is a dependent variable that could be influenced by the independent variable.

Experimental Versus Correlational Studies

Experimental research is not the only research in which the investigator tries to study cause-effect relationships. There are many researchers who find it impossible or unethical to assign people to conditions by a flip of a coin and yet would like to study the causes and effects in those situations. For instance, you might believe that the schools people attend determine how much people learn. It is impossible, however, to assign students to school by a flip of a coin except in some very rare instances. The quality of schools and students' academic achievement are related in complex ways, and it is difficult to make a simple cause-effect statement about the two. Most research on the relationship between schools and academic achievement is, therefore, correlational rather than experimental research. The researchers do not manipulate one variable and look at the subsequent effects on another variable. Instead they *measure* both variables and look at the relationship between the two.

The difficulty in making causal assertions with correlational research is that the relationship between the two variables could result from three possibilities:

1. Perhaps the quality of schools determines the students' academic achievement:

Schools → Achievement

2. Perhaps the students' academic achievements (which they get from their parents' training, their reading at home, and other nonschool activities) determine the quality of schools:

Achievement → Schools

3. Perhaps both the quality of schools and the students' academic achievements are determined by other causes, called third variables, such as parents' income and social status:

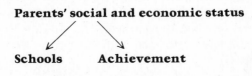

Parents' social and economic status

Schools   Achievement

Deciding which of these possibilities explains the relationship between school quality and academic achievement requires a theoretical model and complex statistical analysis. We will discuss these further in our chapters on quasi-experimental designs and survey research. For now, it suffices to say that when social scientists do nonexperimental research and find a relationship between two variables, they must contend with numerous rival explanations before making their causal statements.

EXPERIMENTAL DESIGNS

We use the following notation to describe different research designs:

X = a treatment, an independent variable, a cause
O = an observation, a dependent variable, an effect
R = a sign that the subjects have been randomly assigned to the treatment conditions.

Design 1. Randomized Two-Group Design

Subjects are randomly assigned to the experimental treatment group (X) or to a no-treatment comparison group (not-X). There is a slight chance that randomization failed and that they would differ on the dependent variable (O_1 and O_2) even if no treatment intervened. This is a small and remote possibility that is taken into consideration in the statistical analysis and the probability or p levels as we mentioned earlier.

This design contains all the bare essentials for an experiment: random assignment, treatment and no-treatment groups, and observations after the treatment. We must have at least two groups to know whether the treatment had an affect, and we must have some assurance that the groups were equivalent before treatment so that we can attribute any posttreatment differences to the experimental treatment. We can rule out several rival explanations or threats to internal validity by using this design. We know the posttreatment differences are not the result of a subject *selection* bias because subjects were randomly assigned rather than personally selected into the two groups. We know the posttreatment differences are not a product of *maturation* because the two groups should have matured (aged, fatigued) at the same rate if they were tested at the same intervals after random assignment.

We can rule out other rival explanations not just by referring to the random assignment but by looking carefully at the experimental procedures to see whether it is plausible that the treatment group might have been exposed to some other events (historical events in the outside world or events within the experimental session) that the no-treatment group did not experience. If not, we can eliminate *history* as a rival explanation. If the two groups were tested or observed under similar circumstances, we can eliminate *instrumentation* differences as an explanation. Once we have eliminated these rival explanations, we can feel reasonably confident that the experimental treatment caused the subsequent difference between the two groups (O_1 and O_2).

Many experimenters use this design or some variation of it, with two or more treatment groups. Glass and Singer's (1972) laboratory studies of the effects of urban stress had this design — but instead of a no-treatment comparison group, they used two alternative treatments: predictable versus unpredictable noise in one set of studies and controllable versus uncontrollable noise in another set. Design 1 is the simplest of the true experimental designs.

Design 2. Before-After Two-Group Design

$$R \begin{array}{ccc} \nearrow O_1 & X & O_2 \\ \searrow O_3 & \text{not-}X & O_4 \end{array}$$

This design has an additional set of tests or observations of the dependent variable called pretests before the experimental treatment. Pretests have several advantages. They provide a check on the randomization and let the experimenter see whether the groups were equivalent before the treatment. If the groups are not equivalent on the pretests, the experimenter can adjust the posttest measures to provide a fairer test of the treatment. Pretests also provide a more sensitive test of the effects of the treatment by letting each subject serve as his or her own comparison. Instead of comparing only O_2 and O_4, the experimenter can compare each subject's pretest and posttest scores (O_1 with O_2 and O_3 with O_4). As subjects' pretest scores all differ from one another and their posttest scores reflect some of these preexisting individual differences, the experimenter gains precision by making these intraindividual comparisons.

To understand the benefits of this pretest design, suppose you and a friend were randomly assigned to different groups in an experiment on weight loss; you were assigned to the no-treatment comparison group and your friend to the weight loss treatment group. If you weigh 130 pounds on the pretest and 130 pounds on the posttest, it is clear that being in the comparison group did not affect your weight. If your friend weighed 160 pounds on the pretest and 150 pounds on the posttest, it is plausible that the treatment caused your friend to lose 10 pounds (assuming we can rule out maturation, history, instrumentation, and all other threats to internal validity). However, if the experimenter did not take pretest measures and looked only at the posttest weights, your friend's 150 pounds compared to your 130 would make the treatment look bad. Therefore, having pretest information in this before-and-after, two-group design gives an experimenter a more precise measure of treatment effects.

The pretest also has some disadvantages, however. It may sensitize subjects to the purpose of the experiment and bias their posttest scores. If this happens for the experimental and control groups alike, their posttest scores should be equally elevated or depressed and pretesting alone would not be a rival explanation for a difference between O_2 and O_4. If however, the pretest affects the treatment group differently from the no-treatment group, this would appear as a difference on the posttest scores and would be indistinguishable from a difference produced by the treatment alone.

Design 2 provides no solution for this problem. Experimenters must, therefore, decide whether this is a plausible occurrence for any particular study, and if it is, they should avoid this design in favor of the simpler Design 1. Schulz (1976) used a variation of this before-after design in his study of the effects of control among retirement home residents. Instead of two groups, he had four, and all had pretests as well as posttests.

$$R \begin{array}{cll} O_1 & X_1 \text{ (control-visitor)} & O_2 \\ O_3 & X_2 \text{ (predict-visitor)} & O_4 \\ O_5 & X_3 \text{ (random-visitor)} & O_6 \\ O_7 & X_4 \text{ (no-visitor)} & O_8 \end{array}$$

The pretests (odd-numbered O's in the preceding diagram) and posttests (even-numbered O's) contained several dependent variable measures: health status, psychological well-being, and activities. The treatments, on the other hand, were all variations of *one* independent variable. Any single independent variable may have multiple values or levels—therefore, the four X's in the preceding diagram represent not four different independent variables but four values of one independent variable called "degree of control over visitors."

Schulz did not find differences between all four groups after the treatment. Instead, he found the first two were similar, and together they had better health than the last two, which were also similar to each other. He concluded that the important beneficial ingredient in degree of control was predictability, for that was what the first two groups had in common. In interpreting his results, Schulz was not bothered by the potential effects of pretesting alone or by the effects of pretesting in combination with the treatments because the pattern of results does not lend itself to either of those interpretations. (Ruling out rival explanations depends on three things: (1) the design of the study, (2) the experimenter's knowledge of what different events (such as intrasession history) the subjects may have experienced, and (3) the pattern of results and whether that particular pattern could plausibly be explained by some events other than the experimental treatments.)

The third design combines Designs 1 and 2. With this design an experimenter can test decisively whether the posttest differences were caused by the treatment, the pretest, or the combination of treatment-plus-pretest.

Design 3. Solomon Four-Group Design

$$R \begin{array}{cll} O_1 & X & O_2 \\ O_3 & \text{not-}X & O_4 \\ & X & O_5 \\ & \text{not-}X & O_6 \end{array} \qquad \begin{array}{c} \textbf{(Design 2)} \\ + \\ \textbf{(Design 1)} \end{array}$$

Design 3 is an expensive design because it requires four groups of subjects to test the effects of only two levels of a treatment. The four groups are needed because in addition to the treatment and no-treatment groups we have pretested and nonpretested groups.

This design offers the separate advantages of Design 1 (no interference from pretesting effects) and Design 2 (greater precision from the pretest scores as base lines against which to measure the effects of the treatment). In addition, it enables the experimenter to see whether the *combination* of pretesting plus treatment produces an effect that is different from what we would expect if we simply added the separate effects of pretesting and treatment. Such combinations, if they are different from the sum of the two individual effects, are called *interaction* effects. They are like what happens when two natural elements combine and interact to produce a new effect — hydrogen and oxygen together produce a new compound, water. The whole is different from or greater than the simple sum of the parts. In many social science problems, interactions are important. We need more than two-group designs to study these and we need more than one independent variable because an interaction results from a combination of two or more causes or independent variables. Designs with two or more independent variables are called factorial designs.

Design 4. Factorial Design

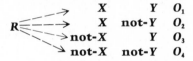

$$
R \begin{cases}
\longrightarrow & X & Y & O_1 \\
\dashrightarrow & X & \text{not-}Y & O_2 \\
\longrightarrow & \text{not-}X & Y & O_3 \\
\longrightarrow & \text{not-}X & \text{not-}Y & O_4
\end{cases}
$$

The X is one independent variable; the Y is another. (In a factorial design, two or more independent variables are always presented in combination.) The entire design contains every possible combination of the independent variables (also known as factors, hence the name, factorial design). If there are more than two independent variables or factors and if each has more than two values, the design rapidly mushrooms because each additional variable or value doubles the number of conditions. We can illustrate this with the following tables, which are the form most commonly used to diagram factorial designs.

Table 2.1 illustrates the combination of two factors or independent variables. In the language of experimental design, we call this a two-by-two factorial design, which means there are two factors and each has two values or levels. If we added a third factor, we would double the number of conditions if the additional factor also had two values, triple it if the new factor had three values, and so on. For instance, if we added the actor's age as another factor and used three age categories — child, adolescent, adult — we would have a 2 X 2 X 3 design, with 12 conditions, shown in Table 2.2. This 12-cell design is much more complex than the original 2 X 2. It is triple the size and, therefore, either requires three times as many subjects or spreads the same number of subjects thinner, with one-third the number in each condition. It also introduces not just one additional factor that may produce effects but three additional interactions.

TABLE 2.1   A 2 X 2 Factorial Design

Factor Y	*Factor X*	
Actor's Behavior	*Actor's Gender*	
	Male	*Female*
Assertive	Assertive Male	Assertive Female
Submissive	Submissive Male	Submissive Female

To describe an interaction, we shall examine a 2 X 2 design like that shown in Table 2.1 (Costrich, Feinstein, Kidder, Marecek, and Pascale, 1975). The actors were confederates of the experimenter — persons who pretended to be regular participants like the subjects but who actually played preassigned parts. Each actor was a member of a discussion group with four to eight other people who were the subjects. An experimenter had instructed the actors to take either an assertive or submissive role in the group discussion, but no one else in the group was aware of this backstage plan. One-fourth of the groups had an assertive male confederate, one-fourth had a submissive male confederate, one-fourth had an assertive female, and one-fourth had a submissive female confederate. At the end of the discussion hour, each member of the group rated each other person on a number of qualities, including their popularity.

TABLE 2.2   A 2 X 2 X 3 Factional Design

Factor Y	*Factor Z*	*Factor X*	
Actor's Behavior	*Actor's Age*	*Actor's Gender*	
		Male	*Female*
Assertive	Child		
	Adolescent		
	Adult		
Submissive	Child		
	Adolescent		
	Adult		

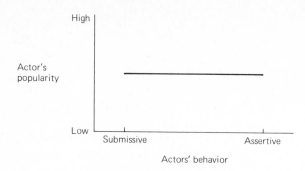

FIGURE 2.1. No effect of actor's behavior on popularity ratings in a discussion group

Notice that the variable Actor's Gender in this study refers not to the subjects who participated but to the stimulus persons whom the subjects rated. This is an important distinction. Subjects' age and gender are characteristics they bring with them rather than experimental conditions to which people can be randomly assigned. The portion of a study that examines such subject variables is, therefore, technically not a true experiment because it does not feature random assignment. The gender of an actor or stimulus person to whom subjects respond is an experimental variable, however, because subjects can be randomly assigned to interact with or observe a male or female actor.

The experimenters combined two independent variables—actor's gender and actor's behavior—because they were particularly interested in the effect of the combination, the interaction. For the sake of simplicity we will disucss only one dependent variable—the observers' ratings of the actors' popularity. The experimenters were not interested in the effects of either the actor's gender or the actor's behavior alone, and they found no overall effects of either of these factors alone as shown in Figures 2.1 and 2.2. Men and women were equally popular, and submissive and assertive actors were equally popular. But the actor's gender *in combination with* his or her behavior did affect the popularity ratings. Assertive men and submissive women were popular; submissive men and assertive women were unpopular. The interaction is diagramed in Figure 2.3.

The horizontal lines in Figures 2.1 and 2.2 show no effect of either the actor's gender or behavior alone. The crossed lines in Figure 2.3 show the **interaction effect.** An interaction effect appears on a graph as a crossover of two or more lines

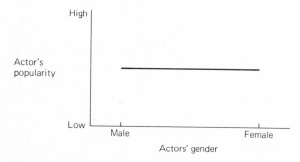

FIGURE 2.2. No effect of actor's gender on popularity ratings in a discussion group

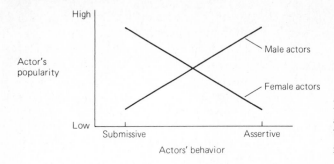

FIGURE 2.3. Effect of the interaction of actor's gender and behavior on popularity ratings in a discussion group

or as a set of nonparallel lines that would cross over if they were extended. An interaction expressed in words rather than graphs appears as a qualified statement. It requires a reference to both independent variables because they work in combination. The interaction shown in Figure 2.3 means that the effect of being assertive or submissive on a person's popularity in a group *depends on* what gender the person is. For men, being assertive causes them to be more popular than being submissive; for women, the opposite is true. When two variables combined produce an effect different from the sum of their individual effects, we call it an **interaction effect.** We could not have arrived at Figure 2.3 simply by summing the effects in Figures 2.1 and 2.2. Neither gender nor behavior alone affected an actor's popularity. The separate effects are called **main effects.** Had men been more popular than women, or vice versa, this would have been a *main effect* of gender; or had submissive actors been more popular than assertive actors, it would have been a *main effect* of behavior. Neither of these main effects was significant, but the *interaction* of actors' gender and behavior produced marked effects.

Interaction effects require more complex theoretical explanations than main effects. In the preceding example, the explanation for the interaction introduces a new concept: out-of-role behavior. Both men and women are less popular in groups if they violate the stereotypes of their gender and step out of role (Costrich, et al., 1975). The researchers designed this study because they had a hunch that out-of-sex-role behaviors would cause people to be less well-liked. They used a factorial design because they were specifically interested in the combined effects of gender and assertiveness. One reason to use factorial designs is to look for interaction effects. Another reason is to be able to generalize the effects of one variable across several levels of another variable. For instance, if you wanted to study the effects of being able to control noise (Variable 1) on people's ability to solve puzzles, you might vary the type of puzzle as a second independent variable. This would enable you to demonstrate that people perform better on not just one but two types of puzzles (Variable 2) when they can control the noise in their environment. You add the second variable not because you expect it to make a difference but to demonstrate that it makes no difference. A third reason to include more than one independent variable in an experiment is to study the separate effect of that variable. You may design a factorial study even if you expect to find only two main effects and no interaction.

Factorial designs, with two or more independent variables, therefore, have several advantages over single factor designs. They permit the investigator to discover interactions as well as main effects. And if there are no interactions, they enable the researcher to generalize the main effect of one factor across two or more values of another factor. If we were interested in the effects of assertiveness training on career advancement, we might not expect any interaction between assertiveness training and the trainee's race, age, or gender; but it would still be wise to include trainees of more than one sex, race, and age. Only then could we generalize and draw conclusions about the effects of assertiveness training that are not limited to men or whites or young people. If we included only young white men in the study, we would not know whether the results hold true for others.

In the past, some social science theories that were thought to be true of people in general were, in fact, true of only one group. For instance, much of the early research on achievement motivation predicted achievement behavior in men but not in women (McClelland, et al., 1953). Only later did researchers point out that the same laws did not explain women's behavior (for example, Alper, 1974). Subsequent research showed that women sometimes feared success, something McClelland had not predicted (for example, Horner, 1972). More recent research, varying both the gender of the subjects and the gender-appropriateness of the task, has found both men and women fear for someone who succeeds at a task that is generally reserved for a person of the opposite sex (Monahan, Kuhn, and Shaver, 1974). Both men and women fear the consequences of violating sex-role stereotypes. Only when the gender of the subjects and the gender-appropriateness of the tasks were included as variables in the research design could the researchers discover these effects. Note that age and race of the subjects were not included as factors. To know whether black as well as white and old as well as young people avoid opposite-sex-labeled tasks, researchers must include these factors as independent variables.

Let us imagine an experiment that included all of these as independent variables. We would have a five-factor design with 32 conditions. We have not drawn the 32-celled table here because it would fill an entire page. You can either imagine or draw a 2 X 2 X 2 X 2 X 2 table, with Age, Race, Sex of Subjects, Sex Appropriateness of Task, and Success versus Failure as the five independent variables, appearing in all possible combinations.

A design of these proportions becomes unwieldy in several respects. It requires a large number of subjects. A rule of thumb for factorial designs is to have a minimum of five subjects per cell. (You shall see in the chapter on statistics and data analysis that the ideal number of subjects depends on several other features of a study, but as a simple rule of thumb we can use the number five.) A 32-cell design, therefore, requires a minimum of 160 subjects. The design also becomes unwieldy in the data analysis. It produces not only five main effects (one for each independent variable) but also ten two-factor interactions (the interaction of age and race, age and sex, race and sex, and so on), six three-factor interactions (the interaction of age, race, and sex; another interaction of age, race, and sex appropriateness of task; another of age, race, and success; and so on), three four-factor interactions, and one five-factor interaction. No investigator would either predict or be prepared to explain all 25 effects. Therefore, it is not practical to include all possible combinations of all these independent variables. Any single experiment would be unwieldy if it included all five independent variables in a factorial design, yet all five should be studied. Chapter 4 on survey research shows how five variables like these are often included in surveys.

Repeated Measures Designs: One Solution to the Numbers Problem

Repeated measures designs are also called *within-subjects* designs. Rather than assign different people to different treatments, the experimenter exposes the same persons to multiple treatments. Each subject is repeatedly treated and tested, and the variations caused by different treatments appear within the same person's performance rather than between different groups of people.

The independent variables we have presented in the preceding examples are of two types: manipulated variables and subject variables. Manipulated variables are designed by the experimenter, and any subjects can be randomly assigned to manipulated treatments. Subjects can be randomly assigned to groups with assertive or submissive confederates; they can be randomly assigned to work on sex-appropriate or sex-inappropriate tasks; they can be randomly assigned to receive visitors whose visits are predictable or unpredictable. Subject variables, on the other hand, come with the subject, such as age, height, personality traits, gender, race, and so on.

Subject variables impose restrictions on research design as well as analysis because they cannot be used as within-subjects or repeated measures factors. It is a rare and ingenious researcher who can have the same group of subjects experience being both old and young or both male and female or both black and white. If an experimenter could do this, it would mean that these subject variables had become manipulated variables. A white novelist did this as a personal experiment (Griffin, 1962). He used medications to turn his skin dark and wrote about his experiences as a white man and then a black man. People who have undergone surgery to change their gender have also experimented with their own subject characteristics. Aside from these personal experiments, however, we have no instances in which a researcher manipulated such subject variables. Subject variables, therefore, cannot be used as within-subjects or repeated measures factors.

When factors can be varied within-subjects, experimenters can use a design that requires fewer subjects. Repeated measures designs are more efficient because they require fewer subjects and provide more sensitive measures of the effects of a variable. For instance, if we wanted to study how quickly men and women can solve puzzles that are labeled "masculine problem" and "feminine problem," we could study this as a between-subjects or within-subjects design. The subjects' gender is a subject variable and must be a between-subjects factor. The label on the puzzle could be either a between-subjects or within-subjects factor. If it were between-subjects, we would have to recruit 20 subjects for our study, using our rule of thumb that there be five observations in each cell of the design. The 20 observations would come from 20 different people. See Figure 2.4.

We could, however, make the sex-labeling of the task a within-subjects factor and have each subject solve both a "masculine" and "feminine" labeled puzzle. In this case, we would need only ten subjects, five men and five women, to get the same number of observations in each cell because each person would solve two puzzles. See Figure 2.5.

The other efficient feature of repeated-measures designs is the precision gained by using each subject as his or her own comparison. Like the pretest observations of

FIGURE 2.4. Illustration of the number of subjects needed for a between-subjects design

		Sex-labeling of the task	
		Masculine	Feminine
Subjects' Gender	Male	5 Men	5 Men
	Female	5 Women	5 Women

Total = 20 Subjects

the before-and-after, two-group design, the repeated measures give us individual base lines for each subject. The five men who solve the "masculine" puzzle in Figure 2.5 may vary widely in the time they require. One may solve the puzzle in ten seconds and another may take ten minutes. If each person takes one minute longer to solve the "feminine" than the "masculine" puzzle, this would not appear as a noticeable difference between the two puzzle groups if we used a between-subjects design, but it would appear as noticeable in a within-subjects design.

Subject variables cannot be used with repeated measures; not even all manipulated variables are suitable as within-subjects or repeated variables. Some manipulated variables would arouse the subjects' suspicions about the purposes of the experiment. For instance, suppose we tried to use the race or gender of job applicants as a within-subjects variable. If we presented prospective employers with two hypothetical job applications and résumés in which everything was identical except the race or sex of the applicant, the prospective employers could see immediately that we were testing to see if they practice race- or sex-discrimination in hiring. Other variables are not suitable if they produce long-lasting effects that would carry over from one testing to the next. For instance, if we tried to compare the effects of alcohol and hallucinogenic drugs on drivers' reaction times, we would not have them drink a large dose of alcohol, give them a driver's test, and then give them hallucinogenic drugs an hour later for a second test. In addition to the obvious ethical problems of administering drugs to experimental subjects (see Chapter 15 on ethics), we also run into practical problems. If we use repeated measures designs, we must be sure the

FIGURE 2.5. Illustration of the number of subjects required for a within-subjects design

		Sex-labeling of the task	
		"Masculine"	"Feminine"
Subjects' Gender	Male	5 Men --------	------ (5)
	Female	5 Women ------	------ (5)

Total = 10 subjects

effects of the first level of a treatment are gone before we try to administer the second. A third limitation is that we must be careful not to confuse the effects of a treatment with the order in which the treatments are administered. If each subject receives treatment A before treatment B, we cannot tell whether the difference in reactions to the two treatments is a result of the treatments or of their ordering — subjects may show fatigue effects or practice effects by the time they receive the second treatment. Any repeated measures design should include at least two orders: treatment A before B for half the subjects and treatment B before A for the other half.

THE STRENGTHS AND WEAKNESSES OF TRUE EXPERIMENTS

We have emphasized the strengths of true experiments. By randomly assigning people to experimental conditions, experimenters can be reasonably confident that the subsequent differences are caused by the treatments and not preexisting differences among groups of people. Manipulated experimental variables, unlike correlated subject variables, enable experimenters to conclude, "This caused that." No experimenter can be 100 percent sure that "this" experimental treatment was the cause of "that" effect, but experimenters can be surer than most other researchers. Experimental designs and procedures maximize the internal validity of research — they enable the researcher to rule out most rival explanations or threats to internal validity. There is a trade-off, however. Experimenters maximize internal validity often at the expense of the external validity or generalizability of the results. Do the findings extend beyond the laboratory? Can the experimenter talk about these phenomena in the world outside, or are they phenomena that appear only in seemingly sterile conditions?

The main criticism of true experiments is that they are poor representations of natural processes. Babbie (1973) lists three disadvantages of controlled experiments: (1) They provide "an artificial test of the hypothesis. The relevance of the experiment to the real world is always subject to question" (p. 33). (2) They may not be generalizable to other segments of the population. Many psychology experiments use college sophomores as subjects, yet they are not intended to be studies of the psychology of college students but studies of people in general. Unless we repeat those experiments with middle-aged people, noncollege educated people, working people, elderly people, or other segments of the population, we do not know whether the findings are generalizable. (3) Experiments provide no useful descriptive data. For instance, if 20 percent of the people in the treatment group agree with a statement about the usefulness of therapy, this tells us nothing about the percent of people who agree with this statement in the larger population *unless* we have recruited the subjects for our experiment by selecting a *representative sample* from the larger population. In theory, this can be done; in practice it is rare. These are important criticisms, but they are not inevitable condemnations of experimental designs because not all experiments contain these limitations and not all nonexperimental research is beyond reproach on the same grounds.

Some laboratory experiments, like Glass and Singer's studies of noise, use remote analogs of the real world variables, like urban stress. The artificial conditions in those experiments may be more effective ways to study the problem than are some more realistic conditions. For instance, the unpleasant intermittent laboratory noise may produce realistic effects, more like the urban stresses that Glass and Singer want to generalize to, than would intermittent traffic sounds. The latter are realistic but relatively mild, and they may have negligible effects. Glass and Singer wanted to recreate in a short time in the laboratory the same effects that are created over weeks, months, or years of living with unpredictable and uncontrollable urban stresses, including city traffic but also including bureaucratic harassment and the other physical and social stresses of urban living. They chose laboratory-generated noise not because they thought it sounded like urban stressors but because they thought it would produce the effects of urban stress, condensed in a short time and a small space. The laboratory noise and laboratory measures of physiological and cognitive effects are all substitutes for the real phenomena — they are analogs and, therefore, artificial. Being artificial is not necessarily a disadvantage, however. Some laboratory analogs are more effective than their realistic but mundane counterparts and, therefore, make the research more persuasive.

Field experiments are less likely to seem artificial. Schulz's study of residents in a retirement home introduced experimental variations that were not part of the daily routine in the home and in that sense may seem artificial, but having visitors is a normal occurrence in retirement homes, and the only abnormal feature was that these visitors had been asked to go there by the researcher. Even this is not entirely artificial, however, because social agencies and volunteer organizations also send visitors to rest homes, hospitals, and other institutions. How generalizable any treatments and effects are can be discovered only by trying to replicate the findings in another setting.

The second criticism of experiments questions the representativeness of the research subjects. Are college students representative of the larger population? For some research questions, yes; for others, no. For much psychological research college sophomores are no different from anyone else. For instance, to study the effects of a variable like amount of piano practice on level of performance in a piano recital, we can assume that what is true for 18-year-old college students is also true of six-year-old elementary school students and 40-year-old workers. To study the effects of a more socially situated variable, however, like politicans' campaign styles, on people's support for candidates, we would be wise to include a more heterogenous group of people than just college students. Or to study the effects of an economic variable like tax incentives for installing solar energy systems, it is necessary to include people with a range of incomes. Often the subjects of research are not individuals but groups or aggregates, such as classrooms, nations, businesses, or price indexes. There are many instances where college sophomores are not the appropriate subjects of a study, but this does not preclude conducting an experiment. If the units, be they classrooms, schools, commercial districts, or housing units, can be randomly assigned to treatment conditions, we can conduct a true experiment.

For many social science questions, the subjects in the research must be more heterogeneous than college students — they must vary in age, income, education, or occupation if these are variables in the research. Sociological research usually raises questions about various groups or types of people — people of different economic, ethnic, educational, and cultural backgrounds. Or, if not different groups of people, sociologists study the effects of different types of situations and social structures. Sociological questions, therefore, cannot usually be studied with college sophomores alone. There is nothing about experimental designs, however, that requires studying college sophomores. Schulz's study of residents in a retirement home was a true experiment with a noncollege population. The only requirment of a true experiment is random assignment; and with manipulable variables, with ingenuity, and with tact, experimenters have been able to use random assignment in many places outside colleges.

The third criticism — that experiments provide no useful descriptive data — like the first two, is often true but need not be. An important difference between experiments and surveys is that surveys contain a random sample of respondents who are *representative* of some larger population. Therefore, if 80 percent of the people in a representative sample say they believe cigarettes cause cancer, we can generalize this to the population. Because the sample is a random selection of people from a population, the distribution of beliefs and preferences in that sample is approximately the same as the distribution in the population. The survey, therefore, provides descriptive data about the population. An experiment, on the other hand, usually does not contain a representative random sample because the purpose of the experiment is not to provide descriptive data about percentages of people in the population who profess certain beliefs. The purpose of an experiment is to provide information about causes and effects.

If an experimenter wanted first to select a random sample of people from a particular population and then randomly assign people in the sample to treatment groups, there is nothing to prevent this. Nothing in the design or logic of experiments would rule against random sampling in addition to random assignment. Experimenters usually have no incentive to select random samples, however, because their purpose is not to describe the frequency with which people say or do one thing versus another. Their purpose is to discover *why* people say or do one thing under some set of circumstances — to discover the causes rather than the frequencies of events.

A researcher who combined the random sampling of a survey and random assignment of an experiment is Fay Cook (1979). She studied the conditions under which people are most willing to support welfare payments. One variable she thought would influence people's willingness to give was the age of the recipient (over or under 65); another variable was the recipient's condition (poor or disabled); third was the extent of the recipient's poverty (none, marginal, high acute, high chronic); and fourth was the cause of the person's poverty (self-caused versus other-caused). She combined all four variables in a factorial design and wrote brief descriptions of people for each of the conditions. For instance, the following describes a young man who was chronically poor and chronically disabled, whose poverty was caused by forces outside of himself:

> James Richards is 32 years old. He has always been very poor without enough income to buy adequate food and clothing. Although he tried hard, he could never get into a

job training program to acquire skills for a steady job. So, all he's been able to find are odd jobs around town.

   A few weeks ago, he was the victim of a hit-and-run driver. The accident left him permanently paralyzed from the waist down. For the rest of his life, it will be extremely difficult for him to take care of himself and his apartment. [Cook, 1979, p. 68]

In addition to constructing such character descriptions, Cook interviewed people about how willing they were to give welfare support to poor or disabled children, adults under 65, and the elderly as well as disaster victims. She conducted interviews, including eight different character descriptions like the preceding one, among 384 residents of Chicago whose age, race, sex, and income were also variables in the research. The experimental design permitted her to say that a welfare recipient's age caused people to offer different levels of support; and the representative sample survey enabled her to determine how much welfare support men and women of different ages, races, and income levels were willing to give. She found people more willing to help the disabled than the poor and more willing to help the elderly than to help children. Children, however, received more support than poor adults under 65 and disaster victims. The last two were the least preferred groups. Cook also found the *respondents'* race, sex, and income affected how much help they would give. Blacks offered more support to the vignette characters overall than did whites, and among blacks, men gave more than women. Respondents' income was inversely related to how much support they were willing to give: low income people were willing to give the most support, and high income people gave the least (Cook, 1979).

   Fay Cook's experiment embedded within a sample survey shows that it is possible to maximize both internal validity and external validity within a single study. It is an admirable and rare but nonetheless feasible way to do research.

SUMMARY

The different research methods that we describe in this book—experiments, surveys, participant observation—are not logically incompatible with each other. Experiments can be done with representative samples and include a survey; surveys can include experiments embedded within the interview. Experimenters can do some participant observation, and participant observers can introduce some experimental manipulations. Seldom are these strategies combined, however, either for lack of time and resources or for lack of knowledge. Researchers often become specialists in one method and use that exclusively. We hope the readers of this book will develop an understanding of and appreciation for various methods. We do not expect the readers to combine all of these methods in all of their research. Instead, we expect them to become adept at choosing the most appropriate methods to answer the questions rather than trying to do everything all at once.

Quasi-Experimental Designs

Science does not begin and end with the true experiment. It is a process of discovery, in which you use the best tools available to answer your questions. When random assignment and laboratory control are unavailable, you may choose from a large assortment of other techniques. The term *quasi experiments* covers a wide range of other research designs. The term first became popular with the publication of a small but influential book by that name, written by Campbell and Stanley (1963), recently revised and expanded (Cook and Campbell, 1979; also Judd and Kenny, in press).

Quasi experiments are research designs that do not have randomly assigned treatment and comparison groups. Instead, the comparisons between treatment and nontreatment conditions must always be made with nonequivalent groups or with the same subjects prior to treatment. If you cannot randomly assign people or groups to treatment conditions, you lose the ability to control what happens to whom. You can still *observe* what happens, when, and to whom, however; and by deciding what and when to measure, you can design one of several quasi experiments. You forfeit control when you do not use random assignment, but you can still conduct research and analyze cause-effect relationships without a true experiment. By judiciously gathering data from additional times and places, you can create a quasi experiment. For instance, Lawler and Hackman (1969) studied the effects of participative decision making on the work attendance of janitors. They could not randomly assign men to participative decision-making groups or control groups and, therefore, had no equivalent control group with which to make comparisons. The researchers did, however, have a long series of absenteeism records from the men prior to their new participatory decision making and could compare absenteeism rates before and after the participatory procedures were introduced. This was not a true experiment because there was no random assignment. It was a quasi experiment, called a time-series design.

In this chapter, we show how you can do research in which you assess causes and effects even if you cannot randomly assign people to conditions. Well-conceived quasi experiments permit you to rule out many of the threats to internal validity that we discussed in Chapter 2. Ill-conceived pre-experiments do not. We begin our discussion with examples of pre-experimental designs so that you can then appreciate what quasi experiments do by contrast. Pre-experiments are research designs that lack random assignment and that contain few data points or *O*'s in our experimental notation. The following are three pre-experimental designs, which are examples of how *not* to do research.

PRE-EXPERIMENTAL DESIGNS

The One-shot Case Study

X O

Suppose you have a hunch that practicing yoga makes people serene. For the moment we will not worry about how we measure or define serenity. We will assume that can be done. To test this idea, you interview people who practice yoga. This is a one-shot case study. The X is practicing yoga; the O is your assessment of each person's serenity. Imagine that the interviews reveal a high level of serenity among men and women yoga devotees. Will you conclude that practicing yoga makes people serene? You cannot—not without some comparisons. The one-shot study, with only one X and one O, includes no comparisons.

This design is so weak that your conclusion is vulnerable to at least three rival explanations. The level of serenity you observed could be the result of:

1. *Selection:* People who study yoga may be serene to begin with, and had they not been able to find yoga instruction, you may have observed the same levels of that attitude. You cannot rule out this very plausible alternative because you have no preyoga measures.

2. *History.* The level of serenity you observe may be a reflection not of those people but of the political and historical climate of the time. Perhaps everyone is becoming more relaxed. Without a comparison you cannot rule out this possibility.

3. *Mortality.* Perhaps other people who once practiced yoga but then discontinued would not show such serenity; the remaining people whom you interview could be a select group of yoga students. Had you been able to interview the others, you might have found no great level of serenity.

With this one-shot, one-group design, the level of serenity you observe is meaningless without some comparison level, and the pre-experimental one-shot case study includes no comparison. If you developed a serenity scale that had a low score of zero and maximum of 75 and if the yoga students averaged 50 on the scale, you would not know whether that was a relatively high or low score because you had no data or standards with which to compare it in this one-shot design.

The One-group Pretest-Posttest Design

$$O_1 \quad X \quad O_2$$

The one-group pretest-posttest design adds one more data point, the pretest O_1 and that permits you to rule out selection as a rival explanation. If the yoga practitioners have a higher score after they studied yoga than before, you know that the high score was not a preexisting characteristic of this group. But can you attribute it to the practice of yoga? No. There are five other rival explanations or threats to the internal validity of this design.

1. *History.* If the posttest observation is made after considerable time, the difference between it and the pretest may be the result of different social climates — the nation may have ended a war, a new presidential candidate may be talking about Eastern philosophies, or popular culture may be advertising new forms of meditation. Any historical changes like these could be rival explanations if they occurred in the time between the pretest and posttest.

2. *Maturation.* If the people you were studying became older, more relaxed, or retired with the passage of time alone, this would be a rival explanation. The longer the time between the pretest and posttest, the more likely it is that such developmental changes could explain the difference.

3. *Testing.* If the first interview sensitized the people you were studying and made them believe they should relax or slow down, the pretesting alone could have produced higher scores on the posttest. The shorter the time between pretest and posttest, the more plausible are testing effects.

4. *Instrumentation.* If you changed your interview questions or scoring system between the first and second observation, these changes in the measuring instrument could account for a difference between pre and post levels of serenity.

5. *Interaction of selection and maturation* (or selection and any of the other threats to internal validity). Even if none of the preceding threats are plausible explanations for the population in general, they may be plausible explanations for the select group of people who study yoga or for that specific group of practitioners whom you interview. For instance, you may decide it is implausible that maturation makes all people serene; some people may become more anxious with age. Nonetheless, you may find it plausible that the kind of people interested in yoga would naturally become serene even if they did not practice it, and this represents an interaction between selection and maturation. Similarly, you may decide that not all people would be sensitized by the pretest interview and try to be calmer on the posttest; but for the group of people you have selected, testing may have that effect. This would be an interaction of selection and testing.

These five rival explanations are potential threats for any pre-experiment of this design. You may be able to rule out one or more of these for any particular case because either the results or the context make that threat implausible. For instance, if you used unobtrusive measures of yoga students' state of tension or relaxation — such as the amount of lip biting or nail chewing they exhibited — you could regard *testing* as an implausible explanation of any changes you observed because the students would have been unaware of, and therefore unaffected by, your testing. Whether a study is vulnerable to these threats depends upon both the design and the details of the procedures and results. Any one-group pretest-posttest study is *potentially* vulnerable to the five threats discussed previously, however, until proved otherwise. This is a generally weak design that you should avoid if you can design something better. The third pre-experimental design has two sets of observations, but instead of observing one group of people twice, it observes two groups once.

The Static-group Comparison

Group 1	X	O_1
Group 2	not X	O_2

The dashed line separating the two groups indicates that people were not randomly assigned to Group 1 and Group 2; instead, these are either naturally occurring groups or groups to which people are assigned for some reason. If we apply this design to our question about yoga, we would interview one group of people who practiced yoga (Group 1) and another group who did not (Group 2). The treatment, yoga, is signified by the X for Group 1. If you conducted this study using the static-group comparison pre-experiment, you would have to contend with the following threats to validity:

1. *Selection.* Selection is the major threat to this design. Because you did not randomly assign people to Group 1 and Group 2, it is very likely that the two groups are different in many ways apart from practicing yoga. You can imagine that if you had interviewed the people in Group 1 just before they learned yoga, they would have scored higher on your serenity scale than the people in Group 2. Such preexisting differences may, in fact, be the cause of learning yoga. Their serenity may have caused them to become yoga students rather than vice versa.

2. *Mortality.* If you conducted your study by interviewing yoga students who belonged to a particular meditation group and found they were different from nonpractitioners, you may err in concluding that yoga makes a person serene. Membership requirements in the meditation group may have caused less serene people to drop out because they did not meet the standards required. Any such differential dropout rates are threats to internal validity.

3. *Selection by history interaction.* Although historical events that both groups are exposed to cannot account for a difference between them, differential exposure to such events would be a threat to validity. If you have reason to suspect that one group experienced some event that the other group did not experience, you have a rival explanation for any difference you observe.

The static-group comparison is a correlational design. The X is a characteristic of people that they bring into the study — such as practicing yoga or attending private school or going to a therapist. The static-group comparison shows what the relationship is between that characteristic (X) and another characteristic (O) such as feeling serene, having academic aspirations, or showing insight into one's self. A correlational study shows whether there is a positive or negative relationship between two characteristics and whether the relationship is strong or weak. A positive relationship appears when people have simultaneously high scores or simultaneously low scores on both characteristics. For instance, a positive relationship between going to a therapist and having insight into one's motives means that people who go to a therapist (have a positive score on that variable) also have insight, and those who do not go to a therapist do not have insight into their motives. A positive relationship between attending private school and having academic aspirations means that those who attend have high aspirations and those who do not have low academic aspirations. This would appear as a positive correlation between those two variables.

A positive correlation does not mean that the variable labeled X causes the variable labeled O. It is just as likely that the causal relationship goes in the opposite direction: having insight into one's motives can cause one to go to a therapist, and having academic aspirations can cause a person to attend private schools. It is also possible that there is no direct causal relationship between the two variables in spite of their positive relationship. Both could be the result of a third variable—being raised in a family that puts great emphasis on education could cause people to attend private schools and to have academic aspirations. If you conduct a correlational study, like the static-group comparison, you often cannot determine which of these three explanations accounts for the positive relationship. The impossibility of disentangling these and other rival explanations is expressed in the adage "correlation does not prove causation." This third pre-experimental design is correlational.

The three pre-experimental designs are examples of how *not to do research if there are alternatives*. Quasi-experimental designs provide an alternative. When you do not have the power to assign people randomly to treatment conditions, you can still gather data and rule out many of the threats to validity by using carefully chosen quasi-experimental designs. There are several books written about quasi experiments (for example, Campbell and Stanley, 1963; Cook and Campbell, 1979; Judd and Kenny, in press) which you can consult to see the full range of designs. In this chapter we discuss three types of quasi experiments, each of which is an extension of a pre-experiment. Each of these achieves its greater interpretability through the addition of more data points or observations to the pre-experimental base.

QUASI-EXPERIMENTAL DESIGNS

Interrupted Time-Series Designs

$$O_1 \; O_2 \; O_3 \; O_4 \; O_5 \; O_6 \; O_7 \; O_8 \; XO_9 \; O_{10} \; O_{11} \; O_{12} \; O_{13} \; O_{14} \; O_{15} \; O_{16}$$

Time-series designs are an extension of the pre-experimental one-group pretest-posttest design ($O_1 \; X \; O_2$). Although that pre-experimental predecessor is subject to many threats to internal validity, the time-series, with its long sequence of O's, provides information to rule out several threats, particularly maturation and testing. If you find a marked difference between O_8 and O_9 and wonder whether the difference is truly a result of the treatment (X) or of maturation, you can inspect all of the intervals before and after that point to look for maturation trends. Presumably, if maturation were occurring, it would show up as a long-term trend, producing similar differences between O_1 and O_2, O_2 and O_3, and so on, along the entire series. If none of the other intervals show such a trend and the only difference lies between O_8 and O_9, maturation is not a very plausible explanation, unless, of course, you are studying some phenomenon that happens to coincide with a particular maturational change such as puberty and that could also plausibly be affected by puberty. Only under such a special set of circumstances and coincidences would maturation pose a threat to the validity of a time-series study.

The same reasoning applies to testing as a rival explanation. If you suspected that the difference between O_8 and O_9 resulted not from the treatment but from the sensitizing effects of the pretest (O_8), you could examine all of the preceding and succeeding intervals to see whether the repeated testing produced similar differences along the entire series. If there were no differences at any other points, it would be highly implausible that the testing at O_8 alone would have created an effect at O_9.

Sometimes the X occurs only once, and its effect is presumed to persist forever or for some specified time. A measles innoculation should last forever; a flu shot may have a limited period of effectiveness. Sometimes the X signals a permanent change in the situation—as when a state changes its divorce laws to permit no-fault divorce or when the federal government introduces new air pollution standards. In cases like these, when the treatment occurs not only at a single point in time but continues in force, the time-series is more rightly diagrammed as follows:

$$O_1\ O_2\ O_3\ O_4\ O_5\ O_6\ O_7\ O_8\ XO_9\ XO_{10}\ XO_{11}\ XO_{12}\ XO_{13}\ XO_{14}\ XO_{15}\ XO_{16}$$

In either case, with a one-shot treatment or a continuing treatment, the virtue of time-series designs is that you can examine the *trends* in the data before the treatment, at the time of intervention, and after the treatment. This allows you to assess the plausibility of maturation as a rival explanation. If maturation is a cause, it should appear as a trend before the treatment as well as afterwards.

How easily you can interpret a time-series and rule out rival explanations depends not on the formal features of the design alone but also on the pattern of results. Some results are relatively easy to interpret—you can rule out most of the threats to validity and conclude the treatment caused the effect. Other patterns are more vulnerable to rival interpretation.

The two features that researchers examine in results from an interrupted time-series design are the slopes of the lines for the pretest and posttest observations and the intercept—the point at which either line would intersect the vertical axis. For instance, Figures 3.1 to 3.3 show a variety of results plotted for interrupted time-series designs—the first (3.1) is readily interpretable and shows an effect of the treatment; the second (3.2) is ambiguous; the third is a clear case of no effect of the treatment (3.3).

With results like those in Figure 3.1, there are not many rival explanations. It is quite obvious that the treatment caused the shift in scores from the pretest level to the posttest level. There are no maturation trends in either the pretest or posttest observations; so maturation alone or maturation by selection interaction are not persuasive alternative explanations. The most problematic and plausible threat is history—some event that coincided with the treatment. How plausible this is depends entirely on the problem under study. If we were studying the effects of a foreign relations film on American students' attitudes toward people of other countries and if the showing of the film coincided with international agreements about sharing the world's energy resources or with an international incident in which Americans

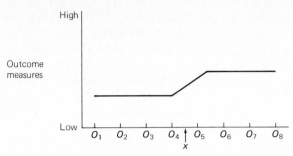

Temporal intervals when outcome measures were taken, with treatment introduced between O_4 and O_5.

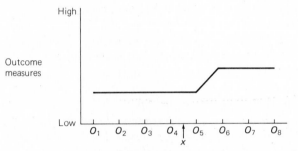

Temporal intervals when outcome measures were taken, with treatment introduced between O_4 and O_5.

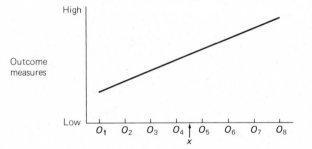

Temporal intervals when outcome measures were taken, with treatment introduced between O_4 and O_5.

FIGURES 3.1, 3.2, 3.3. Some possible outcomes resulting from the introduction of a treatment (X) into a time series of measurements

were suddenly held hostage by another country, these historical events would be plausible rival explanations. If there are no obvious external events that coincide with the treatment and could have produced the same effects, history presents no problem.

  With results like those in Figure 3.2, it is not clear that the treatment caused the shift upward because the shift does not coincide with the treatment; it lags behind by one time interval. In some cases, there may be reason to expect such a lag and, therefore, attribute the effect to the treatment. For instance, a rise in the world's petroleum export prices would not be felt immediately in domestic gas prices at the pumps because there is a six-month oil reserve that was bought at lower prices. Therefore, if you were studying the effects of world export oil price increases on American gas consumption, the effect may lag six months behind the cause. If the time-series observations were made quarterly, at three-month intervals, the effect would appear not in the first observation following treatment but in the second, and the pattern in Figure 3.2 would be a convincing demonstration of the effect of the price increase on consumption. If there is no such plausible storage mechanism and, therefore, no plausible lag for the cause to have its effect, Figure 3.2 is more difficult to interpret, and other rival explanations may be causes. These alternative explanations would likely fall under the heading of history — other events that followed the treatment and produced the effect.

Figure 3.3 is the clearest case of no effect. The higher levels of O after the treatment merely reflect the prevailing trend that also produced increasingly higher levels of O before the treatment. This figure also shows most clearly why the time-series design is far superior to the pre-experimental one-group pretest-posttest design. If the pattern seen in Figure 3.3 were studied with only one pretest and one posttest (points O_4 and O_5), the researcher would be tempted to conclude that the treatment had an effect — causing O_5 to be higher than O_4. Without the other data points, it would be impossible to distinguish between a real effect and the prevailing trend that we see in Figure 3.3.

By the addition of a series of pre- and posttest observations, the time-series design is much more interpretable than the one-group pretest-posttest design. Even though it lacks random assignment and lacks a control group, it is a useful quasi-experimental design because the additional observations allow the investigator to test the plausibility of several rival explanations — maturation, testing, instrumentation, mortality, and regression. The chief threat to internal validity with this design is history.

The interrupted time-series design has several variations. It may include more than one group or subject, making it a multiple time-series design:

$$O_1 \quad O_2 \quad O_3 \quad O_4 \quad O_5 \quad O_6 \quad X \quad O_7 \quad O_8 \quad O_9 \quad O_{10} \quad O_{11} \quad O_{12}$$

$$O_{1'} \quad O_{2'} \quad O_{3'} \quad O_{4'} \quad O_{5'} \quad O_{6'} \qquad O_{7'} \quad O_{8'} \quad O_{9'} \quad O_{10'} \quad O_{11'} \quad O_{12'}$$

This design provides identical information about a second group or subject and permits you to test the most troublesome threat to internal validity that a single time-series design is heir to — *history*. If the treatment coincided with some historical event and if the two groups were presumably exposed to the same historical conditions, the effect of that historical incident should appear in both time series as a difference between O_6 and O_7. For instance, suppose we had tried to assess the effect of a film called *The Death of a Princess* on American and European attitudes toward Saudi Arabians. The film was a fictionalized account of a true story — a Saudi Arabian princess was executed by a firing squad after she had been accused of committing adultery. Saudi government officials protested the showing of this film in Europe and America because they said it misrepresented Arab society and would arouse hostility in viewers. Nonetheless, the film was shown on American and

European television. If we had studied the effects of this—by measuring the anti-Saudi sentiment expressed in newspaper editorials or counting the number of anti-Saudi bumper stickers on cars, we might have found an effect like that in Figure 3.1. Suppose, however, that the showing of the film coincided with a rise in oil prices or an act of terrorism. Any such event that occurred at approximately the same time could account for the rise in hostility as recorded in the media or in our bumper sticker count. How could we determine whether it was the film or the other historical events that produced the effect? If we could find a locale that had been exposed to the same rise in oil prices or had heard of the same act of terrorism but had not been exposed to the film, we could assess the rival explanations. Two towns that had both experienced the rise in oil prices, one of which had received the film broadcast and one of which had not, would provide a test of the rival explanation. If the anti-Saudi sentiment expressed in the former town's newspapers or bumper stickers rose after the film broadcast whereas the level remained constant in the other, we would rule out the rival explanations of *history* and conclude the film produced the effect.

This example presents a hypothetical quasi experiment but a real dilemma. Sometimes the questions that quasi experiments are designed to answer are important political questions with serious implications, but the measures available to answer them are sorely inadequate. A time-series design, in particular, is often based on archival data—such as sales records of the numbers of bumper stickers sold— *eg ELECTION RESULTS* that were never intended to be sensitive indicators of a social variable—such as attitudes toward another nation. Nonetheless, such data may be the only measures available in a long enough series to use in a quasi experiment like the time-series. Chapter 11 on observational and archival data discusses the strengths and weaknesses of such available archival data.

Regression-Discontinuity Designs

Group 1 O_1
- - - - - - - - - - - - -
Group 2 O_2
- - - - - - - - - - - - -
Group 3 O_3
- - - - - - - - - - - - -
Group 4 XO_4
- - - - - - - - - - - - -
Group 5 XO_5
- - - - - - - - - - - - -
Group 6 XO_6

The regression-discontinuity design is an extension of the pre-experimental static group comparison $\dfrac{X \quad O_1}{\text{not } X \quad O_2}$. The static group comparison is weak because *selection* is an ever-present plausible rival explanation for a difference between the two O's. The regression-discontinuity design, with its long series of comparison groups, provides information about the plausibility of such preexisting group differences and enables the researcher to rule out selection as a rival explanation. A researcher can examine the differences between the various nontreated groups to see what the naturally occurring groups' differences are. The groups in a regression-discontinuity design are all ranked or ordered on a criterion, such as financial need, and those above or below a cutoff point receive the treatment, such as a scholarship award.

The regression-discontinuity design is a cross-sectional design; it examines the effects of the treatment by looking *across* many groups of persons and compares those below the cutoff point with those above. The time-series designs are longitudinal designs; they examine the effects of the treatment by looking *along* a single group or person's time line and compare the observations made before the treatment with those after. As diagrammed earlier, the two types of designs look very different. As graphed in Figures 3.4 and 3.5, the two look similar.

Although the statistical analyses are different (the interested reader can consult Cook and Campbell, 1979, and Judd and Kenny, in press, for details), the logic underlying the interpretation of these two designs is similar. In both cases we can project the point just before the treatment and compare the projected estimate with the observed results. If the observed results differ from the projection, that is evidence of an effect of the treatment. In both cases, we assume that if there is a preexisting trend, that trend would normally continue and should not be confused with a treatment effect. For instance, if the child whose time series we show in Figure 3.4 liked school more with each passing year, we expect that trend to continue. The change in the intercept shows that the liking increased to a new level after the academic enrichment program; the program gave the child a boost. The regression-discontinuity design shows the same effect (Figure 3.5). If children who receive higher test scores naturally like school more and if children are selected for an enrichment program on the basis of their test scores, we would expect the trend to continue along the projected line even if there were no real effect of the program. The upward shift of the line, the change in intercept, demonstrates the effect of the program over and above the natural trend.

The time-series design and the regression-discontinuity design achieve their interpretability by the addition of observations. Time series add observations over time—taking the long view forward and backward. The regression discontinuity

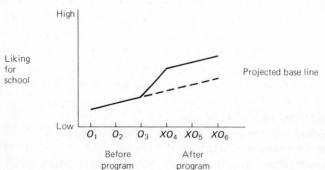

FIGURE 3.4. Time series for one child. Effects of academic enrichment program on children's liking for school.

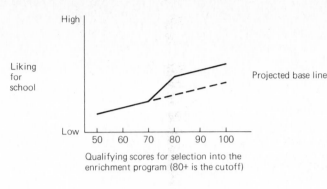

High

Liking
for
school

Low

50   60   70   80   90   100

Projected base line

Qualifying scores for selection into the
enrichment program (80+ is the cutoff)

FIGURE 3.5. Regression-discontinuity for children below and above the cutoff. Effects of academic enrichment program on children's liking for school.

adds observations across different groups, all at one point in time. The added observations in both cases permit us to compare the difference between observations immediately adjacent to the treatment with the differences between pairs of observations before the treatment and pairs after the treatment. The series also permit us to examine naturally occurring trends and to compare those projected trends with the actual results.

Pretest-Posttest Nonequivalent Control Group Design

The pretest-posttest nonequivalent control group design does not include a long series of observations either over time or across groups.

Group 1 O_1 X O_3

Group 2 O_2 O_4

It is not an extension of any of the preexperimental designs; rather, it is a combination of the static group comparison and the one-group pretest-posttest pre-experiment. By combining the features of both, it is more interpretable than either of those. It includes pretest information about the existing group base line levels, and it provides a comparison group. The comparison group is not formed by random assignment, however. It is a preexisting or preselected group, which we choose because it is similar, but it is not equivalent. Nonetheless, the simple addition of a comparison group and a pretest lets us possibly rule out a number of threats to internal validity.

A major advantage of this design over the static group comparison is that we can measure preexisting differences between groups. Figure 3.6 illustrates results that are fairly interpretable, thanks to the added pretest. It is quite likely, as Figure 3.6 shows, that people who install solar panels use energy more sparingly than other people to begin with. Their interest in solar energy is a further expression of their preexisting inclinations. Therefore, if we had only the posttest information, we would not know whether the difference reflected the natural conservation tendencies of the people who installed solar panels or whether it reflected the savings pro-

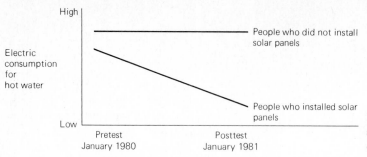

FIGURE 3.6. Effects of solar heating panels on electric use

duced by the panels. When we look at the pretest differences, we see that those who installed the panels were conservers to begin with. They used less electricity even before they installed the panels. This difference became even larger after the treatment, however, and this suggests that the solar installations had an effect.

Are there any rival explanations? You might suspect that the people who became interested in solar energy would naturally have decreased their electric consumption even if they had not installed the panels — because they were conscious of the need to conserve energy and may have used less hot water in January 1981. This design does not provide the information necessary to rule out this possibility — a selection by maturation interaction. Only if we had a longitudinal series of observations could we see whether the treated group was on a natural downward trend both before and after the solar installation.

This example illustrates how you must consider not only the design but also the content of a study and the pattern of results when ruling out rival explanations. For some topics you may not consider it plausible that the treated group would have changed so as to become increasingly different from the control group without the intervention of the treatment.

For some patterns of results, the most plausible explanation is that the treatment produced the effects. Imagine an energy conservation program imposed on people who live in states that use the most air conditioning. Suppose the imposed conservation program consisted of higher electric rates for people in the high consumption states. To study the effects of this program we could compare the electric consumption by people in those states with consumption by people in neighboring states who had not consumed as much electricity for air conditioning. We know that the treatment group initially consumed more electricity than those in the comparison states, so their pretest levels would look like O_1 and O_2 in Figure 3.7. If the posttest showed that the treatment group reduced their consumption below the level of the control group, the most plausible explanation is that the program worked. A crossover like that in Figure 3.7 is more difficult to explain with any of the rival explanations like a maturation by selection interaction. In this example, the constant trend of the control group we may consider the normal trend; the downward trend of the treatment group we can reasonably attribute to the treatment. To explain away the apparent treatment effect by calling it differential maturation (or differential development of energy consciousness), we would have to regard the people in the formerly high-electric consumption states an extraordinary

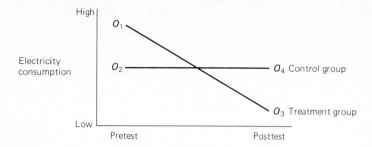

FIGURE 3.7. Electric consumption levels by people living in treatment and control states

group of late-blooming conservationists who not only met but surpassed the conservation levels of the people in the neighboring states. This is so unlikely for this case, and most others, that the crossover pattern shown in Figure 3.7 is usually interpreted as a treatment effect.

WHEN TO DO QUASI EXPERIMENTS

We have said in this chapter and the previous one that if you want to make causal statements, you should conduct a true experiment and avoid pre-experiments. If you cannot use random assignment to design a true experiment, a quasi experiment is the second best choice. A quasi experiment is a fallback position, not as good as a true experiment but far superior to pre-experiments.

There are many social interventions — housing programs, school programs, drug programs, taxation programs — that are important to study but that are not administered with random assignment. To study the effects of such innovations, we must fall back on some quasi-experimental design. Which quasi-experimental design you choose depends upon what kind of data are available. The time-series and regression-discontinuity designs require a large number of data points and are most easily used when studying archival data — data that have been regularly collected like census data, annual price index data, monthly weather reports, and so on. Although these data were originally collected for other purposes, you can use them to test hypotheses about the effects of new social programs. Sometimes, however, archival data gathered for one purpose are not suitable for answering other questions. For instance, if we wished to study the effects of a rape prevention program on the incidence of rape, we might try using a time-series quasi experiment to study the effects of a new preventive program on the number of rapes reported to the police over a 15-year period. We would expect to find a decrease in the number after the program began. In theory this sounds like a good time-series design with useful archival data. In practice, the data would be difficult to interpret because the actual incidence of rape is much higher than the number of rapes reported to the police. The archival data, therefore, would underestimate the overall number of rapes. Also, it is conceivable that the number of rapes reported to the police would increase rather than decrease as a result of the program if part of the program consisted of encouraging rape victims to report the crime.

When existing archival data are unavailable or unsuitable, a researcher could still design a time series and gather data over a number of weeks, months, or years. The longer it would take to gather such data, the less likely it is that you or anyone would want to conduct a time-series quasi experiment because it would be costly in time and effort. The advantage of the time-series design is that it includes a large number of observations to test rival explanations; the disadvantage is that it is costly to gather so much data if it does not already exist in archives.

The same is true for the regression-discontinuity design. It is best suited for studying social programs for which data are regularly available. For instance, school records exist for a large cross-section of students. It is possible, therefore, to study the effects of scholarship awards or special admissions or enrichment programs even though students are not randomly assigned to such treatments. The large number of data points available from a wide cross-section of students lets you design a regression-discontinuity study that is far better than a simple two-group static-group comparison.

The pretest-posttest nonequivalent control group design is not so tied to the availability of archival data. Because it requires less data — fewer observation points — it is a design that you can use when you gather your own data. It can be less costly than either of the other two quasi-experimental designs because you must locate only two groups and observe them only twice.

INTERNAL VALIDITY, EXTERNAL VALIDITY, AND QUASI EXPERIMENTS

Quasi experiments are a compromise — between a true experiment with random assignment and a pre-experiment, which is often uninterpretable. They also represent a compromise between maximizing internal validity and external validity. What true experiments achieve in drawing causal inference and maximizing internal validity, they sometimes sacrifice in external validity. Laboratory experiments sometimes bear no surface similarity to the real world phenomena they are intended to mimic, and even field experiments sometimes lose external validity simply because the subjects know they are experimental guinea pigs subject to random assignment. Quasi experiments often avoid these drawbacks. A time-series analysis of the effects of rape-prevention programs does not create guinea-pig effects because the victims are not even aware of being studied. Quasi experiments can be less intrusive than true experiments because they permit the natural selection processes to occur. People are accustomed to choosing their own treatments or being selected for treatments by some criterion measure such as scholastic promise. They are not accustomed to being randomly assigned to treatments except in the case of an announced lottery.

The subject assignment processes that quasi experiments include are the naturally occurring biased selection processes that exist in the world. These nonrandom sorting processes make it difficult for us to disentangle the treatment effects from other rival effects, particularly selection, but they also give quasi-experimental studies an element of external validity that true experiments lack. They enable us to study the effects that treatments have on that segment of the population that is most likely either to choose or be chosen for the treatment. Not everyone would choose to attend an experimental college or enter psychotherapy or work a four-day week. For treatments like these that people are able to choose for themselves, it does not make sense to rule out the self-selecting bias that would normally exist. We would not want to assign all people randomly to some level of these treatments. We could devise a true experiment from among those people who would normally choose such treatments if we recruited more volunteers than each program could accommodate. If we randomly selected the entrants from among the self-selected applicants, we could devise a true experiment. Most people are not accustomed to entering a lottery for such programs, however, and it would require either deception or education to make a lottery acceptable. We do not advocate deception. We would like to see some public education to make lotteries possible for evaluating some programs — though this would raise people's awareness that they were guinea pigs and may thereby lower the external validity of a study.

SUMMARY

Quasi-experimental designs provide a means to study some naturally occurring social treatments. They are a compromise between a true experiment that has high internal validity and the poor pre-experiments that have almost no internal validity at all. Quasi experiments enable us to rule out some threats to validity because they include more data points than the pre-experiments. The number of quasi-experimental designs that a creative reseracher can construct is limitless. We have presented three types that are extensions of pre-experiments to show how the additional data points make a previously uninterpretable design interpretable. A determined researcher can design yet unthought-of quasi experiments by gathering data from enough subjects at enough times to rule out many threats to internal validity, so that even without random assignment it will be possible to infer causes and effects.

Survey Research Designs

This chapter was written by Leo Rigsby

INTRODUCTION

Frequently in social research we want to be able to answer questions about the distribution of and relationships among characteristics of people or groups as they exist in their natural settings. We might ask, for example, what is the distribution of candidate preferences among the voting age population of the United States? Or what accounts for differences among young people in how well they do in school or how much schooling they receive? Or how do family background or peer group processes relate to educational performance? These are phenomena that influence the interactions of people as they pursue their everyday lives. **Survey research** is the research strategy to study such phenomena. This chapter examines some designs and data analysis strategies that make up survey research.

In doing survey research, one collects data from all or part of a population to assess the relative incidence, distribution, and interrelations of naturally occurring phenomena (Kerlinger, 1964). The term **population** here refers to the aggregation of people to which we wish to generalize. For example, if we ask, "What is the distribution of candidate preferences among voting age populations in the United States?" the relevant population is all potential voters in the United States. If we ask, "What accounts for differences among young people in how well they do in school?" the relevant population might be people in the American population who have reached an age beyond which they are unlikely to seek further education. The relevant population for "How do family background or peer groups processes relate to educational performance?" could be the same as that for the second question. The phrase **naturally occurring phenomena** refers to the processes of life as they occur. This is in contrast to the "manipulated" variables of experiments discussed in Chapter 2. Many variables measured in surveys are what were referred to as subject variables in that chapter.

Survey researchers typically gather their data as verbal responses to predetermined questions that are asked of most or all the research subjects. This is in contrast to the unstructured interviewing done in participant observation. The participant observer's questions at one point may be determined by respondents' answers to previous questions (see Chapter 6). It is because survey respondents answer the same questions that the incidence and distribution of characteristics can be studied. In the planning of surveys, careful attention is given to both the wording of questions and to the way questions are presented to respondents. These important topics are covered in Chapter 8. As survey questionnaires are planned before the data collection begins, surveys cannot explore feelings or interpretations of individual respondents in great depth as could be done in participant observation. On the other hand, the systematic data collected from each respondent allows the exploration of relationships among variables that are measured (for example, education related to income). Such relationships cannot be explored if each respondent or situation is not measured in the same way.

Some survey research attempts to go beyond the reporting of distributions and relationships to their interpretation. Such attempts raise the problem of basing explanations on correlational data; that is, survey researchers may wish to explain what accounts for the distribution of occupations among men and women in the United States. Naturally occurring characteristics and processes (for example, the influence of race and sex on educational attainments) cannot be meaningfully assigned to research subjects and cannot be manipulated in laboratory studies. The only way such phenomena can be studied is as they occur in life processes. To establish the relationships of these characteristics to important life processes, one must employ techniques other than experimentation.

The wide variety of situations and purposes for the application of survey research can be seen in the following examples of its use:

1. Sociologists collect data on a representative sample of male members of the U.S. labor force to study their training and occupational attainments.

2. Public opinion polling organizations conduct studies of the popularity of various presidential candidates among potential voters.

3. Market research organizations conduct studies of smokers to find out what they want cigarettes to be like.

4. Medical researchers survey the nation's population to determine the incidence of disease-related characteristics.

5. Political scientists interview members of the U.S. House of Representatives to gain an understanding of why reorganization reform was adopted.

6. A national women's magazine asks its readers to answer a questionnaire that solicits information about their occupational aspirations.

7. Political sociologists survey a sample of students in large universities to determine whether they support or are against reinstitution of a military draft in the United States.

8. A national broadcast rating organization (using mechanical recording devices instead of questionnaires and interviewers) measures the distribution of television watching each week.

9. A housing researcher surveys mortgage lenders to determine the proportions of their mortgage loans made in poor versus middle class and wealthy neighborhoods.

SOME SURVEY DESIGNS

The most straightforward design in survey research seeks to establish the incidence and distribution of characteristics or the relationships among characteristics. Where survey researchers have these limited goals, they only concern themselves with whether their study populations are representative of the populations to which they wish to generalize and that they have accurately measured the characteristics on which they wish to report. The national public opinion polling organizations like Lou Harris, Associates, and The Gallup Poll frequently conduct studies that fit this model. These organizations often are commissioned by the news media to study public reaction to current issues. For example, recent studies reported in the daily newspapers have covered people's views on nuclear power, the gasoline shortage, whether the military draft should be reinstituted, and what adults consider to be the most pressing problems facing the country. The media report of a typical study done by one of these organizations will consist of respondents' opinions tabulated successively by such personal characteristics as race, region of the country lived in, and kind of occupation. Although such studies require careful planning and execution, they do not raise complex problems of statistical analysis or interpretation. All data are collected in a single interview for each respondent, and very simple tabulations are presented. No explanation of *why* people hold different opinions is attempted. Such studies provide useful information about the bare essentials of public opinions and preferences.

Static Group Comparison Designs

Where more than distributions and simple tabulations are needed, a research design must be conceptualized. A common design for survey research that attempts explanation and interpretation of relationships is very close to one of Campbell and Stanley's pre-experimental designs, the "static-group comparison":

$$X \qquad O$$
$$\text{--------}$$
$$\qquad O$$

If we imagine this design with a naturally occurring X with several levels (for example, sex — female/male, or socioeconomic status — low/medium/high), it becomes the following:

$$X_1 \qquad O_1$$
$$\text{---------}$$
$$X_2 \qquad O_2$$

The design depicts two or more comparison groups defined by their value on X. One would compare the O scores of the comparison groups to assess whether there is a relationship between X and O.

Suppose X in the preceding diagram represents occupation (blue collar, white collar) and O represents income. If the comparison groups differ in income, it is tempting to interpret this difference as the effect of occupation on income. Such an interpretation would be analogous to our interpretation of the effects of X in a true experiment. The difficulty with interpreting the results of a static group comparison is the possibility that there are other differences between two occupation groups that might also affect income. Such differences are alternative plausible explanations for any differences in income between groups. There are three criteria for inferring causation. They are these: (1) that X and O covary, (2) that X precedes O in time, and (3) that there are no alternative explanations of the group differences in O. To say that two variables covary means that there is some tendency for certain values of or levels of one variable to occur with particular values of or levels of the other variable. For example, to say that education and income covary (or that they are correlated) is to say that there is some tendency for lower levels of income to occur with lower levels of educational attainment and that higher levels of income tend to occur with higher levels of educational attainment. The basic correlational design of survey research can almost always meet the first of these three criteria. Readers who have taken statistics courses may recall the uncompromising dictum of statistics teachers: "Correlation does not demonstrate causation." To that truism should be added the statement that causation does imply **correlation.** Thus, the demonstration of a correlation between two variables using different populations and different research conditions certainly lends credence to a causal hypothesis involving the two variables. Each such instance is a test of the hypothesis that could disconfirm it (Campbell and Stanley, 1963, p. 234). In addition, each such instance has to be examined for plausible alternative explanations before even tentative causal interpretation is suggested.

A comment should be made about the assumption of time order in this design. It is actually the case that X and O are measured at approximately the same time; that is, each is likely to be measured by responses in a questionnaire. In this sense it cannot be said that X comes before O in time. The survey researcher must assume that X as measured in the survey has influenced the respondent as part of her or his prior life processes. Sometimes it can be determined in survey research problems that X preceded O in time. For example, for most Americans, the end of schooling comes before the beginning of their first full-time employment. If we used survey data to study the occupational attainments of American workers, we could say that, for most male Americans, educational attainment came before occupational placement. Even so, this time order does not describe part of the population. Some people who ultimately attain college degrees work on a full-time basis at a job they consider to be permanent before they attend or complete college. To the extent that respondents are not uniform regarding the ordering of education and the first job, there is ambiguity in the interpretation of the relationship between them. Such ambiguity is one reason for survey researchers to exercise caution in making causal inferences from survey research.

If one's purposes are limited to assessing the incidence or distribution of characteristics, say, the number or proportion of men and women in a given occupation, the design is perfectly adequate for providing the answer. Even when one wishes to assess the degree of covariation among variables, this design is adequate to the task. Thus, using this design, one could readily gather data from which to calculate the degree of correlation between family background measures (income, parents' educational attainments) and performance in school (grades, grade point average). It is when one wishes to go beyond the calculation of relationships to the interpretation of them that the limitations of the research design are met.

Panel Design

To meet the time order criterion for establishing causation, we can use a second common survey design, namely, the **panel survey design.** This design takes into account time and changes over time by collecting data on the X's and the O's at two or more points in time:

$$X_{1_1} \ X_{1_2} \ X_{1_3} \ O \ldots X_{1_2} \ X_{1_3} \ O \ldots X_{1_2} \ O$$
$$\text{------------------------------}$$
$$X_{2_1} \ X_{2_2} \ X_{2_3} \ O \ldots X_{2_2} \ X_{2_3} \ O \ldots X_{2_2} \ O$$

The first of the two subscripts on the X's indicates the level of the variable, for example, for sex, female and male. A particular variable might take on more than two values, of course. If the variable were age when first surveyed, it could take on as many values as were represented in the range of ages among the respondents surveyed. The second subscript represents the variable identification. In the preceding diagram, information on variables X_1, X_2, and X_3 was gathered on the first interview; X_2 and X_3 on the second; and so forth. What is implied in this diagram is that data on a number of X's and perhaps a number of O's are collected at a number of points in time. Some of the X's are variables whose values are not expected to change like those of sex and race. Others are X's whose values may change for some people, as in the case of employment status and educational attainment. Finally, some of the variables are like O's from experimental research whose values would be expected to change where values of X's have changed, as for income level. One of the early studies of voting behavior in this country used this design to look at such X's as class background, religion, and exposure to political campaign appeals and such O's as intention to vote and candidate preference (Berelson, Lazarsfeld, and McPhee, 1954.)

Studies using panel designs have come increasingly into use for following complex processes like changes in employment and changes in consumer expenditure patterns. For example, the National Longitudinal Surveys of Labor Market Experience is a study using annual or biennial interviews of several groups in the United States population. Different groups are being studied because they encounter different kinds of labor market problems. "For the two cohorts of youth, these problems revolve around the process of occupational choice, and include both the preparation for work and the frequently difficult period of accommodation to the labor market and when formal schooling has been completed. The special problems of the middle-aged men stem in part from skill obsolescence, from the increasing incidence of health problems, and from employment discrimination, all of which are reflected in declining labor force participation rates and in longer-than-average duration of unemployment, if it occurs. For the women, the special labor market problems are those associated with re-entry into the labor force by married women who feel that their children no longer require their continuous presence at home" (Center for Human Resource Research, 1977). This study is funded by the U.S. Department of Labor and is intended to provide a basis for understanding more general issues affecting workers in the U.S. labor force as well as the specific problems facing the groups being studied. Even questions that were not part of the original study design can be included in the annual reinterviews to give flexibility to the research design. Some of the results of the continuing study are used by policy makers in the Department of Labor to formulate changes in the economic policies of the federal government and to evaluate present policies.

Another panel study with comparable national scope and importance is the Panel Study of Income Dynamics carried out by the Institute for Survey Research at the University of Michigan (Morgan and Duncan, 1980). Based on annual interviews with 5,000 American families, this study has collected economic and social data on families and their individual members since 1969. The study has produced massive amounts of data, including information on such things as short-run and long-run unemployment, work hours of family heads, use of food stamps, home ownership, residential mobility, child care, shifting family composition, taxation, income inequality, trends in food expenditure, and the economic effects of higher gasoline prices. Like the National Longitudinal Survey of Labor Market Experience, the Panel Study of Income Dynamics is funded by federal government agencies who are interested in the data to help them make and evaluate economic policy.

In panel design surveys special kinds of detailed analyses of changes in the level of some of the variables can generate useful insights about change processes. However, ruling out alternative hypotheses remains problematic. There are two major problems. First, it may be that the time between interviews in the panel study does not correspond to the time period necessary to tell whether one variable affected another. For example, suppose one were reinterviewing at one-year intervals and found that both consumer debt (for the purchase of a new car) and the number of adults from the household who are employed had increased since the last interview. It would not be clear whether the additional household member had gone to work so that they could buy a new car or whether the new car had been purchased to allow the household member to go to work (or, perhaps, both). The second problem is that there may be other important differences between comparison groups defined by the X's that have not been taken into account.

Cross-sectional, Pseudopanel Design

The time-series or panel design just given, in combination with an idea from Glock's (1967) article on the uses of survey research in sociology, yields a slightly different design that represents another commonly employed design in survey research. It is a design where the variables represent phenomena that have occurred over a period of time:

$A_1 \ B_1 \ C_1 \ D_1 \ E_1 \ldots$
$A_2 \ B_2 \ C_2 \ D_2 \ E_2 \ldots$
$A_3 \ B_3 \ C_3 \ D_3 \ E_3 \ldots$
.
.
.
$A_n \ B_n \ C_n \ D_n \ E_n \ldots$

FIGURE 4.1. Time sequence of the operation of variables included in *The American Occupational Structure* by Blau and Duncan.

A's $\begin{cases} \text{Race-ethnicity} \\ \text{Sex} \\ \text{Father's education} \\ \text{Type of school attended before age 16} \\ \text{Birth order and number of sibs} \\ \text{Composition of respondent's family when he was 16} \\ \text{Size of city of residence when he was 16} \\ \text{Decade respondent was 16} \\ \text{Oldest brother's educational level} \\ \text{Father's occupation when respondent was 16} \end{cases}$

B's $\begin{cases} \text{Respondent's educational level} \end{cases}$

C's $\begin{cases} \text{Respondent's first job} \\ \text{Respondent's marital status} \end{cases}$

D's $\begin{cases} \text{Respondent's residence in 1962} \\ \text{Respondent's job in 1962} \end{cases}$

The horizontal dimension still represents the passage of time, but it is time as conceived by the researcher. Each A_i takes on several values or labels. It is implied that the variables labeled A "happened" earliest and approximately simultaneously, that B variables came later, that C variables came later still, and so on. An example may make this clearer.

Blau and Duncan (1967) studied the effects of a large number of variables on level of occupational placement of American males during the early and middle 1900s. Their theory placed the key variables in a time-order sequence as depicted in Figure 4.1. That figure presents an interpretation of their theory that was derived from the data analysis presented in their book. The set of variables furthest to the left (the A's) summarize influences on the lives of young men prior to the time they begin to make the crucial decisions that determine how much education they will receive and what kind of work they expect to do as adults. Next come the respondents' educational attainments (the B's). The next two variables are the prestige level of the respondents' first jobs and their marital status at that time (the C's). Finally, come the prestige level of the respondents' 1962 jobs and their places of residence in 1962 (the D's). Blau and Duncan argued that family background determined educational level and that family background and educational attainment together determined level of attainment in the first job. They further argued that family background, educational attainment, and the first job determined level of occupational attainment at the time of their study (1962). In none of their analyses were independent variables manipulated or, for that matter, manipulatable. Their research was aimed at discovering and understanding the patterns of educational and occupational attainments of males in the U.S. labor force over the first half of the twentieth century. It is hard to imagine how any important part of that process could have been studied in the laboratory under experimental conditions.

In the preceding pages we have outlined the most common models in survey research. The survey researcher seeks to understand and generalize from "natural" processes that have occurred (for example, educational or occupational attainment) or are occurring (for example, a preelection opinion poll). Frequently, the processes of interest occur over the course of a generation or several generations. A multitude of influences, recognized and unrecognized, may impinge on the processes being studied. This is in contrast to the situation faced by experimental researchers who, with laboratory isolation and control over exposure to stimuli, can greatly simplify the influences affecting the processes they study.

How can survey researchers achieve internal validity under these circumstances? One strategy often employed by survey researchers is to avoid causal statements altogether. This results in descriptions of research conclusions that do not go beyond describing them simply in terms of statistical outcomes (X is related to Y taking into account A and B). This strategy seeks to avoid, rather than to meet, the problem of internal validity. Clearly, however, some caution is necessary in stating the survey conclusions where explanations of social phenomena are given. Not only must data analyses support the conclusions the researcher offers, but they should, where possible, eliminate alternative explanations through appropriate statistical controls. Because of the necessity of being aware of alternative explanations in order to assess their plausibility, it is essential that as much as possible be known about the research problem. A thorough literature search covering the various theoretical approaches should yield the essential rival hypotheses and views of direction of causal connections, and so on. Strong grounding in the substantive literature of the problem area is probably the most crucial step in enhancing the internal validity of survey research. Translating that literature into appropriate measures and statistical operations are the crucial subsequent steps. Next we will discuss the latter process — the logic of statistical controls. The issues of measurement are treated in Part II of this book.

STATISTICAL ANALYSIS IN SURVEYS

Introduction

Survey research covers a broader range of purposes than experimental and quasi-experimental research. In these kinds of research, the major problem is to establish whether X caused Y. Whereas most social research, including surveys, aims at establishing the kind of understanding of social processes that ultimately will lead to general laws explaining the processes, much survey research is aimed at establishing facts and relationships that are prior to the elaboration of causal laws. In many cases, survey research is aimed at establishing whether X and Y covary or under what conditions they covary. To take an example, the studies of voting behavior in the United States conducted at the University of Michigan Survey Research Center (A. Campbell, et al., 1954; 1960; 1966) have, as a total research program, generated a wealth of understanding about the attitudes, social processes, and structural conditions affecting political behavior in the United States. No one of the many studies that has been part of that research program constitutes a test of whether X caused Y. Clearly, however, the aim of the research program is to establish the causes of voting choice — party identification, support for extremist candidates and third parties, and so on.

Assessing the internal validity of such a program of research is a complex task. Many of the specific pieces of research in that program were aimed at establishing that socioeconomic status (SES) and party identification covary, assessing what the conditions are under which they covary, whether they covary with other relevant variables taken into account, and so on. Where the intention is merely to establish relationships and to establish the conditions under which they hold, internal validity is not an issue. As the pieces of research are put together to go beyond just establishing relationships to interpreting them, internal validity becomes an issue. Internal validity of research conclusions may be more meaningfully assessed in reviewing an area of research than in reviewing individual pieces of research. However, internal validity cannot be established on the basis of individual pieces of research that themselves have no validity. Statistical control is a strategy for enhancing the internal validity of individual pieces of research.

Statistical Control

To rule out alternative explanations of variation in or change in the dependent variable, survey researchers use statistical procedures. For example, suppose we found, by examining records of fires in some city (note that surveys don't have to be of people!), that there is a positive and strong relationship between the number of fire trucks called to a fire and the amount of damage in dollars resulting from the fire (that is, the more trucks, the higher the monetary damage). Does this correlation represent a causal connection between trucks and cost of damage? Your intuition would probably tell you that it does not, but let us examine the situation closely. First, we do have a situation where X and Y covary. Second, one could argue that in modern times, where fire insurance requirements for urban fire coverage demand that every covered building be reachable by fire equipment within a specified time limit after an alarm, trucks arrive before the damage is done. (We wouldn't want the reader to reject our point on the basis of disagreement with this dubious assumption.) Thus, the time precedence of a possible causal relationship is satisfied. The most problematic question is whether there are alternative explanations of the observed correlation, such as, the effects of a third variable. One such variable is the size of the fire. Figure 4.2 depicts these two alternative explanations. Alternative A says the number of fire trucks present is the cause of the monetary damage. Alternative B suggests the following three propositions:

1. The severity of fires determines how much damage is done.
2. The severity of fires determines how many fire trucks are called to the scene.
3. These two propositions taken together imply that there will be a correlation between amount of damage and number of fire trucks called.

Intuition compels us to prefer Alternative B. A statistical procedure can help us decide whether our intuition is supported by evidence. The procedure is to examine

FIGURE 4.2. Two explanations of the relationship between number of trucks at fires and the amount of damage done by the fires.

A) number of fire trucks → amount of monetary damage

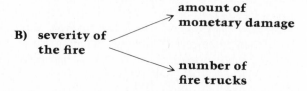

**B) severity of
   the fire**

**amount of
monetary damage**

**number of
fire trucks**

the relationship between number of trucks and amount of damage while taking into account the severity of fires. One way to do this would be to classify fires into two categories, those that are of average or less severity and those that are greater than average in severity. We then calculate the relationship between number of trucks and amount of damage for fires classified as less severe and for those classified as more severe. If Alternative B is correct, there should be very little relationship between trucks and damage when the severity of the fire is taken into account. This is because most of the fires with few trucks and little damage should be among those that are of less severity. Likewise, most of the fires with many trucks and lots of damage should be among those of greater severity. The same point is illustrated in Box 4.1.

A correlation like that between number of trucks and amount of damage is called a **spurious correlation** because it does *not* represent a direct causal con-

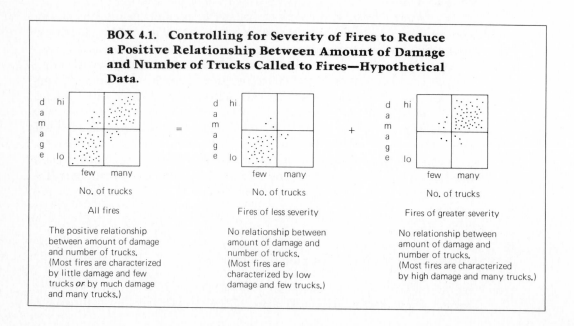

BOX 4.1. Controlling for Severity of Fires to Reduce a Positive Relationship Between Amount of Damage and Number of Trucks Called to Fires—Hypothetical Data.

All fires

The positive relationship between amount of damage and number of trucks. (Most fires are characterized by little damage and few trucks *or* by much damage and many trucks.)

Fires of less severity

No relationship between amount of damage and number of trucks. (Most fires are characterized by low damage and few trucks.)

Fires of greater severity

No relationship between amount of damage and number of trucks. (Most fires are characterized by high damage and many trucks.)

nection between the variables. Calling a correlation "spurious" does not imply that it does not exist or that it has a value of zero. It is induced or created by the common dependence of the variables on an antecedent variable. The correlation simply does not represent a direct causal connection. Note that deciding to call a correlation "spurious" is tantamount to making a causal interpretation. In survey analysis, before we can assert causal connections between variables, we must be sure their correlations are not spurious. To do this, we take into account variables representing the influences of phenomena that could cause spurious correlations. In our preceding example, severity of fire was an uncontrolled correlated variable; when we took it into account, it became a controlled variable, and it explained the spurious correlation.

Presenting Survey Data

Frequently in survey research, the substantive problem is to explore the meaning of some relationship rather than to test a causal hypothesis. This is theory building rather than hypothesis testing. Much of survey research is an effort to generate ideas and explanations rather than to test them. The following discussion of data analysis applies to these efforts as much as it applies to testing hypotheses and eliminating alternatives hypotheses.

A strategy for the detailed examination of basic relationships was developed by Lazarsfeld (Glock, 1967; Lazarsfeld and Rosenberg, 1955; Kendall and Lazarsfeld, 1950). The general paradigm is that a two-variable relationship is established in a research problem. The relationship may then be explored by successively introducing other variables as statistical controls. We will discuss two examples of the process of **elaboration** (the label given by Lazarsfeld to the detailed examination of two variable relationships through the introduction of control variables). The examples illustrate different uses of the elaboration process.

Interpreting a three-variable relationship. Data for the first example come from a study of library users by sociologist Jan Hajda. He was commissioned by the City of Baltimore to study who used the public library and for what purposes. As part of the study, he wanted to know what kinds of people were likely to read books regularly because lending books is one of the important functions of public libraries. A series of tables from that study is reproduced in the pages that follow. The purpose of this segment of the analysis was to gain a better understanding of why being a book reader was related to age.

The data given in Table 4.1 show the relationship between women's age and whether they report being book readers. The title of the table tells us what variables are included in it. Sometimes the title will give information about where the data come from as well. We have given this information below the table after the heading *Source.* In this example, comparison groups are formed by dividing the sample into two age categories. The comparison groups are analogous to "experimental" and "control" groups in experimental research, although age category is a naturally occurring, rather than an experimenter-assigned, variable. In order to be interpretable, these comparison groups have to be formed so that they are mutually exclusive and exhaustive; that is, no respondent should be classified in more than one category,

TABLE 4.1 Women's Reports on Being "Book Readers" by Age

Age	Percentage Having Read a Book Recently	Number of Cases
45 years and older	37%	867
Under 45 years	49	963

Source: Probability sample of Baltimore women studied by Jan Hajda. (Unpublished data cited in Davis, 1968.)

and every respondent should be classifiable into some category. The division of the age dimension into two groups satisfies these two conditions. The table shows the rate of book reading in two comparison groups.

Any percentage or mean is not interpretable in isolation. Only in comparison with some other number can we give meaning to either. Among those 45 years and over, is the 37 percent who are book readers a "high" or "low" percentage? We cannot answer this question without including some other comparison group. A logical and relevant comparison group in this context is the other age category, those under 45 years of age. Therefore, we compare the percentage of book readers (dependent variable) between different age categories (comparison groups) in much the same way we would compare average levels of O (dependent variable) between experimental and control groups (comparison groups).

What does the comparison tell us? Literally, it tells us what the difference in percentages of book readers between the comparison groups is. If we were trying to make a causal interpretation of this relationship, we would say that the difference in percentages is a measure of the "effect" of age on being a book reader. If we think of the percentages as being rates (percent means per 100; 37 percent means 37 of each 100 cases), then the difference between these percentages (49% − 37% = 12%) represents the increment in the rate of occurrence of book readers among younger

TABLE 4.2 Women's Reports on Being "Book Readers" by Age (Raw Data)

Age (Comparison Group)	Number Who Are Book Readers	Number Who Are Not Book Readers	Total Number in Comparison Group
45 years and over	321	546	867
Under 45 years	482	501	983

> **BOX 4.2.   Percentaging a Two-Variable Table.**
> **The percentages given in Table 4.1 are computed from the data given in Table 4.2. All of the data for a given percentage come from a row in this table. The base or denominator of the percentage is the number of cases in the comparison group. The numerator is the number of cases that are both in the comparison group *and* in the designated category of the dependent variable (that is, book readers). Specifically, the 37 percent from the first row of Table 4.1 is 321 (number of respondents 45 years old and over who are book readers) divided by 867 (the number of respondents 45 years old and over). The result of this division is then multiplied by 100 to convert from proportion to percentage. We would compute the 49 percent from the second row of Table 4.1 from the second row of Table 4.2. The percentage of respondents under 45 years old who are book readers is 49 percent. Note that Table 4.1 gives only "percentage who are book readers" and does not give "percentage who are not book readers." This is because, in this case, the dependent variable has only two categories. The "percentage who are not book readers" is redundant information that can be computed by subtracting "percentage who are book readers" from 100 percent.**

as compared to older women. In this sense, we can say that the effect of age (being younger than 45 versus being 45 or older) on being a book reader is 12 percent. The very act of constructing and interpreting percentage tables pushes one in the direction of an informal kind of causal analysis. The reader should note that because a different set of age categories would result in a different estimate of the effect of age, no great importance should be attached to the magnitude of, as opposed to the existence of, the effect.

Researchers whose orientation is toward experimental research may object to the use by survey researchers of the terms *independent* and *dependent* variables. In the experimental paradigm, independent variables are manipulated and dependent variables are measured after the manipulation. There is no such clear time order of occurrence in the case of book reading and age. Why do we say that age is the independent variable and book reading is the dependent variable (in this instance)? The answer, arbitrary though intuitively appealing, is that

1. We are interested in understanding why some people are book readers and others are not.

2. We can imagine an age-"causes"-book-reading link, but less readily can we imagine a book-reading-"causes"-age link.

3. It is well established in social science literature that age differences among people are an important determinant of differences in a wide range of attitudes and behavior, including the use of leisure time (Cain, 1964).

We can construct a plausible scenario that relates age to book reading. It must be clearly recognized, however, that "plausibility" is only one important element in judging the validity of research conclusions. To conclude that "differences among people in age explains part of their differences in reading habits" is a long way from concluding (as one might in an appropriately designed experiment) that age caused book reading. One is very tempted to make just this interpretation, however, and say, "Differences in age cause/explain/account for/predict differences in book reading."

A next logical step in the analysis of survey data is to explore the age-book-reading relationship further. We might ask: Why is book reading related to age? We could posit an explanation and then examine additional tabulations to see whether the data support the explanation. Following the original analysis, we could observe that most people who were 45 and over when the survey was conducted (in the early 1960s) were of high school age before the 1940s. The proportion of the U.S. population who graduated from high school during those years (say, 1920–1938) was less than 30 percent (*The New York Times*, 1969, p. 517). Those who were under 45 would have been of high school age in the late 1940s and the 1950s, a time when higher proportions of those reaching the ages of high school graduation completed four years of high school and even went on to college (50–60 percent). Perhaps differences in age reflect systematic differences in educational attainment, which, in turn, are plausibly more closely related to differences in reading habits. Though there are undoubtedly differences among people who achieved given levels of education, one would expect higher levels of educational achievement to be associated with greater enjoyment of reading, greater capacity for reading, and actually doing more reading. If this argument were true, then it should be the case that, with education taken into account, the weak relationship between age and book reading would diminish. Further, even with age controlled, there should be a substantial relationship between education and book reading. What is implied is the following:

Age--→ educational opportunity ---→ book reading
      and attainment

In Table 4.1, we examined data that support the indirect tie between age and book reading (age → book reading). The data in Table 4.3 are consistent with, and

TABLE 4.3 Level of Educational Attainment by Age

Age	Educational attainment			Total	Number of Cases
	0–8 Years	*9–12 Years*	*Some College*		
45 years old and over	45%	39%	16%	100%	867
Under 45 years	16	63	21	100%	963

Source: Probability sample of Baltimore women studied by Jan Hajda. (Unpublished data cited in Davis, 1968.)

TABLE 4.4   Women's Reports on Being Book Readers by Their Level of Educational Attainment

Level of Educational Attainment	Percent Who Are Book Readers	Number of Cases
0–8 years	14%	546
9–12 years	47	955
Some college	75	349

Source: Probability sample of Baltimore women studied by Jan Hajda. (Unpublished data cited in Davis, 1968.)

lend credence to, the first step in the argument (age → education). Those data show that the modal level of educational attainment for women 45 and older was completion of elementary school (45 percent). Smaller proportions completed successively higher levels of education (39 percent and 16 percent for attending high school or college, respectively). For women under 45 years, however, the modal level of educational attainment was in the high school range (63 percent). The percentage of younger women who received only elementary level schooling was substantially smaller than the percentage of older women receiving only this level of education.

Data in Table 4.4 address the second step of the argument just given. There the relationship between educational attainment and book reading is given. Looking across the comparison groups (defined by educational attainment), we can see that higher levels of educational attainment go with higher rates of book reading. Again one can use differences between percentages as an index of the effect of having higher educational levels on the incidence of book reading. Women who have educational attainments in the high school years are more likely (47% − 14% = 33%) than those with only elementary education to be book readers. Women whose educational attainments are beyond the high school years are more likely (75% − 47% = 28%) than those with high school experience to be book readers.

Next comes the crucial test of the relationships among these three variables. Putting the two links of this argument together implies that if we look at the relationship between book reading and age with education controlled, there should no longer be an effect of age on book reading (that is, there should no longer be differences between age groups in rates of book reading). Table 4.5 gives the relevant data showing that age groups no longer differ in rates of book reading (15 percent versus 14 percent; 47 percent versus 47 percent; and 76 percent versus 74 percent). On the other hand, comparing across educational levels within age groups (read vertically in Table 4.5), we find that educational groups differ as much as in Table 4.4 in the incidence of book reading. Stated in terms of the causal language that we used earlier, the effects of education on book reading are undiminished by controlling age.

The outcome we have just described in the three-variable analysis is called "explanation" because it shows that the level of educational attainment explains the relationship between age and book reading (Lazarsfeld and Rosenberg, 1955). The suggestion of these data (the "explanation") is that (1) these older women are less

TABLE 4.5   Book Reading Among Baltimore Women by Their Level of Educational Attainment and Age

Level of Educational Attainment	Age	
	Under 45	*45 and older*
	(percentage who are book readers)	
0–8 years	15%	14%
	(157)	(389)
9–12 years	47	47
	(617)	(338)
Some college	76	74
	(209)	(140)

Source: Probability sample of Baltimore women studied by Jan Hajda. (Unpublished data cited in Davis, 1968.)

well educated than the younger ones and (2) that differences in education among the women largely account for their differences in book reading.

The mechanics of presenting three-variable analyses.   Earlier we discussed the presentation of two-variable tables. Having completed our substantive discussion of the rest of that analysis, we will return briefly to those additional tables to review some guidelines in presenting data for such analyses.

In terms of presentation of data in tabular form, Table 4.3 has a feature not present in earlier tables. There one of the variables — level of education — has more than two categories. When this is the case for variables being treated as dependent variables, the percentage of the comparison group falling into *each* of the categories of the dependent variable is given. (Recall that in the discussion in Box 4.2 we said that where the dependent variable is a dichotomy, that is, has two categories, only the percentage of the comparison group falling into one of the categories is presented. The other percentage is easily obtained by subtracting the percentage given in the table from 100 percent). In order to make it perfectly clear to those reading the table, a total column is given to show unambiguously which set of categories are the comparison groups. Thus, for the 867 women who are in the "45 years old and older" group, the distribution of educational attainments is 45% + 39% + 16% = 100%. The percentages should always add to 100 percent, or a footnote should state why they fail to do so. Where the dependent variable has more than two categories, it is more convenient for the reader to present all the percentage figures.

In Table 4.5 still another new feature is encountered. This is the presentation of the incidence of book readers by categories of two independent variables simultaneously. In effect, what has occurred is the creation of six comparison groups from the cross classification of a two-category variable (age) with a three-category variable (educational attainment). This creates a 2 × 3 = 6 cell table. The numbers in parentheses to the right of, and slightly below, the percentages is the number of respondents in the comparison group (or in the cell). This comparison group total, as was the case in the two-variable table, is the base of the percentage. The numerator of the percentage is the number of women in the comparison group who are book readers. Providing the base for each percentage along with the percentage itself gives the interested reader all the data that are needed to recreate the original tabulation. The reader will then be able to compute correlation coefficients or to reorder the data in other ways that may be meaningful or useful.

There is a second reason for *always* giving the base on which a percentage is based. This is to enable the reader to make an independent assessment of the stability of percentages and differences between percentages. The stability of a percentage is the degree to which it is unaffected by minor changes in the classification of respondents on the variables involved (say, owing to sampling variations or measurement error). Suppose we were comparing the incidence of book reading among age groups each of which had only ten respondents. A 20 percent difference between the groups in the incidence of book reading would represent a difference between the groups of only two people. Stated in this way, the 20 percent difference between the groups does not seem like a very meaningful difference. On the other hand, if each age group had 1,000 respondents, a 20 percent difference in book readers would represent a difference of 200 book readers. That big a difference in the number of book readers more reasonably represents a "real" difference between the groups in book reading.

Interpreting relationships among variables—a second example. It is common knowledge that jobs that have higher status have higher pay on the average. The data in Table 4.6 may then seem a little surprising, for they show that when annual income is divided near the median for 1959, white-collar workers (professionals, managers, sales workers, and clerical workers) were only slightly (13 percent) more likely to receive $4,000 or more income than blue-collar workers. Although this percentage difference is significant, it is not as great as one might have expected. Perhaps the relationship is masked by the lack of a relevant control. There are several relevant possibilities—sex, urban-rural residence, race, among others. The sex of a worker is something that recent research has shown to be strongly related to both occupational attainment and income (Epstein, 1970). Tables 4.7 and 4.8 confirm

TABLE 4.6   Annual Earnings Among Employed Persons by Occupation (1959)

Occupation	Percentage Earning $4000 or more	Number of cases*
White collar	41%	259
Blue collar	28	355

Source: U.S. Census of the Population, 1960. (Data from the 1 in 1,000 sub-sample of individuals. Unpublished data cited in Davis, 1968.)
*Numbers rounded to the nearest 100,000 people.

TABLE 4.7   Annual Earnings of Employed Persons by Sex (1959)

Sex	Percentage Earning $4,000 or More	Number of Cases
Males	45%	423
Females	8	191

See notes to Table 4.6.

that sex is related to both for employed persons in the United States in 1959. In Table 4.9, the relationship of occupation to earnings is clarified by introducing the workers' sex. There is a strong relationship between occupation and earnings for male workers and a somewhat weaker relationship between these variables for female workers. Our "common knowledge," then, is primarily a function of observations about the relationship between occupation and earnings for male workers. Because female workers are more often in white-collar clerical jobs than male workers and are less often in high-paying jobs, the relationship between occupation and earnings appears not to be as strong as we might have expected. A control for sex clarifies the nature of the occupation-earnings relationship.

A number of books have been written to develop and illustrate the elaboration analysis originally developed by Lazarsfeld (Kendall and Lazarsfeld, 1950; Lazarsfeld and Rosenberg, 1955). We have only briefly touched on this topic. Students who wish to study strategies of survey analysis in greater detail should consult one or more of these books. The books by Davis (1968), Rosenberg (1968), and Hyman (1955) are clearly written and should be available in most college and university libraries.

In survey research, such as that illustrated in the foregoing examples, data analysis is a strategy for exploring the meaning of relationships among variables and for eliminating alternative explanations of relationships. The examples we have just discussed illustrate the exploration of the meaning of relationships. The general strategy is to introduce additional variables as statistical controls in order to observe their effects on the originally observed relationship. Choosing variables to introduce

TABLE 4.8   Occupation by Sex for Employed Persons in 1959

Sex	Percentage with White-Collar Occupations	Number of Cases
Male	36%	423
Female	57	191

See notes to Table 4.6.

as control variables in a data analysis is a theoretical issue. For example, suppose the following sequence of variables described the actual sequence of causation to determine current income for men and women in the American labor force:

family background $\longrightarrow$ educational attainment $\longrightarrow$ occupational attainment $\longrightarrow$ current income

One should not introduce a variable whose influence occurs late in the sequence as a control in studying relationships among variables earlier in the sequence. To illustrate, if one is exploring as a dependent variable differences among men and among women in educational attainment, then occupational attainment and current income would be inappropriate controls. Appropriate controls would be variables representing additional or alternative influences on educational attainment. Unfortunately, it is frequently impossible to order variables into a sequence like this one. Much of the debate and controversy in the social sciences is over the establishment of such sequences. It is important, therefore, to make a thorough review of the literature in any area in which one wishes to conduct research, seeking a synthesis of past results and theoretical ideas. Then one can choose control variables on the basis of careful and explicit consideration of these results and ideas.

For example, only the consistency of the results with the argument and the plausibility of the argument can lead us to conclude that age is an indirect, and education is a direct, cause of book reading. We could have presented the data in a way that would make book readers and nonbook readers the comparison groups. Then we would have talked about how being a book reader affects the incidence of being older or how being a book reader affects the acquisition of higher levels of education. It makes no sense to say book reading causes people to grow old (though one of the early readers of this chapter insists emphatically that the more he reads, the older he gets!). It is plausible, however, that book reading could cause the acquisition of higher levels of education. Because this possibility cannot be ruled out, any interpretation of such observed relationships must be made with caution.

Survey researchers do seek to make causal explanations. They frequently avoid the term *causes* and instead use *predicts, explains, leads to, brings about, produces, determines,* or any of a number of such words or phrases. Yet survey researchers

TABLE 4.9 Annual Earnings by Occupation and Sex-Employed Persons

	Sex	
	Female	**Male**
	Percent Earning	**Percent Earning**
Occupation	**$4000 or more**	**$4000 or more**
White Collar	12% (108)*	62% (151)
Blue Collar	2 (83)	36 (272)

*Numbers rounded to the nearest 100,000 people.

like experimental researchers want to know *why* social phenomena are related and, frequently, how to control or manipulate those relationships. Because survey researchers cannot control the variables they measure and cannot rule out alternative hypotheses through randomization, they can seldom make causal inferences with the assurance of an experimental researcher. To the extent that survey researchers attempt causal interpretations, they must be prepared to defend the internal validity of their conclusions.

SAMPLING

In every piece of research a crucial issue is whether the research conclusions can be generalized beyond the immediate pool of research subjects. This is an important element of external validity that was discussed earlier. The best way to assure that the results can be generalized beyond a single study is to draw a representative sample. As we mentioned in an earlier section of this chapter, survey research is often focused on establishing relationships or measuring the incidence of characteristics of some population rather than assessing causal connections among variables. Because of this, the incorporation of representative sampling may be an essential aspect of the research design in surveys. For this reason generalizability of the results to other populations is more often possible with survey research design than with other kinds of research.

In choosing a study population, we try to choose the research subjects so that they are representative of the population to which we wish to generalize the research conclusions. A "representative" sample is one for which the results (for example, proportions of people holding certain opinions, differences between comparison groups in some behavior, and so on) are what we would have found had we studied the entire population (within acceptable limits). This enhances the external validity (the generalizability) of our research conclusions.

A national public opinion polling organization that wishes to estimate the proportions of the vote that will go to the Democratic and Republican candidates will try to select research subjects that represent the range and frequency of political behavior of the voting population of the United States as a whole. In usual practice it is not feasible to study the entire voting population. The financial resources and manpower that it would take to poll the approximately 125 million adults who are potential voters are enormous. Moreover, a carefully chosen sample can yield estimates of population values (that is, means, proportions, variances, correlations, and so on) that are within acceptable limits of error. For example, in the 1968 election two of the national public opinion polling organizations — the Gallup Poll and the Harris Poll — predicted that Richard Nixon would get 43 percent and 41 percent of the vote, respectively. Nixon's actual percentage of the total vote was 43.4 percent (*The New York Times*, 1969). The polling organizations made their predictions on the basis of carefully drawn samples of approximately 2,000 respondents from a voting age population estimated at about 120 million people, of whom only 73 million actually cast ballots. In the face of the uncertainty of whether potential voters are registered and whether registered voters will actually go vote, the accuracy of the projected vote percentages is very impressive.

Any measure of a population value (for example, average income) that is based on part of, rather than all of, a population is an estimate rather than its actual value, even assuming there is no measurement error. Different ways of choosing the part of the population to be studied will produce different estimates of the population value. Some of these estimates will be closer to the true value than others. Further, for some kinds of samples, the researcher can estimate the degree of variation around the "true" population value.

A rather detailed, but nontechnical, discussion of kinds of samples and of how to draw samples is given in the Appendix. There distinction is made between probability and nonprobability sampling plans. Probability sampling plans have the characteristic that every element or member of the population has a known probability of being chosen into the sample. This does not mean that every member of the population has to have the *same* probability of being chosen. For example, if a researcher wished to compare voting intentions of different income groups, people with very high income levels would be assigned higher probabilities of being chosen in the sample than people whose incomes were nearer the population average. Because people with high incomes are rare, this would assure that there were enough people with very high incomes to provide a meaningful estimate of their voting intentions. Probability sampling plans provide the basis for making statistical inferences to the population from which the representative sample is drawn. Nonprobability sampling plans provide no such basis for making statistical inferences. This means that the external validity, the generalizability, of studies using nonprobability samples is open to serious question.

In spite of the fact that statistical inference to larger populations may be impossible, many studies in the social sciences use research subjects who were not selected by a probability process because the researchers have preexisting access to the study population. For example, research evaluating government programs is logically restricted to program effects on the subject population (frequently with a nonprogram control group selected also for convenient access). Most social psychological experiments use students from lower division psychology classes (Schultz, 1969; Higbee and Wells, 1972; Borgatta and Bohrnstedt, 1974). Other researchers may choose research subjects or groups of subjects (for example, classrooms or schools) because they exhibit particular characteristics. For example, the 20 high schools studied by McDill and his associates were selected from among several thousand schools because they were particularly high or low in their proportion of high achieving graduates, given their social composition (McDill and Rigsby, 1973).

What is to be made of this? Is probability sampling unimportant? How can these researchers legitimate their generalizations? The resolution of this issue is very complex. Generally, social scientists agree that probability sampling *is* important, but they also give various reasons for not using probability sampling. Such reasons must be balanced against the goals and intentions of that piece of research. For example, Campbell and Stanley (1963) and Cook and Campbell (1976) argue that internal validity (which necessitates close control over the research process and isolated laboratory conditions) should have precedence over external validity.

Another reason for not selecting a probability sample is that one may be able to argue that the processes he or she is studying are general, uniform processes, invariant across populations. This is frequently argued in experimental psychology.

This argument implies that the variables in the study are not related to the social processes that create population groups. For example, if wealth, race, and attitudes toward race create neighborhoods that are relatively homogeneous by race and wealth, then the results of a study including variables that are correlated with wealth and race but conducted with research subjects from a single neighborhood could not be generalized to populations that differed in wealth or racial composition or both. Where the research variables are correlated with the processes that create the population, these processes themselves constitute an alternative explanation of any causal inferences made. Thus, in addition to external validity's being threatened by the nonrepresentativeness of the study population, internal validity is threatened by the alternative explanation that may not have been eliminated. The uniqueness of the population represents a threat to the generalizability of the research conclusions as a matter of degree. The more unique the population and the more strongly related its uniqueness to the key research variables, the greater the threat to both internal and external validity.

Sometimes researchers consciously attend to the uniqueness of the research situation and assume that generalization is impossible or irrelevant. For example, ethnographers and participant observers seldom seek generalization, except at the most abstract level, to other populations or situations. In a like manner, one sometimes hears experimentally oriented colleagues say, "We are not interested in generalizing to larger populations. Rather, we want to generalize to theory."

A fourth circumstance where probability sampling may be impossible or unnecessary is in the study of unique historical events (which may, nevertheless, be of general theoretical interest and importance). If a revolution were in process in country X, a survey or other researcher on the scene would be wise to talk to whoever is around and involved, regardless of whether such persons constitute a purposive, random, haphazard, fortuitious, or total coverage sample!

A fifth reason for using a nonprobability sample is that the researcher has limited resources (time, financial, or both) and cannot "afford" to carry out the study with a more appropriate study population. One can never be sure in evaluating such studies whether their conclusions are unique, artifactual results from a specific population or whether the conclusions have broader, scientific usefulness. Although one cannot say that such studies are better not done, one cannot assess the degree to which they add to the store of scientific knowledge. Only where many similar studies address the same research questions in very diverse populations with compatible results is there any basis for assessing external validity. In such situations the judgment can only be made about research conclusions common to the bulk of the studies, not about the specific conclusions of any particular study.

SUMMARY

The strength of survey research is in answering questions of fact and in assessing the distributions of the characteristics of populations. In uses of this kind, issues of internal validity are not raised. There are no causal inferences. Because survey strategies lend themselves easily to extensive, scattered data-collecting sessions (interviews), external validity can be enhanced through the use of probability sampling plans. No other research strategy matches the strength of survey research in its potential for handling external validity. Of course, not all survey research takes advantage of the possibility of using probability sampling. When survey researchers fail to employ probability sampling, the external validity of their research conclusions is as problematic as that from other kinds of research.

When the aims of survey research are broadened to include interpretation and causal analysis of correlations, internal validity becomes important. Because survey research deals primarily with naturally occurring variables that cannot be randomly assigned and manipulated, both the time order of occurrence and alternative explanations of relationships become problematic. On the other hand, many interesting and important social science research problems are not amenable to simulation in the laboratory setting. No experimentally oriented social scientist has yet found a way to simulate the lifetime effects of being reared in poverty versus wealth, of being born female versus male, of being born a black American versus a white American, or of having high versus low education. Where processes such as occupational attainment take place over a lifetime, they cannot reasonably be studied by research techniques other than survey research.

Many of the research areas where survey research is the logical choice are areas where the researcher wishes to make causal inferences. Such inferences can never be made with the certainty in survey research that they can be made with in some experimental research. Certain strategies can be employed to enhance the internal validity of survey research, however. In some research problems, the time order of variables can be determined by collecting data over a period of time. In other research problems, alternative hypotheses can be rendered less tenable through statistical controls. The internal and external validity of *research programs* or long traditions of research can more readily be assessed than the results of single instances of survey research.

Evaluation Research

Evaluation research differs from the other forms of research we have discussed not in its methods but in its purposes, its use, and its relationship to social and political institutions. It is applied research. Most of what we have discussed in previous chapters was basic research. Basic research is conducted to add to our store of knowledge, test hypotheses, build theories, and perhaps find some practical application in the future. But even with no forseeable practical application, basic research is carried on for its own sake. Applied research, as its name suggests, is carried on for practical reasons — to produce findings that are applicable, practical, immediately useful. Evaluation research is a special form of applied research, designed to evaluate programs, usually ameliorative social programs such as remedial education, welfare reforms, innovative teaching methods, health care delivery systems, job training programs, and the like. The results of evaluation research are not meant merely to add to our store of knowledge or develop theories. They are used, often immediately, to decide whether programs should stop or go, whether budgets should expand or contract, whether personnel should be hired or fired — all based on whether the program accomplished what was intended.

Much applied research is marketing research — designed to assess people's preferences for commercial products or for advertising techniques. Although we could classify all such research as evaluation research on the grounds that it is evaluating something (for example, evaluating a product or an advertisement), we do not include it in this chapter. We are concerned instead with evaluations of social programs that have implications for social policy. It is the connection with social policy and budget and personnel decisions that makes evaluation research different from both basic research and other applied research.

SUMMATIVE AND FORMATIVE EVALUATIONS

There are two general categories of evaluation research called *summative* and *formative* research, or *outcome* and *process* research. Summative or outcome evaluations examine the effects of a program and ask, "Does it work?" Formative or process evaluations ask, "What is it?" and "How does it work?" Outcome evaluations use experimental, quasi-experimental, and survey research designs. Process evaluations use techniques more like participant observation (see Chapter 6). Outcome research usually uses statistical analysis of quantitative data. Process research is usually qualitative research and uses case histories rather than statistics to make a point. Outcome evaluations are used to decide whether programs should continue or cease, and for this reason administrators may resist and evaluators find it difficult to implement an outcome evaluation. Process evaluations seem more benign because they are used to help the administrators form their programs, revise them, and improve them. Process evaluators provide feedback to the program director about how the participants react to the program, how the implementors are carrying out the program, and whether the actual program resembles the intended program. They define the program as it appears in action and describe how it works. This feedback often takes place during the early stages of a program, when there is still room for change and improvement — hence, the name *formative* evaluation. By contrast, summative evaluations are done at the end of a program or after it has been in existence long enough to have produced some measurable effects that provide a fair test of the program's success. This chapter focuses on summative evaluations; the chapter on participant observation describes the steps that can be used in formative evaluation research.

Donald Campbell (1969) describes the inevitable conflicts that arise between administrators whose careers depend upon implementing successful programs and evaluation researchers whose careers require that they evaluate other people's programs. He urges program administrators to adopt an "experimental" attitude and use information from evaluators about whether the innovative programs they are administering achieve the intended goal. To have a truly experimental attitude, however, a program administrator would have to be in a position to administer two or more alternative programs, so that the evaluation could be an evaluation of programs rather than personnel. By evaluating programs rather than people, a researcher could gain cooperation from some of the people who would otherwise resist or distort program evaluation. Such social and administrative arrangements are unlikely, however, because it is not always possible to separate a program from its personnel or its administrators; so there may be no "pure" evaluations of programs detached from their directors or implementers.

DIFFERENCES BETWEEN EVALUATION AND BASIC RESEARCH

Results with Immediate Impact

Because it is carried out to evaluate ongoing programs, evaluation research is designed with a shorter time span than basic research. The social problems are not solved immediately, but *decisions* about programs are made immediately because budget allocations and personnel decisions are frequently based on demonstrable "results." Laurence Lynn (1977) points out that "social problems are seldom solved by a single decisive act or policy declaration; rather, policies to deal with them are fashioned incrementally over time in a series of measures which are partial and not necessarily reversible" (1977, p. 72). However, policymakers often have "short time horizons" and wish to see research results to justify continuing or terminating a program. The press for quick and definite answers makes most evaluation research different from basic research.

Although evaluation research is intended to produce immediate results and have an immediate impact, two circumstances often prevent this from happening. The first arises when results are equivocal or contradictory, so that it is not clear what the policy decision should be. There have been many evaluations of preschool Head Start programs, for instance, and they do not all agree about the program's success or failure (Cicerelli, et al., 1969; Campbell and Erlebacher, 1970). Negative income tax or income maintenance programs have also been tried and evaluated in many places, and the results are contradictory (Kehrer, 1978; Kershaw, 1972). If the planners and decision-makers are to use these results, which set should they use?

The second circumstance that interferes with using the results of program evaluation arises when the real effects of social programs are not immediately visible. For instance, Head Start preschool education was originally introduced to "break the cycle of poverty" by educating three- and four-year-old children so that they would become achieving self-sufficient adults. Today's educational planners do not intend to wait 20 or 30 years for an evaluation, however, before they decide whether to continue with the preschool programs. Instead, they use immediate outcomes — the children's subsequent academic achievement in elementary school — and assume that adult occupational achievement will follow from childhood scholastic performance. There is a positive but weak connection between the two.

Weiss (1972) calls these immediate or short-run effects "proximate" goals and the long-term desired effects "ultimate" goals. She says short-run effects suffice when previous research shows a direct and strong connection between proximate and ultimate goals. For instance, "in evaluation of a Smokers' Clinic, it is probably enough to discover that the program led participants to stop smoking. It is not essential to investigate the ultimate incidence of lung cancer" (Weiss, 1972, p. 38). Many of our more ambitious social programs, however, are designed to have long-range effects. Proximate outcomes in such cases are unsatisfactory, but they are all that we have. Later in this chapter we shall describe one evaluation that did assess the ultimate goals — a 30-year follow-up of men who had participated in a program as boys (McCord, 1978).

Vested Interests with Various Criteria for Success

The choice of dependent variables — the criterion for evaluating a program — makes evaluation researchers face this issue: In whose interests is the research? It is not sufficient to say "in the interests of science" because the outcome will influence more than science. Because the results of evaluation research are used to make funding decisions, there are vested interests in the criteria chosen for success. The evaluation may affect some people's jobs, education, or health; and the results may be in the interests of some people and perhaps to the detriment of others.

For instance, in negative income tax experiments across the United States, participants were given income subsidies, and the primary criterion (dependent variable) for evaluating the effect of the program was whether or not there was a decline in *work incentive*. The people and agencies that implemented and evaluated the income subsidy were concerned that the men and women who received a guaranteed minimum income not stop working as a result. They judged the program successful or not on the basis of the number of hours the recipients worked and the amount of money they earned. The same programs could have been evaluated on a number of other grounds — the health of the participants, their increased enjoyment of leisure time activities, their self-esteem, their participation in community activities, or their satisfaction with life. These other criteria were either ignored or deemphasized (Berk and Rossi, 1977). Work disincentive is a relevant criterion, as is the amount of money earned. Nonetheless, the other criteria could also have been used to judge the program's success or failure.

The scientific questions of selecting dependent variables become political questions in evaluation research. Whose criteria will prevail? It is not always clear that one set of criteria is "better" than another. All evaluation research must address the question of whose values, whose criteria for success or failure, will prevail in judging the outcome of a program. Different parties or participants in the research program have different perspectives and different goals. Evaluation researchers, therefore, even more than basic researchers, must ask themselves "Whose side are we on?" (Becker, 1967).

Technical Decisions with Ideological Consequences

The technical issues involved in finding measurable criteria have ideological consequences. "Applied social researchers are more technically proficient in the study of individuals than in the study of organizations, and therefore, social research tends to be more social psychological than social structural" (Berk and Rossi, 1977, p. 81). For instance, we have scales for measuring the alienation of individuals but none for measuring the alienating features of work places that might produce the alienation in employees (Berk and Rossi, 1977). This critique applies to basic research as well as evaluation research, but its consequences are more immediate and apparent in research evaluating social programs.

Evaluation research affects more than a decision of whether a social program succeeded or failed. It also affects our definition of what the social problems and their solutions are. The technical ease with which we can measure problems and outcomes determines which ones we recognize or attend to: "outcomes that can be counted easily tend to be listed as the outcomes desired" (Berk and Rossi, 1977). Crime prevention programs provide a case in point. One criterion for success is reduction in crime rates. This can be accomplished or attempted in several ways. If we consider the events leading to crime as forming a long causal chain, we could intervene at any point along that chain to prevent or reduce crime (Kidder and Cohn, 1979). We could intervene in the childhood experiences of "potential delinquents" and try to prepare them for noncriminal careers (McCord, 1978). Or we could focus on adult employment problems and provide job skills for the unemployed. Or we could seek alternatives to unemployment and layoffs as industrial options. Or we could focus on the doorsteps of victims of crime and promote better home security measures, such as locks and burglar alarms. All of these are plausible starting points for explaining and preventing crime. They all suggest very different goals or solutions for crime prevention programs, too, some of which would be much easier to implement successfully than others. Programs to install door locks and burglar alarms have higher success rates (if we simply count numbers of locks and alarms distributed) than do programs to restore community cohesion or job security; and, as Berk and Rossi (1977) point out, "outcomes that can be counted easily tend to be listed as the outcomes desired" (p. 81). The technical decision—to count burglar alarms installed—has the ideological implications that the way to reduce crime is to prevent victimization.

DESIGNS IN EVALUATION RESEARCH

If we put aside the uses or implications of the research and look only at the research design and measurement problems, evaluation research is very much like basic research. It includes all the same designs and threats to validity; it involves the same measurement issues and problems with operational definitions. We can find examples of evaluation research that use each of the designs or approaches we have discussed in the preceding chapters. There are over 200 evaluations that are "true experiments" with the treatment randomly assigned to recipients (Boruch, 1975). There are many evaluations that use quasi-experimental designs, with nonrandom assignment and comparisons made either with nonequivalent control groups or with the same groups' pretreatment measures. Some evaluations consist of surveys—these are often "needs assessment" studies to determine the demand for social programs such as community mental health centers. And some evaluations use qualitative methods and participant observation (see Chapter 6). In this section we describe two large-scale evaluations, one a true experiment and one a quasi experiment. Many evaluations are done on a much smaller scale, but we present these two because they magnify some of the issues discussed above.

A True Experiment—The Cambridge-Somerville Youth Study

The Cambridge-Somerville Youth Study is a unique piece of evaluation research because it did what many social evaluations ideally should do. It examined the long-term effects of a childhood treatment program. In 1939 a social philosopher and physician named Richard Clark Cabot began a program that he hoped would prevent deliquency among boys in Boston. He located over 500 boys aged five to 13 through recommendations of teachers, clergy, policemen, and welfare agencies. Some of the boys were considered "difficult" or predelinquent, and others were identified as "average." Half were assigned to the treatment program, and the other half were designated "controls." The assignment was made by the toss of a coin, making this a true randomized experiment.

Boys in the treatment program had counselors visit them on the average of twice a month. The counselors worked with both the boys and their families and encouraged the families to seek assistance from the program. The assistance and counseling included tutoring for the boys, medical and psychiatric attention, summer camps, youth activities, and access to other community programs. Boys in the control group participated only by providing information about themselves. The program lasted five years.

Over 30 years later, in 1975 and 1976, Joan McCord and her research team traced 488 of the original 506 members of the experiment "through court records, mental health records, records from alcoholic treatment centers, and vital statistics in Massachusetts. Telephone calls, city directories, motor-vehicle registrations, marriage and death records, and lucky hunches were used to find the men themselves" (McCord, 1978, pp. 284–285). Both the program and the evaluation of the program are remarkable. The program is notable for its truly experimental nature with random assignment and its magnitude — 506 boys were studied for five years. The evaluation is remarkable for its long-term follow-up and its thoroughness — 95 percent of the men were located and their records traced 30 years after their original assignment to the treatment and control groups. In McCord's follow-up she compared the men who had been in the treatment group with "matched mates" from the control group. She used official records and statistics from courts, mental hospitals, and alcohol treatment centers, as well as the men's self-reports from a questionnaire, which was returned by 113 men in the treatment group and 122 in the control group.

The results of these comparisons are surprising and controversial. Many of the records show *no differences* between the men who received "treatment" and those who received none, and in those instances where there were differences, the differences often show the treatment to have been *harmful* rather than helpful. McCord divided the treatment and control samples into those who had been described as "difficult" and "average" at the beginning of the treatment to see whether treatment was more beneficial for boys who originally seemed "difficult"; she again found no beneficial effects. Instead, 34 percent of the "difficult" boys in the treatment group and 30 percent of the "difficult" boys in the control group had juvenile records.

Adult criminal records reinforced the finding of no difference. Equal numbers of both treatment and control group men had been convicted for committing crimes as adults. The one significant difference between the two groups' criminal records showed the treatment to have been harmful: "a higher proportion of criminals from the treatment group than of criminals from the control group committed more than one crime. . . . Among the . . . men with criminal records from the treatment group, 78% committed at least two crimes; among the . . . men with criminal records from the control group, 67% committed at least two crimes" (McCord, 1978, p. 286).

Comparisons of health statistics also made the treatment group look bad. In response to questionnaire items that asked whether they were alcoholic, 17 percent of the treatment group responded yes, compared with 7 percent of the control group. On some other measures, the groups were equal: 21 men in each group had "received treatment in mental hospitals for disorders other than alcoholism" (McCord, 1978, p. 286). But the general mental and physical health of the treament group appeared worse than the controls: (1) of the 24 men in each group known to have died, those in the treatment group died at earlier ages, and (2) in response to questions about stress-related illnesses such as ulcers, asthma, high blood pressure, and the like, more men from the treatment group reported having had at least one of the ailments.

Comparisons of the family relations, occupations, and leisure time activities of the treatment and control groups again showed few differences — and the differences that did exist made the treatment look harmful. Roughly equal percentages of the two groups were married, divorced, remarried, and never married. Approximately equal proportions were unskilled workers. They differed in their numbers of white-collar or professional workers, however: 43 percent of the control group and 29 percent of the treatment group had white-collar or professional jobs. A comparison of the prestige ratings of the occupations of the two groups using National Opinion Research Center ranks showed that the control-group men were in positions with higher prestige (McCord, 1978).

The *only* measure on which the treatment group indicated the program was successful was a questionnaire item that asked for their subjective evaluation of the program: "In what ways (if any) was the Cambridge-Somerville project helpful to you?" "Two-thirds of the men stated that the program had been helpful to them" (McCord, 1978, p. 287). They wrote comments such as: "helped me to have faith and trust in other people," "helped prepare me for manhood," and "better insight on life in general" (McCord, 1978, p. 287).

McCord's evaluation of the Cambridge-Somerville experiment has received much attention and comment, particularly because it contradicts many other beliefs about the value of social programs (for example, Sobel, 1978). The only explanation McCord (1979) has found for the harmful effects of the Cambridge-Somerville experiment is that the men in the treatment group developed unrealistically high expectations. The unsolicited help and attention that they received as boys may have led them to expect more of themselves and of other people than they were able to realize. Critics of McCord's conclusions warn against overstatement; they ask for further research before we decide that programs like the Cambridge-Somerville project be abandoned (for example, Sobel, 1978). As the program was a true experiment, with boys randomly assigned to treatment and control groups, we can be reasonably confident that the effects McCord reported were a result of the treatment and not preexisting group differences. There are no other plausible explanations. The evidence is quite clear, therefore, that the treatment hurt more than it helped. The only redeeming feature of the program appears in the men's subjective evaluations — two-thirds said it had helped them. We will return to this point when we consider the role of client's satisfaction in program evaluation.

A Quasi Experiment—Head Start Preschool Education

Before we describe the evaluations of Head Start programs, we want to note first the social philosophy that underlies such programs. In a review of policy developments in improving education and training for low-income populations, Henry Levin

(1978) notes two types of reasons given for why people who are capable of working are still poor: (1) that they are unwilling to work or incapable of working enough to earn enough to rise above the poverty level, or (2) that there are not enough jobs. "The former explanation assumes that it is the low productivity of workers or their laziness that determines their low incomes. The latter explanation assumes that ... there just are not enough jobs with wages above the poverty level that are made available to such populations" (Levin, 1978, p. 523).

A decade of compensatory education programs in the United States began with the assumption that "if children of poor families can be given skills and motivation, they will not become poor adults" (Economic Report of the President, 1964). This assumption involved "blaming poverty on inadequacies of the poor versus blaming the poverty condition on the inadequacies of society" (Levin, 1978, p. 523). It reflected the personal theory of the program developers or perhaps the prevailing theory of the times. Social programs and their scientific evaluations are not neutral — they contain notions of blame and responsibility, and they represent someone's diagnosis of what the problem and the solution are. Head Start programs for preschool children focus on people instead of on societal conditions, and they are founded on the idea that poverty is caused by poor people's lack of education.

The actual evaluations of Head Start and other preschool programs did not, in fact, use measures of poverty to judge the programs' success or failure. They used children's subsequent academic achievement — a proximate rather than ultimate goal.

The evaluations of Head Start programs began within the agency that sponsored the programs, and they included three types: (1) summative evaluations of the overall effectiveness of all Head Start programs, (2) comparisons of different strategies and curricula within Head Start, and (3) on-site monitoring or process evaluations of individual programs (Williams and Evans, 1972). We will describe the first type of evaluation — summative evaluation of the overall effectiveness of the programs — and discuss some of the criticisms of that evaluation.

The first and most widely publicized evaluation of the overall effectiveness of Head Start was done by the Westinghouse Learning Corporation (Cicirelli, et al., 1969). The evaluation included a sample of 104 Head Start centers from across the country and a sample of children from those centers who were then in first, second, and third grades was chosen. A comparison group was formed of children from the same grades and the same schools who had not been in preschool Head Start programs. These comparison children were selected to be similar to the Head Start children in age, sex, race, and kindergarten attendance. The evaluators tested both groups of children with a series of standardized tests to measure scholastic abilities and self-concepts. They also had teachers rate the children's achievement and motivation, and they interviewed the parents of both groups of children. The comparison group was not formed by random assignment, making this a quasi experiment rather than a true experiment. The researchers tried to match the children in terms of their backgrounds; we shall discuss later how such attempts to "match" fail to eliminate group differences.

The results of this evaluation received wide attention because the findings were negative. The major conclusions were that (1) the summer programs were ineffective in producing gains that persisted in the elementary school years; (2) the full-year programs were marginally effective in producing cognitive gains and ineffective in producing gains in how the children felt about themselves; (3) Head Start children remained below national norms for standardized tests of language and scholastic achievement, but approached national norms on school readiness in grade one. The most positive finding came from parents' testimonials: "Parents of Head Start enrollees voiced strong approval of the program and its influence on their children. They reported substantial participation in the activities of the centers" (Cicirelli, et al., 1969, pp. 7–8). The Westinghouse report concluded that "the Head Start children cannot be said to be *appreciably* different from their peers in the elementary grades who did not attend Head Start in most aspects of cognitive and affective development measured in this study, with the exception of the slight, but nonetheless significant, superiority of full-year Head Start children on certain measures of cognitive development" (pp. 7–8).

The criticisms of this study, even though it was not a true experiment with random assignment, include some of the criticisms made of randomized experiments: "the study is too narrow. It focuses only on cognitive and affective outcomes. Head Start is a much broader program which includes health, nutrition, and community objectives, and any proper evaluation must evaluate it on all these objectives" (Williams and Evans, 1972, p. 257). The authors of the evaluation answered that "in the final analysis Head Start should be evaluated mainly on the basis of the extent to which it has affected the life-chances of the children involved. In order to achieve such effects, cognitive and motivational changes seem essential" (Williams and Evans, 1972, p. 257).

Another criticism was that the test instruments used to measure the cognitive and motivational changes were not developed for disadvantaged children and were therefore insensitive and inappropriate. The evaluators conceded that this was possible, but they said that they "used the best instruments available" (Williams and Evans, 1972, p. 258).

A third criticism is that the study looked only for long-term effects by testing children in first, second, and third grades and ignored the immediate benefits that children may have derived from being in a preschool program. "Rather than demonstrating that Head Start does not have appreciable effects, the study merely shows that these effects tend to fade out when the Head Start children return to a poverty environment" (Williams and Evans, 1972, p. 259). The evaluators admitted that this, too, may be true, but they said the program must be judged not by its short-term effects alone if those effects disappear in a year or two; " . . . the fact that the learning gains are transitory is a most compelling fact for determining future policy" (Williams and Evans, 1972, p. 259).

Of the remaining criticisms, we shall discuss one in detail, for it is a point that pertains to the design of the program and the evaluation—the quasi-experimental design. Because children were not admitted to Head Start by a lottery, the "control" group of comparison children was not equivalent, making this a nonequivalent control group design. The researchers tried to match the Head Start and comparison children on age, race, sex, kindergarten attendance, and parents' social status; but matching does not eliminate the effects of preexisting differences between two populations. Matching is a good strategy *only if* it is followed by random assignment. If the investigators had originally tried to match pairs of children and then from within each pair randomly assigned children to Head Start and the control group, they would have created equivalent groups. But matching alone is no substitute for random assignment.

Researchers may try to match nonequivalent groups either on pretest measures of the dependent variable or on other variables known to correlate with the dependent variable. Both of these strategies fail to eliminate preexisting group differences. Matching on variables known to correlate with the dependent variable always errs in the direction of undermatching and, therefore, fails because we can never know when we have matched on enough variables to be sure the two groups represent the same population. For instance, the Head Start evaluators matched the treatment children with a comparison group on the basis of age, sex, race, kindergarten attendance, and parents' social status. The children may still have differed in the kinds of television programs they watched, in their grandparents' education levels, in numbers of books in their homes, in the achievement levels of their friends, and so on. The numbers of variables on which they were not matched is infinite. As compensatory social programs are usually designed for populations that are defined as disadvantaged, the children from the treatment group had fewer natural "head starts" than the comparison group on many other variables (Campbell and Erlebacher, 1970). Therefore, because they were not matched on grandparents' education, kinds of television programs they watched, and many other variables, the treatment group probably would have scored lower on these unmatched variables. The two groups were undermatched, with the advantage probably going to the control group. Therefore, matching on variables known to correlate with the dependent variable is inadequate because it is always incomplete. The resulting undermatching will usually favor the control group and make compensatory social programs look harmful solely as a result of the failure to equate groups.

Matching on pretest measures of the dependent variable is also inadequate because it opens the way for regression artifacts to operate. To demonstrate how regression artifacts undermine matching on pretest scores, we ask you to take on faith something that is explained more fully in Chapter 7 — that measurement is always imperfect and scores are not 100 percent reliable from one measurement time to the next. Recall that in Chapter 2 we said that students who receive extreme scores on one examination — the lowest and highest midterm scores — will most likely not receive the same scores on a second examination. Partly because students may change how they study for the second examination and partly because our measurement of how much they knew on the first examination was not perfect, their second scores are likely to change. They generally do not change a great deal — they usually do not reverse positions — but the people who scored lowest on the first exam most likely do not all score lowest on the second exam, and the people who received the highest score the first time will not all receive the highest again on the second. Because they received extreme scores on the first test, any change in their positions means they receive less extreme scores on the second, and *regress toward the mean*. Figure 5.1 illustrates this pattern. The dashed line shows what the average posttest score was for each group of people who received a particular score on the pretest. For the people who received 40 on the pretest, the average posttest score was 55, and for those who received 100 on the pretest, the average posttest score was 85.

The fact that extreme scores regress toward the mean does not imply that students become more homogeneous over the course of a semester. If we work backwards and begin with final exam scores, we find the same regression effect of final exams on midterm scores. The students who received the highest scores on the final exam would not all receive identical midterm scores, and those who received the lowest scores on the final would not all receive the lowest scores on the midterm. If we turn Figure 5.1 on its side, we can see that the same regression toward the mean occurs when we look first at posttest scores and second at pretest scores. Regression toward the mean occurs, therefore, not as a result of a homogenization process but as a result of scores being less than 100 percent reliable. Any change of the most extreme scores is of necessity a regression toward the mean.

When we apply this logic to the quasi-experimental study of compensatory

FIGURE 5.1. Scatterplot showing regression toward the posttest mean from pretest scores. The numbers inside the graph (1's, 2's, 3's, and 4) indicate how many students received each score on the two tests.

The dashed line represents the average posttest score for each group of students who received a particular pretest score. The figures in parentheses are those averages. Turning the figure on its side, the same line represents the average pretest score for each group of students who received a particular posttest score. The regression toward the mean operates in both cases.

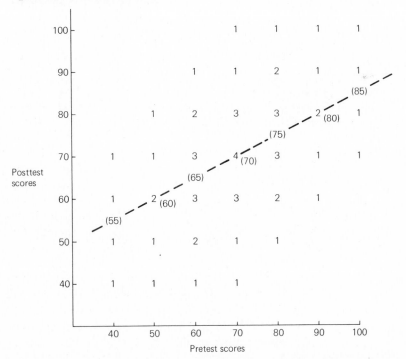

programs like Head Start, regression artifacts can make a program look detrimental in the following way. If children are not randomly assigned to the treatment and control groups but are selected on the basis of some qualifications, we cannot assume that the children in the two groups come from the same population. In fact, the more reasonable assumption is that they come from two different populations or social groups, those who qualify and those who do not. In the case of a compensatory program, those who qualify must usually demonstrate a disadvantage such as having a low income. The children who qualify for the program come from a group considered disadvantaged; the comparison children come from a group considered advantaged. These two groups obviously differ in their income levels and in the many other advantages that accompany income. They also differ in their average pretest achievement levels, a difference that the evaluators may try to remove by "matching" on pretest scores. In the process of matching, a researcher sets the conditions for regression artifacts to operate. Figure 5.2 shows the distributions of pretest scores for two hypothetical groups—one an advantaged comparison, the other a disadvantaged treatment group. The distributions overlap but they have different means or averages. In an attempt to "match" individuals from the two groups, the researcher draws from opposite ends of each group—from the upper end of the disadvantaged group and the lower end of the advantaged group. The crosshatched region of Figure 5.2 shows the "matched" portions of each group.

These two "matched" groups represent extreme scorers from their respective populations. Because the pretest scores are not 100 percent reliable, we know that the posttest scores of these children will not be equally extreme—they will regress in opposite directions, toward their population means. The advantaged group's posttest scores will be slightly higher, for they represent the bottom end of their population; the disadvantaged group's posttest scores will be slightly lower, for they rep-

FIGURE 5.2. Hypothetical distributions of pretest achievement levels of two populations, one considered disadvantaged and one advantaged. Crosshatched areas represent the "matched" groups from the two populations.

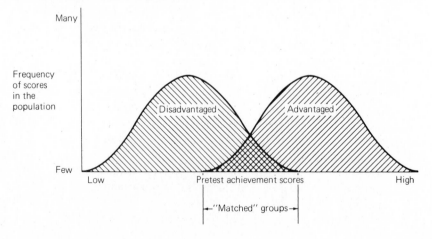

FIGURE 5.3.   Regression toward the mean of posttest scores from the extremes of two populations' pretest scores.

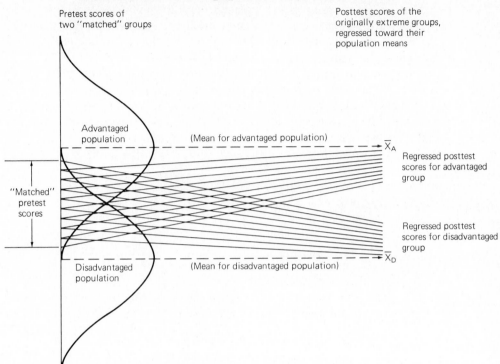

resent the upper end of their population. Figure 5.3 illustrates these regression effects and shows how regression artifacts alone can create a difference on the posttest even if no compensatory program had actually been implemented. Regression effects can make a program look detrimental if the treatment and comparison groups are selected in such a way that they represent opposite ends of two preexisting social groups. The same regression artifacts can also make a program look mistakenly beneficial if the treatment is given to the advantaged group, and a presumably "matched" comparison group is drawn from a disadvantaged group.

Matching, therefore, is inadequate for removing preexisting group differences. Unless we randomly assign individuals from a common pool to treatment and control groups, it is always likely that the two groups represent different populations with different means. Attempts to match on either pretest scores or other variables are destined to be imperfect, and regression toward the mean is a potential explanation for subsequent differences. Critics of Head Start preschool programs have said that compensatory education does not work; critics of the Head Start evaluation have said that evaluation was in error. The nonequivalent control group made the program look ineffective; and "matching" did not remove the bias (Campbell and Erlebacher, 1970).

The two examples of large-scale evaluations of social programs that we have discussed both showed negative results. In the first case, the results are difficult to dispute because the true experimental design makes most other explanations implausible. McCord's conclusion that the treatment in the Cambridge-Somerville experiment was harmful is persuasive. The question that remains unanswered about that evalaution is *why* did the treatment hurt more than it helped? In the Head Start evaluation, the negative results are not convincing because there is a rival explanation — regression artifacts alone could have made the program look ineffective. It may be the evaluation research rather than the social program that failed in this case. A true experiment, with randomization, makes it possible for an evaluator to assess a program with greater confidence that the results represent true program effects. Randomization, however, remains a controversial procedure. We shall consider the case for and against random assignment.

RANDOMIZATION—ARGUMENTS PRO AND CON

Critics have made the following arguments against true experiments:

1. They are not feasible.

2. They have a narrow scope and are limited because they "fail to include qualitative information . . . (and) are unable to recognize subtle human reactions to a social program" (Boruch, 1975, p. 122).

3. They are useless in providing information on how to make a program better.

4. They are unethical because they either deprive the control group of a desirable treatment or subject the experimental group to a questionable treatment.

In response, Robert Boruch, an evaluator, has addressed each of the criticisms as follows (Boruch, 1975).

1. Randomized social experiments are feasible because over 200 social programs have successfully used random assignment (Boruch, 1975). This does not mean that it is easy to implement true experiments, but it is proof that they are feasible. Boruch's list of over 200 experiments shows a wide range of programs that include job training, education, mental health, social welfare, medical care, economic incentives, criminal justice, the mass media, and many others. Random assignment is possible in more places than the critics believed.

The critics may still have a point, however, if we ask whether there are some special conditions that make random assignment particularly difficult and other conditions that make it easy. Boruch (1975) gives us some insight on this: "The examples . . . serve as a basis for examining conditions under which controlled tests appear to be most readily mounted. For example, many such tests compare the effects of various material products, such as two different income subsidy plans, rather than the effects of social programs which are based heavily on personal skills or program staff, such as two rehabilitation programs for the mentally ill." It is conceivable that experimental tests of the latter sort are more difficult to conduct because we do not know enough about designing tests that are especially sensitive to staff skills or that do not threaten the status of program staff. Program administrators often resist random assignment and true experimental designs because they do not want an evaluation which looks foolproof — and they may be right. We may not know enough about designing treatments and measuring the effects of social as opposed to material programs to conduct a truly fair test of an idea; and well-intentioned program administrators do not want to jeopardize a good *idea* by having a rigorous evaluation conducted on an inadequate implementation of that idea.

2. True experiments need not preclude gathering qualitative data, and gathering quantitative data need not preclude discovering "subtle human reactions to a social program." Data in true experiments can be either quantitative or qualitative; what matters is that they be systematic: "systematic and reliable information is essential for dispelling erroneous ideas generated by casual observation, dramatic anecdote, and unchecked impressions. That systematic information may be quantitative, or qualitative, or both" (Boruch, 1975, p. 122; Kidder, 1981).

Another part of the second criticism is that experiments are narrow and limited in scope because they are "one-shot affairs." Boruch replies that "nothing in experimental design methodology demands one-shot tests, and, for a variety of reasons, sequential assessment should ordinarily be the rule rather than the exception" (1975, p. 125). Both the critics and the defenders of experiments are correct. Experiments and evaluations often are one-shot tests and do not follow the program or the participants over many months or years, but they need not be so limited. The 30-year follow-up evaluation of the Cambridge-Somerville experiment is a notable exception. The negative income tax experiments and many evaluations of mental health programs, remedial education programs, and job training programs, however, have not followed participants' progress long after the program. Most summative or outcome evaluations are not longitudinal studies because the answer to the question, "Does it work?" cannot wait for years.

3. The third criticism, that true experimental evaluations are not useful because they provide little guidance on how to make the program better, also has a grain of truth to it. If we discover that job training programs do not succeed in getting higher wages for the trainees, we do not know what will succeed. All we know is that this attempt failed. Experiments do not necessarily provide ideas for innovations, but they do provide clear answers about whether a particular innovation worked or not. Whenever it is possible to compare two innovations, an experimental test will show which one is better. If we accept experiments for what they are — tests of effects — they do enable us to make decisions about whether a program is good and which of several alternative programs is the best.

Another part of the third criticism is that "rigorous evaluations of social programs, including experiments, can destroy any incentive to be creative in program development" (Boruch, 1975, p. 128). Boruch answers that experimental design and evaluation cannot guarantee creativity but that there is also no reason why they must stifle it. The experimental mode is very compatible with creativity — people who are willing to experiment are innovative and creative. And those who experiment generally want to know the results of their experiments.

Barriers to innovation may arise when the results of the innovation threaten the innovator's career, and, in this sense, experimental evaluations can stifle creativity. For this reason, Donald Campbell (1969) says the ideal is to compare two innovations, with the program administrators' jobs guaranteed no matter what the evaluation reveals, so that administrators and evaluators can be impartial judges of the value of social programs. "This is a useful strategy to the extent that multiple comparisons inhibit premature emotional endorsement of what might be thought of as *the* solution to a complex social problem, and that they reduce the staff anxieties usually associated with a test of only one solution" (Boruch, 1975, p. 129).

4. The fourth criticism of randomized experiments concerns the ethics of experimentation, and it takes several forms. On the one hand, critics say that the untreated or control group is unfairly deprived of a potentially good program. On the other hand, critics also say the treated or experimental group (guinea pigs) are unfairly subjected to questionable treatments that may not help and may even harm them. Whether the treatment be helpful or harmful, experimentation is called unfair. Boruch has a simple answer: "failure to experiment . . . [may be] unethical" (Boruch, 1975, p. 135), because we will never know if a treatment is good or bad if we do not put it to experimental test.

In those cases where we know that a program will not be harmful and we doubt only whether it is helpful or simply ineffective, we ideally want to permit as many people as possible to participate. The limit on how many people can participate is usually determined not by any principle of experimental design but by budgets. If this is the case and if more people volunteer or express an interest in a program than can be served, randomization may be the fairest way of deciding who can participate in the program and who will be in the control or comparison group (Brickman, Folger, Goode, and Schul, 1981; Rabinovitz and Wortman, 1976). Some people participate in lotteries for pleasure and profit. They may also be willing to participate in lotteries for access to social programs for which there are more volunteers or applicants than there are places available. A social psychologist who has examined the fairness of lotteries has found that people regard random assignment as fair when all of the people in the pool are equally deserving (Brickman, 1978). If prior screening of people's merits or needs still leaves a pool of people larger than the number who can receive a special program (for example, scholarships), then a lottery seems fair, and a lottery is random assignment.

CLIENT PARTICIPATION IN EVALUATIONS

We began this chapter by saying that evaluation research differs from basic research in the extent to which it affects people's lives, and as a consequence the choice of dependent variables or criteria for "success" is a choice that different parties would make in different ways. If social programs are designed for the recipients or clients, it seems reasonable that the clients' evaluation of the program should be included in the criteria for judging its success.

Malcolm Bush and Andrew Gordon (1978) valued client participation in their research on children's placements in foster homes, institutions, or their families of origin. In going through records, they came across the description of a woman described as a pyromaniac — a mother who set fire to her apartment and whose child was subsequently taken from her and placed in an institution as a ward of the state. When Bush and Gordon interviewed the child, they heard another version of that incident. The child said that during a cold winter, when the apartment heating was inadequate and the mother had repeatedly requested that it be repaired, the mother lit a fire in a wastebasket which tipped over and set fire to the apartment. From an agency's point of view, this was pyromania; from the child's point of view, it was an effort to keep warm. Whichever version of the story you believe, there are at least two — and one is the client's.

Bush and Gordon (1978) advocate including clients' preferences not only in the evaluation of social programs but also in the decision of what treatment they should receive. Letting clients choose their own treatments naturally obviates random assignment, but we present the case because it also tells us something about using client satisfaction as a criterion for program evaluation. Bush and Gordon make three points: (1) that clients have more information about their past and present needs and a greater stake in choosing the right treatment than do "outsiders"; (2) that clients who exercise such choice are more pleased with their treatments (in this case, foster placements for children) than clients who are denied the choice; and (3) that for the choice to be a *real* choice, it must be an "informed" choice. Two factors sometimes limit people's ability to make an informed choice: relative deprivation may make small benefits look good to someone who has previously had no benefits at all, and restricted experience with alternative treatments in the past may limit people's ability to make an informed judgment about which treatment to choose. Some of the children in Bush and Gordon's study who could "only remember one kind of placement, institutions, were very reluctant to choose other forms of care when given a variety of options" (Bush and Gordon, 1978, pp. 26–27). Only when the researchers made it clear to the children what the other placements were like, were the children able to make a real informed choice between living in an institution or a family.

Applying this logic to the McCord study casts doubt on the validity of the participants' subjective evaluations of the treatment. Would two-thirds of them still have said positive things about the treatment had they known about the subsequent criminal records, poor health, lower occupational standing, and earlier deaths of the treatment group? For client satisfaction to be a useful evaluation, it must be an *informed* evaluation, with hindsight about the objective consequences of the treatment and not a simple judgment of whether it made the clients feel good. It is fair and reasonable to include clients as judges and evaluators of the services they recieve, but if they are not fully informed, they may err in their judgments. Like McCord's findings that clients' testimonials were contradicted by objective evidence, McDill and McDill (1969) report inflated and sometimes misguided testimonials in evaluations of educational programs. "Studies of compensatory education programs have one 'universal finding': regardless of the type of program, duration, or actual results, parents are enthusiastic" (pp. 43–44). Perhaps the participants in the Cambridge-Somerville experiment and the parents of children in compensatory education programs are telling us that they appreciate the special attention — the investment of resources, the good intentions. Would they say the same if they knew the objective outcomes? We have yet to see the data from such "informed" subjective evaluations.

There are additional problems with subjective satisfaction ratings. Many surveys of satisfaction have generated extremely high levels of self-reported happiness with a variety of areas "in which it is 'common knowledge' that people are dissatisfied" (Gutek, 1978, p. 49). For instance, some survey data show 85 percent of assembly-line workers are satisfied with their jobs whereas "researchers have concluded that assembly work is among the most powerless, meaningless, unchallenging, monotonous jobs around" (Gutek, 1978, p. 49). Similarly, some survey data report that "a full 92% are satisfied with their marriages. Divorce statistics suggest that satisfaction rates should be lower . . . " (Gutek, 1978, p. 48). Gutek concludes "one reason for distrusting measures of satisfaction is simply that people seem to be satisfied with everything that social scientists ask them about" (p. 48).

Another reason to distrust satisfaction measures is that people's reports of their own satisfaction do not mesh with their reports of what they believe other people's satisfaction must be. For instance, "although 80% of subjects thought they were treated fairly in their encounter, only 42% thought that government agencies in general treat people fairly" (Gutek, 1978, p. 49). This means that people regard their own experiences and perhaps their own satisfaction levels as exceptions to an otherwise bleak picture. Which is more accurate — their report of their own exceptional experiences or their assessment of what they think most people experience? And what does this mean for assessing satisfaction? Gutek describes the most drastic approach to the problem of using clients' satisfaction ratings — "abandoning the attempt entirely: better to assess organizational effectiveness in terms of objective factors, such as recidivism rate, number of cases handled, and the like" (p. 50).

We face a dilemma: We want to take into account clients' evaluations, criteria, ratings of effectiveness, and satisfaction; but those ratings do not always agree with objective indicators. If we resort to objective indicators, we face another problem: "the more any quantitative social indicator is used for professional decision making, the more subject it will be to corruption pressures and the more apt it will be to distort and corrupt the social process it is intended to monitor" (Campbell, 1975, p. 3). Moreover, objective indicators measure something quite different from satisfaction. The relationship between objective indicators such as absenteeism or job turnover and subjective ratings of satisfaction is weak (Gutek, 1978, p. 50). Gutek concludes, therefore, that we should *not* abandon subjective measures because "people live in a subjective world as well as an objective one. . . . Satisfaction may not take the place of objective indicators, but neither can objective indicators take the place of subjective indicators such as satisfaction" (p. 50).

SUMMARY

Evaluation research has all the same problems and solutions in design and measurement as does basic research. It differs from basic research in its purposes and its connection with social policy. The relationship to policy and public welfare presents challenges to evaluation researchers that require personal, political, and philosophical decisions. The biases inherent in the questions asked and the criteria used to determine a program's success or failure do not simply get buried in libraries. They influence decisions and affect people's lives. This makes some social scientists regard evaluation research as both exciting and exasperating.

Participant Observation

6

The research approaches described in the preceding chapters have a lot in common. Experiments, quasi experiments, surveys, and evaluation research all have identifiable designs, and the people engaged in those forms of research speak a common language of research design and measurement. Participant observation is different. It does not contain explicit designs, and the people engaged in participant observation use a different vocabulary. The division between participant observation and the other forms of research is sometimes characterized by the terms *qualitative* and *quantitative*, but these are inaccurate descriptors because participant observers occasionally use numbers and experimenters can use qualitative observational data (see Chapter 11). The division is sometimes also characterized in terms that imply that one form of research is better than the other: experimental research has been called "hard" and participant observation "soft"; experimentation has been called "rigid" and participant observation "rich"; and so on. The differences between participant observation and other forms of research have been exaggerated and the similarities neglected. In this chapter we describe both how they differ and what they have in common (cf. Kidder, 1981).

HYPOTHESIS GENERATION VERSUS HYPOTHESIS TESTING

The research approaches discussed in the preceding chapters are used primarily to test hypotheses. The hypotheses may be abstract, as in Glass and Singer's studies of the effects of urban stress on cognitive performance, or concrete, as in McCord's evaluation of the Cambridge-Somerville experiment. In either case, the research is designed to test some specific predictions or hypotheses. For instance, Glass and

Singer hypothesized that if people are able to control aversive noise, they will perform better on mental puzzles then if they cannot control the noise; their laboratory tests bore out this prediction. This is called the **hypothetico-deductive** method; the researcher begins with a theoretical framework, formulates a hypothesis, and logically deduces what the results of the experiment should be if the hypothesis is correct. **Inductive** research proceeds in the opposite direction; the researcher begins with data and generates hypotheses and a theory, from the ground up (Glaser and Strauss, 1967). Participant observation is generally inductive research.

These distinctions are useful for characterizing the differences between participant observation and the other forms of research, but they are not hard and fast lines. Experimenters and survey researchers also work inductively at times. If their hypotheses are not supported by the data, they begin to explore the data for better explanations, and in the process they generate new hypotheses. Participant observers also begin with some preliminary hypotheses before they gather any data. The difference is that participant observers *revise* their hypotheses, as their research proceeds, with **negative case analysis,** which takes the place of statistical analysis in participant observation.

NEGATIVE CASE ANALYSIS

Negative case analysis requires that the researcher look for data that would disconfirm the hypothesis. When a single negative case is found, the participant observer revises the hypothesis so that it accounts for that case. Donald Cressey's study of embezzlers illustrates how negative case analysis works (Cressey, 1953). He revised his hypothesis five times before he completed his analysis of what leads embezzlers to use other people's money. The following excerpts show how he used negative case analysis to generate his final hypothesis.

> The first hypothesis ... was that positions of financial trust are violated when the incumbent has learned in connection with the business or profession in which he is employed that some forms of trust violation are merely technical violations and are not really "illegal" or "wrong," and on the negative side, that they are not violated if this kind of definition of behavior has not been learned [p. 27].

Cressey developed this hypothesis from previous work on white-collar crime. After he had interviewed only a few inmates convicted of embezzling, however, he revised his hypothesis because the men told him they had known all along that embezzling was illegal. His revised hypothesis was that

> positions of trust are violated when the incumbent defines a need for extra funds or extended use of property as an "emergency" which cannot be met by legal means ... [p. 27].

Although some embezzlers admitted this was true, others said that there had been no financial "emergency," and they had still taken the money. Yet others said that when there had been financial emergencies earlier in their lives, they had resisted taking other people's money. Both of these cases contradicted the second hypothesis, so Cressey developed a third:

> it shifted the emphasis from emergency to psychological isolation, stating that persons become trust violators when they conceive of themselves as having incurred financial obligations which are . . . non-socially sanctionable and which . . . must be satisfied by a private or secret means [p. 28].

When qualitative researchers revise their hypotheses, they test them not only in light of new data gathered in subsequent days or weeks, but also in light of the data already recorded. Each day's observations become recorded on tape or on paper (and tape-recorded data are usually transcribed so that they, too, appear on paper) in the form of field notes, and these notes provide the basis for hypothesis revision and rejection and confirmation. When Cressey developed his third hypothesis, he checked it not only against subsequent interviews but also against previous ones. When he did this, he found "that in a few of them there was nothing which could be considered as financial *obligation*, that is, as a debt which had been incurred in the past and for which the person at the present time felt responsible. Also, in some cases there had been non-sanctionable obligations at a prior time, and these . . . had not been alleviated by means of trust violations" (p. 28). So Cressey revised his hypothesis again:

> emphasizing this time not financial obligations . . . but non-shareable *problems* not only because of an acknowledged responsibility for past debts, but because of present discordance between his income and expenditure as well [p. 29].

This included men who had not developed debts but who have been living above their means and had been afraid to admit this to their families or friends, and it included some who had been maintaining separate households without telling their family and friends. Again, however, there were exceptions, men who said they had experienced the nonshareable problem for a long time before they embezzled — "some stated that they did not violate the trust at the earlier period because the situation was not in sharp enough focus to 'break down their ideas of right and wrong'" (p. 30). This led to Cressey's final revision:

> Trusted persons become trust violators when they conceive of themselves as having a financial problem which is non-shareable, are aware that this problem can be secretly resolved by violation of the position of financial trust, and are able to apply to their own conduct in that situation verbalizations which enable them to adjust their conceptions of themselves as trusted persons with their conceptions of themselves as users of the entrusted funds or property [p. 30].

Cressey developed and tested this hypothesis with all cases of embezzlement found in one state prison. He then tested the hypothesis in three additional ways. He searched the literature on embezzlement and looked to see if his hypothesis was consistent with other studies. He examined 200 cases of embezzlement collected by another researcher, E. H. Sutherland. And he went to a federal penitentiary and interviewed people convicted of federal bank and post office embezzlement. In each of these sources he looked for negative cases that would contradict his hypothesis and concluded the following:

In all of the cases interviewed the process was found to be present, and when cases were examined with a view to answering the question: "Why did these men not violate their trust in an earlier period?" it was seen that in earlier periods one or more of the events in the process had not been present [p. 31].

Cressey's book is atypical because few other published reports reveal so clearly the process of forming, revising, and retesting hypotheses. It is typical, however, in its use of negative case analysis to revise and generate hypotheses.

What makes qualitative research systematic is not standardization but negative case analysis. Cressey revised and developed his hypotheses and his conclusion by testing each revision against data he had already gathered and subsequent data that he continued to gather. Each time he found a negative case, he revised his hypothesis to incorporate the new evidence. He did this until there were no more disconfirmations. To be systematic in qualitative research, therefore, means to make a thorough search for cases that might disconfirm the hypothesis. The search and the data collection are not routinized; in fact, they usually require asking new and different questions in each search. The measurements are not standardized, the data are not uniform, and they do not yield numbers that can be added or averaged. But the *procedure* is systematic.

Negative case analysis, with its continual revision and retesting of hypotheses, is more like what experimenters do when they design subsequent studies. The participant observer in effect does a series of consecutive studies, but does them all within the same piece of research because there is no rule that says he or she cannot change the hypotheses or questions in midstream. The technique, in fact, requires changing the questions to take account of the unanticipated answers and observations that come along.

Negative case analysis is what the participant observer uses in place of statistical analysis. In some respects, it is a more stringent analysis because it tolerates no deviations from the rule. Statistical analysis is necessary when there are deviations from the rule, as there always are in studies with quantitative measures. Not everyone receives the same score, and statistical tests become necessary to see whether group averages adhere to the predicted pattern in spite of individual deviations from the average (see Chapter 13). When negative case analysis has been completed, there are no deviations. This, of course, assumes that the researcher is capable of setting aside all personal or theoretical biases and conducting a tireless and objective search.

Participant observers are not gifted with any greater skills of objectivity than are experimental researchers, and some critics of qualitative research suspect that the social sciences in which participant observation predominates, such as anthropology, are also fields that recruit "counter-cultural romantics and displaced creative novelists" (Campbell, 1974, p. 3). Experimental social psychologists warn that most people err by believing vivid personal testimonials more than dull statistical information, which can make participant observation sound truer than it might be (Borgida and Nisbett, 1977). Participant observers are more vulnerable to criticism on these grounds than are experimenters. The ultimate test of the believability of any kind of research, however, is not its seeming objectivity but its replicability. If no one can replicate or repeat the research and reach the same conclusions, the research is not believable, no matter how vivid the data.

CAUSAL ANALYSIS OF CAREERS

Participant observation is particularly useful for studying socialization into adult roles or careers. These are not only occupational careers as we know them, but also careers in crime and drug use, for example. They include studies of becoming a marijuana user, becoming a parole officer, becoming an embezzler, and becoming hypnotized (Becker, 1963; McCleary, 1978; Cressey, 1953; Kidder, 1972). When the researcher delineates the steps necessary in becoming socialized into any one of these roles, he or she performs a causal analysis. Cressey concluded that to become an embezzler, "the entire process must be present," with all the conditions he described in his final hypothesis.

If we compare this type of causal analysis and conclusion with the causal analyses of experimental research (see Chapter 2), we see that the participant observer does not identify a single cause but a *combination* of steps or links in a causal chain. Only when all of those links are present does the person become a marijuana user or embezzler or parole officer. Experimenters, on the other hand, more often identify one or two causes; many experimental studies are factorial designs with two or three factors. Which is the better way to proceed? Each method has its costs as well as its benefits, and the choice between methods always requires a trade-off.

When an experimenter judiciously selects two independent variables to see whether they are "causes" of some effects in the dependent variable, either separately or in combination, the experimenter has the advantage of knowing that, in this study at least, the presumed causes preceded the effect, so that the resulting relationship cannot mean that the causal relationship goes in the opposite direction. Within the confines of the experiment, it is clear that the manipulated independent variables are the *causes* and the resulting dependent variable shows the *effect*. This does not prove, however, that the causal process works that way outside the laboratory, in the "real world." Outside the laboratory in the natural social world, there may be many other causes that not only produce the same effect but are much more important than the causes isolated in the experimental laboratory. The participant observer has the advantage of being able to see a fuller range of causes and to report on those that appear most important in the natural setting.

The participant observer is in much the same position as the survey researcher and quasi-experimental researcher. They each lack control over which "causes" people are exposed to and instead study groups or individuals who select their treatments or choose their careers or in some other nonrandom fashion become exposed to particular events. Frequently, they also study a complex set of causes rather than an isolated few. Whereas the experimenter talks about main effects and interactions (Chapter 2), the participant observer talks about a series of causes or steps necessary to become an embezzler or a marijuana user without knowing whether this is an interaction effect or a cumulative series of main effects.

In his study of embezzlers, Cressey identified four conditions that must be present if a person is to become an embezzler. The person must

1. Be in a position of financial trust.
2. Have a nonshareable financial problem.

3. Recognize embezzlement as a possible solution for the problem.

4. Develop a way to rationalize embezzlement to make it seem like a "loan" or justifiable use of other people's money.

A participant observation study of becoming a marijuana user describes three conditions that lead to marijuana use for pleasure (Becker, 1963). They are:

1. Learning the technique of smoking to produce effects.
2. Learning to perceive the effects.
3. Learning to enjoy the effects.

This series of conditions must occur in the order listed, and no one condition alone is sufficient to cause marijuana use. Learning to smoke to produce physical symptoms is necessary but not sufficient because the physical symptoms are not always obvious; the novice must learn to perceive them. The following quotation illustrates the learning that takes place:

> I didn't get high the first time ... The second time I wasn't sure, and he [smoking companion] told me, like I asked him for some of the symptoms or something ... So he told me to sit on a stool. I sat on—I think I sat on a bar stool—and he said, "Let your feet hang," and then when I got down my feet were real cold, you know.
>
> And I started feeling it, you know. That was the first time. And then about a week after that, sometime pretty close to it, I really got on. That was the first time I got on a big laughing kick, you know. Then I really knew I was on [Becker, 1963, pp. 49–50].

Without all three conditions present, people do not continue to use marijuana for pleasure. The following quote is from someone who learned to smoke marijuana to produce and perceive effects but did not enjoy them.

> It was offered to me and I tried it. I'll tell you one thing. I never did enjoy it at all. I mean it was just nothing that I could enjoy. [Well, did you get high when you turned on?] Oh, yeah, I got definite feelings from it. But I didn't enjoy them. I mean I got plenty of reactions, but they were mostly reactions of fear [Becker, 1963, p. 54].

Even people who have been regular users may discontinue use if one of the necessary conditions no longer occurs, as in the following instance:

> It was too much, like I only made about four tokes, and I couldn't even get it out of my mouth, I was so high, and I got real flipped ... I walked outside, and it was five below zero, and I thought I was dying ... I fainted behind a bush. I don't know how long I laid there ... all weekend I started flipping, seeing things there and going through hell, you know, all kinds of abnormal things ... I just quit for a long time then [Becker, 1963, p. 57].

Participant observers frequently revise not only their hypotheses but also their topic of study. For instance, in Becker's analysis of becoming a marijuana user, he ultimately narrowed his topic to study people who use marijuana for pleasure. The three steps he identified are the conditions that lead to the use of marijuana for pleasure. There are also other reasons why people may use marijuana, and Becker's analysis would not apply to them. For instance, some people may use marijuana to become or remain members of a social group, and they may smoke even if they perceive no effects. Others may use marijuana not for pleasure but for the thrill of doing something illegal or experiencing terror. In such cases, the fear reported by the people in the preceding quotations might not prevent further marijuana use. In revising their hypotheses, participant observers also redefine their topic of study.

When Kidder (1971) went to India to study the acculturation of foreign sojourners, she began with the idea that Western visitors would gradually learn to see India through the eyes of Indians who had become their "best friends." She revised this idea when she began interviewing sojourners and found that when she asked them for the names of Indians with whom they spent the most time, many had no answer. The friends with whom many sojourners spent time and talked about India were not Indians but other foreigners. The research topic, therefore, changed — from a study of how foreigners become acculturated into Indian society to a study of how they become socialized into a society of sojourners. Kidder interviewed foreign sojourners and recorded her own experiences as a Westerner in India to analyze the process of becoming socialized into the society of sojourners. She found sojourners acquired an identity that they had not anticipated if they had not lived abroad before: they quickly learned that they were wealthy and alien. They adapted to that identity by learning to bargain for goods and select among foods to protect both their wealth and their health. Their newly acquired wealth derived from the difference in cost of living at home and in India; their fragile health derived from their lack of immunity to a new variety of ailments. The final accommodation made by most of the sojourners was to recreate a Western life-style in India. They learned this from other sojourners who taught them how to shop, eat, and socialize. Therefore, the study changed its focus — from an examination of how sojourners became "Indianized" to an observation of how they became "foreignized."

DEGREES OF PARTICIPATION

The examples on the preceding pages represent different degrees of participation by the researchers. Kidder was a participating member of the community of sojourners that she studied in India; Cressey had never been an embezzler. To use participant observation as a research technique, a person may be a fully participating member of the group under observation or primarily an observer, participating only vicariously. Participant observers, like anthropologists, frequently immerse themselves in a setting where they are obviously not bona fide members but can become accepted as trusted friends and observers. The following example illustrates how Carol Stack, a white woman, became accepted in a family and circle of friends in a black community. She studied how family and friendship networks helped residents of that community cope with illness, unemployment, and housing evictions. The following description of how she became a participant observer is from her book, entitled *All Our Kin:*

> I first came by the Walters' home in the summer of 1968 . . . [the family] were sitting in the living room on a red velvet couch, which Magnolia had covered herself. The eight were methodically folding several piles of newspapers for Lenny's five evening paper routes . . . After a lesson from a seven-year-old on how to make the fold, I joined

in . . . I told them I would like to begin a study of family life in The Flats . . . Several months later Magnolia told me that she had been surprised that I sat with them that first day to fold papers, and then came back to help again. "White folks," she told me, "don't have time, they's always in a rush, and they don't sit on black folks' furniture, at least no whites that come into The Flats" [Stack, 1975, p. 10].

Carol Stack got to know Magnolia's daughter, Ruby, who introduced her to life in The Flats and taught her much by example.

> Ruby and I enjoyed comparing our attitudes and approaches toward everything. Although she asked me to bring my white friends over to her house, she was always hypercritical in assessing whether they were anti-Black or whether they "put on airs." Some of my friends she liked very much, yet she encouraged me to break up some friendships, especially if she had reason to doubt a friend's loyalty to me. It seemed at times, by the circumstances and demands that she contrived, that she was testing the loyalty of my friends — using her own standards, of course — just as she tested her own friends. For example, she insisted that I ask my friends to take care of Kevin [Stack's son] or to loan me money. She was in fact teaching me how to get along [Stack, 1975, p. 14].

Such immersion in the lives of the people one studies is very different from the distance maintained by experimenters and survey researchers. The latter often do not know or ask for the names of their research subjects, trying instead to assure them of anonymity and to treat all persons alike. Participant observers do the opposite; they become well acquainted with the people they study and consequently treat no two people alike. Moreover, participant observers are also drawn into interactions by the people they study, as the preceding and following examples illustrate.

> Ruby had a quick, affirmative way of letting others know my presence was acceptable to her, and that it "damn well better be acceptable to them." At one large family gathering, relatives came from out of town to see Ruby's stepfather, who was sick. Ruby sensed their hostility and insecurity toward me. She turned to me and said, "What is your white ass doing sitting down when there is so much cooking and work to do in my kitchen?" I responded, "My white ass can sit here as long as your black ass can." With that, we both got up, went into the kitchen and got to work [Stack, 1975, pp. 15–16].

This degree of immersion in the research setting is at odds with the distance and anonymity of experiments and surveys. Does it make participant observation more vulnerable to distortion? Not necessarily; in fact, the lack of anonymity of respondents may ensure that the researcher observes phenomena as they are and not as the respondent or the researcher wishes they were. Subjects in laboratory experiments and anonymous respondents in surveys may be freer to distort reality than are people whose identities are known and whose actions are observed in their natural setting (Becker and Geer, 1957). The people studied by participant observation are constrained to act as they normally would, particularly if the research continues over many weeks or months. They cannot put on an act and continue to function with their friends, families, or fellow workers. Even if a participant observer could not recognize an act or a distortion, the actor's associates would, and the participant observer would probably hear about it. We have a paradox: the more time a participant observer spends with the people he or she studies, the less influence the observer exerts as a researcher because although the research subjects may wish to appear a particular way in the researcher's eyes, they cannot act in unnatural ways if the observer stays with them very long. The more the participant observer is immersed in the research setting, therefore, the less likely the research subjects are to distort the research.

The participant observer is still susceptible to distortion from his or her own biases. The researcher's biases enter into experimental and survey research too, however, in determining the questions asked and the responses permitted. The formulation of questions in the evaluations of Head Start and the Negative Income Tax Experiments (Chapter 5) expressed particular biases about the causes of poverty and the solutions. Designing an experiment or survey and gathering numerical data do not prevent the researcher's biases from operating. Participant observation may appear more susceptible to the researcher's biases because the data are usually not numerical, but numbers alone do not ward off bias.

THE USE OF NUMBERS

Experimenters and survey researchers are very exacting in their use of numbers. The number of subjects or respondents is an important piece of information because that number enters into the computation of statistical tests (see Chapter 13). The numerical values obtained in quantitative measurement are also carefully calculated and examined (see Chapter 7). Participant observers do not place as much emphasis on numbers, though they occasionally refer to numerical values in discussing both the sample size and the measurement of variables.

Sample Size and Numbers of Observations

A book entitled *The Making of Blind Men* provides some interesting examples of the use of numbers in qualitative research (R. Scott, 1969). It is a study of adult socialization into the world of the blind and shows how agencies for the visually handicapped can make people become helpless and dependent even though there is no necessary connection between being blind and being dependent or helpless. Some agencies also make visually handicapped clients "blinder" than they were to begin with by encouraging them to become dependent on a specially accommodative environment rather than teaching them how to maneuver in the world outside.

In describing his sample, Scott reports the following approximate numbers (emphasis added):

> I spoke with *perhaps a hundred* blind people . . . [p. 12].
>
> I conducted *nearly one hundred* interviews with professional workers in the field of work for the blind . . . [p. 12].
>
> . . . I have analyzed the records and reports of *many* public and private organizations for the blind [p. 11].
>
> I also spent *much time* visiting and observing a representative sample of other organizations, programs and agencies in the blindness system [pp. 12–13].

The use of numbers here is different from their use in quantitative research. Experimenters and survey researchers tell us exactly what the sample size or number of observations is. No surveys or experiments or quasi experiments refer to "perhaps" or "nearly" 100. They tell us whether there were 99 or 100 or 101 interviews because these figures enter into the statistical analysis and they must be exact. Participant observers do not usually perform statistical analyses, and therefore it makes little difference whether they interviewed 99 or 101 people. It is conceivable that if there were 99 observations that fit the hypothesis, the one hundredth or one hundred and first would be a negative case, but the larger the number of cases observed, the less likely it is that an additional case would contradict and therefore change the conclusions. Scott reported that he spoke with "perhaps a hundred" blind people, because he wished to inform the reader that his sample was approximately 100 and not approximately 10 or 20.

A large sample size serves the same purpose in all kinds of research — it makes the results more reliable because it is less likely that additional observations would change the outcome. A large sample size does not always mean that many people were studied. It could mean that a small number of people were studied over a long period of time. This is analogous to a within-subjects or repeated-measures design in experimentation, in which case the researcher reduces the number of people and increases the number of observations obtained from each person.

Measurement

Participant observation need not be all qualitative work; it can include quantitative measures, too. In a participant observation study of parole officers, McCleary (1977, 1978) observed that the officers did not always report parole violations. In fact, he found they "ignore most of the crimes, incidents, and violations that they observe in their caseload" (McCleary, 1977, p. 576). They reported incidents only when the report would benefit them by enabling them to transfer a troublesome parolee from their caseload, threaten a parolee, or protect their own careers. Otherwise, the amount of paperwork that they would create by full reporting would be too costly. It would take an inordinate amount of time, it would limit the parole officer's (PO's) ability to counsel men and give them a "second chance," and it would jeopardize the PO's own job because he or she may have to defend the decisions in a hearing. McCleary used his own observations and reports from parole officers to document that many violations go unreported. He tried to supplement these qualitative data with a quantitative measurement of paperwork. The following excerpt describes his efforts "to collect 'crucial' quantitative data" (McCleary, 1978, p. 39).

> . . . It occurred to me that I could test a number of hypotheses simply by measuring the *quantity* of writing done under certain conditions. This seemed to be a simple task when conceived but later proved to be nearly impossible. I first tried measuring the amount of time PO's spent on paperwork in the office writing reports. I discovered what I already knew, however: That PO's spend little or no time in the office writing reports. Most of this work is done at home. Office time is spent answering phones, interviewing clients, and socializing with office-mates and supervisors. I next considered going into the files in each office and simply counting the number of pages in each

dossier. This figure could then be correlated with the predicted aspects of each case. Given the volume of records in each office, however, there was no way I could do this unnoticed. I settled finally on "use of the Xerox machine" as the best quantitative indicator. Certain types of reports are always copied. Furthermore, the Xerox machines in each office have accounting sheets which each user must sign. It was a simple matter to copy these sheets and then code them as data. This method was both unobtrusive and precise. After a few weeks, I knew how much Xeroxing each PO in every branch office had done. I then attempted a simple statistical analysis, with "use of the Xerox machine" as my dependent variable. The analysis failed to confirm my theories, however. The independent variables that I believed would predict how much report writing each PO would do all proved statistically insignificant. At that point I had two options. I could discard or modify my theories about report writing or I could discredit my quantitative indicators. I was reluctant to discard my theories because, first, I "knew" that they were correct, and second, they were based on a common-sense notion of human nature. The second alternative, discrediting my quantitative indicators, was more attractive. According to Cook and Campbell (1975), a threat to construct validity occurs whenever there is a discrepancy between the construct variable and its operationalization. In this case, I searched for a discrepancy between the "amount of report writing" and "use of the Xerox machine," its operationalization. I knew that Xerox copying was an imprecise measure of report writing because supervisors, POs and secretaries make personal use of the Xerox machine. I had thought that the personal use was minimal, however. To investigate this assumption, I observed the Xerox machines in a few branch offices for an entire day. I discovered that many of the POs who were full-time students copied books, journal articles, and class assignments on the office Xerox machines. In one branch office, over 80 percent of the copying done during my observation period was for personal use. I admit to some pleasure at making this discovery. Had I not been able to discredit this quantitative indicator, I would have been forced to discard a number of theories. The displeasure in this would have come about simply because I "knew" the theories were correct. "Knowing" and quantitative data come together when one "proves" the other [McCleary, 1978, p. 41].

Had it worked, the quantitative measure of "amount of Xerox machine use" would have been a simple, unobtrusive, and objective measure of report writing. As it turned out, it was more a measure of personal copying than of report writing and was, therefore, not a valid indicator for McCleary's purposes. We present this example not to suggest that quantification cannot work in participant observation, but to demonstrate that it is not guaranteed to succeed. Numerical data are no freer from errors than are qualitative observations. They can each be biased. The use of the Xerox machine was an *unintentionally* biased measure. The POs were not purposely inflating the Xerox machine records to make it seem as though they were writing more reports — had they known someone was checking on their Xerox machine use, they probably would have reduced their use since they used it for nonofficial purposes.

THE USE OF ILLUSTRATIONS IN
QUALITATIVE RESEARCH

Participant observers occasionally use numbers to indicate how large their sample of observations was, as in Scott's study of agencies for the blind. They less frequently use numbers to measure a construct as in McCleary's study of parole officers. The most common form of reporting data is to provide illustrative excerpts from recorded notes. For instance, Cressey reported that embezzlers may use other people's money to solve a variety of nonshareable financial problems, and he provided the following quotations from his notes to illustrate the variety of problems.

> *Blackmail:* "I came into contact with a kind of blackmailing mess . . . Some men were trying to get money out of me to keep from exposing an affair with another woman to my wife. That's how I got started using other people's money" [p. 71].

> *Keeping up a front:* "All told, when I ran off to Florida, I owed about $35,000., including the mortgage. If I had been sensible, [my wife] and I would have sat down and figured out a way of liquidating those debts. But I wasn't sensible; I was caught in a maze of what I thought were important activities, and I was most concerned with keeping up that big front" [p. 61].

> *Other personal embarrassments:* "His wife needed some medical attention of an unethical nature, and through a friend he got in touch with a doctor . . . who specialized in this kind of medical practice. Later, this doctor came into the bank and demanded payment of $50. from him. He did not have the money and was afraid of exposure, so he wrote a check, signed his name to it, and gave it to the doctor . . . When the check came back to the bank . . . he destroyed it" [p. 71].

Field Notes

To be able to provide illustrative quotations like these, a participant observer must record detailed notes called **field notes,** of everything he or she hears and observes. This requirement usually strikes the beginning participant observer as an impossible task, which it is, because the term *everything* sets no limits. It can include endless details about the time and location of an interview or observation, with descriptions of the building, the furnishings, the decor, the level of cleanliness, the amount of noise, the numbers of other people present, the facial expressions of the persons being observed, their appearance and dress styles, their behaviors, and so on. Only some of these details will be relevant to the analysis, but when the participant observer begins, he or she does not know what the final analysis will be. The rule, therefore, is to try to remember "everything" and write notes that are as complete as memory allows.

Recording everything that is said is an equally arduous task. Participant observers generally do not record conversations on tape because a tape recorder would inhibit the researcher's participation in many situations. For instance, if Carol Stack had carried a tape recorder into Ruby's home whenever she went to visit, she probably would not have developed the rapport that we described earlier. Occasionally a tape recorder may not intrude; Kidder (1971) studied how people become hypnotized by attending a series of hypnosis workshops where she tape-recorded the hypnotic inductions and the posthypnotic discussions between hypnotists and their subjects. Many of the other participants in the workshop also had tape recorders, which they used to record the lectures that preceded and followed the hypnotic inductions, so Kidder's use of a tape recorder was not unique or obtrusive.

In instances where a tape recorder would interfere with participant observation, the researcher must rely on memory to write the field notes as soon after the observations as possible. The following excerpt of field notes from McCleary's study of parole officers illustrates how a participant observer selects, remembers, and records the materials that become the data from which illustrative examples can be drawn.

A Day in the Life

(What follows is an actual interview written up in the first week of June, 1976. Naturally, the interview as presented here has been edited so as not to include any identifiers. I prefer making notes during the actual conversation. The notes are then used as a mnemonic device for reproducing the conversation. This is not always possible because some POs are annoyed or bothered by note taking. Other POs seem not to mind, or at least, understand the necessity. Bob, the PO who speaks in this interview, has told me this explicitly. Because I was able to take notes, my conversations with Bob are of a better quality than the average. I have shown him this particular interview and he agreed that this is more or less what he said.

(I can give a brief description of Bob here without identifying him. He is a "typical" PO—at least demographically. He has an undergraduate degree in a social science and is currently enrolled in a psychiatric social work graduate program. His future plans are uncertain, but after the M.S.W., he would like to stay with the DC "if possible." By this, Bob means that he expects the DC to promote him to a position where he can utilize his academic credentials.

(Bob is in his late twenties, black, and has lived most of his life in the city. His parole district coincides roughly with the neighborhood he grew up in. Not surprisingly, a number of his childhood friends are now his parolees. Bob has commented on this fact a number of times. He attributes his relative success in life to a positive family, religion, and fortune: "I was one of the lucky ones."

(On the evening of this conversation, I met Bob in a restaurant near his office. We talked for less than an hour about his workday. We then went out into the field, and after two hours, adjourned to a tavern. The conversation at that time was more general. The conversation begins at approximately five in the afternoon, and counting the interruption, lasts until ten at night. Bob speaks:)

"My vice is letting things go until the last minute. You know, never do today what you can put off until tomorrow. Well, today was tomorrow.

"First I had a site investigation report to file. The deadline was today. I got down to the office about nine and Terry was already waiting for the report. His deadline was tomorrow. I gave him my standard excuse and asked him to give me a hand with it. He complained about it, you know how he is, but he agreed to help. Everybody in the office does. So we split the report up. I took the home investigation and he took the employment investigation. He can handle that by phone. All he has to do is call the employer and verify the job. The home investigation is different. You usually can't do that by phone, and even if you could, Terry wouldn't let you. He's a pretty liberal supervisor but that's one rule he won't bend. If he even suspects you didn't visit the home, he'll make you do the report over."

(The PO training manual is explicit on this point: "The PO must conduct this investigation in the residence where the client plans to reside." Supervisors enforce this rule to the letter. The reason for this is that, or so supervisors believe, a knowledge of the home environment often gives the PO some control over his parolee.)

"I had my car this morning. The address was on _____ street, near the el tracks.

I couldn't find a parking place nearby, so I parked in front of a loading zone sign. I've got a little Sheriff's Department card that says "Official Vehicle." I put that on my dash and I usually don't get a ticket. The house was a lower flat, kind of depressed looking. There were vacant lots on both sides and a lot of trash. It was fairly nice looking on the inside, though. The hallway corridor was clean.

"The dude I was investigating planned to live at that address with his sister and brother-in-law. You get problems with those arrangements. Sometimes the relatives don't want the dude but they're either afraid to tell him so or else the dude won't take No for an answer. I get some cases where relatives tell the dude No right out but then the dude thinks they'll change their minds after he moves in. Well, you have to make sure the relatives want the dude."

These field notes read like the script of a play. They contain descriptions of the time, the setting, and the actor; they have an aside by the narrator, McCleary; and they contain the lines spoken by the main actor, Bob. The lines spoken by Bob are approximations because the researcher wrote them from memory rather than from a tape recording. As readers we must generally trust that the quotations and descriptions are fairly accurate. In this case, McCleary tells us that he showed the written interview to Bob who agreed it was accurate.

Not all of the details in these notes became usable data in McCleary's analysis. Nonetheless, it was important for him to have recorded them for two reasons. First, by trying to write down as much as possible, the researcher stands a better chance of having useful data available for analysis later on; deciding which data are useful should be done during the analysis rather than during the writing of the field notes. Second, writing even those details that seem irrelevant at the time helps the researcher recall other details that are clearly relevant; each piece of information acts as a cue for recalling other pieces of the setting and is, therefore, worth recording as a device to activate memory. If you doubt that you could recall and write from memory an hour-long interview, try it. You will probably be surprised by how much you can remember if you try to write "everything."

THE USE OF ANALOGY

In analyzing a social institution or social relationship, researchers sometimes draw analogies between the phenomenon they have studied and another phenomenon that readers are already familiar with. Participant observers are particularly likely to do this. In the chapter about evaluation research we distinguished between outcome and process evaluations. Outcome evaluations address the question, "Does it work?" and that question is best answered with an experiment. Process evaluations address the question, "How does it work?" and this is best answered with participant observation. The studies of adult socialization and career analyses described earlier in this chapter address the question, "How does someone become an embezzler?" or "How does someone become a marijuana user?" or "How does someone become hypnotized?"

In answering questions like these, participant observers frequently find analogies useful. For instance, in her analysis of how people became hypnotized in the workshops she attended, Kidder (1972) showed how the process she observed is similar to attitude change; the workshop participants changed their attitudes about their own behaviors and experiences and learned to redefine hypnosis. The hypnotists brought about the change in several stages. First they convinced the subjects that they had acted as though they were hypnotized. For instance, when a subject asked after the first hypnotic induction:

> " . . . how do you know if you were in a trance or not? I mean, I know I did some things, but I think they were all under conscious voluntary control," the hypnotist replied, "I think you can tell if someone is in a trance by looking at them . . . the facial expressions. I could walk around the room and tell who wasn't and who was, by how they responded. I thought you were, but maybe you didn't *think* you were" [Kidder, 1972, p. 317].

A second hypnotist concurred:

> You were actually the one that I thought went into trance the quickest [Kidder, 1972, p. 317].

In addition to direct persuasion, the hypnotists used other techniques known to produce attitude change. They pointed out that the subjects were not coerced to behave as they had during the trance inductions; therefore, they must have done so because they wished to become hypnotized. When some subjects protested that they had behaved as though they were hypnotized and felt as though they were just "playing the game," the hypnotists pointed out that there must have been some reason for their doing so:

> . . . *Why* did you feel that you wanted to play the game? [Kidder, 1972, p. 319].

The hypnotists negotiated responsibility by persuading the subjects that a hypnotic trance would not be forced upon them but that they could enter a trance if they chose to cooperate:

> Well, let me say this. Earlier hypnosis was done in an authoritarian fashion—now it is much more permissive and we conceive of hypnosis as the achievement of the subject, in which the hypnotist helps . . . [Kidder, 1972, p. 319].

The workshop participants who became hypnotized changed their definitions of their own behaviors and of hypnosis. They agreed that hypnosis was not so different from some relaxed waking states, and they conceded that they had behaved in ways that a hypnotist would call trancelike. The techniques that the hypnotists used are like techniques used in attitude change experiments. Therefore, becoming hypnotized is like changing one's attitude. The analogy makes hypnosis understandable in other terms. It may also seem like an irreverent debunking of hypnosis. Participant observation research sometimes has an air of debunking, as when a researcher compares mental hospitals with refuges for unwanted persons or schools with prisons. Reasoning by analogy is risky because it may draw comparisons between two processes that have never before been described in similar terms or even in the same sentence, and it may identify similarities between the sacred and the profane. Analogies are useful, however, because they enable us to understand new phenomena in familiar terms.

SUMMARY

Participant observation differs from the other forms of research discussed in earlier chapters in several notable ways. The data are usually qualitative rather than quantitative and are recorded as field notes written largely from memory. Participant observers immerse themselves in the research setting and in the lives of the people they study. Although the field notes and research reports use fictitious names, the research subjects are not anonymous to the participant observer. They each become known to the other. Participant observers generate and revise their hypotheses as they gather data, and they use negative case analysis to arrive at conclusions that hold true for every observation, without exception.

The similarities are more subtle and difficult to detect. Like quasi experiments and surveys, participant observation is used to study naturally occurring phenomena. The participant observer does not manipulate treatments or randomly assign people to situations, but participant observers occasionally attempt causal analysis. Studies of careers and adult socialization are causal analyses. They contain descriptions of necessary steps or conditions for becoming an embezzler, a marijuana user, a hypnotic subject, or whatever else the end point may be. Quasi experimenters, survey researchers, and participant observers each gather and analyze their data in different ways, but they face similar problems when they try to perform causal analyses of naturally occurring phenomena.

part 2

Measurement

Reliability and Validity

7

To do any research in social relations, we must be able to measure the constructs we wish to study. *Constructs* are the abstractions that social scientists discuss in their theories, such as social status, power, and intelligence. To measure a construct, we must identify a *variable* that is a concrete representation of the abstraction. For instance, income is a variable that represents social status. No single variable can serve as a complete representation of a construct for reasons that we discuss later in this chapter. Nonetheless, we must identify at least one variable if we are to measure a construct. Variables themselves require further specification in the form of an *operational definition* or set of instructions for translating the variable into a set of categories. For instance, income can be measured in numerous ways, and we require an operational definition to specify whether to measure only wages, whether to include interest and dividends, whether to include assets such as property and savings, and so on. An operational definition, in turn, generates a *scale* or set of categories. A scale may have only two categories, such as "High income" and "Low income," or it can have a large number of categories or gradations. As we progress from constructs to scales, we become increasingly concrete and specific in our language, and our work becomes increasingly open to public scrutiny. Scientific measurement must be open to inspection and replication by other scientists and by informed lay people.

OPERATIONAL DEFINITIONS

An operational definition is the sequence of steps you take to obtain a measurement. The sequence must be repeatable, so that you can instruct someone else to obtain the same measurements. If someone claimed to have found a way to measure people's health by "sensing" the "auras" that surround a person and if that technique were so mystical that no one else could use it and obtain the same readings, that would be an unacceptable operational definition. A thermometer reading of someone's temperature, by contrast, is an acceptable operational definition because it is a straightforward procedure that can be easily repeated. But what is a thermometer reading actually an operational definition of? Is it a measure of health?

Technically, a thermometer reading is a measure of how high the mercury has risen in a tube, which, in turn, is a measure of how warm the mercury is, which is a measure of how warm the inside of the person's mouth is who held the thermometer under his or her tongue. Is that a measure of health? We usually accept it as a measure of whether or not a person has a fever, but even that is debatable. We all have different thermometer readings at different times of day; at what point do we call a temperature a "fever"? At 99°F? Or 100°F? The connection between temperature and "fever" is not entirely clear. The thermometer reading, therefore, is an imperfect measure of whether or not someone has a fever. It is a less than adequate measure of health because the connection between temperature and health is more tenuous than the connection between temperature and having a fever. A person may have a normal temperature but suffer from high blood pressure or diabetes or arthritis and, therefore, not be in perfect health.

Health is a very complex abstract construct with many components: blood pressure, blood sugar levels, white blood cell count, red blood cell count, degree of obesity, cholesterol level, history of cancer, and many other details constitute a person's state of health. A temperature reading, therefore, measures only one component of health. To obtain an adequate assessment of someone's state of health, we must take many readings and ask many questions, as a physician does during a general medical checkup. Any single measurement, such as a red blood cell count, is an operational definition of a component of health, such as degree of anemia. And each such operational definition is more acceptable as a scientific measurement of health than is an "aura" reading because "auras" are not publicly accessible. Almost anyone can learn to measure blood pressure or count red blood cells, and two people can agree in their measurements. Not so with reading auras. Scientific measurement is accomplished with operational definitions that can be used and repeated by any number of people. This is what makes operational definitions objective.

The emphasis on objectivity should not be misconstrued. It does not mean that all measurement or all observations must be quantified. Good observations and measurement can also consist of words rather than numbers. Moreover, it does not mean that a number like 100 on a thermometer or achievement test *is* that person's temperature or level of achievement. If the same person were retested with another instrument or at another moment, the number might change. Each measurement gives an approximation to the true score — and each also contains some error. The emphasis on objectivity does not guarantee truth or accuracy, but it does permit scientists to communicate with one another and with the public. It also permits anyone to challenge and check a piece of research because the operational definitions are instructions for replicating an observation.

Operational definitions are like the procedures we use to teach children about objects and concepts. We point at objects and name them. Because we cannot point with our fingers at abstract concepts, we devise a number of steps, like taking thermometer readings or achievement tests, and point to the final answer as a measure of fever or achievement level.

Early logical positivists were overzealous in their application of operational definitions. They made circular claims such as "intelligence is what the intelligence tests measure," which left no room for debate. Such tautologies help us to understand neither the concept of intelligence nor the test used to measure it. Donald Campbell criticizes the tautological approach, which he calls "definitional operationism" (Campbell, 1969). He says that every observation is affected by a variety of factors that bear no relation to the construct we wish to measure. For instance, answers to census questions about family income or number of adults living in a home are only partly determined by the respondent's true income or family size. They are also determined by "the social interaction of the interview . . . the interviewer's appearance . . . the respondent's fear of similar strangers, such as bill collectors, welfare investigators and the law . . ." (Campbell, 1969, p. 15). Paper-and-pencil measures are as vulnerable to irrelevant influences as are face-to-face interviews or observations:

> A manifest anxiety questionnaire response may in part be a function of anxiety, but it is also a function of vocabulary comprehension, of individual and social class differences in the use of euphoric and dysphoric adjectives, of idiosyncratic definitions of the key terms frequently repeated, of respondent expectations as to the personal consequences of describing himself sick or well, etc. The questionnaire situation is so obviously complex, and the instruments so poorly compensated even for such obvious sources of bias as respondent differences in vocabulary level . . . that it seems now incredible that anyone would have regarded it as definitional of a single theoretical parameter, yet such was the power of the positivist ideology that it once was [Campbell, 1969, p. 15].

Any single operational definition cannot provide the one and only true measure, therefore, because it also taps irrelevant features. In the absence of other operational definitions of the same construct, we do not know how much of the measurement reflects these irrelevant features and how much reflects what we intended to measure.

A second reason for not accepting single operations as definitive measures of concepts is that it would logically preclude our efforts to improve measurement in science. An early critic of "definitional operationism" called it "an obstacle to scientific advance because of its exclusion of criticism" (Adler, 1947, p. 441). Campbell elaborates this:

> One of the great weaknesses in definitional operationism . . . was that it allowed no formal way of expressing the scientist's prepotent awareness of the imperfection of his measuring instruments and his prototypic activity of improving them. Thus, while Boring was defining intelligence in terms of the Stanford-Binet, 1916 edition, Terman was already working on a revision which would make it a less biased instrument. Missed by definitional operationism is the fact that many of the meter readings in any actual scientific activity are discarded because the scientist judges them to be in error, the meter operating imperfectly for some reason or other. Criticism of method and improvements of method are activities rendered nonsensical in a consistent logical positivism [Campbell, 1969, p. 15].

A third reason to be suspicious of any claim that intelligence (or any other quality) is what any single test measures is that without a second independent test to measure the same quality, there is no guarantee that the test is related to anything other than itself. Adler (1947) devised a test to measure something he called "C_N," as follows:

The C_N Test

1. How many hours did you sleep last night?_____
2. Estimate the length of your nose in inches and multiply by 2._____
3. Do you like fried liver? (Mark $+1$ for Yes and -1 for No)._____
4. How many feet are there in a yard?_____
5. Estimate the number of glasses of ginger ale the inventor of this test drank while inventing it._____

Sum = Crude C_N Score

His instructions say, "This test is to be taken daily at the same hour of the day for as long as you can take it. Then you may proceed to calculate your refined C_N rate . . ." (p. 439), and he provides an elaborate formula for the calculation of the refined rate from the crude score. If you should wonder what your C_N score represents, he says that "the test measures C_N and C_N is what the test measures" (p. 439).

Adler created this test to show the futility of trying to hide behind definitional operationism. He adds:

> We are confronted here by a seemingly closed system. All criticism is excluded. C_N *is* what it was defined as, and the test is what defines it. Still C_N does not make sense; we are unable to form a concept of it [Adler, 1947, p. 439].

Unless there are at least two operational definitions of a concept, we have no way of knowing whether a particular definition is appropriate. In the case of the C_N Test, we must have some idea what C_N is to construct a second operational definition, and it is not sufficient to say that "C_N is what the C_N Test measures." That begs the question.

Campbell and Adler have identified the following errors committed by researchers who rely on *definitional operationism*: (1) They do not acknowledge the irrelevant factors and errors that contribute to a score, (2) they do not allow room for improvement, and (3) they do not tell us anything about the concept other than that it is what the test measures. In spite of these problems, however, we do not advocate abandoning operational definitions. Instead, we advocate the use of *multiple* operational definitions. If we agree that each measure is an imperfect indicator of a complex abstract concept like intelligence or social status, we can use multiple measures without violating any claims that one operational definition is supreme. In addition, by acknowledging the imperfection of all our current measures, we leave room for improvement, without which there would be little hope for scientific advance. "We are continuously confronted by the necessity of developing new concepts and new ways of measurement. There is hardly any measurement in sociology [or any social science] that is generally recognized as fully satisfactory" (Adler, 1947, p. 441).

In discussing operational definitions, we have emphasized the imperfections, errors, and fallibility of measurement because, in teaching research methods courses, we have seen students paralyzed by the fear that they have not found the *best* measure for their research. We want to inoculate students against this fear by saying *no* measure is perfect. Students should not conclude that research is impossible, but should realize that any single operational definition is imperfect and that it is therefore wiser to choose two. Two imperfect measures are better than one. Each provides a check on the other, and each has a different set of errors or biases.

RELIABILITY

Classical measurement theory begins with the assumption that all measurement contains some error (Guilford, 1954). Any observed score has two components:

Observed Score = True Score + Error

A reliable measure is one that has a small error component and, therefore, does not fluctuate randomly from one moment to the next. To understand reliability in measurement, consider what it means in a person. If you call someone reliable, you probably mean the person is consistent — if she tells you one thing today, she will say the same thing tomorrow. If a reliable person says she will meet you at noon tomorrow, when you appear at the assigned time and place, that person will be there. A reliable person is also one who, if she begins to tell you a story of something that happened, maintains a consistent account and does not give different versions from one hour to the next. These various definitions of a reliable person imply the person will not say one thing and do another or give different versions of the "truth" at different times.

A reliable instrument also tells the same story from one measurement instance to the next. By contrast, consider an unreliable instrument, an *elastic* ruler. If you tried to measure your height by standing on one end of the elastic ruler and holding the other to the top of your head, you would get a slightly different reading each time you measured because you would pull a little more or less on the ruler each time and it would stretch or shrink accordingly. An elastic ruler has a large error component, and that makes the observed scores unreliable. The larger the error component in relation to the true score, the less reliable the instrument.

Reliability is assessed in several ways, and the elastic ruler would fare poorly on each. The types of reliability assessment are as follows:

Test-Retest Correlation

By using an instrument twice on the same persons or groups, we can compute the correlation between their two scores. This correlation is a measure of the reliability of the instrument. If the instrument is reliable, people should maintain the same relative positions on the instrument. If there have been no major changes in those groups' or persons' lives, the persons who scored high on the first testing should still score high on the second. No one expects to find a perfect correlation for most measures in the social sciences because they all contain an element of error that makes the observed scores fluctuate from one testing session to the next. Even a wooden ruler might not yield identical measures of height from one time to the next because there is some slippage in placing the ruler, because people's posture changes and influences their height, because they may wear different shoes from one time to the next. Repeated readings with a wooden ruler would be more consistent from one time to the next than with an elastic ruler, however. The smaller the error component, the more consistent the readings from one measurement time to the next, and the higher the test-retest reliability of the instrument.

Split-half Correlation

By correlating the results obtained from two halves of the same instrument, we can calculate the split-half reliability. If our elastic ruler were 200 inches long, we could measure people's height by using the first half of the ruler once, from 0 to 100 inches, and then the second half, from 100 to 200 inches. We should get approximately the same number of inches for a single person from both ends of the ruler, but they will not be identical because the elasticity creates errors. The same would happen if we had a 200-item attitude scale. We could give each person two attitude scores, based on the first hundred and second hundred items. The scores would be similar, but not identical, because the items differ and both halves of the scale include some error in their measurement. The split-half reliability of either the ruler or the attitude scale is the correlation between the scores obtained from the two halves. The more similar the scores from the two halves, the higher the correlation, and the more reliable the instrument is.

There are other ways to compute split-half reliability. Rather than correlate totals from the first and second halves of an instrument, we can correlate totals made up of alternate items—odd versus even items. Either calculation gives information about the reliability or consistency of a measure. The correlation coefficients will not be identical because each set of subtotals will produce a different result. Some calculations will product maximally dissimilar halves, as, for instance, summing all items worded in a positive direction for one total and summing all items worded in a negative direction for the other total. Other calculations will produce maximally similar halves, such as summing alternate items provided they do not differ systematically in the direction of wording or tone or content.

Because different ways of halving an instrument produce different split-half reliability coefficients, there is no single answer to the question, "What is the reliability of a test?" Each instrument will have a range of reliability coefficients.

Average Item-total Correlation

By correlating each item with the total score and averaging those correlation coefficients, we obtain another measure of the internal consistency of a test. The total score should be corrected each time so as not to include the score from the item it is correlated with. This gives a measure of how much the answer to each item agrees with the sum of answers to the other items. This reliability coefficient and the following one show whether the instrument taps the same variable with each additional item.

Average Interitem Correlation

Correlating each item with every other item and averaging those coefficients produces another internal consistency measure.

All four measures of reliability—the test-retest, split-half, average item-total, and average interitem correlation—show whether the instrument is measuring a single quality and how precisely it measures it. Using these criteria, we can evaluate Adler's C_N Scale and determine how reliable it is. The test-retest reliability of his scale could be reasonably high. People's answers to one of his five questions may be stable over time—"Do you like fried liver?" would probably elicit the same answers if asked today and a week from now. Answers to the question, "How many hours did you sleep last night?" may change from week to week, but individuals may retain a fairly constant rank ordering, such that those who sleep long hours will give answers ranging between eight and ten hours and those who sleep very little will answer between four and five hours each time they are asked. The test-retest correlation will not be a perfect $r = 1.00$, but it should be substantially greater than zero because most people have regular sleep patterns. The answers to the questions "Estimate the length of your nose in inches and multiply by two" and "Estimate the number of glasses of ginger ale the inventor of this test drank while inventing it" will probably produce wild guesses because few people know the length of their noses—most would probably not even know where to begin measuring if they tried—and no one would know how many glasses of ginger ale Adler had drunk. But they could remember how they guessed the first time, so answers to these two items may also have a high test-retest correlation. The item that asks how many feet are in a yard would elicit the same answer from everyone—three feet—and a test-retest correlation would be zero because there are no consistently high and consistently low scores. With no variation in scores, there is no correlation.

Four of the five items on Adler's C_N Test could yield high test-retest correlations, therefore, and the fifth would have a zero correlation because there would be no variability of scores. The test-retest reliability of the C_N Test as a whole depends on the correlation of the total scores, however, and not on the individual items. For a test that is internally consistent, whose items all measure the same construct, the test-retest correlation of the total score is higher than the test-retest correlation of individual items. For the C_N Test, however, this is not likely to be true because the total scores represent a nonsensical sum with no apparent internal consistency.

The other three measures of reliability are all measures of internal consistency. On each of them, Adler's C_N Test would earn a low reliability rating. Consider the following fictional people and their answers to the C_N Test (Table 7.1).

If the test were internally consistent, a person who scores high on Item 1 should also score high on Items 2 through 5. This is not true in our example. Jane scored higher than Jim on Item 1, but lower on Item 2, higher on 3, and lower on 5. There is no consistency from one item to the next because the items do not mea-

TABLE 7.2   Rank Ordering of Nine French High School Students' Intelligence Scores Obtained with Three Hypothetical Measures.

Operational Definition #1	*Operational Definition #2*	*Operational Definition #3*
English IQ Test	French Translation of English Test	French Interviews
Marie ⟶	⟶ Pierre	Pierre
Pierre ⟶	⟶ Marie	Marie
Jeanne	Jeanne	Jeanne
Jacques	Jacques	Jacques
Lisa	Lisa	Lisa
Charles	Charles	Charles
Carole	Carole	Carole
Robert	Robert ⟶	⟶ Marianne
Marianne	Marianne ⟶	⟶ Robert

The nonoverlapping portions of the circles in Figure 7.1 consist of two components: error and aspects of the construct that are measured by only one operational definition. The disagreements between the measures of intelligence obtained with the English version of the test, the French version, and the interviews with educators arise from both the error and unique components of the underlying variable contained in each operational definition. The error component includes both random and systematic qualities. The systematic qualities include knowledge of English for the English version of the intelligence test and conversational skills and poise for the interview with educators. These are not part of what we mean by intelligence because a French student may be very intelligent but be unable to answer a single item of the English version because she has never studied English. Another student may receive high scores on both written tests but become stage-struck during an interview with French educators. Facility with English and stage presence are irrelevant variables that are included in these two measures of intelligence. If we use only one operational definition, we do not know how much of the observed score represents the construct we intend to measure—intelligence—and how much represents irrelevant qualities like knowledge of English or conversational skills. When we use two or more operational definitions, we can correlate them, calculate the amount of common variance, and know to what extent the measures tap what we intend and to what extent they contain error. The more dissimilar the operational definitions are—like a written test and an interview—the more heterogeneous the irrelevant components. If you use maximally dissimilar operational definitions, the irrelevant components are also dissimilar, and the shared variance reflects the variable intended. The more dissimilar two methods of measurement are, the more meaningful a correlation between them is because the common variance then reflects the underlying variable rather than shared error or irrelevant components.

Reliability and validity estimates lie on a continuum as illustrated in Figure

FIGURE 7.2. Reliability-validity continuum.

Reliability ——————————————→ Validity
Correlation between   Correlation between
Maximally similar   Maximally different
Measures   Measures

7.2. At one end of the continuum are correlations between identical methods of measurement. Test-retest correlations are based on the same test administered twice. At the other end of the continuum are correlations between very different methods of measuring the same variable. A paper-and-pencil test of intelligence and an interview can be distinctly different measures. Reliability estimates are correlations between identical or similar methods; validity estimates are correlations between dissimilar methods.

Both ends of the scale have some practical limits beyond which the correlations are meaningless. If the measures are so similar that they are guaranteed to produce 100 percent agreement, they would not be considered a fair test of the reliability of an instrument. For instance, if a retest were administered immediately after its initial administration and each person simply copied his answers from the first test, the perfect correlation between the test and retest measures would tell nothing about the reliability of the instrument. It would only show that people can copy their answers accurately. At the other end of the continuum, if two measures of intelligence were so different that they did not both bear some resemblance to what most people call "intelligence," their low correlation would be a foregone conclusion. For instance, a test of how well people can sight-read music would probably not correlate highly with an adult intelligence test. Sight-reading music requires intelligence, but it also requires prior training and interest in music, both of which are different from intelligence, so the correlation may be near zero. Finding maximally different methods to measure the same variable is difficult — because the more the methods differ, the less likely they are to tap the same variable.

There are several ways to evaluate the validity of an instrument, each based on finding agreement between two different assessments of the same variable.

Face Validity

Face validity is evaluated by a group of judges, sometimes experts, who read or look at a measuring technique and decide whether in their opinion it measures what its name suggests. For instance, professional speech therapists could look at a test designed to measure degrees of speech impairment and decide whether the test measures what the testers claim. Evaluating face validity is a subjective process, but we could calculate a validity figure by computing the amount of agreement between judges. The higher the percent who say it measures what it claims to measure, the higher the face validity. Every instrument must pass the face validity test either formally or informally. Every researcher who chooses an instrument is a judge who has decided that the test measures the construct he or she wishes to study. Without such minimal face validity, an instrument would not be used.

Concurrent Validity

Concurrent validity is the ability of a test to distinguish between individuals who are known to differ. For instance, if you were developing a test to measure people's political conservatism, the test should distinguish between people who belong to groups we assume differ, such as the Young Americans for Freedom and the Students for a Democratic Society. If members of these groups scored the same, the test would be a measure not of political conservatism but of something those groups shared, such as a distrust of the current political administration.

Predictive Validity

Predictive validity is the ability of a test to identify future differences. For instance, the predictive validity of college entrance examinations is the ability of those tests to identify who will graduate from college and who will drop out or to predict who will receive high grades and who will receive low grades or to predict who will go on to graduate school and who will not. Depending on which of these criteria we choose, the test may have high, moderate, or low predictive validity. Predictive validity is an evaluation of a test's practical worth in foreseeing the future. It is a pragmatic approach to validity.

Construct Validity

Construct validity is an evaluation of the extent to which an instrument measures the theoretical construct the investigator wishes to measure. Unlike face validity, construct validity requires more than expert opinion. It requires a demonstration that the construct in question exists, that it is distinct from other constructs and, therefore, worthy of its own name, and that the instrument measures that particular construct and no others. Construct validation requires *agreement* between scores obtained with two instruments presumably measuring the *same* construct and *disagreement* between two instruments measuring *different* constructs. Agreement gives evidence of *convergent validity*, which is one aspect of construct validation. Disagreement is evidence of *discriminant* validity, the second aspect of construct validation. For instance, if you wished to design a questionnaire to measure attitudes toward women, its convergent validity would consist of agreement between people's scores on the questionnaire and their friends' ratings of those persons' attitudes toward women. To demonstrate that the interview measured attitudes toward women and not political liberalism or attitudes toward people in general, it is necessary to make other comparisons. It is necessary to demonstrate that the people's attitudes toward women are *not* too highly correlated with a distinctly different set of attitudes, like attitudes toward men. Low correlations with tests measuring different constructs demonstrate the *discriminant* validity of the instrument.

There are no criteria for how high the correlations must be to demonstrate convergent validity and how low they must be to demonstrate discriminant validity. What matters is the pattern of correlations: the former should be higher than the latter.

MULTITRAIT-MULTIMETHOD MATRIX

The multitrait-multimethod matrix is a table of correlations that demonstrates the role of both convergent and discriminant validity in construct validation (Campbell and Fiske, 1959). It requires at least two methods to measure at least two different variables. The matrix of correlations looks complicated, but the logic is simple and compelling.

The matrix is based on the principle that the more features two measurements have in common, the higher their correlation will be. Measurements can share two types of features: traits and methods. Traits are the underlying construct the measurement is supposed to tap; they are the content. Methods are the form of the measurement — paper-and-pencil questionnaires, face-to-face interviews, unobtrusive observations, census records, and so on. Ideally, scores should reflect only the intended trait and not be influenced by the method. In reality, the form or method of measurement also affects the score, and some of the variation in observed scores is a product of the method used to obtain the scores. A face-to-face interview about attitudes toward women, for instance, would measure not only attitudes toward women but also people's desire to appear liberal or current in their views. An English language test of intelligence would measure not only students' intelligence but also their English proficiency. A set of police department statistics on murder rates in major American cities would measure not only murder rates but also the efforts of police commissioners and mayors in those cities to be reappointed or reelected. Each attempt to measure a construct, therefore, is contaminated by aspects of the method that are irrelevant to the construct but inevitable in the measurement.

Some irrelevant aspects of methods are known and can be taken into account. For instance, if the statistics from one police department are inflated and those of another depressed for political purposes, the investigator can adjust the figures to reduce the contamination. Interviewers can try to establish rapport with their respondents to elicit honest rather than guarded or socially desirable answers (see Chapter 8). Researchers can also correct for known biases in questionnaires. For instance, people often develop preferences for circling Yes's or No's. Researchers can control these biases by wording items so that half contain positive statements and half negative statements about the topic. A person who believes in the virtue of electoral politics, for instance, would have to agree with the statement "It is important to vote because every vote counts" and disagree with the statement "Voting is wasted effort." If someone answered the questionnaire unthinkingly and chose to disagree with most items regardless of their content, that person's score would not be biased either for or against electoral politics if half the items were positive and half negative. By controlling the direction of wording, researchers can eliminate such response biases from the observed score.

In addition to these known biases and sources of contamination, however, measuring techniques include other features that an investigator cannot control, and scores, therefore, inevitably contain both a trait and a methods component. The multitrait-multimethod matrix lets a researcher assess the extent to which scores reflect the trait and the method contained in every measurement.

Because every score is made up of two elements — a trait and a method — the correlation between two sets of scores depends on how much they share both the

TABLE 7.3 Correlation Coefficients in a Multitrait-Multimethod Matrix.

Coefficients	Elements Contained in the Scores That Are Correlated	
	Traits	Methods
1. Reliability correlation	Same	Same
2. Convergent validity correlation	Same	Different
3. Discriminant validity correlation	Different	Same
4. Nonsense correlation	Different	Different

[handwritten annotations: "HIGH" bracketing rows 1-2; "LOW" bracketing rows 3-4]

trait and the method. Reliability coefficients are correlations between scores that reflect the same trait and the same method. Convergent validity coefficients are correlations between scores that reflect the same trait measured by different methods. The reliability coefficients of an instrument should, therefore, logically be higher than its validity coefficients because the former are based on more shared elements. The multitrait-multimethod matrix introduces two additional correlation coefficients to assess the validity of an instrument. These are both correlations between *different traits.* One is a discriminant validity correlation between different traits measured by the same method, and the other is a nonsense correlation between different traits measured by different methods. Table 7.3 depicts these correlations and their elements.

The first two correlations should be high; the last two should be low. If the third and fourth correlations are as high as the convergent validity correlations, it means the two traits are not different but are the same or highly similar. For instance, if an investigator devised two separate tests, one called Attitudes Toward Women and the other Attitudes Toward Men, the two should not be too highly correlated if they are truly separate attitudes. If the intercorrelations between these tests were like those shown in Figure 7.3, we would be satisfied that they measured two distinct traits or attitudes.

The same-trait-different-method correlation coefficients (.70) are higher than

FIGURE 7.3. Multitrait-multimethod matrix of correlations between attitudes toward women and attitudes toward men.

		Paper-and-Pencil Questionnaire		Observations of Behavior	
		Attitudes Toward Women (ATW)	Attitudes Toward Men (ATM)	Attitudes Toward Women (ATW)	Attitudes Toward Men (ATM)
Questionnaire	ATW	(.90)*	.30		
	ATM	.30	(.90)		
Behavior	ATW	.70	.10	(.90)	.30
	ATM	.10	.70	.30	(.90)

*The correlations in parentheses are reliability correlations.

FIGURE 7.4. **Multitrait-multimethod matrix of correlations between attitudes toward women and attitudes toward men.**

			Paper-and-Pencil Questionnaire		*Observations of Behavior*	
			Attitudes Toward Women (ATW)	*Attitudes Toward Men (ATM)*	*Attitudes Toward Women (ATW)*	*Attitudes Toward Men (ATM)*
Questionnaire	{	ATW	(.90)*	.80		
		ATM	.80	(.90)		
Behavior	{	ATW	.40	.30	(.90)	.80
		ATM	.30	.40	.80	(.90)

*The correlations in parentheses are reliability correlations.

the different-trait-same-method correlations (.30) and the different-trait-different-method correlations (.10). This is justification for saying the tests measure two different traits. If, however, the matrix looked like Figure 7.4, the tests would be invalidated, not because the correlations were too low but because some of the correlations were too high.

The correlations in Figure 7.4 show the two attitudes are very similar because they are highly correlated with one another. The correlation between two different traits measured by the same method (.80) is higher than the correlation between the same trait measured by different methods (.40). These two attitudes have no discriminant validity because they are so highly intercorrelated. If they are truly different attitudes, the correlation between them should not be higher than the convergent validity correlations of the same trait measured by different methods (.40).

Particularly if a researcher is trying to develop a test to measure a newly conceptualized trait, it is important to assess its discriminant validity to demonstrate that it is new and different. Campbell and Fiske (1959) point out that tests have been invalidated not only because of low correlations but also "because of too high correlations with other tests purporting to measure different things" (p. 84). If we obtained the correlations shown in Figure 7.4, we would conclude the two tests measure roughly the same attitude; and rather than talk of "Attitudes Toward Women" and "Attitudes Toward Men," we would rename the scales and call them both "Attitudes Toward People."

SCALES

A scale in social science is a set of categories to differentiate among people on any one variable. There may be as few as two categories in a scale or as many as 100 or more.

Nominal Scales

Nominal scales contain qualitatively different categories to which we attach names rather than numerical meaning. The simplest are dichotomies, with only two values, such as "male" and "female," or "homeowners" and "renters." The categories are qualitatively rather than quantitatively different. If, for the sake of coding and keypunching data, we use numbers like 1 and 2 to stand for "male" and "female," respectively, the numbers have no arithmetic value. The number "2" does not mean that cases placed in that category have more of the quality than cases placed in the category numbered "1." Other examples of nominal scales are the following:

Types of urban stressors:

1 = traffic noises
2 = air pollutants
3 = crowds
4 = bureaucratic harrassment
5 = other

Living arrangements for the elderly:

1 = own home or apartment
2 = relative's home
3 = retirement home
4 = other

The list of alternatives need not exhaust all possible categories, but it should include those categories relevant to the theory and the population tested and should enable the coder to classify every case. For instance, there are many more living arrangements for elderly people than the three just listed. If, however, we designed a study to test the effects of living in one's own home, in someone else's, or in an institution, then the three categories plus the unspecified "other" category would be sufficient for the purposes of that study. The inclusion of "other" enables us to classify every case.

Ordinal Scales

An ordinal scale contains categories that can be ordered by rank on a continuum. The categories have a rudimentary arithmetic meaning such as "more" or "less" of the quantity being measured. For instance, we could order occupations in terms of how much autonomy the workers have in their jobs:

1 = little autonomy (for example, assembly line workers, keypunch operators, and check-out clerks in a large discount department store)
2 = moderate autonomy (for example, construction workers, nurses, and taxi drivers)
3 = much autonomy (for example, independent artists, jewelers, doctors, lawyers)

The scale states that 1 means an occupation permits less autonomy than 3 and that 2 is located in between. An ordinal scale gives only this information and does not provide any information about the distances between the values. The interval between 1 and 2 may be larger or smaller than the interval between 2 and 3. An ordinal scale does not imply anything about the arithmetic values other than that they are in order.

Interval Scales

When numbers attached to a variable imply not only that 3 is more than 2 and 2 is more than 1 but also that the size of the interval between 3 and 2 is the same as the interval between 2 and 1, they form an interval scale. Just because a scale contains values from 1 to 100, it does not automatically follow that the difference between 60 and 70 is the same as the difference between 90 and 100. For instance, if we made up a 100-item vocabulary test on which most people defined between 60 and 70 words correctly and only two people defined 90 and one person defined 100 correctly, the gap between 90 and 100 probably represents a greater difference in vocabulary level than the gap between 60 and 70.

If the intervals represent *equal* quantities of the variable measured, they constitute an interval scale. For every unit increase on the scale, there is a unit increase in the variable. The Fahrenheit scale measures temperature in equal intervals. The temperature difference between 33 and 34 degrees is the same as the temperature difference between 36 and 37 degrees. If this seems obvious, it is because we have grown accustomed to the Fahrenheit scale and take for granted that it represents equal intervals of physical heat and cold. We cannot take it for granted that social science scales represent equal intervals.

Most social science constructs are measured by ordinal rather than interval scales. For instance, if we used families' annual income as a variable to measure the underlying construct "social status," we could not assume that the dollar scale represented equal intervals of social status. The status difference in the interval between $20,000 and $40,000 in annual income is much larger than the status difference in the interval between $120,000 and $140,000. As we go up the income scale, the $20,000 difference makes less and less difference in social status. Two families with incomes of $120,000 and $140,000 are more likely to live next door to each other than are two families with incomes of $20,000 and $40,000, because the $20,000 interval represents a bigger difference in social status at the bottom end of the scale than at the top. Annual income, therefore, is not an interval scale measure of social status.

The numbers on an interval scale can be added or subtracted because the properties of the scale are such that $20 - 10 = 40 - 30$. But numbers on an interval scale cannot be multiplied or divided because the scale does not have a true zero. It has an arbitrary zero. We can multiply and divide the values only if we have a ratio scale.

Ratio Scales

Ratio scales do have a true zero, and as a result the scale values represent multipliable quantities. Physical scales measuring length and weight are ratio scales: a 4-foot length of board is twice as long as a 2-foot piece; ten pounds of feathers weigh twice as much as five pounds. For these physical scales, zero is real and not arbitrary. Although we cannot point to anything that has zero inches or zero pounds, we know what those mean on our rulers or scales, and we do not arbitrarily locate zero at any point on the scale.

Some variables used to measure social constructs look superficially like ratio measures because they have zero as the lowest score. Money as a measure of social status, for instance, gives the appearance of being a ratio scale because the variable has an absolute true zero. A person can be penniless and possess no money. This does not mean, however, that the penniless person has zero social status. A monk who takes a vow of poverty, for instance, has no money but has social status among people who respect religious orders. The most we can assume about social status measured in dollars is that more money represents more status, all other assets being equal.

If we measured happiness by how often a person smiled, we might be tempted to say that someone who smiles ten times is twice as happy as someone who smiles five times. True, ten smiles are twice as many as five smiles. Our scale, however, is to be a measure not of *smiling* but of the construct *happiness*. *Number of smiles* is the variable we have chosen to measure the abstract construct *happiness*, and happiness may not double as smiles do.

Even standardized and copyrighted measures such as IQ scales do not have true zeros. No psychologist would try to argue that someone with an IQ score of 150 is twice as intelligent as someone with an IQ of 75. Although the numbers can be added or multiplied and though a scale may begin with zero, it does not mean that the underlying construct has those properties. It is difficult to imagine any social construct such as happiness, social status, or power for which there is a true zero because it is always possible to imagine a case with a little less of the construct. For instance, if we devised a ten-item scale of happiness for which every answer that represented unhappiness received a zero, someone who answered all ten items with zeros would receive a total happiness score of zero. Does that person truly have no happiness? Is it not possible to imagine someone else who might have even less happiness than that person? Social science constructs have this quality of an infinite regress at the bottom end of the scale. It is always possible to imagine a case of a little less status, a little less power, a little less happiness; and the scale, therefore, does not have a true zero. Without a true zero, a scale does not have ratios—it is not possible to say that a score of ten represents twice as much of the construct as five.

MEASUREMENT PRESUPPOSES THEORY ✱

The preceding discussion implies that we know what the relationship is between the variable we measure and the underlying construct that it represents. How do we know what the relationship is? The relationship between a variable like dollar income and a construct like social status is called the "epistemic correlation" (Carter, 1971). This is not a correlation that we can actually compute—because we have no direct access to the construct *social status*. We can measure it only with variables like dollars or years of schooling. Hence the dilemma: How do we determine the epistemic correlation between a variable and a construct if we can only measure the construct with variables? The solution is twofold.

First, we use what we already know about both income and social status to determine what the relationship is between the two. We have an intuitive theory about the relationship of dollars to status. This is not a theory based on social science research — it is based on common sense and personal observations. For instance, most of us know by the time we are 18 that the social status difference between two families with annual incomes of $140,000 and $120,000 is *not* the same as the social status difference between two families with incomes of $40,000 and $20,000. The first difference is negligible; the second is sizable, even though in both instances the difference is $20,000. Recognizing this commonly accepted fact is one step in deciding what the relationship is between income and status. It is not a direct linear relationship like that shown in Figure 7.5. Intuition and common sense inform us that equivalent increases in dollar income do not produce equivalent increases in social status. This is one way we decide that income is not an interval scale measure of status.

The second step in determining the relationship between a variable like dollars and the construct it represents is to locate another variable that measures the same construct. Education, or years of schooling, is another measure of social status. *If* there were a direct linear relationship between income and status and if there were a direct linear relationship between schooling and status, then there should be a direct linear relationship between income and schooling. If $A = B$ and $A = C$, then B should equal C. But $B \neq C$ in this case. For each additional year of schooling, people do not always receive additional income. There are people with many years of schooling who have lower incomes than people with fewer years of schooling. Therefore, either income or schooling or both have a nonlinear relationship to the construct social status.

What should we assume about the relationship between status and our numerical indicators? The answer comes again from our prior knowledge about what the numbers mean. In the case of income, it is probably reasonable to assume that dollars and status are related in a curvilinear rather than linear fashion. Figure 7.6 illustrates a curvilinear relationship. This relationship means that "small differences in income make less and less difference as one becomes richer and richer" (Carter, 1971, p. 16). We cannot prove that social status has such a curvilinear relationship with income because we have no direct measure of social status. We will probably make fewer errors, however, and reach more insightful conclusions if we assume a relationship like that in Figure 7.6 instead of Figure 7.5.

The relationship between social status and education is probably neither linear like Figure 7.5 nor curvilinear like Figure 7.6, given what we know about the meaning of education. Whereas a visitor from Mars might assume the difference between

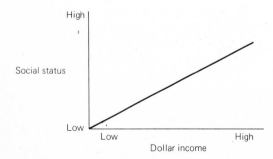

FIGURE 7.5. Direct linear relationship between income and status that is contradicted by intuition and common sense.

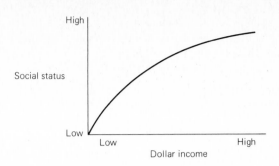

NON LINEAR

INCREASING CONTINUOUS MONOTONE FUNCTION
W/ DERIVATIVE (0) → 1
          ˄ (∞) → 0

FIGURE 7.6. Curvilinear relationship between income and social status. (From Carter, 1971)

14 and 15 years of schooling is the same as the difference between 15 and 16 years, we know that completing 16 years of school means being a college graduate, and that makes a bigger difference than any of the preceding years of schooling. Employers act as though the difference between 15 and 16 years of schooling is bigger than the difference between 14 and 15 years. Education as a measure of social status has plateaus, and college graduation is one of them. Therefore, we should not assume a linear relationship between education and status, nor should we assume a curvilinear relationship like that in Figure 7.6. Instead, we can best approximate the relationship between education and status by using plateaus and assigning status increments to each plateau rather than each year of schooling. Each graduation signals an increase in status: elementary school graduate, high school graduate, and college graduate. Figure 7.7 illustrates this relationship between number of years of education and social status.

FIGURE 7.7. Relationship between number of years of education and social status.

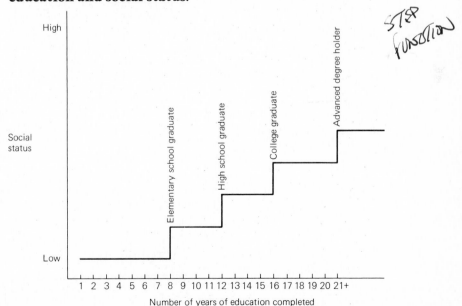

STEP FUNCTION

Fitting quantitative variables to abstract constructs is a bit like using a luminous ruler to measure an elephant on a moonless night. We can obtain clear numbers, but we know that the numbers do not perfectly capture the dimensions of the beast. The ruler does not bend where the elephant bends; it slips when the elephant stamps its feet; and as we grope in the dark, it is hard to tell what portions of the elephant we have measured and which parts remain untouched. When we transfer our numbers onto paper and try to sketch the elephant from the measured inches, part of our sketch is derived from what we already know about elephants — our intuition and common sense knowledge about the shape and size of an elephant.

SUMMARY

We began this chapter by saying operational definitions are essential — without them there would be no scientific measurement. They provide a public process for reproducing and replicating measures. By reproducing and replicating measurements, we can determine how reliable they are. Operational definitions are also full of error, however. They always include irrelevant elements that bear no relation to the construct we intend to measure and exclude portions of the construct that we would have liked to measure. For this reason, no single operation is definitional of the construct. Each is only an approximation, a partial substitute for the underlying construct. In recognition of the fact that no single measure is 100 percent reliable or 100 percent valid, we advocate using multiple operational definitions of a single construct. "When multiple operations provide consistent results, the possibility of slippage between conceptual definition and operational specification is diminished greatly" (Webb, Campbell, Schwartz, and Sechrest, 1966, p. 5). "The most persuasive evidence comes through a triangulation of measurement processes. If a proposition can survive the onslaught of a series of imperfect measures, with all their irrelevant error, confidence should be placed in it" (Webb et al., 1966, p. 3).

The major problem in measurement is that we can never be sure we have measured what we intended to. It is a problem that has both an infinite regress and a solution. The infinite regress is as follows: We are interested in the concept of social quarks and try to measure them in various organizations by developing the Quick Quark Scale. The scale has ten items, and we score each organization for the presence or absence of quarks on each item. For instance, if the people in the organization all call one another by first names, the organization gets a plus for the presence of social quarks on that item. If all employees set their own work schedules, the quark is present; if not, it is absent. We use ten items to assign organizations a quark score ranging from 0 to 10. Having done so, we want to know whether these scores measure the variable we intended. Perhaps they are really measures of the social class of the employees rather than the quark quality of the organization; perhaps they measure the prosperity of the organization; perhaps they measure the authoritarianism of the participants; or perhaps they measure no single variable at all, but a collection of ten discrete qualities.

To determine whether the scale measures social quarks, we compare the scores obtained from this scale with scores obtained from another set of items from another quark scale. In doing this, however, we must trust the second scale, and how can we know that it measures social quarks? We can demonstrate that the second scale measures social quarks by comparing its results with a third scale; the third scale can be trusted by comparing it with a fourth; and so on. The infinite regress occurs because we can never be sure any scale measures what we intended to measure unless we compare it with another, which we admit is also fallible. The solution lies in giving temporary credence to those other measures while we test the goodness of one. Campbell describes the predicament as follows: "We are like sailors who must repair a rotting ship at sea. We trust the great bulk of the timbers while we replace a particularly weak plank. Each of the timbers we now trust we may in its turn replace. The proportion of the planks we are replacing to those we treat as sound must always be small" (1974, p. 6). We can live with the knowledge that each of our measures is imperfect as long as there is some agreement among the imperfect measures. We give up the search for certainty and accept consensus instead.

Questionnaires and Interviews

This chapter was organized and revised by Leonard LoSciuto, with portions adopted from Arthur Kornhauser and Paul B. Sheatsley's Appendix to the third edition.

The situation often arises in social research in which it is impossible or impractical to collect data about people by observation. In these situations interviews and questionnaires are commonly used to gather information. Typical topics of interest are a person's knowledge, attitudes, beliefs, feelings, motivations, anticipations, future plans or past behavior.

In the interview and questionnaire approach, heavy reliance is placed on *verbal reports* from the subjects for information about the stimuli or experiences to which they are exposed and for knowledge of their behavior. The subjects' reports may or may not be taken at face value: they may be interpreted in the light of other knowledge about the person or in terms of some psychological theory, or inferences may be drawn about aspects of the subjects' functioning that they have not reported. Regardless of the amount and kind of interpretation, however, the starting point is the subjects' self-report. Thus, the investigator can ordinarily obtain only material that the subject is willing and able to report.

For many years now, a controversy has existed in the social science literature about the validity of verbal reports. The question is: How do we know a man is *really* hungry when he says, "I am hungry"? There are many weighty issues involved in this question, which we shall not discuss.[1] Let us point out, however,

---

[1] A discussion by Galtung (1967) argued for considering verbal data as important in their own right and not merely because of their relationship with nonverbal behavior. Galtung states that there is nothing intrinsically more valuable about nonverbal behavior, for both may have consequences of varying importance; the verbal behavior may inflict great pain or pleasure, and the nonverbal may have no impact on others. Similarly, neither has a prior claim to superior validity; it is possible to lie or deceive by both word and deed. The *connections* between verbal and nonverbal behavior are thus not necessarily a test of the validity of data gathered about either. What a person says (in a particular social context) need have no relationship with what he or she does (in another social context); both may be important facts about the person and the social context or contexts. To demand consistency between them is to impose a simplicity that violates the complexity of social relations.

that in everyday life we accept many verbal reports as valid. For example, if we ask a friend what she thought of a certain play and she says, "it's terrible," we ordinarily believe that her statement accurately represents her feelings. However, in everyday life we also realize that in certain circumstances verbal reports are not to be trusted. For example, whenever we have reason to suspect that a person's truthful self-report would be embarrassing or would in some way place the person in an unfavorable light, we are likely to entertain some reservations about it. Or whenever we have reason to believe that a person is using a verbal report to ingratiate himself or herself, to gain respect or prestige, to amuse or astonish, or in some other way to create a certain social effect, we are likely to place little confidence in it. In other words, when the circumstances in which the report occurs lead us to suppose that the subject's *motivation* or the pressure to which the subject is exposed is such as to prevent a candid report, we are not likely to give it much *credence.*[2]

Not only may people be reluctant to report openly their beliefs, feelings, motivations, plans, and so on; they may be *unable* to do so. As psychoanalysts have pointed out, we are not aware of many of our important beliefs and motivations and hence cannot report them. Moreover, self-report frequently requires *self-diagnosis.* Even such seemingly simple questions as, "Are you shy with strangers?" or "Would you rather go to a party or stay home and read a good book?" require individuals to make judgments about themselves on the basis of many past events. Feelings, beliefs, and motivations become apparent to the self in an intellectually comprehensible form only as the end result of an involved process of inference. With respect to complex social attitudes, some people have never learned to make the inferences necessary to an adequate verbal report; they cannot indicate, in any systematic or analytic manner, their attitudes toward their spouses, for example, or toward welfare or toward school busing for racial integration.

In sum, self-reports may be inaccurate because people are sometimes *unwilling or unable to remember or to describe* accurately what they *know,* what or how they *feel,* and what they *do.* Nevertheless, all people have a unique opportunity to observe themselves. To the extent that they can and will communicate their knowledge about themselves, they provide the investigator with information that could otherwise be obtained, if at all, only by other, even more fallible methods than self-reports. By and large, it may be reasonable to assume that people will tell the truth about themselves unless we have specific reasons to think otherwise. The researcher who is about to launch a study based on self-reports should identify particularly sensitive topics, if any, and try to take into account the sensitivity through proper interviewing techniques, question wording, and so on.

---

[2]In particular, see Derek Phillips (1971). The research of Parry and Crossley demonstrated how the answers to factual questions are also influenced by the desire to appear "respectable." As summarized by Katz (1951), "They found that people consistently exaggerated their registration and voting behavior. The exaggeration varied from thirteen percent who falsely claimed to have voted in the 1948 election to twenty-eight percent who made fictitious claims to voting in local elections. One third of those who reported contributing to the Community Chest were speaking of pious intentions, not actual contributions. Telephone and home ownership were accurately reported. Similarly, car ownership was not appreciably inflated, but ten percent of those reporting a driver's license did not have one. Again, ten percent claimed to have library cards when in fact they had none."

COMPARISON OF INTERVIEWS AND QUESTIONNAIRES

Although both interviews and questionnaires place heavy reliance upon the validity of verbal reports, there are important differences between the two methods. In a questionnaire, the information one obtains is limited to the written responses of subjects to prearranged questions. In an interview, because the interviewer and the person interviewed are both present as the questions are asked and answered, there is opportunity for greater care in communicating questions and in eliciting information. In addition, the interviewer has the opportunity to observe both the subject and the total situation in which response occurs. Interviews conducted by telephone fall between the questionnaire and the face-to-face interview in the extent to which the interviewer can assess the subject and the subject's situation and in the extent to which a valid questioning process may be ensured. There follow some of the general characteristics of the questionnaire and interview approaches with their respective advantages and disadvantages. A summary of this information is presented in Table 8.1.

Advantages of Questionnaires

The primary advantage of questionnaires is that they are usually *less expensive* to administer. This is because questionnaires are most often simply mailed or handed to large numbers of interviewees (called *respondents*) simultaneously. An interview, on the other hand, usually calls for questioning each individual separately.[3] With a given amount of funds, it is usually possible to cover a wider area and to obtain information from more people by means of questionnaires than by personally interviewing each respondent or interviewing each respondent by telephone.

A second advantage of the mailed questionnaire is that it avoids potential interviewer bias, which is discussed later in this chapter. The way questions are asked and even the general appearance of the interviewer may influence respondents' answers. Though it is certainly possible to minimize such biases in face-to-face surveys, only a mailed survey eliminates them.

Another advantage of questionnaires is that respondents may have greater confidence in their *anonymity* and thus feel freer to express views they fear might be disapproved of or might get them into trouble. Although an interviewer may assure the respondent that he or she will not be identified in any way, the respondent may doubt this. As in most interviewing situations the interviewer knows either the respondent's name or address or other identifying information, it is always possible that this information may be included in the completed interview. If a questionnaire is presented as anonymous and there is no apparent identifying information, the

[3]This is not true, of course, of group interviews, where as many as eight to ten people may discuss the subject matter of an investigation under the direction of an interviewer. However, such interviews are more satisfactory as a source of hypotheses or as a way of gathering information about the group; they do not ordinarily yield systematic information from every individual in the group on each point covered in the interview schedule.

TABLE 8.1 Advantages of Various Survey Methods
(+++ = relatively good; ++ = intermediate; + = relatively poor)

Advantages	Mailed Questionnaires	Mass-Administered Questionnaires	Face-to-Face Interviews	Self-administered Questionnaires in Face-to-Face Contexts	Telephone Interviews
• low cost	+++	++	+	+	++
• speed	+	+++	+	+	+++
• anonymity	+++	+++	+	++	+
• lack of pressure on respondent for immediate response	+++	++	+	++	+
• likelihood of obtaining a good sample from the population	+[1]	+	+++	+++	++[2]
• avoidance of interviewer bias	+++	++	+	++	++
• lack of dependence on motivation and ability of respondents to read questionnaires and write responses	+	++	++	++	+++
• likelihood of establishing rapport with respondent	+	++	+++	++	++
• ability to ask complex questions at length and in depth	+	++	+++	++	++
• ability to get full, detailed answers through clarification and probing	+	+	+++	+	++
• ability to use visual aids	+	+++	+++	++	+

[1]Unless a relatively high response rate can be obtained
[2]Unless no-phone and unlisted phone households are dealt with

149

respondents may feel greater confidence that their replies will not (or cannot) be identified. Studies that have used both methods have sometimes found rather marked differences between the replies to the interview and those to the questionnaire. Edwards (1957) for example, in a survey of attitudes of residents of Seattle toward a proposed state bill providing a cash bonus to war veterans, had interviewers question half of the respondents. The other half were given a sheet marked "Secret Ballot," which they checked, folded, and inserted into a box labeled "Secret Ballot Box." ((This was, of course, an unusually vivid way of emphasizing anonymity.) The interviews showed many more "don't know" replies and fewer unfavorable responses than the ballots. A referendum vote in an election heid a few weeks later provided a check; the proportions obtained from the secret ballot were much closer to those of the actual vote than the results of the direct interview.

Another characteristic of the questionnaire that is sometimes, though not always, desirable is that it may place *less pressure* on the respondent for *immediate response*. Sometimes this is necessary, as when the respondent is expected to report some information that may have to be looked up. When the subjects are given ample time for answering attitude questions, they can consider each point carefully rather than reply with the first thought that comes to mind, as may happen under the social pressure of long silences in an interview. On the other hand, one may wish the questions to be answered in a particular order to avoid putting ideas from later questions into the respondent's answers. In that case, a questionnaire may be developed that encourages — but does not guarantee — a one-at-a-time approach from the respondent. It might have few questions on each page and instructions to complete each page before turning to the next one (Galtung, 1967).

Advantages of Interviews

The foremost advantage of the face-to-face or telephone interview over the questionnaire is that the interview approach almost always *yields a better sample of the population* being studied. If questionnaires are mailed to the general population, *only 10 to 50 percent of them will ordinarily be returned* even after a number of follow-up mailings. The large proportion who do not return such questionnaires may be much different from those who do return them in ways that are central to the study. Because the nonrespondents are often more transient, less educated, and less interested in the survey topic, a very misleading picture might be garnered from a survey on any issue in which more than half of those who were mailed a questionnaire did not respond.[4]

In contrast, the <u>response rate</u> of the face-to-face or telephone interview approach among the general population is often as high as 70 to 80 percent. Most people are willing and able to cooperate in a study when all they have to do is talk. People usually enjoy talking to others who are friendly and who are interested in what they think.

As you might suspect, questionnaires are more likely to be returned if they are attractively designed, short, and clear and easy to fill out and mail back. It also

---

[4]For a more extended discussion, see Parten (1950, Chapter 11).

helps if they are personalized with regard to the cover letter, envelopes, and the questionnaire itself and if some monetary or other inducement can be offered for a reply. At least three follow-up mailings are also recommended to those who do not reply at first (Dillman, 1978). Perhaps the most important considerations affecting return rate are the nature of the people to whom the questionnaire is sent, the interest of these people in the questions, and the sponsorship of the survey. For example, a questionnaire sent to a group of obstetricians by the American Medical Association on the subject of specific obstetric patient care practices may yield a relatively high return rate.[5]

There are some steps to take to reduce the nonresponse problem after it occurs, although the steps should be planned ahead of time. For example, after follow-up mailings are done, one might select a sample of the nonrespondents and try to interview them in person or on the telephone. These methods, of course, apply to any survey in which the response rate is thought to be too low. The methods of follow-up do require, however, that the name and address of the sampled individuals are known, so that anonymity and perhaps some feelings of confidentiality are sacrificed.

It should be emphasized that Dillman (1972, 1978), Erdos (1970), and others report that reasonable response rates can indeed be obtained from mail surveys. The key seems to be the willingness and ability of the researcher to devote special attention to *all* of the preceding considerations in great detail (Dillman, 1978). For example, specific steps in personalizing the mail survey might be to sign cover letters individually and address the survey by hand rather than by computer or typed label. Guiding each such specific step must be a conception of the motives people may have for responding and not responding to the survey. Without such careful, detailed considerations and procedures, nonresponse is likely to be a crucial drawback to mail surveys.

The mass-administered questionnaire does not suffer from response rate problems. Anonymity will also be relatively high, and cost relatively low. However, mass administration by definition requires large captive or volunteer audiences that are unlikely to represent properly a population of interest — unless, of course, you are interested in generalizing your results only to the students in a particular school or the patients in a particular hospital, and so on. People who agree to come to a central spot for an interview will not necessarily be like the many who will refuse to come.

Another important advantage of the face-to-face or telephone interview over the questionnaire is the *inability* of many people to respond properly. It has been estimated that, for purposes of filling out even simple written questionnaires, at least 10 percent of the adult population of the United States is illiterate. For complex questionnaires, the percentage would undoubtedly be considerably higher. Thus, one of the major drawbacks of the usual questionnaire is that it is appropriate only for subjects with a considerable amount of education. Complicated questionnaires requiring extended written responses can be used with only a very small percentage

---

[5]Mailed questionnaires are also sometimes the only way to reach special groups not accessible to conventional interviewers, such as wealthy but secluded persons, business executives, and others who may seek refuge behind secretaries and doorpersons.

of the population. Even many college graduates have little facility for writing, and of those who do, *most lack the patience or motivation to write as fully as they might speak.* Therefore the questionnaire technique is not an appropriate method for large segments of the population. Further, for those for whom it is appropriate, the burden of writing or of maintaining interest is great enough to limit the number of questions that may be asked and the fullness of the responses. On the other hand, interviews can be used with almost all segments of the population. In fact, in contrast with the questionnaire, a frequent problem in interviewing is that of limiting the responses of the verbose individual.

Another advantage of the interview situation is its *greater capacity for correcting misunderstandings by respondents.* In a questionnaire, if the subject misinterprets a question or records his or her responses in a baffling manner, there is usually little that can be done to remedy the situation. In an interview there is the possibility of helping to clarify questions before the responses to them are recorded. This is a limited advantage, however, because in a standard survey the interviewer is usually instructed only to repeat the questions rather than to explain them. This is a good time to point out that most good professional survey interviewers are not trained social scientists. They are most often intelligent lay people with good clerical skills and notable persistence who are working on a part-time basis. They cannot be expected to reword questions on the spot in order to clarify the project director's intent. Even if the interviewers are graduate students or the project directors themselves, on-the-spot rewording is a dangerous practice. If it is done, you will then face the problem of finding out precisely what question each respondent was answering and the additional problem of how to analyze (that is, compare) the data. In most large-scale surveys, therefore, interviewers are trained to be as much like amiable, receptive, and very sensitive tape recorders as possible. Typically, the training of interviewers for a particular study will consist of some home study plus two or three days of intensive in-person grounding in interviewing principles and in the questionnaire itself.

The face-to-face interview has the advantage of *greater permissible length* over both the questionnaire and the telephone interview. Typically, the face-to-face interview will last between one and two hours, whereas mail and telephone surveys will generally be limited to no more than 30 minutes or so. These time limits are not hard-and-fast and are based more on experience and anecdote than on experimental research. For example, earlier writing in the survey field emphasized that telephone interviews should be very short (less than five minutes). Later experimental work such as that of Quinn, Gutek, and Walsh (1980) and the recent experience of others indicate success with much longer telephone interviews. A substantial length differential does exist, however, and the greater length of the face-to-face interview enables more *in-depth coverage* of subject matter. The greater length and the in-person situation also may help the interviewer to develop greater rapport with the respondent, which, in turn, should facilitate responses to *sensitive* questions—those that may be potentially embarrassing or threatening. However, here, too, the work of Quinn, Gutek, and Walsh (1980) has shown that the assumption of greater validity of face-to-face interviews compared to telephone interviews is not always justified.

The interview is more appropriate than the questionnaire for revealing information that is both *complex and emotionally laden* or for probing the sentiments that may underlie an expressed opinion. Under some circumstances, the interviewer may be very artful in getting such information.[6] However, if a verbal report is to be accepted at face value, it must be elicited in circumstances that encourage the greatest possible freedom and honesty of expression. Although, as already noted, an anonymous questionnaire may sometimes be the most effective way of producing such a permissive atmosphere, its usefulness is limited to issues on which respondents have views that can be simply expressed. Especially in the face-to-face interview, the opportunity for *probing* answers to questions exists. Probing techniques are discussed later in this chapter. The inability to explain fully in writing one's asocial or antisocial feelings and behavior, as well as the solemnity and permanent nature of a response that is put on paper in one's own handwriting or (if the questionnaire is not anonymous) under one's own name—all work against involved discussions of socially taboo or socially controversial issues in response to a questionnaire.

Finally, the face-to-face interview situation has the advantage of permitting *visual aids* or *devices* to be used. *Cards* may be shown to respondents so that they may select categories and report which category number or letter applies to them—this allows them to avoid direct answers and increases both item response rates and validity.

A combination of the face-to-face interview and the questionnaire approaches, usually called the *self-administered questionnaire*, is often successful in obtaining high response rates while allowing the respondent privacy in filling out the form himself or herself. If some portions of an interview are thought to be particularly threatening or sensitive—such as questions on drug abuse or sexual behavior—these portions may be turned over to the respondent to answer. The interviewer is available to help, if desired. However, the interviewer does not intervene unless asked to once detailed instructions and examples on how to fill out the questionnaire have been given. Feelings of privacy, confidentiality, and anonymity may be further ensured by allowing the respondent to seal up the answers in an envelope.

Advantages of Telephone Interviews

Telephone interviews typically combine the advantages and disadvantages of both mailed questionnaires and personal interviews. *Low cost and rapid completion with relatively high response rates are the major advantages of the telephone interview* (Sudman, 1967). National polling organizations, for example, usually conduct national surveys of voter sentiment within the last few days of election campaigns and give feedback to candidates about voter opinion within a few hours. This information may aid the candidate in making last-minute appeals to particular segments of the electorate and may be especially important in determining the outcome of

[6]For an interesting discussion of the use of the interview method to obtain information about a socially taboo subject, see Kinsey et al. (1948). The project directors here were the interviewers, and so they were able to memorize the interview and improvise on it when necessary. This is in contrast to the standard survey interview.

close elections (Oberdorfer, 1970). It is also possible to conduct large-scale surveys within a few hours of the occurrence of a traumatic event in order to elicit immediate reactions. Finally, the savings in cost may allow additional interviewing that would be prohibitive for in-person interviews or several waves of mailed questionnaires.

Some social scientists have prejudices against the use of telephone interviewing that are not supported by evidence or hold beliefs that may have been true in the past but are no longer accurate. The major reservation about telephone interviewing has been that *those people who have telephones are not representative of the general population.* This argument is still valid to some degree, particularly in rural areas and in the inner city. A second problem is that *an increasing proportion of telephone subscribers are maintaining unlisted numbers.* If these groups can be identified, appropriate allowances can be made for possible biases in analysis. One study of an urban area (Leuthold and Scheele, 1971) revealed, for example, that those persons with low incomes and high levels of social isolation are least likely to have telephones. The total number of nonsubscribers was estimated to be only about 10 percent of the total population. An additional 9 percent of the population was estimated to hold unlisted numbers (this number is closer to 15 or 20 percent now by most national estimates and much higher in big cities) and hence would not appear in a sample drawn from a telephone directory. Although the frequency of unlisted numbers was not related to class factors in the study, blacks, urban dwellers, and younger people were more likely to hold unlisted numbers. *Random digit dialing techniques* can be used in studies where it is essential to include those with unlisted numbers. Random combinations of numbers are dialed within working telephone exchanges, so that unlisted numbers have the same chance of being chosen as listed numbers. There are some difficulties in that telephone exchanges may contain businesses as well as residences and that random selection of digits will often result in nonworking numbers. Interviewers must often dial four to ten numbers to reach an eligible residential number (Tuchfarber and Klecka, 1975). The techniques may not be worth their costs in areas in which almost all phones are listed.

It is widely believed that telephone interviews that take more than a few minutes result in the conversations being terminated by the respondents. As pointed out in the last section, little evidence can be found to support these beliefs, and what little evidence there is challenges them. Few studies that rigorously evaluate the quality of telephone responses have been done, but the preponderance of evidence is that little difference in the quality of responses to telephone and personal interviews is usually evident.[7]

Telephone interviews, in contrast to face-to-face interviews, involve *no travel* to and from the place where the interview is conducted. Savings in travel time and

[7]Telephone interviews have been believed to be more subject to a tendency for interviewees to respond in the socially desirable direction regardless of the "true" response. This belief is strongly challenged by a study by Colombotos (1969), conducted with several samples of physicians, which showed no differences in this tendency between responses collected by telephone and by personal interviews. In fact, there is growing evidence that the telephone can be used on problems of considerable sensitivity (Hochstim, 1967). Some evidence in this direction is also provided by Quinn et al. cited earlier.

costs more than offset telephone charges. Interviewers may, moreover, find themselves in uncomfortable situations when they are required to travel to unfamiliar sections of a city. It is also generally simpler to supervise, train, and monitor the performance of telephone interviewers than of face-to-face interviewers because it is easier to observe the former in interviewing situations directly. Thus, tighter control of the quality of some aspects of the interviewing process can be maintained by using telephone interviews. Telephone interviews are obviously particularly advantageous in cases where it is necessary to interview groups of individuals who are likely to have telephones, but who are scattered over a large area.

Thus, telephone interviews would appear to be particularly useful in cases where a low budget is combined with a need to conduct interviews quickly, where the interview is relatively short and not very complex, where biases introduced by people who are nonsubscribers (or who have unlisted numbers) are assumed to be relatively unimportant, and where visual aids are not required in the interviewing process.

QUESTION CONTENT

In both questionnaires and interviews, information is obtained by asking questions. Questioning may be aimed at what people know; what they believe, expect, feel or want; or what they have done. We may also ask about reasons for any of the preceding. These major types of question content are discussed in the following pages as pertaining to *facts, attitudes, and behavior*. It should be recognized, however, that questions do not always fall neatly into one or another content type. The distinctions among types are a matter of custom and convenience rather than theoretical rigor.

Content Aimed Mainly at Ascertaining Facts

Often the simplest and seemingly most economical method of obtaining facts is to go directly to the people who are in a position to know them and to ask for the desired information. We expect all individuals to know a variety of facts about themselves and their environment. A sizable proportion of most questionnaires and interviews is directed toward obtaining such information. Questions about age, education, religion, income, nationality, marital status, and occupation are of this type. So are questions about events, circumstances, or policies known to the respondent.

Reported facts must, of course, always be evaluated in terms of credibility, and methodological research indicates that the reported facts are often in error to some degree. For example, Myers (1940) plotted a distribution of ages for United States citizens, as reported in the decennial census, and found a marked "piling up" of reported ages ending in zero (40, 50, 60) and smaller peaks at ages ending in five. As Table 8.2 implies in part, memory is fallible for nonrecurring events, for events in the distant past, for events of little interest, and for events difficult to comprehend. Memory has an ephemeral quality and depends on situational factors; memory can be corrupted in relation to events of significance to the self. These factors require

TABLE 8.2 Inaccuracy of Reports of Facts in an Interview[a]

Subject	Percent of Respondents Giving Inaccurate Reports
Contributed to United Fund	40
Registered and Voted	25
Age	17
Owns Library Card	10
Owns Driver's License	10
Owns Home	4
Owns Auto	3
Has a Telephone	2

[a]Parry and Crossley (1950) used experienced interviewers to solicit information from 900 respondents in one community. The facts reported by the respondents about themselves were later compared with records from appropriate agencies. The following degrees of inaccuracy were found.

caution in accepting recall of events at face value (see Cannell and Kahn [1968, pp. 541–549] for a review).

There are techniques for aiding the respondent's memory, many of which call for relating facts of interest to other facts significant to the respondent. Thus, marital, fertility, occupational, and hospitalization data, for example, are often collected in a chronological or history format, with consistency checks with other questions built in. Sometimes forgotten events can be prodded into consciousness by the interviewer. For example, Cannell, Fisher, and Bakker (1965), in a study of reports of past hospitalization, found an increased failure, over time, to report past hospitalizations. Respondents failed to mention about 30 percent of their hospitalizations that had occurred a year earlier. But on a second interview, after the interviewer urged the person to remember, a high proportion of these hospitalizations was remembered.

When the focus is on description or understanding of an event, a situation, or a community rather than on information about the individual respondent, it is frequently possible to check accuracy through comparison of the reports of several respondents. If respondents occupying widely different positions in the community agree on a statement, there is much better ground for accepting it as true than if only one of these respondents makes the statement (Campbell, 1955; Vidich and Shapiro, 1955). It is also sometimes possible to check reports (such as hospitalizations, for example) against statistical records. Such records, of course, may have their own biases. (See Chapter 11 on the use of available data.)

On the whole, specific facts rooted in the relatively recent past which are *nontrivial, nonsensitive,* and *nonthreatening* to respondents are reported with a high degree of accuracy. This is especially true if attention is given to issues of question wording, format, and interviewer techniques. These issues are discussed in a later section in this chapter.

Content Aimed at Ascertaining Opinions, Feelings, Beliefs, and Attitudes

Although social scientists distinguish among opinions, feelings, beliefs, and attitudes, as do we all, for the purposes of this chapter questions about them may be regarded as similar in that they are relatively *subjective*, that is, not verifiable through outside sources. For convenience, we will refer to them all as *attitude* questions except when a distinction seems necessary.

As Moser and Kalton (1972) have pointed out, there are several reasons why attitude questions are more troublesome than factual questions. For one thing, the respondent *may not even know what his attitude* is—he or she may never have confronted the issue until the interviewer asked him or her. Secondly, attitudes are necessarily *many-sided and situationally determined*. For example, one may favor abortion on medical grounds and disapprove of it on moral grounds. The same person may be against abortion in some circumstances and proabortion in others. Then, there is the problem of *attitude intensity* and, related to this, consistency. Two people may hold similar views toward activities of the Soviet Union, but one may feel more strongly about the view. It is possible also that on any given day, depending on moods and events, one's attitude toward the Soviets may be different from what it was the day before.

A primary result of these vagaries is that attitude questions are more vulnerable to changes in wording, emphasis, and sequence than are questions about facts. In fact, political polls may differ from each other by more than 20 percentage points in public endorsement for a particular candidate or policies merely because a phrase was included in one poll and not in the other. Such evidence has been noted for over 30 years.

Professionals in the survey field are, therefore, very concerned with issues of interview construction and format. Of all such issues, perhaps most debate has centered around the use of *free-answer* (that is, **open-ended**) versus **fixed-alternative** (closed) **questions** to measure attitudes. Because of its importance, this debate is discussed at some length in the following pages. Discussion on other problems of format, wording, and so on, can be found in sections in this chapter that follow. Although these problems are most acute in attitude measurement, they apply to all standardized survey situations.

In a question about capital punishment, a researcher may ask a respondent to describe how he or she feels about the topic and simply write down what is said. This is a free-answer question. Or the respondent might be provided with some fixed alternatives and asked to choose the position closest to his or hers. The major problems with free-answer questions are the *costs* and *confusion* in *coding* them. When left to their own devices, respondents will often give answers that are self-contradictory and/or incomprehensible and that will defy efforts at categorization. Again, respondents may be answering on many different grounds—moral, legal, and so on—as well as with different degrees of knowledge, favorability, and intensity. On the other hand, the fixed-alternative question, though cost-efficient, only works well if those who build the alternatives know what the true range of alternative attitudes in the population really is to begin with. This is important, for if a popular alternative is left out, respondents will not suggest it with enough frequency to allow the error to be identified. They will tend instead to choose among the alternatives given them, even if a "miscellaneous" or "other" category is included.

Often the free-answer format is reserved for questions calling for *reasons* or *explanations.* In order to get full explanatory answers, you usually must ask more than one free-answer question, however. For example, the answer to the question, "Why do you feel the way you do about abortion?" may elicit, among others, answers about educational or personal experiences, understanding of legal restrictions, moral dilemmas, or beliefs about when a human life begins. Answers should ideally be collected from everyone about each aspect. This, unfortunately, will require extra time in interviewing and in coding so that relatively few variables can be explored in such depth. A good general rule is to ask as many questions as are needed in order to understand the key variables thoroughly even if it means sacrificing some information about the others.

An average of answers across a number of items is likely to be a better sample of the respondent's true attitudes than the answer to any one question. The result should be greater reliability or consistency over time for the average than for the single answer. *Content validity* will also be greater because more items allow more coverage of different aspects of the topic. In addition, *statistical validity* may also be greater because greater test-retest reliability permits, although it does not guarantee greater validity. (See Chapter 7.) This approach of using multiple questions sometimes involves the construction of **scales,** in which many questions tapping the same attitudes are asked and a total score derived. (See Chapter 12.) Shuman and Presser (1979), in summing up the results of their recent studies on these two basic forms of questioning, state that fixed-alternative questions should ideally be constructed initially on the basis of numerous free-answer responses. Another approach to this problem is to include many fixed-alternative and a few free-answer questions on key study issues. The latter are particularly valuable when reasons, contexts, and illustrations for attitudes are sought. In fact, both of these approaches are taken in most social science surveys, which consist largely of fixed-alternative questions sprinkled with those of the free-answer variety.

Content Aimed at Present or Past Behavior

Present or past behavior is often the subject of interviews because, for one thing, the respondents are in a uniquely favorable position to observe their own behavior. Further, how a person has behaved in the past in a certain type of situation is, in the absence of contradictory evidence, an indication of what future behavior will be in similar situations.

In asking about present or past behavior, experience has demonstrated that the most valid answers are obtained by *specific* rather than general questions. For example, it is preferable, in a study of consumer behavior, to ask, "Which brand or brands of coffee do you have in the house at the moment? May I see it? Do you usually buy this brand?" than to ask, "Which brand of coffee do you usually use?" Specifying a concrete instance and then asking whether this instance is typical or atypical provide the subject with more cues for recall and, in a sense, bind the person to a reality that acts as an obstacle to distortion in response. Similarly, in the study of prejudice, questions about past behavior in specific situations are likely to elicit more accurate reports than general inquiries about previous behavior. Thus, it is preferable to ask, "For whom did you vote in the last mayoralty election? What made you vote for him or her? Did you know the religion of the candidates? Were you influenced for or against any candidate by knowledge of his or her religion? Do you usually tend to consider a candidate's religion in deciding for whom to vote?" than to ask only the general question, "Do you usually tend to consider a candidate's religion in deciding for whom to vote?"

As with knowledge questions, one must be concerned with the *length of time* over which recall of behavior is required. Appropriate time limits cannot, unfortunately, be suggested from research evidence (Robinson, 1977). Obviously, the shorter the time since the behavior, the better. Telephone surveys on which television ratings are established, for example, often ask for shows being watched "right now" rather than depending on recall.

It is also clear from consumer and media studies that different techniques such as *diaries* in which respondents are asked to log their behavior as it happens often yield somewhat different results from studies that require recall after the event. (See, for example, LoSciuto, 1971.)

Question wording about illegal or antisocial behavior may require delicacy and even euphemisms (Bradburn and Sudman, 1979). Other techniques of use may be long conversational lead-ins to questions, self-administration of key items, efforts to build extra interviewer rapport, and so on. In any case, pretests or pilot studies to establish the appropriate way to ask behavior questions are advisable for each study.

OUTLINE OF PROCEDURES IN QUESTIONNAIRE CONSTRUCTION

Early in planning their research the investigators will weigh the merits of several techniques for collecting the desired data and decide whether to use a questionnaire[8] or some other method. If they choose another method, they may still want to supplement it with a questionnaire. In deciding which part of the research job can best be handled by a questionnaire, the investigators must first discover the extent to which the desired data are already available in census volumes, in published or unpublished reports, or in collections of letters, diaries, or other sources. Then they must decide whether all or parts of the needed data can best be obtained through a formal questionnaire — or through "depth" interviews, long-continued case studies, standardized tests, refined observations, and/or experiment.

An alternative that should be considered is the use of scales or questionnaires previously developed by other researchers. If such instruments have been developed and used, information about the quality of the instruments may be available, including reliability and validity data. Even without such data, consideration of the scales

[8]The term *questionnaire* is used throughout this section to refer to standardized interview schedules as well as forms to be filled out by the respondent.

and questions developed by other researchers may help clarify one's own thinking about possible survey questions. If it is decided to use the questions again, the current research will have the advantage of comparability to the previous work.

Several useful collections of scales have been compiled, notably in the area of attitude measurement. See, for example, the work of Robinson and Shaver (1969), Shaw and Wright (1967), and Miller (1964).

Let us assume, now, that the study director has decided to use a questionnaire. The entire process of its construction can be divided into the following six steps: deciding what information should be sought, deciding what type of questionnaire should be used, writing a first draft, reexamining and revising questions, pretesting, editing the questionnaire, and specifying procedures for its use.

Deciding What Information Should Be Sought

The first step in the research procedure — formulating the precise problem to be answered — provides the starting point for developing the questionnaire. Suppose that the purpose of a study is to determine the attitudes of the public toward the placement of a nuclear reactor. Preliminary consideration of the problem may indicate the need for inquiry into beliefs and opinions about war, relations with the Soviet Union, the respondents' optimism or pessimism, their realism, fatalism, as well as about nuclear energy. The investigators must decide what aspects of the problem are to be dealt with in the particular study.

An excellent test of one's performance in this stage of questionnaire construction — and at the same time a valuable aid — is the preparation of "dummy tables" showing the relationships that are anticipated. By drawing up such tables in advance, the investigators force themselves to definite decisions about what data are required and how they will be used. They can even enter figures representing different possible findings in order to visualize the bearing each would have on alternate hypotheses and to see what new hypotheses they suggest.

The research planners may well run through the possibilities represented by the headings in a classification, stopping at each point to decide what specific material their questionnaire should seek in the light of the specific purpose of their research.

Deciding What Type of Questionnaire Should Be Used

The appropriate form of question depends on the mode of administration, the subject matter, the sample of people to be reached (educational and social level, and so on), and the kind of analysis and interpretation intended.

Each class of questionnaire content may suggest two markedly different kinds of item — those that ask *explicitly* for the information wanted and those in which the desired information is *inferred* from responses directed to other matters. For example, instead of asking the respondents directly about their own social adjustment, they may be asked whether most people are hard to get along with. Questions of "fact" are often asked not to obtain direct information about the facts, which may already be known, but as indirect measures of knowledge or interests. *Opinions* about an issue may be sought because of research interest in the issue ("direct" questions) or in order to throw light on the personality of the respondent ("indirect" questions).

The investigator must also decide whether to use *closed* (that is, fixed-alternative) or *open-ended* (that is, free-answer) questions. The relative advantages and disadvantages of the two types of question and the use for which each is most appropriate have been discussed earlier in this chapter.

The use of *follow-up questions* or *probes* is advisable at many points in the ordinary interview, especially in connection with free responses. The questionnaire should anticipate where these are required and should provide the appropriate wording. Although sometimes a single, fixed follow-up question can be specified, usually several alternatives are needed, depending upon the preceding response. For example, if the answer is too general and indefinite, the follow-up may be one of these: "In what way?" "Just how do you mean?" "Can you give me an example?" If the answer is incomplete, the questions may be, "Any other reasons?" or "Would you tell me a little more about that?" Other follow-ups ask, "What makes you think this?" or "What was there about the picture that made you feel that way?" or "Where were you working at that time?" and so on through an endless variety of questions needed to clarify or amplify the initial response. To the extent that the improvisation of the follow-ups is left to the interviewer, to be adapted to the specific responses, we depart from a standardized questionnaire or interview and border on a "partially structured" interview.

The questionnaire planners also have to decide whether to use a set of *several questions* rather than a single question on particular points to be covered. Several specific questions covering different aspects of a topic often obtain more precise and useful information than does a more general question, even if it is open-ended and accompanied by follow-ups. (This point is discussed in more detail later in this chapter.)

First Draft of the Questionnaire

Probably the best way to begin is to outline or list the topics for the questionnaire, consider carefully what is likely to be the best sequence of topics (not the *logical* sequence, but the best *psychological* sequence from the standpoint of the respondent), and then write the questions.

In addition to the questions deemed essential, the questionnaire writers sometimes find it wise to include a few extra ones aimed at checking the reliability of responses or measuring the influence of changes in wording. For example, two or more roughly equivalent or closely related questions, well separated in the questionnaire, may be asked in order to measure consistency of answers. The effect of different wording may be determined by constructing two parallel forms of questionnaire ("split-ballot technique"), to be used with equivalent samples of the population. The two forms have some of their questions in common, but certain other questions are worded in different ways in order that the effects of these differences may be measured.

At this stage of questionnaire construction, all available suggestions should be utilized. Questionnaires that have previously been drafted on the same or similar problems may prove most helpful. But the wise questionnaire writer will think the questions over and strive not only to improve them but to supplement or replace them in novel ways whenever this can be done to advantage. There are few places in social research where time-consuming, painstaking effort is more rewarding than in the preparation of questions.

Reexamination and Revision of the Questions

In the process of revision, it is invaluable to supplement one's own efforts by the critical reactions of individuals who are familiar with questionnaire methods and with the type of problem at hand. As far as possible, the experts should represent different approaches and reflect different social orientations. Also, representatives of different groups—minorities, racial groups, community groups, and women—should examine the draft to determine if there is any bias reflected in the selection or wording of questions. Every questionnaire will benefit from forthright criticism by persons with different values and a different social outlook. In addition, the questionnaire should be scrutinized for technical defects that may exist quite apart from biases and blind spots due to personal values.

Pretesting the Questionnaire

The **pretest** is a tryout of the questionnaire to see how it works and whether changes are necessary before the start of the full-scale study. The pretest provides a means of catching and solving unforeseen problems in the administration of the questionnaire, such as the phrasing and sequence of questions or its length. It may also indicate the need for additional questions or the elimination of others.

In general, the pretest should be in the form of personal interviews. In mail or telephone surveys, the interviewing pretest can be followed by a trial of the techniques actually to be used. The latter will detect any further problems peculiar to the procedure, such as lack of adequate instructions for filling out answers to questions. Ordinarily, if the preceding steps have been well performed, a few interviews suffice for the pretest. However, it is sometimes necessary to do many interviews in order to make sure that people differing in education, temperament, and opinion will understand the questions and give complete and pertinent answers. The people interviewed on the pretest should be similar in characteristics to those who will be interviewed in the final study.

Those who do the interviewing on the pretest must have a clear understanding of the purpose of the study. They must be informed of the overall aim and the specific intent of each question because they must note whether the question is understood and answered by the respondents in the manner intended. In conducting the interviews, they should be alert to every reaction and comment of the respondent and should record these verbatim. They should be instructed to try out alternative wordings of questions that are not clear.

A valuable part of the pretest interview is discussion of the questions with respondents after they have answered them. The respondent may be asked what the question meant to him or her, what difficulties were experienced in replying, what further ideas were had that were not brought out by the question, how the *respondent* would ask the question, and what his or her feelings were on questions answered, "Don't know."

It is also important to have the interviewers record their own observations, criticisms, and suggestions. What difficulties did they encounter in locating respondents and in interviewing them? What points seemed to cause embarrassment or resistance? Where did they have trouble maintaining rapport? Did the respondent become bored or impatient? On what questions did the respondent request further explanation? Was there enough space for recording answers? And so on.

If substantial changes are necessary, such as adding entirely new questions, a second pretest should be conducted. Sometimes, in fact, a series of three or four or even more revisions and pretestings is required.

Editing the Questionnaire and Specifying Procedures for Its Use

After all the preceding steps have been completed, the questionnaire should be ready for use. All that remains is a final editing by the research staff to ensure that every element passes inspection: the content, form, and sequence of questions; the spacing, arrangement, and appearance of the material; and the spelling out in detail of procedures for using the questionnaire.

The editorial job is directed primarily at making the questionnaire as clear and easy to use as possible. Directions for printing or mimeographing layout should be given precisely, with emphasis on legibility, ample space for replies, and the convenience of interviewers and respondents in following questions and writing answers.

The questionnaire itself should contain simple, clear directions telling the respondent (or interviewer) just what he or she is supposed to do—which questions are to be answered only by certain classes of respondents, which ones the interviewer is to explain, how fully and in what terms the response is to be recorded, where a list is to be shown to the respondent, and so on.

GUIDE FOR QUESTIONNAIRE CONSTRUCTION

What follows is essentially a checklist of points to consider in formulating questions.[9] The investigators may, for special reasons, decide to depart from the rules at various places. But they should move ahead cautiously, with full awareness of what they are and are not doing. The most troublesome errors in questionnaires do not arise from bad judgment after due consideration of doubtful points; they creep in unwittingly, even in "obviously simple" questions.

[9]For a more detailed and highly readable discussion, see Payne (1951).

Decisions about Question Content

Is this question necessary? Just how will it be useful?

Does the subject matter require a separate question, or can it be integrated with other questions?

Is the point already sufficiently covered by other questions?

Is the question unnecessarily detailed and specific for the purposes of the study?

EXAMPLES: Instead of asking the age of each child in the family, it is sometimes sufficient to get the number of children under age 16.

Some studies of public opinion dispense with questions regarding respondents' income, for other information serves well enough for socioeconomic classification (rental level of district, occupation, and such).

Are several questions needed on the subject matter of this question?

Should the question be subdivided?

EXAMPLES: Efforts to cut corners by combining two issues in one question must be avoided — for example, asking for a single answer about feelings toward blacks and Jews; asking views about changes in wages and hours, instead of separating the issues; about nationality of "parents," instead of father and mother separately; and so on.

Does the question adequately cover the ground intended?

EXAMPLES: If the investigator wants information about the total family income, a question about the respondent's "earnings" may be inadequate as it probably will not lead the respondent to mention "other income" or the earnings of others in the family.

A question simply asking people whether they are in favor of having more educational television programs would not reveal whether they wanted these for *themselves* or for the other person — that is, whether *they* would watch.

Is additional related material needed to interpret the answers?

EXAMPLES: Often replies to questions about specific social reforms can be understood better in the light of associated attitudes elicited by other questions — for example, questions that ascertain broad attitudes toward security and opportunity for the poor, antagonisms toward centralized authority, belief in need for social change, and so on.

A question asking for the respondent's opinions about the characteristics of a particular racial group calls for parallel questions about other groups in order to determine whether his or her opinions are specific to that group or reflect a more general view of outgroups or even of people in general.

In opinion questions, is further information needed about the intensity of the respondent's conviction or feeling?

EXAMPLES: In connection with questions on stereotypes, it may be important to find out not only whether the respondent has certain stereotypes but also what feeling tone, if any, is attached to these stereotypes. A person may think that the members of a certain group are "clannish," but may feel that this is reprehensible or admirable or may be indifferent about it. He or she may consider this trait admirable in one group and reprehensible in another.

Techniques for ascertaining intensity of opinion include "feeling thermometers," on which the respondent rates directly that he or she feels "very strongly," "fairly strongly," and so on; scales running from one extreme of intensity to the other (for example, from "Don't care whether I vote for the candidate" to "Positively going to vote for him, even if I have to get out of a sickbed"); asking about the respondent's behavior (for example, how much he or she has discussed the question or read about it, whether he or she has joined organizations, written to newspapers or congressmen).

Another procedure is to call attention to difficulties or sacrifices entailed in the respondent's position (for example, higher taxes) to see whether and how this changes his or her opinion. Similarly, one may mention that many people hold an opposite view and then ask whether he or she thinks these people may be right.

One may ask the respondent to specify what sacrifices or penalties he or she would be willing to undergo if he or she could thus guarantee a desired outcome — for example, how much money he or she is willing to pay a year to get television programs without advertising.

Is further information needed about how important the respondent considers the conditions or issue asked about?

EXAMPLES: Free-answer questions may help to determine how significant the point in question is for the respondent, how much he or she emphasizes personal consequences, what concern he or she manifests over the social effects, and so on. For example: What if there *is* another world war? What difference does it make if police or hospital employees *have* (or are kept from having) a right to strike?

The respondent can be asked to give direct ratings of the relative importance of the issue in question compared with other issues, in order to indicate which of different possible consequences he or she considers probable and whether or not a given condition "matters much" to him or her. For example, does he or she think a Republican victory in the next election will have important consequences, either good or bad; and what possible effects, as given in a checklist, does he or she consider most important?

Do respondents have the information necessary to answer the question?

Is it a matter they can report on adequately?

Does the question call for answers the respondent either cannot give at all or cannot give reliably?

Is the point within the respondent's experience?

Is it too remote or nonvivid or difficult a memory?

Is it unanalyzed or unverbalized experience?

Is it subject to serious errors of observation and/or recall?

Does the question ask for opinions on matters so unfamiliar to the respondent that the opinion does not mean what it seems to?

Can the necessary background information be given to the respondent in the course of the questionnaire or interview, or should the question not be asked at all of respondents lacking the information?

If the question attempts to supply the needed background information, does it give an adequate and unprejudiced statement?

EXAMPLES: Does the question concern childhood behavior and attitudes, incidental recent experiences of no special interest to the respondent, or unanalyzed and inarticulate experiences? If so and if the purpose is to obtain objective information rather than the respondent's subjective impression, official records, refined observations, and experiments should be used when possible. When questioning is used, the respondent should be aided in ways suggested on the following pages.

An opinion-poll question asking about who was to blame for a list of specific strikes found that from one-half to four-fifths of the respondents did not know enough about these strikes to express an opinion. In similar questions that did not directly ask whether people had the information, almost all the respondents expressed opinions regardless of their probable lack of information.

Can the desired information be supplied better by specific respondents other than the one first approached?

EXAMPLE: A mother may be able to report *what* books her child reads, but the child must be questioned to find out how he or she *feels* about reading these books.

It is important in such instances to arrange to have the appropriate persons answer each set of questions — by using separate schedules, by having interviewers see the different individuals, by specifically requesting that the individual who receives the questionnaire have his or her colleagues answer certain of the questions, and so on.

Are alternative questions required on this subject matter to adapt it to different classes of respondents?

EXAMPLES: In television research, those who watch a television program "regularly," "occasionally," or "never" have to be asked different sets of questions. The regular viewers may be queried about their attitudes toward the program; the occasional viewers may be asked, in addition, their reasons for not watching more often; the questions to nonviewers ask whether they watch other programs, whether they know of this program, and so on.

Does the question need to be more concrete, specific, and closely related to the respondent's personal experience?

Is it asked in too general a form?

Can the information be obtained more easily by referring it more closely to the respondent's own behavior?

Does it utilize natural psychological aids to recall, such as having the respondent recall experiences in temporal sequence — working back from the present or working up to the present from a specified time in the past?

EXAMPLES: It is often effective to use behavior indicators instead of, or along with, subjective expressions of feeling. For example, one can ask not only, "How well did you like the book?" but also "Have you recommended it to anyone else? Have you looked for other books by the same author?"

An interview schedule used in an inquiry into homemakers' morning radio listening, instead of asking what hours they usually listened and to what programs, first obtained a list of what they had listened to *today*, then the same for *yesterday* — and only then, as a final step, asked what programs they *usually* listened to during the morning hours.

Is the question content sufficiently general and free from spurious concreteness and specificity?

Ordinarily, the danger lies in questions that are too general; but on occasion the reverse is true, and a highly specific question is improperly used to tap general attitudes or to ascertain overall facts.

Is the subject matter such that a specific question may elicit inaccurate or misleading responses?

EXAMPLE: At times, specific and recent instances may be unrepresentative. As many activities vary seasonally, questions about what the respondent did today or last week may elicit a far less accurate report of his or her general activity than a question about usual or average behavior during previous months (for example, amount of television viewing, miles of driving, or kind of breakfast food eaten).

Do the replies express general attitudes and only seem to be as specific as they sound?

EXAMPLE: This fault occurs most often in attitude or opinion questions. Suppose an investigator concerned with opinions about racial policies in a school system asks, "Do you feel that qualified black teachers have just as good a chance as qualified white teachers to be hired in the schools in this city?" Many people answer such a question on the basis of an assumption that, in general, blacks are (or are not) treated fairly, rather than on the basis of any specific knowledge or opinion about practices within the school system. Thus, although the answers may seem to refer to the particular issue, this may be deceptive. In order to be sure, investigators must ask either a number of questions referring to different specific situations or a general question in addition to the one concerning the specific situation in which they are interested.

Is the question content biased or loaded in one direction, without accompanying questions to balance the emphasis?

Is the question unfair in any way? Would the content be accepted as fair by informed persons with opposite views on the point under inquiry?

Is it likely to obtain answers that will unduly favor one side of the issue?

Does the question introduce unwarranted assumptions about the subject matter?

EXAMPLES: Opinion-poll questions may inquire into negative and vulnerable aspects of working-class families without accompanying questions about positive features and without mentioning parallel negative aspects of middle-class life. By dwelling on what is *wrong* with the working-class life-style, thinking is directed disproportionately to its disapproved features and an unfair picture is obtained.

Many single questions likewise reflect biased selection of subject matter; for example, a question about who pays the advertising costs of consumer goods, with no mention of the possibility that advertising makes it possible to sell the merchandise at a lower price.

Question content sometimes carries a bias simply because of the *timing* of the question. If a community has just experienced a race riot, questions on ending discrimination will give biased results. The same is true of questions on labor relations or international relations following upon some favorable or unfavorable event. Seasonal influences likewise may seriously bias answers to questions, for example, asking about favorite sports or recreational activities during the height of the football season.

Will the respondents give the information that is asked for?

Is the material too private, of an embarrassing nature, or otherwise likely to lead to resistance, evasion, or deception?

What objection might a person have to answering?

Does the question "put the person on the spot" or make the person feel he or she is being quizzed?

Can one get the information in a manner that would not offend, or should it be omitted?

Do any special conditions exist at the time and place of the survey to augment suspicion or resistance?

EXAMPLES: There are obviously matters that people are reluctant to disclose; for example, family quarrels, receipt of charity, one's own limitations and difficulties, antisocial attitudes such as race and religious prejudices, "inside" information about a political or religious organization or labor union, and so on. Either such topics must be avoided in interviews and questionnaires, or forms of inquiry must be employed that will elicit the desired information without unduly disturbing the respondent.

One technique is that used to ascertain whether people read certain types of magazines. The interviewer offered to buy any old magazines that might be lying around the house. This resulted in the report of a considerably larger number of low-prestige magazines than had been found by direct inquiry.

Much of the desired information, however, is subjective and essentially personal; it can be obtained only by questioning the respondent. Here the informal, free-answer type of interview sometimes succeeds where formal questions do not.

Special types of indirect and projective interview questions are sometimes used. Instead of asking a man how much he donated in a charity drive, why he gave, and why he did not give more, such questions might be made to refer to "people you know" or "people like you." This type of question assumes that what the man says about others is likely to be a projection of what is true of himself—a sometimes useful but not altogether safe basis for interpretation. Sometimes a personal question will be answered more frankly if it follows a parallel indirect question about "most people": "And how do you yourself feel about this?"

Even if direct questions are asked, skilled interviewers encounter remarkably few refusals to reply. A great deal depends upon the interviewer's own attitude. If he or she is embarrassed or feels that the question is too personal, such doubts are readily transmitted to the respondent. If the interviewer confidently expects a reply, he or she is likely to get it.

Is the question likely to encounter emotional influences and desires that will lead to falsification of answers?

EXAMPLES: Many people answer even factual questions in a way that tends to exaggerate such matters as their income, education, and social status; reduces their actual age; ennobles their acts and motives.

One can also expect some replies to be thrown off by emotional influences that tend to exaggerate or minimize hardships. A pessimistic tendency has, for example, been noted in farmers' estimates of current crop damages. Where the content of a study is likely to suffer from such distortions, effort should be made to check or corroborate the information by different approaches to the matter within the questionnaire and by reference to outside sources when possible. Information about school and employment, for example, can be checked by seeing that dates and periods of time are consistent, by inquiring into courses of study and details of jobs, and by similar cross-checking techniques. In addition, when justifiable, efforts can be made to check with school authorities and previous employers.

If the question content gives a clue as to who is sponsoring the study or what the purpose is, respondents often feel disposed to express appropriately favorable feelings or at least, in a spirit of politeness, to withhold negative expressions. Hence a general policy of not revealing the sponsor or the specific purpose of the question is advisable.

Another especially interesting influence to be mentioned here is the inclination of respondents at times to answer "for the record." Questions about labor relations are likely to be answered by both industrial and labor leaders with one eye on the possible effects of the opinion study. This "public-relations bias" may also affect the ordinary citizen. For example, when questioned about whether religion is declining in influence or whether religious or racial hatred is increasing, many respondents hesitate to acknowledge what they consider an evil trend lest they give comfort and encouragement to the "enemy."

In the examination of prospective questions, such influences have to be considered and, as far as is feasible, guarded against. The decision may be to omit the questions or to adopt indirect or free-answer methods or some other form of inquiry.

Decisions about Question Wording

Can the question be misunderstood? Does it contain difficult or unclear phraseology?

Are the words simple enough for the least educated respondent?

Are any terms used in a specialized way, and, if so, is the meaning made clear by pictures or otherwise?

Is the sentence structure short and simple? Is there any looseness or ambiguity? What else *could* the question mean to a respondent?

Is the meaning clearly distinguished from other ideas the respondent may *think* the question asks — ideas that may seem more natural or important to him or her?

Could unintended emphasis on a word or phrase change the question's meaning?

EXAMPLES: Questions that ask for "nationality," "occupation," "marital status," and many other items of personal data often cause trouble unless spelled out in detail.

Such terms as "guaranteed wage," "detente," "TVA," and "mass media" are encountered in questionnaires and interviews even though they convey no clear meaning to large sections of the United States public.

Simple familiar words are often employed in a vague, ambiguous manner. For example, the simple question, "What kind of headache remedy do you usually use?" proved ambiguous, for to some respondents "kind" signified *brand* whereas to others it meant *tablets versus powder*. Or what does "Do you usually use eye shadow?" mean? Every day? "Usually" whenever you use *any* makeup? "Usually" for special occasions?

Long or difficult sentences are likely to be misunderstood by many respondents.

Sometimes accenting particular words changes the meaning of a question. An unintended emphasis on the word *should* in the question, "Do you think the United States should accept Russian overtures toward detente?" introduces a moral note and might well cause some respondents to answer in the negative, meaning we *should* not (although in the world of practical politics, it is the thing to do).

If any suspicion of misunderstanding remains after questions have been worded as clearly as possible, good practice calls for follow-up questions by the interviewer to determine just what the respondent meant. The interviewer is instructed to ask such additional questions as, "Just how do you mean that? . . . Would you tell me a little more about what you have in mind there? . . . Will you give me an example of what you mean?"

Does the question adequately express the alternatives with respect to the point?

EXAMPLES: The safe rule is to make each of two alternatives explicit whenever there is the slightest ambiguity about the second alternative. Even when the implication is reasonably clear, a statement of the second alternative may serve to make it more vivid than it would otherwise be and hence to place the two possible answers on a more nearly equal footing. Payne (1951) gives a striking example of the effect of failing to state alternatives explicitly. To the question, "Do you think most manufacturing companies that lay off workers during slack periods could arrange things to avoid layoffs and give steady work right through the year?" 63 percent said companies could avoid layoffs, 22 percent said they could not, and 15 percent expressed no opinion. A carefully matched sample of respondents was asked the question with an alternative explicitly stated: "Do you think most manufacturing companies that lay off workers in slack periods could avoid layoffs and provide steady work right through the year, or do you think layoffs are unavoidable?" When the question was asked this way, 35 percent said companies could avoid layoffs, 41 percent said layoffs are unavoidable, and 24 percent expressed no opinion.

Is the question misleading because of unstated assumptions or unseen implications?

Is the frame of reference clear and uniform for all respondents?

Does the question bring out the basis for the respondent's reply — the frame of reference within which he or she is answering?

What consequences of the proposed action does the respondent see?

Does the question distinguish between what the respondent wishes to have true and what he or she thinks is true?

EXAMPLES: Many questions can be answered only on the assumption that certain other things are true, or the respondent may make certain assumptions in his or her answer. Unless questions designed to probe these assumptions are also included, the replies are subject to grave misinterpretation. The following is an illustration:

> "To which of these groups do you feel you belong — the white-collar class, the working class, or some other class?" This question assumes that the person feels he or she belongs to a "class" based on occupation. One should first determine whether the person feels *any* class identification and, if so, how he or she thinks of "class."

When questions are asked of the general public, the investigator must consider the degree to which the implications of the action are seen, how far the opinions are offhand and superficial, and how far they reflect crystallized views based on public discussion. It is important to ask supplementary questions to ascertain the considerations the respondents have in mind in answering as they do. Free-answer questions may be used which ask for reasons, advantages of the course advocated, and arguments against it; or questions may ask the respondents to react to specific arguments for and against the measure; or questions of the following type may be used: "Are you in favor of (or opposed to) doing this *even if it means* so and so?"

Is the wording biased? Is it emotionally loaded or slanted toward a particular kind of answer?

Does it employ stereotypes? Does it contain prestige-carrying names? Does it employ superlative terms that push the answer one way or the other? (If such elements of bias are present, are they there intentionally — and does the research purpose justify their inclusion?)

Does the question tend to elicit replies that are more biased than those the respondents would give on the same point if they had an opportunity to answer freely and fully?

Would the wording be acceptable to persons with opposite views on the matter?

EXAMPLE: Two parallel opinion questions in 1939 asked whether the United States was likely to be involved in the war. The results show how greatly a difference in wording can affect responses when opinion is confused and undecided. One form asked, "Do you think the United States will go into the war before it is over?" The replies were: "Yes," 41 percent; "No," 33 percent; "Don't know," 26 percent. The other form asked, "Do you think the United States will succeed in staying out of the war?" The replies were: "Yes," 44 percent; "No," 30 percent; "Don't know," 26 percent.

Is the question wording likely to be objectionable to the respondent in any way?

EXAMPLES: Instead of asking the respondent directly what the amount of his or her income is, a question such as the following makes it easier to obtain the information:

> For the purpose of our survey, we need to have a rough indication of the total income of your family after taxes. Would you mind telling me in which of these classes it falls:
>
> Below $4000 a year   From $10,000–$12,500
> From $4000–$7500   From $12,500–$20,000
> From $7500–$10,000   Above $20,000 a year

The same use of lists and classifications may aid in questions about age, religion, and the like.

A change in words may make a question more palatable. Instead of "Did you graduate from high school?" the question can ask, "What grade were you in when you left school?" A good general rule is to avoid placing the respondent on the defensive; always leave the person an easy "out."

Would a more personalized or less personalized wording of the question produce better results?

EXAMPLES: The investigator must judge in each instance whether a personal or an impersonal question will produce better results for the purposes of the particular survey. For example, a question may be asked in such different forms as the following:

> Are working conditions satisfactory or not satisfactory in the plant where you work?
> Do you feel that working conditions are satisfactory or not satisfactory in the plant where you work?
> Are you personally satisfied or dissatisfied with working conditions in the plant where you work?

The most personal form of these questions probably elicits a more individual expression of feelings; the most impersonal, a judgment more tempered by what the respondent supposes other people think or what he or she thinks the objective realities may demand. On the other hand, the impersonal form may, at times, prevent embarrassment and lead to franker replies.

Can the question be better asked in a more direct or a more indirect form?

EXAMPLES: Using the "indirect" procedure, questions are asked, for example, about how radical or conservative certain magazines or people in public life are. The respondent who calls them all conservative indirectly reveals his own "radicalism" and conversely with one who rates them all as radical.

Another type of indirect (or quasi-indirect) questioning is well illustrated in magazine-audience measurement. When respondents are asked directly to identify the articles and advertisements they have seen in a magazine, serious errors arise through false identifications occasioned by confusion and tendencies to exaggerate. Instead of asking the respondents directly to *recall* whether they have seen the pages, they are asked merely to say whether each item "looks interesting." This is followed by the question: "Is this the first time you have seen it?" By first focusing attention on *interest*, more satisfactory answers are secured regarding ads previously seen.

Other examples have to do with information and views that the respondents may be reluctant to give if they are asked about them directly. War veterans who evade (and resent) direct questions about their battle experiences sometimes report these memories with genuine interest if the questioner comes at them obliquely — for example, by asking how well army equipment held up in the field, whether enlisted men were sufficiently trained before going into action, and so forth.

No general recommendations are warranted regarding the use of indirect questions. Their possibilities and limitations have to be examined in each new setting and with the research purposes clearly in mind. Both technical and moral issues are involved: whether the intended inferences can safely be drawn from indirect evidence; whether the particular type of indirection biases the response; whether the questions arouse suspicion of trickery or surreptitious prying — and whether such suspicion is justified.[10]

Decisions about Form of Response to the Question

Can the question best be asked in a form calling for check-answer (fixed-alternative or short answer of a word or two or a number), free-answer, or check-answer with follow-up answer?

EXAMPLES: For most items, fixed-alternative items are valuable because they provide a *frame of reference* and help to clarify the meaning of the question.

For example, here is a free-answer question.

What is your marital status?

Answers to this may be in terms of legal categories, marital problems, plans for the future, opinions about marriage, feelings about personal fitness for marriage, and so on. However, what was probably wanted was the following fixed-alternative question:

Are you currently:
    Married   _____
    Divorced   _____
    Widowed   _____
    Separated, or   _____
    Have you never been married?   _____

[10]For a more detailed discussion of indirect questions, see Chapter 10.

Best results are often achieved by means of a combination of free-answer and fixed-alternative methods or by compromises between them. Thus, single questions may consist of an initial check-answer part immediately followed by free-answer parts that inquire into the meaning of the check response and obtain examples, statements of the respondent's assumptions, the strength of his or her feelings on the point, and so on. For example:

Are people at the head of your company interested in their employees, or don't they care?

Interested	_____
Don't care	_____
Other answer	_____
In what ways do they show that?	

✓ *If a check answer is used, which is the best type for this question—dichotomous, multiple-choice ("cafeteria" question), or scale?*

EXAMPLES: The simple yes-no response (and similar dichotomous choices such as agree-disagree, do or do not) are appropriate for some questions dealing with points of fact and with issues that are clear-cut and on which well-crystallized views are held. Even on direct yes-no questions and simple two-way comparisons, however, it is usually found desirable to include an intermediate response of "doubtful," "undecided," "same," "no difference," "both," or the like. The inclusion of such responses is sometimes considered inadvisable because it provides too easy and attractive an escape for respondents who are disinclined to express a definite view. On the other hand, forcing replies into two extreme categories (particularly if the interviewer is not even supplied with a space for checking an intermediate answer) is likely to cause difficulty for many respondents and to yield results that are less realistic and more misleading than is true when an intermediate reply is provided for.

A graded series of response possibilities frequently gives the investigator additional or more accurate information than a dichotomous response and presents the question more adequately and acceptably to the respondent. In addition, the "graded series" approach usually does not take up significantly more space or response time. The most common multiple-choice responses utilize three, four, or five gradations, but larger numbers are sometimes appropriate. A widely used special form of multiple choice (the so-called "cafeteria" question) asks the respondent to choose from a list of assorted words or statements one or more that best represent his or her own view. The items may or may not be arranged in order from high to low, good to bad, favorable to unfavorable, to constitute a crude scale. Examples of several of these forms follow.

Suppose a person is asked by a close friend to do something that requires a personal sacrifice. In your country, how strong an obligation would a person of your age feel to help his or her friend?

_____not strong at all
_____not very strong
_____rather strong
_____very strong
_____extremely strong

Put a "1" in front of the thing that is most important to have or do in order to get ahead in the world. Put a "2" before the next most important, and so on.

_____pull   _____good luck

_____brains   _____hard work

Of course, you want ALL these things—but which will influence you most when it comes to choosing your next car? Check three items.

_____Appearance   _____Safety

_____Gas Economy   _____Ease of Control

_____Comfort   _____Smoothness

_____Pickup   _____Cost

_____Dependability   _____Speed

_____ . . . . ?

If a checklist is used, does it cover adequately all the significant alternatives without overlapping and in a defensible order? Is it of reasonable length? Is the wording of items impartial and balanced?

EXAMPLES: Poor checklists constitute one of the most common faults in questionnaire construction. The "cafeteria" type of question seems to offer special temptations to careless listing of miscellaneous alternatives.

Many checklists consist of loose and ambiguous qualitative terms—*usually, sometimes, rarely, frequently, occasionally, good, fair, poor.* The difficulty with these terms is that respondents have different standards in mind, so that two persons may report the same facts under different categories. When feasible, it is better to use concrete and objective terms for the different degrees.

Another frequent fault of checklists is that they are incomplete. Several studies have shown that replies may be seriously changed by the omission of one or more significant alternatives from the checklist. Many checklists are defective because they contain alternatives that appear equally true or that are not mutually exclusive; items that do not fit into the continuum formed by the other items (the list does not remain in one dimension); items that are loaded in wording, ambiguous or too extreme; items that contain more than one idea; items that influence responses by being overspecific; items that overrepresent or underrepresent one side of an issue. The following examples illustrate some of these faults:

Which one of these four statements comes closest to what you yourself think about commercials on television?

a. I'm in favor of advertising on television because it tells me about the things I want to buy.

b. I don't particularly mind advertising on television. It doesn't interfere too much with my enjoyment of the programs.

c. I don't like advertising on television, but I'll put up with it.

d. I think all advertising should be taken off television.

(What if the respondent is in favor of advertising on television but not "because it tells me about the things I want to buy"? He or she is almost forced by such lists to say things he or she doesn't mean.)

Why do you think the government wants to keep prices from going higher? Which one of these comes closest to your opinion?

    a. So some people won't be able to get too much while others get too little.
    b. So people won't worry about prices going higher and start to hoard.
    c. So there won't be any necessity for raising wages and salaries.
    d. So there won't be a lot of profiteering.

(Most respondents regarded the alternatives here as equally compelling and were at a loss to choose only one.)

To the question, "To what social class do you belong — middle class or upper or lower?" almost nine-tenths of the respondents answered, "Middle class." But when psychologically more realistic alternatives — middle class, lower class, working class, upper class — were offered in a different question, only 43 percent said, "Middle class"; 51 percent chose "working class."

The sequence of items in a checklist also deserves attention. The first and last items tend to be favored when the list is read to the respondent rather than shown to him or her; the last item tends especially to receive a disproportionate number of responses. It is good practice to have the interviewers rotate the order in which items are presented or to have alternate forms of the questionnaire containing different ordering of the items.

Is the form of response easy, definite, uniform, and adequate for the purpose?

EXAMPLES: Many ways of making answers easy and definite have been referred to under preceding points. Among the most important are the use of check categories instead of asking for precise estimates (as with income, age, and so on) and the obtaining of raw figures rather than averages, percentages, or other derived figures. Thus, it is better not to ask what percentage of income is spent for rent but to get the figures for income and rent separately; to ask not the average distance of recent automobile trips but the distance of each recent trip. It is also becoming standard practice to show the respondent a card with the alternative replies whenever the checklist is at all lengthy or difficult to hold in mind.

Whenever a question schedule contains a long series of blanks for check answers or numerical entries, it is desirable to have clearly indicated columns and to use guidelines or extra spaces to reduce the chances of error in locating responses.

One of the methods that make for easy tabulation is precoding. The answers are anticipated, the code is set up and included on the questionnaire, and the interviewer or respondent merely checks or circles the coded answer. For example:

	Col. No.	Yes	No
1. a. Do you have a television set in working order?	5	1	2
b. Do you usually read a daily newspaper?	6	1	2
c. Do you usually read a weekly newspaper?	7	1	2
d. Do you read any magazine regularly?	8	1	2

This method can be used for all or part of the questionnaire. Its advantage is that a further coding operation is unnecessary and the information can be machine-punched immediately.

The disadvantage of this method is that there may be a tendency to force answers into a code. Some questions are better left as free-answer questions; precoding them would mean inaccuracy and a possible sacrifice of information. For example, question 1.b. (preceding) would yield more information if it were worded "About how many minutes or hours, if any, do you spend reading the daily newspaper? It is always possible to combine code categories after the answers are examined. It is not possible to expand dichotomous answers into more code categories.

Decisions about the Place of the Question in the Sequence

Is the answer to the question likely to be influenced by the content of preceding questions?

Do earlier questions create a certain set or expectation that might influence answers to this question?

Do preceding questions aid the recall of ideas that bear on this question?

Does this question become inappropriate if certain answers were given previously?

EXAMPLES: When both general and specific questions are to be asked on a topic, it is usually advisable to have the general ones come first. Thus, if people are to be asked what improvements they desire in their working relations and also how they like their supervisor, the first question must be placed before the second; otherwise, better supervision will be disproportionately emphasized as a desired improvement simply because it has been freshly called to mind.

Earlier questions may also create a generally favorable or unfavorable mental set toward the topic considered — as when a series of questions about strike and labor troubles precedes questions about attitudes toward unions and their regulation.

A final example illustrates a simple and fairly common pitfall. The second of the following questions obviously becomes inappropriate and awkward if the respondent has given an affirmative answer to the first:

> **a.** Do you think the government is giving the public as much information as it should about our military strength as compared with Russia's?
> **b.** What aspects would you especially like to know more about?

Is the question led up to in a natural way? Is it in correct psychological order?

EXAMPLES: People are often more willing to answer objective questions about situations and behavior than about attitudes, preferences, and motives. Moreover, they may find it easier to formulate their attitudes or motives after the situation or behavior has been clearly specified. Thus it is usually best to start with simple objective questions. Once the respondent has been drawn into the interview, he or she may be more willing to answer questions about personal feelings, motives, and so on. Thus, an interview that was designed to ascertain how people felt about living in a trailer camp began by asking when the respondent had moved to this camp, where he had lived before, how he happened to come to this place. and *then* how he liked it in the camp.

Questioning "along the time line" may be helpful. The respondent can more readily recall objective facts and report reasons and attitudes if he is helped to remember them in their original sequence. For example, in a study of the development of occupational interests, rather than asking simply, "When did you first decide you wanted to be a _____?" and "Why did you choose that occupation?" one might start by asking the respondent if he or she remembers whether as a small child he or she had any ideas about what he or she wanted to do when grown up, what they were, why the occupations he or she favored at that time seemed attractive, and so on, specifying various periods in his or her life.

People often find it easier to answer if questions proceed from the more familiar to the less so, from the more important aspects to those of minor importance, from the relatively specific or immediate to the more general or remote. For example, an inquiry into points of satisfaction and dissatisfaction in work can move smoothly from such matters as the activities involved in the job to surrounding conditions, fellow workers, employment terms (hours, wages, and so on), and on to life outside the plant and to economic and social conditions.

Does the question come too early or too late from the point of view of arousing interest and receiving sufficient attention, avoiding resistance, and so on?

EXAMPLE: Some suspicion may be aroused if a home interview with workers opens abruptly with the question: "Where do you work? In what department?"

An opening question such as, "Do you think the government is giving the public as much information as it should about nuclear reactors?" is likely to arouse some resistance, because the respondent may hesitate to criticize the government to a stranger. The same question would probably be answered more readily at a later point in the interview.

It is usual to place questions asking for personal and identifying data about the respondent at the end of the question form. He or she is ordinarily more willing to tell age, education, marital status, income group, and so on, by this time — and in case he or she is not, at least the replies to the previous questions have not been interfered with by the suspicion or resentment that personal questions occasionally arouse.

THE ART OF INTERVIEWING

This section, like the preceding one, is concerned with **standardized interviews,** containing either closed or open questions. A few of the points apply also to **unstructured** and partially structured **interviews,** but for the most part such interviews require greater skill and a quite different interviewing procedure.

The quality of interviewing depends first upon proper study design. Even the most skilled interviewers will not be able to collect valid and useful data if the schedule of questions is inadequate to the survey's objectives or has been put together clumsily. On the other hand, if they are properly selected and trained, a staff of ordinary men and women using a well-designed standardized questionnaire can elicit the required information.

Within the limits of survey design, however, there is ample room for "the art of interviewing" to come into play. The interviewer's art consists in creating a situation wherein the respondent's answers will be reliable and valid. The ideal usually sought is a permissive situation in which the respondents are encouraged to voice their frank opinions without fearing that their attitudes will be revealed to others and without the expression of any surprise or value judgment by the interviewer.

The first requisite for successful interviewing, therefore, is to create a friendly atmosphere and to put the respondents at their ease. With a pleasant, confident approach and a questionnaire that starts off easily, this is usually not difficult to achieve. From then on, the interviewer's art consists in asking the questions properly and intelligibly, in obtaining a valid and meaningful response, and in recording the response accurately and completely.

Creating a Friendly Atmosphere

The interviewer's introduction should be brief, casual, and positive. The study's interest lies in the actual questions, and the interviewer should get into them as quickly as possible. Lengthy introductions or explanations only arouse the respondent's curiosity or suspicion. The best approach is: "Good morning. I'm working on a local public-opinion survey and would like to get a few of your ideas. For instance . . ."—and read the first question. Frequently the respondent will answer that question and go right ahead with the entire interview with only the most cursory inquiries about the objectives of the survey.

The interviewer's aim should be to interview everyone eligible for the sample. A small proportion of respondents will be suspicious or hostile, and a larger number may require a little encouragement or persuasion; but the good interviewer will find that hardly one person in 20 actually turns him or her down. Many people are flattered to be singled out for an interview. The interviewer should answer any legitimate questions the respondent has and should, if necessary, produce his or her credentials and explain that names are not recorded, that the interview is not a test (there are no "right" or "wrong" answers), and that in a democracy it is important to find out how people feel about important issues—and the only way to find out is to ask them.

The interviewer's manner should be friendly, courteous, conversational, and unbiased. He or she should be neither too grim nor too effusive, neither too talkative nor too timid. The idea should be to *put the respondent at ease,* so that he or she will talk freely and fully. A brief remark about the weather, the family pets, flowers, or children will often serve to break the ice. Above all, an informal, conversational interview is dependent upon a thorough mastery by the interviewer of the actual questions in the schedule. He or she should be familiar enough with them to ask them conversationally rather than read them stiffly, and should know what questions are coming next, so that there will be no awkward pauses while studying the questionnaire.

The interviewer's job is fundamentally that of a reporter, not an evangelist, a curiosity-seeker, or a debater. The interviewer should take all opinions in stride and never show surprise or disapproval of a respondent's answer. He or she should assume an interested manner toward the respondent's opinions and never divulge his or her own. If the interviewer should be asked for personal views, he or she should laugh off the request with the remark that the job at the moment is to get opinions, not to have them.

The interviewer must keep the direction of the interview in hand, discouraging irrelevant conversation and endeavoring to keep the respondent on the point. Fortunately, he or she will usually find that the rambling, talkative respondents are the very ones who least resent a firm insistence on attention to the actual business of the interview.

Asking the Questions

Unless the interview is unstructured or only partially structured, interviewers must be impressed with the importance of *asking each question exactly as it is worded.* Each question has been carefully pretested to express the precise meaning desired in as simple a manner as possible. Interviewers must understand that even a slight rewording of the question can so change the stimulus as to provoke answers in a different frame of reference or bias the response.

Any impromptu *explanation* of questions is similarly taboo. Such an explanation again may change the frame of reference or bias the response, and it is easy to see that if each interviewer were permitted to vary the questions as seemed best to him, the survey director would have no assurance at all that responses were in comparable terms. If any respondent gives evidence of failing to understand a particular question, the interviewer can only repeat it slowly and with proper emphasis, offering only such explanation as may be specifically authorized in his or her instructions and, if understanding is still lacking, note this fact on the schedule.

For similar reasons, the questions must be asked in the same *order* as they appear on the questionnaire Each question sets up a frame of reference for succeeding questions, and it is assumed that each respondent will be exposed to the same stimulus. Frequently, the answer to a later question will be influenced by facts called to mind in an earlier one; to ask the later question first, even though to the interviewer there seems sound reason for doing so, will destroy the comparability of the interviews.

The interviewer, finally, must ask *every* question, unless the directions on the questionnaire specifically direct skipping certain ones. It may sometimes seem that the respondent has already, in answering a prior question, given his or her opinion on a subsequent one, but the interviewer must nevertheless ask the later question in order to be sure, perhaps prefacing the inquiry with some such phrase as, "Now you may already have touched on this, but . . ." Similarly, even if the question seems foolish or inapplicable, the interviewer must never omit asking it or take the answer for granted. Again, he or she may preface the inquiry with some such remark as, "Now I have to ask . . ."

Obtaining the Response

It might be thought a simple matter to ask a respondent the required questions and to record his or her replies, but interviewers will soon find that obtaining a *specific, complete* response is perhaps the most difficult part of their job. People often qualify or hedge their opinions; they answer, "Don't know" in order to avoid thinking about the question; they misinterpret the meaning of the question; they launch off on an irrelevant discussion; they contradict themselves—and in all these cases, the interviewer usually has to *probe*.

Alertness to incomplete or nonspecific answers is perhaps the critical test of a good interviewer, and as no one can foresee all the possible replies that may call for probes, each interviewer must understand fully the overall objective of each question, the precise thing it is trying to measure. Both the written instructions and the oral training should emphasize the purpose of the question and should give examples of inadequate replies that were commonly encountered during the pretest. By the time he or she is actually out interviewing, the interviewer should have formed the automatic habit of asking himself or herself, after each reply that the respondent gives, "Does that completely answer the question I just asked?"

When the first reply is inadequate, a simple repetition of the question, with proper emphasis, will usually suffice to get a response in satisfactory terms. This is particularly effective when the respondent has seemingly misunderstood the question or has answered it irrelevantly or has responded to only a portion of it. If the respondent's answer is vague or too general or incomplete, an effective probe is this: "That's interesting. Could you explain that a little more?" or "Let's see, you said. . . . Just how do you mean that?"

Throughout, the interviewer must be extremely careful not to *suggest* a possible reply. People sometimes find the questions difficult, and sometimes they are not deeply interested in them. In either case, they will welcome any least hint from the interviewer that will enable them to give a creditable response. Interviewers must be thoroughly impressed with the harm that results from a "leading probe," from any remark that "puts words in their mouth." To be safe, the interviewer should always content himself or herself with mere repetition of all or part of the actual question or with such innocuous nondirective probes as are suggested in the preceding paragraph.

The "Don't know" reply is another problem for the interviewer. Sometimes that response represents a genuine lack of opinion; but at other times it may hide a host of other attitudes: fear to speak one's mind, reluctance to focus on the issue, vague opinions never yet expressed, a stalling for time while thoughts are marshaled, a lack of comprehension of the question, and so on. It is the interviewer's job to distinguish among all these types of "Don't know" response and, when appropriate, to repeat the question with suitable assurances. In one case, for example, one might say, "Perhaps I didn't make that too clear. Let me read it again"; in another, one might say, "Well, lots of people have never thought about that before, but I'd like to have your ideas on it, just the way it seems to you." Or, again, the interviewer might point out, "Well, I just want your own opinion on it. Actually, nobody really knows the answers to many of these questions."

Qualified answers to questions that have been precoded in terms of "yes-no," "approve-disapprove," or similar dichotomies are an interviewing problem that is actually in the domain of the study director. As far as possible, the most frequent qualifications of opinion should be anticipated in the actual wording of the question.

If very many people find it impossible to answer because of unspecified contingencies, the question is a poor one. Most qualifications can be foreseen as a result of the pretest, and those that are not taken care of by revisions of the wording should be mentioned in the instructions to interviewers, with directions on how to handle such answers. In some cases, special codes may be provided for the most frequent qualifications; in other cases, the interviewer may be instructed to record them as "Don't know" or "Undecided." In avoiding many qualifications inherent in the response to almost any opinion question, the interviewer may find it helpful to use phrases such as, "Well, in general, what would you say?" or "Taking everything into consideration" or "On the basis of the way things look to you now."

Reporting the Response

There are two chief means of recording opinions during the interview. If the question is precoded, the interviewer need only check a box or circle a code or otherwise indicate which code *comes closest* to the respondent's opinion. If the question has not been precoded, the interviewer is expected to record the response *verbatim.*

On precoded questionnaires, errors and omissions in recording are a frequent source of interviewer error. In the midst of trying to pin the respondent down to a specific answer, keep attention from flagging, remember which question comes next, and the many other problems that engage the interviewer's attention in the field, it is not surprising that the interviewer will sometimes neglect to indicate the respondent's reply to one of the items, overlook some particular question, check the wrong code on another, or ask some other question when it should be skipped.

The better the interviewer, the fewer the mistakes made, but even the best interviewers will occasionally be guilty. The unforgivable sin is to turn in the interview as complete when it contains such errors and omissions. The only certain way for the interviewer to avoid this is to make an automatic habit of *inspecting each interview*, immediately after its completion, before going on to another respondent, to make sure that it has been filled in accurately and completely. If any information is lacking, the interviewer can go back and ask the respondent for it; if the questionnaire contains any errors or omissions, he or she can correct them on the spot; if the interviewer's handwriting is illegible in places or if he or she has recorded verbatim replies only sketchily, he or she can correct the weakness right there. If the interviewer waits until later in the day, or until he or she returns home at night, he or she will have forgotten many of the circumstances of the interview, or perhaps the prospect of editing the whole day's work will seem so forbidding that he or she will skip the matter completely.

The importance of clerical errors and omissions can be impressed upon the interviewer during training by pointing out that the questionnaire is designed as an integral whole and that the omission or inaccurate reporting of a single answer can make the entire interview worthless. Thus, if for each question the responses of persons with different amounts of education are to be shown separately and the interviewer neglects to record the amount of schooling the respondent has had, that whole interview must be discarded in that part of the analysis.

In reporting responses to free-answer questions, interviewers should be aware of the importance of *complete, verbatim* reporting. It will often be difficult to get down everything the respondent says in reply, but aside from obvious irrelevancies and repetitions, this should be the goal. Interviewers should be given some idea of the coding process, so that they can see the dangers of summarizing, abbreviating, or paraphrasing responses. Unless the coder can view the *whole* answer, just as the respondent said it, he or she is likely to classify it improperly or lose some important distinctions that should be made.

Interviewers should be instructed to quote the respondent directly, just as if they were news reporters taking down the statement of an important official. Paraphrasing the reply, summarizing it in the interviewer's own words, or "polishing up" any slang, cursing, or bad grammar not only risks distorting the respondent's meaning and emphasis, but also loses the color of his or her reply. Frequently, the verbatim responses of indiiduals are useful in the final report as illustrations of the nuances of attitudes, and they should not be abbreviated or distorted.

Although tape recorders may be used to record responses verbatim, their presence sometimes inhibits responses. If the interviewer prefers to record responses by hand, a few simple techniques can greatly increase the interviewer's speed and the extent of success in the verbatim recording of responses. It is perfectly permissible to ask the respondent to wait until the interviewer gets down "that last thought (that's pretty interesting)," but in order not to slow up the interview, the following devices will be found helpful for speedy recording. First, an interviewer should be prepared to write as soon as a question is asked and to write while the respondent talks, not waiting until the entire response is completed. (Experienced interviewers often finish their recording of the prior response while they ask the next question and the respondent is considering his reply.) Second, the interviewer should use common abbreviations. Third, he or she should not bother to erase, but should cross out instead. Fourth, the interviewer may depart from the ideal of verbatim recording to the extent of using a telegraphic style; omission of "a," "the," and such parenthetical expressions as "well," "you know," "let's see," will ordinarily not lead to loss or distortion of meaning. But the interviewer should not speed up recording by merely jotting down key words here and there. The connecting words and phrases are easily forgotten, and the recorded answer, even if it means something to the interviewer, may prove incomprehensible to the coders.

It is generally helpful if, on precoded qestions, the interviewer reports verbatim anything the respondent says to explain or qualify the coded response; but he or she should not solicit such comments. The volunteered remarks of respondents often help the study director later in evaluating the meaning of the results and warn him or her of any commonly held qualifications or differences in intensity of opinion.

Sampling

Sampling is an essential part of the interviewer's job. No matter how precise and detailed the original sampling design, its execution will depend upon the training and competence of the interviewers who carry it out. Although the interviewers' responsibility is much greater under quota-sampling conditions, in which they themselves select the respondents to be interviewed, even under probability sampling, where they have no freedom of choice, they must be careful to avoid error and bias.[11]

If the sample is predesignated by name, for example, the interviewer should be given advice on how best to make contact with the assigned individuals and how to overcome any hostility that may be encountered. If a system of substitution is provided for cases in which the originally designated respondent cannot be interviewed, the circumstances in which substitutions are allowed should be described carefully so that the sample will not be biased by too free an exercise of this provision.

If the sample is of an area type—that is, if it involves selection of dwelling units within a given area according to some prearranged plan—interviewers must be thoroughly trained in its execution. It has been found, for example, that biasing errors may easily creep into the listing of dwelling units and into the supposedly random selection of households and of individual respondents within those households.

As pointed out in the appendix, biases are particularly likely under quota sampling, in which the interviewer selects the subjects. It is especially likely to occur when quotas are assigned in terms of economic levels, the definition of which is largely subjective. Unless some restraint is exercised upon the interviewers, they will generally tend to pass up persons who look unpleasant, uninterested, or inarticulate and to seek out individuals they think will give them "good" answers. If housing units are being selected, too many well-kept buildings may be selected. There is also the danger that unless area controls are introduced, too many interviews will be concentrated in one neighborhood, with consequent overrepresentation of particular religious, occupational, or national groups.

It is generally helpful, when a quota-type sample is used, to give interviewers informal quotas in terms of education and to keep a check on this factor as the interviews are returned. Such an additional informal control will ensure some effort on the part of interviewers using quota samples to avoid the usual tendency of including too few respondents in the lowest educational and socioeconomic groups and will permit the study director to caution any members of the staff who seem to be guilty of sampling bias of this type.

Biasing Factors Introduced by the Interviewer

Interviewer "bias"—that is, systematic differences from interviewer to interviewer or, occasionally, systematic errors on the part of many or even all interviewers—may enter not only in the selection of the sample, but also in the asking of questions and the eliciting and recording of responses. Interviewer bias is not simply a matter of prejudiced or untrained interviewers exerting influence on their respondents and deliberately or carelessly distorting the answers they receive. The dangers of bias cannot be overcome simply by hiring "impartial" interviewers. The fact that an interviewer has strong opinions on the subject under survey does not necessarily

---

[11]Different types of samples are discussed in the appendix.

mean that his or her work will be biased, nor does the fact that he or she has no strong stand necessarily make his or her work free from bias.

Much of what we call interviewer bias can more correctly be described as interviewer *differences* that are inherent in the fact that interviewers are human beings and not machines and that they do not all work identically or infallibly. The fact that respondents, too, are human beings, with differing perceptions, judgments, and personalities, simply compounds the differences that would occur even if the interviewers were engaged in evaluating physical instead of human materials. It is not to be expected, therefore, that interviewers will unfailingly bring back complete, comparable, and valid reports. Although a large number of the more obvious types of error and bias can be overcome by appropriate methods of interviewer selection and training, some are bound to remain. Fortunately, however, it is easier for the study director to become aware of the biases of interviewers and thus to discount their effects in his interpretation of the data than it is for the clinician, the experimenter, or the participant observer to detect their own bias when they themselves collect the data.

Assuming an unbiased selection of respondents, bias in the interview situation appears to come about through (1) the respondent's perception of the interviewer and (2) the interviewer's perception of the respondent. We use the term *perception* here in the broad sense, which emphasizes the manner in which the relation between interviewer and respondent is influenced and modified by their wishes, expectations, and personality structure.

There is an abundance of experimental evidence to prove that bias may result, under certain conditions, regardless of anything the interviewer may do to eliminate it. In one study, 50 percent of a sample of non-Jewish respondents told non-Jewish interviewers that they thought Jews had too much influence in the business world, whereas only 22 percent of an equivalent sample voiced that opinion to Jewish interviewers. Similar experiments have shown that blacks will frequently answer differently when interviewed by white people and that working-class respondents are less likely to talk freely to middle-class interviewers. Such effects can occur no matter how conscientiously the interviewer attempts to be "unbiased."

The magnitude of these effects naturally varies with the way in which the respondent perceives the situation. Thus, in one study, it was demonstrated that blacks spoke more frankly with white interviewers in New York than they did in Memphis, Tennessee. The interviewing situation was "objectively" the same in both cities, but respondents perceived it differently. By altering the respondent's perception of the situation (for example, by assuring that the name will not be recorded), these biasing effects can often be reduced, but they can seldom be eliminated.

The study director should keep these matters in mind when selecting the interviewers, and the staff should be warned of the dangers. It is for reasons of this type that interviewers are usually instructed, for example, to dress inconspicuously so that their clothes and appearance will not influence lower-class respondents; to interview the respondent privately so that his or her opinions will not be affected by the presence of some third person; and to adopt an informal, conversational manner in an effort to achieve the best possible rapport.

Not all interviewer effects operate through the respondent's perception of the interviewer, however. Indeed, some respondents appear to be totally immune to even the most flagrant biasing characteristics of the interviewer. Fully as important a source of bias are the interviewer's perceptions of the respondent. No matter how standardized the questionnaire may be and no matter how rigidly the interviewer may be instructed, he or she still has much opportunity to exercise freedom of choice during the actual interview, and it is often the interviewer's perception of the respondent that determines the manner in which he or she asks the question, probes, classifies equivocal responses to precoded questions, and records verbatim answers.

Interviewers do not approach each new respondent in an unstructured fashion; indeed, they often have strong expectations and stereotypes, which are more and more likely to come into play as they continue interviewing. On the basis of their past judgments or of prior answers received from other respondents, they may, for example, quite unconsciously come to associate lack of education with ethnic or religious prejudice; or they may come to anticipate a large number of "no opinion" responses from the housewives they interview. Such expectations will almost inevitably affect their performance. Thus, given the same "no opinion" response from a wealthy businessman and from a housewife, they may probe the former's reply, in the belief that an opinion *must* be lurking there somewhere, whereas they will routinely accept the latter's reply without probing and go on to the next question.

A final source of bias arises from the interviewer's perception of the *situation*. If he or she sees the results of the survey as a possible threat to personal interests or beliefs, for example, he or she is likely to introduce bias. Or if the interviewer regards the assignment as impossible, he or she is almost bound to introduce bias. Such difficulties can best be overcome by proper motivation and supervision.

Because interviewers are human beings, such biasing factors can never be overcome completely, but their effects can be reduced by standardizing the interview, so that the interviewer has as little free choice as possible. Thus, the use of a standard wording in survey questions aims to prevent the bias that would result if each interviewer worded the question in his or her own fashion. Similarly, if interviewers are given standard instructions on probing procedure, on the classification of doubtful answers, and so on, their biases will have less chance to operate.

It should be noted, however, that as the interviewer's freedom is restricted, the opportunities for effective use of his or her insight are correspondingly restricted. Conversely, the more responsibilities the interviewer is given for probing and evaluating the respondent's opinion, the more bias is likely to result. A compromise must generally be made. In a study whose results are to be analyzed statistically and quantitatively and in which large numbers of inexperienced or hastily trained interviewers are relied upon, it is wise to reduce the interviewer's freedom of choice to a minimum by standardizing, so far as possible, every aspect of the interview situation.

As bias, in the sense that different interviewers will not always bring back the same answers from equivalent respondents, can never be entirely eliminated, the study director's main responsibilities are so to select, train, and supervise the staff that any *net* effect of bias will be at a minimum and to be aware of the possibilities of bias at various points so that their effects in the analysis may be discounted.

Many critics tend to exaggerate the significance of "interview bias" — overlooking the fact that social scientists are universally dependent upon data that have been collected by means of oral or written reports and that these reports, no matter how collected, are invariably subject to essentially the same sources of error and bias as are those collected by survey interviewers. The clinician and, frequently, the experimenter depend upon oral reports of feelings, perceptions, behavior, and so on; and they, as well as the sophisticated "participant observer" in another type of investigation, are just as likely to bias their subjects' responses as are the interviewers participating in an attitude survey. The major difference is that when social scientists have to depend upon the reports of interviewers whom they select and train, they become more aware of the dangers and difficulties involved.

So far we have been discussing the standardized interview, in which questions are all predetermined. The alternative answers to the questions are generally also predetermined to a large extent, with few free-answer questions. All questions are read in precisely the same order and in the same way to all respondents to ensure comparability of responses.

Although most large, well-conducted surveys follow this pattern, there are exceptions. Some interviews are relatively less structured, with the interviewer using only a topical guide (if anything) and the answers completely free. In the following section, we discuss the less structured interview.

LESS STRUCTURED INTERVIEWS

For some research problems, a less structured approach than that provided by a standardized interview is appropriate. Largely as a result of the influence of clinical interviewing and anthropological fieldwork, a varied assortment of interviews has been developed in which neither the exact questions the interviewer asks nor the responses the subject is permitted to make are predetermined. Such interviews take various forms and go under various names — the "focused" interview, the "clinical" interview, the "nondirective" interview, and so on. They are commonly used for a more intensive study of perceptions, attitudes, and motivations than a standardized interview, whether with closed or open questions, permits. This type of interview is thus useful when investigators are scouting a new area of research or when they want to find out what the basic issues are, how people conceptualize the topic, what terminology is used by respondents, and what is their level of understanding.

The flexibility of the unstructured interview, if properly used, helps to bring out the affective and value-laden aspects of respondents' responses and to determine the personal significance of their attitudes. Not only does it permit the subject's definition of the interviewing situation to receive full and detailed expression; it should also elicit the personal and social context of beliefs and feelings. This type of interview achieves its purpose to the extent that the subject's responses are spontaneous rather than forced, are highly specific and concrete rather than diffuse and general, and are self-revealing and personal rather than superficial.

The freedom that the interviewer is permitted is, at once, both the major advantage and the major disadvantage of interviews of this type. As a *measurement device*, such an interview procedure is inadequate, for its flexibility results in lack of comparability of one interview with another. Moreover, analysis is more difficult and time-consuming than that of standardized interviews. There can be little doubt of the usefulness, in the hands of a skilled investigator, of such interviews as a source of hypotheses that can later be submitted to a systematic test by more quantitative methods. Partially structured interviews are also used, on occasion, in studies that test hypotheses. However, the lack of comparability from interview to interview and the complexity of analysis usually make them less efficient for this purpose than standardized interviews.

Let us briefly discuss several of the major types of partially structured and unstructured interviews.

Focused interview.   In the focused interview (as described by Merton, Fiske, and Kendall [1956]) the main function of the interviewer is to focus attention upon a given experience and its effects. Interviewers know in advance what topics or what aspects of a question they wish to cover. This list of topics or aspects is derived from a formulation of the research problem, from an analysis of the situation or experience in which the respondent has participated, and from hypotheses based on psychological or sociological theory. This list constitutes a framework of topics to be covered, but the manner in which questions are asked and their timing are left largely to the interviewer's discretion. Interviewers have freedom to explore reasons and motives, to probe further in directions that were unanticipated. Although the respondent is free to express completely his or her own line of thought, the direction of the interview is clearly in the hands of the interviewer.

Merton, Fiske, and Kendall (1956) have described this type of interview.

> First of all, the persons interviewed are known to have been involved in a *particular situation:* they have seen a film, heard a radio program, read a pamphlet, article or book, taken part in a psychological experiment or in an uncontrolled, but observed, social situation (for example, a political rally, a ritual or a riot). Secondly, the hypothetically significant elements, patterns, processes and total structure of this situation have been provisionally analyzed by the social scientist. Through this *content or situational analysis,* he has arrived at a set of hypotheses concerning the consequences of determinate aspects of the situation for those involved in it. On the basis of this analysis, he takes the third step of developing an *interview guide,* setting forth the major areas of inquiry and the hypotheses which provide criteria of relevance for the data to be obtained in the interview. Fourth and finally, the interview is focused on the subjective experiences of persons exposed to the pre-analyzed situation in an effort to ascertain *their definitions of the situation.* The array of reported responses to the situation helps test hypotheses and, to the extent that it includes unanticipated responses, gives rise to fresh hypotheses for more systematic and rigorous investigation.

The focused interview has been used effectively in the development of hypotheses about which aspects of a specific experience (a television program, a moving picture, a lecture, and so on) lead to changes in attitude on the part of those exposed to it. The interviewer, being equipped in advance with a content analysis of the stimulus experience, can usually distinguish the objective facts of the case from the subjective definitions of the situation. Thus, the interviewer is alerted to the possibility of **"selective perception"** and prepared to explore its implications. Suppose, for example, that one is concerned with reactions to a series of newspaper pictures portraying housing conditions in a slum neighborhood, intended for use in connection with a campaign for more stringent housing laws or for slum clearance and urban redevelopment. The pictures show broken stairs, wallpaper peeling off, holes in walls through which rats are reported to enter — in general, conditions that may reasonably be attributed to inadequate maintenance on the part of the landlord rather than slovenliness on the part of the tenants. A respondent, in discussing the pictures, may say, "they show how these low-class people do not take care of their places; there is no use trying to give them decent housing, they just knock it to pieces anyway." The interviewer, knowing that the content of the pictures is not intended to give this impression, can follow up the respondent's interpretation, trying to discover whether there are unconsidered aspects of the pictures that form a basis for this impression or whether it stems from the subject's stereotyped views.

The definition of a focused interview may be broadened to include any interview in which interviewers know in advance what specific aspects of an experience they wish to have the respondent cover in their discussion, whether or not the investigator has observed and analyzed the specific situation in which the respondent participated. For example, in a study of the functioning of a program of part-time work for high school students, we might prepare a set of questions to be covered even though we are not familiar with the specific job setting of each of the students. We might include questions such as the following: "Does the student feel that he or she was given an adequate picture of the job before starting it? Does he or she feel that the job is at a level appropriate to his or her skills?"

Obviously, the more detailed the investigator's knowledge of the situation in which the person being interviewed has participated and the more specific the investigator's hypotheses, the more precisely can the investigator outline in advance the questions to be covered in the interview.

Clinical interview.   Somewhat similar to the focused interview is the clinical interview, the primary difference being that the clinical interview is concerned with broad underlying feelings or motivations or with the course of the individual's life experiences rather than with the effects of a specific experience. In this type of interview, too, the interviewer knows what aspects of feeling or experience he or she wants the respondent to talk about, but again the method of eliciting the information is left to the interviewer's discretion. The "personal history" interview, used in social casework, prison administration, psychiatric clinics, and in social research using individual life histories, is perhaps the most common type of clinical interview. The specific aspects of the individual's life history that the interview is to cover are determined, as in all data-collection instruments, by the purpose for which the information is gathered.

For example, Lee (1957) was interested in the possibility that adolescents who become heroin addicts may be predisposed to addiction by family experiences that lead to certain personal characteristics. On the basis of earlier work with juvenile addicts, Lee and colleagues conducting related studies hypothesized that among boys living in the same neighborhood and thus exposed to roughly the same opportunities for using heroin, addicts are likely to differ from nonaddicts in the following ways: they have relatively weak ego functioning, defective superego functioning, inadequate masculine identification, lack of realistic middle-class orientation, and distrust of major social institutions. Next, the investigators asked themselves what types of family environment might be expected to stimulate or enhance such characteristics. On the basis of theoretical considerations, largely drawn from psychoanalytic thinking, they constructed a list of circumstances or events of family life that might be expected to contribute to each of the five characteristics. For example, it was considered that factors such as the following might be conducive to weak ego functioning: inappropriate handling of childhood illnesses, discordant relationship between parents, the mother figure either passionate or hostile toward the boy, either parent's having unrealistically high or low aspirations for the boy, and so on.

It seemed clear that relatively unstructured interviews would be a more appropriate method of getting the needed information than would a standardized series of questions. Accordingly, the interviewers visited the parents of the boys included in the study — a sample of addicts and a control group of nonaddicts — and encouraged them to talk freely about their sons. The interviewers had no set questions to ask. They were instructed to cover the following major topics: the physical characteristics of the neighborhood and the house, the composition of the family and the household, the health history of the family, the present and early adolescent life situation of the subject, childhood training and socialization, relationships within the family, and relationships between the family and the "outside world." The interview guide indicated a number of subtopics to be covered under each of these major ones; for example, under "childhood training and socialization," the interviewer was to get information about early development, discipline and patterns of handling by parents, early socialization experiences, and early school experiences. Under each of these subtopics, the interview guide listed more specific points to be covered.

Nondirective interview.   In the nondirective interview, the initiative is even more completely in the hands of the respondent. The term *nondirective* originated from a type of psychotherapy in which patients are encouraged to express their feelings without directive suggestions or questions from the therapist. In a more limited sense, nondirection is implicit in most interviewing; that is, although the interviewer is expected to ask questions about a given topic, he or she is instructed not to bias or direct the respondent to one rather than another response. In nondirective interviewing, however, the interviewer's function is simply to encourage the respondent to talk about a given topic with a minimum of direct questioning or guidance. The interviewer encourages the respondent to talk fully and freely by being alert to the feelings expressed in the statements of the respondent and by showing warm, but noncommittal, recognition of the subject's feelings. Perhaps the most typical remarks made by the interviewer in a nondirective interview are these: "You feel that . . ." or "Tell me more" or "Why?" or "Isn't that interesting?" or, simply, "Uh huh."

The nondirective interviewer's function is primarily to serve as a catalyst for a comprehensive expression of the subject's feelings and beliefs and of the frame of reference within which the subject's feelings and beliefs take on personal significance. To achieve this result, the interviewer must create a completely permissive atmosphere, in which subjects are free to express themselves without fear of disapproval, admonition, or dispute, and without advice from the interviewer.

THE SOCIOMETRIC METHOD

Sociometry is concerned with the social interactions among any group of people. The data collection is geared to obtaining information about the interaction or lack of interaction among the members of any group (or among subgroups, or among groups, or among subgroups and individual members). The interaction that is investigated may be behavioral, or it may only be desired or anticipated or fantasized. The content or type of interaction studied may be any one of a variety of social behaviors—sitting next to, eating with, buying from, lending to, visiting, playing with, having as a friend, talking to, living next to, or others.

Sociometric studies most commonly use questionnaires, although observational data or other kinds of records may provide the grist for a sociometric analysis. Essentially, sociometry is not so much a data-collection procedure as it is a focus on a certain type of subject matter and a related method of analysis.

When interest is in actual behavior, one may observe the participants in an action, the nature of the action, and the relationship of the participants to one another; both the *initiation* and the *reception* of social behavior are of interest. When interest is in desired or fantasized interaction or in feelings about interaction with specified individuals, verbal reports are called for. The sociometric questionnaire or interview, as most commonly used, involves simply asking each member of a group to indicate which other members he or she would like to have as a companion in some activity (for example, "eat lunch with") and which ones he or she would not like to have as a companion. Sometimes individuals are allowed to name as many members as they wish; more frequently they are limited to naming a specific number. It is assumed that preferences are more likely to be stated honestly when the subject believes that they will really determine subsequent social arrangements; that is, that he or she will be assigned to sit next to (work with, and so on) the individuals he or she has named. Therefore, when it is feasible, sociometric questionnaires are usually given with a statement that the investigator will arrange circumstances to permit the fulfillment of the individual's preferences if possible.

Sociometric questionnaires are easy to administer and are adaptable to many different types of setting. Studies of the reliability of sociometric data, on the basis of repeated tests, indicate that although there may be considerable variation in specific choices, patterns of group interaction and various scores or indexes derived from the data are quite stable. Despite the ease of administration, however, the analysis of sociometric data is frequently more complex than one anticipates (Proctor and Loomis, 1951).

Sociometric data can provide information about an individual's position in the group, the social subgroupings within the group, the relationships among the subgroups, the group's cohesiveness, and other matters. Data of this type have been used in studies of leadership, of relations among ethnic groups, of the effect of experimental treatments on group structure, of the effect of variations in group structure on the behavior of group members, and of characteristics of individuals who are frequently chosen and those who are seldom chosen.

In a study of friendship choices among members of the Wisconsin state legislature, for example, Patterson (1959) found that legislative leaders tended to be selected as friends by assembly members more frequently than did nonleaders. Patterson interviewed (or contacted by mailed questionnaire) 87 percent of the members of the assembly in a study of informal organization in the legislature. Mailed questionnaires were used as a supplement to personal interviews when legislators could not be reached in person. Each member was asked to nominate his or her closest personal friends in the assembly. Patterson found that the structure of friendships in the Wisconsin assembly tended to parallel voting patterns in the assembly. Expressions of friendship that were directed toward leadership in the assembly were concluded to be helpful in mitigating political conflicts.

One of the first studies of leadership that made use of sociometric techniques was that of Jennings (1943). Girls in a state training school were asked to indicate which girls in the school they would want to live with and which ones they would want to work with; for each of these activities, they were asked to list also which girls they would *not* want as companions. A "choice score" was computed for each girl on the basis of the selections and rejections she received; in terms of these scores, each girl could be described as "over-chosen," "average-chosen," or "under-chosen." It was found that choice score was closely related to leadership in the community; of the 20 members of a Community Council selected a few months before the sociometric measures were taken, 18 were "over-chosen," and the other two were just below the "over-chosen" point. Study of the reasons given for the sociometric choices and rejections led to the conclusion that leadership is not explainable by any particular personality characteristic or constellation of traits; it is determined on the basis of the interpersonal contribution an individual makes in a specific group.

Festinger, Schachter, and Back (1950), in a study of the effect of the location of dwellings on friendship formation, used reports of actual social behavior rather than statements of preference. Studying a relatively self-contained community of married war veterans, they asked each of the wives, "What three people in Westgate or Westgate West do you see most of socially?" (Westgate consisted of 100 single-family houses arranged in nine courts; Westgate West consisted of 17 two-story buildings with five apartments on each floor.) They found that 65 percent of the people named by Westgate West residents lived in the same building as the chooser, 44 percent of them on the same floor. Moreover, people living in the immediately adjacent apartment were named more often than those living two doors away, who in turn were named more often than those living three doors away, and so on. A similar pattern was found in the Westgate community. Thus it was clearly demonstrated that in this community, consisting of new residents homogeneous in age, interests, and socioeconomic status and relatively isolated from the larger community, ecological factors were an important determinant of friendships.

Among the earliest applications of sociometric techniques to the study of relations between racial or ethnic groups were the studies of Criswell (1937). She asked children in mixed black-white classes from kindergarten through the sixth grade in a public school to choose two classmates beside whom they would like to sit. She found that, in this school and within this age range, cleavage between the sexes was far more marked than cleavage between blacks and whites. The white children did not begin to form a "racial" group until the fifth grade—a finding previously reported by Moreno (1934).

Although such studies are extremely useful in revealing interrelationships among members of a given group, one must be cautious about interpreting cleavages as evidence of prejudice. Preference for members of one's racial or ethnic group may simply indicate greater familiarity. For example, the white students in a racially mixed school class may live in the same neighborhood and know one another well, but they may have little acquaintance with the black students, who live in a different neighborhood. If this is true, a nonrandom choice (more white students choosing other white students than would be expected by chance) does not necessarily indicate an avoidance of the black students. This is not to deny that prejudice may be involved somewhere, historically, in the chain of causation—as in the creation of the segregated neighborhoods. But this is different from asserting that the nonrandom choice patterns of the children are necessarily indications of prejudice among the children.

VISUAL AIDS IN INTERVIEWING

Occasionally, visual aids—photographs, line drawings, dolls, cards with information on them, or other materials—are introduced into the interviewing situation. We shall discuss here the use of such techniques in the course of direct interviewing; that is, in situations where the visual material is used simply to substitute for a verbal statement or to make clear what is being asked about and respondents are asked directly for their reactions to it. Such use has been rather limited; more frequently visual materials are used in indirect or projective questioning. This latter use will be discussed in Chapter 10. A second use that is finding increasing acceptance is in measuring attitudes by card sorting.

Perhaps the most common use of visual materials has been in studies of racial awareness and racial attitudes of young children. The device was first used in this way by E. L. Horowitz (1936). He presented children with pictures of groups and of individuals and asked questions similar to those used in many of the sociometric procedures. In one of his tests he used a set of paired photographs depicting identical activities and settings. One photograph in each pair showed five white children participating, whereas the matched photograph showed the same group with a black boy substituted for one of the whites. The subjects were shown each picture and were asked to indicate whether they would care to join in the activity with the children depicted in the picture. From their responses (yes, no, undecided), it was possible to compute a "willingness to join in" score for the series of all-white pictures and for the series of racially mixed pictures; the difference between the scores was taken as a measure of bias.

A number of other investigators have used the Horowitz pictures. In one study (Mussen, 1950) an attempt was made to estimate their validity by comparing scores on the **"ranks"** and **"show me" tests** with actual sociometric choices of other boys in the same cabin in an interracial camp. Scores on the tests correlated significantly with the proportion of choices of white and black boys as cabin-mates, and changes in test scores from beginning to end of the camp period were correlated with changes in proportion of whites and blacks in the sociometric choices.

Picture tests have been used by Helgerson (1943), by Horowitz and Horowitz (1938), and others to discover whether race or other characteristics, such as sex, age, socioeconomic status, and facial expression are more important in determining children's preferences. The technique consisted of pairing pictures in which several variables were contrasted. In a study contrasting the effects of sex and race on preference, for example, the individual would be presented with the following pairs of pictures: a black boy and a white girl, a white girl and a white boy, a black girl and a white boy, a black boy and a black girl. With respect to each pair of pictures, the child would be asked, "Which one would you rather play with?"

Picture tests have also been employed by R. E. Horowitz (1939) and by Clark and Clark (1950) to study young children's awareness of their own race. The technique consisted mainly in showing the children a series of pictures (varying in race, sex, age, and so on) and asking the child, "Which one is you?" or "Which one is most like you?" or "Is this you?"

White and brown dolls have been used in a similar fashion by Clark and Clark (1950) and by Goodman (1952). In both of these studies, the dolls were used not only in connection with questions directed toward children's awareness of their own racial identification but also toward their attitudes: "Which doll do you like best?" "Which doll is prettier?" and so on.

Clark and Clark (1950) used an interesting variation of a pictorial technique to get at children's awareness of their own racial identification and fheir feelings about it. They presented black children with a box of crayons, including a range of shades of brown as well as the colors usually included in children's crayon sets, and two line drawings. Each child was asked first to color one figure "the color that you are," then to make the other one "the color that you like little girls (boys) to be."

The use of pictorial techniques has not been limited, however, to studies of children or of intergroup attitudes. Murphy and Likert (1938) made use of both photographs and motion pictures in a study of the attitudes of college students. The photographs, borrowed from news services, all showed conflict situations—strikes, war, and ghetto riots. In connection with each picture, the subjects were asked to answer such questions as these: "Describe briefly in outline form your reaction to this photograph. . . . In this situation, with whom do you sympathize? . . . What do you like or dislike in this photograph? Why?" After seeing each film, the students were asked to write briefly what they thought about it and then to express their agreement or disagreement with a number of statements related to it.

Visual aids are sometimes helpful in inducing people to discuss matters about which they may feel awkward or embarrassed when questioned directly. Thus, Whyte (1957) reported that in a study of the meaning of work, he had difficulty in getting respondents (skilled glass workers) to talk about certain aspects of their work. They talked freely about working conditions, the union, fellow workers, foremen, and higher management people. But when he tried to learn about their reactions to mental and physical processes involved in the work itself — for example, aesthetic satisfactions, feelings of creativity — they became embarrassed and inarticulate. Therefore he made line drawings of a number of different products on which the men had worked, and asked each respondent to arrange the cards in the order of his preference for the different jobs. Then the respondent was asked to explain why he had ranked the cards as he did. The resulting comments revealed much more about feelings toward the work process itself than had been elicited in the earlier, purely verbal interviews.

Collier (1957) carried out a small-scale experiment to discover the relative effectiveness of a purely verbal interview and one using photographs. In a study of the migration and acculturation of French-Acadians to an English industrial town in one of the Canadian maritime provinces, he was especially interested in the areas of work, home, and community relationships. Two respondents were each interviewed twice by purely verbal techniques in partially structured interviews, a third time with the addition of photographs. In interviews with two other respondents, photographs were used throughout. The photographs were of industrial plants in the town in which the respondents worked, houses and street scenes in the communities in which they lived, and activities in and around the home of the particular respondent; these latter pictures were taken with the cooperation of each respondent and his family. Collier found much greater interest in the interviews with the photographs, much more specific information given in the interview, greater ease of keeping the interview on the topics in which the investigator was interested, and greater ease of judging the extent of a respondent's information about certain matters.

Whether or not visual techniques are likely to be an effective aid in interviewing depends on the circumstances and the research purpose of a given study. Pictorial methods are particularly useful in the study of attitudes of children or of those with limited literacy. Verbal comprehension is needed only to the extent of understanding the general test instructions; as these can frequently be given orally, reading ability is not required. The usefulness of pictorial methods, however, is not restricted to respondents with limited reading ability. Pictures are of value in depicting many types of situations that are difficult to describe; thus, they permit the uncovering of reactions that are difficult to obtain by other methods. Another advantage is that a pictorial test, because it usually has more inherent interest than a written questionnaire, is likely to meet with less resistance.

Against these assets must be counterposed certain liabilities. A picture presents a concrete situation; if we are interested in investigating general attitudes, we may find that responses are influenced by specific details of the pictures we present. Thus, Murphy and Likert (1938), in the study previously described, found that responses to the pictures dealing with unions and strikes seemed to depend on the respondent's interpretation of which side had started the violence shown in a given picture. A related limitation is the difficulty of using pictures to study attitudes toward groups that have no distinguishing visual characteristics (for example, Catholics, socialists, psychologists). Though it is possible to use symbols or names to identify members of different religions, nationalities, or other groupings, the symbols may not have a clear-cut meaning for the respondents; or the respondents may react to the symbols rather than the groups they represent. There is a further difficulty in studies whose design calls for comparison of responses to pictures or photographs that supposedly differ only in the racial (or other) identification of the individuals portrayed. A score based on deviations from random choice assumes that the pictures, for example, of Oriental and white children are of equal attractiveness apart from their racial characteristics. To be sure that this condition has been met is no easy matter.

Card sorting is a technique for measuring attitudes, beliefs, reported behaviors, and values that requires visual materials. Cataldo, Johnson, Kellstedt, and Milbrath (1970) reported one specific use of card sorting in measuring various types of participation and attitudes about governmental services. They presented each respondent with a small flat cardboard "sortboard" on which four boxes labeled "things you do regularly," "things you do fairly often," "things you seldom do," "things you never do" were placed. Respondents were then instructed to place a series of cards with a different activity listed on each card into the specific box that corresponded to their *own behavior* most accurately. These items included such statements as "vote in elections," "engage in political discussions," "join in public street demonstrations."

Once the initial sort had been completed and recorded, respondents were then instructed to sort the same cards once again. This time, however, respondents were instructed to sort the cards according to what they felt had a *responsibility* to do. Accordingly, respondents were instructed to sort the cards into piles: (1) things that you feel are essential to do, (2) things that you feel you have an important responsibility to do, (3) things you feel some responsibility to do, and (4) things you feel you have no responsibility to do. Thus, the two sorts provided information about the respondents' reports of their own behavior as well as reports of their sense of responsibility for different activities.

The advantages of card sorting of this type are many. Cards can be sorted with speed and ease (Cataldo et al. reported conservative estimates of 3.6 minutes required for sorts of 30 cards), and standardized items and responses are derived from the operation. Very simple items can be used so that sorting is not highly demanding and fatiguing for respondents. This fact also makes sorts easy to administer to respondents in the field. Finally, the specific sorts used in the Cataldo et al. study were found to meet reasonable tests of reliability and validity and to be generally free of the more systematic response errors that are frequently found in the measurement of attitudes. Strong tendencies to agree or disagree consistently or to place items at a single location on the "sortboard" were not discovered.

Card sorting does have disadvantages. The most important disadvantage is that an interviewer must be present to instruct respondents on how to complete the sorts as well as to monitor the respondent's behavior while the sort is being conducted. Clerical errors in the field are also somewhat more likely than with ordinary fixed-alternative questions, for a large number of cards are used in most sorts. Card sorts do require literate respondents who have normal eyesight. Finally, single sorts of more than 60 or 90 items are not recommended because fatigue and irritability can be induced by overutilization of this technique just as with any other technique. It is, however, fully feasible to perform a number of single sorts in an interview.

SUMMARY

From this survey of questionnaire and interview procedures, it is apparent that investigators interested in individuals' self-reports have a choice of many different ways of eliciting them. In making such decisions as whether to use a questionnaire or an interview, whether to use a standardized or a less structured form, and whether to supplement the verbal material by visual aids, investigators need to consider the advantages and disadvantages of each approach in the light of the purposes of their study. Although the approaches have been discussed independently, combinations of methods are certainly appropriate in given situations. The structured standardized interview has been emphasized in this chapter because of its utility when a large number of variables need to be studied in a large group of people.

If it is determined that the interview or questionnaire approach is indeed most appropriate for the study in question—that is, if verbal reports are thought to be theoretically relevant and feasible for your purposes—there are some fundamental methodological issues that must then be addressed.

First, there is a need for *representative samples* if generalizations are to be made beyond the group interviewed. *Response rates* must be high, or the representativeness will be destroyed because people who do not participate are likely to be different from those who do.

Second, there is a need for *multiple indicators*, or asking more than one question on key study variables. No one item is likely to be reliable enough or multifaceted enough to stand alone, especially if one is dealing with nonfactual questions.

Implied is that surveyors like all other researchers should test the *reliability* of at least their key measures, when possible, through reasking the same questions, through comparing different interviewers' results, or through other means. *Validity* (except for content or nonstatistical measures of it) is a more difficult problem because the "true" answers or criteria are often not available for checking purposes. Such criteria should be sought and used, when possible.

Related to the above issues is the need for more careful attention to the art and science of *interview and questionnaire construction*. There is expertise and experience to be utilized, some general guidelines to be followed, exhaustive pretesting to be done, and usually several revisions to be gone through before the interview schedules are finalized. It must be realized by the researcher that once the survey questions are finalized, the dependent variables are no longer the abstractions or constructs represented by summary phrases such as "attitudes toward democracy." Rather, the dependent variables are precisely those questions that have been formulated to measure the abstractions—and nothing more.

Scaling

In measurement it is frequently necessary to make distinctions of *degree* rather than of *quality*. We may, for example, wish to know whether Mr. Green feels more intensely about using school busing to attain racial balance than does Mr. Blue. Or we may wish to know whether Mississippi spends more than Ohio per capita on public higher education after the relative wealth of the two states has been taken into account.

Making these distinctions of degree may be thought of as a function of analysis rather than of data collection; that is, it is a procedure done *after* the data are obtained. However, the desire to be able to make such distinctions influences the *form* in which the data are collected. At the very least, it means that the questions asked must be the kind to give information on which judgments of degree can be based. Frequently, the distinctions of degree are introduced into the measuring instruments themselves.

In each of the preceding instances, we are comparing characteristics of two pieces of data along a common scale. These scales serve as measuring devices — whether they concern attitudes, indicators of state wealth and expenditures, or other characteristics — that allow comparisons to be made between cases, whether observations occur at the same time or observations occur at different times.

SCALES VERSUS DIMENSIONS

It is necessary to distinguish clearly between scales and dimensions as both terms are used with considerable frequency in social science research. In speaking of **scales,** we refer to the techniques that are employed in combining one or more measurements in order to form a single score that is assigned to each individual. By **dimension,** we infer from the data of scales that an underlying characteristic is present that describes cases at the conceptual level. We may conceptually define, for instance, liberalism-conservatism; we might then generate some questionnaire items that we believe would measure liberalism-conservatism. If our items formed a satisfactory scale (according to criteria that will be discussed later in this chapter), then we would infer the presence of a broader theoretical dimension, liberalism-conservatism, for that particular sample of responses. Earlier social science research sought to create scales that tapped single dimensions; more recently there has emerged a realization of the multidimensional nature of most scales.

Traditionally individuals have been placed on scales for several reasons. In some instances, there was a goal to reduce the complexity of the data, to calculate a single score that represented several variables, so that analysis could be simplified. In other instances, investigators may have wished to test a hypothesis that several variables actually measured a single, underlying concept so that they might be said to go together on the same "dimension" of a concept. Finally, the goal may have been to reduce error in measurements and thereby to increase the reliability of the final measures that were used in analysis. Scaling techniques are used in many instances to accomplish all three of these goals. Let us elaborate what is meant by each of the tasks.

Assume that there are several variables, all of which are purported to relate to the individual's sense of power or weakness about his or her relations to government and the formation of public policy. We call these items measures of a "sense of political efficacy" (Campbell, et al., 1954; Campbell, et al., 1960). It is a bit cumbersome to test hypotheses about political efficacy by relating each questionnaire item, taken individually, to other variables that are theoretically supposed to relate to political efficacy. Scaling allows us to simplify the analysis by combining several variables into a single value.

To take another instance, say that we are considering a set of 27 congressional roll-call votes that occurred during the last U.S. Congress and that all of them are related to issues of social welfare. If we want to determine which representatives generally vote in a liberal way and which representatives generally vote in a conservative way on issues concerning social welfare, then we have quite a task. We must scrutinize each congressional representative (our units of analysis) on 27 different roll-call votes (our variables). If all of the representatives could be placed on a single scale with respect to the way they voted on the 27 roll calls, that would allow us meaningfully to describe each representative with regard to liberalism-conservatism, and our task would be immensely simplified.

The procedures — discussed in some detail later in this chapter — for converting the values from each variable into a single value for a scale involve using a set of rules to "rescore" each case in the analysis. In this sense, a "new" variable is created by using explicit rules for transforming initial values into scale values.

The extent to which individual variables can be placed on a single scale without losing large quantities of information is governed by the criterion of *dimensionality*. Not all of the scales we discuss make explicit use of the notion of dimensionality, but it is nonetheless an important concept. If all variables measure the same more general characteristics of an attitude or other characteristics of an individual, then we should be able to show that the variables are all highly interrelated. We assume that the variables measure differing amounts of the same thing and consider them to be **unidimensional.** If, however, these relationships are low, we need to investigate the possibility that a number of dimensions exists. Thus, some scaling operations are also tests of a hypothesis that the individual variables that are being combined to form a single scale score also can be organized along a single *dimension*.

It is important to emphasize that the existence or nonexistence of a single dimension reflects a research hypothesis that is just like any other hypothesis. Whether or not it is true is a matter of testing and not a matter for unsupported speculation. What may be true at one time or for one sample, furthermore, may not be true at a later time. As an example, we can again consider the case of political efficacy.

Four political efficacy items were found to form a single dimension in a great deal of research conducted on a variety of populations during the 1950s and early 1960s (Campbell, et al., 1954; Campbell, et al., 1960). Thus, it was assumed that efficacy provided a fairly immutable, highly general, and unidimensional attitude that was found to be useful for explaining a variety of aspects of political participation. Later, more intensive item analysis of the efficacy items based on data that were collected during the 1960s revealed, however, that the four items had, during the turbulent 1960s, split apart so that they represented *two* distinct dimensions rather than a single dimension. Items on one of the dimensions appeared to measure attitudes about one's personal potency to affect political life, whereas items on the other dimension appeared to measure attitudes about politicians' abilities to affect change in policy (Balch, 1974). In short, it was demonstrated empirically that the set of items no longer measured what they had once measured because the way that the items were interrelated had changed. And the dimensionality of the original scale had undergone concomitant change.

Many scaling techniques increase the reliability of measurement by reducing the amount of **random error** that is associated with responses to questionnaire and personal interview items. Error may also be reduced when scaling is performed on aggregations of these kinds of responses in the analysis of such grouped data as census materials, statistical reports of various kinds, and other measures. (Because the way in which random measurement error is reduced by scaling is far too complex to detail in this book, the reader is referred to sources on attitude measurement such as Edwards, 1957; Scott, 1968; Torgerson, 1958; and Upshaw, 1968.)

We can also distinguish among scales on the basis of whether one or more than one variable is used to compute a score on a scale. On some very simple scales, for instance, individuals may rate themselves according to some characteristic, or judges (most frequently specially trained coders) may evaluate individuals, groups, or institutions according to characteristics that they each possess by placing them on a scale. To the question, "Do you consider yourself to be very liberal, liberal, middle of the road, conservative, or very conservative?" individuals rate themselves on the basis of their self-designated liberalism-conservatism by the responses they give. This response then allows each person to be compared with other people who also reply to the question in a meaningful way.

Or consider the task of coders in trying to evaluate a news story as being "favorable, neutral, or unfavorable" (Holsti, 1969, p. 107) in respect to the United States government's participation in resolving Israeli-Arab hostilities. The coders tried to evaluate the contents and manner of presentation of a news story on the basis of a set of rules that they had been trained to use. The unit of analysis may be different (a news story rather than an individual), and the variable may be different (a gross characteristic of a news story rather than an attitude of a person), but both the news story and the individual are placed on scales so that comparisons among cases can be made.

A second very general type of scale is constructed by combining scores on a number of items into a single scale score, as mentioned earlier. Individuals respond to a series of questionnaire items, or United States congressional representatives cast a series of roll-call votes, or measures of a series of states of socioeconomic characteristics are collected. In each instance, each variable is assumed to measure a more general, common dimension so that single-scale scores represent the dimension when the variables are combined into a single score by scaling techniques.

In the case of attitudes about racial integration, for instance, a white man may be characterized according to whether he agrees or disagrees with each of the following: "I would prefer to have blacks as well as whites in my classes; I believe that the quality of my education would be better if blacks were admitted to my school; property values do not decline when black people move into a neighborhood"; and so on. A score that represented a more general attitude about integrationist sentiment might then be constructed by summing the total number of *agree* responses and then subtracting the total number of *disagree* responses. It would be presumed that the single score would represent a more general attitude about racial integration even though each individual item concerned a somewhat different aspect of the problem.

RATING SCALES

A number of types of rating scales have been employed, but one feature is common to all types. The rater places the person or object being rated at some point along a continuum or in one of an ordered series of categories; a numerical value is attached to the point or the category. Scales differ in the fineness of the distinctions they permit and in the procedures involved in assigning persons or objects to positions. These differences will become apparent in our discussion of several of the more common types of rating scales.

Graphic Rating Scales

Perhaps the most widely used is the graphic rating scale. In this type, the judge (the subject, the interviewer, observer, coder, and so on) indicates his or her rating by simply placing a check at the appropriate point on a line that runs from one extreme of the attribute in question to the other. Scale points, with brief descriptions, may be indicated along the line; their function is to serve as a guide to the judge in localizing a rating rather than to provide distinct categories.

Table 9.1 is a scale checked by interviewers of respondents living in interracial housing projects (Deutsch and Collins, 1951).

In this example, the X and Y items were introduced to avoid forcing interviewers to make ratings that they considered inappropriate and to allow them to explain why a rating could not be made.

TABLE 9.1 Respect Felt For Blacks in the Project (Place Check on Appropriate Position on Line, or Circle X or Y.)

Thinks Highly of Blacks in Project without Qualification		*Generally Respects Blacks Living in Project*		*Is Ambivalent; Partly Respects, Partly Feels They Are Inferior*		*Generally Feels They Are Inferior*		*Strongly Feels They Are Inferior*
1	2	3	4	5	6	7	8	9

X: Is indifferent to blacks as a group; doesn't think about them.
Y: Doesn't think of blacks as group; considers them as individuals.

One of the major advantages of graphic rating scales is that they are relatively easy to use. Yet, for the effective use of graphic rating scales, experience has shown that certain precautions must be taken in their design and use: for example, end statements so extreme that they are unlikely to be used should be avoided, and descriptive statements should be placed to correspond as closely as possible with numerical points on the scale. For a more detailed discussion of practices to be followed in the construction and use of graphic rating scales, the reader is referred to Guilford (1954).

Itemized Rating Scales

Itemized rating scales have also been referred to as "specific category scales" (Krech and Crutchfield, 1948) and "numerical scales" (Guilford, 1954). In this type of scale, the rater selects one of a limited number of categories that are ordered in respect to their scale position. The number of scale positions or categories used has varied, depending on the research problem and the kinds of judgments required. Scales with five or seven categories are most frequently employed, but many investigators have used as many as nine or 11 points.

Itemized rating scales, like graphic ones, can be used in connection with data gathered by any of a number of methods. Sherif, Sherif, and Nebergall (1965), for instance, reported findings from a study of pro-Republican and pro-Democratic attitudes during the 1960 United States presidential campaign. Among other things, subjects were asked to react to a set of nine statements about how the election of Republican and Democratic candidates would serve the country's best interests. The statements ranged from unequivocal affirmation of the Republican candidates:

> The election of the Republican presidential and vice-presidential candidates in November is absolutely essential from all angles in the country's interests.

to a neutral position with regard to the candidates:

> From the point of view of the country's interests, it is hard to decide whether it is preferable to vote for presidential and vice-presidential candidates of the Republican Party or the Democratic Party in November.

to unequivocal affirmation of the Democratic candidates:

> The election of the Democratic presidential and vice-presidential candidates in November is absolutely essential from all angles in the country's interests.

In one part of the study, subjects were then instructed to select the statement that was most acceptable to them and the statement that was least acceptable to them. (A number of other tasks were given to subjects in this study. For instance, subjects were instructed to check all the other statements that were acceptable to them and all those that were unacceptable to them. A variety of different scale "scores" were constructed from these data.) Most important for present purposes, however, is the simple rating of the statement that comes closest to the subject's own stand on the election. This statement specifies *where* the subject is located on a scale that concerns Republican and Democratic party attitudes. People who locate themselves on the pro-Republican end of the continuum are assumed to be favorable to Republican candidates, whereas people who locate themselves on the pro-Democratic end of the continuum are assumed to be favorable to Democrats. Similarly, people who find pro-Democratic statements "most objectionable" are assumed to dislike Democratic candidates, whereas people who find pro-Republican statements "most objectionable" are assumed to dislike Republicans. Findings from the study indicate, moreover, that acceptance and rejection are usually mirror images of each other. Few people liked both parties equally or disliked both parties equally.

The verbal descriptions used to identify the scale positions may vary from brief statements indicating only degrees of the attribute to more elaborate descriptions including illustrations of behavior appropriate to the category. The two examples just given provide relatively detailed definitions and illustrations. At the other extreme, Proshansky (1943), in the analysis of descriptions of pictures in a projective test of attitude toward labor, instructed his judges to rate the descriptions in response to a five-point scale on which the two end categories were defined simply as "very favorable" and "very unfavorable," and the middle category as indicating that it was impossible to classify the respondent as either favorable or unfavorable; the second and fourth positions were given no specific definition other than that they were to be used for descriptions that fell between the extreme and the middle position.

The more clearly defined the categories, in general, the more reliable the ratings are likely to be. How much definition is needed depends on the nature of the material, the familiarity of the coders with the concepts involved, and the fineness of distinctions required for the study.

The problems involved in the construction and application of itemized rating scales are for the most part similar to those that characterize other types of rating scales. These problems are treated later in this section.

Comparative Rating Scales

In using graphic and itemized rating scales, raters make their judgments of the individual without direct reference to the positions of other individuals or groups with which the individual might be compared. On the other hand, comparative rating scales—as their name suggests—clearly imply such relative judgments. The positions on the rating scale are expressly defined on the basis of a given population or social group or in respect to people of known characteristics. For example, a questionnaire used in selecting applicants for admission to a graduate school may ask the rater for an estimate of the given applicant's ability to do graduate work, "as compared with the total group of graduate students you have known." Is the applicant more capable than 10 percent of them? 20 percent? 30 percent? Or the rater may be asked to indicate, for example, whether an individual's leadership skill most closely resembles that of person A, of person B, or of person C (all of whom are known to the rater and all of whom have been assessed in terms of their leadership skill). In the first example given earlier, in order to make a valid rating, the judge must have a clear conception of the range and distribution of the abilities of the total graduate student group. Scales of the second type are often difficult to construct, for there may not be sufficient variation in leadership behavior (or whatever attribute is being rated) among the people known to the judges for them to serve as examples for the various points on the scale.

Another comparative or relative rating procedure is the *rank-order scale*. Here the judge is required to rank individuals specifically in relation to one another; the judge indicates which person is highest in regard to the characteristic being measured, which is next highest, and so on, down to the one who is lowest. Ranking in this fashion is used only when the investigator is concerned with a limited group of individuals. The rating an individual receives indicates simply his or her relative rank or position in the group being studied; it would not necessarily be of any usefulness apart from the specific group whose members are being compared.

Self-Ratings versus Ratings by Others

All these types of scales may be used to secure individual's ratings of themselves or someone else's rating of each of them. It seems reasonable to assume that individuals are often in a better position to observe and report their own beliefs, feelings, and fears than anyone else is. This assumption is valid, however, only if individuals are aware of their own beliefs and feelings and are willing to reveal them to others. If a man is unaware, for example, of the fact that he has hostile feelings toward a particular minority group or if he is aware of such feelings but is afraid of the consequences of revealing them, then the self-rating procedure is of little value. Another difficulty arises from the fact that even if individuals are capable of reporting their beliefs or feelings objectively, their concept of what constitutes a moderate or an extreme position may be quite different from those of others making comparable self-ratings.

Despite the hazards involved, self-ratings have proved useful in the measurement of social attitudes. For beliefs and feelings that the individual can be expected to be aware of and willing to report—for example, attitudes toward specific television programs—self-ratings are a useful source of information. With respect to certain attributes of attitudes—for example, intensity and importance—self-ratings have so far proved to be the only satisfactory source of information. Attention by the investigator to such matters as clearly specifying the dimension to be rated and defining the frame of reference or standards against which the ratings are to be made may serve to reduce the possibilities of distortion in self-ratings and increase their usefulness.

Construction and Use of Rating Scales: Some Cautions

As a large element of judgment enters into the use of rating scales, there is considerable room for systematic errors to be introduced by the personal bias of the rater or raters. One rather common systematic error is the **halo effect.** If more than one characteristic of a person is to be judged, raters frequently carry over a generalized impression of the person from one rating to the next, or they try to make their ratings consistent.[1] Thus, if a rater considers a person to be shy and if that same rater believes shy people to be poorly adjusted, he or she is likely to rate the person poorly adjusted as well as shy. It is apparent that the halo effect reduces the validity of the ratings of some traits and introduces a spurious degree of positive correlation among the traits that are rated.

Another frequent type of constant error is the **generosity error.** Here the tendency of the rater is to overestimate the desirable qualities of subjects whom the rater likes. Still other frequent errors have been identified. Thus, raters tend to avoid making extreme judgments and to assign individuals to the more moderate categories. Murray, et al. (1938) have identified the **contrast error,** in which there is a tendency on the part of raters to see others as opposite to themselves in a trait. Murray and his colleagues found, for example, that raters who were themselves very orderly rated others as being relatively disorderly, whereas raters who were themselves less orderly tended to see others as more orderly.

One way of reducing constant errors such as those just described is to train the raters carefully and especially to make them aware of the possibility of such biases. Specific steps may be taken to reduce the likelihood of specific types of error. For example, the tendency to avoid using the extreme positions may be counteracted by giving somewhat less than extreme labels to these positions. People are more likely to check "I am well satisfied with my job" than "I am completely satisfied with my job"; at the other extreme, they are more likely to check "there are many things about my job that I do not like" than "there is nothing about my job that I like." The generosity error may be reduced by using relatively neutral descriptive terms for the scale positions rather than evaluative ones; for example, "does not readily accept new opinions or ways of doing things" rather than "rigid." Halo effects may be reduced or eliminated altogether by having the various ratings of a given person made independently—either by different raters or by the same raters at different times without awareness that they are rating the same person. However, this latter condition can be met only when the ratings are made on the basis of recorded material, such as responses to interview questions, accounts of behavior, or other sources from which identifying information can be removed.

---

[1]The tendency to make ratings consistent is not unlike what Newcomb (1931) has described as a "logical error"; that is, judges often give similar ratings on traits that seem to them to be logically related. Also see the discussion of halo and other effects in Phillips (1971, pp. 12–49).

Systematic errors, of course, reduce the validity of ratings. There may also be random errors that reduce their reliability. One frequent source of unreliability among different raters is the fact that some frame of reference is implicit in any rating; different raters may use different frames of reference in describing individuals in terms of the characteristic in question. For example, the rating of a person as conservative or radical takes its meaning from the rater's reference group—the group norms the rater has in mind when making ratings. Lack of correspondence between ratings by different observers is frequently caused by the fact that they make ratings with different reference groups in mind.

Reliability can be increased not only by careful *training* of raters but also by attention to the construction of the rating scale. *Clear definitions* of the characteristic being measured and of the various positions on the scale, as well as *clear specification* of the reference group, help to reduce unreliability. Whenever possible, the definitions of the scale points should *include concrete illustrations* of question reponses, types of behavior, or communication content. Careful consideration should be given to distinguishing between adjacent positions on the scale; for example, to the difference between "favorable" and "very favorable."

In constructing a rating scale, one must decide how many scale positions or categories are to be used unless one is using a graphic scale on which the rater is free to check any point on a continuous line. There is no simple rule for determining the optimal number of positions. A basic consideration, of course, is the degree of differentiation wanted in the measurement. But regardless of what is demanded by the research problem, other factors must be taken into account: (1) the discriminative ability of the judges or raters, including the extent to which they are trained and experienced; (2) the kind of characteristics to be judged, for example, whether they are complex "inner" attributes or more manifest "outer" attributes; (3) the conditions under which the ratings are to be made, for example, whether they are based on extensive data (long periods of observation of the subject or a great deal of communication content) or on limited data (brief observation or limited communication content). These factors interact in their effect on the degree of fineness possible in the rating scale. If relatively manifest behaviors are to be rated, then a more differentiated scale may be used even with relatively unsophisticated judges, provided they are trained appropriately. On the other hand, if complex attributes are to be judged and experienced judges are not available, it may be necessary to use a less differentiated scale in order to obtain reliable ratings. In any case, all of these factors must be considered in determining the number of distinctions to be included in the rating scale. Very often preliminary testing is necessary before a final decision can be made.

Reliability of ratings is usually enhanced considerably by having several raters working as a team—making independent judgments, comparing their ratings and discussing discrepancies, and making second independent judgments that are then pooled or averaged to give a final score (see Murray, et al., 1938). Much research has demonstrated the superiority of the average, or consensus, of the judgments of several people over that of one individual (see Murphy, Murphy, and Newcomb, 1937) because random errors tend to be canceled out when several independent ratings are combined.

It should be noted that the pooling of independent ratings is more feasible when the rating is being done by coders working from recorded material or by observers of a behavioral situation; it is often not feasible to have more than one rater (interviewer) present in an interviewing situation.

In many studies ratings are made in the process of analysis by coders who have studied the recorded material. Often, however, ratings are made on the spot by an interviewer or observer, for there may be overtones in the subject's manner or behavior that cannot be recorded adequately and therefore cannot be taken into account in a rating made by an analyst who has not had direct contact with the subject. Little systematic evidence of the relative merits of these two procedures is available. However, Maccoby and Maccoby (1954) have suggested that, at least in the case of interviewing, the advantage of the interviewer in being able to observe additional cues may be more than offset by two disadvantages: (1) interviewer ratings are especially susceptible to halo effects, for the interviewer necessarily knows that it is the same individual being rated and because all the ratings of a given individual must be made at the same time; (2) each interviewer tends to develop an individualized frame of reference for ratings, based on the particular sample of respondents he or she has interviewed, whereas the standards of coders working in the same office and subject to frequent checking, if necessary, can be kept more consistent.

It would be rather fruitless to attempt to discuss in any detail what constitutes a good rater because there is very little definitive research on this topic. However, several general conclusions seem warranted. First of all, not only do individuals differ in their ability as raters, but the same individuals may differ in their ability to rate different characteristics. A good rater with respect to one characteristic may be poor with respect to another. In other words, the ability to judge is not general; it is a highly specialized function within the individual. Second — contrary to common expectation — acquaintance with the person to be rated does not lead to increasing **validity** of ratings. Guilford (1954) has pointed out that long acquaintance often results in substantial generosity errors. Third, confidence in one's judgment is not necessarily an indication of its validity. At least one investigation (Kelly and Fiske, 1950) has reported an inverse relation between confidence and the validity of predictions. However, Guilford (1954) cited an early study by Cady, which indicated that judgments of which the rater is confident are much more reliable than those of which the rater is less confident. Fourth, most of the studies of validity of ratings seem to indicate that people who are high on a characteristic generally considered undesirable are poor judges of that characteristic both in others and in themselves.

The simplicity of rating scales commends their use to many. Their simplicity, however, may be more apparent than real. Often so much time is required to establish adequate reliability that the procedure becomes uneconomical. Yet it is also true that, despite the difficulties involved, a rating scale may be the only instrument available for a given purpose, at least in the present stage of development of research techniques. Furthermore, as we indicated earlier, rating-scale methods have a wide range of application; they can be used in connection with communication content, observed behavior, responses to questionnaires, or data collected by almost any other method.

Perhaps the most significant problem in the use of rating scales has to do with their validity. Even a cursory examination of the relevant literature reveals that, whereas evaluation of the reliability of rating scales is common, measures of validity are rarely reported. The reason, of course, is the dearth of available external criteria against which ratings can be compared. As a matter of fact, ratings themselves have often been used as criteria for checking the validity of other types of measuring instruments, such as personality inventories.

This does not mean, of course, that investigators have completely ignored the question of the validity of their rating scales. In effect, they have assumed that their scales were valid when the following conditions were met: (1) the attributes being measured were relatively "objective," so that their meaning would be uniformly understood by the raters using the scales; (2) the ratings themselves were obtained under optimal conditions, including carefully constructed scales, trained judges, and specified common frames of reference. Under these conditions, one may not go too far wrong in assuming that if the obtained ratings are reliable, they are probably also valid. However, if either one of these conditions is not met, then the assumption of validity is hazardous. The first condition has been overlooked by some investigators, who have also assumed that even intuitive, nonobjective ratings can be done accurately. There is little reason to assume that intuitive judgments can be made even by highly trained and intelligent people. For example, Kelly and Fiske (1950) found that ratings by experienced clinical psychologists based on unstructured interviews had little value in predicting performance in situations that were not clearly specified. If the concept of what is being measured is vague, as it is in some rating scales, it is unlikely that the ratings will be clear in meaning. When the concept of what is being measured is ambiguous, the ordering of individuals may actually be quite arbitrary, and even distinctions of *greater* or *less* become meaningless.

QUESTIONNAIRES THAT FORM SCALES

As we have pointed out, a large element of judgment is involved when a rater places an individual on a rating scale on the basis of the individual's observed behavior, answers to open-ended questions, or other responses. In an effort to devise procedures that would make it possible to place individuals on a scale with less likelihood of error, carefully standardized questionnaires have been constructed. In this approach, individuals do not directly describe themselves in terms of their positions on the dimension in question. Rather, they express their agreement or disagreement with a number of statements relevant to it; on the basis of these responses, they are assigned scores. In the process of standardizing the questionnaire, the investigator has established a basis for interpreting scores as indicating positions on the dimension. Because this technique has been used most often in the measurement of attitudes, our discussion will focus on attitude scales.

Attitude scales differ from one another in method of construction, method of response, and basis for interpreting scores. Different types of attitude scales will be discussed in this section.

The separate items or questions in an attitude scale are usually not of interest in themselves; the interest is, rather, in each individual's *total score* or in the subscores that result from the combination of the individual's responses to various items. The total score is assumed to indicate each individual's position on a more general attitude. In effect, any set of items works as well as any other set, provided they give the same final scores on the particular attitude being measured.

In selecting items for inclusion in a scale, two criteria are commonly used. First, the items must elicit responses that are psychologically related to the attitude being measured. For example, in a scale measuring anti-Semitism, the following item has a *manifest* relation to the attitude being measured: "Anyone who employs many people should be careful not to hire a large percentage of Jews" (Adorno, et al., 1950). However, the relationship does not necessarily have to be evident. In fact, there is considerable advantage to using items that, on the surface, have no bearing on the attitude being measured. This may prevent respondents from concealing or distorting their attitudes. Thus, in their study of antidemocratic ideology, Adorno, et al. used many items that had no apparent relationship to this attitude — for example, "When a person has a problem or worry, it is best for him not to think about it, but to keep busy with more cheerful things." This item is one of several that indicate an individual's readiness or lack of readiness to adopt a psychologically insightful view of other people and of himself. The theory is that people who are lacking in psychological insight and understanding have a personality structure (for example, greater repressed hostility, weaker ego, and so on) that predisposes them to an antidemocratic ideology.[2]

The second criterion requires that the scale differentiate among people who are at different points along the dimension being measured. In order to discriminate not merely between opposite extremes in attitudes but also among individuals who differ slightly, items that discriminate at different points on the scale are usually included. Thus, a test of opinions about child-rearing practices, along the dimension "permissiveness-strictness," would contain not only items representing a very strict approach and others representing a very permissive approach, but intermediate items representing moderate strictness, moderate permissiveness, and some middle point. Some types of scales, however, provide for the identification of moderate positions by permitting the expression of various degrees of agreement or disagreement with extreme items rather than by the inclusion of intermediate items.

The way in which a scale discriminates among individuals depends on the construction of the scale and the method of scoring. In some scales the items form a gradation of such a nature that the individual will likely agree with only one or two, which correspond to his or her position on the dimension being measured, and will likely disagree with statements on either side of those he or she has selected. Such scales, in which a person's response specifies that person's position, are sometimes called **differential scales.** In other scales, individuals indicate their agreement or disagreement with each item, and their total scores are determined by adding the subscores assigned to their responses to all the separate items; such scales

---

[2]Such indirect items cannot, of course, be used as measures of the attitude being studied simply on the basis of theoretical assumptions about their relation to the attitude. Before they are accepted as adequate measures, their relation to the attitude must be demonstrated. (This statement is equally true for items that seem to have a *manifest* relation to the attitude being studied.) Thus, in the study of antidemocratic ideology, the hypothesis that items such as the one quoted were related to antidemocratic ideology was tested — and borne out — by analysis of the difference between responses to such items made by people known on other grounds to have a democratic ideology and those made by people known to have an antidemocratic ideology.

are sometimes called **summated scales.** Still others are set up in such a way that the items form a *cumulative* series; theoretically, an individual whose attitude is at a certain point on the dimension being measured will answer favorably all the items on one side of that point and answer unfavorably all those on the other side. Each of these types of scales is discussed in more detail in the following paragraphs. (See also the detailed discussions of attitude scaling in Dawes, Singer, and Lemons, 1972; Edwards, 1957; Horst, 1968; and Scott, 1968.)

Differential Scales

Differential scales for the measurement of attitudes are closely associated with the name of L. L. Thurstone. The methods he devised represent attempts to approximate **interval scales.** An interval scale is one on which the distances between points on the measuring instrument are known and on which equal numerical distances represent equal distances along the continuum being measured. Such a scale enables one to compare differences or changes in attitude, for the difference between a score of three and a score of seven is equivalent to the difference between a score of six and a score of ten and to the difference between any other two scores that are four points apart.

A differential scale consists of a number of items whose position on the scale has been determined by some kind of ranking or rating operation performed by judges. Various methods of securing judgments of scale position have been used: the method of *paired comparisons* (see Thurstone, 1927, 1928); the method of **equal-appearing intervals** (see Thurstone, 1929, 1931; Thurstone and Chave, 1929); and the method of *successive intervals* (see Saffir, 1937). It is beyond the scope of this volume to give the details of these procedures; we shall only present in broad outline Thurstone's method of equal-appearing intervals, which has been the most commonly used.

In selecting the items for the scale and assigning values to them, the following procedure is used: (1) The researcher gathers several hundred statements conceived to be related to the attitude being investigated. (2) A large number of judges — usually from 50 to 300 — working independently, classify these statements into 11 groups. In the first pile each judge places the statements he or she considers most favorable to the object; in the second, those considered next most favorable; and in the eleventh pile; the statements he or she considers most unfavorable. The sixth, or "neutral," position is defined as the point at which there is neither favorableness nor unfavorableness.[3] (3) The scale value of a statement is computed as the median position (or pile) to which it is assigned by the group of judges. Statements that have

---

[3]Throughout this section, for the sake of simplicity, the discussion is worded in terms of scales measuring favorableness-unfavorableness toward some object. A scale may, of course, be concerned with some other dimension; for example, liberalism-conservatism of social, political, or economic views; permissiveness-strictness of views on child rearing; and so on. In the developing of Thurstone scales, the instructions to the judges specify the dimension along which the items are to be placed. Thus, in developing a scale to measure liberalism-conservatism, the judges would be instructed to place in the first pile the items they consider most liberal, in the eleventh those they consider most conservative. The same principles and procedures apply whether the dimension to be measured is favorableness-unfavorableness or some other.

too broad a scatter are discarded as ambiguous or irrelevant. (4) A final selection is made, taking items that are spread out evenly along the scale from one extreme position to the other. It is often possible to construct duplicate forms of the scale from items not used on the original form.

The resulting **Thurstone**-type **scale** is a series of statements, usually about 20; the position of each statement on a scale of favorable-unfavorable attitude toward the object has been determined by the judges' classification. The subjects, in filling out the questionnaire, are asked either to check each statement with which they agree or to check the two or three items that are closest to their position.

Table 9.2 is an illustration of items from a Thurstone-type scale and is taken from MacCrone's study of attitudes toward natives in South Africa (1937).

The scale values, of course, are not shown on the questionnaire, and the items are usually arranged in random order rather than in order of their scale value. The mean (or **median**)[4] of the scale values of the items the individual checks is interpreted as indicating that individual's position on a scale of favorable-unfavorable attitude toward the object.

Theoretically, if a Thurstone-type scale is completely reliable and if the scale is measuring a single attitude rather than a complex of attitudes, an individual should check only items that are immediately contiguous in scale value — for example, items 15 and 17 in Table 9.2. If the responses of an individual scatter widely over noncontiguous items, his or her attitude score is not likely to have the same meaning as a score with little scatter. The scattered responses may indicate that the subject has no attitude or that the subject's attitude is not organized in the manner assumed by the scale. There is no a priori reason to expect that all people have attitudes toward the same thing or that attitudinal dimensions are the same for all.

Several objections have been raised against the Thurstone-type scale. First, many have objected to the amount of work involved in constructing it. Undoubtedly, the procedure is cumbersome, and this is one reason why the procedure is no longer used so much as it was initially. However, Edwards (1957) has expressed the opinion that, in view of newer developments in timesaving techniques, the amount of time and labor involved in constructing a scale by the method of equal-appearing intervals is not substantially different from that involved in constructing a summated scale. In any case, it is doubtful that simple methods for the rigorous construction of scales will ever be developed. The precise measurement of attitudes is perhaps inevitably a complex affair.

A second criticism has been that, because an individual's score is the mean or median of the scale values of the several items he or she has checked, essentially different attitudinal patterns may be expressed in the same score. For example, on the scale of attitudes toward natives of South Africa given earlier, an individual who checks the two moderately "anti" items 15 and 17 receives a score of 8.5 (the median of their scale values). Another individual, who checks items 1, 15, 17, and 22 (per-

---

[4]Thurstone, on the assumption that scales constructed by this method were true interval scales, advocated the use of statistics appropriate to interval scales — the mean and the standard deviation. Other investigators, operating on the more cautious assumption that the intervals are not truly equal, have favored the use of the median as appropriate to ordinal scales.

TABLE 9.2   Attitude toward Natives in South Africa

Scale Value	Item No.	
0.8	11.	I would rather see the white people lose their position in this country than keep it at the expense of injustice to the native.
3.1	3.	It seems to me the white man by placing restrictions such as the "Colour Bar" upon the native is really trying to exploit him economically.
3.8	22.	I consider that the white community in this country owe a real debt of gratitude to the missionaries for the way in which they have tried to uplift the native.
8.4	17.	To my mind the native is so childish and irresponsible that he cannot be expected to know what is in his best interest.
8.6	15.	I do not think that the native can be relied upon in a position of trust or of responsibility.
10.2	2.	The idea of contact with the black or dark skin of the native excites horror and disgust in me.
10.3	1.	I consider that the native is only fit to do the "dirty" work of the white community.

haps because item 22 has a meaning for him that is different from that which it had for the judges), also receives a score of 8.5 (the median of the scale values of these items). The two individuals are rated as having the *same degree of prejudice, even though the latter checked the most unfavorable item in the scale and the former did not.*

A still more serious question has to do with the extent to which the scale values assigned to the items are influenced by the attitudes of the judges themselves. Do the attitudes and backgrounds of the judges affect the position of the various items on the scale? This obviously is a matter that is open to experimental inquiry. A number of early studies supported the view that the scale values assigned did not depend on the attitude of the judges. Hinckley (1932) found a correlation of .98 between the scale positions assigned to 114 items measuring prejudice toward blacks by a group of southern white students in the United States who were prejudiced against blacks and those assigned by a group of unprejudiced northern students. Similarly, MacCrone (1937), in the study of racial attitudes in South Africa referred to earlier, found that the scale positions assigned various items by South Africans of European background and by educated Bantus, natives of South Africa, were similar except for a few items. In studies of the construction of scales measuring attitudes toward a particular candidate for political office (Beyle, 1932), toward war (Ferguson, 1935), toward patriotism (Pintner and Forlano, 1937), and toward Jews (Eysenck and Crown, 1949) there were correlations of .98 or higher between the scale positions assigned to the items by groups of judges with opposed attitudes toward the object of the scale.

Later research, however, has sharply challenged the conclusions of these studies. Hovland and Sherif (1952), using the items employed in the Hinckley study mentioned earlier, found marked differences between the scale values assigned to items by antiblack white judges on the one hand, and those assigned by problack white judges and black judges, on the other. Items rated as neutral or moderately favorable by Hinckley's subjects were likely to be seen as unfavorable by the problack white judges and the black judges. (It should be noted, however, that even in these studies there was high agreement in the *rank order* in which judges with differing attitudes arranged the items along the favorable-unfavorable continuum.) This discrepancy between the earlier and the later findings can be accounted for by the different procedures used. Hinckley followed a rule suggested by Thurstone, that any judge who placed more than one-fourth of the statements in a single category should be eliminated as "careless." Hovland and Sherif, however, found that judges with extreme attitudes tended to place many statements in the same category; checks within their procedure convinced these investigators that this was not a matter of carelessness. Application of the rule followed by Hinckley would have eliminated over three-fourths of their black judges and two-thirds of their problack white judges; when they did eliminate these judges, they found that the scale values assigned by the remaining white judges were very close to those assigned by Hinckley's judges. These findings strongly suggest that Hinckley's procedure had the effect of ruling out judges with extreme attitudes.[5]

However, more recent work (Upshaw, 1965) has shown that the effect of the judges' attitudes is only to impose a linear transformation upon the ratings. Therefore, the nature of the intervals is maintained. It can be safely concluded that the procedure seeking to create equal-appearing intervals does provide an interval scale within the major range of scale values.

Summated Scales

A summated scale, like a differential scale, consists of a set of items to which the subject is asked to react. However, no attempt is made to find items that will be distributed evenly over a scale of favorableness-unfavorableness (or whatever dimension is to be measured). Rather, only items that seem to be either *definitely favorable* or *definitely unfavorable* to the attitude object are used, not neutral or slightly favorable or unfavorable items. Rather than checking only those statements with which they agree, respondents indicate their agreement or disagreement with *each* item. Each response is given a numerical score indicating its favorableness or unfavorableness. Often, favorable responses are scored plus; unfavorable responses, minus. The

[5]Other investigators (Kelley, et al., 1955; Granneberg, 1955) found that other methods of constructing Thurstone-type scales were less subject than the equal-interval technique to the effect of extreme attitudes on the part of the judges. The method of successive intervals showed less difference between white and black judges, and the method of paired comparisons eliminated the differences almost entirely.

algebraic summation of the scores of the individual's responses to all the separate items gives the individual's total score, which is interpreted as representing his or her position on a scale of favorable-unfavorable attitude toward the object. The rationale for using such total scores as a basis for placing individuals on a scale seems to be as follows: The probability of agreeing with any one of a series of favorable items about an object or of disagreeing with any unfavorable item varies directly with the degree of favorableness of an individual's attitude. Thus, one could expect an individual with a favorable attitude to respond favorably to many items (that is, to agree with many items favorable to the object and to disagree with many unfavorable ones), an ambivalent individual to respond unfavorably to some and favorably to others, and an individual with an unfavorable attitude to respond unfavorably to many items.

The type of summated scale most frequently used in the study of social attitudes follows the pattern devised by Rensis Likert (1932) and is referred to as a **Likert-type scale.** In fact, most scales currently used in social science research are Likert-type scales. In such a scale, the subjects are asked to respond to each item in terms of several degrees of agreement or disagreement: for example (1) strongly approve, (2) approve, (3) undecided, (4) disapprove, (5) strongly disapprove.[6] There follow several items from a Likert-type scale, the Mach IV Scale used by Christie and Geis (1970) to measure Machiavellianism, or the desire to manipulate other people.

Subjects were directed to indicate the level of agreement or disagreement with each of the Mach IV items by marking a number that corresponded with strong agreement, agreement, no position, disagreement, or strong disagreement on each item. Items that were found to be highly related to the total scale score (that is, to discriminate well among high and low scorers on Machiavellianism in initial tests) included these:

2.   The best way to handle people is to tell them what they want to hear. (+)

10.   When you ask someone to do something for you, it is best to give the real reasons for wanting it rather than giving reasons which might carry more weight. (−)

18.   It is hard to get ahead without cutting corners here and there. (+)

17.   Barnum was very wrong when he said there's a sucker born every minute. (−)

15.   It is wise to flatter important people. (+)

9.   All in all, it is better to be humble and honest than important and dishonest. (−)

The procedure for constructing a Likert-type scale is as follows: (1) The investigator assembles a large number of items considered relevant to the attitude being investigated that are either clearly favorable or clearly unfavorable. (2) These items are administered to a group of subjects representative of those with whom the questionnaire is to be used. The subjects indicate their responses to each item by checking one of the categories of agreement-disagreement. (3) The responses to the various items are scored in such a way that a response indicative of the most favorable atti-

---

[6]Although Likert used five categories of agreement-disagreement, some investigators have used a smaller and some a larger number of categories. Many summated scales call simply for an expression of agreement or disagreement without indication of degree.

tude is given the highest score. It makes no difference whether *five* is high and *one* is low or vice versa. The important thing is that responses be scored consistently in terms of the attitudinal direction they indicate. Whether approve or disapprove is the favorable response to an item depends, of course, upon the content and wording of the item. (4) Each individual's total score is determined by adding the individual's item scores. (5) The responses are analyzed to determine which of the items discriminate most clearly between the high scorers and the low scorers on the total scale. For example, the responses of those subjects whose total scores are in the upper quarter and the responses of those in the lower quarter may be analyzed in order to determine for each item the extent to which the responses of these criterion groups differ. Items that do not show a substantial correlation with the total score or that do not elicit different responses from those who score high and those who score low on the total test are eliminated to ensure that the questionnaire is "internally consistent" — that is, that every item is related to the same general attitude.

The Likert-type scale, like the Thurstone scale, has been used widely in studies of morale, of attitudes toward blacks, of attitudes toward internationalism, and many other studies. But as indicated by Triandis (1971), just because a scale is called a "Likert-type" scale, we cannot assume it has been constructed through the use of an item analysis, as previously described. Too many researchers use shortcuts and refer to their scales as "Likert-type scales" when only the format is common to that type. But a properly constructed Likert-type scale has several advantages over the Thurstone scale. First, it permits the use of items that are not manifestly related to the attitude being studied. In the Thurstone method, the necessity of agreement among judges tends to limit items only to content that is clearly related to the attitude in question; in the Likert method, any item that is found empirically to be consistent with the total score can be included. Second, a Likert-type scale is generally considered simpler to construct. Third, it is likely to be more reliable than a Thurstone scale of the same number of items (Tittle and Hill, 1967). Within limits, the reliability of a scale increases as the number of possible alternative responses is increased; the Likert-type scale item permits the expression of several (usually five) degrees of agreement-disagreement, whereas the Thurstone scale item allows a choice between only two alternative responses. Fourth, the range of responses permitted to an item given in a Likert-type scale provides, in effect, more precise information about the individual's opinion on the issues referred to by the given item.

The Likert-type scale does not claim to be more than an **ordinal scale;** that is, it makes possible the ranking of individuals in terms of the favorableness of their attitude toward a given object, but it does not provide a basis for saying *how much more favorable* one is than another or for measuring the amount of change after some experience. From the point of view of the level of measurement we would like our instruments to provide, this is, of course, a disadvantage.

Another disadvantage of the Likert-type scale is that often the total score of an individual has little clear meaning, for many patterns of response to the various items may produce the same score. This disadvantage is less marked to the extent that careful item analysis ensures that only items that discriminate between low and high total scores on the scale are included in determining a final score. We have already noted that Thurstone-type scales are also subject to this criticism, but it applies even more strongly to the Likert scales because they provide a greater number of response possibilities. It seems reasonable to suppose that two similar total scores based on different combinations of item responses may reflect different "attitudes." Thus one may raise a serious question whether the Likert-type scale actually conforms to the requirements of an ordinal, much less an interval, scale. Despite the lack of theoretical rationale for scalability, however, pragmatically the scores on the Likert-type questionnaire often provide the basis for a rough ordering of people on the characteristic being measured.

The fact that different patterns of response may lead to identical scores on either a Thurstone or a Likert scale is not necessarily as serious a drawback as it may at first appear. Some of the differences in response patterns leading to a given score may be attributable to random variations in response. Others may arise because specific items involve not only the attitude being measured but also extraneous issues that may affect the response. Thus, some of the differences in response patterns leading to the same score may be thought of as error from the point of view of the attitude being measured rather than as true differences in attitude that are being obscured by identical scores. The fact that the scale contains a number of items means that these variations on individual items unrelated to the attitude being measured may cancel each other out.

Moreover, different ways of getting to the same place may be equivalent from the point of view of the measurement goal that is being served. For example, if one weights addition and subtraction equally in a concept of arithmetic ability, it makes sense to score two individuals as equivalent in arithmetic ability, even though one is relatively strong in addition and the other relatively strong in subtraction. Similarly, it may make sense to say that the net degree of animosity toward a given attitudinal object is the same in two individuals even though the animosity expresses itself differently.

The problem is to determine when the fact that the same score can be arrived at in different ways has consequences for the meaningfulness of the score and when it does not. In part, this problem is one of conceptual clarity; in part, it involves questions of fact. If investigators are not clear about what they are trying to measure and why, this will be only one of many problems with which they will be unable to cope. But even if their concepts are clear, they will still want to know (although, unfortunately, they may not be in a position to find out) the answers to such questions as these: Do the response patterns of individuals remain stable over time? If alternate forms of the test are available, do individuals receive the same scores on different forms? Do different individuals achieving the same score in different ways react in the same way to particular stimuli, problems, or incentives?

Ultimately, what is involved is a question of the validity of the scale. Questions of validity always involve questions of fact, which cannot be settled by armchair argument. The problem of whether different combinations of responses can meaningfully be assigned the same score is one for empirical investigation.

Cumulative Scales

Cumulative scales, like differential and summated scales, are made up of a series of items with which the respondent indicates agreement or disagreement. In a cumulative scale, the items are related to one another in such a way that, ideally, an individual who replies favorably to item 2 also replies favorably to item 1; one who replies favorably to item 3 also replies favorably to items 1 and 2; and so on. Thus, all individuals who answer a given item favorably should have higher scores on the total scale than the individuals who answer that item unfavorably. The individual's score is computed by counting the number of items he or she answers favorably. This score places the person on the scale of favorable-unfavorable attitude provided by the relationship of the items to one another.

Sometimes the items as they appear in the scale are arranged in order of favorableness; sometimes they are randomly arranged. Ordinarily, no attempt is made to determine whether the intervals between items are equal; thus, in practice, cumulative scales are ordinal scales.

One of the earliest scales used in the measurement of attitudes, the Bogardus social-distance scale (see Bogardus, 1925, 1928, 1933) was intended to be of the cumulative type. The social-distance scale, which has become a classic technique in the measuring of attitudes toward ethnic groups, lists a number of relationships to which members of the group might be admitted. Respondents are asked to indicate, for specified nationality or racial groups, the relationships to which they would be willing to admit members of each group. Their attitudes are measured by the closeness of relationship that each is willing to accept. The Bogardus-type scale is illustrated in Table 9.3.

The items used in the Bogardus scale (that is, the column headings in Table 9.3) were selected on logical grounds. It seems reasonable to expect that an individual who circles four in relation to Chinese, indicating that he or she would be willing to accept them to employment in his or her occupation, would ordinarily also circle five and not circle six or seven. (Here, as in other scales, the content of the item must be taken into account in deciding whether a yes response is to be scored as favorable or unfavorable. Because six and seven are essentially statements of exclusion, the *absence* of a circle constitutes the favorable response to these two items.

TABLE 9.3 Bogardus Social Distance Scale

Directions: For each race or nationality listed below, circle each of the classifications to which you would be willing to admit the average member of that race or nationality (not the best members you have known or the worst). Answer in terms of your first feeling reactions.

	To Close Kinship by Marriage	*To My Club as Personal Chums*	*To My Street as Neighbors*	*To Employment in My Occupation*	*To Citizenship in My Country*	*As Visitors Only to My Country*	*Would Exclude from My Country*
English	1	2	3	4	5	6	7
Black	1	2	3	4	5	6	7
French	1	2	3	4	5	6	7
Chinese	1	2	3	4	5	6	7
Russian and so on	1	2	3	4	5	6	7

Thus, neither six nor seven should be circled for a given group if any of the other numerals is circled.) If the individual did *not* circle three (willing to admit to my street as neighbors), one would expect, on logical grounds, that he or she would also not circle two or one.

On the whole, the assumption that these items form a cumulative scale has been borne out. Nevertheless, in practice some reversals do occur. Some individuals, for example, who would object to living in a building with Puerto Ricans would not object to having Puerto Ricans in an informal social club (see Deutsch and Collins, 1951). Although individuals not infrequently show such reversals in replies on the social-distance scale, it is relatively uncommon to find an entire group reversing items. Thus, the social-distance scale has been used rather effectively in comparing the attitudes of different groups of people toward various nationalities. It may be noted that reversals can almost always be interpreted by postulating the intrusion of some factor other than the individuals's own attitude toward the group in question — for example, the respondent's image of how other people would interpret his living in a certain neighborhood or his expectation concerning the impact on real estate values of admitting minority-group members to residence on his street.

With the appearance of the Thurstone and Likert scaling methods in the late 1920s and early 1930s, attention shifted away from cumulative scales. However, during the 1940s there were a revival of interest and a rapid development of techniques for determining whether the items of a scale do, in fact, have a cumulative relationship, regardless of whether they appear cumulative in common-sense terms. This renewed interest was linked to the work of Louis Guttman (1944) and others on the development of unidimensional scales — that is, scales consisting of items that do not raise issues or involve factors extraneous to the characteristic being measured. In fact, it was the goal of Louis Guttman to develop a technique for determining whether a stimulus domain was unidimensional. Other people were the ones who applied his technique as a means of attitude scaling.

A number of investigators had pointed out that the Thurstone and Likert scales, although ostensibly measuring "an attitude," contained statements about various aspects of the object under consideration. Thus, Carter (1945) pointed out that form A of the Peterson scale of attitude toward war (a Thurstone-type scale) had as its most favorable statement, "War is glorious"; as its most unfavorable statement, "There is no conceivable justification for war"; and as its midpoint, "I never think about war and it doesn't interest me." He commented that it is difficult to think of these statements as falling along one dimension. He suggested that such statements as, "The benefits of war rarely pay for its losses even for the victor" and "Defensive war is justified but other wars are not" belong on two different scales, one having to do with the economic results of war, the other with the ethics of war activity. It was argued that combining items referring to different aspects of the object made it impossible to specify exactly what the scale was measuring and also accounted for the scattering of responses, which made it difficult to assign any clear meaning to the score based on the median of the items checked.

There have been several approaches to this problem. We shall discuss here only the technique developed by Guttman, commonly called *scale analysis* or the **scalogram method.** One of the main purposes of this technique is to ascertain

TABLE 9.4   An Example of a Cumulative Scale

	Agrees to				Disagrees to			
Score	4	3	2	1	4	3	2	1
4	X	X	X	X				
3		X	X	X	X			
2			X	X	X	X		
1				X	X	X	X	
0					X	X	X	X

whether the attitude or characteristic being studied (technically termed the "universe of content" or the "universe of attributes") actually involves only a single dimension. In the Guttman procedure, a "universe of content" is considered to be unidimensional only if it yields a perfect or nearly perfect cumulative scale — that is, if it is possible to arrange all the responses of any number of respondents into a pattern like the one in Table 9.4.

The important thing about this pattern is that, if it holds, a given score on a particular series of items always has the same meaning; knowing an individual's score makes it possible to tell, without consulting the questionnaire, exactly which items the individual endorsed. Consider, for example, the following items with which respondents are asked to agree or to disagree.

1.   I do not think public officials care much about what people like me think.

2.   Voting is the only way that people like me can have any say about how the government runs things.

3.   People like me do not have any say about what the government does.

4.   Sometimes politics and government seem so complicated that a person like me cannot really understand what is going on.

If these items were found to form a perfect cumulative scale, then *all* persons with a score of two on the scale would agree with the first two items and disagree with the last two items. We would also know that a person with a score of three would disagree only with the last item, that "... politics and government seem so complicated that a person like me cannot really understand what is going on," and a person with a score of one would agree only with the first item, "I do not think public officials care much about what people like me think."

In practice, perfect cumulative, or unidimensional, scales are rarely or never found in social research, but approximations to them can often be developed. Scalogram analysis uses several criteria for deciding whether or not a particular series of items may be usefully regarded as approximating a perfect unidimensional scale. The most important of these is the reproducibility of the responses — the proportion of responses of a large number of subjects that actually fall into the pattern presented earlier. This pattern contains all the responses to particular items that would be predicted from a knowledge of the individual's total score on the series of items (the individual's "scale type"). Thus, the proportion of actual responses that fall into the pattern provides a measure of the extent to which particular responses are "reproducible" from the total score. Guttman and his co-workers have set .90 as the minimal reproducibility necessary for a series of items to be regarded as approximating a perfect scale. In the initial study, the preceding items were found to have a reproducibility of .94 (Campbell, et al., 1954). Examples of such scales are presented in Stouffer, et al. (1950).

The Guttman technique is a method of determining whether a set of items forms a unidimensional scale; as a number of writers have pointed out, it offers little guidance for selecting items that are likely to form such a scale. Edwards and Kilpatrick (1948) have suggested a method of selecting a set of statements likely to form a unidimensional scale. Called the *scale-discrimination technique*, it seems to be a sensible combination of aspects of the Thurstone and Likert approaches to scale construction, although we must acknowledge that it has not been used by more recent scale constructors. It consists of the following steps: (1) A large assortment of items dealing with the issue of study is collected. Items that are ambiguous, irrelevant, neutral, or too extreme are eliminated by inspection. (2) As in the Thurstone method of equal-appearing intervals, a large number of judges place the remaining items in eleven piles, according to their judged favorableness or unfavorableness toward the issue. The extent to which the judges agree on the placement of each item is determined, and the half of the items on which there is greatest variability or scatter of judgments is eliminated. Each of the remaining items is assigned a scale value corresponding to the median position in which it has been placed by the judges. (3) These items are then transformed into a Likert-type scale by providing for the expression of five or six degrees of agreement-disagreement in response to each item. This scale is administered to a large group of subjects, and their responses are analyzed to determine which of the items discriminate most clearly between the high scorers and the low scorers on the total scale. The resulting "discriminatory coefficients" of the various items are then plotted against their scale values. From the total list of items, twice the number wanted in the final scale are selected. The items selected are those that have the highest discriminatory coefficients in their scale interval; for example, of all the items with scale values between 8.0 and 8.9, those with the highest discriminatory coefficients are selected. An equal number of items is selected for each interval. (4) The items in the resulting list are arranged in order of their scale value. The list is then divided into two equated forms of the questionnaire by assigning all the odd-numbered items to one form and all the even-numbered items to the other.

The Guttman and related techniques represent major contributions to the methodology of questionnaire construction and analysis. However, two qualifications related to the use of unidimensional scales should be kept in mind: (1) Such a scale may not be the most effective basis either for measuring attitudes toward complex objects or for making predictions about behavior in relation to such objects; (2) a given scale may be unidimensional for one group of individuals but not for another. The same scale may be unidimensional at one time, but not at a later time for the same group. As we have indicated earlier, the movement in attitude scale construction over the last decade has been toward the development of scales measuring several dimensions.

Let us consider the first reservation. Suppose we have devised a unidimensional scale to measure attitude toward the economic results of war, another to measure attitude concerning the ethics of war activity and still others to measure whatever other aspects of attitude toward war that can be identified and measured by unidimensional scales. No single one of these scales may give an accurate reflection of an individual's attitude toward the complex concept *war* or provide a basis for predicting how the individual would vote on the question of his or her country's participation in a specific war. A greater degree of theoretical analysis concerning just what aspects of attitudes about war one wishes to measure is required. The analysis must then proceed by concentrating on the more specific measures or by developing multidimensional scales.

As for the second reservation, it is sometimes assumed that unidimensionality is a property of a measuring instrument, rather than of the patterning of an attitude among a given group of individuals. For one group, a number of items may be arranged unidimensionally in a given order; for another group, the same items may fall into a different order; for still another group, they may not form a unidimensional pattern at all. The way in which the experiences of different groups can lead to different patternings of items is illustrated in a study by Harding and Hogrefe (1952). These investigators interviewed three groups of white department-store employees. The members of group I worked in departments in which there was at least one black person in a job equal in status to their own or of higher status than their own; those in group II worked in departments in which all the blacks were in jobs of lower status than their own; those in group III were in departments where there were no blacks. The interviews included six social-distance questions, having to do with: sitting next to blacks in buses or trains, sitting at the same table with a black person in a lunchroom, taking a job in which there were both black and white people doing the same kind of work as the respondent, working under a black supervisor, living in a building in which there were both white and black families, and having a black for a personal friend. The investigators found that these six questions formed satisfactory Guttman-type scales for each of three groups, but that the question about taking a job in which there were both black and white people doing the same kind of work as the respondent fell in a different position for each of the three groups. For group I — the people who were actually in this situation — this question tied with the one about buses and trains for the "most acceptable" position. For group II — those working in departments with blacks, but in positions of unequal status — sitting next to blacks in trains and buses was more acceptable than working with them on an equal status. For those in all-white departments, both sitting next to black people in buses and trains and sitting at the same table with a black person in a lunchroom were more acceptable than working with black people on an equal status.

There is one major limitation common to all three of the preceding scaling procedures; they assign one number — that is, *a point* — to represent the individual's position. Current attitude theory demonstrates the importance of a breadth of acceptable points for the attitude. Sherif, Sherif, and Nebergall (1965) referred to *latitudes of acceptance* and *rejection*; that is, each individual has not only a preferred position on an attitude continuum but also a number of other positions that he or she considers to be acceptable. Furthermore, there may be one attitude position that the person rejects vehemently, but there may be a *range* of positions that are also considered objectionable. Two persons with different latitudes of acceptance may have similar latitudes of rejection.

SOME MODIFICATIONS OF SCALING TECHNIQUES

Not all attempts to quantify attitudes fit into the classification of scales we have described. Especially within recent years, a number of approaches have been developed that use some aspects of scaling procedure but cannot properly be described as differential, summated, or cumulative scales. We shall discuss two such approaches: the Q-sort and the semantic differential.

The Q-Sort

The operations involved in a **Q-sort** are similar to the first steps in the construction of a Thurstone scale by the method of equal-appearing intervals. The subject is presented with a large number of statements believed to be relevant to the topic under investigation and is asked to sort them into a specified number of piles—usually nine or eleven—according to some criterion. In the Thurstone technique, it will be remembered, this sorting process has the purpose of assigning scale values to statements; the criterion for sorting is not the sorter's agreement or disagreement with a statement but his or her judgment of its degree of favorableness or unfavorableness toward the object. In the Q-sort, the purpose of sorting is to get a picture of the individual's own view of, or attitude toward, the object being considered. The criterion for placing statements in the various piles is the extent of the sorter's agreement with them; the pattern into which the person sorts the statements constitutes the data for analysis of the person's position. A restriction not present in the Thurstone sorting procedure is introduced into the Q-sort; this is specification of the number of cards to be placed in a given pile. As a means of simplifying the statistical analysis, the numbers are usually specified in such a way that the sort forms a roughly normal distribution.

Let us consider an example of the use of a Q-sort in the context in which it has most frequently been employed—the study of personality. More specifically, this was a study of individual attachments to the candidate during the presidential campaign of 1968 of Senator Eugene McCarthy (Brown and Ellithorp, 1970). Each respondent was given a set of 60 statements that were printed on individual cards. The following statements, representing some of the theoretically hypothesized linkages between the individual McCarthy supporter and the McCarthy movement, are illustrative:

1. I think that a man like McCarthy, even though he had failed, would have made the country proud. He was a man I could follow.

2. The McCarthy phenomenon has allowed me to hope that changes will be made. I am confident that by 1972 someone will emerge to provide the leadership we need.

3. Maybe we weren't defeated after all. Maybe McCarthy did his job. He got rid of L. B. J., didn't he? Besides, it's not over yet by any means.

Each respondent was then asked to provide his or her viewpoint on each item by sorting the cards along a continuum that was numbered from −5 (most disagree) to 0 (no position) to +5 (most agree) and was printed on a large piece of cardboard. The respondents (34 student McCarthy supporters) ranked each of the 60 items by placing each at some point along the continuum. The 34 sets of rankings were then intercorrelated, and analysis proceeded by factor analysis of the data. In this particular study, three dimensions were found to be present in the data as demonstrated by factor analysis. Respondents did appear to be linked to the McCarthy movement on the basis of at least one of these three dimensions.

The appropriate statistical techniques to be used in the analysis of data from Q-sorts are a matter of some controversy. Some authors have held that *factor analysis*[7] is essential; others have disagreed. In the study of McCarthy's supporters, factor analysis was used.

Although Q-sorts have been used most often in studies such as this, where the emphasis is on self-image or other-person images, the method is applicable to the study of other attitudes. Subjects might be presented with sets of statements about methods of child rearing or about labor-management relations or about Chinese-Americans and then asked to sort them in respect to the extent of their agreement or disagreement with each statement. The resulting data might be used, for example, to compare a given individual's views about different ethnic groups or to compare the views of different individuals about a given group or object.

The Semantic Differential

Osgood, Suci, and Tannenbaum (1957), who developed the *semantic differential*, described it as a method for measuring the meaning of an object to an individual. It may also be thought of as a series of attitude scales. The subject is asked to rate a given concept (for example, *Irish, Republican, wife, me as I am*) on a series of seven-point bipolar rating scales. Any concept — whether it is a political issue, a person, an institution, a work of art — can be rated. The seven-point scales include such bipolar scales as the following: (1) fair-unfair, clean-dirty, good-bad, valuable-worthless; (2) large-small, strong-weak, heavy-light; (3) active-passive, fast-slow, hot-cold.

One may use the individual's responses to determine whether, for that individual, two concepts or objects are alike or different. For example, does the person's picture of "me as I am" coincide with his or her picture of "me as I would like to be," or are the two quite different? In this use, one draws a "profile" of the meaning of each concept to the individual simply by drawing lines between the points checked on each of the scales for a given concept. A technique for measuring the

---

[7]Factor analysis is a method of finding the common element or elements that underlie a set of measures. For a discussion of factor analysis, see Gorsuch (1974), Harmon (1967), or Rummel (1970).

extent of similarity between the two profiles has been developed. Similarly, one may compare two individuals' concepts of a given object by measuring the similarity of the profiles provided by their checks on the various scales.

Used in this way, the semantic differential does not place individuals on an underlying scale representing some dimension of attitude; it simply provides a method of measuring the similarity or difference between their concepts of a given object. However, the responses to subgroups of the scales can be summed up to yield scores that are interpreted as indicating the individual's position on three underlying dimensions of attitude toward the object being rated. These dimensions have been identified by using factor-analytic procedures in examining the responses of many individuals concerning many concepts or objects. It has been found that, more or less consistently, the scales labeled (1) in the preceding paragraph seem to group together; that is, an individual tends to place a given object in a similar position on each of these scales. Similarly, the scales labeled (2) seem to group together; so do the scales labeled (3). The manifest content of each scale does not clearly indicate the underlying attitudinal dimension to which it is relevant; what does it mean, for example, to rate Republican as hot or cold, as clean or dirty? But from the consistent grouping of the scales, Osgood and his colleagues have inferred that the three subgroups measure the following three dimensions of attitude: (1) the individual's *evaluation* of the object or concept being rated, corresponding to the favorable-unfavorable dimension of more traditional attitude scales; (2) the individual's perception of the *potency* or power of the object or concept; and (3) the individual's perception of the *activity* of the object or concept.

Figure 9.1 is an adaptation of one given by Osgood and his colleagues, illustrating the use of the semantic differential in plotting the meaning of several different concepts to a group of Republicans in a study that was made shortly before the 1952 presidential election in the United States. From the diagram one can see, for example, that to these subjects the concept of *Truman* is very different from the concept of *Taft* but is very similar to the concept of *socialism*. (Senator Robert A. Taft was a conservative Republican who was a leading candidate for the Republican presidential nomination in 1952; the nomination went to Eisenhower instead, however.) The concept of *Stalin* is similar to the concept of *Taft* on the potency and activity dimensions but *very different on the evaluative dimension*.

Osgood and his colleagues suggested that the semantic differential makes possible the measurement and comparison of various objects by diverse subjects; they implied that the measuring instrument is not grossly affected by the nature of the object being measured or by the type of person using the scale. If this is really true, the semantic differential would be a solution to many of the problems of attitude measurement. Osgood, Suci, and Tannenbaum provided some evidence that different types of subjects use the scales in similar ways. Thus, they indicated that Taft Republicans, Eisenhower Republicans, and Democrats used the same underlying dimensions in their reactions; so do normal persons and schizophrenic patients; so do Korean exchange students, Japanese exchange students, and United States citizens. This is impressive evidence that the scales are comparable across different types of subjects, although it seems possible that if people with widely different educational backgrounds were compared, the same results might not be obtained.

FIGURE 9.1. Model of the "Semantic Space" for Taft Republicans (adapted from Osgood, et al., 1957). Each of eight concepts is numbered according to the key below. The point at which the line for a given concept starts shows the rating of that concept on the scales *fair-unfair* and *strong-weak*. The length of the line shows the rating on the scale of *active-passive*; a solid line indicates a rating toward the *active* end of the scale; a broken line, a rating toward the *passive* end. Thus, for example, it can be seen that Stalin (4) was rated as very unfair, very strong, and very active; Truman (5) as somewhat unfair, somewhat weak, and somewhat active.

Key

1. **Taft**	5. **Truman**
2. **U.S. Policy on China**	6. **Atom bomb**
3. **Socialism**	7. **United Nations**
4. **Stalin**	8. **Eisenhower**

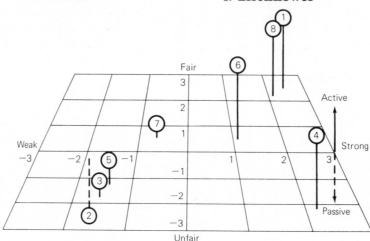

However, Osgood and his colleagues presented considerable evidence indicating that the measuring instrument is not completely comparable across concepts. The meanings of scales and their relation to the other scales vary considerably with the concept being judged. What is good, for example, depends heavily on the concept being judged; "strong" may be good in judging athletes but not in judging odors. The implication of this is that it may be quite difficult to develop rating scales that provide a consistent measurement of the underlying dimensions independently of the concepts being judged.

In completing our discussion of attitude scales, we should point out that the field of scale construction and analysis is in a period of rapid development and change. In addition to the work we have discussed, major contributions have been made by Coombs (1964); Dawes, Singer, and Lemons (1972); Lazarsfeld (1957); Loevinger (1947, 1948); Suppes and his co-workers at the Applied Mathematics and Statistics Laboratory of Stanford University (Davidson, Suppes, and Siegel, 1957); Torgerson (1958); and others.

SUMMARY

In this chapter we have discussed various methods of scaling, that is, of distinguishing among objects or individuals in terms of the degree to which they possess a given characteristic. Here, as in connection with other measurement techniques, we have raised questions about reliability and validity. Although many users of scales have investigated the reliability and validity of their measures, it is probably still true, as one writer (Ferguson, 1957) has remarked, that there has been "more measurement than validation." As we have pointed out earlier, there are understandable reasons for the lack of attention to validity — notably the difficulty of determining what would be appropriate criteria of validity for measures of complex attributes and of gathering the necessary data. However, a number of investigators have demonstrated that, with ingenuity, one may develop useful criterion measures. It is perhaps to be expected that in relatively new research fields, such as the social sciences, more attention should at first be paid to the development of a variety of measuring techniques than to their validation. Nevertheless, it seems clear that research in the social sciences would now be advanced by greater attention to the validity of the instruments used.

Examples and discussion in this chapter have concerned the scaling of attitudes rather than other individual or group properties. This should not be taken to mean that the scaling techniques are not applicable to other characteristics of individuals or collectivities — rather, some way was needed to present scaling techniques in a brief and clear format. The reader is referred to the references on measurement and scaling made in this chapter for many examples of scaling things other than attitudes, as well as examples of more sophisticated scaling techniques.

Indirect Assessment

TWO TYPES OF INDIRECT METHODS

PROJECTIVE METHODS
Projective Methods in the Study of Social Attitudes
Pictorial Techniques
Verbal Techniques
Techniques Using Other Sense Modalities
Play Techniques
Psychodrama and Sociodrama as Techniques

MORE STRUCTURED INDIRECT TESTS
Measures Presented as Tests of Knowledge or Ability
Information Tests
Tests of Ability To Think Critically
Tests Employing Bias in Learning and Memory
Estimation of Group Opinion and Social Norms
Judgments of Attitudinally Relevant Persons or Materials
Measures Based on Selection of Classification Principles
Techniques Involving Perceptual Responses
Measures Based on Physiological Reactions

SUBSTITUTE MEASURES

A NOTE ON VALIDATION

SUMMARY

As we noted in Chapters 8 and 9, techniques that rely on our own report of our behavior, beliefs, and feelings presuppose that we are both *willing* and *able* to give such personal information about ourselves. But this is not always true. People may be unwilling to discuss controversial topics or to reveal intimate information about themselves. They may be reluctant to express their true attitudes if they believe that such attitudes are generally disapproved. Or they may be unable to give the desired information either because they cannot easily put their feelings into words or because they are unaware of their feelings about the matter in question.

To get around these limitations, techniques have been devised that do not depend upon people's self-insight or their willingness to reveal their attitudes or behavior. In this chapter, we deal with techniques that require only minimal cooperation on the part of the individuals being studied. In that sense, the techniques of this chapter are "in between" the techniques in which the individual is presented with some direct questions (discussed in Chapters 8 and 9), or the techniques (to be covered in Chapter 11) that use data already available, providing indirect evidence of attitudes or behavior. Many methods discussed in this chapter involve some degree of deception and some invasion of privacy because individuals are induced to respond under some pretext other than the investigator's true interest and because they are encouraged to reveal matters that they might perhaps wish to conceal. Because of these reasons, these techniques run the risk of being unethical. We want to note that concern at this point even while reminding the reader of the general discussion of ethical issues in social research presented in Chapter 15.

Another question about these techniques is that of their validity as indicators of the characteristics they are intended to measure. Many of these measures are highly ingenious, but few of them have been subjected to any extensive evaluation of either their reliability or validity. Questions of this sort will be discussed as we introduce specific measures as well as more generally at the end of the chapter.

Despite these limitations of indirect tests, there is one point on which they score an unequivocal plus: their great diversity of approach. As we pointed out in Chapter 7, no single measure provides a completely adequate indicator of the concept it is intended to represent; any given measure is subject to other influences in addition to the one the investigator is trying to assess, and our best hope lies in using a number of different measures, angling in on the central concept from different directions. The great variety of indirect techniques that have been devised makes a real contribution in this respect.

TWO TYPES OF INDIRECT METHODS

Indirect tests can be classified in a number of ways. We find it useful to divide them first into two broad classes, differing in their degree of structure. The less structured ones are commonly referred to as **projective methods;** typically, they involve some sort of imaginative activity on the part of the individual in interpreting ambiguous stimuli. Among the second type, the *more structured* ones, we may distinguish the following categories: measures involving bias in performance of objective (or supposedly objective) tasks; measures involving judgments of attitudinally relevant objects or materials; measures based on perceptual responses; measures based on involuntary physiological responses; measures involving overt behavior; and substitute measures. As elsewhere, these are not hard-and-fast classifications; some techniques have more than one of these characteristics, and their placement in one or another category is a matter of judgment.[1]

PROJECTIVE METHODS

Projective methods are based on the assumption that how an individual organizes a relatively unstructured stimulus reflects his or her perception of the world and response to it.

Projective methods were first devised by psychologists and psychiatrists concerned with the diagnosis and treatment of patients suffering from emotional disorders; that remains their major use. For this purpose, the tests attempt to give a comprehensive picture of the individual's personality structure, emotional needs, conflicts, and other feelings. To discuss either the theory underlying these tests or the methods of interpreting them is beyond the scope of this book. They are primarily tools of the clinical psychologist rather than the research-oriented social scientist; moreover, their use requires intensive specialized training. However, in view of their great usefulness in the investigation of certain types of problems in social

[1]For a somewhat different way of categorizing indirect tests, see Kidder and Campbell (1970) or Lemon (1973). Throughout this chapter, we have made extensive use both of those reviews and of Campbell's earlier review (1950) of indirect measures.

psychology, sociology, political science, and anthropology, we shall briefly describe their general characteristics, mention some of the more frequently used tests, and indicate the kinds of social relations research in which they have been used.[2]

It will be sufficient, for our purposes, to note the following characteristics of these techniques. The stimuli are capable of arousing many different kinds of reactions: for example, an inkblot, which can be perceived in different ways; a picture, which can elicit a variety of stories; a set of dolls, which can be arranged in many ways. There are no right or wrong answers, nor is the respondent faced with a set of limited alternatives. The emphasis is on the respondent's perception of the material, the meaning given to it, the way the respondent organizes or manipulates it. The nature of the stimuli and the way they are presented do not clearly indicate the purpose of the test or how the responses will be interpreted. The individual is not asked to talk directly about himself or herself. The ostensible subject matter is the inkblot, the picture, the dolls, and not the individual's own experiences or feelings. However, the responses are interpreted as indicating the individual's own view of the world.

In a projective test, the individual's responses are not taken at face value — that is, with the meaning that the subject presumably would expect them to have — but are interpreted in terms of some preestablished psychological conceptualization of what responses to the specific test situation mean. This underlying conceptualization provides the framework for interpreting the responses. Usually, the system of interpretation considers responses not in isolation but in respect to patterns. The tester attempts to arrive at a psychologically coherent picture of the individual by deriving the full meaning of any particular response from the total record of the person's replies.

One of the most frequently used projective techniques in the clinical setting is the Rorschach Inkblot Test, consisting of ten cards, each with a copy of an inkblot. The subject is asked, "What might this be?" Another commonly used technique is the Thematic Apperception Test, abbreviated TAT. This test consists of a series of pictures about which the subject is asked to tell stories. In some of the pictures the persons or objects are quite clearly represented; in others they are not. Some of the pictures deal with ordinary or usual events; some with situations that are unusual or bizarre.

Techniques such as these are designed to elicit a rich sample of behavior, from which a great variety of inferences can be drawn. Some inferences may have to do with adaptive aspects of the person's behavior, that is, how well he or she carries out the task posed by the test (to tell what an inkblot looks like, to make up a story, and so on). Others have to do with expressive aspects. How the person deals with the materials of the test is taken as reflecting the "style" of his or her personality; for example, an individual's approach to the test may show constriction or expansiveness, intellectual control or impulsiveness, and so on. Inferences about adaptive and

---

[2]The student who is interested in pursuing the subject of projective techniques in the study of personality should consult one of the volumes that give descriptions of the various methods — for example, Anderson and Anderson (1951) or Zubin, et al. (1965).

expressive aspects are generally considered relevant to a description of the individual's personality structure. In addition, from the content of what the individual says, inferences may be drawn about needs, attitudes, values, conflicts, ideologies, and self-concepts. Such inferences rest on the assumption that what the individual perceives in the test materials represents an externalization or projection of processes within himself.

Other commonly used tests are word association, sentence completion, doll play, and figure drawing. In the word-association test, the subject is presented with a list of words; after each, he or she responds with the first word that comes to mind. Both the rate and the content of the person's responses may indicate areas of emotional disturbance. In the sentence-completion test, the first words of a possible sentence are given, and the individual is asked to complete it. Like the word-association test, the sentence-completion method may provide clues to areas of emotional disturbance; any given area may be investigated by presenting the respondent with relevant sentence beginnings. In the doll-play procedure, the subject is given a set of dolls, usually representing adults and children of both sexes, and is either encouraged to play freely with them or to show how they would act in various circumstances. This procedure is, of course, especially appropriate for use with children; it is well suited for eliciting feelings about family relationships. In the figure-drawing test, the subject is asked to "draw a person," to "draw a man," or to "draw a woman." The assumption is that the drawing represents the person's image of himself or herself or of important figures in the person's life (for example, in the case of a young boy, his father and mother) and that unusual features represent areas of conflict or anxiety. In addition to the relatively specific function ascribed here to each of these tests, each of them may be used as a basis for broader interpretations about the individual's personality.

Many of these techniques have been subjected to much investigation; standardized methods of administration, scoring, and interpretation have been published. Nevertheless, questions have been repeatedly raised about their validity, and the research evidence on this point is far from conclusive. This matter will be discussed in more detail in the summary section of this chapter.

Despite these questions about validity, projective tests from which inferences about personality structure may be drawn have been used fruitfully not only in clinical research and practice but in studies concerned with the relation of individual personality to various social and cultural factors. For example, in a study of alienation, Keniston (1965) found TAT stories to be a rich source of clues about differences between alienated and nonalienated college students. Many of the stories told by alienated students had a strange, weird, primitive, magical tone, whereas those told by nonalienated students were more realistic, even conventional; he commented that these archaic themes indicate that the alienated students are, "for better or worse, unusually open to that deepest stratum of personality wherein these images reside." In respect to specific content, he found that stories told by alienated students were more likely than those of nonalienated students to have themes depicting idyllic situations that abruptly and traumatically ended; of dominating and possessive older women who frequently restrained men's sexual activity or aggressiveness; of inner conflict, misery, death, destruction, and disaster.

Projective Methods in the Study of Social Attitudes

When the focus of an investigation is on a specific characteristic or on the content of an individual's attitudes toward some social object rather than on the person's general personality structure, projective techniques in the form in which they are used in the study of personality are not very helpful. Yet a projective approach frequently seems desirable as a way of encouraging in respondents a state of freedom and spontaneity of expression. This is especially likely to be the case when there is reason to believe that respondents cannot easily evaluate or describe their motivations or feelings (for example, when asked to indicate the strength of their motivation toward achievement or toward affiliative social relationships) or when there are topics on which respondents may hesitate to express their opinions directly for fear of disapproval by the investigator or when respondents are likely to consider direct questions as an unwarranted invasion of privacy or to find them threatening for some other reason.

Several clever techniques have been developed for use in such situations. These share some of the characteristics of the projective methods already described. They have the capacity of arousing many different reactions, they encourage a free response on the part of individuals, they do not ask them to talk directly about themselves or their own views or feelings, yet their responses are taken as reflecting their attitudes. In line with the purpose of tapping specific attitudes or characteristics, the test materials usually provide a more specific subject-matter focus than do those used in tests designed to yield information about broad personality patterns; for example, the individual may be presented with a picture in which some of the characters are white and others black or with a photograph that he or she is told represents a union meeting or with a cartoon in which a leader is giving orders to a group.

Of course, if no precautions are taken, the general purpose of the test, or at least the topic with which it is concerned, may be quite apparent. However, two procedures may be used in the construction of a projective attitude test to make its objective or the topic involved less patent. A fictitious purpose may be ascribed, which appears plausible in the light of what is demanded of the subject; and, in addition to the stimuli relevant to the investigator's objective, "neutral" or unrelated stimuli may be included, so that the subject's suspicions are not aroused by having the same theme or issue occur in every stimulus situation that is presented.

When limited time prevents the inclusion of neutral stimuli or when the respondents are highly sophisticated, it may be impossible to conceal the purpose of a projective attitude instrument. But this is not always a serious disadvantage. Although respondents may try to distort their responses to create a favorable impression, they cannot always do so. In telling a story about a man and a woman working on a task together, subjects may still reveal their beliefs or feelings by automatically assigning the woman to an inferior role or by unwittingly attributing behavior to the woman along stereotyped lines.[3] The subjects may not even realize that some of

[3]We do not wish to suggest that there is a simple correspondence between a person's beliefs or feelings and the characters he or she depicts in a story. A subject may depict a woman as being in an inferior social role in a story without feeling that this is the only appropriate role for women.

the beliefs and views they have about women are indicative of bias; they may assume that most people see women as "dependent" or "emotional" because that is the way they are. Of course, it is still true that conscious attempts to distort may reduce the extent of valid information obtained.

When the purpose of a projective test is apparent, one may ask these questions: Why bother with such a test in view of the time and effort involved in its construction and application? Why not simply use a direct interview or questionnaire? There are several reasons for preferring the projective test even though it may be transparent. Each of these must be evaluated for each particular situation.

1. People may find it easier to express themselves if they are not explicitly talking about their own feelings and attitudes even though they realize that what they say may be so interpreted. They may have some distance from the topic if they can ostensibly talk impersonally and some security in not having to say in so many words that this is how they themselves feel.

2. Even when they have the best intentions in the world, the subjects may be unable to describe their feelings and attitudes as accurately as they may be discerned in the projective test situation. Suppose we ask a man, "Why do you usually vote for Republican rather than Democratic candidates?" He may well have been totally insensitive to this aspect of his behavior. He may literally not know. But suppose we ask him what his party preference is and what he considers the good and bad points of the Republican and Democratic parties and candidates to be (Campbell, Converse, Miller, and Stokes, 1960). We may readily determine what the good and bad things about the parties and candidates are that the respondent mentions. It is also a simpler matter to determine with which political party the respondent identifies. Voting preference is very often a consequence of reference group identifications (with one of the political parties) and likes and dislikes about the parties and candidates. Although this is not strictly a projective technique, it is sometimes possible to predict a respondent's vote more accurately than he or she can if one has information concerning his or her partisan feelings. It soon becomes evident, for instance, that many Americans fail to "vote for the man, not the party," when the researcher scrutinizes this kind of data.

3. Sometimes access to certain populations of potential subjects (for example, school children, workers in a factory, and so on) is withheld if the topic under investigation is made explicit to the subjects, but granted if it remains tacit even though obvious. This raises a series of questions concerning the meaning of **"informed consent,"** which are discussed in Chapter 15 more thoroughly.

4. Even though the purpose of a projective attitude test is apparent, it may produce more extensive information than a questionnaire or even an interview with open-ended questions would. In the descriptions of the pictured situations, for example, we may see how attitudes color perception or what aspects of attitude (feelings, beliefs, and so on) are significant for the individual.

The projective techniques that have been devised for the study of social attitudes vary in the effectiveness with which they mask their purpose, in the richness of personality material they reveal, in the ambiguity of the stimulus presented to the subject, and in the skill and effort required to collect and analyze responses. Only a few of the specific adaptations of these techniques have been used in more than one investigation. We shall briefly describe the major techniques because they are relevant to the study of social relations and because they do not usually require the complex skills demanded by the projective methods for the study of personality. They must, however, be used and interpreted cautiously.

We shall group the many specific adaptations of projective tests for the study of social attitudes in terms of certain general materials and methods of approach: pictorial, verbal, play, and psychodramatic techniques.

Pictorial Techniques

Pictorial techniques have long been popular in the projective study of social attitudes and other socially relevant characteristics. The Thematic Apperception Test (TAT) has been the stimulus for several ventures.

The most extensive of these has been the work of McClelland and Atkinson and their co-workers on achievement motivation (Atkinson, et al., 1954; Atkinson, 1958; Atkinson and Feather, 1966; McClelland, 1965; McClelland, et al., 1953; and many others). Using some cards from the original TAT and others specially designed to portray situations in which one might (or might not) see achievement-related themes (for example, two men looking at a machine; a boy seated at a table with an open book before him), these investigators developed standardized techniques for scoring the degree of achievement motivation shown in stories told in response to the cards. Different investigators have used different sets of pictures, but the basic scoring principles remain the same. Dozens of studies show relationships between this measure of achievement motivation and child-rearing practices, vocational aspiration and achievement, and behavior in a wide variety of situations, experimental and otherwise.

Zigler and Child (1969), reviewing some of this literature, raised serious questions about the validity of the measures. They pointed out that one of the problems is the great variety of behaviors that have been considered to reflect achievement orientation; in other words, there is a great deal of ambiguity present in the validating criterion. However, part of the difficulty is attributable to the measuring instrument. The extent of achievement-related themes in stories told in response to the same cards is influenced by the wording of the instructions (for example, whether the respondents are told that the stories they tell are an indication of their creative ability or whether they are led to believe that they are simply helping in the development of the instrument) and by immediate past experiences (for example, whether respondents have just been in problem-solving situations in which they succeeded or failed). Thus, the stories told do not always represent stable characteristics of the individual.

McClelland and Atkinson and their co-workers have also developed a method for scoring TAT stories on the basis of "need for affiliation," that is, concern with establishing and maintaining positive affective relations with other people. Less research has been done with respect to this characteristic than with respect to achievement motivation, and with even less clear-cut results. Part of the difficulty has been with the criterion measures. Most experimental investigations involving affiliation motivation have used as their behavioral indicators choices such as whether to be alone or with others, usually strangers, in an anxiety-producing situation. Such indicators represent a rather different definition of "affiliation" than that used in scoring the stories.

TAT-type pictures have also been used to study more specific social attitudes.[4] Burwen and Campbell (1957) used stories told about TAT pictures as one of many measures in a study designed to investigate the concept of a generalized attitude toward authority. Each measure was used in relation to two kinds of figures: those in positions of authority, either generalized or specific, in relation to the respondent; and those having the same status as the respondent. Both direct and indirect measures were used. The reliability (consistency) of scores based on the TAT cards involving authority figures was .55; this compared with a reliability of .46 for a photo-judging task, .56 for an autobiographical inventory, .59 for a direct attitude questionnaire, .75 for a sociometric questionnaire, and .24 for an adjective checklist; in other words, although the reliability of the scores based on the TAT was not high, it was about as good as that of most of the other instruments used. A much more serious problem was the fact that scores for favorableness of attitude toward authority figures based on the TAT stories correlated .49 with scores for favorableness of attitude toward peers derived from the TAT scores, whereas the correlations between attitude-toward-authority scores based on the TAT and scores of attitude toward boss or father derived from other instruments ranged from only .03 to .14. In general, in this study, the investigators found that the correlations between attitudes toward different figures as measured by similar instruments were higher than correlations between attitudes toward similar figures as measured by different instruments. Given this fact and the diversity of measures they had used, they concluded that attitudes toward authority are probably not so generalized as has often been assumed. More specifically, they concluded that, in order to have any confidence in the meaning of a score based on a specific instrument, such as the TAT, one must include not only items (in this case, pictures) relevant to the concept in which one is interested (in this case, attitude toward authority figures) but also items relevant to some other concept (in this case, attitude toward peers) and compare the two scores.

TAT-type pictures have been used in a number of studies of attitudes toward minority groups, some of which have met this criteron of presenting not only cards that included minority-group figures but also comparable scenes that did not.

Vaughan and Thompson (1961) developed sets of matched TAT-type cards to study the attitudes of white New Zealand children toward Maoris. The matched pairs of cards were identical except that in one the crucial figure was Maori, in the other white. Stories told by white children who had had little contact with Maoris showed significantly more unfavorable attitudes than those told by children who had greater contact. (Maoris are native inhabitants of New Zealand.)

Another pictorial technique makes use of cartoons. Rather than being asked to construct a whole story, the respondent is shown a scene drawn in cartoon form, with the dialogue for one character given; there is a blank balloon for the other character, and the respondent is asked what this second character would probably say. The model for this type of measure is the Rosenzweig Picture-Frustration Test.

---

[4]The construction and use of undisguised attitude scales are discussed in Chapter 9.

In its original form, this was a clinical test; all the pictures portrayed situations of frustration for the second character; the responses given for him are scored in terms of whether they indicated a tendency to place the blame on others or on oneself or not to react in terms of blame. J. F. Brown (1947) adapted this test for use in the study of ethnic attitudes. The Brown adaptation included a number of pictures in which blacks or Jews frustrate whites or non-Jews and others in which whites or non-Jews frustrate blacks or Jews. The respondent fills out a blank space indicating what the frustrated person says in reply. The type of reply is considered by Brown to be indicative of the person's attitude toward the minority group in question.

As with many of the pictorial techniques, the visual cues necessary to portray the different ethnic groups make the purpose of the test apparent to any but the most naive respondents. Nevertheless, Sommer (1954), using a modified form of Brown's version of the test, was able to pick out with considerable success not only individuals who scored high and those who scored low on a self-report scale of attitude toward blacks but also a subgroup who had been instructed to "fake," that is, to respond to the Picture-Frustration Test as if they were unprejudiced, even though their self-report scores showed them to be unfavorable toward blacks.

Fromme (1941) used cartoons in a somewhat different way. He showed people political cartoons, each with four alternative captions that he believed represented a full range of favorable and unfavorable attitudes toward the topic at issue in the cartoon, and asked them to choose the one that best fitted the cartoon. He then used the cartoons and their captions to stimulate discussion and to obtain qualitative insights into political attitudes.

Verbal Techniques

Verbal projective techniques, like pictorial ones, present incomplete or ambiguous stimuli to which the individual must respond in his or her own way. As with the pictorial tests, many of the verbal techniques had their origin in clinical psychological measures.

A simple verbal technique involves sentence-completion. The individual is presented with a series of incomplete sentences, which he is asked to complete, usually under some time pressure to ensure spontaneity of response.[5]

This technique has been used for studying attitudes of many kinds. For example, Kerr (1943) used it in a study of national stereotypes held by English people. Some of the sentence beginnings were:

> The thing I do admire America for is . . .
> The trouble with America is . . .
> When I think of the Russians I think of . . .
> If the British and Soviet armies fight side by side they . . .
> If you invite an American to your home he may . . .

[5]For detailed discussion of the sentence-completion technique as a method of studying personality, see Rohde (1946), Rotter and Willerman (1947), Rotter (1951), and Stein (1947). For a detailed discussion of this approach in measuring ego development, see Loevinger and Wessler (1970) and Loevinger, Wessler, and Redmore (1970).

Burwen, Campbell, and Kidd (1956) used an incomplete-sentence test as one of a number of measures of attitudes toward superiors and subordinates in an air force population, with sentence stems such as

He never felt comfortable in the presence of . . .
Whenever he saw his superior coming he . . .

The test showed moderate internal reliability (.69) but very low correlations with other measures designed to assess the same attitudes.

In another study using a variety of methods, Maher, Watt, and Campbell (1960) compared a sentence-completion test with a direct self-report attitude scale on attitudes toward family and law in a prison population. The scores on the two types of measures have a correlation of .50 for attitudes toward family, .51 for attitudes toward law. Both measures showed the same pattern of relationship to type of crime committed, although the direct measure was slightly more effective in distinguishing among prisoners who had committed different types of crimes.

Sentences must explicitly mention the attitudinal object or group in which the investigator is interested to elicit relevant responses; thus the intent is probably obvious to all but the most naive respondents. This is probably true even if neutral items are interspersed with the crucial ones.

Similar in some respects to the open-ended question (discussed in Chapters 8 and 9) is the so-called projective question. The subject is asked to respond to a vague question (for example, "What are you?"), and the response is taken not at face value but rather from the point of view of the perceptions, beliefs, sentiments, and motives that predispose the individual to answer in the way he or she does. Such questions frequently take the form of asking about a possible event in the future ("What would you do if you inherited a large fortune?"), about an imaginary event ("Suppose that a woman from Mars came down to this planet and you were the first person she saw and she asked what kinds of people there were on earth; what would you tell her?"), or about something the subject clearly is not in a position to know.

Sometimes projective questions take the form of asking about other people's views. The assumption here is that respondents may hesitate to express critical or unpopular views as their own but will put them into the mouths of other people. Smith (1954) gave the following illustration from the field of market research. Instead of asking housewives, "What do you think are the objectionable features of this cleanser?" the interviewer said, "Some women who use this cleanser find a lot of faults with it. I wonder if you can guess what they are objecting to."

Again, as in the case of sentence completion, it must be noted that one cannot always safely assume that respondents' answers to questions of this sort really reflect their own feelings, especially if the questions are of the "most people" form. Maccoby and Maccoby (1954) gave the following striking example:

. . . a young woman being interviewed about her attitudes toward her job situation was asked: "How do most of the girls [*sic*] in the office feel about the supervisor?" She answered, "They think he's wonderful. They'll do anything for him." At which point the interviewer followed with: "And how about you—how do you feel about him?" She made the reply: "I really detest him. I'm trying to transfer out of the unit."

Another verbal technique is that of asking the respondent to describe the kind of person who would behave in a specified way. This approach has been used most frequently in market research, to elicit respondents' "images" of a given product, but it would seem easily adaptable to the investigation of attitudes of other kinds. One use of this approach in market research (Haire, 1950) has become almost a classic. In a conventional survey of attitudes toward Nescafé, an instant coffee (a product that was new at the time), women were asked, "Do you use instant coffee?" If the answer was no, they were asked, "What do you dislike about it?" Most of the replies were along the line, "I don't like the flavor." The investigators, suspecting that this was a stereotype that did not express the underlying reasons for rejection of instant coffee, switched to an indirect approach. Half of the sample of housewives interviewed were presented with the following shopping list made out by a hypothetical woman:

> pound and a half of hamburger
> 2 loaves Wonder bread
> bunch of carrots
> 1 can Rumford's Baking Powder
> Nescafé instant coffee
> 2 cans Del Monte peaches
> 5 lbs. potatoes

The other half of the sample were presented with the same list, except that "1 lb. Maxwell House Coffee (Drip Ground)" was substituted for the Nescafé. Each respondent was asked to read the shopping list and then to write a brief description of the personality and character of the woman who had made it out. The differences between the descriptions of the woman who bought Nescafé and the one who bought Maxwell House coffee were striking. Almost half of the women who read the list containing the instant coffee described its writer as lazy and failing to plan her household purchases well; the woman who bought the drip-ground coffee was hardly ever described in these terms. In addition, the woman who bought the instant coffee was more often described as a spendthrift and a poor wife. A check of the pantries of the respondents showed that most of the women who described the buyer of the instant coffee in these unfavorable terms did not have instant coffee on their shelves; those who did not describe her unfavorably were much more likely to have instant coffee. In other words, it seemed clear that the decision to buy instant coffee was influenced at least as much by attitudes about what constitutes good housekeeping as by reaction to the flavor of instant coffee. These attitudes could not so easily have been elicited by direct questioning. This study was reported in 1950; were it repeated today, we would hope to see a change in the respondents' attitudes toward women and housework.

Techniques Using Other Sense Modalities

Projective techniques using stimuli involving other **sense modalities** have been employed in the study of personality. For example, Grings (1942) developed a technique called the "Verbal Summator" or "Tautophone." A recording of indistinct vowel sounds was presented with instructions such as these: "This is a recording of a man talking. He is not speaking very plainly, but if you listen carefully, you will be able to tell what he is saying. I'll play it over and over again, so that you can get it, but be sure to tell me as soon as you have an idea of what he is saying." Grings reported that the "cover story" was almost always accepted without question and that people managed to produce intelligible verbal content without being aware that it came entirely from themselves.

A visual variation of this approach was Rechtschaffen and Mednick's (1955) Autokinetic Word Technique, which took advantage of the fact that a single dot of light in an otherwise dark room appears to move. These investigators told respondents that the light was spelling out words that they were to read and report. All respondents "saw" words and, when told about the nature of the experiment, were shocked to learn that they themselves had fabricated the content.

As far as we know, these techniques have not been used in the study of attitude or other specific socially relevant characteristics. However, as Kidder and Campbell (1970) suggested, they could easily be put to such use by adding instructions indicating what the man is talking about or instructing that the light is spelling out words about some specified topic, such as pornography, gun control, Mexican-Americans — whatever attitudinal object the investigator is interested in.

Play Techniques

Techniques involving the manipulation of dolls have frequently been used to study children's attitudes. Hartley and Schwartz (1948) investigated children's attitudes toward different religious groups by presenting them with identical sets of dolls against backgrounds containing symbols from the Jewish religion, Catholic religion, or no religion, and asking them to play out situations such as a birthday party, a ride on a school bus, and so on. The results indicated that children recognized the religious symbols and that their play with the dolls reflected attitudes toward different religious groups in a meaningful way.

Dolls are useful in studying how people use space and distance in their relationships with others. K. B. Little (1968) used the spatial placement of dolls and figure silhouettes to study social interaction among five national groups — American, Swedish, Greek, southern Italian, and Scottish. Subjects were asked to place four gray plastic dolls on a piece of newsprint so that they "looked natural" in 19 different situations. Each situation — designed to portray a different quality in acquaintance and affective tone, authority interactions, and intimacy of interaction — was defined for the subject on a typed card.

Little found that native-born persons in each society maintained the same overall ordering of distances among the different types of situation, more intimate situations producing the closest arrangement of the dolls (see also Little, 1965). Two Mediterranean groups — Greeks and southern Italians — however, placed the dolls closer together than did the other groups. The results were interpreted by Little as reflecting the different views that these societies maintain about the appropriateness of spatially close "contact" in social relationships.

Little concluded that the " . . . use of dolls, silhouettes, etc., in free placement, particularly with instructional sets, provides a sensitive and reliable method for assessing not only the schemata themselves but also the marked individual differences that characterize them"(1968, p. 6).

Psychodrama and Sociodrama as Techniques

Like most of the other projective techniques, **psychodrama** and **sociodrama** were originally developed in contexts other than research. These methods require that individuals act out roles, either as themselves (psychodrama) or as somebody else (sociodrama), as they would in a real-life situation. How they play their roles and the history that they create for the characters they portray provide insight into their attitudes. The investigator, in much the same way as an observer, can record the behavior for later analysis, can categorize it on the spot, or can rate it in terms of various scales.

Psychodrama and sociodrama are among the few tools available for the systematic investigation of social *skills*. They make it possible to place persons in situations in which one can observe how skillfully they behave in relation to other people. For example, Stanton and Litwak (1955) presented actual and potential foster parents with situations of interpersonal stress in which they were instructed to behave in a specified way (defined as not showing specified undersirable or neurotic kinds of behavior); for instance, in one scene the prospective or actual foster father was instructed that he was to play the role of a married man having dinner with his parents; the investigator, playing the role of the man's father, treated his son like a child, criticized his wife, and put him in the wrong. These investigators found that ratings based on a half-hour's role playing were better predictors of people's behavior as foster parents (as rated by case workers who had sustained contact with them) than were ratings based on 12 hours of intensive interviewing by a trained social worker.

Stanton, Back, and Litwak (1956) included a role-playing approach in an interview survey of attitudes toward public housing projects on the part of slum dwellers in Puerto Rico. They reported that respondents participated willingly and that the approach was successful in discovering the limits of positive and negative feelings. These investigators stressed the importance of designing the scene specifically to elicit responses relevant to the particular behavior or attitude in which the investigator is interested.

MORE STRUCTURED INDIRECT TESTS

Investigators of social attitudes have been interested in developing tests that would have the advantages of projective techniques — disguising the investigator's purpose — but that would be simpler to administer, score, and interpret. A number of structured disguised tests have been devised.

Many tests of this kind are based on the fact that our attitudes are likely to influence our perceptions, beliefs, judgments, and memory. That this is so has been demonstrated in a number of studies. For example, Bartlett's classic experiment (1932) on the recall of pictorial materials and stories revealed the influence of social attitudes on memory. In one of these experiments, students at Cambridge University twice read a story drawn from the folklore of a culture foreign to them; the story dealt with matters with which they had little familiarity. After varying periods of time, the subjects were asked to repeat the story as accurately as possible. Bartlett found that the reproductions all showed systematic changes, increasing with time, which could partly be accounted for by the cultural frame of reference of the subjects.

We have classified structured indirect tests into the following categories: techniques involving performance on objective (or allegedly objective) tests, techniques involving judgments of attitudinally relevant objects or materials, measures involving selection of classificatory principles, measures involving perceptual responses, measures involving involuntary physiological responses, and measures involving overt behavior in standardized experimental situations.

Measures Presented as Tests of Knowledge or Ability

Findings such as those of Bartlett, cited earlier, have given rise to the development of tests that appear to the subjects to be objective but are so difficult that the subjects' attitudes influence their performance. To the respondent, the task and orientation are similar to those of an achievement or ability test. In contrast with most projective tests, in which the individual is told there are no objectively correct answers, the subject is told there *are* right and wrong responses.

The rationale underlying the use of such tests is essentially the same as that underlying the use of projective techniques: When there is no clear, objectively verifiable basis for choosing among alternative responses to a situation, individuals' responses will tend to reflect their predispositions. Of course, the stronger such predispositions are, the more likely they are to be reflected in the individual's responses.

Kidder and Campbell (1970) have presented a design for constructing such tests:

> Find a task which all your respondents will take as objective and in which all will strive to do well. Stress the importance of accuracy and emphasize the fact that there are right and wrong answers. Make the task sufficiently difficult so that answers will not reflect differential knowledge on the part of the respondents. At the same time, tell the subjects that the test is admittedly hard and they may have to guess when they are in doubt. Load the test with content relevant to the attitude under study. Look for systematic error or for persistent selectivity of performance. If such be found, it seems an adequate basis for the inference of an attitude [p. 349].

Information tests

A number of investigators have used measures presented as tests of information to assess attitudes toward a variety of social objects. Typically, these take the form of multiple-choice tests. They differ in whether a correct answer is included or whether the respondent must choose between *equally wrong* answers differing in implications about the object and, if a correct answer is included, whether it is counted in the scoring.

Such indirect measures are useful in skill-testing situations. For example, in an extensive study of superior-subordinate relationships within bomber crews, Campbell and Damarin (1961) used an indirect measure called a "Test of Leadership Knowledge" along with nine other measures. The respondents were told that the leadership knowledge questions were based on ". . . the findings of scientific research on problems of leadership." Furthermore, the instructions attempted to motivate them to do well by the claim that "some persons will do much better than others on this test, because of their experience in leadership or because of their better understanding of leadership problems. . . ." A sample question read, "The foremen who spend more time supervising their men than in working alongside the men are: the high production supervisors; the low production supervisors; the two groups are equal on this." Scores on the information test correlated significantly with scores on a direct scale of attitudes toward authority, a sentence-completion measure, and the F-scale, which measures authoritarianism; however, they showed no correlation with the six other measures used in the study. In particular, they were not significantly related to ratings by instructors and by other crew members, whereas two direct attitude scales correlated significantly with such ratings.

In general, tests in which attitudes are inferred from measures presented as tests of information have been found to correlate significantly with direct attitude measures and discriminate among criterion groups with known attitudes. However, in all of the studies where direct attitude measures as well as information tests have been used, the direct measures show higher internal consistency. Moreover, in almost all of the studies where both types of measure have been administered to criterion groups, the direct measures have discriminated more effectively. One problem with information tests is the difficulty of devising equally plausible alternative responses that *differ* in their direction away from the correct answer. Another is the ambiguity of implications of information items. For example, an indirect test item may ask the respondent to estimate the proportion of college graduates who are black. One respondent who underestimates the proportion of black college graduates in the United States may do so because of a belief that blacks are inferior in intelligence to whites; another may do so because of a belief that blacks are not given equal educational opportunities. Similarly, one respondent who overestimates the proportion of blacks among those arrested for various crimes may do so because of a belief that blacks have more criminal tendencies and less self-control than whites; another may do so because of awareness that some police discriminate against blacks. Finally, variables of intelligence and of actual knowledge about the topic may contribute to how one answers such information tests.

Thus, although information tests may be a useful part of a battery of measures, they do not seem sufficiently pure or sensitive measures of attitudes to warrant placing great confidence in scores of favorableness or unfavorableness based on them. As Kidder and Campbell (1970) suggested, their greatest value may lie in the opportunity they afford to explore the pattern of individuals' beliefs about an attitudinal object.

Tests of ability to think critically

Syllogistic inference does not always proceed logically; frequently it is affected by the content of the syllogism. G. B. Watson (1925) included as part of his "Measurement of Fair-Mindedness" an inference test composed of statements of fact followed by several conclusions that might be drawn. For example, one statement was:

> Statistics show that in the United States, of one hundred men starting out at an age of 25, at the end of forty years, one will be wealthy, while fifty-four will be dependent upon relatives or charity for support.[6]

This statement was followed by several possible conclusions:

> The present social order cheats the many for the benefit of the few.
> The average young man, under present conditions, cannot count on being wealthy at the age of 65.
> Most men are shiftless, lazy, or extravagant, otherwise they would not need to be dependent.
> The one man is living upon luxuries ground out of the bones of the masses of common people.
> Some day the workers will rise in revolt.
> No such conclusion can fairly be drawn.

The subjects were asked to check only those conclusions that were established by the facts given in the statement without drawing upon any other evidence. They were cautioned to check only those inferences that were certain, not those that were merely probable. Checking anything other than "No such conclusion can fairly be drawn" or the alternative that simply rephrased the original statement (in this case, item 2) was taken as evidence of bias.

Watson's tests of fair-mindedness have been expanded in the Watson-Glazer Tests of Critical Thinking (Glazer, 1941), but the Watson-Glazer tests seem to have been used only as direct measures of the ability to do critical thinking, rather than as indirect indicators of attitudes toward various social groups or social policies; nevertheless, it would seem that they could be used as indirect measures by appropriate scoring.

In fact, Cook (1968) attempted to develop a test along such lines. Using a reading-comprehension format, this test presented a presumably factual paragraph about some social issue, followed by two alternative sentences; the respondent was asked to indicate the extent to which each alternative was supported by the material presented in the paragraph. After a quick reading (the test instructions emphasize speed as well as accuracy), both alternatives seemed relevant; actually, neither was clearly

---

[6]To the student of today, this may not appear to be a factual statement. But at the time the test was devised—before the introduction of social security programs—statistics did show that 54 percent of 65-year-old men were dependent on relatives or charity for support.

supported by the material in the paragraph. The assumption was that the respondents would perceive the alternative that was closer to their own position as receiving greater support from the material they had just read. However, scores on this test showed no significant correlation with scores on a self-report attitude inventory that had been found to correlate with scores on a number of other indirect measures.

A number of investigators have used errors in drawing conclusions from formal syllogisms as indicators of attitudes. For example, Thouless (1959) presented both sound and unsound syllogisms on both sides of the issue in which he was interested — socialism. A sample item read: "Slave labor was inefficient because of the lack of incentive to individual effort. Competitive civilizations have prospered because they have provided incentive to individual effort but under socialism such incentives would disappear. We see, therefore, that socialism is a form of slavery." The respondents were instructed first to read only the underlined conclusion, ignoring the rest, and indicate whether they believed the statement to be true or false. Then they were instructed to go back and read the entire argument and decide whether it was sound or unsound, logical or not. With a sample of adults, ranging in age from 23 to 58, he found that 40 percent of the judgments of the soundness of the argument were erroneous. Of these, 78 percent were in the predicted direction; that is, of judging the arguments for statements with which one agreed as sound or of judging the arguments for statements with which one disagreed as unsound. With a sample of university students, however, only 10 percent of the judgments of soundness were erroneous, and the direction of these errors was not systematically related to the respondents' own views.

Feather (1964) also used both valid and invalid syllogisms on both sides of the issue in which he was interested — religion. He, too, predicted that judgments of the validity of syllogisms would be influenced by the respondents' own attitudes: specifically, that religious persons would err more often in the direction of accepting invalid proreligion statements and rejecting valid antireligion statements and that irreligious respondents would make corresponding errors on the invalid antireligion statements and the valid proreligion statements. His hypothesis was confirmed in the case of his religious respondents but not in the case of the irreligious ones. Further examination of his findings explained this seemingly inconsistent result; on the neutral syllogisms interspersed in the test, irreligious respondents showed greater ability to reason logically (that is, made fewer errors) than the religious respondents.

Reviewing this kind of study, Kidder and Campbell (1970) commented:

> These findings suggest that the usefulness of the syllogisms test as an indirect attitude test may be limited by such factors as education, training in logic, and general critical abilities. At one extreme, it is likely that an uneducated person might not even grasp the distinction between the logical soundness of an argument and its empirical validity. For him, the instructions to judge the soundness of an argument may be no different from asking him whether he agrees or disagrees with the conclusion. Under such conditions the test loses all disguise. If, on the other hand, the subjects possess a high degree of education and training, and can easily distinguish between the logical and descriptive truth of an argument, the test may again fail not because it lacks disguise but because it does not tap attitudes at all. . . . Only for the middle range of respondents, who know enough about the distinction between logical and descriptive truth to follow the instruc-

tions but who still make errors, is the test both an attitude measure and a disguised one at that [p. 360].

Tests employing bias in learning and memory

Since Bartlett's (1932) demonstration of the distortion of memory through cultural influences, there has been interest in the effects of the individual's predispositions and past experiences on learning and memory. E. L. and R. E. Horowitz (1938), in their pioneering work on racial attitudes, included among their many novel measurement techniques several based on the hypothesis that attitudes influence the perception and recall of relevant material. In one, the Aussage Test, a complicated picture was exposed for two or three seconds; then a series of standardized questions testing perception and memory were asked. Another of the tests developed by Horowitz and Horowitz — the Pictorial Recognition Test — involved exposing tests of photographs of black and white faces and then asking the respondents to pick out, from a larger number of such photographs, the ones they had been shown. Some 30 years later, Diller and Cook (1969) repeated this study, with modifications designed to disguise its purpose more effectively. Using whites whose attitudes, as measured on a self-report attitude inventory, were either moderately unfavorable to blacks, neutral, or moderately favorable, they found no differences among the groups either in their accuracy of identification of the pictures as having been seen or not seen before, in their accuracy of recall of the trait descriptions associated with the photographs, or in their favorableness of the descriptions recalled in relation to the white and black photographs.

A number of investigators have considered the effects of attitude on the learning and recall of verbal materials. Levine and Murphy (1943) found that both the learning and the forgetting of controversial material were related to attitude. Strongly pro-Soviet and anti-Soviet groups of United States college students were asked to learn two passages about the Soviet Union, one of which was very favorable. Each group learned more rapidly and remembered longer the passage in harmony with its own attitude. Alper and Korchin (1952) tested college students for recall of a letter about coeducation that was generally unflattering to women. Male students recalled significantly more than female students did, and the females made more distortions in recall.

In another example of the effects of attitude upon memory, Doob (1953) gave respondents a questionnaire with five paragraphs dealing with different topics — advertising, religion, the Tennessee Valley Authority, the function of a liberal arts education, and the conflict between the United States and the Soviet Union — and asked them simply to read the paragraphs and indicate their agreement or disagreement with each one on a five-point scale. Two days later the memory test was administered by reminding the respondents that two days previously they had "read through some statements on various topics" and asking them to list the topics they remembered. Doob then asked them to write out, for each of the topics they had listed, "as many of the arguments and ideas as you can which were advanced in the original statements." The results suggested that different aspects of attitude have different effects on recall. Respondents remembered *more* items from paragraphs to which they had reacted strongly, whether in agreement or disagreement, but they remembered *more accurately* those with which they agreed.

Subsequent studies (Brigham and Cook, 1969; Greenwald and Sakumura, 1967; Waly and Cook, 1966) have not confirmed all of the findings. These more recent studies have used both the materials and conditions of the earlier studies and additional material and variations on the research design. None of the three studies found any relationship among attitude, plausibility, and memory. The Greenwald-Sakumura and Brigham-Cook studies did not find any relationship at all between attitude and memory for items; they did not support either the hypothesis that individuals learn better those items that they agree with or agree with plausible items and disagree with implausible items. In fact, the only clear-cut finding of the Brigham-Cook study was that both pro- and antisegregation subjects tended to remember implausible material better than plausible material regardless of its content. Both Greenwald and Sakumura (1967) and Brigham and Cook (1969) suggested that material possessing *novelty* may be remembered better than familiar material, but neither study tested this hypothesis; in both, it was advanced as an after-the-fact speculation derived from the findings.

Because attitudes influence performance in so many other respects, it would be surprising if they did not affect learning and memory in some way. Indeed, the early studies seemed to show rather marked effects of attitude on learning and memory. The more recent research on this topic, however, suggests that these effects are not nearly so simple and straightforward as they had seemed. The conditions under which attitude influences memory and the nature of the influence are so unclear at the present time that tests based on speed of learning or accuracy of recall seem of doubtful value as indirect measures of attitude. Perhaps further work in this area will uncover principles on the basis of which tests of this sort can be made more trustworthy indicators of attitude.

Estimation of group opinion and social norms

People's estimates of the size of various groups (whether these are objectively defined groups having attitudinal relevance or whether the estimates are of the proportion of some population holding specified views) are influenced by their own attitudes.

Two decades ago, Breed and Ktsanes (1961) asked a sample of church members and a sample of city residents what they would do if their church or schools were desegregated. After this the respondents were asked how they thought others in the study (other church members or other townspeople) would respond. Dividing the respondents into segregationists and integrationists on the basis of how they said they would react, these investigators found that the segregationists either were unaware of or denied the existence of any prointegration opinion in the community. Not a single segregationist said that any of his fellow church members or townspeople would take a tolerant position, whereas in actual fact 27 percent of the respondents did give replies indicating that they would support desegregation.

Such attitudes can affect our perceptions of groups with which we are intimately involved. Campbell (1950) used a test of group opinion in a study of morale among submarine crews. The respondents first completed an anonymous direct "Secret Ballot" test of ship morale. This was followed by an indirect test of group opinion, which read:

> You and the other members of the ship's company have voted on the "Secret Ballot." Your job on this test is to guess the results of that ballot. We want your judgment or guess as to *how your own ship* voted and your guess as to *how the whole squadron voted.* Some people are much better at this sort of thing than are others. It has been said that good leaders are better at knowing what the group thinks. This is one of the problems we are trying to study.

Scores on the three forms of the questionnaire were correlated with other indicators of morale, such as ratings by squadron headquarters and reenlistment rate. Estimates for the whole squadron correlated negatively with most of these other measures. The estimates for own ship correlated positively with seven of the eight other measures, but scores based on the direct "Secret Ballot" measure correlated more highly with each of the other measures.

Weitz and Nuckols (1953), in a study of the relationship between job satisfaction of insurance agents and whether they were dismissed from the job, used both direct questions and those asking for estimates of the reactions of others. The indirect questions were introduced with this explanation:

> We want to get your opinion about the attitudes of other agents toward their job. Below are a number of questions which can be answered by a percentage. Circle the percent figure you believe best answers the question. If you don't know, guess.

The questions were of this form:

> Approximately what percent of the agents in your company think that the training they received was good.
> 0%, 10%, 20%, 30%, 40%, 50%, 60%, 70%, 80%, 90%, 100%.

The direct questions were introduced with this explanation:

> Now we'd like to get your attitude about your own job. Check the word or phrase which you feel best completes the statement for you.

The latter questions were of this form:

> The training I received for my present job was:
> _____poor
> _____adequate
> _____excellent

Although neither the score based on the direct questions nor that based on the indirect questions correlated very highly with job survival at the end of the year, these investigators found that the direct questions about the person's own reactions provided a better basis for prediction than did those asking for estimates of other people's reactions.

Let us summarize the status of the techniques described in this section.

Although such "estimating" techniques have been used successfully in showing that groups with different attitudes differ in their perception of social facts, as measures of attitude they must be used with caution. First, to determine the extent and direction of distortion, the investigator must have some independent measure of group composition or opinion. Second, different individuals within the group may have had different experiences that provide objectively different bases for their estimates. Third, in the absence of firm theoretical or empirical support, it is frequently not clear whether distortion in a given direction reflects a favorable or an unfavorable attitude. Distortion in estimation may reflect either wishes or fears; not enough research has been done to know the conditions under which distortion indicates one or the other.

Judgments of Attitudinally Relevant Persons or Materials

A wide variety of judgements has been shown to be influenced by attitudes; consequently, a number of investigators have attempted to devise indirect attitude measures, using judgments of various sorts. We shall consider measures involving judgments of characteristics of individuals, of the quality of productions, of the favorableness of statements about attitudinal objects and of preferred social policies.

Judgments of characteristics of individuals

For example, Hsu (1949) had women graduate students (unfortunately, only three) sort photographs of males for handsomeness and ten days later for judged membership in the Communist party. The correlations were negative for the two women who were anti-Communist and positive for the one who was relatively pro-Communist.

In a study of self-images of a sample of London voters, Green and Stacey (1966) presented eight photographs of men and asked respondents to indicate which of the men they would most like to be. Later each was asked to indicate which of the photos he thought were Conservative and which were Labor supporters. There was a significant tendency for respondents to attribute their own political affiliation to the photographs they had selected as the ones they would most like to be.

Judgments of productions attributed to different sources

It is a well-established finding that literary passages are judged to be of greater literary merit if they are attributed to a renowned author than to one who is unknown, and news reports are given greater credence (at least by United States college students) if they are attributed to *The New York Times* than to *Pravda*. The principle involved — that the regard in which the supposed source is held influences the judgment of the product — provides a promising lead for another indirect approach to attitude measurement. Laughlin and Laughlin (1968) used this approach in a novel way, employing expressions taken from the jargon of pickpockets and

Ozark mountaineers, such as "in the gales" and "misbobble." Each item was given one of four different definitions and attributed to either a Nobel-Prize-winning physicist, a deep-sea diver, an organizer for the Black Panthers, or an underworld pickpocket. The following definitions of "misbobble" give the flavor of the test:

physicist: "failure of an experiment due to a careless oversight"
diver: "unsuccessful dive due to faulty equipment"
Black Panther organizer: "failure at a rally to sway the audience; use of a poor tactic"
pickpocket: "an unsuccessful attempt to fleece a victim"

There were four versions of the test; in each, any given expression was attributed, with the appropriate definition, to only one source. The respondents rated each item for its expressiveness, creativity, acceptability for adoption into the conversations of a learned person, and acceptability for adoption into formal communications such as speeches or journal articles. There were no differences in the ratings for expressiveness; the pickpocket's use of "misbobble" was considered as expressive as the physicist's. On the other three scales, however, the source to whom the expression was attributed was a significant determinant. Ratings generated from the association of the term with the physicist and diver were all significantly higher than those for the Black Panther organizer and the pickpocket, which did not differ from each other. This is an indication of those respondents' attitudes.

Judgments of favorableness of statements

Ager and Dawes (1965) had a number of judges sort a series of statements about science into six categories on the basis of favorableness. Pairs of statements drawn from various categories were then constructed, and respondents were asked to indicate which of each pair was the more favorable. These investigators predicted that respondents would lump together the statements that were at the opposite end of the pole from their own attitudes and would not recognize fine gradations among them. "Error scores" were computed, based on the discrepancy between an individual's ratings and those assigned by the initial judges. More errors were made at the end of the continuum opposite to the respondent's own position.

Judgments of extremity of statements

Many of the studies involving judgments of favorableness of statements have found that people tend to rate statements at the opposite end of the scale from their own positions as more extreme than statements at the end of the scale with which they agree; people who are favorable toward the attitude object tend to rate unfavorable statements as more unfavorable than do people who themselves are unfavorable toward the object. Dawes (1971) took advantage of this "contrast effect" to construct a test in which respondents were presented with pairs of statements and asked to judge which statement of each pair was more extreme, regardless of the position it advocated. The statements concerned the participation of the United States in the Vietnam War; respondents were self-identified "Hawks" or "Doves." Sample pairs of statements were these:

A. No American can in good conscience oppose our efforts in Vietnam; those who do so are, in a word, cowards.

B. Although mistakes are being made by the United States in Vietnam, we seem to be following a reasonable course there.

A. We should get out of Vietnam now, without concern for "face" or prestige, or any other of those nonsensical abstractions with which we justify our barbarity.

B. As long as the Communists persist in their aggression against South Vietnam, America must resist that aggression.

As predicted, the Hawks tended to rate statements opposing American participation in the war as more extreme than statements favoring it, whereas the Doves tended to rate statements favoring American participation as more extreme than statements opposing it.

In order to test whether this contrast effect reflected simply differences in the use of scale points or genuine differences in perception of the opposing positions on the issue, Dawes (1971) reversed the procedure, asking respondents to write statements that they considered typical of the opinions of people with varying positions on controversial social and political issues and then having judges rate these statements for extremity. The instructions for writing the statements read:

> We are planning to engage in research concerning attitudes toward the Vietnamese War. We are going to use college students in this research, and we will be asking them to endorse or reject the sorts of statements that college students typically make about the war. We are asking your help in obtaining such statements. Please write four statements that you think would be endorsed by the typical Hawk on campus. . . . Now please write four statements that you think would be endorsed by the typical Dove on campus.

Again, subjects were self-identified as Hawks or Doves. Both groups attributed considerably more extreme statements to those with whom they disagreed than to those whose position they shared; the hawkish statements written by Doves were more extreme than the hawkish statements written by Hawks, whereas the dovish statements written by Hawks were more extreme than the dovish statements written by Doves. The differences were even more marked than in the earlier study in which respondents rated statements presented to them. Judges rating the statements for extremity correctly classified about 75 percent of the subjects as Hawks or Doves. In another study dealing with the positions of the supporters of George Wallace and of write-in peace candidates in the election, judges correctly identified about 95 percent of the subjects as Wallace supporters or peace-candidate supporters (Dawes, 1971).

Judgments of social policies

Jones and Cook (1975) found that one's attitude is associated with one's choice between alternative policies that ostensibly have the same goal. Hypothesizing that differences in racial attitudes would lead subjects to select either policies providing opportunities for self-improvement or policies providing for social change when subjects were asked to select specific policies that promised to improve the lot of blacks in the United States, Jones and Cook instructed subjects to read 30 short paragraphs that described problems in housing, hiring practices, and similar issues. Each paragraph was followed by a pair of proposals for correcting the problem mentioned. One proposal was oriented toward self-improvement, whereas the other was oriented toward societal change in remedying the situation.

Subjects in the experiment had been selected from groups known to vary in how much prejudice they manifested. Prejudice was also measured by a lengthy attitude scale. Results showed that attitudes toward blacks and judgments about the relative effectiveness of different social policies were strongly related. More prejudiced subjects tended to select self-improvement policies, whereas less prejudiced ones tended to select societal change policies. The attitude toward a social group mediated selection of a policy in this study. Jones and Cook noted that subjects' policy selections may be based on conflicting "theories" about the status of blacks in society — more prejudiced subjects saw blacks as being personally responsible for their status, whereas more egalitarian subjects saw societal factors as being responsible for the status of blacks.

Measures Based on Selection of Classification Principles

Another indirect approach to the measurement of attitudes, especially of their salience, involves presenting respondents with sets of material and asking them to perform some task, the results of which yield groupings that can be taken as indicating the dimensions important to the respondent in classifying people.

Kuethe (1964) used an ingenious application of this general approach in studying the attitudes of male college students. Materials consisted of a blue felt background and figures cut from felt; the texture of the material made the figures cling where they were placed. In one use of this technique, each subject was presented with three sets of figures: (1) two male figures made of black felt and two male figures of white felt; (2) two male figures of black felt and a female figure of white felt; (3) a male and female figure of white felt and a male figure of black felt. Separate subjects were told to place the figures on the background in any arrangement they chose. Scoring was based on whether the black and white figures were segregated or were mixed together. It was found that whites who scored low in prejudice on a self-report measure of attitude toward blacks tended to disregard color in their grouping of the figures, whereas those who scored high in prejudice tended to separate the black and white figures.

In another variation of this technique, the same investigator presented subjects with different sets of figures, this time all cut from yellow felt; each of the sets included one man aiming a rifle and one or two other figures. He found that subjects who expressed high degrees of "extrapunitiveness" (blaming others for frustrations) on the Rosenzweig Picture-Frustration Test were much more likely to arrange the figures in such a way that the rifle was aimed at another human figure than were those who scored low in extrapunitiveness. The investigator interpreted both measures as indicators of tendency toward aggressive behavior.

Another approach based on the tendency to classify individuals on the basis of their group membership has been suggested by Cook and Selltiz (1964). This technique rests on the finding from studies of learning that when words drawn from various categories are presented in random order and subjects are asked to recall them, the words tend to be recalled in clusters, with several words representing a given category being recalled together even though they were not next to each other in the list presented. To the best of our knowledge, this technique has not been applied to the study of social attitudes. However, it is feasible to adapt it for such use. In studying the salience of race as a basis of classification, for example, names of people from several different occupational categories—baseball players, musicians, political figures, actors—would be presented in random order; one name in each category would be that of a minority group member or a woman. The extent to which different respondents grouped names of minorities or women together in recall would be considered an indication of the salience of race and gender as a basis for their classifying of individuals.

Techniques Involving Perceptual Responses

It has long been recognized that perception, especially of ambiguous stimuli, is influenced by past experience, mental "set," present motivational state, and perhaps other characteristics of the perceiver. Thus, it has seemed reasonable to suppose that perceptual responses might be used as indicators of attitudes.

An early attempt along these lines was created by Cattell (1949, 1950). Among many other indirect measures, he used a "Misperception Test," which involved a one-second tachistoscopic exposure of attitude statements with misspellings. The subject was required to recall the statement and note the misspellings; overlooking of the latter was regarded as a sign of a strong attitude. However, the resulting scores showed little correlation with other measures of the same attitudes.

Much of the recent work on perceptual responses as indicators of attitude has involved the phenomenon of **"binocular rivalry."** In this approach, two different pictures are presented stereoscopically. If the exposure time is short enough, the subject is not aware that there are two slides; rather, the viewer sees either one or the other or some combination of the two as a single image. With longer exposure, the two images may be seen alternately. Bagby (1957), presenting pairs of photographs differing in cultural content (for example, a bullfighter and a baseball player) to respondents from Mexico and the United States, found that Mexicans tended to see the pictures with Mexican content, whereas people from the United States saw those with content representative of their own country.

Cook (1968) has pointed out a number of methodological difficulties with designs based on binocular rivalry, such as the problem of eye dominance, memory of earlier stimuli, and the difficulty in securing unambiguous reports from subjects of what they saw. He concluded that this approach probably is not promising as an attitude measure.

Measures Based on Physiological Reactions

At the opposite extreme from measures relying on an individual's self-report of beliefs or feelings are those relying on physiological responses not subject to conscious control. Although the study of such measures depends, of course, on the subjects' willingness to take part in the measurement situation, the results are completely independent either of their insight into their own reactions or their willingness to report them. A number of investigators have explored the possibility that physiological reactions might serve as indicators of social attitudes. These approaches fall into two groupings: first, measures of involuntary physiological reactions to the presence of a member of the object group or to pictorial representations of situations involving members of the object group; and second, measures involving conditioned responses.

Involuntary physiological reactions to attitudinally relevant stimuli

Physiological changes of various sorts accompany the experience of emotion. Several investigators have attempted to use measures of such changes as indicators of the affective component of attitudes.

One of the most frequently used measures has been change in the galvanic skin response (GSR). Rankin and Campbell (1959), under the guise of a laboratory experiment concerned with changes in GSR in connection with associations to various stimulus words, employed two "experimenters," one white and one black, to attach and adjust the electrodes necessary for measurement. The real interest was in differences in the subjects' GSRs when the experimenter was white as compared with GSRs when the experimenter was black. On the whole, the white subjects showed significantly larger GSRs when the black experimenter adjusted the electrodes than when the white experimenter did. Attempts to relate extent of GSR to attitude toward blacks as indicated by two other measures — a self-report questionnaire and an indirect "information" test — were complicated by the effects of varying experimental arrangements, for example, whether the attitude measures were administered before or after the GSR. On the whole, the correlations between GSR and scores on the direct attitude questionnaire were positive; correlations with the "information" measure were negligible.

Cooper and his associates have recorded GSRs in response to verbal references to racial and ethnic groups. Cooper and Siegel (1956) found greater GSR in response to the names of negatively valued groups than to those of neutrally valued groups. Cooper and Singer (1956) measured GSRs to complimentary and derogatory statements about valued and disliked ethnic groups. They found that GSRs increased in response to both complimentary statements about disliked groups and derogatory statements about valued groups, but that the increase was greater for the former. Cooper and Pollock (1959) found a correlation of .82 between magnitude of GSR response to the names of racial and ethnic groups and rankings of these groups by a direct aptitude measure.

The highly publicized work of Hess (Hess, 1965; and Hess and Polt, 1960) on dilation and constriction of the pupil of the eye has seemed to offer a technique that is not subject to this difficulty. These investigators have reported dilation of pupils in response to pleasurable stimuli and constriction in response to unpleasant stimuli. It should be noted that some ophthalmologists (for example, Loewenfeld, 1958, 1966) have questioned these findings, maintaining that, like other physiological responses, changes in pupil size are determined by intensity and suddenness of emotion and general state of arousal (in addition to such physical factors as changes in intensity of light) rather than by the content of the emotion. Yet Hess's promising findings and the great potential value of a physiological measure that might indicate the direction as well as the intensity of emotion made this technique extremely interesting to social science researchers. Woodmansee (1970) has worked intensively to try to develop a measure of attitudes, using this approach but with essentially negative results. Using stimulus slides showing interracial scenes, he has found essentially no difference between the pupillary reactions of those subjects known to be active in the civil rights movement and subjects known to be strongly antiblack. Neither has he found any correlation between individuals' ratings of the extent to which they liked or disliked the various slides and the extent of pupillary change in response to them. In general, he found (as predicted by Loewenfeld) that all the attitudinally relevant slides, whether pleasant or unpleasant, generated a response of pupillary dilation. In an attempt to obtain the constriction response reported by Hess, Woodmansee shifted to extremely unpleasant pictures: a filthy toilet in a broken-down bathroom; slides made from newspaper pictures of a room in which a gruesome murder of a local undergraduate woman had taken place. Even with these extremely unpleasant stimuli, the pupillary responses were still mostly in the direction of dilation. There are great technical and methodological problems, including the degree of light reflected by different pictures and by different sections of the same picture and the constantly fluctuating nature of pupil size even in a resting state. In view of these difficulties and his inability to replicate the constriction responses to unpleasant stimuli as reported by Hess, Woodmansee concluded that this was not a promising technique for attitude measurement.

Generalization of conditioned autonomic responses

Much work in the field of learning has demonstrated that a response that has been conditioned to a given stimulus tends to generalize to stimuli that are similar. Some attempts have been made to use this principle in the study of attitudes. For example, Volkova (1953) reported a series of experiments in the U.S.S.R. in which subjects were conditioned to salivate in response to the Russian equivalent of the word *good*; subsequently, such statements as "The Young Pioneer helps his comrade" brought considerable salivation, whereas such statements as "The Fascists destroyed many cities" brought little or no salivation. In other words, the salivation response conditioned to the word *good* appeared in response to sentences that represented to the subject something good and did not appear in response to sentences that represented something bad.

SUBSTITUTE MEASURES

Another indirect approach to the measurement of a characteristic involves measuring something else or some combination of other things that is sufficiently highly correlated with the characteristic one wants measured to enable it to serve as a satisfactory substitute. We call this approach "the substitute measure."

Gurr (1968) used three indexes based on aggregate data to measure levels of

"relative deprivation" in his cross-national study of civil strife. The selection of the measures was based on the notion that individual expectations increase as the economic and political productivity of a nation provide increasing amounts of goods and services. They were based on changes in trade values, inflation and cost-of-living indexes, GNP growth rates, and political restrictions or redistribution of valued goods (for example, new taxes, land reform, and so on). But during periods of economic leveling off or decline, expectations are much less likely to be satisfied, and a sense of deprivation becomes widespread in a society. Similarly, a sense of deprivation was assumed to increase with increased restrictions on political activity and freedoms and with major relocations of wealth and other values in a society. Gurr went on to demonstrate that a variety of measures of civil strife were, in fact, related to his measures of relative deprivation.

The phenomenon of relative deprivation could be measured more directly by asking individuals questions about their perceived expectations and how well these expectations are being met. This clearly is not feasible in many instances, such as large, cross-national studies or in much historical research.

Ideally, the method of substitute measurements calls for the combination of a number of measures, each of which has a relatively high correlation with the characteristic for which one needs a measure and a relatively low correlation with each of the other measures in the combination. Gurr, for instance, used several economic and political indicators in his research. In principle, such a measure involves an application of the logic of pragmatic validation. However, such a measure cannot be used as an "after" measure in an attitude change experiment. The experimental factor is designed to change the attitude, not necessarily the variables that were initially correlated with it. If successful, the experimental factor may change the basis of the relationship and, among other things, lower the pragmatic validity of the substitute measure.[7]

A NOTE ON VALIDATION

Many questions have been raised about the validity of indirect techniques, and relatively little research evidence is available to answer them. The validity of direct techniques depending on self-report, such as interviews and questionnaires, is less often questioned, probably because of the "obvious" relevance of the questions to the characteristics they are intended to measure. It is the degree of inference involved in indirect tests — the gap between the subject's response and the characteristic it is presumed to indicate — that intensifies our concern about validity.

In the case of projective techniques, there are additional reasons for questions about validity: the great variety of aspects about which inferences may be drawn

---

[7]This consideration points to the grave weakness of pragmatic validation without support in a body of theory or knowledge of the conditions on which the correlation between test and criterion depends. Under these circumstances, we never know whether the underlying conditions may not have changed, so that the test no longer has the pragmatic validity we think it has; that is, we can only hope that since the test has worked until now, it will continue to work in any given application.

and the heavy reliance on the interpretive skill of the individual analyst.[8] For most of the projective techniques, the rules by which the data are to be transformed into scales of measurement are not specified in detail; nor, for that matter, are the dimensions one is attempting to measure. As a consequence, each group of investigators is forced, in some measure, to develop its own rules. Moreover, the very flexibility of the tests means that they do not always cover the same aspects in the same detail. In other words, at least in their present form, projective tests sacrifice precision and reliability in the interest of breadth and depth.

This variability both in the detail with which various aspects are covered and in the interpretations made by different users introduces a question of the extent to which one can speak of validating "*the* Rorschach" or "*the* TAT." Rather, *specific inferences* made by specific interpreters using these techniques can be validated. Cumulation of evidence of validity in specific respects contributes, of course, to validation of the technique as a whole.

To a considerable extent, projective techniques intended to measure broad aspects of personality must rely on **construct validation** (see Chapter 7) rather than on evidence of high correlation with any single criterion. All studies in which scores or qualitative descriptions based on projective techniques are found to be related to some other variable — and there are many such — contribute to the construct validation of the given technique. Thus, the finding in *The Authoritarian Personality* (Adorno, et al., 1950) that the TAT stories of prejudiced and unprejudiced individuals tended to differ in specified ways helps not only to confirm the basic hypothesis of the study (that prejudice is a function of deep-seated personality trends) but to validate the TAT as an instrument for uncovering such personality trends. Similarly, Keniston's finding that the TAT stories of alienated and nonalienated students differed in other specifiable ways not only helped to throw light on the kinds of early family relationships that entered into the development of alienation, but also contributed to validation of TAT stories as reflecting early family relationships and their unconscious emotional concomitants.

In estimating the validity of an indirect measure, whether of the projective type or a more structured test, investigators may use one or more of the following approaches: They may compare scores on the measure with those on an undisguised test designed to measure the same attitude or characteristic; they may compare the scores with those on another indirect measure of the same characteristic; they may compare scores on a variety of measures, direct and indirect, intended to assess the same characteristic; they may compare the scores of two or more groups that may reasonably be expected to differ in the characteristic the test attempts to measure; they may compare the results obtained by the measuring instrument with observations of actual behavior; or, using a more purely construct validation approach, they may predict the pattern of results to be expected if the test indeed measures the characteristic it is intended to measure.

Comparison of scores with those on an undisguised measure is often the easiest approach to validation and is probably the one most frequently used. Proshansky

---

[8]For a more detailed discussion of problems of interpreting projective tests, see Campbell, Miller, Lubetsky, and O'Connell (1964).

(1943) used this procedure with respect to his projective test of attitude toward labor, with positive results. Most studies that have used only this approach to validation of indirect measures have reported positive results. There is always the possibility, of course, that studies in which no relationship is found between the results of a disguised and an undisguised test are not reported. However, a few investigators have reported at least partial lack of correspondence between results of disguised and undisguised measures that help to clarify what the indirect tests may be measuring and the conditions under which they are likely to be effective. For example, the finding by Thouless (1959) that a sample of adults judging the soundness of syllogisms made many errors, the great majority of which were in the direction of agreement with their own attitudes, whereas university students made few errors and these not systematically related to their attitudes, suggested that this technique measures ability for critical thinking as well as specific attitudes and that it is not likely to be an effective measure of attitudes with respondents who are adept in reasoning ability.

The use of an undisguised test as a **criterion** may seem a rather odd procedure, considering the fact that a major reason for using indirect techniques is to get at information that might not be revealed in response to a direct technique. However, two points should be considered. One is that an indirect technique may be used simply as a more effective way of getting information that the individual could give in response to a direct question, if willing to. When this is the case, it is appropriate to use responses to an undisguised instrument as a criterion for the validity of the indirect technique, provided that the undisguised test is administered under circumstances that make it reasonable to expect minimal concealment of true attitudes. For example, it would be reasonable to use scores on an undisguised test of attitudes toward labor as a criterion against which to compare the results of an indirect test only if the undisguised test were administered under circumstances that assured the subjects of anonymity or if the rapport between investigator and subjects was such that they would feel free to reply frankly; it would not be reasonable to use as a criterion scores on a test administered to workers by their supervisor.

Another point in evaluating the use of an undisguised test as a criterion for a disguised one is that the purpose of the disguised test may be to gain more extensive insight into the nature of an individual's attitude. This more extensive knowledge may not mean a different estimate of how favorable or unfavorable an individual is toward a given object, but rather an understanding of the specific pattern of the individual's beliefs about the object or how the attitudes are related to other factors. It is not unreasonable to assume that if a projective technique gives evidence of measuring some aspect of an attitude validly (as indicated by its consistency with the results of a validated undisguised technique), it may also measure other aspects of attitude validly; nevertheless, the consistency should not be taken as conclusive evidence of validity in measuring these other aspects.

Another reason for comparing scores on a disguised measure with those on a validated direct measure is that this may tell us whether further attempts to refine the disguised measure are likely to be profitable. This is the approach that has been followed by Cook (1968) in his development of measures of attitudes toward social groups. The goal of this program was not to demonstrate the particular effectiveness of any single measure, direct or indirect, but rather to develop as wide a variety of measures as possible. In such a program, it was important not to waste time and effort on approaches that were not likely to produce effective indicators of attitudes. Thus the first step in work with any proposed measure in this program was to develop and pretest the instrument itself for feasibility. Were the instructions and test items clear? Did respondents accept the explanation given; to use one of Cook's examples, did they believe that they were being approached by a bona fide textbook publisher with a genuine request to pose for photographs? Were there technical difficulties — such as problems of eye dominance — that had to be overcome before meaningful responses could be secured? The next step was to administer the disguised test to individuals who had already taken, in another connection, a self-report attitude test known to be reliable and valid or to administer the self-report test after respondents had taken the disguised test. If the scores on the indirect measure show no relation to those on the self-report measure, it is concluded that that particular indirect approach is not promising, and work on it is dropped unless there is some special reason (such as reports of successful use by other investigators) to think the technique warrants further work.

In Cook's program, if scores on the indirect measure *did* correlate significantly with those on the self-report measure, the next step was to administer the indirect measure (usually together with other measures) to criterion groups that could be expected to differ in the attitude being measured. As Cook was working primarily with measures of racial attitudes, the following criterion groups were used: civil rights activists or active members of organizations such as CORE, who are assumed to be highly equalitarian in their racial attitudes; students in elective courses on race relations, on the assumption that students who voluntarily expose themselves to material that is likely to be favorable toward minority groups tend to be equalitarian, though less so than those who are actively engaged in some aspect of the civil rights movements; and members of organizations known to have exclusionist policies, on the assumption that members of these groups tend to be antiblack. If scores of these groups differed significantly, this was considered as evidence for the validity of the test. The "criterion group" approach has been used by a number of investigators. For example, Hammond (1948) administered his information test of attitudes toward labor to union members and members of business clubs; Rankin and Campbell (Campbell, 1950) also administered their information test of attitudes toward blacks to blacks and whites, Northern and Southern students, and groups of students known to differ in socioeconomic background and in general political views.

The approach of comparing scores on an indirect measure with observations of actual behavior has been used less often, partly because of the difficulty of determining what kinds of behavior in what kinds of situations would provide an adequate criterion for the characteristic or attitude being measured, partly because of the difficulty of securing measures of such behavior. Nevertheless, some researchers have used this approach. Haire (1950) used it in the instant coffee study by having interviewers ask to see what brand of coffee the interviewees actually had in their pantries, and he found a high correspondence between responses to his indirect measure and behavior as indicated by actually having or not having instant coffee on the pantry shelf. Evans and Chein (1948), in their study of relations between white and black children, found high correspondence between scores on a doll game they developed and children's reports of their own behavior, but little correspondence with observation of actual behavior in test situations. Lansing and Heyns (1959) compared TAT-derived scores of need for affiliation with real-life communicative behavior such as making telephone calls and writing letters, finding high correspondence of the TAT scores with frequency of local telephone calls (but not with long-distance calls).

Among those who have followed the construct validation approach of predicting patterns of findings are Getzels (1951), who predicted and found a greater discrepancy between first- and third-person sentence completion on topics subject to strong social norms than on more neutral topics; and Vaughan and Thompson (1961), who predicted and found that white New Zealand children who differed in the extent of their contact with Maoris also differed in the amount of their favorable or unfavorable references to Maoris in stories they told about pictures showing white and Maori children.

One of the most stringent approaches to validation is the multimethod approach, in which a number of different techniques intended to assess the same attitude are compared. Cattel, et al. (1949, 1950), one of the early users of this approach, found disappointingly low correlations among his various attitude measures. Even more stringent is the "multitrait multimethod" approach urged by Campbell and Fiske (1959). This approach requires that the various techniques be applied with respect to at least two attitudinal objects or characteristics; to be considered valid as an indicator of the attitude or characteristic it is intended to assess, scores on that measure must not only correlate significantly with scores on other instruments intended to assess the same characteristic but should not correlate significantly with scores on measures using a similar technique but intended to tap a different characteristic or attitude. This approach has been used primarily by Campbell and his associates (for example, Burwen and Campbell, 1957; Campbell and Damarin, 1961). Typically, studies using this approach have found quite low correlations among measures using different approaches to assess the same attitude and sometimes rather high correlations between instruments using similar approaches to assess *different* attitudes. When this happens, one must consider whether the difficulty lies in the measuring instruments or whether the characteristic they are intended to measure is not unitary.

We would not, of course, expect all the instruments designed to measure a given characteristic — or even any two of them — to give exactly the same results, for none is a pure measure of any single attitude, characteristic, or ability. Just as direct self-report measures are subject to influence by such "extraneous" characteristics as a desire to give socially approved responses or a tendency to agree (or disagree) with statements regardless of their content, so each class of indirect measures is subject to other influences than the attitude or characteristic it is intended to measure. It may turn out that the major contribution of disguised measures is not that they give "truer" results than self-report measures, but that they provide a variety of approaches, each presumably reflecting different influences in addition to the characteristic the test is intended to measure, with the result that the investigator, by using a combination of instruments, may arrive at a more trustworthy assessment of the characteristic in question than any single measure — disguised or undisguised — could provide.

SUMMARY

Indirect methods of collecting data are used where the researcher doubts that subjects are willing or able to give accurate information about themselves. The diversity of indirect measures is great, but few have been subjected to an intensive evaluation of their reliability and validity.

There are two basic types of indirect methods. The less structured types are called projective methods; these usually involve presenting the subject with a set of ambiguous stimuli. The responses are interpreted as reflecting the individual's personality structure, emotional needs, conflicts, and aspirations. Projective methods include various pictorial techniques (including drawings and photographs) as well as verbal techniques, such as word-association and sentence-completion methods. Doll play and figure drawing serve as projective techniques for children.

More structured indirect methods, the second type, are simpler to administer, score, and interpret than are most projective techniques. Some of these rely on the fact that perceptions and memories are influenced by our attitudes. For example, a "test of knowledge" may really reflect our attitudes toward the topic.

Because of the assumptions behind the inferences used in indirect methods, their validity is of special concern. It should be recognized that at the present time, projective tests sacrifice precision and reliability in the interest of breadth and depth of exploration.

Observational and Archival Data

NATURALISTIC RESEARCH
Three Dimensions of Naturalness
Are the Observations Reliable, Valid, and Ethical?

SYSTEMATIC OBSERVATION
An Example of Systematic Observation
A Definition of Systematic Observation
Steps in Conducting a Systematic Observation
Types of Systematic Observation
Issues in Systematic Observation
Conclusions about Systematic Observation

PARTICIPANT AND ECOLOGICAL OBSERVATION
An Example of Participant Observation
A Definition of Participant Observation
Conclusions about Participant Observation
A Definition of Ecological Observation
Conclusions about Ecological Observation

ARCHIVAL RECORDS
Examples of Archival Research
Types of Archival Research
Issues in Archival Research
Conclusions on Archival Research

SUMMARY

This chapter was written by Marianne LaFrance.

In the detective novel *The Seven-Per-Cent Solution* (Meyer, 1974), two great observers of the human scene join forces—Sigmund Freud brings his capacity to uncover mental depths while Sherlock Holmes notices and deduces. But it is Holmes who teaches Freud a crucial lesson. He chastises Freud for seeing but not observing and notes that "the distinction is an important one and sometimes makes a critical difference" (Meyer, 1974, p. 147).

The distinction alluded to by Sherlock Holmes is the critical difference between everyday seeing and social scientific observation. Scientific observation is a deliberate quest, conducted with diligence and forethought, as contrasted with the informal and essentially passive perceptions of everyday life. It requires a great deal of ingenuity and skill both to see and to observe. This chapter presents some of the strategies social scientists have developed to make this possible.

Many of the observations made by social scientists appear to be mundane at first glance. For example, it has been noted that some restaurant diners salt their food before tasting it and others salt only after they have had a first bite (McGee and Snyder, 1975); that some house owners construct fences around their property whereas others leave their grounds unmarked (Edney, 1972); and that some billiard players show their tongues while making difficult shots whereas others keep them out of sight (Smith, Chase, and Lieblich, 1974). These observations become scientific when the data are gathered systematically and are related to other data also systematically gathered for the purpose of uncovering a general principle of human behavior. As to salting food, McGee and Snyder (1975) predicted that the more individuals ascribe stable traits to themselves, as opposed to seeing their behavior as varying with context, the more likely they are to salt their food before tasting it. Results confirmed their prediction. People who see their behavior changing depending on the situation are more likely to taste the food before seasoning it. In a comparable fashion, Edney (1972) found that people who lived in "defended" houses, with fences

263

and "No Trespassing" signs, had lived there longer than those in undefended houses and expected to continue to live there longer. And finally, Smith, Chase, and Lieblich (1974) observed that tongue showing occurs when one is engaged in some demanding activity and signals an unwillingness to interact. Good billiard players showed their tongues more often on hard than on easy shots and showed the tongue less than did unskilled players overall.

Observation thus becomes scientific when it (1) serves a formulated research purpose, (2) is planned deliberately, (3) is recorded systematically, and (4) is subjected to checks and controls on validity and reliability.

This chapter describes some major types of scientific observation. They are (1) systematic observation of natural behavior, (2) participant observation and ecological inquiry of natural settings, and (3) archival research of natural treatments. All three types share a common heritage in field research in contrast to the laboratory experimental methods described in Chapter 2. Although not restricted to field settings, all three emphasize "naturalness" in one or more aspects of their procedures.

NATURALISTIC RESEARCH

Naturalistic research does not describe a single approach. Rather, naturalistic or field research encompasses a variety of research strategies that share a common concern with describing human behavior that is representative of the way it exists in real life. This means studying behavior as it would have occurred in the ordinary way and in the circumstances that would have spontaneously given rise to it. The aim, of course, is to be able to generalize results beyond the immediate research context.

Different social science approaches emphasize different aspects of naturalness. Ethologists (Blurton Jones, 1972; Rajecki, 1977) have mainly been interested in *natural behavior*; ecological psychologists and advocates of participant observation (Bogden and Taylor, 1975; Garfinkel, 1967) have primarily been concerned with using *natural settings*; and analysts of archives (Holsti, 1969) have been particularly attentive to *natural treatments* or events. Whatever the particular emphasis, several benefits are seen to accrue from a concern with naturalness. Among these benefits are the finding of new or previously unrecognized behavior, the discovery of important empirical relationships, and an increase in the generalizability of the research findings. This chapter is directed toward showing you how to observe everyday behavior in a systematic way so that you see differences that you might not see otherwise.

Three Dimensions of Naturalness

In contrast to experimental methods, naturalistic methods call for as little investigator intervention as possible into the field of study. In the purest conception of naturalistic research, observation would be made of a naturally occurring behavior (for example, smiling) as it happened in its natural setting (for example, bowling alley) as the result of a natural event (for example, getting a strike) (Kraut and Johnston, 1979) while the observer remained unobtrusive. According to Tunnell (1977), the three primary dimensions of naturalistic research are natural-behavior, natural-setting, and natural-treatment.

Natural behavior. Natural behavior points to the dependent variable in an investigation. "A natural behavior is one that is not established or maintained for the sole purpose or primary purpose of conducting research" (Tunnell, 1977, p. 426). For example, putting salt on one's food or "No Trespassing" signs on one's property are natural behaviors because they would have occurred even in the investigator's absence. Consequently, survey or interview responses that occur as the result of an interviewer's questions would not be considered natural behavior, nor would responses where subjects are aware that their specific behaviors are under scrutiny. The concern in both these cases is that the responses are the result of being questioned or observed and not spontaneously generated. An example of a study using systematic observation of a natural behavior but using neither a natural setting nor a natural treatment is a study by Byrne, Ervin, and Lamberth (1970). Subjects, paired on the basis of high or low similarity of responses to an attitude questionnaire, spent 30 minutes together on a "coke date." When subjects returned from the date to the laboratory, interpersonal attraction was assessed by means of a natural behavior, namely, the physical distance between the two persons as they stood together in front of the experimenter's desk. Closer distances were seen to be indicative of greater attraction, the attraction being caused by differences in initial similarity of the people.

Natural setting. A concern with natural setting involves the recording of behavior in a context that is not established for the sole or primary purpose of conducting research. Examples of natural settings would be shopping centers, private homes, racetracks, schools, beaches, churches, bars, hospitals, airports, and so on. To return again to the food salting and house defending studies, which were described earlier, the observations took place in the natural settings of restaurants and neighborhoods respectively.

Much of the work conducted by ecological psychologists (for example, Barker, 1968) has been devoted to identifying and describing the publicly available behavior settings in a number of small towns. Participant observation also assumes that an important way to understand most areas of social life is to go to the settings in which that social life is lived (Bogden, 1972).

Natural treatment. The third dimension of naturalness describes a naturally occurring incident that has some social-psychological consequences. The event is natural because people would have encountered it with or without the presence of a researcher. Examples of natural treatments include natural disasters, economic fluctuations, heat waves, and surgery.

One example of a study that investigated the impact of a natural treatment was an archival study by Carlsmith and Anderson (1979). They examined the relationship between the air temperature (natural treatment) and the incidence of urban riots. The findings strongly suggested that the conditional probability of a riot increases directly with increases in ambient air temperature. Obviously, the investigators did not create differences in mean daily temperature. They were, however, able to make use of differences in "treatment" because records are kept of weather by date. These records were then correlated with concurrent records of urban rioting.

In summary, natural behavior, natural setting, and natural treatment describe different facets of naturalistic research. Although they are independent from each other, they need not be kept separate in practice. In fact, ecological psychologists place high priority on incorporating all three into any research plan (Barker, 1968). They are described separately here so that you will be in a better position to make choices among the various research strategies they represent. You may want to begin thinking at this point whether you are more interested in exploring the display of a particular natural behavior (for example, how frequently people touch each other) or the effect of different natural settings (for example, indoor versus outdoor concerts) or the impact of a natural treatment (for example, graduating from school).

Systematic observation, participant and ecological observation, and archival research emphasize different naturalistic features; nevertheless, all three must be evaluated against the standards of good social science. Are the data obtained valid measures that can be reliably assessed? Are the variables "plausible response measures within the setting, discriminable from other behaviors, easy to observe and score, compatible with other measures, defensible in terms of psychometric canons, sensitive to variations in independent variables, and valid indicators of psychological processes" (Weick, 1968, p. 380)? In other words, are the behaviors selected for observation likely to occur in the setting you have selected? Can they be distinguished from other behaviors that are going on at the same time? Can the selected behavior be seen and coded reliably? Are the coded behaviors similar in meaning to other behaviors reflecting the same theory? Can the scores be quantified and compared across people? Are the observed behaviors likely to show differences as a function of hypothesized events? And lastly, do the coded behaviors reflect what they are supposed to reflect? There is, in addition, one other major standard against which all three must be evaluated, and that has to do with the ethics involved in the investigation of human behavior.

Are the Observations Reliable, Valid, and Ethical?

Reliability. Social scientific observations are reliable to the extent to which they show consistency and stability in their scoring. The most familiar meaning of **reliability** is the degree to which two or more observers agree on their observations. It is usually measured as the percentage of scored units during which the records of two observers are the same. Reliability thus sets the limits on what a piece of research can show. If two or more observers are not in accord in terms of what they see, then what it means remains beyond reach. Reliability thus precedes questions of validity. Consequently, interobserver agreement must always be obtained and reported.

Reliability needs to be more than interobserver agreement, however (Mitchell,

1979). Researchers are obliged to show as well that the behaviors on which the observations are based are stable over time. The reason for having such reliability, usually assessed through test-retest comparisons, is to show that the data being analyzed reflect dependable processes. The concern here is comparable to interobserver agreement. If the observed behavior is highly variable across situations or time (either because of observer inconsistency or behavioral instability), then valid conclusions about its *general* character, causes, and impact cannot be made.

Validity. Whatever the form of the observations, whether they represent checkmarks on a highly refined coding sheet or handwritten field notes, **validity** refers to the extent to which the recorded observations represent what they are supposed to represent. Two observers may agree in their observations, thus constituting reliability, but they both may err in that the behaviors noted are not relevant to, or accurate signs of, that which they are designed to be. Observations are valid to the extent that they reflect what they are presumed to reflect and not something else. It is not possible directly to "see" many processes involved in social relations, such as attraction, prestige, and leadership. Social scientists have to look for observable signs of these phenomena. The question is whether these "signs" correctly represent the process we are interested in knowing more about. Attraction might thus be coded as how closely people stand together (measured in inches), prestige as the amount of afforded office space (measured in square feet), and leadership as the number of verbal directives given to others. These measures would be valid if they accurately corresponded to the underlying dispositions, namely, attraction, prestige, and leadership respectively. If they reflect something else, then the validity of the measures is in question. The ultimate validity may thus depend on how well the observed information predicts some relevant outcomes, that is, interpersonal distance predicting long-term friendship, office space predicting others' respect, and verbal directives predicting group productivity.

Ethics. The investigation of natural behaviors in natural settings under natural conditions is generally done unobtrusively and hence without participant awareness. Consequently, subjects have usually not given permission for the recording, nor do they usually have access to the information once obtained, nor do they usually have veto power over its use. The ethical issues are complex and need to be addressed whenever unobtrusive means are employed. Among the considerations are whether subjects would refuse consent if given the opportunity and what effects are likely to result for these or similar people as a function of the data being made public. Is there a potential risk to these people as a function of doing research on them? The essential issue in naturalistic research is whether the subjects' privacy has been invaded and whether this was warranted (Diener and Crandall, 1978).

SYSTEMATIC OBSERVATION

Sometimes an observer can tell a great deal of what is going on between two people by watching what they do rather than listening to what they say. With the recent advances in the field of nonverbal communication, social scientists now have access to a variety of natural behaviors reflecting social processes (LaFrance and Mayo, 1978). For example, facial features can convey a variety of feeling states, and observational systems range from global ratings of positive versus negative facial expressions (Ickes and Barnes, 1978) to highly codified and objective systems for scoring minute facial movements from film or videotape records (Ekman and Friesen, 1978).

Eyes have been held to be mirrors of the soul, and social science has provided some of the evidence (Argyle and Cook, 1976). Observations of eye contact by dating couples from behind one-way mirrors in laboratory settings have been related to self-reports of love (Rubin, 1970), whereas the amount of gaze behavior during listening, coded in a number of naturalistic settings, has been shown to be culturally variable (LaFrance and Mayo, 1976). For example, Rubin found that couples who scored higher on a scale assessing love for the partner looked at each other more than those scoring lower on the scale. As to cultural differences, LaFrance and Mayo found that white listeners look more at a person who is speaking than do black listeners.

An Example of Systematic Observation

A person's posture can also indicate a stance taken toward someone or something. The following describes one study on postural arrangements in a group in considerable detail to illustrate for you some of the elements in systematic observation. In this investigation (LaFrance, 1979), an effort was made to test a notion put forward by Scheflen (1964) that hypothesized that people who share similar postures in an interaction usually turn out to share a similar viewpoint as well.

The study involved videotaping a number of college classrooms twice during a six-week summer session, once during the first week of the course, and again during the final week. At both times, students filled out a self-report questionnaire assessing their attitudes toward the class. Two questions guided the study: (1) would similar postures by students and instructors relate to their feelings of involvement in the class? and (2) what was the nature or this relation — does posture sharing affect involvement or is the reverse relation true?

Courses were selected for small class size (maximum 20 students) so that all participants could be videotaped simultaneously from an overhead wide-angle camera. The videotapes were then coded by two trained observers working independently. The observational procedure entailed noting separately each person's body position at ten equally timed intervals across an hour of class time, resulting in one observation every six minutes. Three body areas (left arm, right arm, and torso) were coded, using graphic symbols derived from a master sheet depicting the range of possible postures. For example, if a student's right arm were bent at the elbow such that the elbow was resting on the desk and the right hand was touching or supporting the person's head, the coded symbol was $\diagdown\!\diamond$. The second step of the coding procedure involved placing each student's noted body position alongside the body positions noted for the instructor and scoring whether or not each body part was a mirror image of the other person's body part. For example, a student's left arm was scored as sharing if it were in the same position as the right arm of the facing instructor. The third step included correlating each student's posture-sharing score with the rating of his or her involvement in the class on a seven-item bipolar scale.

TABLE 11.1   A Sampling Coding System for Arm Posture Used in Study of Participants in College Classrooms from LaFrance (1979).

Symbol		Verbal Description
Right Arm	Left Arm	
↓	↓	arm straight, extended downward
|	|	arm straight, extended forward
←	→	arm straight, extended laterally
⊥	⊥	arm bent at elbow, lower arm forward and parallel to floor, perpendicular to upper arm
⤬	⤪	arm bent at elbow 45° angle across front of body.
⌐→	←⌐	arm bent at elbow, forearm across body
↗	↖	arm bent at elbow, forearm upward
		arm bent at elbow, forearm up & hand touching head
		arm bent at elbow, hand behind head or neck
<	>	arm bent at elbow, elbow out from body with hand at waist or hip

A Definition of Systematic Observation

Systematic observation involves the selection, recording, and encoding of a set of natural behaviors usually but not necessarily in their natural setting for the purpose of uncovering meaningful relationships. The study investigating the relation between posture sharing and feelings of involvement exemplifies each of these components. In the first place, the study entailed *selection*. Postural arrangements were selected for observation, and other elements of the situation such as smiling or gazing were ignored. The selection was deliberate and settled upon before the investigation began.

Secondly, the study involved the separate operations of *recording* and *encoding*. Once a set of behaviors has been selected for investigation, the researcher needs to establish *when* the observations are to be made and in *what form* they are to be gathered. Both decisions are implicated in the recording of the observations. In the posture sharing study, the initial decision was to videotape-record the whole class period twice for each course. The choice of videotape rather than in vivo recording was based on the desirability of obtaining a permanent record that could be repeatedly examined. This enhances the accuracy of the observations and allows discrepancies between observers to be resolved. In addition, the videotaping was done according to the principle of nonintervention as well. No attempt was made to impose any particular sort of narrative on the shooting. A comprehansive wide-angle overhead position was chosen and sustained throughout each class. The taping began before the class began and finished after it was over.

The videotape was then systematically examined, and a record was made of the postures displayed by all participants in each class. Instead of recording every posture for every student for every second, a decision was made to record the postures according to a method of *time sampling*. The aim was to obtain records of posture sharing that could be compared across classes (because each was observed the same number of times according to the same schedule) without the greater time investment required of continuous and hence complete recording.

The latter method of coding is called **continuous real time measurement** (Sackett, 1978). Continuous measurement occurs when every onset of a behavior (frequency) or elapsed time of a behavior (duration) is recorded during the observational session. For example, had continuous measurement been used in the posture sharing study instead of time sampling, then a judgment would have been made every time there was mirroring between each student's posture and his or her respective instructor's posture. A judgment of sharing would start a stopwatch, which would be stopped when the mirroring temporarily ceased. When mirroring again occurred, the timing would restart.

Continuous measurement conducted this way yields two types of measurement information, namely, the *frequency* of occurrence and the *duration* of the behavior. Frequency represents the number of onsets over the observational session, and duration taps the total number of seconds in which the behavior occurred, which is obtained by summing all durations across the observational session. Both frequency and duration measures could be used to compare across different length sessions by adjusting the scores to take account of the varying length. Suppose that Person A shares posture with an instructor five times for a total of 30 seconds during a 50-minute class. Person B also shares posture five times, lasting a total of 60 seconds during a 100-minute class period. It is necessary to adjust these scores to make them comparable, given different class lengths. This can be done by calculating the *rate of occurence* for the frequency measure $\left(\text{rate} = \dfrac{\text{frequency}}{\text{session length}} \right)$, and percentage duration for the duration measure $\left(\% \text{ DUR} = \dfrac{\text{duration}}{\text{session length}} \right)$ (Sackett, 1978). When you compare posture sharing for Person A and Person B, you will see that Person B's *rate* is half that of Person A's but that they have the identical *percentage duration* of one percent.

As you recall, the posture sharing study used *time sampling* instead of continuous measurement to record postures for the classroom participants. More specifically, that study used **time-point sampling** as contrasted to **time-interval sampling.** In the first of these, recording is done instantaneously at the end of set time periods, such as every ten seconds or every sixth minute or every hour on the hour, with the number and spacing of points selected to be appropriate to the session length. This is like freezing time and recording then whether or not a particular behavior is present. Through the use of film or videotape, the time point is literally accomplished through stop action on one frame. In contrast, time-interval sampling, like continuous measurement, records behavior in real time; but, as in time point sampling, each observed behavior, such as posture sharing, is scored once and only once during successive intervals of the session (for example, 60 seconds) regardless of the number of actual occurrences in each interval. Both time sampling methods are particularly apt when there is a large number of behaviors to code or long observational sessions to be recorded or quick changes in the relevant behaviors. Time sampling tends not to be appropriate for behaviors that occur infrequently or that may be missed or when the sequence of the behavior amid other behaviors is significant or when actual frequencies or durations are important to know. Consequently, continuous recording in real time is the method of choice when these concerns are paramount in the research.

Following recording, the next step entails encoding the observations. Encoding is the process of simplifying the observations through some data reduction method such as categorization and quantifying the categories so that statistical analysis can be done. In our present example, the actual postures displayed were compared (each student to his or her instructor) to determine whether they were sharing posture or not. The presence or absence of posture sharing thus constituted the category for the simplification of the data. A count was then taken of how much sharing each student showed by adding the number of occurrences across the ten observation points. This was correlated with how much involvement they had reported experiencing in the class, which was the average rating given on six, seven-point scales.

Table 11.2 presents data for two students (A and B) and their professor as they might appear on the recording sheet. The first column represents the timing for the observation points. The next two columns, moving to the right, show both arm positions for the professor, the symbols being derived from the master coding sheet given in Table 11.1. Both arm positions for student A and Student B are also given in the table, and beside those respective columns the presence or absence of mirroring is given for each time point. For example, the "Right Arm" column for Student A provides two sources of information. The first records the symbols at each observation point for the position of the Student A's right arm. Next to this column is the one demonstrating the encoding of the posture into one of two values: "1" if the *right* arm of the student was in the same position as the *left* arm of the professor, and "0" if it was in any other position. Summing down each arm's column gives the mirroring score for that arm, and summing across *and* down gives each student's total mirroring score on both arms.

Table 11.3 presents total scores on posture mirroring and self-reported involvement for two students (A and B) of one class. Each student thus has two scores: their mirroring score and the average self-report score. The values for all students in one class are statistically correlated to yield the degree of relationship between posture mirroring on the one hand and self-reported involvement on the other hand.

Sometimes recording and encoding can involve a single operation as when an observer counts whether or not a specific, preestablished behavior has occurred when making a "live" observation. The data are thus already encoded by virtue of being recorded. Sampling according to time-point procedures in vivo would yield this type of situation. In contrast, the recording of a single or multiple behavior through continuous time measurement would allow different types of encoding to

TABLE 11.2 Record of the Arm Postures for Two Students and their Professor during One Hour of Class Time.

Observation Points		Professor		Student A				Student B			
		Right Arm	Left Arm	Right Arm		Left Arm		Right Arm		Left Arm	
Start: Word				Posture	Mirror	Posture	Mirror	Posture	Mirror	Posture	Mirror
Time	Tape Foot Counter										
Minute 6	49	(symbol)	(symbol)	(symbol)	1	(symbol)	1	(symbol)	0	(symbol)	0
'' 12	103	(symbol)	(symbol)	(symbol)	0	(symbol)	0	(symbol)	0	(symbol)	0
'' 18	150	(symbol)	(symbol)	(symbol)	0	(symbol)	0	(symbol)	0	(symbol)	0
'' 24	204	(symbol)	(symbol)	(symbol)	1	(symbol)	0	(symbol)	0	(symbol)	1
'' 30	261	(symbol)	(symbol)	(symbol)	1	(symbol)	0	(symbol)	0	(symbol)	0
'' 36	323	(symbol)	(symbol)	(symbol)	0	(symbol)	1	(symbol)	0	(symbol)	0
'' 42	385	(symbol)	(symbol)	(symbol)	1	(symbol)	1	(symbol)	0	(symbol)	0
'' 48	456	(symbol)	(symbol)	(symbol)	1	(symbol)	0	(symbol)	0	(symbol)	0
'' 54	529	(symbol)	(symbol)	(symbol)	1	(symbol)	0	(symbol)	1	(symbol)	0
'' 60	615	(symbol)	(symbol)	(symbol)	1	(symbol)	1	(symbol)	1	(symbol)	1
Total					7		4		1		2

Class Code_____
Observer Code_____
Date of Obs. _____
Date of Coding_____

TABLE 11.3 Summary Data for Two Students Including Scores on Posture Mirroring and Self-Reported Involvement.

	Posture Sharing Scores			*Average Rating on 6, 7-point Scales*
Subjects	*Right Arm*	*Left Arm*	*Total*	
Student A	7	4	11	6.2
Student B	1	2	3	3.4

be done, such as frequency, rate, duration, percentage duration, and sequential analysis. The distinction between recording and encoding is a critical one in that the same recorded observations may be encoded according to different systems. In this at least, observations do not speak for themselves. The question that you the researcher have in mind will guide you as to how best to encode the observations. Take gaze behavior; for example, two pairs may look at each other for comparable total duration, thus looking very similar; however, the first pair may have accomplished this through one or two relatively extended periods of eye contact, whereas the second pair brought it about through frequent but brief looks.

Steps in Conducting a Systematic Observation

To reiterate, our posture sharing study selected joint postural display at its starting point, recorded the postures as they happened in the context of a naturally occurring situation, encoded them in terms of whether they were similar or not, and tabulated the degree of joint display along with the degree of self-reported involvement in order to test a hypothesis suggesting a positive relationship between these two variables. Let us now present a series of steps in any study using systematic observation. Try to keep either the posture sharing phenomena in mind or a behavior of your own choosing, and follow the steps as we proceed.

Step one: choosing a natural behavior to observe. The first step appears in many ways the easiest but may turn out to be the hardest because it requires making a choice among a surfeit of possibilities. The selection of a particular behavior to observe or a particular social transaction to record can originate from many sources, including the research literature, portrayals by novelists or film makers, or personal curiosity, to name a few. Whatever the source for the behavior, it is important to be specific, explicit, and limited. Do not observe "people in a restaurant"; observe instead "how much people talk while eating out." Instead of observing generally "how people behave in doctors' waiting rooms," observe how "fidgety" they are. Bypass a curiosity with classroom interaction or playground behavior in general, and select either a particular behavior, such as talk time, or a particular transaction, such as the end of class or recess time. Be choosy, selective, and modest. The simplest of behaviors can themselves turn out to be rich in detail and complexity.

Related to this issue of choosing a natural behavior is formulating the specific question to guide the observations. As with the behavior, the question should be precise, explicit, and, initially, simple. Start out with questions like these: "Do people of Group X do more of behavior A than people of Group Y?" or "Do people engage in posture sharing more in seminars than in lectures?" The question ought to spring from a more general issue but should be unambiguous and straightforward.

Step two: selecting an appropriate observational setting. The selection of an appropriate setting in which to make your observation should be based on two primary considerations: The first is theoretical and the second is practical. On the theoretical side, the observational setting should be chosen because the behavior in question is likely to occur there and under typical circumstances. Where is the behavior going to appear with some frequency and normalcy? As we have noted a number of times, settings exert a powerful influence on the incidence of behavior. Select the setting that makes the most sense in terms of your question (Yarrow and Waxler, 1979). The second consideration in selecting a setting is practical. Choose a setting that allows you access from which you can make reliable observations and in which your presence is relatively unobtrusive. A professional football game is accessible but generally would not permit coding of finegrain observations of players' facial expressions. If you are coding fine, small behaviors, select a setting that allows you to be close to your subject; if you are coding large group behaviors, then pick a vantage point with greater distance.

Step three: deciding on the mode of recording observations. Consider the relatively straightforward problem of observing a single behavior, like smiling, by a group of children on a playground. Decisions have to be made as to whether (1) the observations are to be coded live or captured on a permanent record such as videotape for later coding, (2) whether distinctions ought to be made between types of smiles, and (3) whether distinctions should be made between smiles varying in intensity, and so on. These questions are posed to alert you to the need to specify via examples in concrete language and/or pictorial display what constitutes the presence or absence of the behavior before the actual recording begins. These examples of coding categories should be present for referral during the coding. Related to this issue is the development of your coding sheet. This sheet, such as the one provided in Table 11.2, needs to include all the information that would allow an uninformed person to identify the data after it has been collected as well as aid in the actual collection itself. Standard coding sheets should be drawn up at the beginning and should be used by all observers for all subjects across all observations.

Step four: determining the sampling strategy. The sampling strategy is based on the nature of the data that you want to have when all the observations are complete. Do you want to have measures of the actual frequency or duration of particular behaviors, or do you need only a common base that allows you to compare relative amounts of a particular behavior across different settings or groups of people? Actual frequency and/or duration scores require continuous real time observation, whereas the question as to the relative display between groups would make time-point sampling or time-interval sampling feasible sampling strategies. Continuous real time coding requires the largest investment of observer time but makes possible a variety of encoding plans, including measures of frequency, duration, and rate, as well as behavioral sequences and patterns. A permanent record obviously allows different sampling strategies because the same record can be approached repeatedly in different ways.

Also implicated in the sampling strategy are the questions of who and how many are to be observed and for how long and whether the observer should score one or more than one subject at a time. Again, a permanent record such as was used in the posture sharing study allowed all the people who were visible to be coded because the tape could be rerun repeatedly. In contrast, during live observations, choices have to be made. If more than one subject is to be observed at the same time, then multiple observers may be necessary. But if more than a few subjects are observed, this technique becomes impractical. Another solution is the use of **focal individual sampling** (Sackett, 1978). During a given sampling period, one person's behavior is scored. Behaviors not involving the focal subject are ignored. During the next preestablished sampling period, another preordained person is observed. This method generates behavior samples for each person but may not be acceptable if only a few or short intervals can be scored for each participant.

Step five: training observers. Observers are not alike — some observers see "more" than others (Yarrow and Waxler, 1979). In addition, observers can make two types of errors: those of omission and those of commission. In the former case, instances of the behaviors under study are missed, and, in the latter case, more instances are included than were fully present. Observers need to be trained to avoid these errors. Before the actual recording begins, observers need to practice on identical behaviors in identical situations to reach acceptable levels of reliability. Furthermore, reliability checks need to be made on occasion during the ongoing research in order to guard against a phenomenon known as *observer drift*. In observer drift, a recorder may begin observations with high accuracy but over time, owing to fatigue or habituation or experience, the categories begin to change systematically so that behaviors initially ignored start to be included or behaviors initially tabulated are increasingly neglected. Some small error is expected even with the best of observers, but the critical errors have to do with systematic change in observations over time. One should not assume that high reliability at the beginning of a study goes with high reliability at the end of the study. Reliability also assumes that at least two observers are present during some of the observation time.

Step six: analyzing the data. After the coding system has been found or created, after good reliability has been achieved, and after the observations have been recorded on a sufficient number of subjects, two issues remain. The first concerns the measures to use to summarize the findings, and the second concerns the choice of an appropriate statistical test for evaluating the research hypotheses. Chapter 13 on data analysis describes how to organize your data so that they can be maximally informative. In addition, there are some new statistical methods that go beyond the analysis of significant differences (Bakeman, 1978; Gottman, 1978) into the study of behavior streams and sequences. Nevertheless, the questions that guided the data collection and the form of the recorded observations will necessarily constrain the kinds of information that will be forthcoming. In other words, before beginning the actual recording, your sights ought to be on this final step of analyzing the data. Such foresight will help you obtain precisely the kind of data that can be analyzed.

Types of Systematic Observation

Although systematic observation is naturalistic to the extent that the behaviors are already part of the subjects' existing repertoires, nevertheless, there are considerable differences in how these behaviors are recorded and encoded. At one end of the continuum are methods that are relatively unstructured and open-ended in terms of recording. The observer tries to provide as complete and nonselective a description as possible. On the other end of the continuum are more structured and predefined methods that itemize, count, and categorize behavior. Here the investigator decides beforehand which behaviors will be recorded and how frequently observations will be made. The investigator using structured observation is much more discriminative in choosing which behaviors will be recorded and precisely how they are to be coded.

Relatively unstructured methods: natural history approaches.   The most unstructured and nonselective method of observation would be a complete descriptive account of everything that surrounded an event. This is not only an impossible goal but also not a desirable goal. The basic principle of any observational technique is that it summarize, systematize, and simplify the representation of an event rather than provide complete replay of it. Even films and videotapes do not provide exact reproduction, for they are subject to biases introduced by camera angle, lighting, microphone placement, and lens used (Michaelis, 1955). Nor is a "complete" description ever a perfect carbon copy owing to investigators' expectations, language structure, or other cultural biases that may unintentionally affect what is recorded. These issues will be discussed further but are noted here to alert the reader to the fact that all observational techniques involve selection and editing. The issue is to make one's techniques as explicit and available as possible.

Yet natural history and ethological approaches opt for as little prior categorization as possible. Ethologists attempt to enter a scene with a focus on discovering what is there. The object is to derive as detailed and comprehensive a description as possible about the nature of an animal's or person's behavioral repertoire. A basic assumption for ethologists is that the natural world is best approached through careful exploratory studies aimed at the generation of hypotheses rather than the testing of them (Blurton Jones, 1972).

Consequently, ethologists concentrate on molecular behaviors, that is, behaviors that are tied to specific motor or muscular phenomena and avoid descriptions that involve inference. For example, the ethologist would *not* describe someone as looking "very pleased." That would entail too much interpretation. The ethologist would instead describe such details as facial expression, body movement, speech content, and the behavioral results of such a display rather than allude to some underlying state or intention. For example, Eibl-Eibesfeldt (1970) has used a camera with a right-angle lens, which allows a film to be taken of a person while the camera is apparently orienting 90 degrees in the other direction. Such observations led to the discovery of the "eyebrow flash" that occurs during greetings wherein both eyebrows are raised maximally and simultaneously and that is completed within one second. Other ethological observations have discriminated between different types of smiles and the occasions for their use (Brannigan and Humphries, 1972) and the natural "fidgetiness" by patients in dentists' waiting rooms (Barash, 1974).

Structured methods: checklists.   The major difference between unstructured and structured observational methods is that in the latter the investigator knows what aspects of social activity are relevant for his or her purposes before starting and deliberately sets forth a specific and explicit plan to record these activities.

Most structured observational methods require that an observer be present to code the appearance of the behavior, but some newer technological devices can record even in an observer's absence. For example, television meters note how many and what television programs are turned on, pedometers calculate the territory covered by people on foot during any given day, and clap meters gauge the level of an audience's reaction (Schwitzgebel, 1968). Pressure-sensitive floor mats have been used to record the differential use of space in public areas such as art galleries (Bechtel, 1967), and ultrasonic motion detectors attached to chairs have been used to record subjects' spontaneous movements in reactive situations (Dabbs, 1975). But note here that "observers" are still necessary to encode the recordings after the information has been collected.

There are, in addition, some semiautomatic recording devices now available to ease the task of observing in situ. For example, Parke and Savin (1975) examined the interactional patterns between parents and their two-to-four-day-old infants during feeding. A wide range of behaviors were assigned a three-digit numerical code and were recorded in sequence as they happened, using a *Datamyte* keyboard recording device. The Datamyte is a ten-key device that permits behavior with assigned numerical values to be put into the system by keys. The keys are tone-related and record different auditory patterns onto a cassette tape. This, in turn, produces a print-out of numerical values indicating behaviors in order and in time of occurrence.

Checklists or category systems can range from simply noting whether or not a single behavior has occurred to multiple behavior systems. As an example of the first, Bryan and Test (1967) recorded whether or not individuals donated money to a Salvation Army kettle in a study dealing with donations and modeling behavior, and Strayer and Strayer (1976) classified initiation of antagonistic behavior by children in a playground into one of several categories: bite, chase, hit, kick, push-pull, and wrestle. The construction of a reliable and valid checklist is crucial to its usefulness as an observational tool. First, a critical feature of a good checklist is the explicitness with which the behavior is defined. For example, in observing antagonistic behavior, observers would need to know when a friendly tap becomes a "hit." This is accomplished more easily when the behaviors are classifiable on objective grounds than on inferential ones. The observer would code a behavior as a "hit" only if it actually met the explicit description for the act and not if it only appeared that the child "wanted" to hit. Second, each behavior of interest must be able to be classified into one and only one category. A behavior would be either a "push-pull" or "wrestle" but not both. Third, the total set of categories for classifying a particular kind of behavior such as fighting or greeting should be exhaustive of the type but limited in distinctions. The code should cover the sphere of interest but be sufficiently finite to allow meaningful assessments to be made.

Group process and classroom interaction are enduring targets for checklist observational systems. Two such systems are Bales' (1970) Interaction Process Analysis for studying group interaction and Flanders' (1970) system for analyzing teacher behavior. In the former, each act by a group member is categorized into *one* of the 12 categories (Bales, 1970, p. 92) shown in Figure 11.1.

FIGURE 11.1. Category system for interaction in groups.

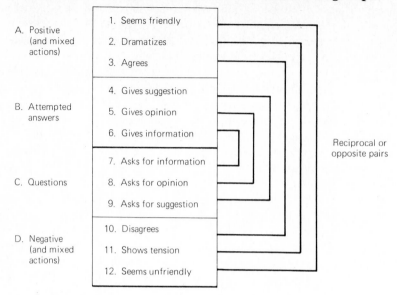

In Flanders' system, classroom behavior is classified according to the ten categories shown in Figure 11.2.

Bales' checklist system uses a modified version of continuous time sampling; that is, each act by a person is coded into one of the 12 possible types, and an act is defined as "a communication or an indication, either verbal or nonverbal, which in its context may be understood by another member as equivalent to a single simple sentence (p. 68)." Flanders, in contrast, uses very small interval time-point sampling in order to maintain a rendering of the original behavioral sequence in the classrooms. An observer codes ongoing behavior into one of Flanders' ten categories every three seconds. (See Figure 11.2.)

Teacher Talk	Response	1. Accepts Feeling 2. Praises or Encourages 3. Accepts or Uses Ideas of Pupils
		4. Asks Questions
	Initiation	5. Lecturing 6. Giving Directions 7. Criticizing or Justifying Authority
Pupil Talk		8. Pupil-Talk Response 9. Pupil-Talk Initiation
Silence		10.

FIGURE 11.2. Category system for classroom behavior.

Structured methods such as the checklist approaches are particularly good tools for testing specific hypotheses after the behaviors of interest have been described and their reliability and validity established. One significant problem with the use of checklist approaches, however, is the tendency by researchers to become too attached to a particular transcription system with the result that they try to transform every context and every situation into the form of a coding system that is available regardless of its suitability to the setting or appropriateness in terms of specified categories. On the other hand, you should be alert to the possibility that a review of the literature may turn up an observational system that is relevant and appropriate to your needs. For example, Boyer, Simon, and Karafin (1973) have compiled a test of 73 different systems of observing young children.

Issues in Systematic Observation

An ancient truism is that a watched pot never boils. Systematic observation reveals some of the truth of this statement in that watched people never act as they would if they were not being watched. An important decision to be made in any systematic observation of natural behavior concerns the obtrusiveness of the observer. Should the observer be visible or concealed? One of the main reasons investigators choose to conceal the fact that observations are taking place is because they fear that the subjects' behaviors will be influenced by their knowledge that they are being observed. This possible change in behavior is important because it limits the confidence the investigator has in the naturalism of the data; that is, the data collected may apply only to other situations in which people are aware that their behavior is being systematically observed. This, of course, is not desirable, for social science aims to produce generalizable information and not information that pertains only to the specific situation under which it is collected. This problem of observer influence has been labeled *reactivity* (Webb, et al., 1966) or *observer interference* (Weick, 1968). More specifically, in situations where observers are visible, subjects tend to suppress negative behaviors (Samph, 1976), increase desired behaviors (Zegiob and Forehand, 1978), and reduce overall activity (White, 1977). As we have indicated previously, there is also the nonmethodological issue of concealed observation, namely, the ethical nature of observing people without their knowledge or consent.

Conclusions about Systematic Observation

Like other methods in social relations, systematic observation of natural behavior demands rigorous training of observers, sensitive description, careful sampling, and appropriate caution in interpretation. The method is unique because it is able to elucidate everyday behavior in terms of the frequency, duration, form, and sequence in which it actually occurs. It is especially informative about human activity that cannot be talked about (owing to ignorance or inability) or will not be talked about (owing to fear or embarrassment).

The primary essence of systematic observation is a concern with natural behavior. The behavior may occur in a natural setting or in a laboratory and be elicited by a natural treatment or an experimentally arranged one.

PARTICIPANT AND ECOLOGICAL OBSERVATION

Systematic observation places high emphasis on natural behavior; participant observation and ecological observation stress the importance of natural settings. In fact, advocates of these methods argue that the best way to predict the behavior of a human being is to know where he or she is. "In a post office, he behaves post office, at church he behaves church" (Willems, 1969, p. 16). The guiding principle is that behavior settings exert a great influence over people, and hence research must begin at actual sites and not in arranged or contrived circumstances. For participant observers, how people see and explain their settings is at the heart of the inquiry, but the inquiry must take place at the site. Ecological researchers go a step further in attempting to describe the setting itself and then the activities conducted in that setting.

An Example of Participant Observation

People tend to be curious about natural settings that are off the beaten track, and mental hospitals are prototypic examples of such settings. In a recent foray into this terrain, Rosenhan (1973) and seven of his colleagues feigned certain symptoms of mental illness to gain admission to several hospitals. These "pseudopatients," three women and five men, included three psychologists, a pediatrician, a psychiatrist, a painter, a homemaker, and a psychology graduate student. All used pseudonyms, and those allied with mental health lied about their real occupations. With these exceptions, all presented their life histories as they actually happened and after admission to the hospitals behaved as they normally would.

All pseudopatients were admitted, and all except one received the diagnosis of schizophrenia. The participants engaged in routine activities, took notes on their observations, and worked at being discharged. This took some effort — the length of hospitalization averaged 19 days with a range of seven to 52 days. Among other observations, Rosenhan (1973) reported that whereas other patients detected that the pseudopatients were not real inmates, members of the hospital staffs sustained the initial view that the observers were disturbed. Once they had labeled the new arrivals as mentally ill, the staff interpreted all actions by the pseudopatients as consistent with the label.

A Definition of Participant Observation

Participant observation has been defined as a "period of intense social interaction between researchers and subjects in the milieu of the latter, during which time data, in the form of field notes, are unobtrusively and systematically collected" (Bogden, 1972, p. 3). As you read in Chapter 6, participant observation is used to generate theory rather than to test it. The object is to describe the complexities found in the situation with a minimum of a priori theorizing. Consequently, one of the most notable aspects of participant observation is the absence of standardized operating procedures (Williamson and Karp, 1977).

In contrast to checklist approaches, participant observation involves a much less formalized procedure although there are some common steps. These include (1) selecting a research site, (2) gaining access and taking a role, (3) making notes, and (4) formulating an analysis.

In the Rosenhan study, the sites were mental hospitals. The choice of the locale was clear at the outset whereas the relevant behaviors for observation were left intentionally open. This latter step is extremely difficult to accomplish, and many question whether it can be done at all. Kaplan (1964) refers to Nietzsche's label "the dogma of immaculate perception" to describe this tactic. Participant observers wish to be open to discovery; nevertheless, surprises are most evident against the backdrop of explicit expectations.

The second step requires selecting the level of visibility and involvement to be taken by the participant observer vis-à-vis the research setting. Rosenhan wanted his participants to remain totally disguised as opposed to candidly exposed, and they did this by becoming total participants. The rationale for this strategy is obvious. Rosenhan assumed that the mental health staff would not acknowledge admitting normal people and calling them insane. His choice of this covert stance, however, raises serious ethical questions. Other choices would have been to participate as a known researcher or to participate as a complete observer, where researchers abstain from any direct interaction in the situation (Gans, 1976).

Having made entry into the field and having decided upon the type of relationship the observer is to have with the subjects, the researcher next focuses on the recording and analysis of the observations. Lofland (1971) noted that participant observation, unlike most other research methodologies, usually combines simultaneous data collection (recording) and data analysis (encoding).

Because the observer is often not able or does not wish to write full notes while at the site, the observer should be trained to make mental notes of what is observed in situ, then notes jotted down immediately after leaving the scene, and finally full field notes, which are the conversion of the jottings and mental notes into a running log of observations. These should be written as soon as it is feasibly possible, to guard against memory loss and conceptual distortion.

The excerpted field notes in Chapter 6 illustrate one participant observer's method of recording his data. In participant observation it is difficult to give any hard-and-fast rules precisely because the nature of participant observation is exploratory, and it is assumed that the perceptions are likely to change during the course of the observation. There are, however, a number of elements common to many natural settings that should not be overlooked. These include details about the participants, the setting, the purpose for the gathering or transaction, and the social behavior that occurs.

Good participant observation field notes include actual quotes, clear distinctions between "fact" and "impression," incorporation of unusual or inexplicable events, explicit rendering and bracketing of feelings and hunches, and comments on the benefits and costs of the data gathering methods.

The final step in particpant observation is the most difficult. The researcher generates a theory that incorporates the categories and provides the linkages among them. These key linkages are at the heart of the final report. This creativity is at one and the same time the strength and weakness of participant observation. At its best, it signals a novel and insightful perspective; at its worst, it is a biased and slanted view.

The proponents of participant observation (Filstead, 1970; Habenstein, 1970; Lofland, 1971; and McCall and Simmons, 1969) note that they usually provide a more "inside" account of the phenomenon under investigation than would a method depending on prearranged categories. In addition, the researcher is free to alter the definition of the problem as more knowledge is gained about the situation (see Chapter 6). This flexibility is usually obtained with more structured methods only during initial pilot testing of the observational system, not after the research has begun.

Conclusions about Participant Observation

One advantage of participant observation is the depth of information obtained. This depth is gained by the investigator's firsthand knowledge of the situation being studied. Participant observation has received, however, a great deal of criticism. The attacks on these methods have focused on problems of reliability (usually only one observer is present in each setting), lack of statistical analysis (to sort out chance occurrences from "real" effects), and bias of the observer. These methods provide rich detail but make verification difficult.

A Definition of Ecological Observation

As noted earlier, both participant observation and ecological inquiry stress the importance of observing behavior in natural settings. They diverge somewhat in the attention they actually give to description of settings. For example, ecological psychologists are very concerned with analyzing and categorizing behavior settings in terms of such dimensions as their geographical character (rural, urban), their practical functions (drugstore, garage), their nonpsychological objects (chairs, blackboards), their primary behavioral displays (singing, discussing), and their temporal domain (morning, evening). For example, ecological studies by Barker and those of his students (Barker, 1968; Barker and Schoggen, 1973; Bechtel, 1977; Wicker, 1979) comprehensively described all the behavior settings of a particular community, which were then organized in hierarchies of types and subtypes. The final step in this **behavior setting survey** is the description of the settings in terms of whichever of their many attributes and characteristics may be of interest.

Individuals are known then by the settings they inhabit as they conduct their daily lives. For the ecological psychologist, the life-style of an individual can be accurately grasped by listing the behavior settings that he or she inhabits. Listing the behavior settings is a technique called **behavior range.** For example, the behavior range for a particular person or group of persons is informative about how active the person or persons are in community life, what interests they have, and where they spend most of their time.

Another method used by ecological psychologists is called a **specimen record.** In specimen records, a skilled observer provides a narrative account of specific actions of one person, such as a child in a noncontrived setting over a substantial time period. The record is made of everything that happens in the behavior and situation of a person. This includes whatever he or she says and does and whatever is done or said to him or her, including the manner in which actions are carried out (Wright, 1967). The observer's task is to capture in plain language a full word picture of the goal-directed behaviors of the child along with those concrete aspects of the situation that are relevant to the child's behavior (Schoggen, 1978). The most desirable method for doing this is dictation during the observation into a shielded microphone attached to a portable recorder.

Conclusions about Ecological Observation

Ecological psychologists strive for theoretical neutrality and recording impartiality in their observations. As in participant observation, the goal is discovery and disclosure about ecologically valid base rate data rather than hypothesis testing. As we noted earlier, there is no such thing as a neutral record of raw experience. Records are formulated in the concepts of one theory or another. Though clearly a matter of degree, ecological methods are potentially more accessible and replicable than those of participant observation because of the emphasis on observing specific actions rather than underlying processes. Although the yield from ecological methods has heretofore not measured up to the costs in terms of the time commitment required, there are some recent attempts to reduce the number of factors necessary to describe behavior settings. Price and Blashfield (1975) factor analyzed Barker's descriptors and reduced the number to nine interpretable factors.

ARCHIVAL RECORDS

At the beginning of this chapter we made the distinction between seeing and observing. We carry that distinction now into another domain, namely, that of statistical records. Data on unemployment rates, hospital admissions, traffic fatalities, population growth, mean daily temperature, consumer price indices, and all matters of statistical tabulation are an incomprehensible mass of numbers to the untrained eye. For persons trained to see, such records, referred to as archival data, present an opportunity to observe the effects and course of real world events.

Many laboratory experimantal manipulations are restricted in their impact, size, duration, and naturalness. Ethical and procedural realities constrain the kind of treatments that we can impose upon subjects. Natural disasters, job changes, births and deaths, and urban riots cannot be staged within the confines of social science laboratories; but they are recorded in a variety of public documents. These events are natural treatments, and archival records of their occurrences can be used to chart their impact.

Examples of Archival Research

Data from available records were used in a series of studies by Gurr (1968) to explain violence in modern societies. The hypothesis guiding this archival study was that violence results from feelings of relative deprivation. Relative deprivation occurs when there is a discrepancy between what people expect to receive and what they are actually able to achieve. The challenge for this study was to find, in existing records, indices that could be translated into signs of relative deprivation (natural treatment) on the one hand and magnitude of violence on the other hand.

Eleven hundred observations of strife collected on 114 nations during the period 1961–1965 were drawn primarily from reports in *The New York Times Index*, *Newsyear* (the annual volumes of *Facts on File*), and the *Africa Digest*. These sources were supplemented by reports of incidents of strife in the *Annual Register of Events in Africa*, and *Hispanic-American Report*, as well as country and case studies. All of these are publicly available reports.

In addition to deriving quantitative measures of strife, including the number of participants involved, the number of casualties suffered, and the number of days the strife lasted, Gurr developed several quantitative measures of relative deprivation, including economic downturns and increases in political suppression. Economic downturns and political suppression are "natural" treatments in the sense of happening without any intervention by social science researchers. Gurr found that these natural events were associated with increases in civil strife.

Another creative use of existing records to assess the effects of natural treatments was made by Durkheim (1951) in his study of suicide. Durkheim's primary hypothesis was that a basic cause of suicide is lack of integration into a social group. He examined three major kinds of social group integration: religious, familial, and political. He found suicide rates were lower among Catholics than among Protestants, lower among married people than among single people, lower among those with children than among those without children, and lower during periods of national fervor. All of these findings, he argued, supported the hypothesis that belonging to a cohesive social group (the natural event) is a deterrent to suicide.

Characteristics of archival research.   Archival studies such as Gurr's work on civil strife and Durkheim's on suicide are singular in a number of respects. First, they rely entirely on the analyses of data collected for purposes other than those of particular studies in social relations. Consequently, they require familiarity with known sources of data such as *The New York Times Index* and skill in uncovering less well-known material such as cemetery records. Second, archival studies often call for ingenuity in translating existing records into quantifiable indices of some general concepts. Objective public records of relative deprivation and social integration do not exist. Gurr's and Durkheim's resourcefulness is evident in using existing material as indicating more general social psychological processes. Third, archival studies are particularly susceptible to alternative interpretations for the natural events and/or their effects. What is required then is care in using multiple measures as Gurr did or ruling out other explanations as Durkheim did. For example, Durkheim examined a number of alternative hypotheses — that suicide is the result of psychopathic states of imitation, of racial or hereditary factors, or of climate. He then demonstrated that the statistics are not in accord with any of these hypotheses. For example, in considering the hypothesis that suicide is influenced by climate, he started with the observation that in all countries for which statistics are available over a period of years, the incidence of suicide increases regularly from January until June and then declines until the end of the year. This observation had led other writers to conclude that temperature has a direct effect on the tendency to suicide. Durkheim examined this possibility in great detail and demonstrated that the data did not support it. He argued, for example, that if temperature were the basic cause, suicide would vary regularly with it; but this is not the case. There are more suicides in spring than in autumn, although the temperature is slightly lower in spring. Moreover, suicide reaches its height not in the hottest months (July and August) but in June. By a series of such analyses, Durkheim demonstrated that the seasonal regularities in suicide rates could not be accounted for by temperature and suggested the alternative hypothesis that social activity is seasonal and that the rate of suicide is related to the extent of social activity.

Types of Archival Research

Every literate community generates a considerable amount of recorded data, both numerical and verbal, on the behavior of its members. Although these data have been accumulated primarily for purposes of administration and description, social science researchers can make good use of them to assess natural treatments.

Statistical records. Many available statistical data refer to socioeconomic information about age, sex, family size, occupation, residence, and other characteristics. Health statistics give birth and death rates and the like; federal, state, municipal, and private economic institutions collect and publish data on wages, hours of work, productivity, absenteeism, strikes, financial transactions, and so on. Many voluntary organizations have records not only of their own membership but of groups of people whom they serve. In addition, a small but steadily increasing body of data is being collected by various institutions on psychological characteristics such as IQ, personality, anxiety, and attitudes. For example, schools, hospitals, social service agencies, personnel departments in businesses, and similar institutions nowadays frequently administer psychological tests of various kinds to their entire populations.

Brenner (1973) used available statistics to examine the relation between economic factors and mental health. He found a positive correlation between rates of unemployment and mental hospital admissions and concluded the state of a country's economy can affect the state of its citizens' mental health. Kasarda (1976) has argued that the data provided in various national censuses offer opportunities for secondary analyses that are limited only by the imagination of the researcher. Among these opportunities Kasarda has mentioned the chance to analyze educational attainment, ethnic and racial segregation, poverty, marriage and divorce, social mobility, and commuting patterns.

Available statistical records are now being used as **social indicators** to chart the status and change in the quality of life (Andrews and Withey, 1976). The United States government has published reports in 1973 and 1976 detailing various social indicators of human well-being, including employment levels, housing availability, and crime rates. These reports are compiled to monitor present social conditions and to chart societal changes. Therein lies one of the singular advantages of using existing records. Many of these are collected regularly, thus enabling the user of archival data to measure relations between social variables across time. For example, is the socioeconomic standing of various racial or sex groups declining, rising, or sustaining the status quo, and to what other social factors is there a systematic tie?

Written documents: public or personal.   Verbal documents also provide a rich source of data. For example, public documents such as the inaugural addresses of United States presidents can be analyzed to detect prevalent motivational themes. Donley and Winter (1970) determined the degree to which achievement and power themes were present in each of the inaugural addresses of presidents. Presidents' motives, as shown by their first official statement, corresponded to the subsequent accomplishments of their administrations. Similarly, Tetlock (1979) drew material from public speeches pertaining to policy decisions by the United States government. The speeches associated with decisions later judged to have been faulty were contrasted with speeches associated with well-worked-out policy decisions. An existing coding scheme was applied to assess the degree to which less differentiated and less integrated modes of information processing prevailed in the poor decisions as opposed to the good decisions. Results showed speeches in the former case were more simplistic and biased.

Personal documents, including autobiographies, letters, diaries, school essays, and the like are also open to social scientific observation once obtained. For example, Schneidman (in Gerbner, et al., 1969) used the thinking, reasoning, and cognitive maneuvering in suicide notes to understand better the mental processes of suicide victims.

By and large, the rationale for the use of personal documents is similar to that of observational techniques of natural behavior. What the latter may achieve for overt behavior, the former can do for inner experiences: to reveal to the social scientist life as it is lived without response interference. However, personal documents are relatively rare, and hence the scope of their usefulness for research is rather limited.

Even when available, personal documents have to be used with caution. Authenticity cannot always be assured. A document can be produced in the form and manner of a personal record by someone else, and not only the authorship may be in doubt, but also the circumstances under which the document was written may not be known. The social scientist must inquire into the motives and situations that induced their production.

Mass communications.   In addition to statistical records and autobiographical documents, every literate society produces a variety of material intended to inform, entertain, or persuade the populace. Such material may appear in the form of literary productions, newspapers and magazines, or — more recently — film and radio and television broadcasts. Mass communications provide a rich source of data for investigating a variety of research questions. They may be used to throw light on some aspects of the culture of a given group, to compare different groups in terms of some aspect of culture, or to trace cultural change. For example, Scott and Franklin (1972) investigated the way that sex has been portrayed in seven high circulation periodicals in 1950, 1960, and 1970. Analyzing each sentence that referred to sex in a sample of issues of *Reader's Digest, McCall's, Life, Look, Saturday Evening Post, Time,* and *Newsweek,* the authors concluded that few changes in liberal (or permissive) references to sex occurred during the period. A slight increase in the total number of references to sex was revealed by the analysis, and, although conservative (or restrictive) references to sex declined from 1950 to 1960, no further decrease in the proportion of references that were conservative occurred between 1960 and 1970.

A similar analysis of magazines was conducted to assess the inclusion and portrayal of blacks in advertisements (Cox, 1971). Five magazines (*Life, Saturday Evening Post, New Yorker, Ladies Home Journal,* and *Time*) were analyzed for all their issues in 1967 and the first half of 1968 and compared with the issues of these same magazines during 1949 and 1950. Only one-half of one percent of the ads in 1949 and 1950 included blacks, and that portion in 1967 and 1968 had increased to slightly over 2 percent. Gains were more apparent with respect to portrayal. In the 1949–1950 period, 95.5 percent of blacks were presented as having occupations below skilled labor, whereas the proportion had dropped to 30.9 percent in the 1967–1968 period.

Both the preceding studies document trends in communication content in the mass media. Other questions susceptible to this kind of analysis include tracing the development of research ideas, disclosing international differences, comparing different media, assessing coverage against objectives, exposing propaganda techniques, uncovering stylistic features, identifying psychological motivations, and assessing responses to events or ideas (Berelson, 1952; Holsti, 1969).

All utilize a technique called **content analysis**, which is "any technique for making inferences by systematically and objectively identifying specified characteristics of messages" (Holsti, 1969, p. 601). This is similar to the definition of systematic observation of natural behavior. Both techniques require objectivity of coding categories in order to assure reliability, systematic application of these coding systems across a representative sample of material in order to control observer bias, and consistency in theoretical aims so that the findings can be related to some relevant variable or variables.

The steps of content analysis are very similar to the steps in conducting a systematic observation of a natural behavior. They are (1) choosing the phenomenon to be coded, such as the presence and portrayal of elderly people in the print media. (2) Selecting the media from which the observations are to be made — the issue here, as in systematic observation, is the selection of media that are typical or representative of what is available and with which people have contact. The issue is to find out what is out there and not to select so as to enhance or inhibit the possibility of obtaining particular findings. (3) Deriving the coding categories is a third step. As was the case with systematic observation, content analysis categories can range from a simple binary system in which the presence or absence of people of a certain age are noted to multicategory systems using mutually exclusive and exhaustive categories in which distinctions are made on a range of phenomena such as the status of the portrayed character (for example, high, middle or low), background physical attractiveness (attractive, neutral, unattractive), or evaluation of context (positive, neutral, negative). (4) Deciding on the sampling strategy is another step. The distinctions here again are roughly comparable to the decisions involved in systematic observation. The task is to choose among strategies that code every reference to the phenomenon in question or to select a discontinuous though regular method of sampling, such as every other issue of several magazines over a year's period. (5) A fifth step is training the coders. Reliability of content analysis is an important consideration and particularly so when inferences are required in order to decide, for example, whether the portrayal of an elderly person is cast positively or negatively. (6) Lastly, we have analyzing the data. Sometimes with content analysis the most straightforward analysis is the straightforward representation of the data in summary form, such as numbers represented and percentage representation.

One type of category system for content analyzing newspapers has been used by Harold D. Lasswell and his associates (1949). Lasswell developed a system of "symbol analysis," which was employed during World War II in several branches of the United States government. In this system, newspaper content was studied for the appearance of certain symbols, such as "England," "Russia," "democracy," "Jews," "Stalin," and so on. The frequency with which these symbols appeared was noted, as well as whether their presentation was favorable, unfavorable, or neutral (or "indulgent," "deprivational," "neutral"). Favorable references were sometimes further divided into those stressing "strength" and those stressing "goodness" or "morality"; negative references were divided into "weakness" and "immorality" categories.

Sampling material from mass communications is a step requiring much time and thought. The first task is to define the universe — newspapers, magazines, radio, or television. But even if we limited ourselves to newspapers, it would not be satisfactory to list all the newspapers published in a given country and draw every tenth or twentieth one. Even if we were also to introduce controls to ensure that newspapers representing different geographical areas, political orientations, economic groups, and ethnic groups were included in the proportion in which they are represented in the total population of newspapers, there would be a problem. The difficulty arises from the fact that newspapers vary tremendously in size and influence, and a realistic sample should not weigh an obscure journal equally with a metropolitan daily. The situation is not the same as that of drawing a representative sample of a voting population, each member of which has equal influence at the polls — namely, one vote.

Graber (1971) wished to represent a cross-section of the newspapers used by the general public as sources of information in the study previously mentioned. She developed a complex sampling scheme that reflected where these newspapers would be found. First, it was decided that newspapers in each of the major regions in the country should be included in the sample. Cities in each region were then divided into three groups by population: over one million, 500,000 to one million, and less than 500,000. It was decided to draw three-fourths of the sample from the most populous states in each region and the remainder from the less populous states to reflect "voting power" on the basis of population.

Further decisions narrowed even more the potential newspapers that could be included in the sample. Half of the newspapers were selected from states in which the Democratic party was stronger; and half, from states in which the Republican party was stronger. Newspapers were selected, moreover, to represent monopolistic as well as competitive newspaper market situations. Finally, two types of newspapers, appealing to either special or general audiences, were included in the sample of newspapers for study. Graber then coded all of the campaign stories in the newspapers included in the sample.

Frequently, then, the sampling procedure in communication analysis consists of three stages: sampling of sources (which newspapers, which radio stations, which films, and so on are to be analyzed), sampling of dates (which period is to be covered by the study), and sampling of units (which aspects of the communication are to be analyzed). With respect to the sampling of units, decisions are often arbitrary and based on tacit assumptions about which feature of a medium best characterizes it. For example, is it the headline, the human interest story, the editorial, or some other feature that best indicates the policy of a newspaper?

To avoid such arbitrariness, content analysts frequently follow one of two possibilities: they analyze on the basis of several different units (for example, they take samplings of headlines, of human interest stories, of editorials, and then count how many times a given subject is mentioned in each); or they disregard these "natural" units completely, dividing the issues of a newspaper mechanically into lines or inches of space from which they draw a sample. Note here the similarity to the distinctions among types of time sampling.

Issues in Archival Research

Archival records afford the opportunity to assess the impact of natural events; they also elicit particular problems of interpretation. For example, records are available that might allow a connection to be drawn between ice-cream sales and crime rates. Suppose we were to replicate previous work showing a positive relation between these two variables (Kasarda, 1976). Could we then conclude that ice-cream intake influences the propensity to commit a crime? Although the correlation is positive, it is considered a spurious relationship in that both variables are related because they are both the result of an unidentified third variable, namely, weather conditions. Both ice-cream sales and crime are affected by increasing temperature; neither one affects the other. The user of archival records must control for spuriousness by controlling for or ruling out other plausible explanations for the obtained relationship.

A second major issue for users of archival records has to do with the adequacy of methods employed for the initial data collection. Careful sampling and measurement are required of all good social science; but because many public records are often collected not in the interests of good social science, attention needs to be drawn to possible sources of systematic error such as overreporting in expense accounts, for example, and underreporting in income for tax declarations. Other errors include procedural inconsistencies, sampling biases, recording and clerical errors, and changing definitions of categories.

Conclusions on Archival Research

The use of already collected data to assess the effects of natural treatments has the advantage of being economical, at least in the data collection stage. The researcher is spared the time and cost involved in data collection and recording. This may be offset, however, by the effort involved in finding and translating the relevant statistics to meaningful variables (encoding) as well as the search for material that would allow for the culling out of alternative interpretations. But such data have other advantages in social research. A major one is the fact that much information of this sort is collected under natural conditions (natural in the sense of being part of the everyday operation of modern life) and that it is often collected repeatedly, thus making possible the determination of trends over time. Still another advantage is that the gathering of information from such sources does not require the cooperation of the individuals about whom the information is being sought, as does the use of questionnaire and interview formats. Moreover, archival data are particularly well suited for the study of large-scale or widespread natural phenomena not amenable to investigation in other ways.

SUMMARY

Naturalistic research emphasizes the importance of ecologically valid observations. Consequently, the concern is with nonmanipulational designs and with nonfabricated behaviors. Naturalistic research methods accept the necessity for internal validity but go further in recognizing that internal validity is only a first step toward the development of an externally valid set of scientific constructs.

In this chapter, we have discussed various naturalistic ways of doing research: systematic observation, participant and ecological observation, and the use of archival records. Despite considerable differences among these approaches in specific procedural details, all are similar not only in their naturalistic underpinnings but also in their attention to the tenets of good social relations research — namely, reliability, validity, and ethicality.

Throughout we have suggested particular benefits and costs contingent upon the use of each strategy but have repeated the common element in all three, specifically, their nonintervention quality. When the social researcher employs one or more aspects of naturalness, whether it be natural behavior, natural setting, or natural treatment, the investigation may yield findings that are more realistic and generalizable than if all three elements are ignored.

According to the framework offered in this chapter, systematic observation stresses natural behaviors, participant and ecological observation highlight natural settings, and archival research emphasizes natural treatments. Despite this tripartite division, there is no necessary barrier to the combination of two or more emphases into a single design. Many field experiments combine systematic observation of natural behavior in natural settings, and many evaluation studies survey responses to natural treatments in natural settings.

One major advantage of using naturalistic methods is that the resulting observations are more likely to be authentic and well-grounded than with methods depending upon interventions into the natural course of events. Consequently, there is greater faith that the observed behaviors are representative of life as it is lived rather then life as it could theoretically be lived.

Another feature of naturalistic research is a potential increase in the external validity of the findings. Naturalistic methods have greater generalizability than more experimental techniques. External validity, of course, assumes the establishing of internal validity, but once this has been accomplished, external validity is often relegated to second-class status.

External validity is not one thing, however (Tunnell, 1977). Research findings may be generalizable to three relatively independent domains: to other comparable *behaviors*, to other comparable *settings*, and to other comparable events *(treatments)*. These three dimensions of naturalness thus can cue the researcher as to the likely area or areas to which the findings may generalize.

part 3

Results

Data Processing

12

Data processing involves the conversion or reduction of information that one collects from observations in social research into a form that permits statistical tabulation, ease of storage, and access for future use. Usually, this means that scientific observations will be translated into numerical form, placed on IBM cards that facilitate data analysis, and stored in a way that allows the information to be used in statistical analysis by a computer.

The problems that are associated with data processing concern ways of minimizing error, techniques of converting observations into numerical form (or coding and data reduction), and procedures and facilities for storing and retrieving information. It is useful to specify some basic characteristics of a set of data that are relevant to any study to appreciate more thoroughly what conversion of data implies and the kinds of errors that may occur in data processing.

THE DATA MATRIX[1]

It is useful to view a set of information that is collected in a study as being arranged in the form of a large **matrix** or, to use a more ordinary illustration, in a form that resembles the layout of mailboxes in a campus post office. A set of boxes is arranged along a wall in a large rectangular shape so that a number of rows and columns appear. People find their mailboxes by ascertaining the appropriate row and column among the boxes, although we rarely think of "finding our mailbox" in this way because we have become so accustomed to walking right up to the same place

---

[1]Many of the ideas in this section follow the very important work of John Galtung (1967).

each day, perhaps checking the number on the front of the box and then dialing the correct combination to open it.

Now, let us step back from the set of mailboxes for just a moment. Each box in the large, rectangular wall of boxes can be located by specifying the column and row in which the box occurs. We call such a configuration of mailboxes a "matrix" of mailboxes. Now let us imagine how we could put social science data in the same matrix form. Imagine that we have interviewed 1000 individuals from a cross-section of the adult electorate in the United States regarding their attitudes on current social and political issues. On our survey we asked 100 questions, including many about attitudes on a variety of topics ranging from abortion to amnesty to school busing to local and national political candidates. We have asked about the respondent's age, education, background, income, occupation, past voting record, and political party preference.

Let us place each of the thousand people whom we interviewed along the rows of the matrix so that each person is assigned one and only one row. The rows represent the units of analysis, which in this case are individuals whom we have interviewed. The first case (or individual in this instance because we are discussing the results of a survey study) is placed in the first row, the second case in the second row, the third case in the third row, and so on until the thousandth case is placed in the thousandth row of our data matrix. If we were assigning each person a row of mailboxes, then we would require a post office that had mailboxes stacked one thousand rows high, possibly stretching the post office analogy a bit far.

We now assign one and only one column to each of the characteristics that we have collected in our survey. As information on 100 different aspects of each individual who was interviewed was collected, we need one hundred columns to accommodate all of the information from our survey. We call each different kind of information a variable. Each column in the data matrix represents one variable. Let us say that the first variable concerns the report of which candidate the respondent voted for in the last presidential election. Thus, information about respondents' votes would be placed in column one for each case. Column two is assigned information about the respondents' preference for the upcoming presidential election. Each variable is assigned one column in this manner until the hundredth variable, let us say, the respondents' income level, is assigned column 100.

The value of a particular variable may be defined as the particular kind of observation that appears for a given case. If, for instance, the first respondent reported a vote for Nixon in 1972, then the value of the first variable for the first respondent would be "Nixon vote." If the second respondent reported casting a McGovern vote, then the value for the second respondent on the first variable would be "McGovern vote." If the third respondent reported not voting at all, then the value on variable one for that respondent would be "not voting." The values of variables are the *results* of our observations for each case. These values are recorded in the appropriate box in our data matrix for each case and variable (the intersection of the case and variable).

Values are usually represented by numbers in most research (integers, or whole numbers without decimals, are nearly always employed for these purposes) for ease in statistical analysis on computational machines, although numerical representation of values is not absolutely necessary if one were of a mind to tabulate values by hand. In an age of computers few would be so presumptuous as to fail to use labor-saving devices. Thus, numerical representation is practically a necessity for few computer programs are written to deal with nonnumerical coding, and no other reasons come to mind to use anything other than numerical coding of values. Different variables may take on a very wide range of values. The things people say that they like or dislike about the graduated income tax, for instance, may require a code that allows for as many as 100 alternative responses, whereas sex is nearly always coded as a dichotomy to represent males and females. Political partisanship often can be presented as having three values: Democrat, Republican, and Independent, although partisanship is often represented as having nine values: strong Democrat, weak Democrat, leaning Democrat, Independent, leaning Republican, weak Republican, strong Republican, apolitical, and other party. Regardless, the particular values involved in a study should reflect the uses to which an investigator wishes to put the information. Thought should be given to the fineness or detail of the values early in the research project because a more refined analysis (such as the nine values of partisanship rather than three) cannot be instituted at a later point in the study.

The **units of analysis,** or cases, in a data matrix need not be comprised of characteristics of individuals. For example, Eulau and Eyestone (1968) used 77 city councils from the San Francisco Bay area as the units of analysis. Each council was viewed as a relatively small but relatively structured group, the members of which regularly interact. The researchers gathered information on a large number of variables for each council.

Distinctions among several kinds of characteristics or variables and several units of analysis will be helpful in thinking about the data matrix. First, it is useful to distinguish among units of analysis in regard to the levels that they imply. Individuals most frequently serve as units of analysis. But larger aggregates of people and groups are also frequently found as units of analysis in the social sciences. Groups of varying sizes and structures have characteristics, just as the individuals who make up the groups, and much fruitful knowledge has been acquired by analyzing and theorizing about such aggregate formations. It is imperative to remember, however, that groups and other aggregates of people do not have the same characteristics as individuals, except in metaphorical senses. People, for instance, have IQs, but groups do not; nor do groups have attitudes, or pulses, or memories. On the other hand, groups have numerical size, structure, and cohesiveness in ways that are meaningless when applied to individuals.

Units may also vary in respect to structure. Perhaps the basic distinction is between units that have no perceptible structure and units that can be characterized by structure in a meaningful way. By structure, we mean that the individuals (or subgroups) that comprise a group interact in some regular way. The interaction may be based on rules or legal codes, as in the case of courtroom procedures and the interaction of judge, jury, defense and prosecutor or in the case of legislative, executive, and judicial branches of the United States government. Or the interaction may be based on norms and other "rules of the game," as in the case of the interaction that occurs in the local bridge club, fraternity meetings, and on dates. Or the interaction may be based on some combination of these factors—as, indeed, most behavior in a complex, industrial society is—as in the interaction that occurs within a political machine or party organization, the working out of responsibilities by a crew of astronauts, or the enforcement of the law by the local police.

Units that have structure can be characterized on the basis of that structure. We speak of the authoritarian or democratic character of family decision making in different cultures or in this society at different times or in different social class groups. Or we may speak of the dictatorial or democratic character of the local high school football coach or the extent to which a college faculty is "integrated" in the sense that its members interact and communicate with one another or the degree to which a state legislature is dominated by leaders who are professional or traditional in inclination. Other aggregates have no structure in this sense. They frequently are characterized by size or rates of various types, such as mortality or percentage of Republican party ballots. Social and demographic characteristics, such as racial, ethnic, and religious composition, income and educational distributions, family size, and condition of housing, are frequently used as variables when the unit of analysis involves relatively unstructured aggregates of people.

Second, it is useful to discuss how variables relate to the unit of analysis in a study. Two distinct types of variables may be distinguished on the basis of the level of analysis referred to by the variable. We call these types *structural* and *contextual* and we will define them after we note the interrelationships between levels. As one moves from lower to higher levels of analysis, the units shift from individuals to small groups to larger groups to entire societies to supranational regional aggregations. The major relation among these "levels of analysis" is that lower levels are included within higher levels. Individuals, for instance, are included within small groups, and small groups are included within large groups, and larger groups are included within nations. The structure of the unit at the higher level of analysis is comprised not just of units of analysis at lower levels but also of the interactions between them. The structure of a small group is comprised of individuals and the interactions among individuals. So, too, is the structure of Congress or Sears, Roebuck and Co. or the Southern Baptist Church.

With regard to the main unit of analysis employed in a study, **structural variables** are characteristics that are formed by combinations of units at lower levels of analysis. The structure is comprised of the units and the way they are related (or "structured"). In contrast, **contextual variables** are characteristics of units at higher levels of analysis that encompass (or form the "context" for) the unit of analysis with which we are concerned. An example should help clarify what we mean by structural and contextual variables.

Assume that a Mr X Lives in Chicago and that he is contemplating how to cast his ballot for national office on election day. A number of facts might be relevant in explaining how Mr. X votes. First, Mr. X identifies with the Republican party. Second, Mr. X holds a number of beliefs, values, and attitudes, all of which are interrelated and most of which strongly favor the Republicans. Third, Mr. X lives in a ward that is strongly Democratic in aggregate voting preference and that has a strong, well-integrated political organization. If Mr. X votes Republican, as much current theory would predict under these circumstances, then it would most likely be because of his partisan identification and because of his pro-Republican ideology.

If Mr. X votes Democratic, then it might be because of community pressures on him or special favors that he might receive from the fact that the Democrats control the local party "machinery." Sustaining his Republicanism through his vote or defecting to the Democrats may, of course, also arise from a host of other factors.

In this example, *ideology is a structural variable*. An ideology is comprised of an organized set of individual cognitions that occur at a lower level of analysis than the individual level. When we speak of a pro-Republican ideology, we are characterizing this system of beliefs, values, and attitudes. To say that Mr. X holds a strong pro-Republican ideology is to attribute a structural characteristic to him because the ideology is formed from the attitudes operating at a lower, more specific level. In contrast, the Democratic character of the ward is a *contextual variable*. The ward itself is a legally defined territory that encompasses many people, including Mr. X. The fact that the ward tends to vote Democratic is one kind of contextual characteristic in this case because it encompasses a level above that of Mr. X's vote. The Democratic organization within the ward is another contextual characteristic that may be ascribed to Mr. X, because the "machine" is operative within the ward in which Mr. X lives. Note that this contextual characteristic has structure, whereas the first contextual characteristic has no particular social structure.

This example shows why it is fruitful to link contextual and structural variables with other variables in a study. It is also imperative not to make the assumption that what is true at one level of analysis is also true at some other level of analysis (Alker, 1965). Groups do not necessarily behave the same way individuals do; nor do groups necessarily behave for the same reasons that individuals do. Individuals within groups do not necessarily behave in the same ways or for the same reasons as do the groups to which they belong. Such assertions appear commonsensical, and indeed, they are. Nonetheless, very common fallacies arise frequently because levels of analysis are confused. The *ecological fallacy* and *individualistic fallacy* are, perhaps, the most common.

Assume that a set of data about voting trends and income for counties is correlated and that we find counties that have greater income tend to be more Republican whereas counties with lower income tend to be more Democratic. We call it the **ecological fallacy** to assume on the basis of these "group level" data that the individuals within the counties necessarily behave in a way that is analogous to the way that their counties behave. Wealthier individuals may well be inclined to cast Republican ballots, and less affluent individuals may well be inclined to cast Democratic ballots. But unless the relationships are actually exceedingly strong, the individual and the ecological (group) associations are by no means necessarily related.

Assume that data about individual relationships are available that suggest that if people possess more pacifist attitudes, there will be an easing of tensions and diminution of conflict in their small group, whereas more aggressive attitudes within the members of a group will lead to an escalation of tensions and conflict. We call it the *individualistic fallacy* to assume from these relationships among individuals that pacifist attitudes among national leaders will necessarily lead to easing of tensions and the diminution of conflict or that aggressive attitudes will lead to an escalation of tensions and conflict. We would require evidence at the level of the nation in order to reach this conclusion because what is true for individuals in small groups may or may not be true for larger groups with differing structures and contexts.

But we are not always in a position to collect data at the level of analysis to which we wish to generalize. What then? On the assumption that some evidence is better than sheer speculation unsupported by systematic observation, we go right ahead. We commit either an ecological or individualistic error, construct our argument based on the respective fallacy, and *then make the weakness of the evidence we are using* explicit. In some instances, we may be able to circumscribe the extent of ecological or individualistic error by complex statistical or theoretical means that are beyond the scope of this book to describe. But in all cases we should make the weaknesses of our argument clear and elaborate possible alternative arguments that cannot be eliminated because of these shortcomings.

Finally, social scientists use many different kinds of data in their analyses. The preceding discussion should make it clear that survey data based on interviews of individuals are only one kind of observation that is fruitful in the social sciences.

DATA REDUCTION

Data reduction is the translation of information from one form to another form to simplify problems of analysis, storage, and dissemination to other scholars. Possibly amorphous material is put in the form of a data matrix in the reduction process. Galtung (1967) described the data reduction process as including the presentation of a stimulus of some type in the presence of an object that responds and thereby makes an impression on a recording instrument. The impression is then recorded in a way that makes it amenable to analysis, usually by computer. The observation is called a **datum** when it reaches the end of the data-processing operation. Different kinds of observations on varying units may stretch the meaning of this formulation or cloud its meaning somewhat, so a simpler paradigm will be used.

The analyst first observes a set of behaviors that have been identified by some theoretical notions: then the analyst records these observations by placing values into a data matrix at the appropriate places. At this stage or at some later stage, information in the matrix is "coded" into a form that is compatible with computer analysis. One must be eternally vigilant at each stage of data reduction to avoid errors or to minimize their impact in biasing the results of a study.

Coding Information

The first stage of coding information, the construction of a **coding frame** or code book, is based on the original design ideas that are the basis of a study. The coding frame is an outline of what is coded and how it is to be coded. The rationale for decisions on how to code each kind of information that is encountered in a study is based on four considerations: (1) What information that is arranged in which specific categories is required to test the hypotheses in the study? (2) In what ways can the information in the study be best coded to allow the most thorough use by oneself and by other scholars for other specific purposes at later times? (3) What conventions will allow us to minimize errors in processing information? (4) What limits on the extensiveness and intensiveness of coding information from a study do resource limitations place on the coding process?

A coding frame is a set of rules used to classify observations of variables into values that are transformed into numbers. The rules define what particular value categories a variable may be assigned in the classification process and, essentially, "what counts for what" in the context of the study. It is precisely at this point — when coding categories are being formulated initially — that theoretical concerns must be brought fully to bear on the way coding categories are designed. Unless coding categories follow directly from the way we have conceptually defined the terms that we wish to test, a great deal of error in basing inferences on later statistical analysis is likely to result from poor formulation of categories. At the extreme, this error could render the data meaningless and make the inferences based on them irrelevant to theoretical concerns. At the very least, a rationale of some kind should be worked out for each category (or value in terms of data matrix) to which each variable in a study may be assigned.

Two more general maxims guide the formulation of all such classifications. They are as follows: (1) Coding categories must be mutually exclusive; the same value should not be coded in more than one category for a single variable. (2) Coding categories should allow an exhaustive classification of all values that appear in a study. No values should be omitted for consideration, or "left out." Let us use a simple example to illustrate.

Assume that we wish to study the relationship between gender and liberalism or conservatism among people in a metropolitan area. We draw a sample, design a study, conduct fieldwork, and ask a question that presumably measures liberalism and conservatism. Such a question to measure liberalism and conservatism might be: "Do you consider yourself to be very liberal, liberal, middle of the road, conservative, very conservative, or don't you think of yourself in these terms?" We then ask each interviewer to observe the respondent's gender directly rather than ask because gender can be classified easily and such observations shorten the number of questions that must be asked.

The interviewer classifies whatever the respondent answered to the question by checking a box on each interview schedule in order to code the liberalism-conservatism responses. Note that the interviewer may be "filtering out" a very great amount of extraneous information, for respondents may have lengthy replies in addition to the simple response that is required for the question. A number is associated with the appropriate box, so that the interview is "precoded" according to the response that is judged most fitting by the interviewer. If the coding frame is well defined, and interviewing instructions are clear about the rules for classification of responses to the question, and the interviewers are well trained, then each response will be classified in one and only one category. Assuming that boxes for "don't know" and "other" responses are provided, then literally all possible responses that have any meaning in terms of the conventional social science usage of liberalism and conservatism (and those that do not) can be classified by the interviewer.

It is also true that provision of boxes for "male" and "female" produce mutually exclusive and exhaustive categorization for the interviewers' observations concerning the gender of the respondents. It is important to understand that information is being interpreted and "censored" at each stage of the study. Not only does the initial delimitation of categories, or values, rule out many alternative categories, but the interviewers, as mentioned earlier, interpret what they have been told in terms of their comprehension of the categories. Additionally, staff coders at later stages will make further interpretations of the information that is present on the coding forms. For example, the response alternatives to the first question could just as well have omitted the "very liberal" and "very conservative" categories so that everyone would be classified without respect of perceived degree of liberalism or conservatism. We assume that some theroetical reason that guided the design of the study required two degrees rather than one degree of intensity on this measure. We further assume that respondents can regularly and meaningfully discriminate between two degrees of liberalism and conservatism in their self-classifications.

Other, even more difficult coding decisions must be planned in designing a coding frame. Not all questions are so neatly and easily handled by precoding as the preceding example suggests. Frequently, the investigator does not have a set of theoretical presuppositions that is well developed enough to specify what all the alternative responses to a question are likely to be. Frequently, the investigator does not even possess a reasonably good hunch about what the more precise patterns of response to more general questions are likely to be. This is particularly true in new or rapidly developing areas in the social sciences. In these instances, "second guessing" what respondents are likely to say is not a very adequate way of handling coding problems (because the guesses may be ill-founded) although prior specification of response alternatives, based on an extensive pretesting procedure, might meet many of the problems by informing the investigator what the major outlines of responses to general questions are likely to be. Ask yourself, for instance, where students who live in dormitories obtain most of their information about national and local affairs. If you say television, we would speculate that you are more likely than not incorrect because radio is much more common in dormitory rooms than is television.

When we use open-ended questions (discussed in Chapter 8), we have the problem of not being able to specify what the responses to questions are likely to be in advance because of ignorance about a problem area. Rather than precoding responses, the interviewer records the verbatim responses of respondents to his or her questions. This places the burden of coding information entirely on the shoulders of an office staff and requires that a coding frame be designed in part at least at a later time. Construction of a coding frame for many open-ended questions is usually an eclectic process. It is in part derived inductively from the actual responses to questions in a survey, but the formulation of more general categories for responses must coincide with the theoretical requirements of the concepts that we wish to measure as defined by the study design. General categories for classifying responses are delineated by the rationale for using a question in the survey. Some modification of these more general categories may be required once responses are in, but not a great deal of modification to the theoretically generated categories is anticipated at this stage. More specific categories for classifying responses are normally formulated with an eye to the actual responses and also to original design considerations to a somewhat lesser extent. It is at the more specific level of coding responses to open-ended questions that modification of preexisting ideas about what responses are going to be is most likely required. Consider the following example.

The Survey Research Center at the University of Michigan normally conducts pre- and postelection surveys at the time of presidential elections (Muehl, 1961). One question has to do with images that people associate with the political parties and candidates. These are measured by asking "What do you like about the (Democrats, Republicans)?" and "What do you dislike about the (Democrats, Republicans)?" A variety of general dimensions, of course, could be developed to encompass responses to these questions. But general classification of responses is in terms of personal aspects of each major party candidate, domestic policy, foreign policy, the parties as managers of government, and group-related attitudes because these categories are assumed to be very meaningful in the citizen's voting decision (Campbell, et al., 1960).

Whether *specific* responses, for instance, hawkish or dovish positions on the Korean or Vietnamese wars, are coded is in part a question of time and in part a question of what we wish to measure in the design of the survey. These items are also coded at at a much more specific level by the Survey Research Center. The more specific the classification of open-ended questions, the more likely that coders will have to construct coding frames in an inductive way "from the data."

Once a coding frame has been established for a study, filling in the data matrix is a matter of applying the frame to the observations. Needless to say, all the problems involved in communication arise in this process, and space does not permit an extended discussion of more specific rules and conventions of coding. A number of excellent treatments of coding are available and should be consulted in detail *prior* to the design of a study, as well as during the study (Benson, 1969; Parten, 1966; Riley, 1963).

It is not necessarily any easier to code information from higher or lower levels of analysis. Consider the design of a code for occupations, for example, at the individual level. Hundreds of occupations that many have never heard of appear in large populations. How, for instance, might one code a "water witcher"? How many readers know what a "water witcher" does, for that matter? Or consider a study that involves governmental bureaus, agencies, and departments. Precisely what is considered an expenditure is by no means always clear and in some instances, can vary by millions or even billions of dollars. Studies of patterns of expenditures must tackle this very sticky problem of formulating rules so that coders can make decisions about what is and what is not an expenditure. Do you know, for instance, how much is being spent this year on national defense? How did you arrive at this figure? How certain are you that you are correct? How many different estimates can you find?

The ambiguities of complex data require that we first impose a general set of theoretically defined categories on an otherwise unorganized and confusing set of observations. Then we may use both theoretical suppositions and inductive generalizations from the data to construct a set of value categories that will meet the twin criteria of mutual exclusiveness and classification of all possible responses. Perhaps the most important thing to remember about the process is that you should always have a reason that you can state explicitly for making decisions about coding operations.

Two additional precesses — editing and reliability checking — also must be mentioned in this discussion of coding. An editor should review all information before coders process it — regardless of the kind or source of information that is being processed — to ensure that it is legible and meets with the overall requirements of the study. In survey studies, for instance, interviewers may attach notes to point out idiosyncracies of some responses. The editor, rather than the coder, should make all nonstandard decisions concerning how material is to be coded. Or an editor should make sure that all documents to be coded contain the appropriate information. The editor's job is to ensure clarity and the appropriateness of information so that coders will make only standardized decisions that can be based on the coding frame explicitly. Space does not allow full discussion of this extremely important process here, but other, more thorough discussions are available (Parten, 1966).

Checking reliability in the coding process itself is also vital. Coders should make the same decision about how material is to be coded each time they confront the same material, and different coders should classify the same material in the same way. Systematic monitoring of the coding staff is essential. This, of course, includes tests of the extent to which coders can classify the same material the same way at different times and the extent to which different coders agree on the proper classification of the same material. (The results of these tests should be included in reports describing the study.) Even when the research group is performing its own coding operations on smaller projects, group members should continually monitor the group's performance in these ways.

Punching and Verifying

Once information has been coded, the contents of the data matrix must be converted to a medium that permits it to be analyzed easily and stored and retrieved in the simplest, most efficient manner that resources allow. In most instances, this means that the data matrix is to be made suitable for processing by computer. A plan for how this conversion is to occur is called a **card design.**

The most common medium used by beginning students to convert information to computer-compatible form is the IBM card, a heavy piece of paper that forms a matrix that contains 80 columns and 12 rows. (See Figure 12.1.) Once coding has been completed, information is placed on IBM cards by assigning specific sets of contiguous columns to specific variables. The set of columns that is assigned to a variable is call a *field.* Fields may vary in width but must be large enough (contain enough columns) to allow one column for each digit of the largest number that is coded for that variable assigned to the field. Numbers are placed in the field by assigning one digit to each column, beginning at the right of the field and then working to the left. This is called *right-justifying* the number and is equivalent to lining numbers up right-justified on decimals when adding a column of figures or presenting a column of percentages.

Only the bottom ten rows (printed 0 through 9 on most IBM cards) are used for storing numerical data. Numbers are stored on a card by punching holes (with and only with a keypunch machine designed for this purpose) in the row that contains the number that is to be stored and in the column that corresponds to the field assigned to a variable. If column five has been assigned to the variable gender, for

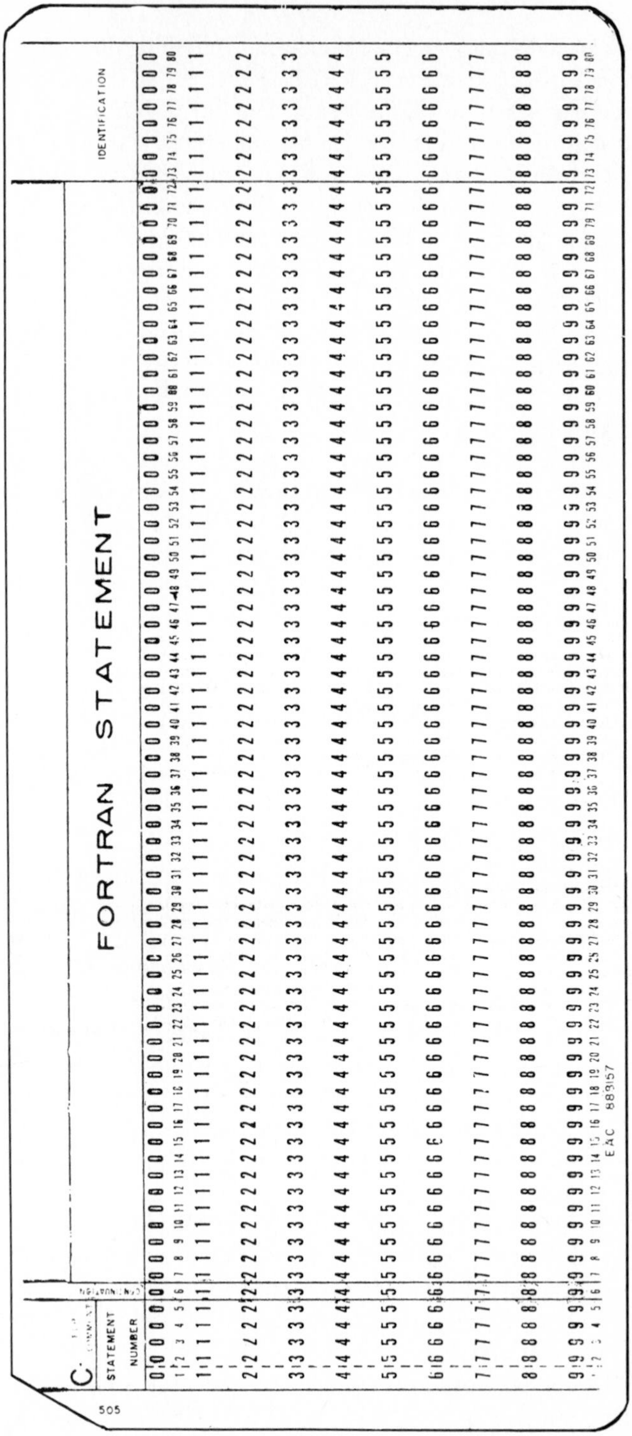

FIGURE 12.1. IBM card

instance, and we wish to record a "1" on a card (let us say, for a male), then we punch a rectangular hole in the row that is labeled "1" in column five. In other words, beginning with 0 at the top of the IBM card, each row represents a different number through 9. As the size of the field increases beyond a single column to two or to three columns or even further, the largest number that can be represented in a field increases as well. We can, for example, punch numbers 0 through 9 in a single-column field, numbers 00 through 99 in a two-column field, numbers 000 through 999 in a three-column field, and numbers 0000 through 9999 in a four-column field. There is no practical limit to the size of a field, although computers will only process numbers up to a certain (very large) size. In general, numbers of the magnitude that social scientists use will cause no problems.

There also is no practical limit to the number of IBM cards that may be used to record information for a given unit of analysis. This means that the investigators can use as many data fields as they find convenient in coding and storing data. It is *never* a good idea to crowd data overly or to try to use the same field to punch more than a single variable. Nor is it desirable to use alphabetic codes (or any other non-numerical code) for coding information that could just as well be put in numerical form. It is of course perfectly permissible to punch textual or lingual information on IBM cards provided that the *purpose of the analysis* is related to textual processing. This is not true, however, in most social science analysis despite the fact that an increasing amount of textual analysis is being conducted in the humanities and the social sciences. The computer can read alphabetic characters without difficulty; most statistical analysis programs cannot.

Keypunching information from coded material is fraught with error. It is necessary to **verify** (or check) the data once they have been keypunched. A verifier is a machine that looks very much like a keypunch except that it does not punch holes. Information is verified by passing punched cards through the verifier, punching the number that should appear in each column in the appropriate field by checking the coded material for that field. If the number that is punched does not match the number that appears on the card, a light comes on and the verifier stops. This alerts the operator that something is wrong with the information that has been punched in the field on the card originally. Machine verification is an important element in maintaining high quality in information. It is an unfortunately common practice to verify information visually by eyesight. But human beings are notoriously subject to error, and this is especially true when very tedious precise work is being done. There is no substitute for verification of information by machine if the goal of quality control is to be maintained in social science data.

Information may also be introduced into a computer in a number of other ways. Some keypunches record information on magnetic tape rather than on paper cards. Other devices punch holes in paper tape, which is then read into the computer. Still, the punched card is probably the most common medium for interacting with computers, at least at the initial stages of data reduction.

Note that the data matrix has been converted to an alternative form once punching is completed. Units of analysis are now represented by one or more cards, and variables are represented by data fields that have been assigned to the cards for each unit. The values are the numbers (and/or other characters) that are punched in each field. It is meaningful to speak of storing and retrieving the data matrix once it has been placed in this form.

Punched and verified data are stored several ways. The most efficient and common way is to record the card images on magnetic tape by using a computer. Information that represents an image of each card is stored electronically in a way that is analogous to the way that a tape recorder records voices and other sounds. Card images can also be stored on computer disks — devices that resemble records — but this equipment is normally very expensive. Similarly, cards are fairly often kept in pressurized drawers in their original format.

Editing the File

The process of data reduction is not completed when the original punched and verified data are written on a magnetic computer tape or otherwise tentatively placed in storage because it is still likely that error exists in the file. This may be error due to the original recording of information or coding the information or in punching and verification of the information (although if information is machine verified, it is unlikely that error originated at the punching and verifying stage). Two kinds of further checks should be conducted at this time to limit further the amount of error that appears in the data matrix.

First, marginal distributions should be computed for each column in the data matrix. We should count each of the values for all of the cases on each variable taken one at a time. This tabulation is used to illuminate what are undefined codes (sometimes called "wild codes") or values that do not appear in the coding frames. For example, we might find row 4 had been punched for the column on gender of respondent. As only the numbers 1, for *male;* 2, for *female;* and 3, for *not reported* were in the code, this punching of "4" is an undefined code. Presumably, it should not happen that a value that has been omitted from the coding frame is coded for a variable. But human beings make errors in keypunching, and thus any undefined code indicates an error and should be corrected by returning to the original punched card, the original coding form, and, if necessary, to the original source, to insert the appropriate value in the data matrix.

Once all undefined codes have been corrected in a column-by-column basis in the data matrix, the contents of each row in the data matrix should be checked for abnormal patterns of data for individual units of analysis. Marginal distributions for each of the rows in the data matrix (on a case-by-case basis) should also be computed for the presence of certain responses. If an abnormally high number of "don't know," "inappropriate," or otherwise unexpected responses occurs for a case, error may be present. If data have been recorded, coded, and punched and verified correctly, then the analyst is faced with the decision of whether to omit the case from the analysis entirely. The outcome of this decision depends on the investigator's theoretical rationale for including the case and the variables for which no data appear in the study initially.

Second, hypotheses about the relationship between certain columns in the data matrix are generated. These hypotheses concern relationships that we would expect to be present. For example, it is uncommon (but not impossible) for women over 50 years of age to have newborn babies. It is uncommon (but not impossible) for men without high school or university educations to earn high incomes. It is also difficult (but not impossible) to understand how a person could answer a question one way at the beginning of an interview and another way at the end of the interview or how the sum of the votes for elective offices in precincts would fail to equal the total number of votes in a ward. These are relationships that would lead us to ask questions about the adequacy of our data reduction process (and perhaps about other things as well) if these relationships were not valid.

In editing a data set, we inspect cases that do not act "as we expect them to." We recheck the original information, coding, and punching and verifying for these cases to ascertain whether error has entered the processing of the deviant cases. In general, the more of this cross-checking we do, the cleaner a data set is likely to be. We systematically look for the deviant cases. The one plausible alternative explanation for the appearance of a deviant case that we must check at this stage is that an error has been made in data reduction. Although one can always argue that a data set is never "completely clean" and therefore is never completely free of errors of data reduction, the analyst has a responsibility to make the data set as clean and free of error as is conceivably possible given the analyst's resources and common sense. This involves an explicit *plan* of checks and cross-checks that is then executed when data reduction is at the editorial stage. These steps should be noted in subsequent written material that is based on the data matrix.

Storing Data

The problems with data reduction do not end until the entire data matrix has been put in a form so that analysis is simple and access to the contents of the rows and columns of the data matrix is easy. Usually, this means that data are punched on IBM cards, the cards placed in a pressure cabinet, the code book and other documentation put in a file, and the study forgotten. In other cases, materials for a study are simply thrown in a box or thrown out because the study has been completed. All of these practices are unfortunate because they limit the usefulness of studies that have consumed much labor and public goodwill. Some argue that social scientists have an obligation to make their data available to others in a meaningful way. And analysts themselves are never certain that they will not want to go back to perform yet further analyses of a data set at some later point in time. All these considerations suggest that attention must be paid to storing data sets and the necessary documentation for these data sets.

A number of practical considerations can guide the storage of the data matrix. First, the medium of punched cards is a simple and efficient way to translate data from coding forms to the computer, but punched cards are not a very effective medium for longer-term storage of social science data. Being made of porous paper, punched cards are very sensitive to the climate in the room in which they are stored, especially to even moderate levels of humidity that may be present. They warp easily. In normal humidity, for example, cards lying out on a desk begin to warp within a few days. Thus, special cabinets that place constant pressure on IBM cards should be used whenever relatively short-term storage is contemplated.

But even these drawers are not an effective mode for storing IBM cards during longer periods. They will not eliminate warping entirely, they are expensive, they require large amounts of space (even to store moderate numbers of cards), and they are heavy (too heavy for the weight tolerances in many older buildings). Cards themselves are relatively bulky (although not nearly so bulky as the original data sheets) and are difficult to send to other social scientists or to move very far. More than a few cards are very difficult to carry even to the local computer center a few blocks away.

Thus, magnetic tape is a much more effective medium for longer-term storage of social science data. As mentioned earlier, a single tape weighing but a few pounds can store the contents of many cabinets full of IBM cards, can be easily carried about (with reasonable precautions concerning heat and magnetic objects in the vicinity of the tape), and inexpensively mailed to colleagues at other locations about the world. Disk storage is also feasible at most modern computer installations but is expensive for longer-term storage (and very expensive in comparison to magnetic tape for shorter-term storage as well).

Magnetic tape is by no means a panacea for all the problems of data storage and retrieval. The use of tapes may result in recording or transmitting errors. Tapes do cost money, and they are subject to breakage. Tapes also must be kept away from magnetic objects. Very large volumes of data, the U.S. Census for instance, require very large numbers of tapes even though tape is a relatively efficient mode of storage. The census is distributed on more than 2000 magnetic tapes, although it may be considerably compressed at some installations.

Dangers of breakage, recording and transmitting errors, and other problems suggest that second copies, or *backup* tapes, should always be made. It is judicious to keep backup tapes in a different building to avoid disasters that might destroy one set of tapes. Finally, it is all too simple to record new information on top of the old information that one thought had been safely stored for posterity. This, of course, destroys the stored data set. In some instances, data sets can be easily replaced. In other instances, data reflecting many human years of work and thousands of dollars of expense may be completely destroyed in a few milliseconds.

The second and equally important matter involved in data storage is documentation. Data without descriptions are simply meaningless values from a data matrix that resemble punched holes in cards or electronic blips on a tape or disk but signify nothing more. No matter how well preserved a data set may be, without adequate documentation, the data are worthless for any purpose of social science. All too frequently, inadequate attention is given to documentation for social science studies. The basic test of documentation is whether it provides other reasonably competent social scientists with all the information that they need to use the data to test hypotheses and draw meaningful conclusions.

Documentation for data sets should include full and complete descriptions of each column or variable in the data matrix and of all the values that are assigned to each variable. This usually means that each item in a study is fully described along with the values that are given to the item and the numerical (or other) codes that may be associated with these values. Important qualifications, conventions, and clarifications should be noted whenever these are significant for a variable or specific value on a variable. Similarly, the units of analysis should be fully described, important caveats noted in detail, and full background information given on the nature of the study, at least in the form of references to other publicly available materials.

Such central characteristics of data sets as full descriptions of the nature of samples (in surveys or aggregate data that are based on surveys), the geographical characteristics of areas, what units may be included or excluded, the universe of content on which units of analysis are based, and time of data collection should be included with the documentation for social science data. It is a great benefit if initial descriptive statistics, such as marginal distributions for each variable, also appear on the documentation so that other analysts may ascertain if some kinds of error are involved in the secondary analyses.

Finally, documentation should fully and completely describe any additional transformation of data from one form to another that has occurred during the data-processing stages. This would include the construction of indexes of various kinds from combinations of variables or the application of an equation to a single variable, the collapsing of value categories so that fewer values result than were initially present, and data transformations that might be used to constrain undesirable distributional characteristics in some forms of data, such as **kurtosis** or **skewness.** Finally, documentation should contain warnings to others concerning any kind of error that might have occurred in the original collection or reduction stages that might affect results of analysis. Statistics about coding reliabilities and other evidence for the reliability and validity of variables should be included in this material.

It is *essential* to maintain adequate records of what data sets are stored in which locations, regardless of the mode of storage. Although this concern is seemingly a trite and obvious detail, readers might be surprised at the sloppiness that is often confronted in the maintenance of information about the way that data are stored. These records should clearly state what data sets are stored where, and how each data set is stored. (For example, if data are stored on magnetic tape, it is necessary to know a variety of characteristics about the tape and the specific way that the data have been recorded on the tape.) It is also important to record where backup data sets are and how they can be obtained in case the working data set is destroyed for some reason. All material should be dated so that someone referring to the records can ascertain precisely when a data set had been processed. This could aid an analyst in avoiding errors later.

SUMMARY

We have discussed general considerations that are important in data processing in this chapter. One of the most important concepts in data processing is the idea of the data matrix. Data processing involves converting raw, unorganized information into a matrix form so that the units of analysis are arranged along the rows, the variables along the columns, and the specific values for each case and variable in the boxes that appear at the respective intersections of rows and columns.

This information is then processed (or "reduced") by mechanical means so that it becomes compatible with the requirements of computer programs and so that it is easy to comprehend and to distribute to other social scientists. We emphasize checking, locating, and correcting errors at each stage of processing. This includes verification of each operation, editing of the final results, and the preparation of full and complete documentation concerning the study. The ultimate test of success in adequately documentating a study is whether other knowledgeable social scientists can meaningfully use the data that are processed.

The data matrix underlies all of these processes. The specific definitions of values change and the medium of storage changes as data are processed. But the basic characteristics of the data matrix remain the same. Analysis simply involves comparison of values in columns or rows or in combinations of columns and rows.

Data Analysis

13

This chapter was written by Michael Milburn.

After the data have been collected, social scientists turn their full attention to analysis and interpretation, a process consisting of a number of closely related operations. It is the purporse of *analysis* to summarize the completed observations in such a manner that they yield answers to the research questions. It is the purpose of *interpretation* to search for the broader meaning of these answers by linking them to other available knowledge. Both these purposes, of course, govern the entire research process; all preceding steps have been undertaken to make them possible.

However, one should not regard analysis and interpretation as simply the final steps of a linear research process that begins with hypothesis generation, research design, and data collection. Research is actually a circular process, so that data analysis, particularly the exploratory data analysis techniques discussed in this chapter, can serve to stimulate further hypotheses to be tested. Data analysis is not necessarily a final boring task at the conclusion of a stimulating research project (although many people treat it that way). It can be a very creative and exciting enterprise, particularly when one encounters interesting and unanticipated results. The procedures discussed in this chapter will be of use to social scientists of various disciplines including psychology, sociology, and political science.

EXPLORATORY DATA ANALYSIS[1]

In Chapter 6 we showed how participant observers work back from their data, generating hypotheses and then testing those hypotheses with further data analysis. With the techniques of exploratory data analysis, experimenters and survey researchers can do the same.

[1] The terminology in this section follows that of Erickson and Nosanchuk (1977).

This chapter is meant to be an introduction to some of the techniques of exploratory data analysis. These procedures can be done easily by hand with just a pencil and some paper and involve nothing more difficult than counting, with an occasional addition or division. They are discussed in more detail in a very readable book by Erickson and Nosanchuk (1977) and in considerable depth by Tukey (1977), who originally suggested these series of techniques, which he has called "exploratory data analysis." Those of you who find this chapter interesting are urged to find copies of these two books.

Stem-and-leaf Displays

The first step in data analysis, once the data have been collected, is to try to get some sense of the data. If we were interested in explaining alcoholism, a significant social problem, the first thing we might do would be to collect some data on the magnitude of the problem. Presented in Table 13.1 are the data that we will be discussing in

TABLE 13.1 Estimated Number of Male and Female Alcoholics (per 100,000) by State* (1970)

State	Males	Females	State	Males	Females
Maine	7200	1600	W. Vir.	5700	800
N.H.	6000	1600	N.C.	3800	500
Vt.	7900	800	S.C.	4900	900
Mass.	10800	1600	Ga.	4700	700
R.I.	11000	1500	Fla.	6300	1200
Conn.	8600	1700	Ky.	6200	700
N.Y.	9500	2100	Tenn.	5500	600
N.J.	8500	1800	Ala.	3200	700
Pa.	7800	1400	Ark.	5300	800
Ohio	7500	1500	La.	7200	1100
Ind.	6900	1300	Miss.	4000	900
Ill.	9200	1500	Okla.	3600	800
Mich.	7900	1300	Texas	4900	1000
Wis.	9300	1300	Mont.	6600	1000
Minn.	5900	1100	Idaho	3600	400
Iowa	5000	800	Wyo.	3400	1300
Mo.	9100	1600	Colo.	7100	1600
N. Dak.	6000	1100	N. Mex.	5100	1300
S. Dak.	4300	1000	Ariz.	5200	1200
Nebr.	5000	1400	Utah	3100	1100
Kans.	4300	800	Nev.	11700	1700
Del.	7300	1100	Wash.	5000	900
Md.	7500	1000	Oreg.	4500	800
Va.	4100	800	Calif.	11400	2200

Source: U.S. Bureau of the Census, *Statistical Abstract of the United States: 1978*, 99th ed. Washington, D.C., 1978.
*Rounded to the nearest hundred.

this section: the estimated number of alcoholics per 100,000 population in each of 48 states (Alaska and Hawaii were excluded because of highly unreliable data), broken down by gender. The numbers are rounded to the nearest hundred. With exploratory techniques, exact precision is not necessary; in fact, too much detail actually gets in the way because what we are after is the "big picture."

What are your first impressions from looking at the table? It looks as if the number of male alcoholics is generally higher than the number of female alcoholics, but it is hard to get too far beyond that by just scanning the numbers. What would be helpful is some pictorial representation. A very useful kind of tabulation is called a "stem-and-leaf," a procedure suggested by John Tukey.

Table 13.2 shows a stem-and-leaf of the data for estimated number of male alcoholics from Table 13.1. How was this obtained? The first step is to scan the data and pick out the high and low values to figure the range of the data. They run from 3000 to about 11,000, so the 1000's place is a good "stem," and we write those numbers down from 3 to 11 (highest on the top) and draw a line to the right of them. Next we add the leaves that will represent our actual data values, using the 100's place as the leaf. The number of male alcoholics in Maine is 7200, so we write a "2" next to the "7," to the right of the line. The number in New Hampshire is 6000, so we add a "0" next to the "6." And so on, until we have added 48 leaves (be sure to count them to check). Note at the bottom what units our stem and leaves are in. Now we examine what we have done.

Immediately, our sense of this "batch" of numbers is much clearer. Most of the states clump together in the 3000 to high 7000 range, with a few values straggling up to the 11,000's. It certainly seems somewhat lopsided toward the lower half of the scale. From this stem-and-leaf we have a sense of both the range of the data and the distribution of the data within that range, i.e., whether the values are evenly distributed or tend toward some central value or "clump" together.

Now you might say at this point, "But I could have done all that with just setting up categories and tallying the numbers in each category." This is true, but the important difference is that with a stem-and-leaf, the data are *recoverable*. You can determine what each of the values are, not just that they fall within a given

TABLE 13.2   Stem-and-leaf of Male Alcoholics

11	074
10	8
9	5231
8	65
7	298593521
6	090326
5	900753120
4	33197095
3	826641

Stem = 1000's
Leaf = 100's
N = 48

TABLE 13.3 Stem-and-leaf of Female Alcoholics

2^3	12
1^9	787
1^6	6665455646
1^3	3331101021003321
0^9	88888977789898
0^6	564

Stem = 1000's
Leaf = 100's
N = 48

range. The importance of this characteristic will become readily apparent in the following pages when we discuss *summary values.*

Before we turn to that, we should take a look at the data for the estimated number of female alcoholics in the different states. Before looking back to Table 13.3, you should try doing a stem-and-leaf of the data yourself.

If you decided to use 1000's as your stem, then you probably found that your stem-and-leaf was not particularly revealing — with all the leaves on just three stems. One possible solution to this is to increase the number of stems by decreasing their range, letting one stem have leaves for 0, 1, 2, and 3; a second stem with leaves 4, 5, and 6; and a third with 7, 8, and 9. Table 13.3 shows a stem-and-leaf done in this fashion.

The stem is again the 1000's place, but each digit is broken down into three stems, with an exponent indicating the highest value of the leaf that goes on that stem (0^9 for 700–999, and so on). This is much more revealing. One rule of thumb is that at least six stems should have leaves. The data for the females appear to be much better behaved than for the males, with the highest number of leaves falling in the middle of the plot. The level is clearly much lower than for the males, the highest value for the females (2200) being less than the lowest value for the males (3100). To enable us to make comparisons between the two batches, it will be helpful to have some summary values. We turn to that now.

Numerical Summaries

Although it is important to have some pictorial representation of a batch of data, such as a stem-and-leaf display, it is also useful to have some numerical summaries of the batch as well. In this section we will introduce two very useful summaries: the **median,** a measure of the "level" or middle of the batch; and the *interquartile range*, a measure of "spread" or how much variation there is in the data. These summaries help describe the data, enable comparisons between batches, and are useful in further exploratory steps.

Level: the median.   The median is very easily determined from our stem-and-leaf display following a simple modification. Draw a new stem-and-leaf, ordering the leaves in ascending order from left to right for each stem. This gives a "cleaned"

TABLE 13.4   "Cleaned" Stem-and-leaf, Male Alcoholics

11	047
10	8
9	1235
8	56
7	122355899
6	002369
5	000123579
4	01335799
3	124668

Stem = 1000's
Leaf = 100's
N = 48

stem-and-leaf (Table 13.4), which makes counting very easy. To determine which value is the median, divide the number of observations by two, and take the number that the result of this division "grows to." *Grows to* is a fairly simple idea also suggested by Tukey. Any number that is not an integer (for example, 10.5, 10.01, 12.9) grows to the next highest integer, so 10.5 grows to 11 as does 10.01, and 12.9 grows to 13. Any integer grows to that number plus one-half, so 15 grows to 15.5, 20 grows to 20.5, and so on. Do not confuse "grows to" with "rounding," because they are slightly different.

For our example of male alcoholics in Table 13.4, what is the median? We have 48 data values, so $\frac{48}{2}$ = 24. Twenty-four grows to 24.5, so the number we are after is the average of the twenty-fourth and twenty-fifth data values. Counting down from the top (or up from the bottom) the twenty-fourth is 6000, as is the twenty-fifth; thus, their average is 6000, the median (abbreviated Md). So the middle or typical number of male alcoholics is 6000 per 100,000 population in a state.

Now, you may ask, why did we go through all that? Why not just add all the values and get their average, the *mean*? First, the median is much simpler to calculate—all you need to do is count. It can easily be obtained by hand. The mean requires a lot of addition, during which it is very easy to make a mistake, and a calculator is also a necessity. Secondly, and very importantly, the median is a *resistant* measure. It is relatively unaffected by extreme values in a batch, values that are sometimes very far away from most of the other data. For our example of male alcoholics, the median is 6000, but the mean is 6429. The mean estimates the middle of the batch to be higher because of the few high values around 11,000.

To give you a better sense of what resistant means, suppose that the rate for Nevada (11,700) was instead 40,000. It occasionally happens in batches of data that one finds an extreme value like this, i.e., one which is very different from all the other values in the batch. The median for the batch would still be 6000, but the mean would now be 7019, simply by changing *one* value. The mean is thus a very nonresistant measure, that is, its size (its summary of the batch) can be easily affected by only one extreme value. For a measure which "represents" a batch, if we want one which tells us about the typical or middle value, the median is generally better than the mean. This discussion is intended to illustrate that care should be taken in drawing conclusions from summary values (like the mean), which are not resistant.

Spread: the interquartile range (dq).   In addition to determining the level of a batch of data, another important characteristic to obtain information about is the spread. The spread is a measure of the variation among the values of a batch, i.e., whether they are wide apart or close together. A measure of the spread of a batch facilitates comparisons with other batches. A useful measure of spread is called the *interquartile range or dq.* It is calculated by taking the difference between the quartiles, the values that "quarter" the data. Divide the number of data values by four, and take the number that this value grows to. For our example, $\frac{48}{4} = 12$, which grows to 12.5. Counting values down from the top to get the upper quartile (q_U), the value is $7850 \left(\frac{[7800 + 7900]}{2} \right)$. Similarly, the lower quartile (q_L) equals 4800. Thus the interquartile range is $7850 - 4800 = 3050$. $z \ dq$

A nonresistant measure of spread, nonresistant because it relies on the mean rather than the median, is the standard deviation. Like the mean, it requires considerably more calculation than does the *dq*. To calculate the standard deviation of a batch of numbers (denoted by X_i, i taking on the values of 1 to N), one takes each value, subtracts the mean ($\overline{X}$) of the batch of numbers from it, and then squares that difference. All these differences squared are then added up and divided by N, the number of data values. Then take the square root of this quotient. The formula for the standard deviation follows:

$$SD = \sqrt{\frac{1}{N} \sum_{i=1}^{N} (X_i - \overline{X})^2} \qquad = \left(\xi x^2 - (\xi x)^2 \right)^{1/2}$$

The "Σ" merely represents summation, so that the data values from 1 to N will be included in the calculation. The standard deviation squared is called the *variance*. You can see that the *dq* is easier to calculate.

In our example for the data on male alcoholics, the standard deviation is 2275.2, lower than the *dq*. To illustrate the result of using nonresistant measures again, if the value for Nevada were 40,000 instead of 11,700, the standard deviation (*SD*) would be 6839.9, a sizable jump from changing just one value (the *dq* would still be the same). When the *SD* is larger than the *dq*, this is an indication that there are some values in the batch that are very different from the rest, often called *outliers*. These will be discussed in the next section on hypotheses generation.

If we take the median, the quartiles, and *dq*, all the summary values can be written down for quick reference as they are in Table 13.5. The *X*s stand for the extreme values of the batch (always useful to keep in mind), the upper value has subscript *U* and the lowest value has subscript *L*.

At this point, if you have not already done so, you should try your hand at these techniques. Take the data for the rate of female alcoholics, do the stem-and-leaf and the "cleaned" stem-and-leaf, compute the median and the interquartile

TABLE 13.5 Summary Table for Male Alcoholics

X_u =	11,700	
q_u =	7,850	
Md =	6,000	MEDIAN
q_L =	4,800	
X_L =	3,100	
dq =	3,050	
N =	48	

range, and lay out a summary table like Table 13.5. Then you can compare the results you get with those in Table 13.6.

You should now have a reasonable grasp of some simple exploratory techniques. By hand, in just a few minutes, you should be able to display a batch of data and the summary values for it. Now, you may ask, how does this help us understand the problem of alcoholism?

Already, many questions arise from looking at the summaries of these two batches of data. Why is the alcoholism rate for men so much higher than for women? Why is there so much more variation (the *dq* is higher) in the rates for men than for women? Perhaps the causes of alcoholism are different for men and women because of the different life situations (work, and so on) that they have, or perhaps the same causes are just operating more weakly for women than for men. One possible way to address this question would be to examine the relationship between the number of male and female alcoholics in each state. If the states with a higher rate of male alcoholics also have a (relatively) high rate of female alcoholics, then one would be led to the conclusion that the same process is operating to produce alcoholism in both sexes. We will defer an examination of this relation until later in the next section when we talk about relationships between variables. Let's move now to a discussion of data analysis and hypothesis generation.

TABLE 13.6 Cleaned Stem-and-leaf and Summary Table for Female Alcoholics

2^3	12	
1^9	778	x_u = 2,200
1^6	4455566666	q_u = 1,500
1^3	0000111112233333	Md = 1,100
0^9	77788888888999	q_L = 800
0^6	456	X_L = 400
		dq = 700
		N = 48

stem = 1000's
Leaf = 100's

HYPOTHESIS GENERATION

We talked at the beginning of this chapter and in chapter 6 about the circular nature of research — that data are not an end step but can be an initial step in developing hypotheses to test. Ideally, a scientist uses a theory from which to develop hypotheses, then tests these hypotheses as an evaluation of the theory. "But where does the scientist get the theory?" you might ask. The way most often is through observation and exploration with some intelligent guesses thrown in. Let us see how we might use procedures we have already discussed to generate some hypotheses to explain the rate of alcoholism.

Examining Displays

One source of hypotheses is the examination of the high and low values in a particular batch. The characteristics of the units with those high and low values may provide some clue to the factors influencing the variable under study, in our case, alcoholism. We will discuss two different types of extreme values: outliers and *adjacent* values.

Outliers. Extreme values that are very far from the center of a batch of numbers are important to pay attention to. They often represent highly unusual values that should be given special consideration, they may represent errors in the data collection process, or they may be values that have no particular relevance to the process under study and so should not be allowed to bias the conclusions and hypotheses one obtains from the batch.

Before defining more precisely what constitutes an outlier, we must introduce one more term suggested by Tukey: a *step*. A step equals 1.5 *dq*. This gives us a metric to apply to outliers. A value is called an *outlier* if it is more than one step higher than the upper quartile or lower than the lower quartile. A value is called a *far outlier* if it is more than two steps higher or lower than one of the quartiles.

We can now apply this to our example. The *dq* for our data on male alcoholics was 3050. So a step is $1.5 \times 3050 = 4575$. The upper bound for outliers is thus 12,425 (that is, $7850 + 4575$), and the lower bound is 225 (that is, $4800 - 4575$). Are there any outliers in our batch? A quick glance at Table 13.5 assures us that there are not because the extreme values in the batch are within our upper and lower bounds. As there are no outliers, we don't have to go any further to determine the bounds for far outliers.

You should try the same computations for the female alcoholic data. Before you do, would you guess that there will be any outliers? Most likely there won't be because we have seen from our earlier explorations that the data for females are better behaved (more symmetrical) than are the male data. A few quick calculations will assure you that there are no outliers for the female alcoholic data either.

Adjacent values. We know now that there are no outlying values for us to consider, but these are not the only extreme values we should pay attention to. Tukey suggests that *adjacent* values should be examined as well. He defines adjacent values to be those that are the closest to being outliers but are within the bounds.

What are the adjacent values for our data on male alcoholics? The top values are 11,700 (Nevada), 11,400 (California), and 11,000 (Rhode Island). The lower adjacent values are 3100 (Utah), 3200 (Alabama), and 3400 (Wyoming). What are the characteristics that might differentiate the high and low alcoholism rate states? One possibility is population density (if we put aside the inconsistent Nevada for the moment). California and Rhode Island will be high, whereas Utah, Alabama, and Wyoming are all low population density states. Another possibility might be per capita income. Utah, Alabama, and Wyoming are basically rural states that depend on farming, ranching, and the like, whereas California and Rhode Island have a reputation for "old" wealth (for example, the mansions at Newport).

Right now we are engaged in total speculation. This is often an important part of research. We should now proceed to explore some of our speculations. This means we first need to collect some more data. Table 13.7 provides the aggregate data by state for per capita income and population density. Now we can begin examining

TABLE 13.7   Population Density and Per Capita Income, by State (1970)

State	Population per Square Mile*	Per Capita Income**	State	Population per Square Mile	Per Capita Income
Maine	30	3300	West Virginia	70	3000
New Hampshire	80	3700	North Carolina	100	3200
Vermont	50	3400	South Carolina	90	3000
Massachusetts	730	4300	Georgia	80	3300
Rhode Island	900	3900	Florida	130	3700
Connecticut	620	4900	Kentucky	80	3100
New York	380	4600	Tennessee	90	3100
New Jersey	950	4700	Alabama	70	2900
Pennsylvania	260	3900	Arkansas	40	2800
Ohio	260	3900	Louisiana	80	3000
Indiana	140	3700	Mississippi	50	2500
Illinois	200	4400	Oklahoma	40	3300
Michigan	160	4000	Texas	40	3500
Wisconsin	80	3700	Montana	0	3400
Minnesota	50	3800	Idaho	10	3200
Iowa	50	3600	Wyoming	0	3700
Missouri	70	3700	Colorado	20	3800
North Dakota	10	3100	New Mexico	10	3000
South Dakota	10	3100	Arizona	20	3600
Nebraska	20	3700	Utah	10	3200
Kansas	30	3700	Nevada	0	4600
Delaware	280	4500	Washington	50	4000
Maryland	400	4300	Oregon	20	3700
Virginia	120	3700	California	130	4400

Source: U.S. Bureau of the Census, *Statistical Abstract of the United States: 1978*, 99th ed. Washington, D.C., 1978, pp. 13, 449.

*Rounded to nearest ten.

**Rounded to nearest hundred.

the relationships that may or may not exist between our variables. Before we do, though, you should do a quick stem-and-leaf of the data in Table 13.7 so that you have a general idea of what is going on in these two new batches.

Relationships Between Variables

So far we have talked about explorations of a single batch of numbers at a time. Now we will go beyond this simple description and begin to look at relationships between variables. The tool we will use is called a scattergram, sometimes called an *X* by *Y* plot.

Scattergrams. Constructing a scattergram is fairly easy, and it is an extremely important step in understanding relationships between variables. Tukey (1977) makes several suggestions for drawing plots, some of which we will briefly mention here. Interested readers are encouraged to find Tukey's text.

First, obtain some graph paper. Ten squares to an inch is the best for drawing our scales and locating intermediate points on the scales. Also get some tracing paper. Plots on tracing paper are much easier to read than those on graph paper because one does not have all the vertical and horizontal lines pulling one's eye away from the data. The vertical (*Y*) and horizontal (*X*) axes should be drawn on the borders of the tracing paper, not down the middle, again so that these lines do not detract from the data.

Now we are ready to begin. Earlier we raised some questions about the relationship in each state of the number of male and female alcoholics. Table 13.8 presents a plot of these two batches of data, each point representing a state with its

TABLE 13.8   Relationship Between the Number of Male and Female Alcoholics

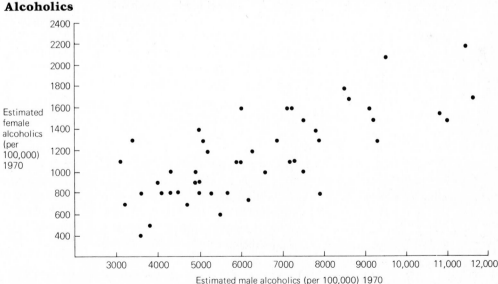

**TABLE 13.9   Descriptive and Predictive Line Fit to the Data by Eye, Showing
the Relationship Between the Numbers of Male and Female Alcoholics**

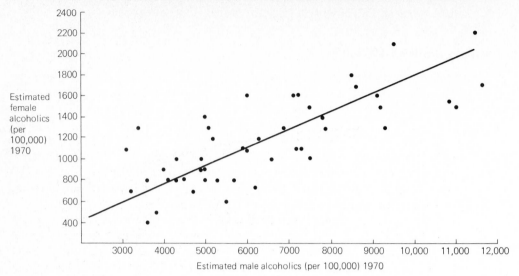

position on the X-axis (horizontal) determined by the rate of male alcoholics in the
state and its Y-axis (vertical) location determined by the number of female alcoholics. What does this tell us?

There appears to be a clear upward trend in the points from the lower left-
hand corner of the plot to the upper right. This suggests that some relationship exists
between the number of male and female alcoholics in a state. As the rate of male
alcoholics goes up, so does the rate of female alcoholics. To summarize this relationship, a straight line is most commonly used. How and where on the plot the line
should be drawn are subjects of considerable complexity. For now, we will very
simply fit a line to the data by eye. Try taking a pencil and a straight edge and draw
a line through the points in Table 13.8 that you feel best represents the points. Now
compare the line you drew to the one in Table 13.9, which is also an eye-fit to the
data. They should be fairly close because the relationship is a fairly clear one. One
measure of the strength of the relationship between two variables is the ease with
which you draw a line to fit the data points.

Fit and residuals.   What does this line tell us? It is both descriptive and predictive.
This line summarizes the relationship, and it gives us, for any rate of male alcoholics, the *predicted* rate of female alcoholics. For a value of X, say 6000, the predicted
value is obtained by drawing a vertical line, parallel to the Y-axis, from the point
denoting 6000 on the X-axis up to the fit line. Then a horizontal line is drawn,
parallel to the X-axis, over to the Y-axis. The point at which this horizontal line
intersects with the Y-axis is the predicted number of female alcoholics. This procedure is shown in Table 13.10.

How good is this prediction? If all the data points fell right on the line, our

TABLE 13.10   Residuals Measured by Vertical Distance from the Fit Line

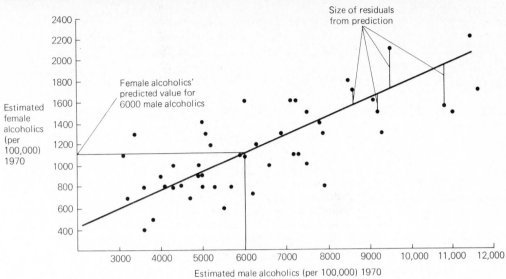

prediction would be perfect. As you can see, all the data points are not on the line; in fact, most of them are definitely off the line, some by a big distance. This reflects an important aspect of the data: they can be considered as having two parts, a *fit* and a *residual*, so that

data = fit PLUS residual

The fit (our summary line) is an *incomplete description* of the data. The difference between our incomplete description of the data and the data themselves is the residual, which may be either positive or negative.

If data points are close to the line, their residuals will be very small. If they are far away, the residual will be quite large. The residual for any point is determined by dropping a line from the point (parallel to the Y-axis) to the fit line, as is shown in Table 13.10. Residuals that are large should be considered carefully. They indicate observations for which our predictions are bad, so they may point to special processes that may be operating for that case.

You should take some time now to draw your own scattergrams and fit lines of the relationships between per capita income and alcoholism rate and between population density and alcoholism. The scattergrams using the male alcoholic data are given in Tables 13.11 and 13.12. What conclusions can you draw from these scattergrams? Make a note of your thoughts to compare with our later discussion of these relationships. Now we turn to some slightly more technical statistical ideas.

Least squares.   The size of the residual for any particular observation will vary considerably depending upon how the line through a set of points is drawn. Without some specific criterion, different people could draw different lines through the same

TABLE 13.11   Per Capita Income and Male Alcoholism Rate (per 100,000)

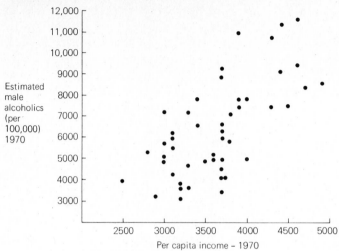

data and come to very different conclusions. We will talk about one specific procedure for fitting a line called least squares, because it fits the line for scatterplot that minimizes the sum of *squared* residuals. We need to consider several formulas to find the least squares line. First, consider the formula for a line:

$$Y = a + bX$$

In this equation, b represents the *slope* of the line (how many units Y increases for each unit increase in X), and a represents the *Y-intercept* (the point where the line intersects the Y-axis when X is zero). The slope is a very important aspect of a linear

TABLE 13.12   Population Density and Male Alcoholism Rate (per 100,000)

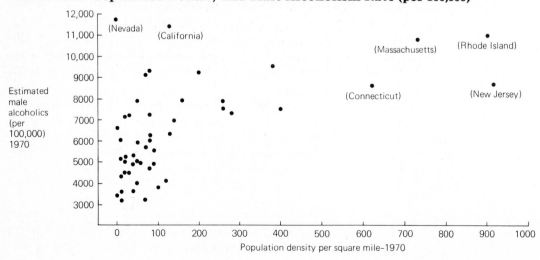

relationship between two variables because it indicates the *effect* that the *X* variable has on the *Y* variable; the larger the slope for a given relationship, the greater the change will be in *Y* for one unit change in *X*. This is sometimes referred to as the *effect size*.

If we can calculate values for *a* and *b* in our formula for the fit line, we will be able to draw it easily by finding two points on the line and drawing the fit line through them. One point is easy: the *Y*-intercept (*a*) is just the value of *Y* with *X* being zero (a point on the *Y*-axis). The second point takes a little more calculation: pick some value of *X*, substitute it in the equation for the line, and solve for *Y*. The procedure should be clear; now all we have to do is calculate what values we will use for *a* and *b*.

Without going through the proofs, it can be shown that the values for *a* and *b* for the line that minimizes the sum of the squared residuals are calculated thus:

$$a = \overline{Y} - b\overline{X}$$
$$b = \frac{N \sum X_i Y_i - (\sum X_i)(\sum Y_i)}{N \sum X_i^2 - (\sum X_i)^2}$$

$$2 \quad \frac{N \varepsilon(x\,y) - (\varepsilon x)(\varepsilon y)}{N \varepsilon x^2 - (\varepsilon x)^2}$$

The value for *a* is easy to calculate once we find *b* ($\overline{Y}$ is simply the mean of the *Y* values; $\overline{X}$ is the mean of the *X*'s). Calculating *b* may look difficult, so you should do it one part at a time. The first term, $N\sum X_i Y_i$, means that one should take each point, multiply its *X* and *Y* values together, sum all these products together, and then multiply the sum by *N* (the number of points). The second term of the numerator, $(\sum X_i)(\sum Y_i)$, is very easy: just add all the *X* values together; then add all the *Y* values together; then multiply these two sums together. Subtract the second term $(\sum X_i)$ $(\sum Y_i)$ from the first term $(N\sum X_i Y_i)$, and that is the numerator.

Now all that is left is the denominator. The first part, $N\sum X_i^2$ is calculated by taking each *X* value, squaring it, summing all the squared values together, and then multiplying this sum by *N*. The second term, $(\sum X_i)^2$, is easy: take the sum of the *X*'s you calculated in the numerator and square it. Again subtract the second term from the first term, and that is the denominator. Divide the numerator by the denominator and that is *b*.

A simple example of this procedure is provided for the data shown in Table 13.13. Two points we can use to draw the fit line are (0, 6.0) and, for example, (4, 2.4) [that is, (−.9) (4) + 6.0]. These points (not data points) are circled on the scattergram in Table 13.13. Thus the line *Y* = 6.0 + (− .9) *X* best fits the six points in Table 13.13, according to the criterion of least squares. Note that, in this case, the relationship is negative; that is, as the values of *X* go up, the values of *Y* go down.

You should now try calculating a least squares line for the relationship between the rate of male alcoholics and either per capita income or population density. If you find all these calculations are tedious by hand, you might try using a calculator. There are some reasonably inexpensive models now available that will calculate a least squares fit line for you.

Correlations. The concept of residuals is very important to an understanding of the strength of a relationship between two variables. Table 13.14 shows two scattergrams, each with a similar line (same slopes) summarizing the variables' relation-

TABLE 13.13   Fit Line Drawn Using the Least Squares Procedure

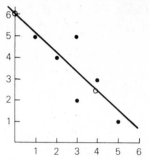

Point	X	Y	XY	X^2
1	1	5	5	1
2	2	4	8	4
3	3	2	6	9
4	3	5	15	9
5	4	3	12	16
6	5	1	5	25
	$\Sigma X = 18$	$\Sigma Y = 20$	$\Sigma XY = 51$	$\Sigma X^2 = 64$

$$b = \frac{N\Sigma X_i Y_i - (\Sigma X_i)(\Sigma Y_i)}{N\Sigma X_i^2 - (\Sigma X)^2}$$

$$= \frac{(6)(51) - (18)(20)}{(6)(64) - (18)^2}$$

$$= \frac{306 - 360}{384 - 324}$$

$$= -\frac{54}{60}$$

$$= -.9$$

$$a = \overline{Y} - b\overline{X}$$

$$= (\frac{18}{6}) - (-.9)(\frac{20}{6})$$

$$= 3 + (.9)(3.33)$$

$$= 6.0$$

TABLE 13.14   Two Scattergrams Depicting Relationships of Different Strengths

**Scattergram Depicting a
Strong Correlation**

**Scattergram Depicting a
Weak Correlation**

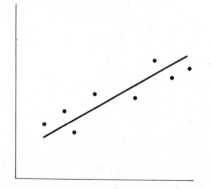

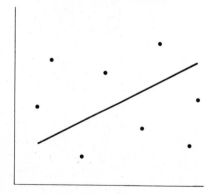

A

B

ships. Which relationship, A or B, appears stronger to you? The relationship in A should have been your guess because of the size of the residuals.

You can see that in Table 13.14A, the data points are very close to the line, so the residuals from the prediction (the fit line) are quite small. Thus, the variation in variable Y (the range from high to low values) is almost totally "explained" by changes in variable X. In Table 13.14B, however, the story is much different. The residuals from the fit line are much larger, so that the predictions of variable Y that one would make from variable X will be much less accurate than in Table 13.14A.

A common confirmatory statistic (based on the mean, not a resistant measure) to summarize the strengths of different relationships is called the **correlation coefficent,** abbreviated: r. It is one measure of association between two variables and ranges from 0 (no relationship) to $+1.0$ (perfect positive relationship) or -1.0 (perfect negative relationship). After you work with correlations for awhile, you develop a good feeling of what correlations of different sizes mean. That may take awhile, so we can give you a few rules of thumb. A correlation of less than .15 (either positive or negative) generally means that there is not much relationship between the variables at all. For a correlation between .15 and .30, the relationship would generally be considered weak, and between .30 and .50, you would call the relationship moderate. A correlation between .50 and .70 would be called a strong relationship, and over .70 (either positive or negative) the relationship would be called very strong.

The formula for computing the correlation is

$$r = \frac{N\Sigma XY - (\Sigma X)(\Sigma Y)}{\sqrt{[N\Sigma X^2 - (\Sigma X)^2][N\Sigma Y^2 - (\Sigma Y)^2]}}$$

As you can see, it is a fraction that looks very similar to the formula for b. In fact, $b = r\dfrac{SD_y}{SD_x}$. If you know one of them and the standard deviations of the two variables you are using, you can easily compute the other. The numerator of the fraction to compute r is called the *covariance* of X and Y. It is the cross-product of X and Y corrected for the difference in their means. The covariance will be big if the high values of X are always associated with the high values of Y, as in Table 13.14A. This numerator will be lower if high values of X are sometimes multiplied by low values of Y, as in Table 13.14B. The denominator of the fraction simply multiplies together the variance of X with the variance of Y. This is essentially the "total" variation.

A mistake that is often made is to think of a correlation as a percent, that is, that a correlation of .40 means that 40 percent of the time X and Y go together, and 60 percent of the time they do not. This is *not* what a correlation means. One can have a correlation of .40 without once having an observation fall directly on the line summarizing the fit between them. The correlation is simply a ratio of the covariance of two variables over their variance.

To obtain a percent measure of the total variation of the Y variable that is "explained" or predicted by the X variable, simply square the correlation coefficent. The result is called, as you might predict, R^2. You should consider it as follows:

$$R^2 = \frac{\text{Explained Variation (by fit line)}}{\text{Total Variation}}$$

Thus, a correlation of .40 means that 16 percent of the variation in the Y-variable is accounted for by the X-variable. A correlation of .70 means that about half (49 percent) of the variation in the Y-variable is predictable by the X-variable.

What about the unexplained variation? What accounts for *it?* There may be a number of things. The Y-variable may be a function not just of one variable, but of several. If you predicted Y with more than one independent variable by calculating the *multiple correlation,* the R^2 might rise. There also may be errors of measurement in your variables that reduce the accuracy of your predictions. There also may be just random human behavior (sometimes called "free will") that prevents social scientists from perfectly explaining individuals' behavior. Depending upon the source of the unexplained variance in a particular X by Y relationship, a researcher may be able to do more or less toward explaining it. Most social scientists are accustomed to explaining considerably less than all the variation in a particular phenomenon being studied. A correlation does not have to be large, i.e., reflect that a large amount of variation is accounted for, to be "statistically significant." If a correlation based on sample data is statistically significant, this simply means that it is unlikely that the "real" correlation in the population being surveyed is zero. Whether a correlation is statistically significant or not is largely a function of the sample size. The larger the sample, the more likely it is that a correlation calculated from that sample will be statistically significant. With a large enough sample, a correlation of .10 (1 percent of the variation) will be significant. Clearly, one should not necessarily attribute a great deal of importance to a correlation simply because it is statistically significant.

Interpreting Relationships

The data in Table 13.12 of the relationship between population density in a state and rate of male alcoholics is a useful example for the caution that must be taken in interpreting a correlation coefficient. If one calculates the correlation, one finds that $r = .554$. However, a careful look at the scattergram suggests that this relationship is not at all as strong as the size of the correlation implies. If you examine the range of population density from 0 to 200, not much of a relationship is apparent at all. There are a few states for the high population densities that also have high alcoholism rates, but there are also states with low population densitites that have high alcoholism rates. The correlation appears high because of the least squares criterion, which is used to calculate the confirmatory regression line that fits the data. The line is pulled the way it is by data from just four states: Massachusetts, Rhode Island, Connecticut, and New Jersey. Without these states, the line would be very different.

However, it is important to note that all the states with high population density have high alcoholism rates. None have low rates of alcoholism. This suggests that population density may have an effect on alcoholism, but it clearly is not the only factor because something different appears to be going on in Nevada and California. To follow up an investigation of the effects of population density, you would probably find it useful to collect data on smaller units, perhaps aggregated by city.

This illustrates a very important rule for the interpretation of a correlation. When you are analyzing a set of data, never calculate the correlation between two variables and then rush to publish your results when you find some strong correlation. *Always* examine the scattergram of any relationship before you draw any conclusions.

The relationship pictured in Table 13.11 is much easier to interpret. There are no points that are far away from the general direction of the data, which seems fairly clearly to be that as per capita income goes up, the rate of alcoholism goes up. The correlation between the two variables is .67 which is fairly strong. Can we now conclude that the more income a person has, the more likely he or she is to be an alcoholic? No, we cannot. We have found a relationship between the number of alcoholics in a state per 100,000 population and the per capita income in that state, but there are several difficulties complicating our interpretation of this *statistical* relationship as a *causal* relationship.

The first problem is that an association between two variables does not necessarily mean that there is a causal relationship between them, as we discussed in Chapter 2. Given that an association or correlation has been found to exist between two variables, X and Y, it may be that X causes Y, or it may be that Y causes X, or it may be that some third variable, say Z, causes both X and Y and the relationship between X and Y is not causal but *spurious*. The process of determining whether relationships between variables are causal or spurious occupies a considerable amount of the time spent in research. In our example, it may mean that higher per capita income causes more alcoholism in a state. It may also mean that if there are more alcoholics in a state, this will cause a higher per capita income (perhaps alcoholics are driven to work harder). Finally, it may be that some third variable like population density causes both a higher rate of alcoholism (more stress, perhaps) and a higher per capita income (more competition encourages people to work harder). One cannot tell, without more careful research, which of the explanations of the alcoholism-income association is more likely.

There is an additional, more subtle problem that prevents us from concluding that the more income a person has, the more likely it is that he or she is an alcoholic. This problem is the *ecological fallacy* (see Chapter 12), a term first suggested by Robinson (1950). The problem is that the levels of our conclusion and our data do not match; our conclusion is on the *individual* level (the more money a person makes, the more likely it is that he or she drinks) and our data are on the *aggregate* level (rate of alcoholism by state, per capita income by state). It may be that the same relationship exists on the individual level as on the aggregate level, but one cannot be sure without collecting data on individuals.

So, you might say, why have we bothered with analyzing the aggregate data at all? Why don't we always just deal with data on individuals? For several reasons. Aggregate data are generally cheaper and easier to obtain, often already collected in easily obtainable sources. Individual level data can only be obtained by surveys, which can be very expensive. Additionally, one may be interested in aggregate data, such as the behavior of nations or state governments. Finally, conclusions can be drawn about individual behavior from aggregate data if particular precautions are taken. The issues involving this type of inference are too complex to be discussed here, but the interested reader is referred to Langbein and Lichtman (1978), who present a fairly detailed analysis.

CONFIRMATORY DATA ANALYSIS

Finally, we come to a point where we are ready to stop exploring data for hypotheses and actually test some hypothesis. This means that we want to be able to say with a given degree of certainty (that is, some known probability) that, for example, two or more groups are different. The groups could be existing groups like male and female alcoholics, or they could be groups in an experiment that we conduct, that is, a treatment group and a control group. Or we might want to say, again with some known probability, that the correlation between two variables is different from zero. To be able to do this, we must plan our procedures more carefully than in our earlier exploratory steps. The first step we must attend to is sampling.

Random Sampling

When we, as social scientists, collect data from some sample of individuals, for example, a public opinion poll, we are not primarily interested in the characteristics of the sample per se, but in what that sample can tell us about the real world, that is, some **population.** We can draw conclusions about some population only if the sample we obtain data from is representative of this population or, more technically, is a *probability sample* drawn from the population of interest. This means that any person in the population we are studying must have some known probability of being included in our sample. The most familiar kind of sample is called a simple random sample, where each element in the population has an *equal* probability of being included in the sample. An example may help to explain this.

Suppose that we are interested in determining whether the percent of male and female alcoholics in the country differs. To decide this, we must obtain a random sample of men and women in the United States and question them about whether they have experienced problems with alcohol. It would not be legitimate if we simply went to the main street in the town where we lived and asked people randomly about their problems with alcohol. This would obviously not be a sample of people from the United States because a person from another town would have a zero probability (or close to it) of being included in our sample. Thus we could not generalize our results to the United States. Additionally, we could not even generalize our results to our town because different people in the town would have different (and unknown) probabilities of being included in our sample (some may work at night and sleep during the day; some may just stay inside their homes [drinking?] all day and not come out; and so on).

The main point to remember is that to make a generalization about some population, you must have some probability sample drawn from that population. There is an additional requirement that the units in a sample must be *independent;* that is, choosing one person to be in the sample does not alter the probability of any other person's being included in the sample. For example, it would be a mistake to pick some man out of the phone book randomly and then include some other person in his household (his brother, wife, and so on) in the sample as well.

Hypothesis Testing

Suppose that we have studied samples of people living either in rural or urban England and that our results show differences between the two samples. One may ask whether the differences that have been obtained reflect true differences between rural and urban English citizens or whether the two samples might have differed to this extent by chance even though the total rural and urban populations are alike in their book reading habits. Through statistical procedures, one is able to answer such a question in terms of a statement of probability.

When we are contrasting samples or studying the differences between experimental and control groups, we usually wish to test some hypothesis about the nature of the true difference between the larger populations represented by the samples. Most commonly, in the social sciences, we are still concerned with relatively crude hypotheses (for example, that urban residents read more books than rural residents); we are usually not in a position to consider more specific hypotheses (for example, that they read *twice* as much). Suppose our data show that our sample of urban English adults reads twenty books a year, on the average, and that our sample of rural English adults reads on the average only fifteen. Clearly, the findings within our samples are in line with the hypothesis: urban residents read more books than rural residents. But we know that the findings based on our samples are not very likely to be exactly the same as the findings we would obtain if we had interviewed all the adults in England. Now we want to estimate whether, if we had interviewed the total population, we would still have found more frequent book reading on the part of urban residents. Remember, the samples we examine are not our main interest in hypothesis testing. We only use samples to make estimates about the *populations* (e.g., adults living in urban sections in England) that we want to be able to make statements about.

Before we look at a specific statistical test, let's examine some potential results of our surveys of the reading habits of English adults. Table 13.15 presents three possible sets of results, each curve called a *frequency distribution*. In each of the three sets, A, B, and C, there are two distributions, one graphing our sample of urban residents and the other our set of rural adults. You should notice that in each of the three possible cases, the mean number of books read by the urban sample is 20, and the average number of books read is 15 for the rural sample. What is the difference between A, B, and C? Clearly, the difference is how much variation there is *within* each of our samples and, consequently, how much overlap there is between the urban and rural distributions.

If you were asked to judge the likelihood that there really is a difference between the reading rates of urban and rural English adults, from which of the three sets of results in Table 13.15 would you be most confident in saying that there is a difference in the populations? (There will almost always be differences in the means of samples from different groups. What we want to know is whether these sample differences reflect differences in the populations from which they are drawn.) Clearly you would be most confident in concluding a difference if the results you obtained looked like those in A. It is this type of judgment that statistical tests allow

TABLE 13.15   Three Possible Frequency Distributions of Numbers of Books Read by Rural and Urban Adults

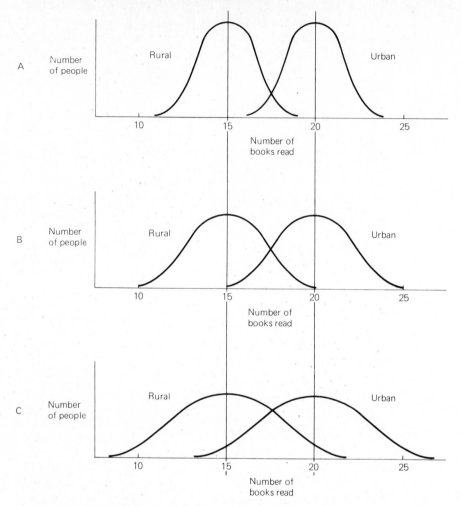

us to make: the probability that a difference between two samples reflects a real population difference and is not due to chance. This we do, ordinarily, by testing the *null hypothesis*—in this case, the hypothesis that in the English population as a whole, rural and urban residents do *not* differ in frequency of book reading.

The null hypothesis   It may seem odd that, when interested in one hypothesis (that there *is* a difference between the two populations represented by our samples), we should test its opposite (that there is *no* difference). But the reason is not too difficult to follow. There is a direct analogy with criminal trials. A jury must make a decision whether or not a defendant is guilty of the crime of which he or she is accused. Before the trial begins and any arguments or evidence is heard, the defendant is entitled (in the U. S. legal system) to a "presumption of innocence," that the defendant did *not* commit the crime. The prosecutor would like the hypothesis of "guilty" confirmed by the jury, but the prosecutor must provide enough evidence to overrule this presumption of innocence beyond a reasonable doubt. Our legal system recognizes that it is not possible to prove the lack of innocence, (i.e., the guilt) of a defendant conclusively, without *any* doubt whatsoever. So the requirement is set that the prosecution must prove guilt beyond a *reasonable* doubt.

Social scientists are engaged in a task quite analogous to that of the prosecutor. When they collect data they wish to prove that their experimental hypothesis is correct, so they start out with the presumption that their hypothesis is not true, e.g., in our example that rural and urban English adults read the same number of books. This presumption is called the *null hypothesis*. We must demonstrate that this presumption is unlikely to be true before we can conclude that, in fact, there is a difference between the reading habits of adults living in rural or urban areas in England.

For our example of English reading habits, the question we want to answer, our experimental hypothesis, is: "Is there a difference between reading habits of English adults in rural areas and adults in urban areas?" Consequently, our null hypothesis (H_o) would be that there is no difference. This is generally written: $H_o = \mu_1 = \mu_2$. The Greek letters μ_1 and μ_2 represent the population means of our two groups: rural and urban adults.

Type I and type II error   After we have collected our samples and examined them, there are two possible decisions we can make: accept the null hypothesis and conclude that there is no difference in the reading habits of our two samples; or, reject the null hypothesis and conclude that there is a differece between our two samples. There are also two possible states of the world (i.e., the population we are interested in making statements about): there may actually be a difference between the reading habits of urban and rural English adults, or there may be no difference between them. The combination of the two actual states of the world and the two different conclusions we may draw from our samples provides four possible outcomes. These outcomes are displayed in Table 13.16.

TABLE 13.16   Type I and Type II Errors

Research Conclusion	REAL WORLD	
	Difference	No Difference
Conclude Difference (reject the null hypothesis) based on samples	Correct decision	Type I error
Conclude No difference (do not reject the null hypothesis)	Type II error	Correct decision

The two columns of Table 13.16 represent the two states of the real world: either that there is a difference between our two groups or there is not. The two rows of the table represent the two possible choices we as researchers can make on the basis of our sample data: reject the null hypothesis or do not reject the null hypothesis. There are thus four possible outcomes depending on our decision and the state of the world. If we conclude, on the basis of a difference between our two samples, that there is a difference in the populations from which those samples were drawn, and if a difference really exists (the upper left-hand cell of our table), then, great! We've made the correct decision. Likewise, if we conclude that there is no difference between urban and rural English adults and, in fact, there is no difference (the lower right-hand cell) we've also made the correct decision.

There are two additional possibilities, however. If we conclude, on the basis of a difference between our two samples, that there is a difference between the two groups we are studying and there is, in fact, no difference between the two groups (the upper right-hand cell), then we have made what is called a Type I error, a false positive. It is entirely possible, because of sampling error, to choose two samples which differ from each other when the two populations they are drawn from are the same. Similarly, if we conclude from our samples that there is no difference between the groups we are studying, and there is a difference (the lower left-hand cell) then we have again made an error, this time called a Type II error, a false negative.

The risk of making the Type I error is determined by the *level of significance* we accept in our statistical testing. Thus, if we decide that we will conclude that the populations truly differ whenever a test of significance shows that the obtained difference between two samples would be expected to occur by chance not more than five times in 100 if the two populations were, in fact, alike, we are accepting five chances in 100 that we will be wrong in rejecting the null hypothesis. We can reduce the risk of a Type I error by making our criterion for rejecting the null hypothesis more extreme; for example, by rejecting the null hypothesis only if the statistical test indicates that the sample difference might have appeared by chance only once in 100 times, or once in 1000 times, or once in 10,000 times. Unfortunately, however, the chances of making Type I and Type II errors are inversely related. The more we protect ourselves against the risk of making a Type I error (that is, the less likely we are to conclude that two populations differ when, in fact, they do not), the more likely we are to make a Type II error (that is, to fail to recognize population differences that actually exist). Once we have determined the degree of Type I risk we are willing to run, the only way of reducing the possibility of Type II error is to take larger samples and/or to use statistical tests that make the maximum use of available relevant information.

The inverse relationship of the risks of the two types of errors makes it necessary to strike a reasonable balance. In the social sciences, it is more or less conventional to reject the null hypothesis when the statistical analysis indicates that the observed difference would not occur more than five times out of 100 by chance alone. If the statistical analysis indicates that the difference between the two samples might have appeared by chance more than five times out of 100, the null hypothesis is not rejected. But these conventions are useful only when there is no other reasonable guide. The decision as to just how the balance between the two kinds of error

TABLE 13.17

Sample 1 (Urban)	Sample 2 (Rural)
19	14
13	8
17	12
20	15
21	16
24	19
25	20
26	21
18	10

$\overline{X}_1 = 20.3$ $\qquad\qquad$ $\overline{X}_2 = 15.0$

$s_1^2 = 17.5$ $\qquad\qquad$ $s_2^2 = 20.25$

$n_1 = 9$ $\qquad\qquad$ $n_2 = 9$

$$s_p = \sqrt{\frac{(n_1 - 1)s_1^2 + (n_2 - 1)s_2^2}{n_1 + n_2 - 2}}$$

$$= \sqrt{\frac{(9 - 1)17.5 + (9 - 1)20.25}{9 + 9 - 2}} = 4.345$$

$$t = \frac{\overline{X}_1 - \overline{X}_2}{s_p \sqrt{\frac{1}{n_1} + \frac{1}{n_2}}}$$

$$= \frac{20.3 - 15.0}{4.345 \sqrt{\frac{1}{9} + \frac{1}{9}}} = 2.59$$

Is this statistically significant? We decide that by looking at a table of critical values for *t*, but there are two more things to discuss before we can make that determination: whether our test is one-tailed or two-tailed and what the number of degrees of freedom is.

Whether a *t*-test is one-tailed or two-tailed depends upon our initial hypothesis. If we had some strong theoretical reason for arguing, before we collected the data, that urban adults would read more books than rural adults (i.e., if we could predict the *direction* of the difference in advance), then our test would be one-tailed. However, if we really didn't know which group would turn out to have read more books (i.e., all we are predicting is that there will be a *difference* between the two groups), then our test is a two-tailed test. A two-tailed test is somewhat exploratory in nature. If we can predict the direction of the difference in advance and perform a one-tailed test we are acting in a more confirmatory way, so our *t*-value, to be statistically significant, does not have to be as large as it does if we were making a two-tailed test.

TABLE 13.18   T-Test Critical Values (16 d.f.)

	Level of significance for one-tailed test					
$p =$	.10	.05	.025	.01	.005	.0005
	Level of significance for two-tailed test					
$p =$	.20	.10	.05	.02	.01	.001
$t =$	1.337	1.746	2.120	2.583	2.921	4.015

Once we have determined whether our *t*-test is one-tailed or two-tailed, we must determine the degrees of freedom. The number of degrees of freedom is equal to the number of observations we have minus the number of parameters we have estimated from the data. In our example we have estimated two parameters: $\overline{X}_1$ and $\overline{X}_2$, the two sample means (the sample variances are based on the means, so they don't count as additional parameters). Thus for our example we have the two sample sizes n_1 plus n_2 minus two for the sample means or $9 + 9 - 2 = 16$.

Now we are ready for the final step. By convention in the social sciences, to call a difference "statistically significant" it should be possible to obtain a difference as big as the observed difference by chance at most only 5 times out of a hundred (i.e., the probability of Type I error is .05). The values of *t* which correspond to these Type I probability levels (called critical values) for both one- and two-tailed tests with 16 degrees of freedom are presented in Table 13.18. The larger the value of *t*, the less likely it is that it would occur by chance if there is really no difference between the groups. As you can see, a *t* value for a one-tailed test which is large enough to occur by chance only five times out of a hundred (1.746) could occur by chance ten times out of a hundred if a two-tailed test were being conducted. So, as we observed earlier, one needs a larger value of *t* to be "statistically significant" if one is using a two-tailed test. Given the size of the *t*-test for our example of book reading in England, it is clear that the differences between our samples will permit us to conclude that there is a significant difference between the book reading habits of urban and rural adults. The value $t = 2.59$ is above the critical values for the .05 level (1.746 for a one-tailed test or 2.120 for a two-tailed test).

One further point should be mentioned. The fact that a result is *statistically significant* does not necessarily mean that it is *socially* or *psychologically significant*. Many statistically significant differences are trivial. For example, given enough cases, an average difference in intelligence between men and women of less than one IQ point may be statistically significant, but it is difficult to see any real import in the finding. On the other hand, there are cases where a small but reliable difference has great practical importance. For example, in a large-scale survey designed to give information about a population, a difference of one-half of one percent may represent hundreds of thousands of people, and knowledge of the difference may be important for policy decisions. One must constantly be concerned with the social and psychological meaning of one's findings as well as their statistical significance.

SUMMARY

We have tried in this chapter to introduce you to a concept of data analysis as more than simply a final tedious step in the research process. The techniques of exploratory data analysis—and we have only introduced you to a few of the many available procedures—are important for developing a fuller understanding of the data one is interested in and for generating possible hypotheses to explain the behavior of the data. We must always remember, however, that the data one explores represent the behavior of people; and it is ultimately social behavior, not numerical behavior, in which we are interested.

Writing the Research Report

14

This chapter was written by Daryl J. Bem.

SOME SUGGESTIONS ON PROCEDURE AND STYLE
Accuracy and Clarity
Work from an Outline
Write Simply. Use Examples. Use Friends as Reviewers
Be Compulsive. Be Willing to Restructure
Person and Voice
Tense
Gender
Where to Find Additional Guidance

You have conducted a study and analyzed the data. Now it is time to tell the world what you have learned, to write the research report. Even if your report is not for a professional audience, we suggest that you adopt the format used for research articles in the professional journals. This format not only permits readers to read the report from beginning to end, as they would any coherent narrative, but also to scan it for a quick overview of the study or to locate specific information easily by turning directly to the relevant section. Despite the standardized format, your individual style will find ample opportunity for expression.

The report is divided into the following sections:

1. Introduction. (What problem were you investigating and why?)
2. Method. (What procedures did you employ?)
3. Results. (What did you find?)
4. Discussion. (What do your findings mean? Where do we go from here?)
5. Summary or Abstract. (A brief summary of points 1–4.)
6. References (An alphabetical list of books and articles cited in the report.)
7. Appendix (Optional). (Copies of questionnaires, scales, or stimulus materials used in the research or tables of data too extensive or too peripheral to include in the body of the report.)

In this chapter we provide a step-by-step procedure for filling in the details of this outline, as well as some stylistic suggestions for achieving maximum clarity in your report.

SOME PRELIMINARY CONSIDERATIONS

Which Report Should You Write?

There are two possible reports you can write: (1) the report you had in mind when you designed your study or (2) the report that makes the most sense after you have seen the results. They are rarely the same, and the correct answer is (2).

According to the popular view of the research process, an investigator begins with a formal theory, derives one or more hypotheses from that theory, designs and conducts a study to test these hypotheses, analyzes the data to see if they were confirmed, and then chronicles this sequence of events in the research report. If research actually proceeded according to this plan, then most of the research report could be prepared before the data are collected. The "Introduction" and "Method" sections could be completely written beforehand, and the "Results" section could be prepared in skeleton form, leaving spaces to be filled in by the specific numerical results obtained. The investigator could even prepare two possible discussion sections, one for positive or confirming results, the other for negative or disconfirming results. Research, however, does not usually go according to this plan—even when that was the plan the investigator had in mind to begin with. Accordingly, we suggest you begin thinking about your report by thinking about your data.

As we noted in Chapter 13, data analysis consists of more than simply checking to see if your original hypotheses were confirmed or disconfirmed. It also involves exploring the data thoroughly to see if there are any interesting results that may not have been originally anticipated. For example, by looking at the data separately for men and women, you might discover an unexpected sex difference. You may even find some results that are far more informative than the confirmation or disconfirmation of your original hypotheses. Statistical tests can help you decide just how much faith you should put in such discoveries. Perhaps you will only be able to mention these findings tentatively in your report and to suggest further research for following them up. On the other hand, you might be justified in deciding to center your report around these new findings and to subordinate or even ignore your original hypotheses.

This is not advice to suppress negative results or findings unfavorable to your theory. If your study was genuinely designed to test hypotheses derived from a formal theory or if the original hypotheses are of wide general interest for some other reason, then the confirmation or disconfirmation of these hypotheses should remain the central focus of your report. In particular, the integrity of the scientific enterprise requires an investigator to report negative or disconfirming results no matter how personally disappointing this outcome might be.

But this requirement assumes that somebody out there cares about the disconfirmation of the hypotheses. Many, if not most, studies in social relations are launched from some personal speculations or idiosyncratic questions of the "I-wonder-if . . ." variety. If your study is of this type, then nobody is likely to care if you were wrong. Contrary to the conventional wisdom, science does not care how clever or clairvoyant you were at guessing your results ahead of time. Your report should not be a personal history of your stillborn thoughts. Scientific integrity does not require you to lead your readers through all your wrongheaded hunches only to show — *voilà!* — they were wrongheaded.

Your overriding purpose is to tell the world what you think you have learned from your study about human behavior. That may or may not be the same as telling the world about what you used to think about human behavior when you began this investigation. If your results suggest an instructive or compelling framework for the presentation of your study, then adopt that framework, making the findings that tell us the most about human behavior the centerpiece of your presentation. An appropriate metaphor here is to think of your data as a jewel. Your job is to cut and polish this jewel, to select the facets to highlight, and to craft the best setting for it. Good report writing is largely a matter of good judgment; despite the standardized format, it is not a mechanical process.

And so, think about your report by thinking about your data. You may even find that the easiest way to begin is to write the "Results" section first.

The "Hourglass" Shape of the Report

An experimental report is usually written in the "shape" of an hourglass. It begins with broad general statements, progressively narrows down to the specifics of your particular study, and then broadens out again to more general considerations. Thus:

The introduction begins broadly:	"Humanity has long been thought of as basically evil."
It becomes more specific:	"Aggression has been seen as innate; altruism, as learned."
And more so:	"But studies of various animal species show that altruism often occurs . . ."
And more so:	"Indeed, Brewer reports that worker ants often sacrifice their own lives in order . . ."
Until you are ready to introduce your own study in conceptual terms:	"Two classes of behavior were selected, one antisocial, one prosocial . . ."
The method and results sections are the most specific, the "neck" of the hourglass:	(Method) Fifteen nursery school children were given M&M's and then observed. . . . (Results) Table 1 shows that 13 of the 15 children were more cooperative . . ."

The discussion section begins with the implications of your study:	"These results show that not all prosocial behavior needs to be learned . . ."
It becomes broader:	"Clearly we need a more symmetric approach to anti- and prosocial behaviors . . ."
And more so:	"Humanity, then, can be viewed as both evil and good; both predestined and free; capable of great sin, but capable of great goodness as well."

This example may be a bit more grandiose in its opening and closing statements than would be appropriate for a professional journal article; but if your study is carefully executed and conservatively interpreted, you deserve to indulge yourself a bit at the two broad ends of the hourglass. Being dull only appears to be a prerequisite for publishing in the professional journals.

INTRODUCTION

What Is the Problem Being Investigated?

The first task of the research report is to introduce the background and nature of the problem being investigated. Even if your study were only asking a simple empirical question about human behavior or were directed toward a practical problem or policy issue, you must still place the question or issue into a larger context so that readers know why it is of any general significance. Here, for example, is an introduction to an article entitled "Does Sex-biased Job Advertising 'Aid and Abet' Sex Discrimination?" By Sandra and Daryl Bem (1973):

> Title VII of the 1964 Civil Rights Act forbids discrimination in employment on the basis of race, color, religion, national origin—and sex. Although the sex provision was treated as a joke at the time—and was originally introduced in an attempt to defeat the bill—more than 40% of the complaints warranting investigation in the first year of the Act were sex discrimination complaints. Nearly 6,000 charges of sex discrimination were filed in 1971 alone.
>
> Title VII extends as well to practices that aid and abet discrimination. For example, the Act forbids job advertisements from indicating a preference for one sex or the other unless sex is a bona fide occupational qualification for employment. In interpreting this provision, the Equal Employment Opportunities Commission (EEOC) has ruled that even the practice of labeling help-wanted columns as "Male" or "Female" should be considered a violation of the law.
>
> Nevertheless, a large number of employers continue to write advertisements that specify a sex preference, and many more write advertising copy clearly intended to

appeal to one sex only. Moreover, many newspapers continue to divide their help-wanted advertisements into sex-segregated columns.

Do these advertising practices aid and abet discrimination in employment by actually discouraging applicants of one sex or the other from applying for jobs for which they are otherwise well qualified? The two studies reported in this article sought to answer this question empirically. Both were conducted and presented as part of legal testimony, the first in a suit filed by the EEOC against American Telephone and Telegraph Company, the second in a suit filed by the National Organization for Women against *The Pittsburgh Press.*

Note how this introduction conforms to the "hourglass" shape of report writing by beginning with the 1964 Civil Rights Act in general and then successively narrowing the focus to the sex provision of the act, the aiding and abetting clause, and finally to the specific practices that are the subject of the experiments to be reported.

The same reporting strategy is employed if your study was designed to contribute to some aspect of psychological or sociological theory. In this case, you need to summarize the theory or conceptual framework within which you are working. But no matter how theoretical or esoteric your study is, an intelligent nonprofessional — perhaps your grandmother — should still be able to grasp the nature of the problem and understand why he, she, or anyone should care. Here are four rules of thumb for helping that reader out:

1. Write in English prose, not psychological or sociological jargon.

2. Don't plunge the unprepared reader into the middle of your problem or theory. Take the time and space necessary to lead the general reader up to the formal or theoretical statement of the problem step by step.

3. Try to open with a statement about human behavior, not the behavior of behavioral scientists or their research. (This rule is almost always violated in the professional journals. Don't use them as a model here.)

4. Use examples to illustrate theoretical points or to help introduce theoretical or technical terms. The more abstract the theory, the more important such examples become.

EXAMPLES OF OPENING STATEMENTS:

Wrong: Recent research in the forced-compliance paradigm has focused on the effects of predecisional choice and incentive magnitude.

Wrong: Festinger's theory of cognitive dissonance has received a great deal of attention during the past 15 years.

Right: The individual who holds two beliefs that are inconsistent with one another may feel uncomfortable. For example, the person who knows that he or she enjoys smoking but believes it to be unhealthy may experience a discomfort arising from the disharmony or inconsistency between these two thoughts or cognitions. This feeling of discomfort has been called *cognitive dissonance* by social psychologist Leon Festinger (1957), who suggests that individuals will be motivated to remove this dissonance in whatever way they can . . .

The Literature Review

After you have set the stage in your opening statement, summarize the current state of knowledge in the area of investigation. What previous research has been done on this problem? What are the pertinent theories of the phenomenon, if any? You should have familiarized yourself with previous work on the topic before you designed your own study, and hence most of your literature search should have been done by the time you are ready to write your report. Nevertheless, your results may have led you to recast your study in a slightly different framework or to introduce a new aspect of the problem. In this case, you may need to cite references you had not previously consulted. Suppose, for example, that you did discover an unanticipated sex difference in your results. You should then go back to the literature to see if other investigatores have found such a difference or to see if there are any related findings that might explain your unexpected result. If you plan to make the sex difference a central feature of your report, then you should discuss the topic of sex differences in the introduction, including citations to the relevant previous findings. If you plan to mention the sex difference only as a subsidiary finding, however, then postpone any discussion of sex differences until the discussion section. (You should now begin to appreciate why you cannot really begin your report until you have a clear view of the results already in mind.)

In reviewing previous work, you need not describe every study ever done on your problem. Cite only articles pertinent to the specific issues with which you are dealing; emphasize their major conclusions, findings, or relevant methodological issues and avoid unnecessary detail. If someone else has written a review article that surveys the literature on the topic, you can simply refer your own readers to the review and present only its most pertinent points in your own report. Even when you must describe an entire study, try to condense it as much as possible without sacrificing clarity. One way of doing this is to describe one variation of the procedure in chronological sequence, letting it convey the overview of the study at the same time. Here, for example, is a description of a very complicated experiment on attitude change designed to test Festinger's theory of cognitive dissonance (Festinger and Carlsmith, 1959):

> Sixty male undergraduates were randomly assigned to one of three conditions. In the $1 condition, the subject was first required to perform long repetitive laboratory tasks in an individual experimental session. He was then hired by the experimenter as an "assistant" and paid $1 to tell a waiting fellow student (a confederate) that the tasks were fun and interesting. In the $20 condition, each subject was hired for $20 to do the same thing. Control subjects simply engaged in the tasks. After the experiment each subject indicated on a questionnaire how much he had enjoyed the tasks. The results showed that $1 subjects rated the tasks as significantly more enjoyable than did the $20 subjects, who, in turn, did not differ from the control subjects.

This kind of condensed writing looks easy. It is not, and you will have to write and rewrite such summaries repeatedly before they are both clear and succinct. The preceding paragraph is the eighth draft.

Books and articles are cited in the text of the report by giving the author's last name and the date of publication. For example: "According to Festinger (1957), people find cognitive dissonance uncomfortable. Not everyone, however, agrees with this conclusion (e.g., Abelson, 1968; Bem, 1967; Kermit, 1979). Nevertheless, direct evidence for internal discomfort has actually been demonstrated in at least one study (Zanna, Freud, & Theophrastus, 1977)." Note that footnotes are not used for references or citations.

Your Study

As you come to the end of the introduction, it is often useful to introduce your own study in brief overview. The purpose is not to discuss procedural details, but to provide a smooth transition into the method section, which follows immediately. The following example could have ended the introduction to the previously cited sex-biased advertising study:

> The question, then, is whether or not such advertising practices discourage potential applicants from applying for jobs. The present study sought to answer this question by asking male and female high school seniors to read several telephone job advertisements and to rate their interest in each job. The interest ratings were analyzed to see if advertisements written in nonsexist language would increase the interest that men and women would show in jobs stereotyped for the "other" sex.

METHOD

What to Include

Readers need to know in considerable detail how the study was carried out. What was its basic design? If the study was an experimental one, just what were the experimental manipulations? (For example, was "threat" established by telling the subjects that they were about to take a very difficult test, which would determine their grades in a course, or by shouting, "Fire!"?) At what point or points were the measurements taken?

If the data were collected by means of questionnaires or interviews, exactly what questions were asked? (The questionnaire or interview schedule is often given in an appendix.) How much and what kind of experience had the interviewers had, and how were they trained for this particular study? If the measurements were based on observation, what instructions were given to the observers?

Readers also need to know how the observations or replies to questions were translated into measures of the variables with which the study was concerned. (For example, which questions were taken into account in estimating "alienation"; or what kinds of bystanders' behavior were classified as "helping"?)

Regarding the sample used in the study, readers should be told: Who were the subjects? How many were there? How were they selected? These questions are crucial for estimating the probable limits of generalizability of the findings. Are elaborate conclusions being drawn on the basis of responses of ten college sophomores, selected because they happened to be friends of the investigator? Were only women interviewed? If so, is there any basis for extending the findings to people in general? Intensive study of a small number of cases that do not constitute a representative sample of any specifiable population may be quite valuable. Nevertheless, the number and characteristics of the participants on which the findings are based should be clearly stated so that readers can draw their own conclusions about the applicability of the findings to other groups.

If you conducted a fairly complex experiment in which there was a sequence of procedures or events, it is often helpful to describe the study as it was seen from the subject's point of view. First give an overview of the study, including a description of the subjects, setting, and the variables assessed; but then describe the sequence of events in chronological order so that the reader is carried through the experience as a subject was. Provide summaries or excerpts of what was actually said to the subject, including any rationale or "cover story" that was given. Show sample items from questionnaires, labels on attitude scales, pictures of apparatus or stimulus materials, and so forth, even if you also include the complete questionnaires or rating scales in an appendix to your report. If you administered a standard personality test, describe its general properties, and give a sample item even if it is a fairly familiar instrument (for example, "Subjects then filled out the Marlow-Crowne Social Desirability Scale, a true-false inventory that taps the degree to which a person describes him or herself in socially desirable terms (e.g., 'I have never lied')." The purpose of all this is to give the readers a "feel" for what it was like to be a subject. This often bears importantly upon the interpretation of your results, and readers should be in a position to arrive at their own judgments about your conclusions.

Name all operations and variables with easily recognized and remembered labels. Don't use abbreviations (The AMT5% group) or empty labels (Treatment 3). Instead, tell us about the sex-biased ads and the sex-neutral ads, the success group versus the failure group, the teacher sample versus the student sample, and so forth. It is also better to label groups or treatments in operational rather than theoretical terms. It is difficult to remember that it was the High Dissonance group that was paid $1 and the Low Dissonance group that was paid $20. So tell us instead about the $1 group and the $20 group. You can remind us of the theoretical interpretation of these variables again later when it is necessary. And, finally, it is often helpful in a complicated experiment to end your description with a one or two sentence summary of the procedure and its purpose.

An Example

The following example is excerpted from the method section of the sex-biased advertising study cited earlier.

METHOD

SUBJECTS

One-hundred twenty seniors from a racially integrated high school in the San Francisco Bay area served as subjects. Half were male and half were female. Few planned to go on to any 4-year college. Students who were not planning to go on to college were purposely sought as subjects so that they might be both appropriate for and interested in jobs like those advertised by the telephone company. (As seniors, many would even be preparing for jobs like these in the near future.)

PROCEDURE

Each student was given a booklet containing 12 job advertisements and was asked to indicate on a 6-point scale how interested he or she would be in applying for each job. The scale ranged from "very uninterested" to "very interested" and was labeled at each point. The 12 advertisements included four telephone jobs and eight nontelephone jobs. In order of appearance, the jobs were: appliance sales, telephone operator, photographer, travel agent, telephone frameman, dental assistant, taxicab driver, telephone service representative, assistant buyer, keypunch operator, telephone lineman, and public relations/advertising.

The cover sheet introduced all 12 jobs as follows: "All of the jobs have a starting salary of between $100 and $120 per week with regular raises after that. None of the jobs requires any previous training or experience beyond high school graduation; all of them provide paid on-the-job training." The phrase, "An Equal Opportunity Employer m/f," appeared at the end of every job advertisement.

SEX-BIASED JOB ADVERTISEMENTS. One-third of the booklets advertised the telephone jobs in the sex-biased format used by AT&T. In other words, these ads were copied verbatim from AT&T ads and brochures furnished to us by the EEOC. The four sex-biased telephone advertisements were worded as follows:

Telephone Operator:

WHO SAYS IT'S A MAN'S WORLD?

Behind every man's telephone call, there is a woman. She's a smart woman. She's efficient. She has to be. She places the complex long distance calls people cannot place themselves or helps them locate telephone numbers.

Hers is a demanding job. But we make it worth her while. We can make it worth your while too. Not only do we pay a good salary to start, but also offer group life insurance, group medical coverage, good vacations with pay and free pensions.

A stepping stone to management positions.

Pacific Telephone

An Equal Opportunity Employer m/f

[The other advertisements and conditions were similarly described and illustrated.]

SUMMARY OF PROCEDURE. The same four telephone jobs were thus presented in three different formats: the sex-biased format used by AT&T, a sex-unbiased format, and a sex-reversed "affirmative-action" format. All 8 nontelephone ads were worded in sex-unbiased fashion and remained constant in all booklets. In other words, only the wording of the telephone jobs changed from condition to condition. For purposes of analysis, a subject was defined as "interested in applying" for a job if he or she checked any of the following three categories: "slightly interested," "moderately interested," "very interested." A subject was defined as "not interested" if he or she checked "slightly uninterested," "moderately uninterested," or "very uninterested."

Ethical Issues

The subjects or participants in our studies are human beings and should be accorded respect and gratitude for their partnership in the research enterprise. Accordingly, after you have described your procedures, it is appropriate to tell us how you compensated them for their time and effort and how you dealt with any ethical problems. If the research design required you to keep subjects uninformed or even misinformed about the procedures, how did you tell them about this afterwards? Did you obtain written consent from your subjects for their participation? Were they free to withdraw their participation at any time? Were they subjected to any embarrassment or discomfort? Were you observing people who were not aware of that fact? What steps were followed to protect the anonymity of your subjects or participants? If your study raises any of these ethical issues, you should be prepared to justify your procedures and to assure readers that your subjects were treated with dignity and that they left your study with their self-esteem intact and their respect for you and behavioral science enhanced rather than diminished.

RESULTS

In short articles or reports of fairly simple studies, the results and discussion sections are often combined into a single section titled "Results and Discussion." The results are discussed as they are presented, and the section ends with two or three paragraphs that state the conclusions reached, mention qualifications imposed by problems encountered in executing or analyzing the study, and suggest what further research might be appropriate. Most empirical studies can be handled in this fashion.

If, however, you need to present many different kinds of results before you can integrate them or draw any inferences or if you wish to discuss several different matters at length in the final discussion, then you should separate the results and discussion sections. Even in this case, however, there is no such thing as a pure results section without an accompanying discussion. You cannot just throw numbers at readers and expect them to retain them in their memory until they reach the discussion section. In other words, the results section is still part of an integrated linear narrative about human behavior. It, too, is to be written in English prose, not numbers and statistical symbols.

Setting the Stage

Before you can present your main results, there are two preliminary matters that need to be handled. First, you need to present evidence that your study successfully set up the conditions for testing your hypotheses or answering your questions. If your study required you to produce one group of subjects in a happy mood and another in a sad mood, then here is the place to show us that mood ratings made by the two groups were significantly different. If your study involved a mail survey, here is where you need to tell us how many people returned the survey and to discuss the possibility that those who did not respond differed in some important way from those who did. If you divided your subjects into groups, you need to assure us that these groups did not differ on some unintended variable that might bear upon the interpretation of your results (for example, social class, race, sex, age, intelligence). If your study required observers to record behavior or judges to score written materials, then you should present quantitative evidence for interobserver agreement or interjudge reliability. If your study required that you misinform the subjects about the nature of the procedures, you should have some evidence that they were not suspicious, that subjects who participated earlier had not informed subjects who participated later, and that your "cover story" produced the state of belief required for the test of your hypotheses. If you had to discard certain subjects, either at the time of the study or later in the data analysis, you need to tell us why and how many and to discuss the possibility that this limits or qualifies the conclusions you can draw.

Not all of these matters need to be discussed at the beginning of the results section. Some of them might already have been mentioned in the method section (for example, interjudge reliabilities of scoring), and others might better be postponed until the discussion section, when you are considering alternative explanations of your results (for example, the possibility that some subjects became suspicious). In some cases, you may not have any hard evidence to cite, and you may have to fall back upon plausible argument: "The possibility that those who did not return the survey were politically more conservative than those who did seems unlikely because surveys were returned in approximately equal numbers from the dormitories, the cooperatives, and the fraternities. If the survey had alienated conservatives, we would have expected a smaller return from the fraternities; moreover . . ."

The decision of what to include at the beginning of the results section to assure the reader that you have successfully set the stage for adequately testing your hypotheses or answering your questions is very much a matter of judgment. It is an important step, but don't overdo it. Get it out of the way as quickly as possible, and then get on with your story.

The second preliminary matter to deal with at the beginning of the results section is the method of data analysis. First you need to describe any overall procedures you followed in converting your raw observations into analyzable data. How were the responses to your mail survey coded for analysis? How were observers' ratings combined? Were all measures first converted to standard scores? (Some of these, too, may have been discussed in the method section and need not be repeated. Similarly, data-combining procedures that are highly specific can be postponed. For example, if you combined three measures of anxiety into a single composite score for analysis, you can tell us about that later when you are about to present the anxiety data.)

Next you need to tell readers about the statistical analysis itself. If this is quite standard, then it can be described in very few words (for example, "All data were analyzed by two-way analyses of variance with sex of subject and mood induction as the independent variables"). If your analysis is unconventional or requires certain statistical assumptions that your data may not meet, however, then you need to discuss the rationale for it, perhaps citing an article or book for the reader who wishes to check into it further.

And finally, this is the place to give readers an overview of the entire results section if it is complicated or divided into several parts. For example: "The results are presented in three parts. The first section presents the behavioral results for the men, followed by the parallel results for the women. The final section presents the attitudinal and physiological data for both sexes combined."

Presenting the Findings

The general rule in reporting your findings is to give the forest first and then the trees. This is true of the results section as a whole: Begin with the central findings, and then move to more peripheral ones. It is also true within subsections: State the basic finding first, and then elaborate or qualify it as necessary. Similarly, discuss an overall measure of aggression or whatever first, and then move to its individual components. Beginning with one of your most central results proceed as follows:

1. Remind us of the conceptual question you are asking. (For example, "It will be recalled that the men are expected to be more expressive than the women." Or "We turn first to the question: Are the men or the women more expressive?") Note that this is a *conceptual* statement of the question.

2. Remind us of the actual operation performed or the actual behavior measured. (For example, "Do the men produce more tears during the showing of the film than the women?") Note that this is an *operational* statement of the question.

3. Tell us the answer immediately and in English. "The answer is yes." Or "As Table 1 reveals, men do, in fact, cry more profusely than the women."

4. Now, and only now, speak to us in numbers. (Your grandmother can now skip to the next result in case she has forgotten her statistics or her reading glasses.) "Thus the men in all four conditions produced an average of 14 cc more tears than the women, $F(1,112) = 5.79$, $p < .025$."

5. Now you may elaborate or qualify the overall conclusion if necessary. "Only in the Father-Watching condition did the men fail to produce more tears than the women, but a specific test of this effect failed to reach significance, $t = 1.58$, $p < .12$.

6. As shown in the preceding examples, every finding that involves a comparison between groups or a relationship between variables should be accompanied by its level of statistical significance. Otherwise, readers have no way of knowing whether the finding could have emerged by chance. But despite the importance of inferential statistics for deciding which results are to be presented as genuine findings, they are not the heart of your narrative and should be subordinated to the descriptive results. Whenever possible, state the result first and then give its statistical significance, but in no case should you ever give the statistical test alone without indicating its meaning in terms of the substantive results. Do not tell us that the three-way interaction with sex, esteem, and parent condition was significant at the .05 level unless you tell us immediately and in English that men are less expressive than women in the negative conditions if father watches — but only for men with low self-esteem.

7. In selecting the descriptive indices or statistics, your purpose should be to show us the behavior of people as vividly as you can, to be as descriptive of the actual behavior observed as possible. If children in your study hit a Bobo doll, tell us how many times they hit it or the percent of children who hit it. If an aggression score represents the mean on a 5-point rating scale, remind us that 3.42 lies between "slightly aggressive" and "quite aggressive." Just as the method section should give us a "feel" for the procedures employed, so, too, the results section should give us a "feel" for the behavior observed.

8. Every set of findings that is sufficiently important to be stressed should be accompanied by a table, graph, or figure showing the relevant data (unless the entire set of findings can be stated in one or two numbers). The basic rule here is that readers should be able to grasp your major findings *either* by reading the text *or* by looking at the figures and tables. This implies that tables and figures must be titled and labeled clearly and completely, even if that means constructing a very lengthy title or heading (for example, "Mean number of tears produced in male and female subjects by the heart operation movie as a function of subject sex, parental observation, and self-esteem"). Within the text itself, you must lead the reader by the hand through the table to point out the results of interest: "As shown in Column A of Table 2, men produce more tears (7.58) than women (6.34) . . . Of particular interest is the number of tears produced when both Father and Mother were watching (rows 3 and 4) . . ." Don't just wave in the general direction of the table and expect the reader to ferret out the information.

9. End each section of the results with a summary of where things stand. "Thus, except for the Father-Watching condition, which will be discussed later, the hypothesis that men cry more than women in response to visually-depicted grief appears to receive strong support."

10. Lead into the next section of the results with a smooth transition sentence: "Men may thus be more expressive than women in the domain of negative emotion, but can we assume that they are also more willing and able to express positive emotions? Table 3 shows that we cannot . . ." (Note, again, that you should give the reader the "bottom line" immediately.) As the results section proceeds, you should continue to summarize and "update" the reader's store of information frequently. The reader should not have to keep looking back to retrieve the major points of your plot line.

By structuring the results section in this way, by moving from forest to trees, by announcing each result clearly in prose before wading into numbers and statistics, and by summarizing frequently, you permit the reader to decide just how much detail he or she wants to pursue at each juncture and to skip ahead to the next main point whenever that seems desirable.

After you have demonstrated that your quantitative results are statistically reliable, it is often useful to become more informal and to describe the behavior of particular individuals in your study. The point is not to prove something, but to add richness to your findings, to share with the readers the "feel" of the behavior: "Indeed, two of the men used an entire box of Kleenex during the showing of the heart operation, but yet would not pet the baby kitten owned by the secretary."

An Example

The following example is from the results section of the same sex-biased advertising study cited earlier.

RESULTS

Do sex-biased job advertisements discourage men and women from applying for "opposite-sex" jobs? As shown in Figure 14.1, our results clearly suggest this to be the case.

Consider first the results for women. When the jobs of lineman and frameman were advertised in a sex-biased format, no more than 5% of the women were interested. When these same jobs were advertised in a sex-unbiased format, 25% of the women were interested. And when the ads for lineman and frameman were specifically written to appeal to woman, nearly half (45%) of the women in our sample were interested in applying for one or the other of these two jobs ($X^2 = 8.53$, $p < .01$, one-tailed). In other words, sex-biased advertisements do discourage women from applying for so-called male

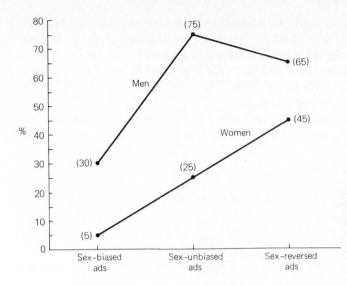

FIGURE 14.1 Percent of men and women who were interested in applying for either of the "opposite-sex" jobs. (Each data point represents 20 subjects.)

jobs; more women would be interested in applying for such jobs if the ad's sex bias were removed; and even more women would be interested if affirmative-action ads were specifically written to recruit them.

The results for men show a similar, but not identical, pattern. As can be seen in Figure 1, men are generally more interested in the jobs of operator and service representative than women are in the jobs of lineman and frameman. (This difference may be due, in part, to the fact that Pacific Telephone does employ male operators in the Bay Area.) Despite this fact, the results clearly indicate that sex-biased job advertisements still tend to discourage men from applying for jobs as operator and service representative ($X^2 = 9.09$, $p < .01$, one-tailed). For when the sex bias is removed, the percentage of men interested in applying for one or the other of these jobs jumps from 30% to 75%. Wording these ads in sex-reversed "affirmative-action" format does not further increase the percentage of men who are interested. [Neither does it significantly reduce it, however ($X^2 < 1$, n.s.).] It may be that 75% is the maximum one can expect for any particular job and that a sex-reversed format *would* serve to to further increase male interest for "female" jobs with lesser initial interest.

The results thus indicate that sex bias in the content of a job advertisement does serve to aid and abet discrimination by discouraging both men and women from applying for "opposite-sex" jobs.

DISCUSSION

As we noted earlier, the discussion section is often combined with the results section; for more complex studies or studies with more extended or abstract implications, it often appears separately. In either case, the discussion forms a cohesive narrative with the introduction, and you should expect to move materials back and forth between the introduction and discussion as you rewrite and reshape the report. Topics that are central to your argument will appear in the introduction and, possibly, again in the discussion. Points you have decided to subordinate may not be brought up at all until the discussion section. The closing discussion is also the "bottom" of the hourglass-shaped format and thus proceeds from specific matters about your study to more general concerns (about methodological strategies, for example) to the broadest generalizations you wish to make.

Begin by telling us what you have learned from the study. Open with a clear statement on the support or nonsupport of the hypotheses or the answers to the questions you first raised in the introduction. Do not, however, simply reformulate and repeat points already summarized in the results. Each new statement should contribute something new to the reader's understanding of the problem. What inferences can be drawn from the findings? These inferences may be at a level quite close to the data or may involve considerable abstraction, perhaps to the level of a larger theory regarding, say, emotion or sex differences. What are the theoretical and practical implications of the results?

It is also appropriate at this point to compare your results to those reported by other investigators and to discuss possible shortcomings of your study, conditions that might limit the extent of legitimate generalization or otherwise qualify your inferences. Remind the reader of the characteristics of your subject sample, the possibility that it might differ from other populations to which you might want to generalize; of specific characteristics of your methods that might have influenced the outcome; or of any other factors that might have operated to produce atypical results. But do not dwell compulsively on every flaw! In particular, be willing to accept negative or unexpected results without a tortured attempt to explain them away. Don't make up long, involved, pretzel-shaped theories to account for every hiccup in the data. There is probably a $-.73$ correlation between the clarity of an investigator's results and the length of his or her discussion section. Don't contribute to this shameful figure.

But suppose that, on the contrary, your results have led you to a grand new theory that injects startling clarity into your data and revolutionizes your view of the problem area. Doesn't that justify a long discussion section? No! In this case you should rewrite the entire report so that you *begin* with your new theory. As we noted earlier, your reporting task is to provide the most informative and compelling framework for your study from the opening sentence. If your new theory does that, don't wait until the discussion section to spring it on us. A research report is not necessarily a chronology of your thought processes.

The discussion section also includes a discussion of questions that remain unanswered or new questions that have been raised by the study along with suggestions for the kinds of research that would help to answer them. Indeed, suggesting further research is probably the most common way of ending a research report.

Common, but dull! If you are following the hourglass-shaped format of the research report, then the final statements should be broad general statements about human behavior, not precious details of interest only to behavioral scientists. Consider: "Thus further research will be needed before it is clear whether the androgyny scale should be scored as a single continuous dimension or partitioned into a 4-way typology." No, no! Such a sentence may well be appropriate somewhere in the discussion, but please, not your final farewell. Why not: "Perhaps, then, the concept of androgyny will come to define a new standard of mental health, a standard that will liberate men and women rather than incarcerate them." Yes, yes! End with a bang, not a whimper!

SUMMARY OR ABSTRACT

A research report often concludes with a very brief summary that restates in barest outline the problem, the procedures, the major findings, and the major conclusions drawn from them. This is called the "Summary." Most journals have now replaced the summary with an **abstract,** an even briefer summary that appears at the very beginning of the article rather than at the end.

An abstract is only about 125 words or less. It permits potential readers to get a quick overview of the study and to decide if they wish to read the report itself. It is very difficult to write because it is so condensed, and it will require slaving over every word to attain clarity. You cannot summarize everything in an abstract — or even in a more extended summary at the end of your report if you choose that format. Instead, you must decide what you wish to highlight, and this implies that you should write the abstract or summary last, after you have a firm view of the structure and content of your complete report.

The title of your report itself serves as part of the abstract or summary. It, too, should convey the content of your study as accurately and as clearly as possible so that a potential reader can decide whether or not to go further. The most informative titles are those that manage to mention both the dependent and independent variables (for example, "Emotional responses of men and women to visual stimuli as a function of self-esteem and being observed by parents"). Here is how the report of the sex-biased advertising study begins.

Does Sex-biased Job Advertising "Aid and Abet" Sex Discrimation?

ABSTRACT

Two studies are reported which indicate that both sex-biased wording in job advertisements and the placement of help-wanted ads in sex-segregated newspaper columns discourage men and women from applying for "opposite-sex" jobs for which they might well be qualified. Both studies were originally conducted and presented as part of legal testimony in actual sex discrimination cases.

Title VII of the 1964 . . .

REFERENCES

All books and articles cited in the text of a research report are listed at the end of the report under the heading "References." They are arranged alphabetically according to the author's last name, a format that parallels the way in which they are cited in the text. The following examples include all the nonfictitious references cited in this chapter.

The following three references are to journal articles cited in this chapter. The italicized numbers are volume numbers; they are followed by the page numbers.

Bem, S. L., & Bem, D. J. Does sex-biased job advertising "aid and abet" sex discrimination? *Journal of Applied Social Psychology*, 1973, *3*, 6–18.

Festinger, L., & Carlsmith, J. M. Cognitive consequences of forced compliance. *Journal of Abnormal and Social Psychology*, 1959, *58*, 203–210.

Martyna, W. What does "He" mean? *Journal of Communication*, 1978, *28*, 131–138.

The following three references are to books cited in this chapter.

The American Psychological Association. *Publication manual* (2nd ed.). Washington, D.C.: American Psychological Association, 1974.

Festinger, L. A. *A theory of cognitive dissonance*. Stanford: Stanford University Press, 1957.

Strunk, W., Jr., & White, E. B. *The elements of style* (3rd ed.). New York: Macmillan, 1979.

The following example, not cited in this chapter, illustrates a reference to an article by Zimbardo that appears in a book edited by Arnold and Levin.

Zimbardo, P. G. The human choice: Individuation, reason, and order versus deindividuation, impulse, and chaos. In W. A. Arnold & D. Levin (Eds.), *Nebraska symposium on motivation* (Vol. 17). Lincoln: University of Nebraska Press, 1969.

APPENDIX

The appendix to a research report contains copies of materials used in the research that would be too extensive to include in the report itself. These might include questionnaires, attitude scales, stimulus materials, or photographs and drawings of experimental apparatus or the research setting. These are materials that would help someone else duplicate your experiment in detail. A second appendix might contain tables of data or additional data analyses that are too extensive or too peripheral to include in the report itself. This is information that would enable an interested reader to explore your data in fine detail or to answer questions about your results that you omitted or that may not even have occurred to you.

Because journal space is at a premium, most journal articles do not have appendixes. Readers who have questions about the data or who wish to replicate the experiment themselves usually communicate directly with the original investigator. Dissertations, theses, and research reports done for class assignments, however, usually do include such appendixes. In fact, it is often useful in research reports done for class assignments to include an appendix containing the raw data themselves. Often an instructor will be able to spot findings in the data that may have been overlooked or to suggest alternative ways of organizing or analyzing data. In short, whether or not an investigator includes appendixes in a report depends a lot upon who the readers will be and the likelihood that they will find the supplementary materials useful. But as we noted earlier, the report itself should still be self-contained; a reader should not have to consult an appendix to understand the methods or results. For example, even if your entire survey questionnaire is contained in an appendix, you should still provide a few sample items from it in the method section.

SOME SUGGESTIONS ON PROCEDURE AND STYLE

Accuracy and Clarity

The overriding criteria for good scientific writing are accuracy and clarity. If your report is interesting and written with flair and style, fine. But this is still a subsidiary virtue. First strive for accuracy and clarity.

Work from an Outline

Even though the standardized format we have described here will go a long way toward organizing your report, you will be able to produce a more coherent report with a minimum of rewriting if your first organize the main points in outline form, examine the logic of the sequence, check to see if important points are omitted or misplaced, and so forth. As we suggested earlier, it is sometimes helpful to begin with the "Results" section, and it is also useful to think of your introduction and final discussion as part of the same conceptual narrative.

Write Simply, Use Examples, Use Friends as Reviewers

As we noted earlier, it should be possible for a nonprofessional to read your report and comprehend what you did and why — even if he or she knows nothing about statistics, experimental design, or the substantive area of your research problem. This is achieved by writing simply, with a minimum of jargon, and using frequent examples to illustrate and introduce technical concepts. The more abstract the subject matter, the more you need examples to tie it back to the reader's own experience and previous level of knowledge.

Read over your own writing, trying to take the viewpoint of an intelligent but nonprofessional reader. Ask at each point, "Do I know yet what this concept means?" "Is this clear?" The ability to take the role of a "naive" reader or listener is the most important skill in writing or teaching. It is not easy. And because it is not easy, you should use your friends as reviewers, especially those who are unfamiliar with the subject matter area. If they find something unclear, do not argue with them or attempt to clarify the problem verbally. If they have read carefully and conscientiously, they are always right: *By definition, the writing is unclear*. Their suggestions for correcting the unclarities may be wrong, even dumb. But as unclarity detectors, readers are never wrong.

Be Compulsive. Be Willing to Restructure

The best writers rewrite nearly every sentence in the course of polishing their successive drafts. The probability of writing a sentence perfectly the first time is vanishingly small, and good writing requires a high degree of compulsiveness and attention to detail. But whether or not one worries about writing style in the course of producing the first draft is to some extent a matter of individual taste. Some experienced writers spend a long time over each sentence, carefully choosing each word. But when the purpose is to convey information rather than to achieve a literary production, it is probably true for most people that time is saved in the long run by writing the first draft as quickly as possible. Once it is on paper, one can go back and rewrite sentences and paragraphs, fortified by the knowledge that at least a first draft of the report has already been produced.

In writing and rewriting, it is important to remember that a badly built building cannot be salvaged by brightening up the wallpaper. Rewriting often means restructuring, not just tinkering with sentences or paragraphs. Sometimes it is necessary to restructure totally an experimental report, even to go back and do more data analysis, just to iron out a bump in the logic of the argument. Don't get so attached to your first draft of the report that you are unwilling to tear it apart and rebuild it. Rewriting often means restructuring.

Person and Voice

In the past, scientific writing employed the third person, passive voice almost exclusively ("The experiment was designed by the authors to test the hypothesis that . . ."). This is dull and clumsy and is no longer the norm. It is now permissible to use the first person and desirable to use the active voice. Do not refer to yourself as "the author" or "the investigator." Do not refer to yourself as "we" unless there really are two or more authors or investigators involved. You may refer to yourself as "I" as long as you do it sparingly; constant use of the first person tends to distract the reader from the subject matter, and it is best to remain in the background. Leave the reader in the background, too. Don't say, "The reader will find it hard to believe that . . ." or "You will be surprised to learn . . ."

Perhaps you are wondering what you *can* do. You can let people and their behavior serve as the subjects of sentences: "Individuals appear to cling to their prejudices even when . . ." "Racial prejudice, then, diminishes when persons interact . . ." You may also refer to the reader indirectly from time to time: "Consider, first, the results for men . . ." You may also refer to yourself and the reader as "we" in some contexts: "We can see in Table 1 that most of the tears are produced . . ." "In everyday life, of course, we tend to put great emphasis on a person's gender . . ."

Tense

Use the past tense when reporting the previous research of others ("Bandura reported . . ."), how you conducted your study ("Observers were posted behind . . ."), and specific past behaviors of your subjects or participants ("Two of the group members talked . . ."). Use the present tense for results currently in front of the reader ("As Table 2 shows, the emotional film is more effective . . .") and for conclusions that are more general than the specific results ("Sex-biased advertising, then, leads qualified applicants to ignore . . .").

Gender

Because of the increased awareness that language can perpetuate stereotypes, authors of journal articles are now expected to avoid writing in a manner that reinforces questionable attitudes and assumptions about people and sex roles. The most awkward problems arise from the common use of masculine nouns and pronouns when the content refers to both sexes. The generic use of "man," "he," "his," and "him" to refer to both men and women is not only misleading in many instances, but research shows that readers visualize and think of male persons when these forms are used (Martyna, 1978). Sometimes the results are not only sexist, but humorous in their naive androcentrism: "Man's vital needs include food, water, and access to females" (quoted in Martyna, 1978).

Unfortunately, the language has not caught up with this new awareness, and the available alternatives are not wholly satisfactory. In most contexts, the simplest alternative is the use of the plural. Instead of saying, "The individual who displays prejudice in his personal relations is probably . . . ," substitute "Individuals who display prejudice in their personal relations are . . ." If it is stylistically important to focus on the single individual, the use of "he or she," "him or her," and so forth is acceptable but clumsy if used very often or more than once in a single sentence: "The individual who displays prejudice in his or her personal relations is . . ." Alternatives like *he/she* or *s/he* are unpronounceable and grate on the eye. They should be avoided. Eventually, our society will probably adopt one of the neutral forms currently being suggested (for example, "e" or "tey"), but none of them has yet won wide acceptance. You may find it instructive to look back over this book for examples of how we have dealt with the pronoun problem during this time of transition.

Stylistic matters aside, however, you must be accurate in your use of pronouns when you describe your research or that of others. Readers must be explicitly informed about the sex of experimenters, observers, subjects, and participants. When referring to males, use male pronouns; when referring to females, use female pronouns. Under no circumstances should an investigator omit or hide sex identity in an attempt to be unbiased. Knowledge of sex is often critically important.

The problems of gender reference become easier when we move away from pronouns. Words like *man* and *mankind* are easily replaced by terms like *people*, *humanity*, *humankind*, and so forth. Instead of manning projects, we can staff them, hire personnel, or employ staff. The federal government has already desexed occupational titles so that we now have letter carriers rather than mailmen; in private industry we have flight attendants rather than stewardesses. And in life, children need nurturing or parenting, not just mothering. In all these cases, you will find it easy to discover the appropriate sex-neutral term if you simply think in terms of the activity or task rather than the person doing it.

And, finally, we come to plain old stereotyping, hidden assumptions about the roles that men and women play that can sneak into our prose. (The following examples are taken from the *Publication Manual* of the American Psychological Association [Change Sheet #2, 1977].) The author who notes that "research scientists often neglect their wives and children" fails to acknowledge that women as well as men are research scientists. Why not "Research scientists often neglect their families"? Of if the author specifically meant male research scientists, this should have been said explicitly. Often stereotypes show up in the asymmetry of the words used: *Man and wife* rather than *man and woman* or *husband and wife* assumes that the man is defined by his personhood, the woman by her relationship to a man. Referring to adult male persons as *men* and adult female persons as *girls* is another common sexist practice.

Adjective use can also connote bias. Thus, we have ambitious men and aggressive women or cautious men and timid women—where the use of different adjectives denotes not different behaviors on the part of men and women, but our biased interpretations and evaluations of their behaviors.

Even verbs can carry hidden bias: "The client's husband lets her teach part-time." Here the author intended to communicate the working status of the woman but inadvertently revealed a stereotype about husband-wife relationships. The author should have said, "The client teaches part-time." If the bias is not the author's, but the client's or her husband's, then that should be clearly indicated: "The client's husband 'lets' her teach part-time." Or "The husband says he 'lets' the client teach part-time." Or "The client says her husband lets her teach part-time." Or "The client says sarcastically that her husband 'lets' her teach part-time." The client and her husband are allowed to say such things. You are not.

And, finally, try to avoid sex-role stereotyping when you select examples. Beware of your own unconscious assumptions about the sex of doctors, homemakers, nurses, athletes, and so forth. Why not: "The athlete who believes in her ability to succeed . . ."? Let our writing promote the view that woman's vital needs are the same as man's: food, water, and access to equality.

Where to Find Additional Guidance

There are two documents that can provide additional information concerning the preparation of your research report. The *Publication Manual* (revised edition, 1974) published by the American Psychological Association provides highly specific information about the exact format used in the professional journals, as well as general advice on format and style of the kind we have included in this chapter. If you are actually preparing a report for a journal, then you should consult the *Manual*, as well as look at articles in the relevant journal itself.

There are many books on how to write expository prose, covering grammar, word usage, punctuation, and style. One of the best is *The Elements of Style* (3rd edition, paperback, 1979) by Strunk and White. It can be read in an hour and is highly entertaining as well. (But beware; it explicitly argues for continuing the use of generic masculine pronouns.)

Enough advice. Go write your report.

Ethical Implications

15

WHY ETHICAL ISSUES ARISE IN RESEARCH WITH HUMAN BEINGS

BALANCING THE COSTS OF QUESTIONABLE PRACTICES AGAINST THE POTENTIAL BENEFITS OF THE RESEARCH

QUESTIONABLE PRACTICES INVOLVING RESEARCH PARTICIPANTS
Involving People in Research without Their Knowledge or Consent
Coercing People to Participate
Withholding from the Participant the True Nature of the Research
Deceiving the Research Participant
Leading the Research Participants to Commit Acts That Diminish Their Self-respect
Violating the Right to Self-determination: Research on Behavior Control and Character Change
Exposing the Research Participant to Physical or Mental Stress
Invading the Privacy of the Research Participant
Withholding Benefits from Participants in Control Groups
Failing to Treat Research Participants Fairly and to Show Them Consideration and Respect

RESPONSIBILITIES TO RESEARCH PARTICIPANTS AFTER COMPLETION OF THE RESEARCH
Clarifying the Nature of the Research
Removing Harmful Aftereffects
Maintaining Anonymity and Confidentiality

ETHICAL ISSUES IN THE UTILIZATION OF RESEARCH
Preventing the Misuse of Research Results
Promoting the Utilization of Research Results

SUMMARY

This chapter was written by Stuart Cook.

WHY ETHICAL ISSUES ARISE IN RESEARCH WITH HUMAN BEINGS

Other chapters of this book reflect the fact that research investigators have on occasion involved their subjects in research without asking them whether or not they wished to participate. Similarly, some investigators have withheld from their subjects certain information about the research in which they were taking part, at least until after the data had been collected. Others have given their subjects misleading information — sometimes to direct their attention away from the true purpose of the experiment and sometimes to create in them a psychological state, such as anxiety, that is required by the research plan. Still others have led their subjects to say or do things that violated their moral standards and about which they were later ashamed.

The fact that such things sometimes happen in research on social relations is a matter of great concern to social scientists. An indication of this is the fact that scientific societies have formulated codes of ethics for the treatment of research participants (for example AAA, 1973; APA, 1973; APSA, 1968; ASA, 1971). In addition, individual social scientists have published books and articles on this topic (for example, Barber, Lally, Markarushka, and Sullivan, 1973; Katz, 1972; Kelman, 1968).

What happens to those who take part in research is of concern also to legislative bodies and government agencies. Federal and state legislatures have explored invasion of privacy, behavior control, and experimenting with humans in public hearings. The U.S. Department of Health, Education, and Welfare has issued regulations on the protection of human subjects all recipients of federal research grants and contracts must follow. The White House, through its Office of Science and Technology, issued a set of ethical guidelines titled "Privacy and Behavioral Research" (1967). In 1974 the U.S. Congress established a National Commission for

Protection of Human Subjects of Biomedical and Behavioral Research, charging it with the responsibility to recommend needed legislative action.

It is important, on the one hand, to take seriously this concern about the possible mistreatment of human participants in research and, on the other, to keep it in correct perspective. An infamous historical event, that is, the so-called medical experiments carried out by Nazi German physicians in the concentration camps during World War II, sensitized the world to the general problem and gave rise to the Nuremberg code of medical ethics for human experimentation. The concern aroused by these medical "experiments" has been renewed by the wide publicity given to more recent experiments in which patients have suffered damage in the course of well-intentioned efforts to try out new drugs or new surgical procedures.

While it is such developments in the medical sciences that have fueled the movement to protect research participants, the ethical issues in social research are no less real. They arise inevitably from the kinds of questions behavioral scientists ask and the methods used to obtain meaningful answers. They may be evoked by the research topic itself, the nature of the setting in which the research is conducted, the kinds of persons serving as research participants, the procedures required by the research design, the method of collecting data, the type of data collected, or the nature of the research report. As a matter of fact, certain types of ethical difficulties occur repeatedly in social relations research. Each type will be discussed in this chapter. As these discussions proceed, it will become clear that, while a questionable practice may sometimes be eliminated, at other times to do so is tantamount to abandoning the proposed research. Hence, in a later section there will be found a discussion of the question of balancing the costs of questionable practices against the potential benefits of the research investigation in which they occur.

Sometimes such an assessment will result in the research being abandoned. Such an action has serious implications. While scientists have an obligation to protect the participants in their research, they also have an obligation to contribute to knowledge. The need for knowledge relevant to the promotion of human welfare and the solution of social problems is particularly acute. Scientists who are trained to provide such knowledge violate the trust placed in them by society, if they do not take part in efforts to satisfy this need. Thus, when they consider abandoning a study (or using methods they think are not the best) they experience a value conflict: They must choose between their obligation to conduct research and their obligation to protect the welfare of their research subjects. This chapter discusses the latter obligation. *The reader should remember that the former is no less binding.*

Sometimes, on the other hand, the balancing of costs and benefits of the research investigation will result in a decision to carry it out. In this event the investigator incurs obligations to the research participant following completion of the research. These obligations—for example, to clarify the nature of the research including the reasons for deception, to remove any harmful aftereffects of questionable practices used in the research, and to guarantee the subject's anonymity and the confidentiality of the data—together with suggestions for ways of meeting them are discussed in a later section of this chapter titled "Responsibilities to Research Participants after Completion of the Research."

In this chapter we show how social scientists have tried to balance the costs of using questionable practices and the benefits of conducting research. Before we proceed, however, we want to introduce a radical critique of how ethical issues are generally handled. A social psychologist with a different point of view from that represented in this chapter has made the following observations:

> The issues . . . can better be dealt with in terms of power than ethics. Professional ethics have a major function of regulating members of a profession so that successful criticism from outside the field is minimized. The apparent power balance in social research almost always lies with the social scientist. There is self-deception on our part about this. We do not like to realize the power differential. We prefer to think we are common partners in the scientific enterprise when, in fact, the people we study often would not be there at all if they did not need the money or were not required to be there or were aware of what we are doing. We can "remind participants of their autonomy and freedom," but this is self-deceptive for us. If others truly experience their autonomy, then reminding them of it is superfluous; if they are, in fact, at a disadvantage in the situation, then such a reminder is hypocritical . . . We act as if there were not a question of power. We put our position in terms of defending freedom of inquiry. But its effect is often indistinguishable from defending privilege on more respectable terms. This is the same paternalistic assumption that those with greater power often make — to make their position more acceptable to themselves — that they are acting for the greater good. But we who have the power say what is the general good [Jack Sawyer, personal communication].

Although the remainder of this chapter does not address the issues as they are raised by Jack Sawyer, we want to alert you that the question of who has power is a central macro-ethical issue, with several components. The ethical issues that we do address are formulated within a framework in which the researcher generally has the power to ask questions and determine the scope of the answers. As this is how most social science research is conducted, we want to inform you of the many ways researchers balance the costs and benefits of their work.

BALANCING THE COSTS OF QUESTIONABLE PRACTICES AGAINST THE POTENTIAL BENEFITS OF THE RESEARCH

As noted at the beginning of the chapter, questionable practices with research participants come about partly because of the nature of the questions being asked about human behavior, partly because of the use of procedures designed to avoid obtaining misleading results, and partly because of the methods used to collect research data. Sometimes these practices can be avoided or minimized by the use of alternative research procedures. Often, however, they cannot. When the latter is true, social scientists face a conflict between two values or rights. The first is the right of science and society to inquire and to know. The second is the right of the individual research participant to have dignity, privacy, and self-determination. A decision not to conduct a planned research project limits the first of these rights. A decision to conduct the research despite its questionable practices with research participants limits the second.

Because the distinctive contribution of sicentists to society is the development of knowledge and the informed application of that knowledge to human welfare, many feel an ethical obligation to conduct research and to defend it against attempts to censor it. One of the scientist's four commandments, according to a former president of the American Association for the Advancement of Science, is "fearlessly to defend freedom of inquiry" (Glass, 1965). The same thought is expressed by those who characterize scientific inquiry as the pursuit of knowledge for the sake of knowledge, regardless of its consequences.

Other scientists qualify this point of view extensively as it applies to research on human beings. The right to inquire and to know, they say, does not include the right to abridge individual dignity, privacy, and self-determination. Claims to the contrary are equivalent to saying that a good end (acquisition of knowledge) justifies the use of bad means (questionable practices with research participants). This price for knowledge, they argue, is too high.

In any research investigation the initial obligation of the researchers is to weigh carefully the potential contributions of the proposed research against the costs to participants exposed to the questionable practices. If the researchers judge the theoretical or practical benefits too limited to justify the costs, they should not conduct the research. If they judge the converse to be true they should proceed; a decision not to act when the action is warranted is as morally reprehensible as a decision to act when action is not warranted.

Weighing the potential benefits of research against its anticipated costs is necessarily subjective. Though it is possible to enumerate many of the points to be considered, we believe that the balancing process itself must remain a matter for the individual investigator. Some argue that, in reality, an investigator has no way to measure the value of a project against its costs to others who have not freely and knowingly consented to suffer those costs. However likely this may be, there seems no alternative to making the effort.

Among the potential benefits of a given research project are the following:

1. Advances in scientific theory that contribute to a general understanding of human behavior. An example might be a better understanding of the power of social influence to induce compliance and obedience.

2. Advances in knowledge of practical value to society. An example might be research on methods to increase the effectiveness of governmental leaders.

3. Gains for the research participant, such as increased self-understanding, satisfaction in making a contribution to science or to the solution of social problems, needed money or special privileges, knowledge of social science or of research methods, and so on.

The possible costs to the participant of various questionable practices in research include affronts to dignity, anxiety, shame, embarrassment, self-doubts, loss of trust in social relations, loss of autonomy and self-determination, and lowered self-esteem. In attempting to assess both the actuality and the seriousness of such costs, social scientists have turned to the research participants themselves. They have sought information in several ways. Some investigators, for example, have described studies involving questionable practices and asked respondents to judge the ethical quality of various aspects of the studies, including deception. Others have asked that questionable practices be rated on such dimensions as psychological discomfort or invasion of privacy. One such study revealed that college students are quite concerned about exposure to pain, are only moderately concerned about various kinds of psychological stress, and show little concern about data gathering procedures that would appear to invade their privacy (Farr and Seaver, 1975). Another discovered that the extent to which an experimental procedure was judged unethical was influenced by the frequency with which it produced undesirable behavior (that is, obedience to requests to harm others and commit crimes) but not by the frequency of emotional suffering that resulted (Schlenker and Forsyth, 1977). A third reported that the frequency with which college students judged experiments involving deception and stress to be unethical decreased if they were given information about the value of the research (Glaskow, Sadowski, and Davis, 1977). Of special interest is the fact that social scientists give more negative ratings than do college students to procedures that involve stress, cause physical pain, lower self-esteem, and/or produce undesirable behavior.

The evidence from these studies makes it clear that social scientists cannot be sure how the participants in their studies will feel about questionable practices to which they are exposed. Moreover, the scientists may anticipate stronger negative feelings toward some practices than will be found to occur. One group of investigators have made an innovative suggestion that would seem to surmount some of this uncertainty. They propose that a sample from the potential pool of research subjects be provided with information about a projected study and asked whether they would consent to participate. Included in the information provided would be a description of the procedures the subjects would experience and estimates of the type of behavior, desirable and undesirable, that they might display. In a study of the feasibility of this idea, these investigators found that they could predict quite well from the reactions of their sample the percent of actual research participants who had, in fact, expressed regret at having participated in a stressful experiment. The predictions held equally well for persons who had and had not been debriefed (Berscheid, Baron, Dermer, and Libman, 1973).

Aside from these direct costs to research participants, there are potential costs to society and future scientific work. For example, some research — in particular the type in which confederates enact roles in natural settings — may contribute to a social climate of suspicion, distrust, or manipulation. Other research, including that employing covert recording of intimate personal behavior, might turn society against social science and reduce future financial support of social research. It should be noted that scientists differ in how seriously they take these latter possibilities. For example, with respect to the possibility that questionable practices in research may contribute to a social climate of suspicion and mistrust, doubters make two points: (1) research could add, at most, a trivial amount to the manipulation and deception that pervade a society plagued by high-pressure salespeople, dishonest repair-people, and thieves; (2) participants in experiments distinguished readily between the deception in experiments and that of everyday life; from the former they draw no implications regarding the latter.

The process of balancing potential benefits against possible costs involves questions of degree as well of kind. Is a potential contribution to scientific theory or to the solution of a social problem *important enough* to warrant high costs to the research participants? For example, granting that research in which the research participant followed orders to give another person dangerous electric shocks promised to be an important contribution to knowledge, was it of enough significance to justify leading research participants to commit acts that might diminish their self-respect? A parallel question may be asked about the research on cooperating interracial groups. Were societal needs for knowledge about the social management of desegregation great enough to justify involving students in research without telling them of its true nature? Some times there is general agreement on the answer to such questions; this often happens, for example, when the research is planned as an analogue to an important social phenomenon. Usually, however, it is difficult to foresee the importance of a single research investigation. When this is the case, the investigator's decision about proceeding with the research becomes more difficult.

Parellel questions may be asked about questionable practices with research participants and the harm they do. How serious is a given questionable practice? How likely is it to harm the research participant? How serious might the harm be? Will it be fleeting or long range?

Answers to these questions are subject to considerable disagreement. A few examples of positions taken by some but rejected by others will illustrate. Studies involving active deception (providing misinformation) are of greater concern than those involving passive deception (withholding information). Field experiments introducing some new element into the environment (for example, feigned heart attack) are more serious than those simply varying some ongoing activity (for example, introducing alternative methods of charitable solicitation). Feigning an illness in a public place is a more questionable practice than feigning a minor accident. The induction of stress caused by fear for one's life (for example, smoke seeping under a door into a locked room) is potentially more harmful than is inducing stress by false feedback of poor performance on a test. An invasion of privacy involving eavesdropping on conversations in a crowded lobby is less offensive to research participants than is covert observation of more intimate relationships. Inducing participants to perform acts that reduce their self-esteem is to be viewed less seriously when they yield to pressure to change an opinion than when they yield to pressure to mistreat another.

Some social scientists are influenced in their judgments of the seriousness of questionable practices in research by comparing them to similar practices in everyday life. For example, some experimenters point out that the stress involved in research is trivial compared to that experienced in reality; this leads them to feel that inducing stress experimentally is ethically a minor matter. In the same vein, others see invasion of privacy as it occurs in research to be benign and harmless because they contrast it to more threatening invasions carried out by credit bureaus, police, and potential employers. Deception for research purposes is compared to everyday deception that has as its purpose taking advantage of others for personal gain; this makes research deception seem of little consequence.

Though there is no question about the validity of the above comparisons, the inferences drawn from them are difficult to defend. They have the character of justifying a lesser evil because a greater one exists. As such they should carry little, if any, weight in the balancing of arguments for and against conducting a given research investigation.

Judgments about the seriousness of questionable practices and their cost to research participants may hinge on yet another consideration, namely, whether the cost can be promptly alleviated. This argues that a deception that can be corrected immediately after an experiment is less serious than one that cannot. Similar arguments would apply to stress and to acts that lower self-esteem; they could be regarded as less serious costs in an experiment if effective remedial actions are taken when the experiment is finished.

In balancing potential contributions against possible costs to participants, investigators must recognize a personal bias. It is reasonable, and to be expected, that they attach importance to the research they hope to carry out. If they did not, it is unlikely that they would have planned it. This means that if the research involves questionable practices, they should not trust themselves to make an objective assessment of relative benefits and costs. Rather, it is wise for them to seek consultation in this process.

Helpful consultation may be obtained from a number of sources. For example, colleagues doing similar research will constitute a valuable resource; they may well have faced a parallel decision in which they balanced factors similar to those under consideration.

However, colleagues may fall short on one score. Being in the same field as the experimenter, they may share too strongly the experimenter's values. Understanding the theoretical potential of the research, they may rate its contribution as higher than would others from a different background. This suggests that it would be wise to consult, also, with persons from other disciplines, with intelligent laypeople, and with individuals like those who would be serving as research participants. Those in the last category will be especially valuable in helping the investigator assess the human costs of the experiment; this is particularly true if they are different from the researcher in age, education, and socioeconomic class. It is informative to carry out a pilot project and discuss with the participants their feelings about the research experience.

Sometimes, because of the potential for harm to the research participants, there is a need for consultants with special backgrounds. For example, if physical stress were being employed, a medical advisor should be consulted. Or if mental stress were involved, it would be appropriate to call in a specialist in the area of personality or psychopathology. In general, the amount and variety of consultation should increase with the seriousness of the questionable practices being considered.

Consultation on ethical issues may be sought either from individuals or from an ethics advisory group. The former procedure is more flexible in that advisors appropriate to the issues raised by a specific experiment may be sought out. However, this approach is more time-consuming because it requires seeking out new advisors for each occasion. Time is saved by constituting a standing advisory group. This may be done by a group of experimenters with similar research interests or by an administrative unit such as an academic social science department. An advantage of the advisory group is that it will accumulate useful experience with ethical issues. On the other hand, if the range of studies about which it is consulted is too great, it may be unhelpful in some cases.

It is important to distinguish an ethics advisory group from institutional committees set up to monitor the "protection of human subjects." The function of these committees is to fulfill the ethical and moral responsibility of the university, hospital, prison, or clinic in which they operate. Typically, they give institutional clearance to the ethical aspects of an experiment. Often they have the additional responsibility of periodic review of ongoing studies to ensure that changes in research procedures have not introduced new concerns for the participants' welfare. Rarely do they have the time or expertise to advise researchers on the ethical decision they must make.

Neither the use of ethical advisors nor ethical clearance by an institutional advisory committee changes the fact that the ethical responsibility for the welfare of research participants remains with the individual investigator. Hence, the researchers may decide to proceed with the study even though the weight of advice suggests that the costs to the participants outweigh the study's potential contributions. Or, conversely, the investigator may decide not to proceed despite advice that supports doing the project. To take any other position than this risks establishing a climate in which investigators seek to present their research plans in a manner that will secure endorsement rather than in a form conducive to securing helpful ethical analysis and advice.

In summary, a few general guidelines may be offered. These, of course, represent an oversimplification of the relevant considerations. The first consideration is whether the research problem is of sufficient importance and likely enough to produce results that will outweigh the possible cost to the research participant. When there is uncertainty, priority must be given to protecting the research participant's dignity and welfare. The participants should emerge unharmed from the research experience; if temporary harm is a possibility, satisfactory arrangements for its prompt alleviation should be available. When questionable practices are employed, they should be of such a nature that the participant, when informed of them, may be expected to find them reasonable and suffer no loss of confidence in the integrity of the investigator. The participant should gain some identifiable benefit from the research. The research experience should be such that after its completion the participant would be willing to take part in further research of a similar nature. The conditions of the research should be such that investigators would be willing for members of their own families to take part. The investigator should have made plans to deal with any anticipated long term aftereffects of the research.

QUESTIONABLE PRACTICES INVOLVING RESEARCH PARTICIPANTS

The questionable practices encountered in social science research may be grouped into ten categories as follows:

1. Involving people in research without their knowledge or consent.
2. Coercing people to participate.
3. Withholding from the participant the true nature of the research.
4. Deceiving the research participant.
5. Leading the research participants to commit acts that diminish their self-respect.

6. Violating the right to self-determination: research on behavior control and character change.
7. Exposing the research participant to physical or mental stress.
8. Invading the privacy of the research participant.
9. Withholding benefits from participants in control groups.
10. Failing to treat research participants fairly and to show them consideration and respect.

Involving People in Research without Their Knowledge or Consent

In some of the most significant research in the area of social relations the research subjects never know that they have been participants in a research project. There are various reasons for this: Sometimes it is impossible or impractical to tell them. Sometimes the investigator decides that the information would lead the participants to display unnatural behavior and thus distort the research results. But for whatever reason, the investigator involves the participant in research without the latter's consent and hence has infringed upon participant's right to make his or her own decision whether or not to participate. The investigator must always seek ways to avoid the prospect of involuntary participation. If unsuccessful, the investigator must then carefully weigh the benefits of the research against its ethical costs.

There are several types of studies in which this problem arises. They are considered separately below. The reader will note that many of these studies give rise to additional ethical issues such as invasion of privacy.

Observational studies of group life.   In a famous study often used to illustrate observational methods of data collection the investigator undertook to study "street-corner" groups of young men (Whyte, 1943). To gain access to needed information, he made friends with the group members and took part in their activities.

In another study the purpose of the investigators was to explore the manner in which a middle-class teacher related to lower-class children. The observations needed for the study were made by a person who the children thought was a student teacher.

This **participant observer** method has been used to study workers in factories, members of tribal groups, residents of small towns, and so on. Key people in such settings usually know of the research. Often, however, others who are observed do not.

Sometimes it is not possible to use the observer method because rules prohibit it or because the presence of a third party or stranger would modify the behavior under observation. An example is provided by a study of the jury system (Meltzer, 1953). The investigators wished to learn how juries functioned and whether the jury system was effective in dealing with the complexities of modern litigation. As by law no one is permitted to be present at jury deliberations, the investigators found it necessary to devise a substitute method of observation. They secured the permission of the judge and the lawyers for both the plaintiffs and the defendants to use hidden microphones to record jury deliberations in five trials.

Studies in which research is added to ongoing programs or operations. An often cited instance of involving uninformed participants in research by adding research to ongoing operations occurred when a social scientist ran for mayor of his home town (Hartmann, 1936). Without the knowledge of the voters he distributed "emotional" campaign leaflets in some precincts and "rational" ones in other comparable precincts. From the size of the favorable vote in the two sets of precincts he inferred the relative effectiveness of the two types of appeal.

Involving students in educational research without their knowledge is quite common. In one such experiment teachers added "motivating" comments to the papers of some students before returning them; no such comments were entered on the papers of comparable students (Page, 1958). The outcome was assessed by means of the students' performance on a later test. In other educational studies students who have received different types of instruction or who are in classrooms differing in ethnic composition have been compared to determine the effect of such differences on achievement, attitudes to school work, and ethnic attitudes.

Field studies. In **field studies** the investigator presents contrasting experiences to two or more groups of persons or to the same individuals at two different times. The outcome is often an action that can be counted or whose onset can be timed. A test of restaurant discrimination against blacks in the neighborhood of the United Nations headquarters in New York City, done 20 years ago, still provides an example (Selltiz, 1955). The experimenter sent a same-sex white pair and a same-sex black pair of diners to the same restaurants. In a substantial proportion of the restaurants the black diners received inferior service, as indicated by delays in serving, out of the way seating, and other inconveniences. The study highlights the purpose of not informing the research participants. Had the restaurant personnel known that an experiment was in progress it seems unlikely that they would have shown such discrimination.

Some of the most dramatic of social science experiments have dealt with altruistic and helpful behavior in natural settings. The experimenters have set up opportunities for people to contribute or to help others. The influence of such factors as size of onlooker group, the helping behavior of a "model," and the ethnic membership of the person needing help have been examined. Some examples of helping behavior employed in field experiments are these: putting contributions into a Salvation Army kettle (Bryan and Test, 1967), helping a woman with a flat tire (Bryan and Test, 1967), helping a person with an epileptic seizure (Darley and Latané, 1968), or helping an ill person on a subway train (Piliavin, Rodin, and Piliavin, 1969).

Discussion. As already noted, the questionable practice common to all these studies is that they engage persons in research without their knowledge or consent. Thus in varying degrees they limit the right of free choice and in so doing raise an ethical problem.

With few exceptions, social scientists believe that to seek consent in the types of studies described would completely change the behavior being studied and, hence, would render the research meaningless. The choice, it appears, is either to abandon the research or to carry it out despite its ethical question marks. This precipitates a value conflict between the scientists' obligations to add to knowledge and their responsibility to protect their research participants.

Although it is true that these studies generate the same ethical concern, it is possible to separate them on the basis of how much they impose upon research participants' time, patience, and welfare by involving them in activities in which they otherwise might not have engaged. If the extent of such imposition is minimal, the cost to the participants seems minor. If the imposition is substantial, the cost increases correspondingly; for example, experimenters who artfully disguise their confederates as injured, bloody survivors of a car wreck, seeking aid at night from rural residents, push the costs to research participants to a high level.

In contrast, observational studies and the studies in which research is added to ongoing programs cause little concern in this respect; participation in the research would not alter the experiences of the participants to a significant degree. In field experiments, on the other hand, the participants' experiences are arranged by the investigator. Such experiments differ in an important way: whether the experiences are commonplace and unimportant, such as a car dallying at a green light, or are potentially more disturbing, such as an epileptic seizure on a sidewalk. In summary, the less the research procedure inconveniences the participants or involves them emotionally, the less severe the ethical question over engaging them in research without their knowledge or consent.

Apart from the fact that the studies of the type cited limit participants' rights to consent to activities in which they are to be involved, these experimental procedures concern social scientists because of the possibility of their cumulative impact on society. Some fear that as the research procedures become known through the mass media and through textbooks, many people will react to *real* crisis situations by thinking that they are "just another experiment." The degree of indifference to needs for help in everyday life is already serious; might it become worse if the public became convinced that people in trouble might be playacting? It should be noted that some social scientists do not believe that there is any danger of this happening. They feel that such fears overestimate just how much people know about what goes on in social science and how much impact social research has on everyday affairs.

Concern for another kind of impact on society is reflected by the sequel to the jury-recording study cited previously. Members of Congress reacted to the jury recordings as a threat to fundamental institutions. When news of the study came out, a congressional investigation resulted. Following the investigation legislation was passed establishing a fine of a thousand dollars and imprisonment for a year for whoever might attempt to record the proceedings of any jury in the United States while the jury is deliberating or voting.

Coercing People to Participate

The fact that scientists studying human behavior need people to take part in their research occasionally causes questionable practices to happen. Under some circumstances, as indicated in the preceeding section, they meet this need by involving subjects in research without their knowledge or consent. Typically, however, the potential research participant knows that research will take place.

Ideally, consent should be obtained only after a potential subject has been given adequate information about the research in question. What we shall examine in this section is the point that consent to participate may be free or it may be wholly or partially coerced. The latter happens in several ways: For example, an investigator may be in a position to *require* individuals to participate. Sometimes an employer or an institution may require participation of persons over whom they have authority. At other times an investigator will offer such strong incentives that the potential participant is unable to resist, such as the case when $20 is offered to a poor person. In all such cases, the ideal of complete freedom of choice is abridged.

In extreme cases, as when persons are ordered by their employer or commanding officer to report for research, coercion is clear. In less extreme cases, however, it may be difficult to distinguish between coercion and legitimate persuasion or between coercion and a fair exchange of rewards and services.

When the freedom of individuals is restricted at their place of work or residence, such restrictions are likely to carry over into research done in these settings. Thus, employees, patients, prisoners, or soldiers may be required to participate in research projects. If a branch of the military service needs to find the sources of a morale problem, soldiers will be expected to take part in research without objecting. Or if an industry wishes to experiment with methods that may increase productivity, workers will be expected to participate. Similar expectations may hold for patients in mental hospitals with respect to research on therapeutic methods or prisoners with respect to procedures for rehabilitation.

It may be the case, however, that the potential participants are not in sympathy with the research objectives and would not take part if allowed to decide for themselves. The worker in the factory may see productivity research as a step toward greater exploitation, and the prisoner may feel that society, not he or she, needs changing. Under such circumstances, investigators face a difficult conflict between their desire, and often their obligation, to conduct potentially significant research and the questionable practice of engaging people in research who have been completely or partially coerced into participating.

Three variations of this conflict may be distinguished; the ethical issues they pose are somewhat different. The first arises in research projects in which some feature of the program or the organization in question is being studied with a view to increasing its effectiveness. The second occurs in research that is meaningful only if carried out with the cooperation of the particular type of person residing in an institution, for example, a study of any type of mental illness. The third is encountered in research that utilizes participants from institutional and organizational settings but has no special relationship to the program or to the people in the setting, for example, when prisoners are research participants in a study of group problem solving.

Research related to organizational programs.   Research dealing with variations in the program of an organization provides the clearest justification for coerced participation. Under these circumstances it will often be true that the research participants will feel no additional abridgment of their freedom beyond that already surrendered in the situation; that is, they will accept the research as one more aspect of their responsibilities. This is less likely to be the case when major changes in work arrangements or therapeutic regimes are introduced and studied. At such times persons included in (or perhaps those excluded from) the innovative program may object. This happened in a mental hospital when the staff decided to experiment with a treatment program that involved working with patients in groups. When a number of patients objected, they were given the alternative of being transferred to a less attractive locked-ward section of the hospital. However, whether or not there are objections, investigators may not shift responsibility for the ethical decision to the institution or organization. If they are unable to arrange for uncoerced consent from research participants, investigators must assess for themselves the costs and benefits of proceeding with the research.

Research intended to be of value to particular types of persons. Research requiring the participation of persons who might be found in a given organizational or institutional setting presents a more difficult dilemma. Research staff members working in such settings feel a professional obligation to contribute to knowledge about the kinds of problems the institution deals with and about methods that might alleviate such problems. If they are to succeed, they must have the cooperation of the patients or prisoners in their research activity. They may believe that such persons are obligated to take part in research programs that in the long run are oriented to their own welfare and to the welfare of others in their same situation. Believing this, the researchers might understandably feel warranted in employing strong incentives to obtain consent; that is, they might justify the use of social pressure or granting of special favors.

But the residents in the institution may not have this sense of obligation to the research. They may doubt its relevance to themselves and object to the time, the discomfort, and the possible curtailment of privileges. Or, as noted earlier, they may believe they have no problem—that the problem resides in the institution or in society. A soldier with a record of imprisonment or repeated violations of army regulations becomes a candidate for resocialization research in which he or she is deprived of all comforts and privileges, winning them back only by exhibiting specified examples of cooperative and compliant behavior. Some enter such a program with apparent willingness; others do so only as an alternative to the threat of lengthy imprisonment and dishonorable discharge. For the latter, as with the mental patients mentioned earlier, the coercion to consent is clear, and, indeed, the researcher may judge it justifiable. For those apparently willing to participate, the coercion is less evident but undoubtedly present; it is to such instances that the investigator must be especially alert.

Research utilizing persons especially vulnerable to requests to participate. When the problem studied has no special relationship to the program or the persons in the organization or institution, the question of free consent hinges on the incentives the investigator employs. The potential participants are approached, not because of any presumed obligation to participate, but because they have the time and are likely to consent. Owing to their circumstances, financial incentives and social approval, upon which depend later favors, take on special force. For example, a prisoner may need money for cigarettes or may be building a record of good behavior for early parole.

In such cases, those incentives that ordinarily would represent a poor exchange of rewards for services rendered by participants now acquire irresistible strength and, in effect, coerce consent.

Problems paralleling those just mentioned arise in the use of incentives to secure research participation among disadvantaged groups in the population. Poor people will find it difficult to resist participation when money is offered. For this reason an employment service is a dependable place to recruit; persons looking for jobs can be counted on to volunteer for research paying the minimum hourly wage. Similarly, persons needing money for special purposes, such as addicts in search of money to buy drugs or alcohol, are usually more than willing to take part.

Questionable incentives may also be used to induce participation of persons who do not have special needs or organizational connections. Appeals to sympathy for the investigator may be made; the plea, "If you help me I can finish my dissertation and get a job," is frequently used. Shame may be employed, as in "Women are afraid of electric shock, but most men can take it." Altruistic contributions may be stressed; for example, "You can help science learn more about the process of negotiation, and this may help head off another world war." When potential participants are inexperienced and have unquestioned respect for the social scientists who approach them, false and exaggerated claims may coerce participation and represent a misuse of interpersonal trust. It does not follow, of course, that a modest description of the potential value of proposed research is out of order. To the contrary, it is one of the elements needed for an informed decision to participate.

Discussion. Complete or partial coercion to participate in research occurs either as a result of the power of institutions and organizations over individuals or as a result of the use of incentives too strong for the potential participant to reject. It is essential for the investigator to be aware of the power this gives over the decisions made by potential research participants and to recognize the special responsibility to protect their freedom to decide. In some cases, it would be reasonable to assume that the potential participant has an obligation to assist in the research. This assumption is dangerous for two reasons: First, it may not be shared by the individuals in question, and second, it may serve as a convenient rationalization that consent is unneccessary. It will be tempting to conclude that if the organization is willing to limit freedom to consent, the investigator need not feel responsible; such a position is ethically unacceptable.

In some cases, it will seem to be to the obvious advantage of persons to participate. They have time on their hands, the research will be an interesting variation from their usual routine, or they can make good use of the money paid for participation. Although all of this may be true and represents legitimate considerations, investigators must strive to provide as much freedom of choice under such circumstances as they would if none of these conditions prevailed—for example, if the potential participants were busy and in less need of money or social approval.

None of the preceding should be taken as negating the appropriateness of a modest and persuasive description of the potential value of proposed research and the use of rewards, financial and otherwise, in exchange for research participation. What it implies, instead, is that such incentives should be employed with full awareness of their potential for limiting a research participant's freedom in choosing to take part.

The special case of coercion to participate in research in universities and colleges: "the subject pool." A widespread practice is to require that students enrolled in a college course, such as introductory psychology, serve as research participants for a specified number of hours. Typically, each student chooses among a number of alternative experiments for which brief descriptions are available.

The research participation requirement is a special case of the use of institutional authority to limit the freedom of consent. It will be of particular interest to readers of this chapter, for most have been exposed to it in the course of their own education. The ethical considerations involved have been debated extensively and opinions on the practice vary widely. A thorough account of this debate has been published in *Ethical Principles in the Conduct of Research with Human Participants* (APA, 1973).

An argument that is frequently offered for the research participation requirement is that participation in ongoing research provides a more realistic and valuable educational experience than taking part in laboratory experiments especially arranged for training purposes. Another argument is that teachers have the right to require students to make a contribution to the advancement of the science they are studying. Current students profit from contributions of time and effort made by student research participants who have preceded them, it is argued, so it is right to expect them to make a parallel contribution to those who study social science in the future. A third argument is that if the research participation requirement did not exist, recruitment of people to serve in research would become much more difficult and often prohibitively expensive. Some potentially valuable research would not get done. Also, the participants who would remain available as volunteers for research would be self-selected, introducing probable biases in the conclusions drawn from research.

The position that prevails at most universities and colleges at the moment is that the spirit of uncoerced consent can be maintained and the recruitment of students to serve as research participants continued if the recruitment procedure preserves a substantial amount of free choice and otherwise protects the participants from undue coercion. When these precautions are combined with procedures that assure an educational benefit to the participant, the demands of uncoerced consent appear to be satisfied. For this reason a number of university departments have developed detailed procedures to guarantee the accomplishment of educational objectives and to minimize the element of coercion. For a review of these procedures the interested reader is referred to *Ethical Principles in the Conduct of Research with Human Participants* (1973).

Withholding From the Participant the True Nature of the Research

Unlike others who are involved in studies without their knowledge or consent, some individuals may willingly participate in a research project but not be told of its true intent. Usually, their participation is explained to these subjects in terms that, although true, tell only part of the story. Misleading explanations of this kind have acquired the label "cover story"; they cover up the experiment's true nature. Their function is to satisfy the participants' curiosity about what is transpiring. Most often the participants are not misled as to the nature of the experiences they will have or the discomforts to be encountered. The ethical problems of studies that do involve such deception are discussed in several of the sections to follow.

When subjects consent to take part in research without being told its true characteristics, they are not giving what is commonly called their *informed consent*. This term had its origins in relation to medical treatment and research and designates patients' rights to consider a type of treatment or research participation with full knowledge of the risks to their personal safety. As applied to social science research, the term has acquired connotations extending considerably beyond this original usage.

Withholding information about research in which a person consents to participate is a questionable practice for reasons previously noted: the right of free choice has been curtailed and, as result, human dignity has been diminished. Social scientists are obliged to avoid such acts if at all possible. If they cannot, they must give careful consideration to the ethical costs of carrying out the research and the values to be served in so doing.

Studies in which the true purpose is not revealed.   One example is a study of a UNESCO publicity campaign (Star and Hughes, 1950). The research in this case was planned around the fact that the campaign was to take place. Respondents were interviewed about UNESCO, some before and others after the publicity campaign. None was told of the connection between the interviews and the plan to evaluate the effectiveness of the campaign.

Social scientists studying the effects of variations in teaching methods have withheld information under similar circumstances. One such study was interested in students' racial attitudes; it compared the effects of being on cooperative interdependent classroom teams with the usual kind of intergroup contact that happens in the traditional classroom setting (Weigel, Wiser, and Cook, 1975). The junior and senior high school students who were the research participants did not know the research was underway. When attitudes were to be assessed at the end of the school year, the investigators approached the students in their homes posing as public opinion pollsters interested in the views of teen-agers on social issues, a true but incomplete description of the purpose of the interview.

The information withheld.   In the examples cited, the research participants are not told of the purpose of the research; that is, they are parties to answering a research question about which they are not informed. Moreover, if their normal routine has been altered, as was true in the educational experiment, this fact also is withheld. Also, they are not told in advance of the probable uses to which the research results will be put, even though in the case of practical application to educational or social policy they may be opposed to such applications. Although they are not deliberately misled as to the experiences they will have in the course of the research, even here the emphasis may be somewhat different from their expectations based on the vague description they receive. In studies other than those described still other information may be concealed: for example, when persons are selected for research because they are low achievers, have inferiority feelings, or are prejudiced, they will not be told this. Or if they are to be exposed to stressful experiences such as failure or fright, this is almost certain not to be mentioned.

Discussion.   There are two versions of the ethical ideal that are relevant to with-holding information from a research participant. One is that all information about the research should be provided. Illustrative wording for this version is found in a bill proposed to the New York State Legislature in 1971:

> ... there shall be made known to him the nature, duration, and purpose of the exper-iment; the method and means by which it is to be conducted; all inconveniences and hazards reasonably to be expected; and the effects upon his health or person which may possibly result from participation in the experiment.

Most social scientists consider this version of **informed consent** to be both unnecessary and impractical. They feel that some aspects of a research plan are of little interest or concern to participants and that other more technical aspects are beyond their comprehension. Moreover, developments occur in the course of some research that could not be anticipated and, hence, could not be described to partici-pants in advance. As a result, these social scientists favor a statement of principle that omits these undesirable features. Wording from the ethics code of one of the social science disciplines reflects this:

> Ethical practice requires the investigator to inform the participant of all features of the research that reasonably might be expected to influence willingness to participate, and to explain all other aspects of the research about which the participant inquires (APA, 1973).

Experience of researchers indicates that if they operate according to this second version of informed consent, they will find that most research participants are con-cerned about what will happen to them in the research, how long the research will take, and any inconveniences or risks that are involved. In contrast, most participants *are unconcerned* about the nature of the research question being asked and are as likely to be willing to answer one kind of question as another. (However, partici-pants do judge research involving pain, stress, or undesirable behavior as more eth-ical if they believe the research topic to be an important one. See section entitled "Balancing the Costs of Objectionable Practices against the Potential Benefits of the Research".)

Special questions arise over how the research results will be used. For example, some potential subjects would not willingly participate in research intended to increase war-making efficiency. Members of religious groups or ethnic minority groups would not wish to take part in the research if results were expected to reflect discredit on their group. A researcher finds it difficult to respond to such concerns for two reasons. First, it is not always possible to predict the applied value of the research. Second, once the research results become public, the researcher has no way to control the use to which others put the findings. (This issue will be discussed at great length later in the chapter.)

One approach to informed consent would limit its applicability to research in which the research participant has been put "at risk." Guidelines for the protection of human subjects disseminated by the U.S. Department of Health, Education, and Welfare of the federal government define this concept as follows:

> Subject at risk means any individual who might be exposed to the possibility of harm (physical, psychological, sociological, or other) as a consequence of participation of the subject in any research development or demonstration activity which goes beyond the application of established and accepted methods necessary to meet his needs.

Risk is recognized by the guidelines to be a matter of professional judgment by the investigator and by ethics review committees at the investigator's institution. If the research does not involve risk, the investigator is not obliged to secure informed consent. This orientation highlights the origin in medical treatment and research of the informed consent concept. In social science research, by comparison, concern for the research participant's dignity, self-esteem and self-determination becomes central. Hence, the ethical ideal is to obtain informed and uncoerced consent regardless of the risk factor.

Another approach is derived from the version of informed consent (described previously) that would inform research participants only of the features of the research that reasonably might be expected to influence their willingness to participate. An early example of this developed in the area of research in the then new psychoactive drugs. Any such drug has at least two effects: One is pharmacological and the other psychological, or suggestive. To control the latter, the drug researcher compares the effect of the real drug with that of a fake drug or placebo. To tell research participants which of the two they are receiving greatly reduces the value of the research. To avoid this and yet give informed consent, drug researchers developed the practice of informing individuals that they would be involved in research in which they would receive either a drug (in varying strengths) or a **placebo** but would not be told which until the research was over. The analogy in social research is to tell participants what experiences they will encounter in the experiment, whether there are inconveniences or possible harm involved, and that they *may* or *may not* be deceived. They are assured, in addition, that when the research is over, they will be given a full account of the results and have their questions answered.

None of these various approaches takes care of all the considerations that lead to withholding information from research participants. When investigators decide that information must be withheld if the research is to be meaningful, they face a value conflict between abandoning the research and proceeding with it despite the ethical question that it involves.

Deceiving the Research Participant

In the research discussed in the preceding sections, the participants have been misled by withholding information from them, either about the fact that research was in progress or about the nature of it. In the research to be discussed in this section, the investigators have felt it necessary to take the additional step of giving the participants incorrect information.

The distinction between *deceiving others passively by telling only part of the truth* versus *actively* by telling an untruth has little, if any, moral standing, in our opinion. Nevertheless, social scientists take the latter more seriously because it brings an additional element into the picture, namely, a violation of participants' assumptions that they can trust what the researcher says. The ideal in the relationship between scientist and research participant is that of openness and honesty. Deliberate lying in the interest of manipulating the participant's perceptions and actions goes directly against this ideal. Yet often the choice appears to be between carrying out such deception and abandoning the research.

Deception is employed for a number of reasons. Three of the more common ones are illustrated below:

Deception to conceal the true purpose of the research. A study of the effect of status differences between ethnic groups on the nature of social interaction within and across ethnic lines illustrates this type of deception (Katz, Goldston, and Benjamin, 1958). The investigators anticipated that members of a lower-status ethnic minority would be more passive and submissive in racially mixed groups than would members of a majority ethnic group. They studied this by setting four-person racially mixed groups to work on tasks requiring cooperation and discussion. Believing that a description of their hypothesis would distort the research participants' behavior, they "employed" the research participants to try out a group of tasks described as being under development for use as vocational aptitude tests.

A second example comes from a study of the effects of the expectations by teachers on gains in IQ of children in their classes (Rosenthal and Jacobson, 1966). Twenty percent of children in each of 18 classroom were identified as having scored high on a test designed to predict academic "blooming" or intellectual gain. This was false; these children had been selected at random. Results showed the predicted bloomers increasing in IQ significantly more than equally able comparison children. Clearly, such a study with its sweeping implications for education would have been impossible had the teachers not been deceived.

Deception to conceal the true function of the research participants' actions. Many studies have been carried out with the general aim of discovering whether subjects convince themselves in the process of giving arguments for a position they do not believe in or extolling the virtues of a product that they know is of little value. Considerable evidence is available that this happens, but there is much disagreement as to why. In one of the experiments attempting to solve this puzzle, the investigators succeeded in getting a group of college students to believe that they were thinking up arguments in favor of a program they opposed, namely, to send other college students to the Soviet Union for four years in order to study the Soviet system of government and the history of communism (Elms and Janis, 1965). The researchers accomplished this by representing themselves as staff members of the U.S. State Department (or, alternatively, the Soviet Embassy) who needed the arguments for a pamphlet. Their purpose in doing this was to direct the students' attention away from the effect of this activity on their own opinions.

Deceptions similar to the preceding are regularly practiced by social scientists investigating theories of cognitive consistency or *cognitive dissonance.* In order to engage research participants in actions counter to their opinions (presumably creating cognitive dissonance), investigators have devised various misleading reasons for engaging them in the production of oral or written counterattitudinal arguments, such as participation in debates in which they represent the side opposed to their own position (see, for example, Scott, 1959).

Other deceptions to conceal the true function of the participant's actions take the form of announcing that the participant is interacting with one other person — usually a peer — when in fact the "other person" is the experimenter or a confederate of the experimenter or even a computer! The purpose of such deception is to present the research participant with a *standardized experience* and *one that can be varied in a controlled manner along a discussion being studied.* One example of this procedure is found in a study in which the investigators were interested in the reaction of one opponent to a conciliatory initiative from another — a phenomenon of importance in international negotiation (Pilisuk and Skolnick, 1968). The research participant was informed that she was engaged in competitive-cooperative interaction (the so-called prisoners' dilemma game) with someone in another room: in fact, the responses from the latter were preprogrammed and originated with the experimenter.

Deception to conceal the experiences the research participant will have. In many studies research participants cannot be told in advance about the critical experiences they are to have. Instead they must be led to encounter this experience as a natural, unplanned development. One example comes from an experiment in which the research participants were to be induced to lie to a second person. From cognitive consistency theory it was deduced that a person who received a large bribe to lie would feel less need to reduce the dissonance between his beliefs and his public "lie" than would one who lied for a trivial bribe; the latter presumably would be under more pressure to reconcile his own beliefs with the untruthful account he gave to a second person (Festinger and Carlsmith, 1959). Since telling the participants what was in store for them would have completely changed the nature of their experience in the experiment, the investigator decided to recruit persons instead for a study of "measures of performance."

Discussion. With few, if any, exceptions, social scientists regard deception of research participants as a questionable practice to be avoided if at all possible. It diminishes the respect due to others and violates the expectations of mutual trust upon which organized society is based. When the deceiver is a respected scientist, it may have the undesirable effect of modeling deceit as an acceptable practice. Conceivably, it may contribute to the growing climate of cynicism and mistrust bred by widespread use of deception by important public figures, as symbolized by the newly coined expression *credibility gap.*

Within this band of general agreement among social scientists, however, two positions may be identified. One is that deception is an inadmissible affront to individual autonomy and self-respect and is inconsistent with the scientific objective of discovering the truth. The other, more widely held, is that deception is occasionally a legitimate means to be used in the service of a higher value, namely the development of a meaningful, "nontrivial" science of human behavior.

Several alternatives to the use of deception have been considered. One of these is to provide the research subjects with no information about the purpose of the experiment or about what will happen to them in the course of it, promising them full information when the experiment is over. In some cases, this would seem a feasible alternative. In others, it would not, because of the well-recognized tendency of research participants to formulate their own hypotheses as to what is happening. Such hypotheses influence the participants' behavior and introduce unknown and untraceable error into the research results.

A second alternative is to provide the participants with full information about the experiment's purpose. One study has suggested that such information would not affect the research findings. In this study the investigators examined the influence of exposure to prior judgments of others upon the research participants' estimates of the comparative length of three curved lines (Gallo, Smith, and Mumford, 1973). The investigators reported that participants who were told that the study was concerned with discovering the extent to which people were conformers showed results similar to those of participants to whom the purpose of the study was not disclosed. (The latter were led to believe they were in a study of distance perception.) However, a second study of the effects of giving participants full information reached opposite conclusions. In this study results obtained with participants who knew the purpose of the experiment (that is, a conditioning study in which verbal approval was used to increase the frequency of use of selected pronouns) were opposite to those of participants who were given a misleading interpretation of the study's purpose. Perhaps we will learn eventually which questions can be answered without deception. Meanwhile, most social scientists would fear that disclosure of purpose would distort research results and, accordingly, would hesitate to take this approach.

A third alternative is to tell the participants about the general experimental procedure (but not the hypothesis) and secure their cooperation in role-playing the behavior they would have supposedly shown had they gone through the experiment. In several cases, this alternative has been used with apparent success. For example, one experimenter asked research participants to role-play a strategy meeting of leaders of a fictitious organization (Kelman, 1967). As expected, participants in these sessions formed different attitudes toward the organization depending upon the type of action they role-played toward it. Another investigator asked research participants to pretend to be in an experiment in which the investigator was asking them to administer dangerous electric shocks as a learning incentive to a second person (Mixon, 1972). He found that role-playing participants, if instructed in such a way as to create the impression that the experimenter was responsible for pain and potential injury to the learner, behaved much as had the participants in the original experiment. However, when the instructions indicated that the role-players rather than the experimenter were to assume the responsibility, the behavior of the role-playing participants was very different from that shown by the true research subjects. On the other hand, there are numerous demonstrations that the results of role-played experiments differ from those in which the investigator has concealed his true purpose in order to involve the research subjects in direct and personal reactions to the conditions being studied (Miller, 1972).

Of course, differences in results leave unanswered the question of whether role-played or traditional experiments provide more meaningful and generalizable research results. This is still under debate. Some social scientists argue that role-played experiments can take into account the meaning attached by people to things they experience and thus provide results more applicable to everyday social phenomena. Others note that whereas role-players can say what they *should* or *might* do under real-life conditions, they are unable to predict what they *would* do. The reason for this, according to scientists who take this position, is that the role-player will not know which of the many aspects of the situation he would respond to in real situations. (For a debate on this issue see Forward, Canter, and Kirsch, 1976; and Cooper, 1976).

It seems probable that their commitment to the development of a significant and relevant science of human behavior will lead many social scientists to continue to deceive research subjects. In some cases the research participants' rights will be curtailed in ways that they may not find troublesome, as in studies where they are given misleading information regarding the purpose of the study or the function of their own behavior within the study. In other cases, as in studies where they are misled regarding the nature of what they will be asked to do or what they will be exposed to during the research, their freedom will be abridged more extensively, and, hence, the moral cost of the experiment, if conducted, will be correspondingly greater.

Leading the Research Participants to Commit Acts That Diminish Their Self-respect

An ethical dilemma tinged with irony confronts the social scientist studying the determinants of such topics as honesty, helping behavior, and resistance to dictatorial and authoritarian influence. These are matters that touch the highest of human ideals. Yet in their investigation social scientists use procedures calculated to induce behavior that conflicts with these ideals. To study honesty, for example, one creates opportunity for research participants to lie, cheat, and steal. To study helping behavior, one puts unsuspecting individuals in situations in which they may refuse to help when it is badly needed. To study resistance to authority one pressures participants to obey orders they regard as wrong and harmful.

The following paragraphs illustrate four of the more common types of undesirable behavior induced for research purposes.

Cheating, lying, stealing. Moral character is a topic of considerable interest to social scientists as well as to the rest of us. For example, among studies of this topic are some that have been conducted to determine whether honesty is a general characteristic or, instead, whether people are honest in some situations but not in others. Other studies have sought to discover the correlates of variations in honesty.

An example comes from a study in which college students were recruited to take part in a theft: this study was stimulated by the actual burglary of a political campaign headquarters — the now famous Watergate burglary in 1972 (West, Gunn, and Chernicky, 1975). The experimenters noted that whereas participants in the burglary explained their behavior in terms of environmental influences external to themselves, observers in the mass media tended to attribute their behavior to defects in their personal character. As these differences in the perceived causes of evildoing are predicted by a theory about the determinants of causal attribution, the experimenters felt it would be important to check the theory in a controlled situation that paralleled the real burglary. As a part of this experiment they offered inducements to college students to help with the theft of records from a business firm. The inducements included performing a patriotic service for a department of the federal government: A substantial number of the students agreed to take part (the actual burglary was never carried out).

Harming others.   Of equal interest has been the topic of harming others and its consequences for subsequent social interaction. Attempts have been made, for example, to discover the conditions under which one individual will obey (or defy) orders to harm another. One approach to studies of this type has been to have the experimenter "order" the research participant to administer painful and dangerous electric shocks to a second person (Milgram, 1965). The purpose of the shocks was presented as a means of punishing the person for his errors, so that he would be motivated to learn (the second person is an experimental confederate). Although emotionally upset, many research participants nevertheless showed the "blind obedience" some had thought to characterize only those persons living under ruthless political dictatorships.

Yielding to social pressure to deny one's own senses or convictions.   Another major topic in social relations is that of conforming to social influence. Human behavior of this sort underlies some of the best as well as some of the worst aspects of group life. The experimental study of conformity has generally led investigators to expose research participants to social pressures that lead them to say things they disbelieve and to do things to which they are opposed, that is, to distrust and deny their own perceptions and feelings. In the best known of such experiments, some college students heard their peers (all confederates) give incorrect reports of the length of lines shown on a wall in front of them (Asch, 1951). Some of these students were unable to resist the cumulative influence of these reports and, in their turn, also reported seeing the lines as different from their true length. Other experimenters have exposed research participants to an incorrect position announced by a group of peers on well-known factual items such as, "In thousands of miles, how far is it from San Francisco to New York?" or to a deviant position on high-consensus opinion items such as, "most people would be better off if they never went to school at all" — after which the participants' own answers and opinions were obtained (Krech, Crutchfield, and Ballachey, 1962). A common finding is that under certain conditions, research participants take positions opposite to those they would ordinarily hold.

Failure to help when help is needed.   In the earlier discussion of involving people in research without their knowledge or consent, several studies of helping behavior were cited. One of these was intended to explore the hypothesis that a person is more likely to give help if he or she is alone than if one of a number of potential helpers. To study this, researchers trained a confederate to fake a realistic and frightening epileptic seizure with the research participant out of sight but nearby (Darley and Latané, 1968).

In another study of this kind, investigators had a man with a cane (or, alternatively, a liquor bottle) drop to the floor of a New York City subway train. Even though the man with the cane was almost always helped and the drunk often helped, most people left the scene with the knowledge that it was not they who had given assistance (Piliavin, Rodin, and Piliavin, 1969).

Discussion.   For some social scientists, practices such as those just described are the most questionable of all those used in research with human participants. These are practices that are to some extent responsible for the fact that research participants behave in ways that cause them shame, embarrassment, or regret—in some cases because they have violated their own moral standards and those of their group or community and in other cases because they have shown themselves to be less worthy and self-directed than they believed themselves to be.

However, this view of the matter is strongly challenged by other social scientists. Some argue vigorously that it is the participant, not the researcher, who is responsible for the participant's actions. It is the subject, they say, who chooses to cheat or not to cheat, to harm or not to harm another person, to yield or not to yeild to social pressure. Others go further: They take the position that it is a service to people to give them an accurate perception of what they are like and, in particular, of their potential for committing an action even though they disapprove of it. According to this position, to help people maintain self-esteem based on false premises about themselves is a disservice to them, and the researcher should have no qualms about exposing an incorrect self-image if that stands in the way of further growth of the individual in question.

Two shortcomings of this position may be recognized. The first is that researchers have no right to impose their educational services on others who have not requested them. The second is that the process of recognizing and changing one's personal weaknesses is complex and sensitive. To be constructive, it must take place in a supportive or a therapeutic context rather than in a brief and threatening laboratory confrontation.

If we grant that practices threatening the research participant's self-respect are undesirable and yet appreciate the importance of the topic being studied with the aid of such practices, we may wish to ask whether degrees of undesirability may be distinguished among practices in common use. Agreeing to harm others, for example, may be judged by some to be potentially more distressing than failing to help others. However, if the harm is minor and the need for help is great, it may lead us to reverse this order.

Some researchers argue that the reactions of research participants who have been led to commit acts that threaten their self-respect should determine whether such practices should be continued. A number of investigators have done follow-up studies on this point (Milgram, 1964; Ring, Wallston, and Corey, 1970). In general, these studies indicated that research participants report only minor and temporary disturbances and that they feel they have gained useful self-understanding from their experiences.

Violating the Right to Self-determination: Research on Behavior Control and Character Change

The questionable practices described in the preceding sections are sometimes the backdrop for an aspect of social research that raises an even more serious problem: Do scientists have the right — even if they have the power — to produce significant changes in the behavior or the personalities of other people? Or, in so doing, are they violating the individual's own right to self-determination in action and character?

It should be noted that this issue is independent of the nature of the behavior or character change produced in research. In the preceding section, for example, the investigator created conditions that led participants to commit undesirable acts such as cheating and harming others. However, the right to self-determination is violated just as clearly when the change produced is of a sort that onlookers might judge desirable, for example, a change in the direction of greater readiness to help others or a greater capacity to resist temptation to be dishonest.

The origin of the questionable practice of violating the research participant's right to self-determination is the social scientist's obligation to produce a science that is adequate for the task of guiding the development and modification of social behavior. Two examples, one of research involving behavior control and the other dealing with major changes in a significant attitude, will illustrate this.

Low academic achievement in metropolitan public schools is a national problem of great concern. Observers disagree as to its causes. Among the explanations suggested are such factors as poor motivation, inadequate teacher-pupil communication, and classes so large that remedial instruction for individuals is impractical. One group of investigators sought to improve academic achievement by a method that involved small-group cooperation, peer tutoring, and positive reinforcement (Hamblin, Hathaway, and Wodarski, 1971). The participating teachers organized their students into classroom teams. The amount of reward (credits that could be exchanged for various privileges) received by all the members of a given team depended not on their individual classroom performance but rather on the average performance of the three *lowest* achievers on their team. As a result of this new "social system," the better students on a team began to tutor the poorer ones, and the academic performance of all students, but especially that of the poorer students, showed improvement.

The second example is a study of racial attitude change (Cook, 1970). The investigator selected white female college students with extremely negative attitudes toward blacks to serve as research participants. For several hours a day, for 20 days, each participant worked cooperatively in an equal-status relationship with a black of equivalent education (an experimental confederate); a third co-worker in the cooperating work group was a white (also a confederate) who endorsed racial equality and desegregation. Several months after each participant left the experiment, her racial attitude was checked by another researcher in a different place in the city. Forty percent of the participants now showed markedly different racial attitudes, having changed in the direction of racial equality and desegregation.

In neither of these experiments did the research participants know of the changes the research procedures were expected to produce. Moreover, the changes would not have occurred had they depended on the free choice of the research participants (that is, the control participants did not change). They occurred only because the investigators had discovered the influences that would lead them to change or, as some would put it, the way to manipulate them.

Positions taken by social scientists on the conflict between the right to self-determination and research efforts to make significant changes in research participants vary considerably. Some have placed primary emphasis on self-determination and freedom of choice and made proposals intended to preserve as much of this freedom as possible in research projects (for example, Kelman, 1968). Others point to the everyday prevalence of behavior control by employers, educators, and government; they go on to argue that the focus should be on developing a type of control that operates for the individual's gain rather than for his or her disadvantage (for example, Skinner in the debate between Rogers and Skinner, 1956). Still others minimize the difference between the two positions, pointing to the illusory nature of much apparent freedom of choice (for example, Hoagland, 1963). They point out that salespersons and political figures often make us "choose" to acquire things or do things that we would be better off not having or doing. Hence, apparent freedom to choose or to act may itself be a result of control by others.

As yet, little concern has been shown regarding the implications of violating the research participant's right to self-determination. The principal reason for this is that social science has only begun to learn how to change people in ways that are fundamental to their conduct and outlook. As knowledge of the major determinants of basic (and sensitive) behaviors and traits accumulates, the value conflict will become more salient, both for scientists and for everyone. The fact that other methods of behavior control are being developed contemporaneously — including electrical brain stimulation, psychoactive drugs, and programs of scientifically tested reinforcement — will add to the concern. In the not-too-distant future it will be necessary for all researchers to clarify their own positions on this issue.

Exposing the Research Participant to Physical or Mental Stress

Human reactions to stress and behavior under stressful conditions are important topics in social relations. Examples of problems in this area include crowd behavior in emergencies, the relation of anxiety to the desire for social affiliation, and persuasibility under conditions of lowered self-esteem. The investigation of these and related questions has led social scientists to induce a wide variety of unpleasant emotional states in their research participants. These range from concern about one's economic security to a belief that one has seriously harmed another person.

That such practices create ethical questions is a matter of general agreement. Although it is true that in everyday affairs people induce stress in others (for example, parents threaten their children; doctors threaten their patients) the assumption is that the person who is being shamed, deprived, made anxious, or punished will profit personally from this experience. Such a justification is absent from most research (although it is occasionally present in research on therapeutic methods).

Stressful experiences are usually presented to research participants without forewarning. It is standard practice to "debrief" the participants at the close of the experiment about the deception that was used in producing the stress.

Some examples of experiments making use of different types of stress are as follows:

Horror. A researcher who believed he had discovered that the pupil of the eye would constrict when viewing unpleasant material and dilate when viewing material that was pleasing, wished to determine whether this would provide a physiological measure of feelings and attitudes (Hess, 1965). As one check on this possibility he photographed the eyes of his research participants while they examined gruesome pictures of the remains of emaciated victims in Nazi concentration camps. Other investigators whose research required the arousal of emotional reactions have shown their research participants pictures of mutilated persons or the distorted faces of persons who have drowned.

Threat to sexual identity. Among youth, experiences that raise questions about sexual identity are likely to arouse considerable emotion. This fact was used by an experimenter studying the effect of a communication from a prestigious source on attitude change. The nature of the experiment was such that it required an attitude to which the research participants had a strong emotional committment. This requirement was met by a "self-referring attitude," that is, self-perceived masculinity or femininity (Bergen, 1962). In one part of this experiment the "director of personality assessment" of a psychiatry department of a university medical center gave the male participants test feedback indicating femininity and feedback indicating masculinity to female participants. Clear-cut emotional disturbance was observable in these individuals.

Failure. Exposing research participants to preplanned failure is commonplace. Among the research topics in which it has been employed are motivation, level of aspiration, learning, problem solving, self-esteem, persistence, coping, and other aspects of personality. Research related to the continuing debate about reward and punishment as incentives for school achievement provides an example. In this study, five grading systems were used on the first midterm examination in a college course, and the results assessed in terms of performance on a second midterm examination (Goldberg, 1965). Under one of the grading policies ("strict"), the lowest 30 percent of students received an *F*. Under another ("lenient"), the lowest 30 percent received a *D* or *C*. After the second midterm, new grades for the first midterm were issued; these conformed to customary grading practices. Meanwhile some students had anxious moments — which was the experimenter's intent. (The results showed that the different grading policies produced no differences in performance on the second test.)

Fear. A dramatic use of this type of stress was made in a study of the effect of prior organization on group behavior (French, 1944). Organized and unorganized groups were assembled for what they believed to be group discussions. After the discussions got under way, smoke was observed to be seeping under the door. When the group members began to leave the room, they found that the door had been locked.

Among the most extreme uses of fear have been those employed in studies of soldiers in emergencies simulating combat. In these studies investigators were looking for selection and training procedures that they believed would save lives in real emergencies (Berkun, Bialek, Kern, and Yagi, 1962). Among the stress-producing situations they used were realistically faked ditching of aircraft in the ocean, reports of accidental radioactive fallout, fake forest fires surrounding an occupied outpost, and misdirected artillery shells exploding close by. During several of the emergency situations the research participants had the task of repairing a malfunctioning radio which was needed to send the message they believed would save their lives.

Emotional shock. An illustration of this type of stress comes from a study designed to test driver reaction to a sudden hazardous situation. The research participant was driving. As he passed a construction job, a realistic dummy fell into the path of the car too late for the driver to avoid hitting it.

Discussion. It is a questionable practice to expose research participants to physical or mental stress without their informed consent, and it is entirely unacceptable to submit them to experiences that may cause them serious or lasting harm. However, as the preceding examples indicate, the degree of stress involved in experiments varies widely. Some stressful experiences are less upsetting than others, and some are more frequently encountered than others in everyday life. The goal should always be for researchers to try to achieve their objectives with less extreme stress experiences.

It may be possible in some instances for investigators to plan research around naturally occurring emotional stress. Everyday examples are patients awaiting injections, surgery, or their turns in a dentist's chair. Good examples of such research may be found in the work of investigators studying the effects of prior information and modeling in reducing emotional reactions to stressful events in hospital settings (see, for example, Vernon, 1973).

There will remain, however, a sizable difference of opinion among scientists regarding research in which the experimenter exposes others to physical and emotional discomfort. Some will be convinced that a scientist has no moral right to do this, whereas others will believe just as strongly that scientists must do this in order to study those matters that in everyday life cause excitement, raise concern, are motivating, lead to conflict, and, in general, are most important to understand.

Invading the Privacy of the Research Participant

Research on some topics in social relations leads investigators to engage in a number of ethically ambiguous practices that we have grouped under the label of *invasion of privacy*. Included are several data-collection procedures such as participant observation, covert observation (sometimes utilizing one-way mirrors, and audiotape and videotape recording), interview and questionnaire inquiries into intimate personal matters, and disguised indirect tests in which the test takers are unaware of what they are revealing.

The recent concern attached to the invasion of privacy derives not from its use by scientists but from its abuse by police, private detectives, credit bureaus, and the government. Wiretapping of telephones, secret tape recording of conversations, "security" interviews with neighbors and acquaintances, checks on personal financial records, and the planting of intelligence agents in political organizations are types of "snooping" and spying that have become all too familiar.

In part, the objection to these procedures is that typically they are used to the disadvantage of the person whose privacy is invaded; for example, they may be employed as a basis for potential criminal prosecution. Another objection, however, is to their abridgment of the "right to privacy." This is one's right not to have personal information or private affairs disclosed publicly and to determine for oneself how much of one's beliefs, actions, and personal attributes to disclose. For almost all of us, this would include privacy for intimate and affectionate relationships between adults and between parents and children. Many would also include privacy in matters of personal hygiene. For many, financial status and the nature of one's religious and political beliefs should be considered as private. For some, the right to privacy also covers things that, though done in public, are not expected to be the focus of attention by others, for example, a conversation with a friend in a crowded lobby.

Studies involving some degree of invasion of privacy fall into five groups: those using techniques of participant observation, those involving covert observation and recording procedures, those asking personal questions in interviews or questionnaires, those employing disguised indirect tests, and those obtaining information from third parties.

Participant observation. Many of the more interesting aspects of human behavior do not lend themselves to laboratory experimentation. Examples include delinquency in street gangs, family influence in voting for president, homosexual practices, the activities of "doomsday" groups, and the customs of primitive tribes. One of the ways scientists have approached the study of such matters is to become a party to the ongoing activity and, unknown to the other participants (or to no more than a few of them), to make systematic notes about what they observe. The study of street-corner groups mentioned earlier was conducted in this way (Whyte, 1943).

A researcher interested in developing a more adequate description of the different types of male homosexuality assumed the role of a lookout for pairs of men who were engaged in oral sexual practices in public restrooms. A year later the same men were interviewed in their homes as part of a large social health survey without being informed that the interviewer had had any previous knowledge of their activities (Humphreys, 1970).

Other investigators interested in cognitive consistency theory studied the adjustment of members of a group to the failure of their prediction that the earth would come to an end on a certain day (Festinger, Riecken, and Schachter, 1956). To do this, they began attending the group's meetings; to avoid suspicion, they represented themselves as having had psychic experiences in the past.

The procedures used in the preceding studies may be distinguished from two similar procedures about which ethical questions are rarely raised. One is the conduct of a study in a situation where one is both a true participant and a scientist, a real patient in a hospital or a real taxi driver. The other is open prearranged observation in settings ordinarily considered private, such as observations of families carried out in their homes. In the latter, the participants rapidly grow accustomed to the observer and return to uninhibited, normal activity.

Covert structured observation.   When social scientists are convinced that the act of open and obvious data collection will change the behavior being observed, they may conceal an observer or use concealed recording equipment. Sometimes this is accomplished by having the observer pose as an apparent bystander. For example, an investigator who was interested in the part played by informal private negotiation in proceedings at the United Nations took note of small international subgroups conversing in hallways and lobbies, recording the nationalities involved, who initiated the contact, and its duration (Alger, 1966). Other investigators, studying sex differences in interests, walked through crowded theater lobbies at intermission time, eavesdropping to discover the topics of conversation in all-male and all-female groupings (Carlson, Cook, and Stromberg, 1936). Sometimes the concealment of the observer is quite literal as was the case in a study designed to check on egocentricity in conversations; the observers hid under dormitory beds (Henle and Hubbell, 1938).

Often **covert structured** (or concealed) **observation** is best accomplished behind one-way mirrors. Typically the research participant is told of the observation but given a false reason for it. For example, in a study in which the social interaction of members of interracial groups was being observed, the research participants were led to believe that the observation was related to the possible revision of a task on which their group was working (Katz, Goldston, and Benjamin, 1958). In another study in which the interaction of mother and child was under observation, the mother thought that only the behavior of the child was being recorded (Bishop, 1951). What is questionable about procedures such as these, of course, is that what people do in areas supposedly not under observation reveals aspects of themselves that they may have elected to keep private. This raises again the issue of what is to be considered private. More will be said about this later.

In some research the nature of the question and the setting are such that no method of collecting information other than by concealed recording seems likely to produce uninhibited and uncensored data. This was the basis for using a concealed audio recording in a study of the ability of a family to survive an extended stay in an underground fallout shelter.

The recording of concealed observations makes invasion of privacy an even more questionable practice. The fact that a tape or film exists broadens the potential audience for the behavior in question and, hence, increases the potential for embarrassment and discomfort should confidentiality not be observed. To the extent that the behavior recorded can be used against the research participant, the danger in this practice is increased still further.

Asking personal questions in interviews and questionnaires. Many problems in social relations are studied by asking research participants to respond to questions on interviews or questionnaires in regard to their beliefs, feelings, actions, past experiences, or hopes for the future. Some of these questions deal with intimate relationships; the well-known Kinsey studies of sexual practices were one such example. Others deal with illegal practices; studies of social and cultural factors in the backgrounds of drug users are illustrative. In studies of the development of personality characteristics, researchers have asked children to describe the child-rearing practices of their parents, for example, to agree or disagree with "dad always seems too busy to pal around with me." Researchers in other studies have asked questions about personal habits, including whether to agree or disagree with "I enjoy soaking in a bathtub" or "Sometimes I tell dirty jokes when I would rather not."

Disguised, indirect, or projective tests. Data-collection instruments of this sort are used by social scientists primarily for two reasons. The first is to measure personality traits or behavioral tendencies about which the research participants either are unaware or, if aware, do not know their position on the trait continuum and, hence, are unable to provide accurate self-description. The second is to measure some characteristic about which it is assumed that respondents are motivated to conceal the truth and give self-descriptions they know to be incorrect. In either case, the investigator is obtaining from research participants information they do not know they are revealing and, in this sense, is invading the privacy of the subject's inner life. In some cases the information would be held back if the participant knew what was happening.

An example of using indirect tests to measure a characteristic about which the respondent is unable to give an adequate self-description is the use of stories told about pictures in the Thematic Apperception Test to assess strength of achievement motivation (McClelland, Atkinson, Clark, and Lowell, 1953). Studies of child-rearing practices have used this technique to assess the impact of different methods of child rearing on the development of this attribute.

In the literature on attitudes there are many examples of measurement of characteristics, when it is feared that the respondents may inhibit or censor answers that correctly describe the characteristics. In one study, for example, groups differing in racial attitude were readily distinguished from each other by asking them to rate the plausibility or convincingness of one set of arguments for segregation and another set of arguments for desegregation (Selltiz and Cook, 1966). The participants were asked explicitly not to indicate their own agreement or disagreement with the arguments but rather to judge their effectiveness as support for whichever policy was endorsed by the argument. The indirect detection of racial attitude was possible because their attitudes led the respondents to judge as more convincing those arguments that supported the policy in which they believed; that is, those with favorable racial attitudes thought arguments for desegregation to be stronger than those with less favorable attitudes.

Obtaining information from third parties.   The information in some research can better be provided by third parties than by the research participants themselves. For example, the impact of an experimental program, such as training in human relations, on the effectiveness of a baseball manager's communication with his players, is best determined by obtaining information from the players. Similarly, the effectiveness of a program intended to prepare mentally retarded persons for work on assembly lines can best be determined by information obtained from the persons in charge. When the consent of the research participant has been obtained, such contacts with third parties present no problems However, when the investigator fears that the act of obtaining such consent might put the research participants on guard and influence their behavior (a reasonable possibility in the first example just given), the investigator may decide to proceed without requesting consent. In both of these illustrations, the behavior inquired about is public, and for this reason some scientists would not find the use of third-party informants questionable. However, third parties can also provide information in such matters as the religious practices of their acquaintances, their study habits, or their use of alcohol and other drugs. Getting information such as this by interviewing the respondents themselves introduces the danger that responses will be distorted in the direction of "proper" behavior. The cooperation of third parties can often be obtained by pointing this out and by promising that information supplied to the interviewer will be held in confidence. When the investigator follows this course, an invasion of privacy occurs. When, if ever, this may be justified is discussed later in the chapter.

Discussion.   The examples just given suggest that privacy may be invaded in two ways: (1) by the observation of acts that an individual may prefer to keep private and (2) by the fact of being observed systematically in the absence of knowledge that this is happening. In the first case, an individual may dislike to reveal certain information regardless of the method by which this happens. In the second, such people may object to being observed when they were not expecting to be, whether the activity involved was a casual conversation in a public place or a more intimate relationship in their home.

   Threats to privacy vary in strength on these two dimensions. With respect to the first, observation of normally public activity such as working, eating, and recreation will meet little, if any, objection, whereas observation of activity customarily occurring in private settings, such as the home, the toilet, or the bedroom, will meet a great deal. With respect to being observed systematically, several degrees of invasion of privacy may be discerned. At the least objectionable extreme we may place observation about which participants are aware in general but about the focus of which they have been misled. More objectionable is observation about which the participant is entirely uninformed; this is true in some (but not all) participant observation. More objectionable yet is concealed observation but without audio or video recording. Most objectionable of all is concealed observation with audio or video recording. Needless to say, the two dimensions will cumulate in determining the extent to which privacy is invaded; for example, secret videotaping of extremely intimate activity will be experienced as intolerable.

The preceding comments are concerned with human "cost" of invading privacy. Thus, although it may be granted that any invasion of privacy is a questionable practice in research, it is also clear that some types of invasion are more costly than others and, if undertaken, require correspondingly greater justification.

Not all of the statements made about invasion of privacy in this discussion are matters of general agreement. It may be argued, for example, that activities occurring in public places should be considered open to systematic observation for research purposes just as they are to unsystematic observation by curious bystanders. This argument would open to concealed observation anything that happens in work settings, waiting rooms, restaurants, and public means of transportation. Some social scientists have extended this position to cover events that happen in private when the parties involved are engaged in governmental or industrial activities in which they are accountable to the public.

Another argument minimizes the seriousness of observing aspects of behavior about which the research participant has not been explicitly warned. It is enough, according to this argument, to make it known that observation is occurring; one may object to observing additional behavior as deceptive but not as an invasion of privacy.

A third argument is that participant observation does not invade privacy, although it may be judged undesirable in violating the mutual trust usually assumed in social relationships. As already noted, this argument seems more compelling when the research observer is a legitimate participant, that is, a real patient, taxi driver, or production line worker. If, however, invasion of privacy is used to cover the fact of being systematically observed in the absence of knowledge that this is happening, then the legitimate versus planted status of the participant observer seems of little consequence.

As noted earlier, invasion of privacy takes on many of its negative connotations from the purposes for which it is used in everyday life. In research, by contrast, data from an intimate question or from a concealed observation are rarely of interest for themselves or in relation to the specific individual to whom they refer. Rather, individual observations merge into measurement indexes or scale scores, and these, in turn, into group averages. This difference is not appreciated by persons unfamiliar with research, and for this reason such persons view procedures of the sort discussed in this section more negatively than the scientists utilizing them. Those who keep this in mind and inform concerned segments of the community in advance will reduce the danger of misunderstanding and hostile reaction. To illustrate, one pair of investigators, who explained their study by letter to both parents and children and obtained their consent in writing to participate, encountered no objection when they asked high school students the question, "Have you ever engaged in sexual intercourse with someone of the opposite sex?" (Jessor and Jessor, 1975).

Withholding Benefits from Participants in Control Groups

Ordinarily the fact that a study has a control group composed of subjects who are not exposed to the experimental experience raises no ethical issues. But there are two exceptions. One occurs when the experimenter or others who know of the research become convinced of the value of a new program or treatment and believe that it would benefit all of the research participants, including those in the control group. The other occurs when the subjects in the control group are deprived of some recognized benefit to which they had earlier had access in order to provide a more accurate assessment of the value of the new program or treatment.

Such circumstances are most likely to be encountered when the study deals with the effects of some remedial or supportive measure such as a new therapy, a promising educational innovation, a new preventive health measure, or an economic benefit. At such times, even though research participants have been chosen for a control group purely by chance, investigators may feel concerned that they are being deprived of something that is important to their present or future welfare. Even if researchers do not develop such a concern, it may be expressed by others who, in some cases, may be in positions of authority.

Examples of studies in which potential benefits have been withheld from control groups. An example from outside the area of social relations research will help to point up the reality of this dilemma. In the early 1970s the news media uncovered the fact that several decades earlier a government-supported experiment had been carried out to evaluate the effectiveness of a new treatment of syphilis. The reporters discovered that the health of a number of persons in the untreated **control group** had deteriorated as a result of the disease; it was clear in retrospect that had these individuals also received the new treatment they would now be in better health.

Two experiments will illustrate the parallel concern with deprived control group participants in social relations research. The first took place in the early 1960s near the beginning of the period in which social scientists began their efforts to find ways to overcome the retardation in school achievement found among children from economically and educationally disadvantaged homes. One approach was to attempt to discover compensatory methods for preparing preschool children for their first year of school work. (The governmental program with this objective was called Head Start.) Basing their reasoning on the nature of the intellectual deficiencies shown by the disadvantaged children, the experimenters devised remedial educational experiences. One group of children received this training for three summers and one for two summers preceding school entrance (Klaus and Gray, 1968). Children from equally deprived homes were assigned to control groups, one such group coming from the hometown of the experimental group and another from a similar town near by. Although doubt has been raised about the effectiveness of the Head Start program in general, the experimental program in Klaus and Gray's study produced differences in average IQs between experimental and control groups that persisted at least through the fourth grade. As in the previous study, there is in this experiment a strong indication that a long-term disadvantage to some children hinged on the chance factor of their assignment to the control group. Again, however, it must be remembered that the same failure to receive adequate preparation for school attendance is characteristic of many thousands of children born into disadvantaged circumstances.

The second experiment dealt with the effect of a guaranteed annual income upon a person's incentive to work (Kershaw, 1972). In this experiment approximately 600 men in four-person families received government payments bringing their income up to a level between $3000 and $4000 per year. This continued for three years. The amount received varied, always being only enough to bring them up to a specified level. Another 600 men, neighbors in the same communities, constituted a control group. Although in equal need, none received the supplemental government payments. Persons in both groups were selected randomly. (Results indicated no reduction in work incentive among those receiving payments.)

Occasionally, the concern about what the control group participants are being deprived of is sufficiently strong to cause those who have authorized the experiment or who are cooperating with the experimenter in carrying it out to withdraw their support. One instance of this occurred in the course of study dealing with the phenomenon caricatured by the expression "some of my best friends are Jews." This refers to the recurrent observation that liked or admired persons from a disliked ethnic group are categorized as "good" exceptions to the disliked groups. As a result, the experience of knowing them usually has little effect on attitude change. A group of researchers developed the hypothesis that this "compartmentalization" and isolation of new experience contradicting old prejudices might be prevented by encouraging the development of cross-racial friendships under conditions in which the ethnic identity of the newly made friends was repeatedly verbalized (Chein, Cook, and Harding, 1948). The experiment was conducted in a recreational center with trained group workers as leaders of experimental and control groups. In the experimental groups the staff workers were to call attention to ethnic identity whenever the children in the groups were having satisfying and enjoyable interchanges; they were not to do this in the control groups. Midway through the research the experimenters observed that the experimental procedure was being employed in the control groups as well as in the experimental groups. In a conference about the matter, the group leaders confessed that they had become convinced that the experimental procedure was a valuable antidote to prejudice and felt morally obliged, therefore, to use it with *all* the children with whom they worked.

Discussion.   What has just been said suggests that withholding potential benefits from subjects in a control group creates an ethical question in only a small proportion of the cases in which it happens. These are the instances in which control group participants are deprived of benefits that would be available normally were the research not under way. In other cases, the deprivation associated with assignment to control groups is no different from that prevailing outside the experiment and, hence, cannot be attributed to the research.

Despite this, many researchers will feel they have incurred some responsibility for control group participants in studies where it turns out that substantial benefits and advantages have accrued to members of their experimental groups. It will sometimes be possible to fulfill this sense of obligation by applying the newly tested procedures to control group participants at the close of the experiment. This is likely to be expensive and time-consuming; hence it must be anticipated when the study is being planned and budgeted.

Finally, the social scientist must remember that persons without scientific training, who may not understand the necessity for control groups in research, will not be sympathetic to experiments in which beneficial experiences are withheld from some participants. This fact should also be anticipated, and the investigator must be prepared to explain the long-range value of such experiments in the event criticism is encountered.

Failing to Treat Research Participants Fairly and to Show Them Consideration and Respect

Although social scientists obtain data from individuals or from their interactions in groups and organizations, the purpose is to establish generalizable principles of human behavior. A given research participant is but one among many persons whose thoughts and actions are studied in a single project. One consequence of this is an insidious tendency to treat the participants as research objects and forget their human sensitivities.

One extreme and, fortunately, rare indication of this tendency is to treat research participants unfairly and with a lack of consideration and respect. A minor example is to arrive late for research appointments, an affront to participants who have often gone to considerable inconvenience in scheduling the time of their own appearance. A more serious example is not to fulfill commitments to the participant. Subjects who have been promised large sums of money to take part may, instead, be paid at the going hourly rates; in such cases the experimenter "persuades" the participant that the misleading promise was necessary to the success of the research and that the research project does not, in fact, have the money for the promised larger payment. Or a promise to furnish postexperimental reports of the research may not be carried out. Sometimes such promises are "fulfilled" with reports that are incomprehensible to a reader not familiar with technical terms. A final example is the failure to provide personal benefits that participants have been led to expect, such as improved self-understanding. Sometimes the benefits that are not delivered may have been promised to groups to which the research participants belong, groups such as ethnic minorities or poverty level neighborhoods.

Although the questionable practices just enumerated are generally thoughtless rather than ill-intentioned, they cannot be excused. In this sense, they differ from the questionable practices discussed earlier in the chapter, all of which followed from the nature of research procedures to which the investigator was committed.

Discussion. A number of steps may be taken to minimize unfair and inconsiderate behavior toward research participants. The first, perhaps, is to recognize the situational context in which such behavior takes place and which facilitates its occurrence. An aspect of this context is a mutually accepted difference in status between experimenter and research participant. For example, the experimenter is often a professor whereas the participant is a student. Or the difference may be that the experimenter is well educated and of comfortable economic status whereas the participant is economically disadvantaged. The experimenter is typically well established and successful whereas the participant may be mentally ill, a drug addict, or a delinquent. The experimenter often represents organizational authority when the participant is a worker or a soldier. Often without being aware of the fact, the two parties generalize this difference in status to their behavior in the research setting. For example, the experimenter may assume that the research participant will display a compliant and submissive orientation and the research participant, sharing this assumption, does so.

Although resolutions by the experimenter to do otherwise are appropriate, they are likely to underestimate the seductive power of the status relationship just described. Unless experimenters build a number of practices into their research routine, they are likely to find that from time to time they have again unintentionally treated the research participant in ways that they regret. Among these practices are the following.

However simple the arrangements with the research participants, it is helpful to put them in writing. This is not a legalistic step; rather it is intended to remind the experimenter to be sure that participants understand the nature of their commitment, on the one hand, and the nature of the benefits they may anticipate from the research experience, on the other. In the case of children or other less competent participants such as the mentally ill or retarded, this obligation is not fulfilled by arrangements made with legal guardians; the participants themselves are also due explanations at a level they can comprehend.

To avoid promising benefits beyond those that can be delivered, researchers will find it wise to adopt the deliberate policy of underselling. This is not to suggest that it is inappropriate for researchers to describe the potential scientific and social importance of their research as they see it or to promise interest and excitement in participating if they know this to be forthcoming. In contrast, to say that the research will produce increased self-understanding or that it will improve life circumstances for a social group to which the participant belongs is a promise hard to keep and should be avoided. If money or other rewards are promised, they must not be exaggerated, and, of course, they must be honored in a literal sense. In those cases where the research calls for studying the consequences of overreward, the experimenter should go no further than to explain the research problem and invite the participants to return the overpayment. Even this should be done at a point in time when the participants are no longer under direct social pressure in the experimental situation.

The investigator can remind participants of their autonomy and freedom in the research situation by telling them in writing two things. One is that they are free to withdraw from the study at any time. As such withdrawal introduces bias into the research results, the experimenter should explain this problem to any participant who is considering such action. The second piece of information is the name and address of someone administratively superior to the researcher to whom the research participant can report dissatisfaction with the treatment received. The participant should, of course, be encouraged to make a prior complaint to the experimenter and should be assured that relief will be forthcoming from this source.

The final step should occur in the experimenter's postexperimental contact with the participant. This is the point at which most can be done to show full consideration and respect. One objective is to do whatever possible at this time to assure that the participants have gained something from their experience. Sometimes the gain will be limited largely to the promised material reward. Often, however, interesting and useful information may be communicated about scientific theory, research methods, or social problems. In addition, and of great importance, is the opportunity to clarify the sense in which the participant has made an important contribution to scientific inquiry. Procedures for doing this will be discussed in greater detail in a later section.

RESPONSIBILITIES TO RESEARCH PARTICIPANTS AFTER COMPLETION OF THE RESEARCH

Even though the conduct of a research project has generated no ethical questions in its treatment of research participants, the investigators incur certain obligation that must be fulfilled following its completion. Among these are the following: they must follow through on any commitments made to the participants when soliciting their cooperation, they must give them such additional information about the research and its results as they desire, and they must assure subjects anonymity and keep in confidence subjects' responses.

In addition, when the research has involved one or more of the ethical questions reviewed earlier in the chapter, the investigator incurs other obligations. For example, if the methodological requirements of the study have necessitated concealment or deception, the researcher must clarify to the research participant the reasons for this and restore a relationship of mutual trust and respect. This is discussed in the following subsection titled "Clarifying the Nature of the Research." If the research procedure has involved discomfort or stress or has diminished the participant's dignity or self-esteem the investigator must do everything possible to alleviate such consequences. This responsibility is discussed in the subsection titled "Removing Harmful Aftereffects." When there are circumstances that may make it difficult to protect the research participant's anonymity and the confidentiality of data, the investigator must make sure that the participant understands this in advance. In the subsection titled "Maintaining Anonymity and Confidentiality" this problem is reviewed.

Clarifying the Nature of the Research

The obligation to reveal concealment or deception, that is, to "debrief," is widely accepted although its advisability and practicality may be questioned under certain conditions (see further on in this chapter). This obligation does not depend for its moral justification upon a favorable outcome of the debriefing process. Nevertheless, it is reassuring to know that, if done properly, misconceptions that might otherwise have persisted can be removed. This has been demonstrated in a number of studies in which the research participants were falsely told that they had unfavorable personality traits, for example, immaturity, poor social skills, low intelligence. With minor exceptions, debriefing has eliminated the negative effects of the false reports; this has been true for effects measured by physiological and behavioral methods as well as by self-description (Holmes, 1976a). Indications are that debriefing is more effective when it includes a discussion of the tendency for the negative impact of false information to perseverate than when this tendency is not discussed (Ross, Lepper, and Hubbard, 1975).

In clarifying the true nature of research that has involved concealment or deception, the investigator should strive to achieve the following:

1. Convey to the participants the investigator's sense of the potential value of the research.

2. Give the participants an appreciation of the contributions they have made to the research.

3. Provide the participants with an educational experience that includes an understanding of behavioral science research as used in the study in which they have taken part.

4. Develop in the participants an understanding of the necessity (as the investigator sees it) of employing questionable practices to obtain meaningful answers to the research question asked in the study.

5. Immunize the participants against the tendency for negative impressions of self that are developed in experiments to perseverate even after attempts have been made to correct them.

6. Convince the participant of the investigator's regrets over the need to employ questionable practices and concern over the participant's feelings about having been subjected to these practices.

7. Give the research participants a perspective on their experiences that minimizes any feeling that they might have been manipulated, made fools of, shown to be gullible, or revealed character weaknesses.

To accomplish these objectives, time must be set aside for a full discussion of the research participants' questions about their own behavior. Such a discussion will provide an opportunity to clarify confusion and correct misinformation and will help to minimize feelings of annoyance and resentment. It will help to detect and alleviate any harm suffered by the research participants. Perhaps it will also restore respect for and trust in the investigator and protect social science against the reputation of being secretive and manipulative in character.

Though recognizing the desirability of revealing questionable practices to the participant, some investigators feel that under many circumstances the disadvantages of doing this outweigh the advantages. For example, if research participants are being drawn from a small community, such as a college or other small institution, the early participants in a study may inform later ones of the experimental deception even though they have pledged secrecy. Such actions lead to serious question about the validity of the research and argue for the desirability of not debriefing. Even when participants who have been debriefed do not reveal what they have been told to others who are to take part in the same study, there remains the problem that potential participants in other studies hear of the deception and may become generally suspicious. If, as is likely, this leads them to guess that something unannounced is afoot in every study in which they take part, this will influence the outcome of all research in this setting in unpredictable ways.

To take another example, there are circumstances in which revealing deception may negate a positive outcome experienced by the research participants. Suppose, for example, that an individual had been induced by experimental arrangements to help a team member who was having difficulty. We know that the individual assumes that he or she has helped at his or her own initiative and derives satisfaction from so doing (Blanchard and Cook, 1976). Some social scientists have suggested that debriefing a participant under these conditions may reduce his self-esteem and possibly do more harm than good.

Such an analysis has led to a search for a compromise by means of which postexperimental discussions would be held with participants in some studies but not in others. One suggestion for such a compromise would be to debrief only when the experimental experience went beyond the limits of the participant's ordinary, everyday experience (Campbell, 1969). This would make debriefing unnecessary in all field experiments and in many laboratory experiments. It would still be called for, however, in obedience studies where the research participants were persuaded to harm others, in compliance studies where they were led to deny their own perceptions, in studies where they were influenced to believe fictitious facts about important topics, and in a number of other research areas. As will be evident, difficulties would arise in choosing those studies in which postexperimental discussions with participants were advisable and those in which they were not.

Still other disadvantages to dispelling deception have been pointed out. Among them is the argument that it gives publicity to the fact that deception is practiced by respected people such as scientists. Two answers may be given to this argument. One is that deception in research will be revealed in other ways, including textbooks. The other is that the deception may be discovered by the participant; it is better to avoid this danger and to reveal the deception under conditions in which it can be interpreted and justified and its consequences for the deceived person dealt with.

If debriefing is to be undertaken, it may be carried out in either of two ways. One is factual in emphasis whereas the other is feeling-oriented. The emphasis in factual debriefing is on providing information about a study's purpose and its methods, as well as the questionable practices used and why they were necessary. Appreciation for taking part is expressed, an apology may be made, and an offer to answer questions is extended. It is sometimes difficult during factual debriefings to avoid the atmosphere that the deception in the study was clever; the participants themselves often introduce this idea. Another danger is that in the debriefing the participants' attention may become fixed on the fact that they were easily fooled. Shame and embarrassment may inhibit their asking questions. Following the debriefing resentment, self-doubts, and loss of self-esteem may surface. These feelings may be accompanied by disillusionment and loss of trust in social relationships.

The feeling-oriented debriefing covers essentially the same content as the factual. It differs primarily in achieving each objective of the debriefing through discussion. An effort is made to be sure that the research participants think about and understand the value of the research and their contribution to it, why an answer to the research question required studying natural rather than self-conscious behavior, how this necessitated deception and other questionable practices, and, finally, the manner in which they themselves were deceived. The investigators' regrets about employing questionable practices and their concern for the participants' reaction to this are brought into the discussion. The investigators attempt to promote uninhibited discussion by the research participants by assuming that these subjects have negative reactions to having been deceived, subjected to stress, or led to commit acts that lowered their self-esteem. The discussion may conclude with a balancing of these negative feelings against each participant's estimate of the potential value of the research (for example, Blanchard and Cook, 1976).

Removing Harmful Aftereffects

One of the advantages of postexperimental discussions with research participants is that they provide an opportunity for the investigator to detect and deal with negative aftereffects of the research experience. Anxiety and feelings of inadequacy may develop inadvertently in the course of research that was thought by the investigator to be entirely free of such possibilities. For example, poor performance by a research participant in a learning or problem-solving experiment may be interpreted by the participant as indicating a general inadequacy. Similarly, one's submissiveness or vacillation in a decision-making study may confirm one's own preexperimental apprehensions about lack of self-confidence. Or, after answering questions in a personality inventory, the participant may come to the conclusion that his or her responses indicate some kind of abnormality or uncertainty about masculinity or femininity.

Unexpected reactions to research experiences may be encountered also in children. An experiment that involved recording **galvanic skin responses** from the palm of the hand will illustrate this. As it happened, the wires to the GSR electrodes used in the experiment had a red plastic exterior. Also, the pen on the moving recorder, which could be seen by the research participant, wrote in red ink. An eight-year-old child participating in the study became emotionally upset and left the building. Later the experimenter discovered that the juxtaposition of the red wires and the red ink had meant to the child that blood was being withdrawn from the hand to which the electrodes were attached.

Although reactions such as these are probably rare in the type of research described, they will occur more often when research experiences are stressful. As noted in the earlier discussion of questionable practices, research participants may be exposed to experiences such as failure, fright, or embarrassment. They may be put into situations in which they cheat, lie, or steal. They may be persuaded by the experimenter to harm others by reading to them derogatory evaluations of their personalities or by administering painful punishment. Or they may be led to believe that they have been responsible unintentionally for serious injury or possible death.

Of great concern are those reactions that manifest themselves later. Accounts of such reactions are not uncommon. One such report involved a male college student who was convinced by means of a fake physiological response displayed to him on an oscilloscope that he had homosexual tendencies. Although he was debriefed, the experience initiated (or perhaps reinforced) a concern that two years later brought the student to a psychotherapist.

On the other hand, studies of the effect of debriefing in preventing the occurrence of longterm negative effects of stressful experiments are reassuring. However, in all such studies the type of debriefing employed went beyond a simple explanation of the deception employed and attempted, in addition, to minimize possible stress reactions, for example, by assuring the research participants that their behavior had been normal or had reflected positive personality characteristics or would not be expected to generalize beyond a laboratory situation. One such study employed both a questionnaire and a psychiatric interview, finding not only no evidence of trauma but also a considerable amount of satisfaction at having participated in the experiment (Milgram, 1964). Another compared a form of debriefing that concerned itself with ameliorating stress with a debriefing focused only upon correcting deception; the former was found to be more effective in reducing emotional upset and in promoting a positive evaluation of the experiment (Ring, Wallston, and Corey, 1970). A third compared a stress-reduction debriefing with no debriefing, finding a clear advantage for the former (Holmes, 1976b). Of special interest is the fact that the latter study measured stress arousal reactions physiologically as well as by participant self-description. This fact lessens somewhat a concern that research participants, rather than accurately reflecting their true emotional condition, may be giving supportive answers in a desire to respond reassuringly to a considerate investigator.

If, in considering whether or not to conduct a study, the investigators cannot be reasonably confident of their abilities to reverse potential negative effects on the participants, they should decide against proceeding with their project. When they decide to proceed, they incur the obligation to detect and remove the negative effects as soon as possible. This has several implications. In long-term or multiple-session research, it indicates the need for a system to monitor the participants' reactions during the course of the research. It implies the use in all studies of a postexperimental discussion session of a kind that facilitates discovery of emotional disturbances when they are present. Finally, in many cases, it requires procedures for long-term follow-up to detect and remove disturbances that develop after the research has come to an end.

Precautions taken in a study of the effects of exposure of adults to pornographic materials will illustrate each of the preceding procedures. As exposure was repeated periodically over a considerable period of time, the emotional condition of the participants was monitored by having them fill out mood scales each day. In addition, they were provided with names and addresses of psychiatrists associated with the project and urged to consult them immediately if they felt the need. After the completion of the study each participant was examined carefully for evidence of disturbance. In addition, to check for the possibility that harmful effects might develop later, all participants were reinterviewed after eight weeks.

Detecting and removing negative aftereffects in field experiments will generally be impossible; for example, the passerby who fails to help a fake heart-attack victim is not accessible to follow-up. The limitation further increases the investigator's uncertainty about costs to the research participant and requires additional assurance that the experiment under consideration promises important benefits.

A type of negative aftereffect that presents a special dilemma is that which occurs as a consequence of terminating a beneficial experimental program. An example has been described by investigators who were studying the outcomes of providing retirement home residents with a predictable and controllable adjunct to their otherwise routinized and dependent existence (Schulz and Hanusa, 1978). (The experimental program consisted of visits by undergraduates on a schedule that could be predicted and controlled by the person visited.) The study found a statistically significant improvement in health status and zest for life among those participating in the experimental program. This had the effect of arresting and reversing the typical decline in physical and psychological status characteristic of aged individuals receiving institutional care. However, to the alarm of the investigators a follow-up approximately three years after termination of the study found a greater mortality rate among the individuals who had participated in the experimental program than among those who had not. They worried that this may have been due to the contrast between the experimental program and the postexperimental return to a life of uneventful dependence following its termination. Although other evidence supported an alternative interpretation in this case, the investigators presented their ethical dilemma as one that must confront all social scientists who experiment with programs of great potential value to their research subject. It is parallel, for example, to the ethical question faced by those who conducted the guaranteed annual income experiment, discussed earlier (Kershaw, 1972). In that study income maintenance payments to poverty-stricken research participants were terminated after they had had three years to become accustomed to them.

Maintaining Anonymity and Confidentiality

The obligation to protect research participants' anonymity and keep research data in confidence is an all-inclusive one and should be fulfilled unless specific arrangements to the contrary are made with the participants themselves. Moreover, the more intimate and sensitive the responses and the less open the procedures by which they were gathered, the greater is the transgression in releasing them to others. When measures are obtained covertly and deal with private matters, the investigator incurs an especially heavy responsibility to keep them in confidence.

A questionable practice not mentioned earlier is the use of secret procedures to identify persons who assume they are providing research data anonymously. An example is the device of putting stamps in precoded precisely measured locations on return envelopes containing **"anonymous" questionnaires;** from the location of the stamp the name of the person returning the questionnaire can be determined. The purpose of these procedures is always the same, namely, to obtain frank and truthful responses which the respondent might be ashamed or afraid to give on a signed questionnaire. The name is needed to make possible comparison of these responses with background data or with opinions or actions measured in some second situation. The investigator who proceeds in this way undoubtedly will not reveal the research participant's identity to others. Nevertheless, the deviation from ethical principles is so blatant in such procedures that, in our opinion, only the promise of substantial scientific or social gain could possibly justify their use.

Sometimes the problem just described can be circumvented with the cooperation of the research participants. For example, if their test or interview responses at two points in time must be compared, this can be accomplished anonymously through the use of code numbers supplied by the participants themselves. Such numbers may be derived from the year, month, and day of birth of a close relative. An even simpler procedure is the use of a separate identification sheet with the assurance that a code number to be assigned by the investigator will be entered on all materials and that the investigator will personally keep confidential the lists of names and associated code numbers.

The use of code numbers for data records that are to be filed and retained for later use is desirable as a routine procedure. Among its advantages are that it symbolizes to everyone associated with the research the emphasis placed on anonymity and confidentiality. In addition it protects against deliberate efforts by others to use research data for purposes other than those intended. This may be of critical importance if access to the data is demanded by those in authority, such as institutional administrators or the courts (see further on in this chapter).

Whenever data are collected only one time and no comparison with data from other sources or with follow-up data collected later is planned, it is wise for the investigator not to collect names. Questionnaires, for example, may be anonymously mailed in or deposited anonymously at some collection point.

Maintaining anonymity and confidentiality would be greatly simplified were it not for the many plausible requests and demands for access to research data by others. These include third parties such as parents and friends, institutional administrators such as school principals, professional associates such as other research investigators, and compilers of data banks.

Requests from third parties. When parents give consent to the participation of their children in research, it seems entirely reasonable to them for the investigator to provide them information on the things the child said and did in the course of the study. Similarly, friends who feel quite close to and concerned about a research participant will see no reason why the friend's responses cannot be shared with them. Were such disclosures to be made, they would often violate implicit assumptions by the research participant that only the investigator would learn of the subject's opinions or behavior. In some cases what was revealed might cause the participant embarrassment and discomfort. Hence, however well-intentioned the third party's request, and however harmless might appear the information requested, the investigator must not release information without the participant's explicit permission. In the case of parents, it is advisable to have a clear-cut understanding about the confidentiality of their children's research behavior before the research begins.

Requests from institutions. When research is carried out on employees, students, prisoners, soldiers, or members of any institution, administrative personnel of that institution may wish access to the research data. Typically they will want the information in order to be more helpful to the research participants—perhaps to give them more effective guidance, to supplement their personal files, and so on. Occasionally, there will be other reasons, such as to learn from the data in order to increase the institution's morale or effectiveness, to locate troublemakers, or to assist in the investigation of theft or other crime. When the researchers are staff members of the institution, they may come under pressure or even under a direct order to release information. It is prudent to anticipate this and, if possible, to work out in advance arrangements for confidentiality that will be honored by administrators. When this is not possible, the investigators must either inform research participants of their inability to protect their anonymity or, if they do not do this, they must be prepared to suffer the punitive consequences of defying the institution's request.

Requests from professional associates. Sometimes one investigator will collect data from the same research participants that another has already used. A merging of data from the two studies may make it possible to answer interesting questions that neither study could answer alone. In some institutional settings this possibility may be anticipated by maintaining cumulative research files containing data on individuals who served as research participants in several different studies.

This situation raises two ethical problems. The first is taking data provided by an individual for one purpose and using it for a second purpose of which the subject has no knowledge and with which he or she might not wish to cooperate. This is a questionable practice akin to that of involving persons in research without their knowledge or consent. The second is the threat to anonymity and confidentiality created by files to which a number of people have access. A suggestion for controlling the latter problem is to have a designated person charged with the responsibility for keeping the list of names and corresponding code numbers and of providing an investigator with merged sets of data identified by code number only.

Requests from data banks. The seriousness of the problem discussed in the preceding paragraphs is multiplied many times by the so-called data banks. A data bank is any collection of coded information about individuals that is kept in a form that makes the information easily retrievable, often by automated means. The potential of data banks for social science research is only beginning to be realized. They make it possible to reanalyze large collections of data and to analyze new data in the context of much data already stored on the same individuals. Among the major data banks are those maintained by agencies of the government. Here one may find records of employment, earnings, taxes paid, and census data on topics such as housing and age. If we wished to do a long-term follow-up of the effects of a job training program, for example, we would find in the data bank of the Social Security Administration records of the trainees' later earnings and unemployment payments.

Occasionally, social scientists are asked to contribute to data banks, sometimes to permit supplementary analysis of their data by others interested in similar questions and sometimes to supplement data already available on the same individuals (for example, welfare recipients). The dangers in doing this are recognized and are receiving much attention both from scientists and the federal government. Many methods of coding and disguising data so that individuals may not be identified are in use, and others are being developed. No investigators who supply information to a data bank should do so without assuring themselves that a sophisticated system of this type is in operation. If it is possible to contact research participants, they should inform them regarding precautions taken to protect anonymity and confidentiality and seek their permission to use their data in this way.

Potential loss of anonymity and confidentiality through court order. Even more threatening to the maintenance of anonymity and confidentiality than the various requests and demands enumerated above is the fact that the confidentiality of research data is not recognized in law. This means that a court may order the release of such data for use in criminal prosecutions and, in addition, may require the social scientists to testify about individuals who have been research participants. This may happen whenever the data involve illegal behavior such as drug use, violation of sex laws, and participation in illegal demonstrations. For example, a court order was obtained by a prosecutor to have the director of an experimental drug therapy program furnish photographs of all male participants. The purpose of the order was to assist legal authorities in detecting persons responsible for an armed burglary; the prosecutor's action was based on the fact that drug users are known to steal in order to buy the drugs their habit requires.

Researchers who may face court orders to surrender data have several alternatives. One is to advise their research participants of this possibility so that they can take this into account when deciding whether to participate. Another is to render the data files anonymous in a manner already described; often this will not be feasible because the study is one that continues over time. A third is to code the data and send the name-code list outside the country for safe keeping. Refusal to produce the list can be expected to lead to punitive action by the courts, and the investigators must reconcile themselves to this possibility.

Loss of anonymity and confidentiality through reports and publications. In research focused on the social life of a group or a community, problems of maintaining anonymity arise when a report is written. Even though pseudonyms for both the groups and individuals in the group are used, experience indicates that the true identity of the group or community soon becomes known. When this happens, it is often possible for group members or residents of the community to identify key individuals in the report. If detailed accounts are given of the behavior of such individuals, their mode of operating, and their relationships with others in the community, the effect can be embarrassing and, in some cases, disruptive to the life of the community and damaging to the reputation and well-being of the individuals.

Scientists differ considerably in their points of view on this matter. Some have argued that details and anecdotes damaging to individuals should not be included in reports, or, if they are, that they should be adequately disguised. Some take the position, in addition, that as the report should focus on general principles, such modification or omission of details about individuals represents little, if any, loss in the value of the report. Others, however, have argued that truth must come first, in other words, that the obligation to truth is higher than the obligation to protect anonymity.

One implication of this latter position has been stated earlier. Investigators who adopt it must have a clear understanding with individuals in the research project that details of what the researchers observe and learn will be published. If the researchers do not plan to show subjects what they will write and provide the subjects an opportunity to modify or withdraw it, this too should be made clear.

It must be noted, however, that not all social scientists feel that such warnings are necessary. On the contrary, some take the position that publicly accountable behavior — defined as anything that transpires in the course of one's job or in the conduct of public office — must be open to observation and study and that anonymity and confidentiality for such behavior should never be promised. A difficulty with this position is that a trusting relationship is very likely to develop in which the research participant assumes confidentiality even though this has not been promised. The investigator has an obligation to be alert to such a development and not take advantage of it.

Anonymity for valued groups.   It may happen that an individual who participates in research remains anonymous, but that his or her data have contributed to averages reported for a group to which the person belongs. For example, a boy may take part in a study for anti-Semitism not knowing that he is contributing to a comparison of parochial and public schools on this variable. Or he may not know that his score on an achievement test will be used with others to derive an average achievement score for his ethnic group. When a man's attitude toward a political candidate is solicited, he may not realize that his answers will contribute to an average attitude score for the department in a factory where he works.

The question of whether research participants should have a veto over such uses of their data — that is, to be told in advance of the uses planned or, alternatively, allowed to withdraw their data after learning of these uses — precipitates a severe value conflict. On one side is the value of autonomy for individuals in determining what research purposes they will contribute to. On the other is the value that truth should not be suppressed and the faith that truth will be used to good ends rather than bad.

Whether the investigator should ever elect to violate anonymity and confidentiality.   It has happened that in the course of research an investigator discovers alarming information about a research participant. For example, the participant may be planning to injure others or may be contemplating suicide. The subject may have participated in an armed robbery or a rape. Or a test used in the research may show that several participants are emotionally disturbed and need immediate help.

One can do little other than present this conflict. However strongly scientists may value their commitment to anonymity and confidentiality, they may on some occasion face a situation in which what is for them a higher value must prevail.

ETHICAL ISSUES IN THE UTILIZATION OF RESEARCH

The preceding sections of the chapter examined the ethical issues that arise in the social scientists' relations with their human research participants and the special

obligations they incur when they decide to proceed with research involving questionable practices. The remaining discussion deals with other ethical issues, namely,
those concerned with the utilization of social research. Certain of these issues focus
on researchers' responsibility for preventing misuse of their findings, especially in
instances where the research involves disadvantaged cultural groups or is conducted
in developing countries. Others deal with their responsibility for promoting the utilization of research. Although social scientists agree as to the importance of these
issues, they disagree on their solution. In view of this, the following discussion will
present unresolved problems to which thoughtful social scientists will continue to
give serious attention for the foreseeable future.

Preventing the Misuse of Research Results

Concern about the misuse of research results may arise in a number of ways. Some
examples follow:

Misuse for aggression.   An investigator who undertook a study of the behavioral
effects of a chemical substance discovered that the material lowered the readiness of
persons to protest or resist when attacked. This led to the realization that the
research might be applied by military forces for war-making purposes and aroused
doubts in the investigator as to whether the research should be continued.

Misuse in other cultures.   Another investigator was commissioned by a major religious group to study the performance of missionaries working in an underdeveloped
area in the hope of determining what accounted for differences in their success in
making converts. In the course of this research the researcher developed doubts that
a Western religion was meaningful for the people with whom the missionaries were
working. As a result, he seriously considered the possibility that the study should
be discontinued.

Misuse in explaining social problems.   A social scientist hoping to understand the
causes and possible remedies for juvenile delinquency collected data on the personal
attributes and family backgrounds of research participants. The results were limited
necessarily to factors in these two areas; they included such findings as the relative
prevalence of fatherless homes among delinquents and their low level of ability to
"postpone gratification," that is, to work for a larger but postponed reward. To the
investigator's dismay, he discovered that others interpreted these findings as revealing basic causes of delinquency and concluded from them that delinquency might
be reduced by remedial work with individuals and families. In contrast, the
researcher's own interpretation was that the basic causes were to be found in the
economic and educational deprivations that led to the broken homes in which the
delinquents grew up and to their ineffective personalities. However, his research did
not bear on such an interpretation. This led him to conclude that he had made a
misleading rather than enlightening contribution to knowledge about the origins of
delinquency and to decide that he should abandon further research of this type.

Misuse in explaining group differences. Many studies have been done comparing the achievement test scores of blacks and whites. Some social scientists argue that these studies were important and desirable. According to their view, the comparisons not only documented the regrettable inadequacies in the school achievement of black children but also spurred a search for the causes and remedies of this condition. Others, however, argue that such studies should never have been done. They reason that whites will inevitably interpret the results as indicative of inherited black inferiority although the test scores may, in fact, reflect any of a number of environmental determinants of low achievement, such as low educational level of parents or inferior prior schooling. Having made an interpretation of racial inferiority, the whites, according to this argument, will use this interpretation to support segregation and other discriminatory social policies.

Misuse for exploitation. Concern about the possible misuse of research sometimes focuses on its application by the organization or institution in which the research was done. One such example comes from industry. One of the well-established findings in social relations research is that when workers participate in decisions about how their jobs are to be performed, their morale usually increases. Moreover, this increase in morale is sometimes accompanied by an increase in productivity. This discovery has spawned a great interest in participative management and new leadership styles. Some social scientists interpret the application of this research as highly desirable; from it, they point out, workers gain a new sense of self-direction and personal significance. Others see this same application as misleading and harmful. They feel that employers support such research only to make workers happier and more resistant to unionization. This, in turn, makes it possible for the employers to continue their exploitation, if the higher productivity can be converted to higher profits rather than to increased wages.

Misuse in the political life of other nations. Another example comes from research on social change in developing nations. A study was planned to explore the sources of internal conflict in such nations as well as ways of preventing and coping with guerrilla activities when these threatened (Horowitz, 1967). The study was openly planned and fully described in public documents. Its financial sponsor was the United States Army Research and Development Office. Unknown to the project leadership, a staff consultant in Chile misrepresented the implications of the source of financial backing for the study. When the source was publicized, the press of Chile charged that the study was a covert operation of the United States military forces. In the resulting uproar, the study was canceled.

More recently, a parallel charge has been made about the purpose of American anthropological field research in Thailand (Wolf and Jorgenson, 1970). It is evident from these two examples that when a military unit with the responsibility for combating guerrilla activities sponsors research on matters potentially related to its mission, the assumption will be made that it plans to apply the research results. The individual investigator involved in the research may oppose this, be sympathetic to it, or find it a matter of indifference. However, in such cases, social scientists not participating in the study will also become concerned. To many of them, the use of data from basic research for counterinsurgency operations should be prohibited — even though some researchers are willing to go along with this objective.

Discussion. Three concerns about the potential misuse of research findings emerge from these examples. One is that the results will be misinterpreted, either intentionally or unintentionally, and hence used to support the wrong policies; the potential misuse of delinquency research and of racial comparison studies are of this type. Another is that the research results, although interpreted correctly, will be used for a purpose of which the investigator disapproves; the studies of the behavioral effects of a chemical and of the effectiveness of a missionary program are of this type. The third concern arises when the application is evaluated differently by different people. The research on worker participation in industrial decision making and on coping with guerrilla activities illustrates this. What is at issue in the latter case is not the appropriateness of applying the research findings to bring about increased worker satisfaction and productivity or decreased guerrilla activity; rather, it is a judgment as to whether such an outcome is to the long-range advantage or disadvantage of people affected by the research.

Faced with such concerns, the reactions of social scientists will vary considerably. Some will take the position that their responsibility ends with the effective conduct and proper interpretation of their research. Others will show their concern for the possible misuse of their research by anticipating probable misinterpretations and attempting to counter them in publications and public statements. Still others will, in addition, feel responsible to oppose actively any misinterpretations of their work about which they learn. A fourth group will be so concerned with the possible misuse of the findings of a given research project that they will decide against carrying it out.

It seems certain that concern for possible misuses of social research findings will take on added importance with time. The critical factor will be the success with which social science is applied to everyday affairs. As this increases, the ability to make use of social science findings will represent a powerful resource. When this happens, social scientists must confront the question of who uses their product and to what ends.

Promoting the Utilization of Research Results

In deciding whether or not to promote the utilization of their research results, social scientists confront one or more of three ethical issues. One of these is whether an investigator has the responsibility for promoting such utilization; this is the counterpart to the issue of his or her responsibility for preventing the misuse of results. A second has to do with the timing of the application of research findings — in particular, whether the application may be premature. The third has to do with rectifying what many regard as an undemocratic imbalance in the utilization of research knowledge — an imbalance characterized by the greater availability of social science to those with educational and financial resources than to those without.

Responsibility for encouraging research application. The proposition—that the research scientist is responsible for encouraging the application of his research results—draws support from two directions. The first is from the public. Support of social science by society is based not so much on an interest in knowledge for the sake of knowledge as it is in an interest in its practical utilization. The social scientist is looked to primarily for his or her help in alleviating and preventing social problems and social conflict. The second direction is from the social scientist himself or herself. Many people enter the social sciences, in part, because of their concern for human welfare. It is natural for them to ask whether their work contributes to its development. However, as noted in the discussion of preventing misuse of research results, there is widespread opposition to the idea that the scientist has any special responsibility for research utilization. According to this view, the scientist's function is the production of knowledge. This knowledge is available to all, and it is the responsibility of practical people in society to apply it.

Degree of certainty prior to research application. Among investigators who feel responsible for encouraging utilization of their research there will still be differences of opinion on a second issue, that is, that of timing. Some will feel that the possibility of utilization should be examined in connection with every study. Others will disagree, feeling that such attempts at application are premature. They argue that a theory based on many studies is the only sound basis for applying science. According to this view, attempts to base application on the results of single studies will mislead people who do not have scientific training and is, hence, an ethically questionable practice. To some extent this difference of opinion may be minimized by considering the nature of the research. Immediate application will be justified when, for example, the researcher is studying a complex programmatic activity in a natural setting. One reason for this is that the similarity of the program studied and the setting in which it was studied to other programs is great enough to make generalization appropriate. By comparison, laboratory studies aimed at devleoping an aspect of a theory will suggest little by way of immediate application. The results of such studies, in combination with other research, may later provide the social scientist with a basis for developing innovative programs or new social institutions. However, not until such programs or institutions are evaluated will it be timely to foster application under field conditions.

Unequal access to research applications. The third ethical issue has to do with the potential for differential utilization of research findings by different components of society. Large industries and government agencies have the resources to be alert to scientific developments and utilize them. Schools and public service agencies, owing to financial restrictions, have this capacity to a significantly lesser degree. Community groups and organizations with low levels of economic and educational resources are the least well-equipped to make use of potentially applicable research knowledge. Social scientists have recognized this and many have attempted to correct it (for example, Levin, 1970). As yet, however, their efforts have met with only slight success.

SUMMARY

Ethical concerns can arise from several aspects of the research process. For example, they can be generated by the kinds of questions studied by researchers and by the methods used to obtain answers. The procedures used when subjects are chosen, the ways that they are treated, and the uses to which the data are put are all of concern. Whereas researchers have an obligation to contribute to knowledge, they have an equally binding obligation to protect the welfare of their research subjects.

This chapter has reviewed ten types of questionable practices that may be encountered in social research. For each of these the concerns were raised, several examples were presented, and the issue was discussed.

Sometimes ethically questionable practices can be avoided or minimized by the use of alternative research procedures. However, they often cannot, and in this case, social scientists face a conflict between two values. The potential contributions of the proposed research must be weighed against the costs to participants who were exposed to the questionable practices. If the possible benefits are too limited to justify the costs, the research should not be done. It is suggested that investigators consult with colleagues or other types of consultants in seeking to determine the relative costs and rewards of research that involves questionable practices.

Appendix

An Introduction to Sampling

The Appendix was written by Isidor Chein.

In this appendix we have not attempted to develop a manual of sampling procedures. Nor have we attempted to review statistical formulas and procedures appropriate for the handling of data obtained in sampling studies. We have aspired, without resorting to mathematical analysis and within the limits of available space, to give the reader some basis for an intelligent appreciation of the considerations involved in sampling.[1]

SOME BASIC DEFINITIONS AND CONCEPTS

A **population** is the aggregate of *all* of the cases that conform to some designated set of specifications. Thus, by the specifications *people* and *residing in the United States*, we define a population consisting of *all* the people who reside in the United States. We may similarly define populations consisting of *all* the shop stewards in a factory, *all* the households in a particular city district, *all* the boys in a given community under 16 years of age who deliver newspapers, or *all* the case records in a file.

By certain specifications, one population may be included in another. Thus, the population consisting of all the *men* residing in the United States is included in the population consisting of all the *people* who live in the United States. In such instances, we may refer to the included population as a *subpopulation*, a *population stratum*, or simply as a **stratum** (pl. strata). A stratum may be defined by one or more specifications that divide a population into mutually exclusive segments. For instance, a given population may be subdivided into strata consisting of males under 21 years of age, females under 21 years of age, males from 21 through 59 years, and

[1] For more comprehensive discussions of sampling and appropriate statistical treatments see Cochran (1963) or Kish (1965).

so on. Similarly, we may specify a stratum of the United States population consisting of white, male, college graduates who live in New England and who have passed their seventy-fifth birthday; or we may have some reason for regarding this group of individuals as a population in its own right—that is, without reference to the fact that it is included in a larger population.

A single member of a population is referred to as a population *element*. We often want to know how certain characteristics of the elements are distributed in a population. For example, we may want to know the age distribution of the elements, or we may want to know the proportion of the elements who prefer one political candidate to another. A **census** is a count of all the elements in a population and/or a determination of the distributions of their characteristics, based on information obtained for each of the elements.

It is generally much more economical in time, effort, and money to get the desired information for only some of the elements rather than for all. When we select some of the elements with the intention of finding out something about the population from which they are taken, we refer to that group of elements as a *sample*. We hope, of course, that what we find out about the sample is true of the population as a whole. Actually, this may or may not be the case; how closely the information we receive corresponds to what we would find by a comparable census of the population depends largely on the way the sample is selected.

For example, we may want to know what proportion of a population prefers one candidate to another. We might ask 100 people from that population which candidate they prefer. The proportion of the sample preferring Mr. Jones may or may not be the same as the corresponding proportion in the population. For that matter, even the actual distribution of votes in an election may not correctly represent the distribution of preferences in the population. Unless there is a 100 percent turnout, the actual voters constitute only a sample of the population of people eligible to vote. A very high proportion of the people who prefer Mr. Smith may be overconfident with respect to their candidate's chances and neglect to come to the polls; or they may be living in a rural area and be discouraged from coming to the polls by a heavy downpour. The election results may properly determine which candidate will take office, but they will not necessarily indicate which candidate is preferred by a majority of the population.[2] Similarly, the early returns in an election

---

[2] It has been a common practice to predict the outcome of an election on the basis of a preelection sample survey which, at best, answered only the question of preferences. The results have occasionally been disastrous. The fiascos are by no means attributable simply to the failure of the samples to represent the distribution of preferences in the population at the time the polls were taken. In one instance (the United States presidential election of 1948), the preelection surveys showed that a large proportion of people were undecided, and there are clear indications that an unanticipated consolidation of opinion in this group helped to confound the predictors. As already indicated in the test, the fact that different proportions of those who prefer different candidates may actually vote complicates the translation of preference estimates into election forecasts.

There are also measurement problems involved. Preferences measured one way may or may not correspond to preferences measured another way. Thus, behavior in the voting booth does not necessarily correspond to preferences expressed to an interviewer. The former is generally accepted at face value as the more valid measure, but we have no certainty that this is the case. An 18-year-old voting for the first time may, for instance, follow his or her parents' preference rather than his or her own, at the last

may be taken as a sample of the population of returns; and, as everyone knows, they can be thoroughly deceptive.

In the case of elections and in the case of early returns in a national election, there probably is not much we can do to guarantee that the samples will correctly represent their populations. We usually accept on faith that the outcome of an election does reflect the popular will. And if we are misled by the early returns with respect to the final outcome, then, at least, our errors are soon corrected. There are, however, situations in which we can to some extent control the properties of the sample. In these situations, the way we go about drawing the sample can, if not guarantee, then at least increase the likelihood that the sample returns will not be too far from the true population figures for our purposes. We can never guarantee that the sample returns do reflect the population with respect to the characteristics we are studying unless we have simultaneously conducted a complete comparable census. We can, however, devise sampling plans which, if properly executed, can guarantee that, if we were to repeat a study on a number of different samples selected from a given population, our findings would not differ from the true population figures by more than a specified amount in more than a specified proportion of the samples.

For instance, suppose that we frequently want to know what percentage of the population agrees with certain statements. On each of these occasions we might put such a statement to a sample, compute the percentage who agree, and take this result as an estimate of the proportion of the population who agree. We can devise a number of sampling plans that will carry the insurance that our estimates will not differ from the corresponding true population figures by, say, more than 5 percent on more than, say, 10 percent of these occasions; the estimates will be correct within 5 percentage points (the **margin of error** or *limit of accuracy*) 90 percent of the time (the probability or confidence level). We can similarly devise a number of sampling plans that will produce correct results within 2 percentage points 99 percent of the time; or within any other limits of accuracy and any assigned probability. In practice, of course, we do not repeat the same study on an indefinite number of samples drawn from the same population. But our knowledge of what would happen in repeated studies enables us to say that, with a given sample, there is, say, a 90 percent probability that our figures are within 5 percentage points of those that would be

---

moment, and it is possible that there may be enough of such instances to affect materially the outcome of an election. Similarly, other kinds of subjectively felt pressures or momentary impulses may take effect in the election booth. Practical politicians seem to feel that the position of their candidate's name on the ballot affects his or her chances, as do the names of other candidates running for other offices on the same ticket; such effects may have a bearing on voting behavior without affecting preferences.

Further complications arise from the gerrymandering of election districts and other factors (for example, the electoral college system), which have the effect of giving different voters different weights in determining the outcome of an election. Perhaps the moral of this footnote will be clear: The usefulness of findings obtained from a sample may depend in large measure on factors that are extraneous to the sampling issues per se. Nor is it easy to draw a hard and fast dividing line between the factors that are extraneous and those that are not. Thus, what is extraneous to the sampling of one population (for example, eligible voters) may be intrinsic to the sampling of another (for example, actual voters); the ambiguity arises when we sample one population with the intention of learning something about the other.

shown by a census of the total population using the same measures. Having set our level of aspiration for accuracy and confidence in the findings, we would select from the available alternatives the sampling plan that could be most economically carried through. Needless to say, the higher the level of aspiration, other conditions being equal, the higher the cost of the operation.

A sampling plan that carries such insurance may be referred to as a *representative sampling plan.* Note that in this usage the word *representative* does not qualify *sample,* but *sampling plan.* What a representative sampling plan can do is to ensure that the odds are great enough that the selected sample is, for the purposes at hand, sufficiently representative of the population to justify our running the risk of taking it as representative.

The use of such a sampling plan is not the only kind of insurance that can be taken out to decrease the likelihood of misleading sample findings. Another involves taking steps to guarantee the inclusion in the sample of diverse elements of the population and to make sure (either by controlling the proportions of the various types of elements or by analytical procedures in the handling of data) that these diverse elements are taken account of in the proportions in which they occur in the population. We shall consider this type of insurance at greater length in our discussion of quota sampling and of stratified random sampling.

It should perhaps be emphasized that the dependability[3] of survey findings is affected not only by the sampling plan and the faithfulness with which it is carried out, but also by the measurement procedures used. This is one reason why sample surveys of a large population can, in practice, produce more dependable results on some matters than can a census. There simply are not enough highly skilled interviewers available to get anything beyond the most superficial information in a national census; a survey on a smaller scale puts less of a drain on the available supply of interviewers and also more readily permits a relatively intensive training program. Similarly, a smaller-scale survey may make it economically feasible to spend more time with each respondent and, hence, make it possible to use measurement devices that could not be seriously considered (except on a sampling basis[4]) in connection with a census of a large population.[5]

---

[3] Throughout this appendix, the terms *accuracy, dependability,* and *precision* are used interchangeably. Although technical distinctions are sometimes made among these words, in most discussions of sampling they are used as synonyms.

[4] It is not uncommon nowadays to collect certain items of information on a sampling basis in the course of conducting a census for other items of information.

[5] There is another reason why sampling surveys may produce more dependable information than censuses. In practice, no census ever reaches all the population elements; in effect, what is supposed to be a census is actually a sample, albeit a sample that includes a very high proportion of the population elements. If the unreached elements differ markedly from those that are reached, the result may be quite different from the true population value even though the unreached elements may be a relatively small proportion of the population. Not all of those unreached are inaccessible; they vary along a continuum of accessibility, depending on the amount one is prepared to invest in trying to reach them. In a relatively small-scale survey, one may be able to afford a greater investment in trying to reach the comparatively inaccessible elements. During a census one may also pursue the known unreached on a sampling basis (for example, by having interviewers return one or more times to dwellings where no

The basic distinction in modern sampling theory is between *probability* and *nonprobability* sampling. The essential characteristic of probability sampling is that one can specify for each element of the population the probability that it will be included in the sample. In the simplest case, each of the elements has the same probability of being included, but this is not a necessary condition. What is necessary is that for each element there must be some specifiable probability that it will be included. This point will be considered more fully in connection with the discussions of simple random samples and stratified random samples. In nonprobability sampling, there is no way of estimating the probability that each element has of being included in the sample, and no assurance that every element has *some* chance of being included.[6]

Probability sampling is the only approach that makes possible representative sampling plans. It makes it possible for the investigators to estimate the extent to which the findings based on their sample are likely to differ from what they would have found by studying the population. Conversely, if they use probability sampling, they can specify the size of the sample (or the sizes of various components of complex samples) that they will need if they want to have a given degree of certainty that their sample findings do not differ by more than a specified amount from those that a study of the total population would yield.

The major advantages of nonprobability sampling are convenience and economy — advantages that may outweigh the risks involved in not using probability sampling. Precise comparisons of the relative costs of the two approaches to sampling are, however, not available (see Stephan and McCarthy, 1958). Moreover, the comparative costs will vary depending on the number of surveys that are contemplated. Thus, if a number of surveys of the same population are to be carried out, the cost of preparing and maintaining lists from which to sample (generally a necessary step in probability sampling) can be distributed over all of them.

Major forms of nonprobability samples are accidental samples, quota samples, and purposive samples. Major forms of probability samples are simple random samples, stratified random samples, and various types of cluster samples.[7]

---

one is at home on the first visit or by sending more highly skilled interviewers to talk with respondents who have refused to give the desired information), but there is also an issue of the relative proportion of unknown unreached in the two procedures, and this depends on what one can afford to invest in exploring the terrain (for example, discovering dwelling units in unsuspected places).

[6] If there is a class of elements that have no chance of being included, this implies a restriction on the definition of the population. If the nature of this class of elements is unknown, then the precise nature of the population is also unknown. If there is no assurance that every element has some chance of being included, this uncertainty implies that there can be no assurance as to the precise nature of the population that is being sampled.

[7] The reader should be warned that *accidental sampling* and *random sampling* are technical terms, as defined in the text. The words *accidental* and *random* may have quite different connotations in ordinary everyday usage. These meanings should not be confused with those assumed in the technical usage. Thus, it may be no "accident" (everyday usage) that a sampler picks the cases he or she does in an "accidental sample" (technical usage). In everyday usage a "random sample" may not connote any nonpurposive sample or what is technically defined as an accidental sample. The justification of the technical usage would take us too far afield and will not be attempted here.

NONPROBABILITY SAMPLING

Accidental Samples

In accidental sampling, one simply reaches out and takes the cases that are at hand, continuing the process until the sample reaches a designated size. Thus, one may take the first hundred people one meets on the street who are willing to be interviewed. Or a college professor, wanting to make some generalization about college students, studies the students in his or her classes. Or a television station, wanting to know how "the people" feel about a given issue, interviews conveniently available shoppers, store clerks, barbers, and others who are presumed to reflect public opinion. There is no known way (other than by doing a parallel study with a probability sample or with a complete census) of evaluating the biases[8] introduced in such samples. If one uses an accidental sample, one can only hope that one is not being too grossly misled.

Quota Samples

Quota sampling (sometimes misleadingly referred to as "representative" sampling) adds insurance of the second type referred to earlier — provisions to guarantee the inclusion in the sample of diverse elements of the population and to make sure that these diverse elements are taken account of in the proportions in which they occur in the population. Consider an extreme case: Suppose that we are sampling from a population with equal numbers of males and females and that there is a sharp difference between the two sexes in the characteristic we wish to measure. If we did not interview any females, the results of the survey would almost certainly be an extremely misleading picture of the total population. In actuality, females and minority-group members are frequently underrepresented in accidental samples. In anticipation of such possible differences among subgroups, the quota sampler seeks to guarantee the inclusion in the sample of enough cases from each stratum.

As commonly described, the basic goal of quota sampling is the selection of a sample that is a replica of the population to which one wants to generalize — hence the notion that it "represents" that population. If it is known that the population has equal numbers of males and females, the interviewers are instructed to interview equal numbers of males and females. If it is known that 10 percent of the population lies within a particular age range, assignments are given to the interviewers to assure that 10 percent of the sample will fall within that age range.

The question of the kinds of characteristics that must be taken into account will be considered in more detail in the course of our discussion of stratified random sampling. It is enough, for the moment, to say that in the sampling of preferences, opinions, and attitudes, experience indicates that it is wise to take into account such bases of stratification as age, sex, education, geographical region of residence, socio-

---

[8] *Bias* refers to the difference between the *average of the estimates* of a population value that would be obtained from a very large number of samples selected by a given procedure and the *actual* population value, assuming identical measurement processes.

economic status, and ethnic background. Not all these are equally visible; the usual practice is to *set* the quotas for the interviewers in regard to the more manifest traits and to get information in the course of the interviews on the less manifest ones. The latter information permits correction of the inadequacies of the sample by adjustments introduced during analysis, a procedure that will be illustrated in the following paragraphs. It also calls attention to omissions, if any should occur, of important segments of the population.

It often happens, in practice, that the various components of the sample turn out not to be in the same proportions as the corresponding strata are in the population. The interviewers may not have carried out their instructions exactly; instead of interviewing equal numbers of males and females, 55 percent of the people they interviewed may have been males. Disproportions between the sample and the population are most likely to occur, of course, in the less manifest traits that have not been included as part of the specifications for the interviewers' quotas. Suppose it is known that, in a given population, 40 percent have not gone beyond grammar school; suppose, however, that only 20 percent of the people interviewed fall in this category. The inadequacy in the sample can be corrected in the analysis by weighting the different strata on the basis of their proportions in the population. This may be done by multiplying or dividing the obtained results by the appropriate figure.

Let us say that the total sample consisted of 1,000 persons, of whom 800 had attended college and 200 had not. Suppose we asked this sample whether they had seen a certain television program, and they responded as follows:

	No College	*Some College Attendance*	*Total*
Yes	20	400	420
No	180	400	580
Total	200	800	1000

In other words, one-tenth of the people without a college education and half of those with such education said they had seen the program. If we wished simply to report the figures for the educational groups separately, no adjustment would be needed. But if we wanted to estimate the proportion of the total population that had seen the program, our sample findings would be misleading. The program had been seen by 42 percent of the people in our sample. But our sample underrepresented people in the lower educational category, overrepresented those with a college education. To derive an estimate of the correct figure for the total population, we must calculate what the responses would have been if 40 percent of the people in the sample had had only high school education, 60 percent had at least attended college (the proportions we have assumed for the population). One way of doing this is to multiply the responses of the no-college group by two (to bring the 20 percent in the sample up to 40 percent), and of the college group by three-fourths (to reduce the 80 percent to 60 percent). This would give 40 yeses in the no-college group and 300 in the college group, or 340 for the total group; thus we would estimate that 34 percent of the population had seen the program, rather than the 42 percent we would have estimated if we had not weighted the strata in terms of their actual proportions in the population.

From this example it should be clear that the critical requirement in quota sampling is not that the various population strata be sampled in their correct proportions, but rather that there be enough cases from each stratum to make possible an estimate of the population stratum value, and that we know (or can estimate with reasonable accuracy) the proportion that each stratum constitutes in the total population. If these conditions are met, the estimates of the values for the various strata can be combined to give an estimate of the total population value.

However, despite these precautions in the selection of the sample and the corrections in the analysis, quota sampling remains basically similar to the earlier described accidental sampling procedure. The part of the sample in any particular class constitutes an accidental sample of the corresponding stratum of the population. The males in the sample are an accidental sample of the males in the population; the 20-to-40-year-olds in the sample constitute an accidental sample of the 20-to-40-year-olds in the population. If the instructions received by the interviewers and their execution of these instructions produce correct proportions of the compound classes (for example, white males in the 20-to-40 age range), the sample cases in these classes are still accidental samples of the corresponding compound strata in the population. The total sample is thus an accidental sample.

There is by now, however, enough experience with quota sampling to make it possible to minimize the risks of at least certain types of unfortunate accidents. It is known that interviewers, left to their own devices, are especially prone to certain pitfalls. They will interview their friends in excessive proportion. But their friends are likely to be rather similar in many respects to themselves. Now consider the possibility that, in certain matters, people who do interviewing and others like them are atypical of the population at large. If these matters are involved in the survey, the sample results are likely to be inaccurate. Once we are aware of the danger, however, we can take steps to discourage the practice.

If interviewers fill their quotas by stopping passersby and inviting them to be interviewed, they will tend to concentrate on areas where there are large numbers of potential respondents: the entertainment centers of cities, college campuses, business districts, bus and air terminals, the entrances of large department stores and factories. Such samples will overrepresent the kinds of people who tend to gravitate to these areas. A concentration on many varieties of such areas will presumably be better than a concentration on only one, but, even so, such samples will underrepresent the kind of people who seldom leave their immediate neighborhoods and especially those who seldom leave their homes. Often this will make no difference, but it is conceivable that, on some matters at some times, there may be sharp differences between the overrepresented and the underrepresented population segments. When this is the case such a sample would, of course, yield misleading results. Again, to be forewarned is to be forearmed.

If the interviewers fill their quotas by home visits, they will tend to proceed along lines of convenience and striking appearance. Thus, concentrating on certain times of the day, they will tend to miss the kinds of people who are not at home at such times (for example, working men and women during the daytime). Similarly, they will tend to avoid the upper stories of buildings without elevator service! They will tend to favor corner buildings and to avoid dilapidated buildings and buildings situated behind others. Such sampling tends to build in a systematic socioeconomic bias (that is, in each residential area, to overrepresent those people living in nicer looking homes) and possibly other biases as well.

The point to be noted about selective factors such as these is that they are not easily corrected during the analysis of the data. For many populations we know in advance the true relative proportions of the two sexes and of the various age groups and so can correct for disproportions in the sample, but what true proportion of what definable population is most likely to be found at an airport terminal during the course of a survey? The major control that investigators have available in connection with such variables is in the sampling process itself. They can try to make sure that important segments of the population are not entirely unrepresented in their sample, try to benefit from their experience and sample in such a way that many possibly relevant variables are not too grossly distorted in their sample, and hope that whatever disproportions remain will not have an undue bearing on the opinions, preferences, or whatever it is that they seek to know.

Purposive Samples

The basic assumption behind purposive sampling is that with good judgment and an appropriate strategy one can handpick the cases to be included in the sample and thus develop samples that are satisfactory in relation to one's needs. A common strategy of purposive sampling is to pick cases that are judged to be typical of the population in which one is interested, assuming that errors of judgment in the selection will tend to counterbalance each other. Experiments on purposive sampling suggest that, without an objective basis for making the judgments, this is not a dependable assumption. In any case, without an external check, there is no way of knowing that the "typical" cases continue to be typical.

Purposive samples selected in terms of assumed typicality have been used in attempts to forecast national elections. One such approach is as follows: For each state, select a number of small election districts whose election returns in previous years have approximated the overall state returns, interview all the eligible voters in these districts on their voting intentions, and hope that the selected districts are still typical of their respective states. The trouble with the method is that when there are no marked changes in the political atmosphere, one can probably do as well by forecasting the returns from previous years without doing any interviewing at all; when changes are occurring, one needs to know how the changes are affecting the selected districts in comparison with other districts.

PROBABILITY SAMPLING

Probability samples involve the first kind of insurance against misleading results that we discussed earlier—the ability to specify the chances that the sample findings do not differ by more than a certain amount from the true population values. They may also include the second kind of insurance—a guarantee that enough cases are selected from each relevant population stratum to provide an estimate for that stratum of the population.

Simple Random Samples

Simple random sampling is the basic probability sampling design; it is incorporated in all of the more complex probability sampling designs. A simple random sample is selected by a process that not only gives each element in the population an equal chance of being included in the sample, but also makes the selection of every possible combination of the desired number of cases equally likely. Suppose, for example, that one wants a simple random sample of two cases from a population of five cases. Let the five cases in the population be *A*, *B*, *C*, *D*, and *E*. There are ten possible pairs of cases in this population: *AB*, *AC*, *AD*, *AE*, *BC*, *BD*, *BE*, *CD*, *CE*, and *DE*. Write each combination on a disc, put the ten discs in a hat, mix them thoroughly, and have a blindfolded person pick one. Each of the discs has the same chance of being selected.[9] The two cases corresponding to the letters on the selected disc constitute the desired simple random sample.

There are, in the tiny illustrative population of five cases, ten possible samples of three cases: *ABC*, *ABD*, *ABE*, *ACD*, *ACE*, *ADE*, *BCD*, *BCE*, *BDE*, and *CDE*. Using the same method, one can select a simple random sample of three cases from this population.

In principle, one can use this method for selecting random samples from populations of any size, but in practice it could easily become a lifetime occupation merely to list all the combinations of the desired number of cases. The same result is obtained by selecting each case individually, using a list of random numbers such as may be found in most textbooks of statistics. These are sets of numbers that after careful examination have shown no evidence of systematic order. Before using the table of random numbers, it is first necessary to number all the elements in the population to be studied. Then the table is marked at some random starting point (for example, with a blind pencil stab at the page), and the cases whose numbers come up as one moves from this point down the column of numbers are taken into the sample until the desired number of cases is obtained. The selection of any given case places no limits on what other cases can be selected, thus making equally possible the selection of any one of the many possible combinations of cases. This pro-

---

[9] In this illustration, each of the discs (that is, each combination of two cases) has one chance in ten of being selected. Each of the individual cases also has the same chance of being selected—four in ten because each case appears on four of the discs. There are, however, very many ways of giving each case the same chance of being selected without getting a simple random sample. For example, suppose we were arbitrarily to divide an illustrative population of ten cases into five pairs as follows: *AB*, *CD*, *EF*, *GH*, *IJ*. If we write the designations for these pairs on five discs, blindly pick one of the discs, and take as our sample the two cases designated on this disc, then every case has one chance in five of being picked but, obviously, not every possible combination has the same chance of being selected as every other—in fact, most of the combinations (for example, *AC*) have no chance at all as they have not been included on the discs.

cedure is, therefore, equivalent to selecting randomly one of the many possible combinations of cases.[10]

Without going into the mathematical argument, it is possible only to illustrate the underlying principles of probability sampling. Consider, for this purpose, a hypothetical population of ten cases as follows:

Case	A	B	C	D	E	F	G	H	I	J
Sex	F	F	F	F	F	M	M	M	M	M
Age	Y	O	Y	O	Y	O	Y	O	Y	O
Score	0	1	2	3	4	5	6	7	8	9

The first five cases are females; the last five, males. The cases designated Y are younger, and the O's are older. Age and sex will be considered later, in relation to stratified sampling. The score represents some attribute of the individual, such as his or her performance on a test of mechanical aptitude.

The mean score for this population of ten cases is 4.5. Assuming that this were not known, the problem would be to make an estimate of the population mean on the basis of the scores of the elements in the sample that is drawn. According to the definition of simple random sampling, the method of selecting the sample must give

---

[10] The procedure of selecting a random sample should not be confused with the procedure of sampling from a list or a file of cases by taking every *k*th (for example, every fourteenth or every sixty-third) case. The latter procedure is called *systematic* sampling. Systematic samples may be either probability or nonprobability samples, depending on how the first case is selected. Suppose one wants to select every sixtieth case. To get a probability sample, the first case has to be selected *randomly* from the first 60, and every sixtieth case thereafter is selected. If the first case is not selected randomly, the resulting sample is not a probability sample because most of the cases have a zero probability of being included in the sample. Although to the uninitiated, systematic sampling seems to be the most natural and rational way to go about sampling from a list, it involves complications not present in a simple random sample. When the first case is drawn randomly, in a systematic sample, there is in advance no limitation on the chances of any given case to be included in the sample. If we are selecting a sample of 100 cases from a population of 6,000, before the first case is selected each case has one chance in 60 (100 in 6,000) of being included in the sample, whether we are using simple random or systematic sampling. But in a systematic sample, once the first case is selected, the chances of other cases are altered. Suppose the first case drawn is Number 46. Selecting every sixtieth case thereafter means that numbers 106, 166, 226, and so on will be drawn; the cases between these numbers now have no chance of being included.

This means that a systematic sampling plan does not give all possible combinations of cases the same chance of being included; only combinations of elements 60 cases apart in the list have any chance of being selected for the sample. The results may be quite deceptive if the cases in the list are arranged in some cyclical order. Suppose, for example, that the 6,000 cases are houses in a community that was built according to a systematic plan and that they are listed in order of streets and numbers. Corner houses would then appear at regular intervals throughout the list; say, the first house and every twentieth house thereafter is a corner dwelling. A sample consisting of cases 1, 61, 121, and so on would be made up entirely of corner houses, one consisting of cases 2, 62, 122, and so on would contain no corner houses. But corner houses are usually larger and more expensive than those within the block, and their occupants may accordingly differ systematically in certain characteristics. Thus, any sample made up entirely of corner houses or entirely lacking in corner houses would give misleading results if the study concerned characteristics in which occupants of the two types of dwellings differ.

equal probability to every combination of the desired number of cases—in other words, over the long run, with repeated sampling, every combination should come up the same number of times. We can, therefore, figure out what will happen in the long run in our illustrative population by the simple device of considering all the combinations; that is, we take every combination of the desired number of cases and compute a mean for each combination. What results is a distribution of sample means—known as a **sampling distribution.** For example, there are 45 possible combinations of two cases in our hypothetical population of ten cases. One, and only one, combination (cases *A* and *B*) will yield a sample mean of .5; there are five combinations (*A* and *J*, *B* and *I*, *C* and *H*, *D* and *G*, *E* and *F*) that will yield sample means of 4.5; and so on. Similarly, there are 210 possible samples of four cases. One

TABLE A.1   Mean Scores of Samples from Illustrative Population of Ten Cases with Population Mean Score of 4.5 (Simple Random Samples)

	Number of Samples		
Sample Means*	*Samples of 2 Cases*	*Samples of 4 Cases*	*Samples of 6 Cases*
.5	1		
1.0	1		
1.5–1.75	2	2	
2.0–2.67	5	10	2
2.75–3.25	3	25	10
3.33–4.00	8	43	52
4.17–4.83	5	50	82
5.00–5.67	8	43	52
5.75–6.25	3	25	10
6.33–7.0	5	10	2
7.25–7.5	2	2	
8.0	1		
8.5	1		
Total No. of Samples	45	210	210
Mean of Sample Means	4.5	4.5	4.5
Percent of Sample Means Greater Than 4.00 and Less Than 5.00	11	24	39
Percent of Sample Means Greater Than 2.67 and Less Than 6.33	60	89	98

*With the small number of different scores in the illustrative population, there are only a limited number of possible sample means. Thus, for samples of two cases, there is no combination that can yield a mean of 2.25; but there are three samples of four cases (*ABDF*, *ABCG*, *ACDE*) with a mean of 2.25. Similarly, a mean of 2.67 is not possible for one sample of six cases. For convenience of tabulation and in order to help bring out the characteristics of the sampling distributions, the means of the samples have been grouped.

of these combinations (*A, B, C,* and *D*) will yield a sample mean of 1.5; one (*A, B, C,* and *E*), a sample mean of 1.75; and so on.

Table A.1 shows the sampling distributions for sample means based on simple random samples of two, four, and six cases from our illustrative population.

Notice that for samples of any given size the most likely sample mean is the population mean;[11] the next most likely is figures close to the population mean; the more a sample mean deviates from the population mean, the less likely it is to occur. Also, the larger the sample, the more likely is it that its mean will be close to the population mean.

It is this kind of behavior on the part of probability samples (not only with respect to means, but also with respect to proportions and other types of statistics) that makes it possible to estimate not only the population characteristic (for example, the mean) but also the likelihood that the sample figure differs from the true population figure by a given amount.

One interesting feature of simple random sampling ought to be mentioned, even though it is hard for most people to believe it without mathematical proof. When the population is large compared to the sample size (say, more than ten times as large), the variabilities of sampling distributions are influenced much more by the absolute number of cases in the samples than by the proportion of the population that is included; that is, the magnitude of the errors that are likely depends more on the absolute size of the sample than on the proportion of the population that it includes. Thus, the estimation of popular preferences in a national preelection poll, within the limits of a given margin of error, would not require a substantially larger sample than the estimation of the preferences in any one state where the issue is in doubt. Conversely, it would take just about as large a sample to estimate the preferences in one doubtful state with a given degree of accuracy as it would to estimate the distribution of preferences in the entire nation. This is true despite the fact that a sample of a few thousand cases obviously includes a much larger proportion of the voters in one state than the same-size sample does of the voters in the nation.[12]

---

[11] This point is obscured in Table A.1, for the case of samples of two, by the grouping of means. Actually, there are five possible samples of two cases with means of 4.5; there are four possible samples with means of 4.0; and so on.

[12] For the benefit of those who may have some knowledge of analytical statistics but who may nevertheless react with startled incredulity when explicitly confronted with the principle of the indifference of sample statistics to the *sampling fraction* (that is, the proportion of the population included in a sample), it may be pointed out that the sampling fraction is not even mentioned in the relevant formulas given in most statistics textbooks. Thus, the familiar formula for the standard error of the mean is $\sigma \sqrt{N}$, where σ is the estimated standard deviation of the population and N is the number of cases in the sample. This formula is derived from the mathematics of simple random sampling and, as given, omits a term. Correctly, the formula should be multiplied by $\sqrt{(1-f)}$, where f designates the sampling fraction. Obviously, the smaller the value of f, the less difference this multiplier makes. In sampling from an infinite population, f equals zero; in sampling from a finite population, it is never quite zero, but is generally too small to have any practical consequences and may hence be disregarded. This is the principle discussed in the text. It should be remembered, however, that when a large population is being sampled, taking account of the sampling fraction may considerably reduce the estimate of the probable margin of error of the sample findings. When the population is small, one must include a large proportion in the sample in order to achieve a small margin of error.

Stratified Random Samples[13]

In stratified random sampling, as in quota sampling, the population is first divided into two or more strata. Again, the strata may be based on a single criterion (for example, sex, yielding the two strata of male and female) or on a combination of two or more criteria (for example, age and sex, yielding strata such as males under 21, males 21 and over, females under 21, females 21 and over). In stratified random sampling, a simple random sample is taken from each stratum, and the subsamples are then joined to form the total sample.

To illustrate how stratified random sampling works, we may return to the previously described population of ten cases. Consider samples of four with equal proportions of males and females (that is, samples made up by combining subsamples of two males with subsamples of two females). To satisfy this last condition, many samples of four that were possible under the conditions of simple random sampling are no longer possible — for example, samples consisting of cases A, B, C, D or of cases A, B, C, F or of cases D, F, G, I — because they do not have two males and two females. In fact, there are now exactly 100 possible samples as compared to the 210 previously possible. As before, we have computed the mean score for each of the possible samples and thereby obtained the sampling distribution of the mean. Table A.2 compares the sampling distributions for samples of four obtained on the basis of simple random sampling, stratified sampling using sex as a criterion for stratification, and stratified sampling using age as a criterion.

It will be noted that there is a marked improvement over simple random sampling when the sampling is based on a stratification of our hypothetical population by sex; with this kind of stratification we get a marked increase in the number of samples that give means very close to the population mean and a marked reduction in the number of sample means that deviate widely from the population mean. When the population is stratified by age, however, there is no such marked improvement in the efficiency of sampling; in fact, the means of individual samples are somewhat less likely to be very close to the population mean.

In general, stratification contributes to the efficiency of sampling if it succeeds in establishing classes that are internally comparatively homogeneous with respect to the characteristics being studied — that is, if the differences between classes (for example, between males and females) are large in comparison with the variation within classes (for example, among the males and among the females). In our illustrative population, the difference in scores between the sex groups is relatively large, that between age groups relatively small; that is why stratification by sex is effective in this case and stratification by age ineffective. The general principle is that, if one has reason to believe that stratifying according to a particular criterion or set of criteria will result in internally homogeneous strata, then it is desirable to stratify. If the process of breaking the population down into strata that are likely to differ sharply from one another is costly, then one has to balance this cost against the cost of a comparable gain in precision obtained by taking a larger simple random sample.

---

[13] For reasons of simplicity of presentation, some points already made in the discussion of quota sampling will be repeated here.

TABLE A.2   Mean Scores of Samples of Four Cases from Illustrative Population of Ten Cases with Population Mean Score of 4.5 (Simple and Stratified Random Samples)

	Number of Samples		
*Sample Means**	*Simple Random Samples*	*Samples Stratified by Sex*	*Samples Stratified by Age*
1.50–1.75	2		1
2.00–2.50	10		7
2.75–3.25	25	3	8
3.50–4.00	43	25	26
4.25–4.75	50	44	16
5.00–5.50	43	25	26
5.75–6.25	25	3	8
6.50–7.00	10		7
7.25–7.50	2		1
Total No. of Samples	210	100	100
Mean of Sample Means	4.5	4.5	4.5
Percent of Sample Means Greater Than 4.00 and Less Than 5.00	24	44	16
Percent of Sample Means Greater Than 2.50 and Less Than 6.50	89	100	84

*Again, the means of the samples have been grouped. See note to Table A.1.

The issues involved in the decision whether to stratify have, basically, nothing to do with trying to make the sample a replica of the population; they only have to do with the anticipated homogeneity of the defined strata with respect to the characteristics being studied and the comparative costs of different methods of achieving precision. Both simple and stratified random sampling involve representative sampling plans.

Except for a slight saving in arithmetic, there is no reason for sampling from the different strata in the same proportion; that is, even with respect to the criteria selected for stratification, it is not necessary that the sample reflect the composition of the population. Thus, in sampling from a population in which the number of males equals the number of females, it is permissible (and may sometimes be desirable) to sample nine, or five, or two, or some other number of females to every male. When this is done, however, it is necessary to make an adjustment in order to find the mean score (or the proportion of elements with a given characteristic, or whatever measure is desired) for the sample that will be the best estimate of the mean score of the total population of males and females. This is accomplished by "weighting" the figure for each stratum in such a way that it contributes to the score for the total sample in proportion to its size in the population, as in the quota sampling illustration previously mentioned. When the various strata are sampled in constant proportion, one is spared this bit of arithmetic since the various strata are already properly weighted.

There may be several reasons for sampling the various strata in different proportions. Sometimes it is necessary to increase the proportion sampled from classes having small numbers of cases in order to guarantee that these classes are sampled at all. For example, if we were planning a survey of retail sales volume in a given city in a given month, simple random sampling of retail stores might not lead to an accurate estimate of the total volume of sales because a few very large department stores account for an extremely large proportion of the total sales, and there is no guarantee that any of these large stores would turn up in a simple random sample. In this case, we would stratify the population of stores in terms of some measure of their total volume of sales (for example, the gross value of sales during the preceding year). Perhaps only the three largest department stores would be in the topmost stratum. We would include all three of them in our sample; in other words, we would take a 100 percent sample of this stratum.[14] Any other procedure in such a situation would greatly reduce the accuracy of the estimate, no matter how carefully samples were taken from other strata. Again, of course, figures from the various strata would have to be appropriately weighted in estimating the total volume of sales in the city.

Another reason for taking a larger proportion of cases from one stratum than from others is that we may want to subdivide the cases within each stratum for further analysis. Let us say that in our survey of retail sales we want to be able to examine separately the volume of sales made by food stores, by clothing stores, and by other types. Even though these classifications are not taken into account in selecting the sample (that is, the sample is not stratified on this basis), it is clear that we need a reasonable number of cases in each volume-of-sales stratum to make possible an analysis of different types of stores within each stratum. If a given stratum has relatively few cases, so that sampling in the proportion used in other strata would not provide enough cases to serve as an adequate basis for this further analysis, we may take a higher proportion of cases in this stratum.

One of the major reasons for varying the sampling proportions for different strata cannot be fully explained without going into the mathematical theory of sampling, but the principle involved can be understood on a more or less intuitive basis. Consider two strata, one of which is much more homogeneous with respect to the characteristics being studied than the other. For a given degree of precision, it will take a smaller number of cases to determine the state of affairs in the first stratum than in the second. To take an extreme example: suppose that there is reason to know that every case in a given stratum has the same score; we could then determine how to represent that stratum in the total sample on the basis of a sample of one case. Of course, in such an extreme case we are not likely to have this information without also knowing what the common score is. But in less extreme cases

---

[14] Note that in such a procedure, the cases in the total population do not all have the same chance of being included in the sample. Each of the three largest stores has a 100 percent chance of being included, whereas each of the stores in another stratum may have only one chance in ten. But the probability of inclusion of each case can be specified, thus meeting the basic requirement for probability sampling.

we can often anticipate the relative degrees of homogeneity or heterogeneity of strata before carrying out the survey. For example, if with respect to certain types of opinion questions, men differ among themselves much more than women, we would accordingly plan our sample to include a larger proportion of men. If it is the case that women may be expected to be more alike than men in these matters, they do not have to be sampled as thoroughly as do the men for a given degree of precision.

In general terms, we can expect the greatest precision if the various strata are sampled proportionately to their relative variabilities with respect to the characteristics under study rather than proportionately to their relative sizes in the population. A special case of this principle is that, in sampling to determine the proportion of cases possessing a particular attribute, strata in which we can anticipate that about half the cases will have the attribute and half will not should be sampled more thoroughly than strata in which we would expect a more uneven division. Thus, in planning a stratified sample for predicting a national election, using states as strata, we should not plan to sample each state in proportion to its eligible population; it would be wiser to sample most heavily in the most doubtful states.

One final point about stratified sampling: There may be reason to believe that certain criteria will provide very effective bases for stratification (that is, using these criteria, we would get strata that differ markedly from one another), but, as pointed out in the discussion of quota sampling, the relevant data may become available only in the course of the survey. In this case we cannot use the criteria in the sampling design, but we can apply the logic of stratified sampling theory in the analysis of the data. Thus, we can take a simple random sample, ascertain the information necessary for stratification during the course of the interviews, and use this information in grouping the cases according to their respective strata and weighting them appropriately in the analysis of the data.

For example, suppose that we want to survey the attitudes of the students in a certain school toward some issue and that we have some reason to believe that the proportions of for, against, and undecided are likely to be different among the black and the white students. Suppose, further, that we have a complete listing of the student body but no identification of the race of the individual students, even though we know that 30 percent of the students are black and 70 percent are white. We could draw a simple random sample of the students and ascertain the race of each respondent while recording his or her views on the issue. The data might then come out as follows:

	Number in the School	*Number That Turn Up in the Sample*	*Number in the Sample Who Are*		
			For	*Against*	*Undecided*
Blacks	300	40	30	8	2
Whites	700	160	50	40	70
Total Number	1000	200	80	48	72
Percentage of Sample			40	24	36

Projecting from the sample to the total numbers in the two racial groups, we would get the following results:

	For	*Against*	*Undecided*
	Estimated Number Who Are		
Blacks	225	60	15
Whites	219	175	306
Total Number	444	235	321
Estimated Percentage of Total Student Body	44.4	23.5	32.1

These figures are easily arrived at. Thus, three-fourths of the black sample are for some issue and three-fourths of 300 is 225. In this case, the corrected percentages are not dramatically different from the total-sample percentages, despite marked differences between the black and white groups. This results from the facts that the disproportion between the sampling fractions in the two groups is not very great (13 percent of the blacks are included in the sample as compared to 23 percent of the whites) and that the black group constitutes a relatively small porportion of this population. Despite the relatively small differences in the results of the two procedures (that is, the uncorrected and corrected percentage estimates) in this example, the assured precision is greater with the second.

From the viewpoint of the theory of probability sampling, it is essentially irrelevant whether the stratification is introduced in the sampling procedure or in the analysis of the data, except insofar as the former makes it possible to control the size of the sample obtained from each stratum and thus to increase the efficiency of the sampling design. It can be shown that any stratum of a simple random sample of a population is itself a simple random sample of the corresponding population stratum. Thus, not only is our total sample of the student body a simple random sample of the total population, but the 40 blacks in the sample are a simple random sample of all the blacks in the school, and the 160 whites are a simple random sample of the white students. In other words, our procedure of drawing a *simple* random sample and then dividing it into strata is equivalent to having drawn a *stratified* random sample using, as the sampling fraction within each stratum, the proportion of that stratum that turned up in our simple random sample. Thus, even though we are not in a position to stratify in advance, we can take advantage of the increased efficiency of stratified sampling.

Cluster Sampling

Except when dealing with small and spatially concentrated populations, there are enormous expenses associated with simple and stratified random sampling — for example, in the preparation of classified lists on population elements and in sending interviewers to scattered localities. The more widely scattered the interviews, the greater are the travel expenses, the greater is the proportion of nonproductive time spent in traveling, and the more complicated — and hence expensive — are the tasks of supervising the field staff. There are also other factors that often make it difficult or impossible to satisfy the conditions of random sampling. For example, it may be easier to get permission to administer a questionnaire to three or four classes in a school than to administer the same questionnaire to a much smaller sample selected on a simple or stratified random basis; the latter may disrupt the school routines much more. For such reasons, large-scale survey studies seldom make use of simple or stratified random samples; instead they make use of the methods of cluster sampling.

In cluster sampling, one arrives at the ultimate set of elements to be included in the sample by first sampling in terms of larger groupings *(clusters)*. The clusters are selected by simple or stratified methods; and, if not all the elements in these clusters are to be included in the sample, the ultimate selection from within the clusters is also carried out on a simple or stratified random-sampling basis.

Suppose, for example, that we want to do a survey of seventh-grade public school children in some state. We may proceed as follows: prepare a list of school districts, classified perhaps by size of community, and select a simple or stratified random sample. For each of the school districts included in the sample, list the schools and take a simple or stratified random sample of them. If some or all of the schools thus selected for the sample have more seventh-grade classes than can be studied, we may take a sample of these classes in each of the schools. The survey instruments may then be administered to all the children in these classes or, if it is desirable and administratively feasible to do so, to a sample of the children.

Similarly, a survey of urban households may take a sample of cities; within each city that is selected, a sample of districts; within each selected district, a sample of households.

Characteristically, the procedure moves through a series of stages — hence the common term, **multistage sampling** — from more inclusive to less inclusive sampling units until we finally arrive at the population elements that constitute the desired sample.

Notice that with this kind of sampling procedure it is no longer true that every combination of the desired number of elements in the population (or in a given stratum) is equally likely to be selected as the sample of the population (or stratum). Hence, the kinds of effects we noticed in our analysis of simple and stratified random sampling of our hypothetical population of ten cases (the population value being the most probable sample result and larger deviations from the population value being less probable than smaller ones) cannot develop in quite the same way. Such effects do, however, occur in a more complicated way,[15] provided that each stage of cluster

---

[15] The complication arises from the fact that there are two sources of sampling error: the sampling of the larger sampling units and the sampling of population elements within the larger units. To illustrate the point that cluster sampling does have the same kinds of effects as simple and stratified random sampling, let us consider the simple case in which the second source of error is eliminated by studying all the population elements in the sampled larger units. Each larger unit has its score (consisting, say, of the mean score of its elements). But this leaves us with simple or stratified random sample of the population of larger units — no different, in principle, from a simple or stratified sample of population elements. Hence, it is clear that the trends we noted in connection with random samples will tend to occur on this level. Now, if instead of taking 100 percent samples of the elements in each larger unit, we were to take a simple or stratified random sample of the elements in each unit, the larger units become the populations from which these samples are drawn — and the tendencies we noted will again occur.

sampling is carried out on a probability sampling basis. One pays a price, however, in terms of sampling efficiency. On a per-case basis, effective cluster sampling is much less efficient in obtaining information than comparably effective stratified random sampling — that is, for a given number of cases, the probable margin of error is much larger in the former case than in the latter.[16] Moreover, the correct statistical handling of the data is apt to be more complicated. These handicaps are, however, more than balanced by the associated economies, which generally permit the sampling of a sufficiently larger number of cases at a smaller cost. The comparison of cluster sampling with simple random sampling is somewhat more complicated. Stratified sampling principles may be used to select the clusters, and what is lost in efficiency because of the clustering effects may be regained by this stratification. Depending on the specific features of the sampling plan in relation to the object of the survey, cluster sampling may be more or less efficient on a per-case basis than simple random sampling. But again, even if more cases are needed for the same level of accuracy, the associated economies generally favor cluster sampling in large-scale surveys.

COMBINATIONS OF PROBABILITY AND NONPROBABILITY SAMPLING

If sampling is carried out in a series of stages, it is, of course, possible to combine probability and nonprobability sampling in one design; that is, one or more of the stages can be carried out according to probability sampling principles and the balance by nonprobability principles. We shall consider two examples.

The investigators may select clusters by probability cluster sampling techniques, but, at the final stage, select the elements as a quota sample. Thus, it is possible to select a probability sample of counties in a state; within each of these counties, a probability sample of neighborhoods; and within each of the selected neighborhoods, a quota sample controlled for, say, age and sex.

The advantage of such a design is that the major economies of quota sampling occur in obtaining the particular cases for the sample. It is relatively inexpensive to select the areas within which the final stage of sampling will take place by probability sampling, and we thereby gain the advantages of probability sampling, at least for the areas. There is some evidence, for instance, that quota samples built up in selected areas are more successful in controlling for such variables as socioeconomic status than quota samples in which the control of these variables depends on the judgments of the interviewers (Kish, 1965).

It may be remarked, in passing, that quota samples are, in practice, nonprobability cluster samples. Our earlier description of quota sampling may have made it appear to be the nonprobability analogue of stratified random sampling; that is, it may have seemed that specified proportions of cases with given characteristics were

---

[16] Thus, these tendencies toward the greatest probability of achieving a sampling result that is the same as the population value and toward progressively larger deviations becoming progressively less probable will occur with respect to both sources of error that are involved in cluster sampling.

selected from the total population. But in practice there are always restrictions on the geographical areas within which the sampling takes place. Hence, the traditional national quota sample has typically involved a nonprobability sample of areas as well as a nonprobability sample of elements within these areas. By using probability sampling to select the areas, however, one can gain an extra measure of security at relatively little cost.

The second example of combining probability and nonprobability sampling involves the opposite strategy. The investigator takes a probability sample of elements within a nonprobability sample of areas. The areas are selected as a purposive sample. For example, a number of counties may be selected on the grounds that they have, for years, tended to produce election results typical of their respective states; within each of the "typical" counties, the investigator selects a probability sample of eligible voters.

One way of looking at this kind of design is to regard the typical counties as defining a population. If a probability sample of this population is taken, the mathematical theory of probability sampling is completely applicable, and one can state the probable limits of error in the relation of the sample results to the true population values. One can then generalize the inferences regarding this restricted population to the national population, subject to the assumption that the typical counties are still typical of their respective states. So long as this assumption is valid, it seems likely that such a sampling plan will produce the most dependable sampling results at the least cost; but then, of course, with each application of this sampling design, we must hope that the assumption is in fact valid. The results of such a sampling plan can, however, always be stated in a form that makes it clear where the possibilities of error lie. Thus, a conclusion might read: There is a 19 to 1 likelihood that from 60 to 74 percent of the eligible voters in these typical counties prefer candidate A. If nothing has happened to make these counties atypical in this election, these results may be taken as reflecting the national distribution of preferences. If the actual distribution of votes follows the distribution of preferences at the time of the survey, it seems likely that candidate A will be elected. The election postmortem can establish how well the vote was predicted in the typical counties and whether they were indeed still typical.

SPECIAL APPLICATIONS OF NONPROBABILITY SAMPLING

It has already been noted that the major advantages of nonprobability sampling are convenience and economy. It is likely, therefore, that many future sampling operations will be conducted according to nonprobability principles as long as researchers are convinced that these sampling procedures work reasonably well despite the fact that they do not provide any basis for estimating how far the sample results are likely to deviate from the true population figures. Investigators, in other words, will continue to use nonprobability methods and to justify their use on the ground of practical experience, even while conceding the superiority in principle of probability sampling. Moreover, many practical samplers will argue that, in many cases at least, this superiority exists only on paper. They will point out that there is a difference between the sampling plan and its actual execution; there can be many a slip in the carrying out of the plan that would nullify its theoretical advantages. Interviewers, for instance, may fail to follow their instructions in selecting respondents, or they may omit some of the questions in interviewing some of the respondents (and, thereby, produce samples of somewhat different and not strictly comparable populations in relation to the various questions in the same interview schedule); some of the selected cases may refuse to be interviewed or not be available; compromises may be made by allowing interviewers to substitute other respondents when those designated for the sample are not found at home;[17] and so on. The sample actually obtained may, hence, not be the probability sample it was planned to be.

Moreover, there are circumstances in which probability sampling is unnecessary or inappropriate. One such circumstance arises from the fact that one does not necessarily carry out studies of samples only for the purpose of being able to generalize to the populations that are being sampled. If one uses samples for other reasons, ability to evaluate the likelihood of deviations from the population values is irrelevant. For example, if the goal is to obtain ideas, good insights, and experienced critical appraisals, one selects a purposive sample with this in mind. The situation is analogous to one in which a number of expert consultants are called in on a difficult medical case. These consultants—also a purposive sample—are not called in to get an average opinion that would correspond to the average opinion of the entire medical profession. They are called in precisely because of their special experience and competence. Or the situation may be viewed as analogous to our more or less haphazard sampling of foods from a famous cuisine. We are sampling, not to estimate some population value, but to get some idea of the variety of elements available in this population.

---

[17] It is sometimes claimed that one advantage of quota over probability sampling is that the former avoids the problem of refusals or unavailability. This is not correct. To be sure, the procedures of quota sampling may—and commonly do—bypass the problem by ignoring such cases and allowing the interviewers to make substitutions. Ignoring a problem is not equivalent, however, to solving it. The existence of cases that one cannot interview implies a restriction on the sampled population. Probability samplers generally acknowledge the restriction; quota samplers generally say nothing about it.

In probability sampling, when the restriction is accepted, the sound practice is either not to replace the dropouts at all or to replace them by selecting new cases by the same procedures that were used in selecting the original sample rather than by, say, using the nearest neighbor who is at home instead of the original case who is not at home. When the sound practice is followed, the resulting sample is a probability sample of the restricted population. This follows from the mathematically provable principle to which we have already referred: any segment of a probability sample is itself a probability sample of the corresponding segment of the population. If the restriction is not accepted, the sound practice is, of course, to make intensive efforts to recover the dropouts.

Another expedient involves the use of data acquired in the course of the survey to transcend the restriction (see Politz and Simmons, 1949 and Simmons, 1954). Briefly, the logic of the Politz and Simmons procedure may be described as follows: Dropouts resulting from the failure to find the selected respondent at home are consequential only if the probability of being at home has some bearing on the subject matter of the survey. Let us then find out from those who are at home what the probability would have been of the interviewers finding them at home if he or she had called at the same time of day during, say, the preceding five days. We can then relate this probability to the responses to the survey questions and correct the survey findings on the basis of this information.

Another example of sampling for ideas rather than for the estimation of population values is provided by the field of market research known as motivation research. The typical problem of motivation research is to find out something about motives, attitudes, and associations that are evoked by certain products, brand names, and package designs, but that may not be obvious even to the respondents themselves. The results of such studies are turned over to advertising agencies, which make use of them in developing advertising campaigns. Characteristically, the motivation researchers are quite happy with accidental samples or with purposive samples selected in such a way as to maximize the likelihood of differences among the elements in the sample. They are looking for ideas to transmit to the advertising people, not for correct estimates of population distributions. One might argue that they would be better off if they could establish, not merely the variety of motives that are likely to become associated with certain products, but also the precise distributions of these motives. At present, however, it seems to be problematical whether the additional information would be worth the extra cost of getting it. At any rate, so long as these researchers deceive neither themselves nor their clients into believing that they are getting the second kind of information, no one can take exception to their application of accidental sampling.

Sometimes there is no alternative to nonprobability sampling. If one is trying to find out something, for example, about the attitudes of people in the People's Republic of China, one has no realistic choice but to rely on informants who have recently spent some time there (each of whom reports on the accidental sample involved in his or her contacts) and on immigrants, who are themselves far from typical. The choice here is between data that do not permit a statistical assessment of the likelihood of error and no data at all. Similarly, if one is trying to reconstruct a picture of a dying or recently deceased culture, one has no choice except to rely on relatively articulate informants for certain types of information. This does not mean that one is not concerned with the possibility of error, but one places one's reliance on the internal consistency of the data and its coherence with other things that one knows.

Another special case justifying the use of nonprobability samples arises from the fact that there are many important considerations in research in addition to the sampling design. It may be necessary to balance one consideration against another — for example, a better sampling design against a more sensitive method of data collection. Ackerman and Jahoda (1950), for example, studied the characteristics of patients in psychoanalytic treatment who had given expression to anti-Semitic sentiments. With complete protection of the anonymity of the patients, some 40 analysts served as informants. The sample of psychoanalysts was, of necessity, an accidental one and, consequently, so was the sample of patients. Supposing that the investigators could have solved the problem of obtaining a probability sample of all psychoanalytic patients in a given area, should they have done so? Assume that this would have required giving up the psychoanalysts as informants and substituting a relatively superficial direct interview.

Similarly, in a study of factors related to the use of narcotics by boys in juvenile street gangs, Chein (1956) used group workers as informants (also with complete protection of the anonymity of the individual gang member). These workers had spent months winning the confidence of the boys, convincing the latter that they were not confederates of the police, social reformers, or other things reprehensible in the eyes of the boys; and they had been working closely with the gangs for many more months — in some instances, for several years. As these informants were available only for the gangs that were being worked with, the sample of gangs — and hence of gang members — was an accidental sample. Assuming that (1) it would have been possible to get a probability sample of gang members and that (2) the information obtained through the group workers was much more dependable than would have been information obtained through direct interview, what should the investigators have done?

The answer to such a question is not easy. The first thing to do, of course, is to assure oneself that the dilemma is real. If convinced that it is, one must then decide whether the problem is, under the circumstances, worthy of investigation at all. If the answer is still in the affirmative, one must decide, in terms of the research purpose, whether it would be better to gather more adequate information based on a not very sound sample or less adequate information based on a sounder sample.

We come, finally, to another special and controversial case of nonprobability sampling. Many studies in behavioral science are carried out on accidental samples of subjects. The data are treated, however, in a manner that is appropriate only to probability samples. For example, statistical tests of significance that presuppose random sampling are applied to the data.

One claimed justification of this practice is completely spurious. The investigators argue that they are interested not in estimating population values, but in studying relationships among variables. For example, the question, "what are the effects of variations in routines of memorizing on the retention of the memorized materials?" does not seem to have reference to any population. Relationships, however, are subject to sampling error just as averages and proportions are. If a great many samples are taken from a given population, certain relationships may appear among some of the variables in some of the samples and may not appear or may appear in different degree in others. Hence the results for a given sample may be quite misleading. If the samples are probability samples, we may legitimately estimate the probability of being in error by more than a specified amount; if they are not, we cannot legitimately make such estimates. Moreover, the answer to the question may be quite different for different populations of subjects (for example, subjects differing in educational experience), for different populations of materials to be memorized (for example, nonsense syllables versus meaningful poems), and for different populations of associated conditions (for example, presence or absence of distracting activities). Relationships never exist in a population vacuum.

A second justification of the practice is more subtle. The investigators, in effect, argue that they are not concerned with estimating true population values (of means, proportions, differences under different experimental conditions, correlation coefficients, and so on) for any *particular* population, the characteristics of which are specified in advance. They may, therefore, postulate hypothetical populations of which the study samples are, to all intents and purposes, probability samples. For example, suppose that we wanted to study the effects of variations in routines of memorizing (under conditions of no distraction and with valued prizes offered for speed of memorizing) on the retention of poetry. We have available an accidental sample of the population of college sophomores and use this sample for our study. Now we postulate that the population elements in our sample are also elements of another population in which ease of access to the elements is uncorrelated with the relationships under study. Under this condition, our sample may be regarded as a quasi-probability sample of this hypothetical population.[18] When we apply statistical tests of significance to the findings of the study, we are, in effect, generalizing to this hypothetical population rather than to the population of college sophomores.

An implication of this line of reasoning should be spelled out. The relationships we have found by such a procedure (and let us assume, for the sake of argument, that they are very striking) hold for we know not whom. The defining properties of the hypothetical population are completely unspecified. One obvious characteristic is that the cases are readily available. Is the relevant characteristic of the population, then, that of being readily available? Elementary school children may also be easily accessible; so may residents of a home for the aged; so may workers in a factory. Would comparable studies of these groups produce the same results? Or is it possible that ease of access has nothing to do with it? Supposing we were to change the conditions under which individuals make themselves available as the subjects of an experiment (for example, by providing financial and other kinds of rewards), would we obtain the same findings on our new samples? It is only by the multiplication of such studies that we can begin to specify the properties of the population for which our findings hold. And as we find samples for which the findings do not hold, we may begin to speculate about why they hold in some and not in others, formulate hypotheses, and select samples on bases that are relevant to the testing of these hypotheses. The point we are making is that the scientific quest does not end with the statement that a finding is or is not statistically significant. We still have the task of specifying the populations for which it is or is not significant. If we have no special reason for wanting to estimate the degree and character of relationships in an already specified population, it may be easier to begin the quest on nonprobability samples and to make use of the fiction of hypothetical populations of which our samples are quasi-probability samples to provide guidelines (for example, statistical tests of significance) for the evaluation of the findings. But it is imperative for us to remember that at this point our scientific quest has barely gotten under way.

The application to accidental samples of statistical procedures appropriate to probability sampling highlights the issue that we do not, at the end of such a study,

---

[18] For convenience, we have cast the present argument in terms of a population of persons. Actually, the issue is somewhat more complex. In the illustration cited, we have not mentioned the uncontrolled conditions of the experiment. Some of these involve attributes of the persons. In terms of the point made in the following paragraph, we will not know at the end of the experiment whether the findings hold for the entire population of sophomores or for some subpopulation of sophomores (for example, psychology majors who volunteer for experiments for some special reason) or indeed whether the attribute *sophomore* is at all relevant in the specification of the population. There are, however, invariably other uncontrolled conditions in an experiment that may or may not affect the outcome. Thus, we have not only an accidental sampling of sophomores, but also an accidental sampling of the conditions under which the experiment could conceivably be conducted. The true hypothetical population is, hence, not merely a population of persons, but a population of persons under conditions. The task of specifying the population prescribed in the following paragraph really applies to this "true" hypothetical population.

know the properties of the population to which we may legitimately generalize. Once the issue has been raised, however, it becomes apparent that we would not necessarily be much better off if we were to start with a probability sample of a well-defined population in the first place. Suppose, for example, that, instead of carrying out our study on an accidental sample of sophomores, we were able to use a probability sample of all of the sophomores at a particular college. To be sure, we would then be able to generalize to this population, within the limits of the estimated margin of error. But is this the population to which we really want to generalize? Do we still want to know whether the specified characteristics of the population are relevant to the relationship we are studying? Do we not, for example, want to know whether the discovered relationship holds only for the sophomores at our particular college? Suppose that it does not. Does this not then point to the possibility of defining a more inclusive population for which the relationship holds, and would we not want to know the specifications of this more inclusive population? Suppose, on the other hand, that it does hold only for the sophomores at our particular college. Would we not then want to know what is so unique about our population of sophomores? And would not the tentative formulation of possible uniqueness of our population suggest hypotheses that we would want to explore — hypotheses that might suggest population specifications that cut across our initial population and that include elements not included in our initial population? In either case, would we not want to press toward the discovery of the specification of a population within which the trend that we have discovered in our population to be statistically significant becomes a virtual certainty?

It should perhaps be added that we are not, in these last few paragraphs, preaching a paralyzing spirit of agnosticism that would prohibit anyone from coming to any conclusions. The progress of science and the scientific tenability of conclusions at any point in time are, after all, based on the coherence and consistency of many bits of fallible evidence, the articulation of theory, and the interlocking of the individually fallible bits of evidence with theory. It has been emphasized elsewhere in this book that science offers no possibilities of absolute proof. The scientist can, at most, aspire to the soundest conclusions that can be reached in the light of the best evidence that can be brought to bear on any issue. At the same time, science would only degenerate into dogma if one did not constantly remain alert to the sources of ambiguity and fallibility in the available evidence and the semantic gaps that may lie concealed in the generalizations that are drawn; if one did not attempt to weigh the possible alternatives that may be compatible with the evidence, particularly in the light of the sources of fallibility and ambiguity; if one did not attempt to pinpoint the gaps in knowledge; and if, even though one has dismissed some alternative on the ground that it is not sufficiently plausible to merit serious consideration or dismissed some manifest gap in knowledge as not sufficiently germane to merit intensive exploration, one would not be constantly prepared to reopen these issues and remain sensitive to the possibility of reopening them. In the light of these considerations, what we have attempted to do in these last paragraphs is merely to look at a considerable body of contemporary research and research practice in the perspective of sampling theory. If there is any preachment implied, it is only another lesson in scientific humility.

Glossary

Abstract   A brief summary of the content and purpose of an article or report.

"Anonymous" questionnaires   A questionable practice in which, in order to identify the person who responded to a mailed questionnaire, the researcher codes or marks the return envelope in some way. The respondent believes the response to be "anonymous."

Behavior range   A technique used in ecological research that involves listing the different physical settings occupied by an individual in a specified period of time, such as a typical day or week.

Behavior setting survey   A technique used in ecological research that describes particular settings or environments in terms of their important characteristics, such as the predominant activities in evidence.

Binocular rivalry   Based on the fact that the two eyes view objects from somewhat different locations, the tendency for one eye to be dominant over the other, leading to one image being seen rather than another.

Card design   A plan for allocating data to an IBM card for analysis, retrieval, and storage.

Census   A count of all the elements of a population and a determination of the distributions of their characteristics.

Coding   The act of categorizing raw data into groups or giving the data numerical values.

Coding frame   A statement of what is to be coded and how it is to be coded, to prepare data for analysis.

Cognitive dissonance   A state in which the person holds two beliefs, or cognitions, which are inconsistent with each other.

Constructs   The abstract concepts used in social science theories such as social status, power, and intelligence

Construct validation   Determination that a measurement taps the construct in question, that it is distinct from other constructs, and that it has the properties described by theories which employ that construct.

Content analysis   A research method usually applied to mass communications, such as newspapers or television, for purposes of identifying specified characteristics of the material.

Contextual variables   In data analysis, the characteristics of units at higher levels of analysis that encompass the unit of analysis with which we are concerned.

Continuous real time measurement   A method of recording used in systematic observation in which every onset of a specified behavior is coded as well as the actual elapsed time of the behavior so as to yield measures of frequency (the total number of onsets of the behavior) and duration (the total amount of time taken up by the behavior).

Contrast error   The tendency to rate objects, qualities, or persons, as more different than they really are, based upon a comparison with previous ratings.

Control group   In an experiment, those subjects to whom no experimental stimulus is administered, but who resemble members of the experimental group in all respects.

Correlation   Covariation of two variables in a group of people, that is, the tendency for certain values of or levels of one variable to occur with particular values of or levels of another variable.

Correlation coefficient   A measure of association between two variables; it can range from 0 (no relationship) to -1.00 (perfect negative relationship) or $+1.00$ (perfect positive relationship).

Covert structured observation   Observations of predetermined aspects of people's behavior made without their knowledge.

Criterion   A proved, accepted, valid measure of some variable.

Datum   Singular; plural is data. A piece of information ready for analysis.

Dependent variable   The presumed effect; the variable that is measured to see how it has responded to a treatment or cause.

Differential scale   A type of attitude scale that seeks to pinpoint each respondent's attitude along a continuum.

Dimension   An inferred continuum, along which different responses can be placed at different points.

Ecological fallacy   The assumption that relationships that hold at the group level also hold for specific individuals within these groups.

Elaboration   The detailed examination of an established relationship between two variables that is carried out by introducing additional variables as statistical controls.

Epistemic correlation   The relationship between a variable like dollar income and a construct like social status; the epistemic correlation must be surmised; it cannot be computed because there is no direct measure of the construct.

Equal-appearing intervals   A goal of Thurstone's method of attitude-scale construction; the identification of a series of attitude statements that differ in their favorability or unfavorability toward an object, such that they mark off the dimension in equal units.

Experimental group   In an experiment, those research participants exposed to the stimulus condition under study.

Experimental variable   A variable manipulated by the experimenter; a treatment condition to which subjects are assigned.

External validity   The generalizability of a research finding, for example, to other populations, settings, treatment arragements, and measurement arrangements.

Field notes   The written or tape recorded notes that contain descriptions of the people, setting, actions, and dialogues for each period of participant observation.

Field study   A study for which the data are collected from persons acting out their typical roles in the everyday world, rather than as subjects in the laboratory.

Fixed-alternative   In a questionnaire or interview, a question in which the responses of the subject are limited to stated alternatives.

Focal individual sampling   A method of recording used in systematic observation in which during a given sampling period all individual behaviors of a particular person are scored as well as all social interactions involving this individual. Behaviors not involving this person are completely ignored.

Free-answer   *See* Open-ended.

Galvanic skin response   A measure of the flow of electricity between two electrodes placed at different points on the skin; sometimes called the electrodermal response.

Generosity error   The tendency for raters to bend over backwards to give favorable ratings to others, out of concern that a too severe rating would harm the ratee's opportunities.

Halo effect   A rating error in which the rater lets his or her general, overall impression of another influence the rating he or she gives the other person on some specific characteristic.

Hypothesis   A tentative explanation of a relationship or a supposition that a relationship may exist. The hypothesis generates an empirical study that seeks to confirm or disconfirm it.

Hypothetico-deductive method   The process of logical reasoning from premises to conclusions; used in deriving predictions from a theory.

Independent variable   The presumed cause; the variable that is manipulated or measured to see what effects it has on other variables.

Induction   The process of making inferences from some specific observations to a more general rule. Used in constructing a theory on the basis of some observed facts.

Inductive method   The process of making inferences from some specific observations to a more general rule. Used in constructing a hypothesis or theory from data.

Informed consent   The principle of research ethics that requires investigators to inform research subjects of all questionable features of the research before the subjects decide whether to participate.

Interaction effect   The combined effect of two or more independent variables on a dependent variable above and beyond the sum of the two main effects.

Internal validity   The conclusiveness with which the effects of the independent variables are established in a scientific investigation, as opposed to the possibility that some confounding variables may have caused the observed results.

Interval scale   Any measuring device that not only is capable of placing people in their rank order on a characteristic, but also can measure the differences between them in regard to that characteristic.

Kurtosis   A quality of the distribution of a set of data, dealing with whether or how much the data "pile up" around some central point.

Likert-type scale   A type of attitude scale that poses statements and asks the respondent to indicate how much he or she agrees or disagrees with each statement.

Main effect   The effect of any one independent variable on a dependent variable.

Margin of error   The variance within which results are accurate; the limits of accuracy.

Matrix   A two-dimensional organization. Each dimension is composed of several positions or alternatives. Any particular "score" is a combination of the two dimensions.

Median   A measure of central tendency; the middle score of a sample, separating the upper half of the cases from the lower half.

Multistage sampling   A sampling procedure that moves through a set of stages from more inclusive to less inclusive sampling units.

Multitrait-multimethod matrix   A table of correlations among two or more traits measured by two or more methods, used to determine the validity of the measurements.

Naturally occurring phenomena   Processes and variables measuring processes that occur in the normal course of events. For example, the relationships of sex and race with occupational attainment would reflect naturally occurring processes. Sex and race are naturally occurring variables.

Negative case analysis   The systematic search for disconfirming instances in the analysis of participant observation data; used to generate and revise hypotheses.

Observer drift   A problem of reliability in systematic observation research in which observers become less accurate in their observations over time.

Open-ended   A type of question on an interview that does not limit the respondent's response to any preselected alternatives.

Operational definition   Procedures used by a researcher to manipulate or measure a concept.

Ordinal scale   A measurement that rank orders individuals on a particular characteristic, but cannot distinguish *how* different each is from the others.

Panel survey design   A survey research strategy where respondents in a survey are interviewed more than once at points separated in time with the aim of studying change in respondent characteristics over time.

Participant observer   The case when a researcher, in order to study the behavior of a group or organization, joins that group or organization and acts as a typical participant. Others in the organization are usually unaware of the researcher's true role.

Placebo   A substance that has no effects upon a person when ingested. Used for a control condition in a variety of studies.

Population   A designated part of a universe from which a sample is drawn; also, the aggregation of people or other research subjects to which one wishes to generalize his or her research.

Pretest   The administration of a measure prior to other testing in a study. One function of a pretest is to identify, or verify the identification of, differing groups on some measure.

Probability sampling   The type of sampling from a population in which one can specify, for each element of the population, the relative likelihood that it will be included in the sample.

Projective methods   Those tests that provide the respondent a series of ambiguous stimuli to which to respond. The assumption is that the respondent will project his or her values, needs, and attitudes into the responses to these stimuli.

Psychodrama   A therapeutic technique in which a group of people act as they would in a real-life situation. May be used to reflect the people's social attitudes.

Q-sort   A scaling device in which the subject sorts statements into a number of piles — usually 9 or 11 — based on some criterion, such as their degree of personal applicability.

Random assignment (or randomization)   A process of assigning people or groups to experimental conditions such that each person has an equal chance of being assigned to any particular condition as is done with the flip of a coin.

Random digit dialing   A technique that assures the inclusion of unlisted telephone numbers in the sampling frame. Random sequences of digits are dialed within working exchanges.

Random error   That deviation from a true score that is the result of transitory aspects of the person, the situation, or the measuring instrument.

"Ranks" test   A measure of attitudes toward different racial groups, administered to children. The subjects are asked to put in order of preference as playmates a series of photographs of children of different races.

Rapport   A state of empathy or harmony between interviewer and respondent.

Relative deprivation   The concept that one's position is not evaluated in absolute terms, but rather in relation to the position of others or in relation to unfulfilled expectations.

Reliability   The consistency in results of a test, including the tendency of a test or measurement to produce the same results when it measures twice some entity or attribute believed not to have changed in the interval between measurements.

Repeated measures design   A research design in which each group or person is repeatedly tested after exposure to more than one experimental condition.

Response rate The number of completed interviews or questionnaires divided by the number of eligible respondents in the sample.

Sampling The selection of a sample of individuals or measurements from the total population to be studied. Sampling may involve elaborate selection procedures if the inferences from the sample are to be sound.

Sampling distribution The distribution of the means of many different samples of different sizes. This sampling distribution is used to determine the degree of possible error in samples of different sizes.

Scale A measuring instrument composed of several items that have a logical or empirical relationship to each other.

Scalogram method A method of attitude measurement which determines if all the attitude statements can be placed on a single dimension.

Selective perception Hearing or seeing only what one *wants* to see or hear, rather than what was actually communicated.

Sense modalities Ways of perceiving the environment—hearing, vision, touch, and so on.

"Show me" test A measure of attitude toward children of different races. The child acting as subject is asked to identify which classmate reflects each of certain qualities or behaviors, such as "always talks too loud in class."

Skewness A quality of the distribution of a set of data dealing with whether the data are or are not symmetrically distributed around a central point.

Social indicators Statistical records of such phenomena as incidence of crime or unemployment tallies that are used to chart the status and change in the quality of life.

Social desirability A response set to answer questions about oneself in the socially approved manner.

Sociodrama A device in which a group of people are given a series of roles to act out as if in a real-life situation. By observing how the person acts out a certain role, we may understand his or her social attitudes better.

Sociometry The study of social interactions and social preferences among a group of people. Sociometry identifies friendship and work-relationship preferences within a group.

Specimen records A technique used in ecological research in which observers provide a narrative running account of all the actions performed by one person over an extended period of time.

Spurious correlation An observed correlation between two variables that exists because both are caused by a common variable.

Standardized In referring to interviews, those in which the questions and the choices for answers are predetermined.

Statistical test of significance A determination of whether a difference between conditions or a relationship is so large that the possibility of its happening by chance is minimal.

Stratum Some subdivision of a population, based on one or more specifications.

Structural variables In data analysis, those characteristics that are formed by combining units from lower levels of analysis.

Subject variable A variable that is a property of a person; a condition or characteristic that a subject brings to a study, such as age, gender, and group affiliations.

Summated scales Those attitude scales on which respondents indicate their agreement or disagreement with each item; the scores for their responses are summed to obtain a total score reflecting their attitude.

Survey research The research strategy where one collects data from all or part of a population to assess the relative incidence, distribution, and interrelations of naturally occurring variables.

Threats to validity   Alternative explanations for the occurrence of an effect.

Thurstone scale   A type of attitude scale in which judges first rate the favorability of statements about an attitude object, then subjects select those statements with which they agree. The goal is to form an equal-interval scale of statements.

Time-interval sampling   A method of recording observations in which each observed behavior is scored once and only once during successive intervals of a session (for example, 30 seconds) regardless of the actual number of occurrences in the interval.

Time-point sampling   A method of recording observations in which recording occurs instantaneously at regularly spaced points during the session (for example, every tenth second).

True experiment   A study of the effects of conditions to which subjects were randomly assigned.

Type I error   A conclusion that there *is* a true difference between two populations when in fact there is *not*.

Type II error   A conclusion that two populations are *not* different from each other when in fact they *are*.

Unidimensional   Reflecting the presence of only one dimension, as opposed to multidimensional.

Unit of analysis   The specific variable being used in data analysis — in social research, the unit of analysis might be something as specific as "the answer to Question 1" or as broad as the size of a city.

Unstructured   In referring to interviews, those in which neither the questions nor the answer categories are predetermined.

Validity   The capacity of a measuring instrument to predict what it was designed to predict; stated most often in terms of the correlation between scores on the instrument and measures of performance on some criterion. The accuracy of observations.

Variable   A concrete representation of an abstract construct; a means of measuring a construct. Income, for instance, is a variable used to measure the construct of social status.

Verify   To check; used to refer to the step of checking that the information that has been punched on an IBM card is accurate and complete.

References

Ackerman, N. W., & Jahoda, M. *Antisemitism and emotional disorder: A psychoanalytic interpretation.* New York: Harper, 1950.

Adler, F. Operational definitions in sociology. *American Journal of Sociology* 1947, *52*, 438–444.

Adorno, T. W., Frenkel-Brunswik, E., Levinson, D. J., & Sanford, R. N. *The authoritarian personality.* New York: Harper, 1950.

Ager, J. W., & Dawes, R. M. Effect of judge's attitudes on judgment. *Journal of Personality and Social Psychology,* 1965, *1*(5), 533–538.

Alger, C. F. Interaction in a committee of the United Nations General Assembly. *Midwest Journal of Political Science,* 1966, *10*, 411–447.

Alker, H. R., Jr. *Mathematics and politics.* New York: Macmillan, 1965.

Alper, T. G. Achievement motivation in college women: A now-you-see-it-now-you-don't phenomenon. *American Psychologist,* 1974, *29*, 194–203.

Alper, T., & Korchin, S. J. Memory for socially relevant material. *Journal of Abnormal and Social Psychology,* 1952, *47*, 25–37.

Altmann, J. Observational study of behavior: Sampling methods. *Behaviour,* 1973, *49*, 228–267.

American Anthropological Association. *Professional ethics.* Washington, D.C.: American Anthropological Association, 1973.

American Political Science Association Committee on Professional Standards and Responsibilities. Ethical problems of academic political scientists. *P.S., Newsletter of the American Political Science Association,* 1968, *1*(3).

American Psychological Association. *Ethical principles in the conduct of research with human participants.* Washington, D.C.: American Psychological Association, 1973.

American Sociological Association. *Code of Ethics.* Washington, D.C.: American Sociological Association, 1971.

Anderson, H. H., & Anderson, G. L. *An introduction to projective techniques and other devices for understanding the dynamics of human behavior.* Englewood Cliffs, N.J.: Prentice-Hall, 1951.

Andrews, F. M., & Withey, S. B. *Social indicators of wellbeing.* New York: Plenum, 1976.

Argyle, M., & Cook, M. *Gaze and mutual gaze.* Cambridge, England: Cambridge University Press, 1976.

Asch, S. E. Effects of group pressure upon the modification and distortion of judgments. In H. Guetzkow (Ed.), *Groups, leadership and men.* Pittsburgh: Carnegie Press, 1951.

Atkinson, J. W. (Ed.). *Motives in fantasy, action, and society.* New York: Van Nostrand, 1958.

Atkinson, J. W., et al. The effect of experimental arousal of the affiliation motive on thematic apperception. *Journal of Abnormal and Social Psychology,* 1954, *49,* 405–410.

Atkinson, J. W., & Feather, N. T. (Eds.) *A theory of achievement motivation.* New York: Wiley, 1966.

Babbie, E. R. *Survey research methods.* Belmont, Calif.: Wadsworth Publishing Co., 1973.

Bagby, J. W. A cross-cultural study of perceptual predominance in binocular rivalry. *Journal of Abnormal and Social Psychology,* 1957, *54,* 331–334.

Bakeman, R. Untangling streams of behavior: Sequential analysis of observational data. In G. Sackett (Ed.), *Observing behavior: Volume II: Data collection and analysis methods.* Baltimore: University Park Press, 1978.

Balch, G. I. Multiple indicators in survey research: The concept "sense of political efficacy." *Political Methodology,* 1974, *1,* 1–43.

Bales, R. F. *Personality and interpersonal behavior.* New York: Holt, 1970.

Barash, D. P. Human ethology: Displacement activities in a dental office. *Psychological Reports,* 1974, *34,* 947–949.

Barber, B., Lally, J. J., Makarushka, J. L., & Sullivan, O. *Research on human subjects: Problems of social control in medical experimentation.* New York: Russell Sage Foundation, 1973.

Barker, R. G. *The stream of behavior.* New York: Appleton-Century-Crofts, 1963.

Barker, R. G. *Ecological psychology: Concepts and methods for studying the environment of human behavior.* Stanford, Calif.: Stanford University Press, 1968.

Barker, R. G., & Schoggen, P. ·*Qualities of community life.* San Francisco, Calif.: Jossey-Bass, 1973.

Bartlett, F. C. *Remembering.* Cambridge: Cambridge University Press, 1932.

Bechtel, R. Hodometer research in architecture. *Milieu,* 1967, *1,* 1–9.

Bechtel, R. *Enclosing behavior.* New York: Dowden, Hutchinson & Ross, 1977.

Becker, H. S. Becoming a marihuana user. *Outsiders.* Glencoe, Ill.: The Free Press, 1963, pp. 41–58.

Becker, H. S. Whose side are we on? *Journal of Social Problems,* 1967, *14,* 239–247.

Becker, H. S. & Geer, B. Participant observation and interviewing: A comparison. *Human Organization,* 1957, *16*(3), 28–32.

Bem, S. L., & Bem, D. J. Does sex-biased job advertising "aid and abet" sex discrimination? *Journal of Applied Social Psychology,* 1973, *3,* 6–18.

Benson, O. *Political science laboratory.* Columbus, Ohio: Charles E. Merrill, 1969.

Berelson, B. *Content analysis in communication research.* Glencoe, Ill.: Free Press, 1952.

Berelson, B., Lazarsfeld, P. F., & McPhee, W. N. *Voting: A study of opinion formation in a presidential campaign.* Chicago: University of Chicago Press, 1954.

Bergin, A. E. The effect of dissonant persuasive communications upon changes in a self-referring attitude. *Journal of Personality,* 1962, *30,* 423–438.

Berk, Richard A., & Rossi, Peter H. Doing good or worse: Evaluation research politically examined. In M. Guttentag & S. Saar (Eds.), *Evaluation Studies Review Annual,* Vol. 2, Beverly Hills, Calif.: Sage Publications, 1977.

Berkun, M. M., Bialek, H. M., Kern, R. P., & Yagi, K. Experimental studies of psychological stress in man. *Psychological Monographs,* 1962, *76* (15, Whole No. 534).

Berscheid, E., Baron, R. S., Dermer, M., & Libman, M. Anticipating informed consent: An empirical approach. *American Psychologist,* 1973, *28,* 913–925.

Beyle, H. C. A scale for the measurement of attitude toward candidates for elective governmental office. *American Political Science Review*, 1932, 26, 527–544.

Bishop, B. M. Mother-child interaction and the social behavior of children. *Psychological Monographs*, 1951, 65 (11, Whole No. 328).

Blanchard, F. A., & Cook, S. W. Effects of helping a less competent member of a cooperating interracial group on the development of interpersonal attraction. *Journal of Personality and Social Psychology*, 1976, 34, 1245–1255.

Blau, P. M. & Duncan, O. D., *The American occupational structure.* New York: Wiley, 1967.

Blurton Jones, N. (Ed.). *Ethological studies of child behavior.* London: Cambridge University Press, 1972.

Bogardus, E. S. Measuring social distances. *Journal of Applied Sociology*, 1925, 9, 299–308.

Bogardus, E. S. *Immigration and race attitudes.* Lexington, Mass.: Heath, 1928.

Bogardus, E. S. A social distance scale. *Sociology and Social Research*, 1933, 17, 265–271.

Bogden, R. *Participant observation in organizational settings.* Syracuse, New York: Syracuse University Press, 1972.

Bogden, R., & Taylor, S. J. *Introduction to qualitative research methods.* New York: Wiley, 1975.

Borgatta, E. F., & Bohrnstedt, G. W., Some limitations on generalizability from social psychological experiments. *Sociological Methods and Research*, 1974, 3, 111–120.

Borgida, E., & Nisbet, R. F. The differential impact of abstract versus concrete information on decisions. *Journal of Applied Social Psychology*, 1977, 7, 258–271.

Boruch, R. F. On common contentions about randomized field experiments. In R. F. Boruch & H. W. Riecken (Eds.), *Experimental tests of public policy.* Boulder, Col.: Westview Press, 1975, pp. 108–145.

Boyer, E. G., Simon, A., & Karafin, G. R. *Measures of maturation: An anthology of early childhood observational instruments.* Philadelphia: Research for Better Schools, 1973.

Bradburn, N., & Sudman, S. *Improving interview method and questionnaire design.* Chicago: Jossey-Bass, 1979.

Brannigan, C. R., & Humphries, D. A. Human non-verbal behavior, a means of communication. In N. Blurton Jones, (Ed.), *Ethological studies of child behavior.* London: Cambridge University Press, 1972.

Breed, W., & Ktsanes, T. Pluralistic ignorance in the process of opinion formation. *Public Opinion Quarterly*, 1961, 25, 382–392.

Brenner, M. H. *Mental illness and the economy.* Cambridge, Mass.: Harvard University Press, 1973.

Brickman, P., Folger, R., Goode, E., & Schul, Y. Micro and macro justice. In M. J. Lerner (Ed.), *The justice motive and social behavior.* Plenum, 1981.

Brigham, J. C., & Cook, S. W. The influence of attitude on the recall of controversial material: A failure to confirm. *Journal of Experimental Social Psychology*, 1969, 5, 240–243.

Brigham, J. C., & Cook, S. W. The influence of attitude on judgments of plausibility: A replication and extension. *Educational and Psychological Measurement*, 1970, 30(2), 283–292.

Brown, J. F. A modification of the Rosenzweig picture-frustration test to study hostile interracial attitudes. *Journal of Psychology*, 1947, 24, 247–272.

Brown, S. R., & Ellithorp, J. D. Emotional experiences in political groups: The case of the McCarthy phenomenon. *American Political Science Review*, 1970, 64, 349–366.

Bryan, J. H., & Test, M. A. Models and helping: Naturalistic studies in aiding behavior. *Journal of Personality and Social Psychology*, 1967, 6, 400–407.

Burwen, L. S., & Campbell, D. T. The generality of attitudes toward authority and nonauthority figures. *Journal of Abnormal and Social Psychology*, 1957, 54, 24–31.

Burwen, L. S., Campbell, D. T., & Kidd, J. The use of a sentence completion test in measuring attitudes toward superiors and subordinates. *Journal of Applied Psychology*, 1956, 40, 248–250.

Bush, M. & Gordon, A. C. Client choice and bureaucratic accountability: Possibilities for responsiveness in a social welfare bureaucracy. *Journal of Social Issues*, 1978, 34(4), 22–43.

Byrne, D., Ervin, C. R., & Lamberth, J. Continuity between the experimental study of attraction and real-life computer dating. *Journal of Personality and Social Psychology*, 1970, 16, 157–165.

Cain, L. D., Jr., Life course and social structure. In R. E. L. Faris (Ed.), *Handbook of modern sociology*. Chicago: Rand McNally, 1964, pp. 272–309.

Cairns, R. B. (Ed.). *The analysis of social interactions: Methods, issues and illustrations.* Hillsdale, New Jersey: Erlbaum, 1979.

Campbell, A., Converse, P. E., Miller, W. E., & Stokes, D. E. *The American voter.* New York: Wiley, 1960.

Campbell, A., et al. *The voter decides.* Evanston, Ill.: Row, Peterson, 1954.

Campbell, A., et al. *Elections and the political order.* New York: Wiley, 1966.

Campbell, D. T. The indirect assessment of social attitudes. *Psychological Bulletin*, 1950, 47, 15–38.

Campbell, D. T. The informant in quantitative research. *American Journal of Sociology*, 1955, 60, 339–342.

Campbell, D. T. Prospective: Artifact and control. In R. Rosenthal & R. L. Rosnow (Eds.), *Artifact in behavioral research.* New York: Academic Press, 1969.

Campbell, D. T. Reforms as experiments. *American Psychologist*, 1969, 24, 409–429.

Campbell, D. T. Qualitative knowing in action research. Kurt Lewin Award Address, Society for the Psychological Study of Social Issues, Meeting with the American Psychological Association, New Orleans, September 1, 1974.

Campbell, D. T. Assessing the impact of planned social change. In G. M. Lyons (Ed.), *Social research and public policy.* Hanover, N.H.: Public Affairs Center, Dartmouth College, 1975.

Campbell, D. T., & Damarin, F. L. Measuring leadership attitudes through an information test. *Journal of Social Psychology*, 1961, 55, 159–176.

Campbell, D. T., & Erlebacher, A. How regression artifacts in quasi-experimental evaluations can mistakenly make compensatory education look harmful. In J. Hellmuth (Ed.), *The disadvantaged child* (Vol. 3), *Compensatory education: A national debate.* New York: Brunner/Mazel, 1970.

Campbell, D. T., & Fiske, D. W. Convergent and discriminant validation by the multitrait-multimethod matrix. *Psychological Bulletin*, 1959, 56, 81–105.

Campbell, D. T., Miller, N., Lubetsky, J., & O'Connell, E. J. Varieties of projection in trait attribution. *Psychological Monographs*, 1964, 78 (15, Whole No. 592).

Campbell, D. T., & Ross, H. L. The Connecticut crackdown on speeding: Time-series data in quasi-experimental analysis. In N. E. Tufte (Ed.), *The quantitative analysis of social problems.* Reading, Mass.: Addison-Wesley, 1970.

Campbell, D. T., & Stanley, J. C. Experimental and quasi-experimental designs for research on teaching. In N. L. Gage (Ed.), *Handbook of research on teaching.* Chicago: Rand McNally, 1963.

Campbell, D. T., & Stanley, J. C. *Experimental and quasi-experimental designs for research.* Chicago: Rand McNally, 1966.

Cannell, C. F., Fisher, G., & Bakker, T. Reporting of hospitalization in the health service interview. *Vital and Health Statistics,* Ser. 2, No. 6, 1965.

Cannell, C. F., & Kahn, R. L. Interviewing. In G. Lindzey & E. Aronson (Eds.), *Handbook of social psychology* (Vol. 2, 2nd ed.). Reading, Mass.: Addison-Wesley, 1968.

Carlsmith, J. M. & Anderson, C. A. Ambient temperature and the occurrence of collective violence: A new analysis. *Journal of Personality and Social Psychology,* 1979, *37,* 337–344.

Carlson, J., Cook, S. W., & Stromberg, E. L. Sex differences in conversation. *Journal of Applied Psychology,* 1936, *20,* 727–735.

Carter, H. Recent American studies in attitudes toward war: A summary and evaluation. *American Sociological Review,* 1945, *10,* 343–352.

Carter, Lewis F. Inadvertent sociological theory. *Social Focus,* 1971, *50,* 12–25.

Cataldo, E. F., Johnson, R. M., Kellstedt, L. A., & Milbrath, L. W. Card sorting as a technique for survey interviewing. *Public Opinion Quarterly,* 1970, *34,* 202–215.

Cattell, R. B., & Luborsky, L. B. T-technique demonstrated as a new clinical method for determining personality and symptom structure. *Journal of General Psychology,* 1950, *42,* 3–24.

Cattell, R. B., Maxwell, E. F., Light, B. H., & Unger, M. P. The objective measurement of attitudes. *British Journal of Psychology,* 1949, *40,* 81–90.

Center for Human Resource Research. *The national longitudinal: Handbook.* Columbus, Ohio: College of Administrative Science, The Ohio State University, 1977. (This handbook contains a 21-page bibliography of technical publications about the surveys and of publications reporting results of the surveys.)

Chein, I. Narcotics use among juveniles. *Social Work,* 1956, *1,* 50–60.

Chein, I., Cook, S. W., & Harding J. The field of action research. *American Psychologist,* 1948, *3,* 43–50.

Christie, R., & Geis, F. L. *Studies in Machiavellianism.* New York: Academic Press, 1970.

Cronbach, L., et al, *The Dependability of Behavioral Measurements: Theory of Generalizability for Scores and Profiles.* New York: Wiley, 1972.

Cicirelli, V., et. al. *The impact of Head Start: An evaluation of the effects of Head Start on children's cognitive and affective development.* A report presented to the Office of Economic Opportunity pursuant to Contract B89–4536, June 1969. Westinghouse Learning Corporation, Ohio University. (Distributed by Clearinghouse for Federal Scientific and Technical Information, U.S. Department of Commerce, National Bureau of Standards, Institute for Applied Technology. PB 184–328).

Clark, K. B., & Clark, M. P. Emotional factors in racial identification and preference in Negro children. *Journal of Negro Education,* 1950, *19,* 341–350.

Cochran, W. G. *Sampling techniques* (2nd ed.). New York: Wiley, 1963.

Collier, J., Jr. Photography in anthropology: A report on two experiments. *American Anthropologist,* 1957, *59,* 843–859.

Colombotos, J. Personal versus telephone interviews: Effect on responses. *Public Health Reports,* 1969, *84*(9), 773–782.

Cook, F. L. *Who should be helped?* Beverly Hills, Calif.: Sage Publications, 1979.

Cook, S. W. *Studies of attitude and attitude measurement* (mimeograph). AFOSR Technical Report, 1968. Boulder: Institute of Behavioral Science, University of Colorado.

Cook, S. W. Motives in a conceptual analysis of attitude-related behavior. In W. J. Arnold

& D. Levine (Eds.), *Nebraska symposium on motivation, 1969.* Lincoln: University of Nebraska Press, 1970.

Cook, S. W., & Selltiz, C. A. A multi-indicator approach to attitude measurement *Psychological Bulletin*, 1964, *62*, 36–55.

Cook, T. D. & Campbell, D. T. *Quasi-Experimentation: Design and analysis issues for field settings.* Chicago: Rand McNally, 1979.

Cook, T. D. & Campbell, D. T. The design and conduct of quasi-experiments and true experiments in field settings. In M. D. Dunnett (Ed.), *Handbook of industrial and organizational psychology.* New York: Rand McNally, 1975.

Coombs, C. H. *A theory of data.* New York: Wiley, 1964.

Cooper, J. Deception and role playing: On telling the good guys from the bad guys. *American Psychologist*, 1976, *31*, 605–610.

Cooper, J. B., & Pollock, D. The identification of prejudicial attitudes by the GSR. *Journal of Social Psychology*, 1959, *50*, 241–245.

Cooper, J. B., & Siegel, H. E. The galvanic skin response as a measure of emotion in prejudice. *Journal of Psychology*, 1956, *42*, 149–155.

Cooper, J. B., & Singer, D. N. The role of emotion in prejudice. *Journal of Social Psychology*, 1956, *44*, 241–247.

Costrich, N., Feinstein, J., Kidder, L. H., Marecek, J., & Pascale, L. When stereotypes hurt: Three studies of penalities for sex-role reversals. *Journal of Experimental Psychology*, 1975, *11*, 520–530.

Cox, K. Social effects of integrated advertising. *Journal of Advertising Research*, 1971, *10*, 41–44.

Cressey, D. R. *Other people's money: A study in the social psychology of embezzlement.* Glencoe, Ill.: The Free Press, 1953.

Criswell, J. H. Racial cleavages in Negro-white groups. *Sociometry*, 1937, *1*, 87–89.

Dabbs, J. M., Jr. *Physiological and physical activity measures of attitudes.* Paper presented at the Navy-Smithsonian Conference on Survey Alternatives, Santa Fe, New Mexico, April 1975.

Darley, J. M., & Latané, B. Bystander intervention in emergencies: Diffusion of responsibility. *Journal of Personality and Social Psychology*, 1968, *8*, 377–383.

Davidson, D., Suppes, P., & Siegel, S. *Decision making: An experimental approach.* Stanford, Calif.: Stanford University Press; 1957.

Davis, J. A. *Elementary survey analysis.* Englewood Cliffs, N.J.: Prentice-Hall, 1968.

Dawes, R. M. *Measures and indicators of attitude.* New York: Wiley, 1971.

Dawes, R. M., Singer, D., & Lemons, F. An experimental analysis of the contrast effect and its implications for intergroup communications and the indirect assessment of attitudes. *Journal of Personality and Social Psychology*, 1972, *21*, 281–295.

Deutsch, M., & Collins, M. E. *Interracial housing: A psychological evaluation of a social experiment.* Minneapolis: University of Minnesota Press, 1951.

Diener, E., & Crandall, R. *Ethics in social and behavioral research.* Chicago: University of Chicago Press, 1978.

Diller, J. V., & Cook, S. W. *Differential recall recognition for faces of liked and disliked groups: A failure to confirm* (mimeograph). Boulder, Colo.: University of Colorado, 1969.

Dillman, D. A. Increasing mail questionnaire response in large samples of the general public. *Public Opinion Quarterly*, 1972, *36*, 254–257.

Dillman, D. A. *Mail and telephone surveys.* New York: John Wiley & Sons, Inc., 1978.

Donley, R. E., & Winter, D. G. Measuring the motives of public officials at a distance: An exploratory study of American Presidents. *Behavioral Science*, 1970, *15*, 227–236.

Doob, L. W. Effects of initial serial position and attitude upon recall under conditions of low motivation. *Journal of Abnormal and Social Psychology*, 1953, 48, 199–205.

Duncan, G., & Morgan, J. N., et al. *Five Thousand American Families—Patterns of Economic Progress: Analysis of the Panel Study of Income Dynamics, Vol. 7.* Ann Arbor, Mich.: Institute for Social Research, 1979.

Durkheim, E. *Suicide.* J. A. Spaulding & G. Simpson (Trans.). Glencoe, Ill.: Free Press, 1951.

Edney, J. J. Property, possession and permanence: A field study in human territoriality. *Journal of Applied Social Psychology*, 1972, 2, 275–282.

Edwards, A. L. *Techniques of attitude scale construction.* New York: Appleton-Century-Crofts, 1957.

Edwards, A. L., & Kilpatrick, F. P. A technique for construction of attitude scales. *Journal of Applied Psychology*, 1948, 32, 374–384.

Eibl-Eibesfeldt, I. *Ethology: The biology of behavior.* New York: Holt, Rinehart and Winston, 1970.

Ekman, P., & Friesen, W. V. The repertoire of nonverbal behavior: Categories, origins, usage and coding. *Semiotica*, 1969, 1, 1–20.

Ekman, P., & Friesen, W. V. *The facial action coding system (FACS).* Palo Alto, Calif.: Consulting Psychologists Press, 1978.

Elms, A. C., & Janis, I. L. Counter-norm attitudes induced by consonant vs. dissonant conditions of role-playing. *Journal of Experimental Research in Personality*, 1965, 1, 50–60.

Epstein, C. F. *Women's place: Options and limits in professional careers.* Berkeley and Los Angeles: University of California Press. 1970.

Erdos, P. L. *Professional mail surveys.* New York: McGraw-Hill, 1970.

Erickson, B. H., & Nosanchuk, T. A. *Understanding data.* Toronto: McGraw-Hill Ryerson, 1977.

Eulau, H., & Eyestone, R. Policy maps of city councils and policy outcomes: A developmental analysis. *American Political Science Review*, 1968, 62, 124–143.

Evans, M. C., & Chein, I. *The movie story game: A projective test of interracial attitudes for use with Negro and white children.* Paper presented at the meeting of the American Psychological Association, Boston, September 1948.

Eysenck, H. J., & Crown, S. An experimental study in opinion-attitude methodology. *International Journal of Opinion and Attitude Research*, 1949, 3, 47–86.

Farr, J. L. & Seaver, W. B. Stress and discomfort in psychological research: Subject perceptions of experimental procedures. *American Psychologist*, 1975, 30, 770–773.

Fawl, C. L. Disturbances experienced by children in their natural habitats. In R. G. Barker (Ed.), *The stream of behavior.* New York: Appleton-Century-Crofts, 1963.

Feather, N. T. Acceptance and rejection of arguments in relation to attitude strength, critical ability, and intolerance of inconsistency. *Journal of Abnormal and Social Psychology*, 1964, 69(2), 127–136.

Ferguson, L. W. The influence of individual attitudes on construction of an attitude scale. *Journal of Social Psychology*, 1935, 6, 115–117.

Ferguson, L. W. More measurement than validation. *Contemporary Psychology*, 1957, 2, 237–238.

Festinger, L. A. *A theory of cognitive dissonance.* Stanford: Stanford University Press, 1957.

Festinger, L., & Carlsmith, J. N. Cognitive consequences of forced compliance. *Journal of Abnormal and Social Psychology*, 1959, 58, 203–210.

Festinger, L., Riecken, H. W., & Schachter, S. *When prophecy fails.* Minneapolis: University of Minnesota Press, 1956.

Festinger, L., Schachter, S., & Back, K. *Social pressures in informal groups: A study of human factors in housing.* New York: Harper, 1950.

Filstead, W. J. Introduction. In W. J. Filstead (Ed.), *Qualitative methodology: Firsthand involvement with the social world.* Chicago: Markham, 1970.

Flanders, N. A. *Analyzing teaching behavior.* Reading, Mass.: Addison-Wesley, 1970.

Forward, J., Canter, R., & Kirsch, N. Role-enactment and deception methodologies: Alternative paradigms? *American Psychologist,* 1976, *31,* 595–604.

French, J. R. P., Jr. Organized and unorganized groups under fear and frustration. *University of Iowa Studies of Child Welfare,* 1944, *20,* 229–308.

Fromme, A. On the use of certain qualitative methods of attitude research: A study of opinions on the methods of preventing war. *Journal of Social Psychology,* 1941, *13,* 425–459.

Gallo, P. S., Smith, S., & Mumford, S. Effects of deceiving subjects upon experimental results. *Journal of Social Psychology,* 1973, *89,* 99–107.

Galtung, J. *Theory and methods of social research.* New York: Columbia University Press, 1967.

Gans, H. On the methods used in this (The West End: An Urban Village) study. In M. P. Golden (Ed.), The research experience. Itasca, Illinois: F. E. Peacock, 1976.

Garfinkel, H. *Studies in ethnomethodology.* Englewood Cliffs, New Jersey: Prentice-Hall, 1967.

Gerbner, G., et al. (Eds.). *The analysis of communication content: Developments in scientific theories and computer techniques.* New York: Wiley, 1969.

Getzels, J. W. *The assessment of personality and prejudice by the method of paired direct and projective questions.* Unpublished doctoral dissertation, Harvard University, 1951.

Glaser, B. G. & Strauss, A. L. *The discovery of grounded theory.* Chicago: Aldine, 1967.

Glaskow, D. R., Sadowski, C. J., & Davis, S. F. The project must count: Fostering positive attitudes toward the conduct of research. *Bulletin of the Psychonomic Society,* 1977, *10,* 471–474.

Glass, D. The ethical basis of science. *Science,* 1965, *150,* 1254–1261.

Glass, D. C., & Singer, J. E. *Urban stress: Experiments on noise and social stressors.* New York: Academic Press, 1972.

Glazer, E. M. *An experiment in the development of critical thinking.* New York: Bureau of Publications, Teachers College, Columbia University, 1941. (Teachers College Contributions to Education, 843)

Glock, C. Y., Survey design and analysis in sociology. In C. Y. Glock (Ed.), *Survey research in the social sciences.* New York: Russell Sage Foundation, 1967.

Goldberg, L. R. Grades as motivants. *Psychology in the Schools,* 1965, *2,* 17–24.

Goodman, M. E. *Race awareness in young children.* Reading, Mass.: Addison-Wesley, 1952.

Gorsuch, R. L. *Factor analysis.* Philadelphia: Saunders, 1974.

Gottman, J. M. Nonsequential data analysis techniques in observational research. In G. Sackett (Ed.), *Observing behavior, Vol. II: Data collection and analysis methods.* Baltimore: University Park Press, 1978.

Graber, D. The press as opinion resource during the 1968 presidential campaign. *Public Opinion Quarterly,* 1971, *35,* 168–182.

Granneberg, R. T. The influence of individual attitude and attitude-intelligence interaction upon scale values of attitude items. *American Psychologist,* 1955, *10,* 330–331. (Abstract)

Green, R. T., & Stacey, B. G. A flexible projective technique applied to the measurement of the self-image of voters. *Journal of Projective Techniques and Personality Assessment,* 1966, *30*(1), 12–15.

Greenwald, A. B., & Sakumura, J. S. Attitude and selective learning: Where are the phenomena of yesteryear? *Journal of Personality and Social Psychology,* 1967, *7,* 387–397.

Griffin, J. H. *Black like me.* New York: American Library (Signet) 1962.

Grings, W. W. The verbal summator technique and abnormal mental states. *Journal of Abnormal and Social Psychology,* 1942, *37,* 529–545.

Guilford, J. P. *Psychometric methods* (2nd ed.). New York: McGraw-Hill, 1954.

Gurr, T. R. A causal model of civil strife: A comparative analysis using new indices. *American Political Science Review,* 1968, *62,* 1104–1124.

Gutek, B. A. Strategies for studying client satisfaction. *Journal of Social Issues,* 1978, *34*(4), 44–56.

Guttman, L. A basis for scaling quantitative data. *American Sociological Review,* 1944, *9,* 139–150.

Habenstein, R. W. Occupational uptake: Professionalizing. In R. W. Habenstein (Ed.), *Pathways to data: Field methods for studying ongoing social organizations.* Chicago: Aldine-Atherton, 1970.

Haire, M. Projective techniques in marketing research, *Journal of Marketing,* 1950, *14,* 649–656.

Hamblin, R. L., Hathaway, C., & Wodarski, J. S. Group contingencies, peer tutoring, and accelerating academic achievement. In E. Ramp & B. Hopkins (Eds.), *A new direction for education: Behavior analysis.* Lawrence: The University of Kansas, 1971.

Hammond, K. R. Measuring attitudes by error-choice: An indirect method. *Journal of Abnormal and Social Psychology,* 1948, *43,* 38–48.

Harding, J., & Hogrefe, R. Attitudes of white department store employees toward Negro co-workers. *Journal of Social Issues,* 1952, *8*(1), 18–28.

Harmon, H. H. *Modern factor analysis* (2nd ed.). Chicago: University of Chicago Press, 1967.

Hartmann, E. W. A field experiment on the comparative effectiveness of "emotional" and "rational" political leaflets in determining election results. *Journal of Abnormal and Social Psychology,* 1936, *31,* 99–114.

Helgerson, E. The relative significance of race, sex, and facial expression in choice of playmate by the pre-school child. *Journal of Negro Education,* 1943, *12,* 617–622.

Henle, M., & Hubbell, M. B. "Egocentricity" in adult conversation. *Journal of Social Psychology,* 1938, *9,* 227–234.

Hess, E. H. Attitude and pupil size. *Scientific American,* 1965, *212,* 46–54.

Hess, E. H., & Polt, J. M. Pupil size as related to interest value of visual stimuli. *Science,* 1960, *132,* 349–350.

Higbee, K., & Wells, G., Some research trends in social psychology during the 1960s. *American Psychologist,* 1972, *27,* 963–966.

Hinckley, E. D. The influence of individual opinion on construction of an attitude scale. *Journal of Social Psychology,* 1932, *3,* 283–296.

Hoagland, H. Potentialities in the control of behavior. In G. Wolstenholme (Ed.), *Man and his future.* Boston: Little, Brown, 1963.

Hochstim, J. R. A critical comparison of three strategies of collecting data from households. *Journal of the American Statistical Association,* 1967, *62,* 976–989.

Holmes, D. S. Debriefing after psychological experiments. I. Effectiveness of postdeception dehoaxing. *American Psychologist,* 1976a, *31,* 858–867.

Holmes, D. S. Debriefing after psychological experiments. II. Effectiveness of postexperimental desensitizing. *American Psychologist,* 1976b, *31,* 868–875.

Holsti, O. R. *Content analysis for the social sciences and humanities.* Reading, Mass.: Addison-Wesley, 1969.

Horner, M. W. Toward an understanding of achievement-related conflicts in women. *Journal of Social Issues,* 1972, *28*(2), 157–175.

Horowitz, E. L. The development of attitude toward the Negro. *Archives of Psychology,* 1936, No. 194.

Horowitz, E. L., & Horowitz, R. E. Development of social attitudes in children. *Sociometry,* 1938, *1,* 301–338.

Horowitz, I. L. (Ed.) *The rise and fall of Project Camelot.* Cambridge, Mass.: MIT Press, 1967.

Horowitz, R. E. Racial aspects of self-identification in nursery school children. *Journal of Psychology,* 1939, *7,* 91–99.

Horst, P. *Psychological measurement and prediction.* Belmont, Calif.: Wadsworth, 1968.

Hovland, C. I., & Sherif, M. Judgmental phenomena and scales of attitude measurement: Item displacement in Thurstone scales. *Journal of Abnormal and Social Psychology,* 1952, *47,* 822–832.

Hsu, E. H. An experimental study of rationalization. *Journal of Abnormal and Social Psychology,* 1949, *44,* 277–278.

Humphreys, L. *Tearoom trade: Impersonal sex in public places.* Chicago: Aldine-Atherton, 1970.

Hyman, H. H. *Survey design and analysis: Principles, cases, and procedures.* Glencoe, Ill.: Free Press, 1955.

Ickes, W., & Barnes, R. Boys and girls together — and alienated: On enacting stereotyped sex roles in mixed-sex dyads. *Journal of Personality and Social Psychology,* 1978, *36,* 669–683.

Jennings, H. H. *Leadership and isolation* (2nd ed., 1950). New York: Longmans, 1943.

Jessor, S. L., & Jessor, R. Transition from virginity to nonvirginity among youth: A social- psychological study over time. *Developmental Psychology,* 1975, *11,* 473–484.

Jones, S. H., & Cook, S. W. *The influence of attitude on judgments of the effectiveness of alternative social policies* (mimeograph). Boulder: University of Colorado, 1975.

Judd, C. M. & Kenny, D. A. *The Design and Analysis of Social Research in Applied Settings.* Cambridge: Cambridge University Press, (in press).

Kaplan, A. *The conduct of inquiry: Methodology for behavioral science.* San Francisco: Chandler, 1964.

Kasarda, J. D. The use of census data in secondary analysis: The context of ecological discovery. In M. P. Golden (Ed.), *The research experience.* Itasca, Illinois: F. E. Peacock, 1976.

Katz, D. Social psychology and group process. In C. P. Stone (Ed.), *Annual review of psychology.* Palo Alto, Calif.: Annual Reviews, 1951.

Katz, I., Goldston, J., & Benjamin, L. Behavior and productivity in biracial work groups. *Human Relations,* 1958, *11,* 123–141.

Katz, J. *Experimentation with human beings.* New York: Russell Sage Foundation, 1972.

Kehrer, K. C. The Gary income maintenance experiment: Summary of initial findings. In T. D. Cook, et al. (Eds.), *Evaluation studies review annual,* Vol. 3, 1978, Beverly Hills, Calif.: Sage Publications.

Kelley, H. H., Hovland, C. I., Schwartz, M., & Abelson, R. P. The influence of judges' attitudes in three methods of attitude scaling. *Journal of Social Psychology,* 1955, *42,* 147–158.

Kelly, E. L., & Fiske, D. W.   The prediction of success in the VA training program in clinical psychology. *American Psychologist*, 1950, 5, 395–406.

Kelman, H. C.   Human use of human subjects: The problem of deception in social psychological experiments. *Psychological Bulletin*, 1967, 67, 1–11.

Kelman, H. C.   *A time to speak: On human values and social research*. San Francisco: Jossey-Bass, 1968.

Kendall, P. L., & Lazarsfeld, P. F.   Problems of survey analysis. In R. K. Merton & P. F. Lazarsfeld (Eds.), *Continuities in social research*. New York: Free Press, 1950.

Kendon, A.   Some relationships between body motion and speech: An analysis of an example. In A. Siegman and B. Pope (Eds.), *Studies in dyadic communication*. New York: Pergamon, 1970.

Keniston, K.   *The uncommitted: Alienated youth in American society*. New York: Harcourt, 1965.

Kerlinger, F. N.,   *Foundations of Behavioral Research*. New York: Holt, Rinehart and Winston, 1964.

Kerr, M.   An experimental investigation of national stereotypes. *Sociological Review*, 1943, 35, 37–43.

Kershaw, D. N.   A negative income tax experiment. *Scientific American*, 1972, 227, 19–25.

Kidder, L. H.   *Foreign visitors: A study of the changes in selves, skills, and attitudes of westerners in India*. Unpublished doctoral dissertation, Northwestern University, 1971.

Kidder, L. H.   On becoming hypnotized: How skeptics become convinced: A case of attitude change? *Journal of Abnormal Psychology*, 1972, 80(3) 317–322.

Kidder, L. H.   Qualitative research and quasi-experimental frameworks. In M. B. Brewer & B. E. Collins (Eds.), *Knowing and validating: A tribute to Donald T. Campbell*. San Francisco: Jossey-Bass, 1981.

Kidder, L. H., & Campbell, D. T.   The indirect testing of social attitude. In G. F. Summers (Ed.), *Attitude measurement*. Chicago: Rand McNally, 1970.

Kidder, L. H. & Cohn, E. S.   Public views of crime and crime prevention. In I. H. Frieze, D. Bar-Tal, & J. S. Carroll (Eds.), *New approaches to social problems: Applications of attribution theory*. San Francisco: Jossey-Bass, 1979.

Kinsey, A. C., et al.   *Sexual behavior in the human male*. Philadelphia: Saunders, 1948.

Kish, L.   *Survey sampling*. New York: Wiley, 1965.

Klaus, R. A., & Gray, S. W.   The early training project for disadvantaged children: A report after five years. *Monographs of the Society for Research in Child Development*, 1968, 33 (4, Whole No. 120).

Kraut, R. E. & Johnston, R. E.   Social and emotional messages of smiling: An ethological approach. *Journal of Personality and Social Psychology*, 1979, 37, 1539–1553.

Krech, D., & Crutchfield, R. S.   *Theory and problems of social psychology*. New York: McGraw-Hill, 1948.

Krech, D., Crutchfield, R. S., & Ballachey, E. L.   *Individual in society: A textbook in social psychology*. New York: McGraw-Hill, 1962.

Lansing, J. B., & Heyns, R. W.   Need affiliation and frequency of four types of communication. *Journal of Abnormal and Social Psychology*, 1959, 58, 365–372.

LaFrance, M.   Nonverbal synchrony and rapport: Analysis by the cross-lag panel technique. *Social Psychology Quarterly*, 1979, 42, 66–70.

LaFrance, M., & Mayo, C.   Racial differences in gaze behavior during conversation: Two systematic observational studies. *Journal of Personality and Social Psychology*, 1976, 33, 547–552.

LaFrance, M., & Mayo, C. *Moving bodies: Nonverbal communication in social relationships.* Monterey, California: Brooks/Cole, 1978.

Langbein, L. I., & Lichtman, A. J. *Ecological Inference.* Beverly Hills, Calif.: Sage Publications, 1978.

Laughlin, P. R., & Laughlin, R. M. Source effects in the judgment of social argot. *Journal of Social Psychology,* 1968, *78,* 249–254.

Lawler, E. E. III., & Hackman, J. R. Impact of employee participation in the development of pay incentive plans: A field experiment. *Journal of Applied Psychology,* 1969, *53,* 467–471.

Lazarsfeld, P. F. *Latent structure analysis* (mimeograph). New York: Bureau of Applied Social Research, Columbia University, 1957.

Lazarsfeld, P. F. and Rosenberg, M. *The language of social research: A reader in the methodology of social research.* Glencoe, Ill.: Free Press, 1955.

Lee, R. S. *The family of the addict: A comparison of the family experiences of male juvenile heroin addicts and controls.* Unpublished doctoral dissertation, New York University, 1957.

Lemon, N. *Attitudes and their measurement.* New York: Wiley, 1973.

Letters of an Indian Judge to an English Gentlewoman. London: Futura Publications Ltd., 1978

Leuthold, D. A., & Scheele, R. Patterns of bias in samples based on telephone directories. *Public Opinion Quarterly,* 1971, *35,* 249–257.

Levin, H. Psychologist to the powerless. In E. F. Korten, S. W. Cook & J. I. Lacey, (Eds.), *Psychology and the problems of society.* Washington, D.C.: American Psychological Association, 1970.

Levin, H. M. A decade of policy developments in improving education and training for low-income populations. In T. D. Cook, et. al. *Evaluation studies review annual,* Beverly Hills, Calif.: Sage Publications, 1978, pp. 521–570.

Levine, J. M., & Murphy, G. The learning and forgetting of controversial material. *Journal of Abnormal and Social Psychology,* 1943, *38,* 507–517.

Likert, R. A technique for the measurement of attitudes. *Archives of Psychology,* 1932, No. 140.

Little, K. B. Personal space. *Journal of Experimental Social Psychology,* 1965, *1,* 237–247.

Little, K. B. Cultural variations in social schemata. *Journal of Personality and Social Psychology,* 1968, *10*(1), 1–7.

Loevinger, J. A systematic approach to the construction and evaluation of tests of ability. *Psychological Monographs,* 1947, *61* (4, Whole No. 285).

Loevinger, J. The technic of homogeneous tests compared with some aspects of "scale analysis" and factor analysis. *Psychological Bulletin,* 1948, *45,* 507–529.

Loevinger, J., & Wessler, R. *Measuring ego development* (Vol. 1). *Construction and use of a sentence completion test.* San Francisco: Jossey-Bass, 1970.

Loeviner, J., Wessler, R., & Redmore, C. *Measuring ego development* (Vol. 2). *Scoring manual for women and girls.* San Francisco: Jossey-Bass, 1970.

Loewenfeld, I. E. Mechanisms of reflect dilation of the pupil: Historical review and experimental analysis. *Documenta Ophthalmologica,* 1958, *12,* 185–448.

Loewenfeld, I. E. Comment on Hess' findings. *Survey of Ophthalmology,* 1966, *11,* 293–294.

Lofland, J. *Analyzing social settings: A guide to qualitative observation and analysis.* Belmont, Calif.: Wadsworth, 1971.

LoSciuto, L. A. A national inventory of television viewing behavior. In E. A. Rubenstein,

G. A. Comstock, and J. P. Murray (Eds.), *Television and social behavior*, Vol. 4. Washington, D.C.: U.S. Government Printing Office, 1971.

Lynn, L. E., Jr. Policy relevant social research: What does it look like? In M. Guttentag & S. Saar (Eds.), *Evaluation studies review annual* Vol. 2. Beverly Hills, Calif.: Sage Publications, 1977.

Maccoby, E. E., & Maccoby, N. The interview: A tool of social science. In G. Lindzey (Ed.), *Handbook of social psychology* (Vol. 1). Reading, Mass.: Addison-Wesley, 1954.

MacCrone, I. D. *Race attitudes in South Africa.* Oxford: Oxford University Press, 1937.

Maher, B. A., Watt, N., & Campbell, D. T. Comparative validity of two projective and two structured attitude tests in a prison population. *Journal of Applied Psychology*, 1960, *44*, 284–288.

Martyna, W. What does "He" mean? *Journal of Communication*, 1978, *28*, 131–138.

McCall, G. J., & Simmons, J. L. *Issues in participant observation: A text and reader.* Reading, Mass.: Addison-Wesley, 1969.

McCleary, R. How parole officers use records. *Social Problems*, 1977, *24*(5).

McCleary, R. *Dangerous men: The sociology of parole.* Beverly Hills, Calif.: Sage Publications, 1978.

McClelland, D. C. *Personality.* New York: Dryden, 1951.

McClelland, D. C. Toward a theory of motive acquisition. *American Psychologist*, 1965, *20*, 321–322.

McClelland, D. C., Atkinson, J. W., Clark, R. A., & Lowell, E. L. *The achievement motive.* New York: Appleton-Century-Crofts, 1953.

McCord, J. A thirty-year follow-up of treatment effects. *American Psychologist*, 1978, *33*, 284–289.

McCord, J. Treatment that did not help. Paper presented at the American Psychological Association Meetings, New York, September 1979.

McDill, E. L., McDill, M. S., & Sprehe, J. T. *Strategies for success in compensatory education: An appraisal of evaluation research.* Baltimore, Md.: Johns Hopkins Press, 1969.

McDill, E. L., & Rigsby, L. C. *Structure and process in secondary schools.* Baltimore, Md.: Johns Hopkins Press, 1973.

McGee, M. G., & Snyder, M. Attribution and behavior: Two field studies. *Journal of Personality and Social Psychology*, 1975, *32*, 185–190.

Meltzer, B. A. A projected study of the jury as a working institution. *The Annals of the American Academy of Political and Social Sciences*, 1953, *287*, 97–102.

Merton, R. K., Fiske, M., & Kendall, P. L. *The focused interview.* Glencoe, Ill.: Free Press, 1956.

Meyer, N. *The seven-per-cent solution.* New York: E. P. Dutton, 1974.

Michaelis, A. *Research films in biology, anthropology, psychology, and medicine.* New York: Academic Press, 1955.

Milgram, S. Issues in the study of obedience: A reply to Baumrind. *American Psychologist*, 1964, *19*, 848–852.

Milgram, S. Some conditions of obedience and disobedience to authority. *Human Relations*, 1965, *18*, 57–76.

Miller, A. *Political issues and trust in government: 1964-1970.* Paper presented at the meeting of the American Political Science Association, Washington, D.C., September 1972.

Mitchell, S. K. Interobserver agreement, reliability, and generalizability of data collected in observational studies. *Psychological Bulletin*, 1979, *86*, 376–390.

Mixon, D. Instead of deception. *Journal of the Theory of Social Behaviour*, 1972, *2*, 139–177.

Monahan, L., Kuhn, D., & Shaver, P. Intrapsychic versus cultural explanations of the "fear of success" motive. *Journal of Personality and Social Psychology*, 1974, *29*, 60–64.

Moreno, J. L. *Who shall survive?* (rev. ed. 1953, Beacon House). Washington, D.C.: Nervous and Mental Disease Publishing, Series No. 58, 1934.

Morgan, James N., et al. *Five thousand American families—patterns of economic progress.* Analysis of the Panel Study of Income Dynamics. Vols. 1–7. Ann Arbor, Mich.: Institute for Social Research, 1974–1979.

Moser, C. A., & Kalton, G. *Survey methods in social investigation* (2nd ed.). New York: Basic Books, 1972.

Muehl, D. (Ed.). *Content analysis at the Survey Research Center: A manual for coders.* Ann Arbor, Mich.: Institute for Social Research, 1961.

Murphy, G., & Likert, R. *Public opinion and the individual.* New York: Harper, 1938.

Murphy, G. L., Murphy, L. B., & Newcomb, T. M. *Experimental social psychology.* New York: Harper, 1937.

Murray, H. A., et al. *Explorations in personality.* Oxford: Oxford University Press, 1938.

Mussen, P. H. The reliability and validity of the Horowitz faces test. *Journal of Abnormal and Social Psychology*, 1950, *45*, 504–506.

Myers, J. L. *Fundamentals of experimental design.* Boston: Allyn & Bacon, 1966.

Myers, R. J. Errors and bias in the reporting of ages in census data. *Transactions, Actuarial Society of America*, 1940, *41*, 395–415.

Newcomb, T. M. An experiment designed to test the validity of a rating technique. *Journal of Educational Psychology*, 1931, *22*, 279–289.

New York Times encyclopedic almanac, The, 1970. New York: The New York Times, 1969.

Oberdorfer, D. Political polling and electoral strategy: The 1968 election. In E. C. Dreyer & W. A. Rosenbaum (Eds.), *Public opinion and behavior: Essays and studies* (2nd ed.). New York: Duxbury, 1970.

Office of Science and Technology, Executive Office of the President. *Privacy and behavioral research.* Washington, D.C.: U.S. Government Printing Office, 1967.

Osgood, C. E., Suci, C. J., & Tannenbaum, P. H. *The measurement of meaning.* Urbana: University of Illinois Press, 1957.

Page, E. D. Teacher comments and student performance: A 74-classroom experiment in school motivation. *Journal of Educational Psychology*, 1958, *49*, 173–181.

Parke, R. D., & Savin, D. B. *Infant characteristic and behaviors as elicitors of maternal and paternal responsivity.* Paper presented at the Biennial Meeting of the Society for Research in Child Development, Denver, 1975.

Parry, H. J., & Crossley, H. M. Validity of responses to survey questions. *Public Opinion Quarterly*, 1950, *14*, 61–80.

Parten, M. B. *Surveys, polls, and samples.* New York: Harper, 1950.

Parten, M. B. *Surveys, polls, and samples: Practical procedures.* New York: Cooper Square Publishers, 1966.

Patterson, S. C. Patterns of interpersonal relations in a state legislative group: The Wisconsin Assembly. *Public Opinion Quarterly*, 1959, *23*, 101–109.

Payne, S. L. *The art of asking questions.* Princeton, N.J.: Princeton University Press, 1951.

Phillips, D. *Knowledge from what? Theories and methods in social research.* Chicago: Rand McNally, 1971.

Piliavin, I. M., Rodin, J., & Piliavin, J. A. Good samaritanism: An underground phenomenon? *Journal of Personality and Social Psychology,* 1969, *13,* 289–299.

Pilisuk, M., & Skolnick, P. Inducing trust: A test of the Osgood proposal. *Journal of Personality and Social Psychology,* 1968, *8,* 121–133.

Pintner, R., & Forlano, G. The influence of attitude upon scaling of attitude items. *Journal of Social Psychology,* 1937, *8,* 39–45.

Politz, A., & Simmons, W. An attempt to get the "not-at-homes" into the sample without call-backs. *Journal of the American Statistical Association,* 1949, *44,* 9–31.

Price, R. H., & Blashfield, R. K. Explorations in the taxonomy of behavior settings: Analysis of dimensions and classifications. *American Journal of Community Psychology,* 1975, *3,* 335–351.

Proctor, C. H., & Loomis, C. P. Analysis of sociometric data. In M. Jahoda, M. Deutsch, & S. W. Cook (Eds.), *Research methods in social relations* (Vol. 2). New York: Dryden, 1951.

Proshansky, H. M. A projective method for the study of attitudes. *Journal of Abnormal and Social Psychology,* 1943, *38,* 393–395.

Quinn, R. P., Gutek, B. A., & Walsh, J. T. Telephone interviewing: A reappraisal and a field experiment. In press: *Basic and Applied Social Psychology,* 1980.

Rajecki, D. W. Ethological elements in social psychology. In C. Hendricks (Ed.), *Perspectives on social psychology.* Hillsdale, N.J.: Erlbaum, 1977.

Rankin, R. E., & Campbell, D. T. Galvanic skin response to Negro and white experimenters. *Journal of Abnormal and Social Psychology,* 1959, *51,* 30–33.

Rechtschaffen, A., & Mednick, S. A. The autokinetic word technique. *Journal of Abnormal and Social Psychology,* 1955, *51,* 346.

Riley, M. W. *Sociological research* (Vol. II): *Exercises and manual.* New York: Harcourt, 1963.

Ring, K., Wallston, K., & Corey, M. Mode of debriefing as a factor affecting subjective reaction to a Milgram-type obedience experiment: An ethical inquiry. *Representative Research in Social Psychology,* 1970, *1,* 67–88.

Robinson, J. P. *How Americans use time: A social psychological analysis of everyday behavior.* New York: Praeger, 1977.

Robinson, W. S. Ecological correlations and the behavior of individuals. *American Sociological Review,* 1950, *15,* 351–357.

Rogers, C. R., & Skinner, B. F. Some issues concerning the control of human behavior. *Science,* 1956, *124,* 1057–1066.

Rohde, A. R. Explorations in personality by the sentence completion method. *Journal of Applied Psychology,* 1946, *30,* 169–181.

Rosenberg, M. *The logic of survey analysis.* New York: Basic Books, 1968.

Rosenhan, D. L. On being sane in insane places. *Science,* 1973, *79,* 250–258.

Rosenthal, R., & Jacobson, L. Teachers' expectancies: Determinants of pupils' I.Q. gains. *Psychological Reports,* 1966, *19,* 115–118.

Ross, L., Lepper, M. R., & Hubbard, M. Perseverence in self-perception and social perception: Biased attributional processes in the debriefing paradigm. *Journal of Personality and Social Psychology,* 1975, *32,* 880–892.

Rotter, J. B. Word association and sentence completion methods. In H. H. Anderson & G. L. Anderson (Eds.), *Projective techniques.* Englewood Cliffs, N.J.: Prentice-Hall, 1951.

Rotter, J. B., & Willerman, B. The incomplete sentence test as a method of studying personality. *Journal of Consulting Psychology*, 1947, *11*, 43–48.

Rubin, Z. Measurement of romantic love. *Journal of Personality and Social Psychology*, 1970, *16*, 265–273.

Rummel, R. J. *Applied factor analysis.* Evanston, Ill.: Northwestern University Press, 1970.

Sackett, G. Measurement in observational research. In G. Sackett (Ed.), *Observing behavior:* (Vol. II) *Data collection and analysis methods.* Baltimore: University Park Press, 1978.

Sackett, G. *Observing behavior:* (Vol. I) *Theory and applications in mental retardation.* Baltimore: University Park Press, 1978.

Sackett, G. *Observing behavior:* (Vol. II) *Data collection and analysis methods.* Baltimore: University Park Press, 1978.

Saffir, M. A. A comparative study of scales constructed by three psychophysical methods. *Psychometrika*, 1937, *2*, 179–198.

Samph, T. Observer effects on teacher verbal classroom behavior. *Journal of Educational Psychology*, 1976, *68*, 736–741.

Scheflen, A. E. The significance of posture in communication systems. *Psychiatry*, 1964, *27*, 316–331.

Schlenker, B. R. & Forsyth, D. R. On the ethics of psychological research. *Journal of Experimental Social Psychology*, 1977, *13*, 369–396.

Schoggen, P. Ecological psychology and mental retardation. In G. Sackett (Ed.), *Observing behavior:* (Vol. I) *Theory and applications in mental retardation.* Baltimore: University Park Press, 1978.

Schultz, D. P., The human subject in psychological research. *Psychological Bulletin*, 1969, *72*, 214–228.

Schulz, R. Effects of control and predictability on the physical and psychological well-being of the institutionalized aged. *Journal of Personality and Social Psychology*, 1976, *33*(5), 563–573.

Schulz, R. & Hanusa, B. H. Long-term effects of control and predictability-enhancing interventions: Findings and ethical issues. *Journal of Personality and Social Psychology*, 1978, *36*, 1194–1201.

Schwitzgebel, R. L. Survey of electromechanical devices for behavior modification. *Psychological Bulletin*, 1968, *70*, 444–459.

Scott, R. *The making of blind men: A study of adult socialization.* New York: Russell Sage Foundation, 1969.

Scott, W. A. Attitude change by response reinforcement: Replication and extension. *Sociometry*, 1959, *22*, 328–335.

Scott, W. A. Attitude measurement. In G. Lindzey & E. Aronson (Eds.), *Handbook of social psychology* (Vol. 2, 2nd ed.). Reading, Mass.: Addison-Wesley, 1968.

Selltiz, C. The use of survey methods in a citizens' campaign against discrimination. *Human Organization*, 1955, *14*, 19–25.

Selltiz, C., & Cook, S. W. Racial attitude as a determinant of judgments of plausibility. *Journal of Social Psychology*, 1966, *70*, 139–147.

Sherif, C., Sherif, M., & Nebergall, R. E. *Attitude and attitude change: The social judgment-involvement approach.* Philadelphia: Saunders, 1965.

Shuman, H. & Presser, S. Open and closed questions. *American Sociological Review*, 1979, *44*, 692–712.

Siegel, S. *Nonparametric statistics for the behavioral sciences.* New York: McGraw-Hill, 1956.

Smith, G. H. *Motivation research in advertising and marketing.* New York: McGraw-Hill, 1954.

Smith, W. J., Chase, J., & Lieblich, A. K. Tongue showing: A facial display of humans and other primate species. *Semiotica,* 1974, *11,* 201–246.

Sobel, S. B. Throwing the baby out with the bathwater: The hazards of follow-up research. *American Psychologist,* 1978, *33,* 290–291.

Sommer, R. On the Brown adaptation of the Rosenzweig P-F assessing social attitudes. *Journal of Abnormal and Social Psychology,* 1954, *49,* 125–128.

Stack, C. B. *All our kin: Strategies for survival in a black community.* New York: Harper Colophon Books, 1975.

Stanton, H. R., Back, K. W., & Litwak, E. Role-playing in survey research. *American Journal of Sociology,* 1956, *62,* 172–176.

Stanton, H. R., & Litwak, E. Toward the development of a short form test of interpersonal competence. *American Sociological Review,* 1955, *20,* 668–647.

Star, S. A., & Hughes, H. M. Report on an educational campaign: The Cincinnati Plan for the United Nations. *American Journal of Sociology,* 1950, *55,* 355–361.

Stein, M. I. The use of a sentence completion test for the diagnosis of personality. *Journal of Clinical Psychology,* 1947, *3,* 47–56.

Stephan, F. F., & McCarthy, P. J. *Sampling opinions: An analysis of survey procedure.* New York: Wiley, 1958.

Stouffer, S. A., et al. *Measurement and prediction.* Studies in social psychology in World War II (Vol. 4). Princeton, N.J.: Princeton University Press, 1950.

Strayer, F. F., & Strayer, J. An ethological analysis of social agonism and dominance relations among preschool children. *Child Development,* 1976, *47,* 980–989.

Strunk, W., Jr., & White, E. B. *The elements of style* (3rd ed.). New York: Macmillan, 1979.

Sudman, S. *Reducing the cost of surveys.* Chicago: Aldine-Atherton, 1967.

Symposium on Operationism. *Psychological Review,* 1945, 241–294.

Tetlock, P. E. Identifying victims of groupthink from public statements of decision makers. *Journal of Personality and Social Psychology,* 1979, *37,* 1314–1324.

Thouless, R. H. Effect of prejudice on reasoning. *British Journal of Psychology,* 1959, *50,* 289–293.

Thurstone, L. L. The method of paired comparisons for social values. *Journal of Abnormal and Social Psychology,* 1927, *21,* 384–400.

Thurstone, L. L. An experimental study of nationality preferences. *Journal of Genetic Psychology,* 1928, *1,* 405–425.

Thurstone, L. L. Theory of attitude measurement. *Psychological Bulletin,* 1929, *36,* 222–241.

Thurstone, L. L. The measurement of social attitudes. *Journal of Abnormal and Social Psychology,* 1931, *26,* 249–269.

Thurstone, L. L., & Chave, E. J. *The measurement of attitude.* Chicago: University of Chicago Press, 1929.

Tittle, C. R., & Hill, R. J. Attitude measurement and prediction of behavior: An evaluation of conditions and measurement techniques. *Sociometry,* 1967, *30,* 199–213.

Torgerson, W. S. *Theory and methods of scaling.* New York: Wiley, 1958.

Triandis, H. C. *Attitude and attitude change.* New York: Wiley, 1971.

Tuchfarber, A. and Klecka, W. *Demographic similarities between samples collected by random digit dialing vs. complex sampling techniques.* A paper delivered at the 30th Annual Conference of the American Association for Public Opinion Research. Itasca, Ill., May 1975.

Tukey, J. W. *Exploratory data analysis.* Reading, Mass.: Addison-Wesley, 1977.

Tunnell, G. B. Three dimensions of naturalness: An expanded definition of field research. *Psychological Bulletin*, 1977, *84*, 426–437.

United States, President, *Economic report of the President together with the annual report of the Council of Economic Advisers, transmitted to the Congress.* January 1964. Washington, D.C.: U.S. Government Printing Office, 1964.

Upshaw, H. S. The effects of variable perspectives on judgments of opinion statements for Thurstone Scales: Equal appearing intervals. *Journal of Personality and Social Psychology*, 1965, *2*, 60–69.

Upshaw, H. S. Attitude measurement. In H. M. Blalock, Jr., & A. B. Blalock (Eds.), *Methodology in social research.* New York: McGraw-Hill, 1968.

Vaughan, G. M., & Thompson, R. T. New Zealand children's attitudes toward Maoris. *Journal of Abnormal and Social Psychology*, 1961, *62*, 701–704.

Vernon, D. T. A. The use of modeling to modify children's responses to a natural potentially stressful situation. *Journal of Applied Psychology*, 1973, *58*, 351–356.

Vidich, A. J., & Shapiro, G. A. Comparison of participant observation and survey data. *American Sociological Review*, 1955, *20*, 28–33.

Volkova, B. D. Some characteristics of conditional reflex formation to verbal stimuli in children. *Sechenov Psychological Journal (USSR)*, 1953, *39*, 668–674.

Waly, P., & Cook, S. W. Attitude as a determinant of learning and memory: A failure to confirm. *Journal of Personality and Social Psychology*, 1966, *4*, 280–288.

Walker, T. G., & Main, E. C. Choice shifts in political decision making: Federal judges and civil liberties cases. *Journal of Applied Social Psychology*, 1973, *2*, 39–48.

Warwick, D. P., & Lininger, C. A. *The sample survey: Theory and practice.* New York: McGraw-Hill, 1975.

Watson, G. B. *The measurement of fairmindedness.* Teachers College Contributions to Education, 176. New York: Teachers College, Columbia University, 1925.

Webb, E. J., Campbell, D. T., Schwartz, R. D., & Sechrest, L. *Unobtrusive measures: Non-reactive research in the social sciences.* Chicago: Rand McNally, 1966.

Weick, K. E. Systematic observational methods. In G. Lindzey & E. Aronson (Eds.), *The handbook of social psychology* (Vol. 2). Reading, Mass.: Addison-Wesley, 1968.

Weigel, R. H., Wiser, P. L., & Cook, S. W. The impact of cooperative learning experiences on cross-ethnic relations and attitudes. *Journal of Social Issues*, 1975, *31*(1), 219–244.

Weiss, C. H. *Evaluating action programs.* Boston: Allyn & Bacon, 1972.

Weitz, J., & Nuckols, R. C. The validity of direct and indirect questions in measuring job satisfaction. *Personnel Psychology*, 1953, *6*, 487–494.

West, S. G., Gunn, S. P., & Chernicky, P. Ubiquitous Watergate: An attributional analysis. *Journal of Personality and Social Psychology*, 1975, *32*, 55–65.

Westie, F. R., & DeFleur, M. L. Autonomic responses and their relationship to race attitudes. *Journal of Abnormal and Social Psychology*, 1959, *58*, 340–347.

White, G. D. The effects of observer presence on the activity level of families. *Journal of Applied Behavior Analysis*, 1977, *10*, 734.

Whyte, W. F. *Street corner society.* Chicago: University of Chicago Press, 1943.

Whyte, W. F. On asking indirect questions. *Human Organization*, 1957, *15*, 21–23.

Wicker, A. W. *An introduction to ecological psychology.* Monterey, Calif.: Brooks/Cole, 1979.

Willems, E. P. Planning a rationale for naturalistic research. In E. P. Willems & H. L. Raush (Eds.), *Naturalistic viewpoint in psychological research.* New York: Holt, 1969.

Williams, W., & Evans, J. W. The politics of evaluation: The case of Head Start. In

P. H. Rossi & W. Williams (Eds.), *Evaluating social programs: Theory, practice and politics.* New York: Seminar Press, 1972.

Williamson, J., & Karp, D. *The research craft: An introduction to social science methods.* Boston: Little-Brown, 1977.

Wolf, E. R. & Jorgenson, J. G. Anthropology on the warpath in Thailand. *New York Review of Books,* 1970, *15*(9), 26–35.

Woodmansee, J. J. The pupil response as a measure of social attitudes. In G. Summers (Ed.), *Attitude measurement.* Chicago: Rand McNally, 1970.

Wortman, C. B., & Rabinovitz, V. C. Randomization: The fairest of them all. In L. Sechrest, et al. (Eds.), *Evaluation Studies Review Annual.* Vol. 4. Beverly Hills, Calif.: Sage Publications, 1979.

Wright, H. F. *Recording and analyzing child behavior.* New York: Harper & Row, 1967.

Yarrow, M. R., & Waxler, C. Z. Observing interaction: A confrontation with methodology. In R. B. Cairns (Ed.), *The analysis of social interactions: Methods, issues, and illustrations.* Hillsdale, New Jersey: Erlbaum, 1979.

Zegiob, L. E., & Forehand, R. Parent-child interactions: Observer effects and social class differences. *Behavior Therapy,* 1978, *9,* 118–123.

Zigler, E., & Child, I. L. Socialization. In G. Lindzey & E. Aronson (Eds.), *The handbook of social psychology* (Vol. 3, 2nd ed.). Reading, Mass.: Addison-Wesley, 1969.

Zimbardo, P. G. The human choice: Individuation, reason, and order versus deindividuation, impulse, and chaos. In W. A. Arnold & D. Levin (Eds.), *Nebraska symposium on motivation* (Vol. 17). Lincoln: University of Nebraska Press, 1969.

Zubin, J., Eron, L. D., & Shumer, F. *An experimental approach to projective techniques.* New York: Wiley, 1965.

ADDITIONAL REFERENCES

Hartley, E. L. & Schwartz, S. *A pictorial doll play approach for the study of children's intergroup attitudes* (mimeograph). New York: American Jewish Congress, 1948.

Kuethe, J. L. Prejudice and aggression: A study of specific social schemata. *Perceptual and Motor Skills,* 1964, *18,* (1), 107–115.

Miller, D. C. *Handbook of research design and social measurement.* New York: David McKay, 1964.

Robinson, J. P. & Shaver, P. R. *Measures of social psychological attitudes.* Ann Arbor, Mich.: Institute for Social Research, 1969.

Scott, J. E. & Franklin, J. L. The changing nature of sex references in mass circulation magazines. *Public Opinion Quarterly,* 1972, *36,* 80–86.

Shaw, M. E. & Wright, J. M. *Scales for the measurement of attitudes.* New York: McGraw-Hill, 1967.

Name Index

Subject Index